P9-CRT-280

Assessing Infants and Preschoolers with Special Needs

Mary McLean
Cardinal Stritch College

Donald B. Bailey Jr.
University of North Carolina

Mark Wolery
Allegheny-Singer Research Institute

Merrill,
an imprint of Prentice Hall
Englewood Cliffs, New Jersey Columbus, Ohio

Library of Congress Cataloging-in-Publication Data
McLean, Mary E.
Assessing infants and preschoolers with special needs / Mary McLean, Donald B. Bailey, Jr., Mark Wolery.—2nd ed.
p. cm.
Rev. ed. of: Assessing infants and preschoolers with handicaps / Donald B. Bailey, 1989.
Includes bibliographical references and index.
1. Handicapped children—Education (Preschool)—Evaluation. 2. Handicapped children—Identification. 3. Handicapped children—Psychological testing. I. Bailey, Donald B. II. Wolery, Mark. III. Bailey, Donald B. Assessing infants and preschoolers with handicaps. IV. Title.
LC4019.2.M45 1996
371.91—dc20 95-43484
CIP

Cover photo: ©Diana Ong/Superstock
Editor: Ann Castel Davis
Production Editor: Linda Hillis Bayma
Photo Editor: Anne Vega
Design Coordinator: Jill E. Bonar
Text Designer: Susan Frankenberry
Cover Designer: Anne D. Flanagan
Production Manager: Laura Messerly
Electronic Text Management: Marilyn Wilson Phelps, Matthew Williams, Karen L. Bretz, Tracey Ward

This book was set in Humanist 777 by Prentice Hall and was printed and bound by Quebecor Printing/Book Press. The cover was printed by Phoenix Color Corp.

Photo credits: Courtesy of Children's Hospital, Columbus, Ohio, p. 165; Scott Cunningham/Merrill/Prentice Hall, pp. 23, 202, 268, 519; Barbara Schwartz/Merrill/Prentice Hall, pp. 1, 123, 305, 462; Anne Vega/Merrill/Prentice Hall, pp. 46, 69, 96, 334, 398, 435; Tom Watson/Merrill/Prentice Hall, p. 491. Photo on p. 234 supplied by the authors.

Printed in the United States of America

10 9 8 7 6 5 4 3

ISBN: 0-02-379394-5

Prentice-Hall International (UK) Limited, *London*
Prentice-Hall of Australia Pty. Limited, *Sydney*
Prentice-Hall of Canada, Inc., *Toronto*
Prentice-Hall Hispanoamericana, S. A., *Mexico*
Prentice-Hall of India Private Limited, *New Delhi*
Prentice-Hall of Japan, Inc., *Tokyo*
Simon & Schuster Asia Pte. Ltd., *Singapore*
Editora Prentice-Hall do Brasil, Ltda., *Rio de Janeiro*

PREFACE

In the years between publication of the first edition of this book and preparation of the second edition, much has happened in the field of early intervention/early childhood special education. In preparing this second edition, we have attempted not only to update the information provided in the original edition, but also to incorporate current practices in the field that are preferred in the identification and assessment of young children with special needs.

One of those practices is the incorporation of family-centered philosophy into all aspects of assessment. Family-centered practices are discussed as procedural considerations in Chapter 3, a chapter on cultural competence has been added (Chapter 4), and a chapter on assessing family concerns, resources, and priorities has been added (Chapter 8). The reader will discover, however, that an emphasis on facilitating collaborative relationships with family members is present throughout the book.

Obtaining information about a child's functioning in typical environments rather than only in clinical settings is another practice emphasized throughout the book. While the chapters that deal with particular developmental domains do present descriptions of tests, other forms of assessment are also included, and the emphasis is on describing a process of information gathering. This process will lead to making a decision about further evaluation or eligibility or program planning and must be based on information that is reflective of the child's typical behavior.

Collaborative decision making among the professionals and parents who make up the assessment team is another practice reflected throughout the book. Although development has been divided into domains for the purpose of communicating information about assessment strategies, the reader should be assured that for the purposes of decision making, it is most important to have the perspective of the whole child in the context of the child's family and typical environment.

This book is organized in a manner that is similar in format to the first edition. The first four chapters provide basic information on the assessment process. Chapter 1 includes information on the legal basis and recommended practices in assessing young children with special needs. Chapter 2 provides the foundation of information on tests and measurement. Chapter 3 reviews procedural considerations in assessment of young children. Chapter 4, written by Eleanor Lynch and Marci Hanson, provides the reader with information on ensuring cultural competence in assessment.

The next five chapters cover special concerns in the assessment of young children. Chapter 5 presents information on Child Find, screening, and tracking. Chapter 6, written by Beth Langley, presents detailed information on assessing the sensory processes in young children. Chapter 7, written by Karen O'Donnell, provides information on neurobehavioral assessment of newborns. Chapter 8, which is new to this edition, addresses assessment of family concerns, resources, and priorities. Chapter 9, written by Joan Karp, provides information on assessing the environments in which young children function.

Chapters 10 through 15 are organized according to developmental domains. Chapter 10, written by Katherine McCormick, addresses cognitive development. Chapter 11, written by Susan Harris and Irene McEwen, provides information on assessing motor skills. Chapter 12, written by Elizabeth Crais and Joanne Erwick Roberts, addresses communication skills. Chapter 13, written by Sam Odom and Leslie Munson, addresses social interaction skills. Chapter 14, written by Karin Lifter, presents information on assessing play skills. Chapter 15, written by Eva Horn and Amy Childre, provides information on assessing adaptive skills.

In Chapter 16, the process of using assessment information to plan instructional programs for infants and young children is addressed. The final chapter of the book, Chapter 17, provides information on assessment for the purpose of monitoring child progress.

As indicated in the preface to the first edition, reading this book will not make one competent in the assessment of infants and young children. The instructor who has chosen to use this text is advised to carefully plan field-based experiences for students who are learning to assess children, work with families, and engage in collaborative decision making as a member of an assessment team. There is no substitute for quality field experiences.

ACKNOWLEDGMENTS

We would like to recognize the contributions of many individuals who were involved in the preparation of this second edition. We are grateful to the chapter authors who contributed their expertise and their time to the revision of this book. Many of them were primarily motivated by their desire to have a new edition of this book for their classes! We are grateful for their hard work.

We would like to acknowledge the contributions of these reviewers of the manuscript: David W. Anderson, Bethel College; Martha Cook, University of Alabama; Lin Douglas, Central Washington University; Blanche Jackson Glimps, Marygrove College; and Marilyn Sass-Lehrer, Gallaudet University.

We dedicate this book to our spouses and children, and especially to Meaghan Grace McLean, whose arrival delayed the completion of this book but was nonetheless joyfully received.

Mary McLean
Donald B. Bailey
Mark Wolery

CONTENTS

CHAPTER

1

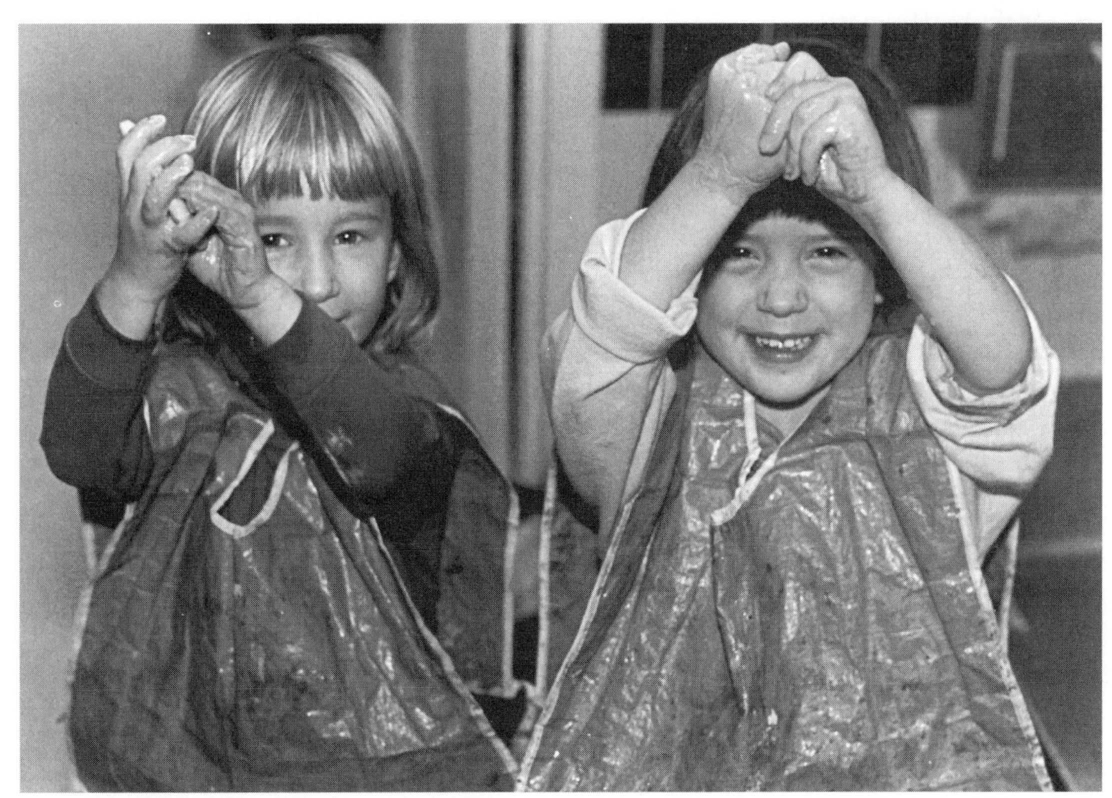

Assessment and Its Importance in Early Intervention/Early Childhood Special Education

Mary McLean
Cardinal Stritch College

Assessment is an important and ongoing responsibility of professionals who serve young children and their families. Assessment provides insight into the course of development for young children. It determines which children have a need for special services, defines the services to be provided, and measures the success of early intervention efforts. Parameters of assessment are determined by federal and state legislation and regulations and are influenced by current thinking relative to best practice. Professionals working in early childhood settings must have a solid understanding of assessment concepts and practices, must have skills in the clinical application of these concepts and practices, and must keep up with new instruments, new regulations, and new trends.

Over the past 25 years, the field of Early Intervention/Early Childhood Special Education (EI/ECSE) has grown dramatically, establishing itself as a discipline related to but also different from parent disciplines of Special Education and Early Childhood Education. The knowledge base for assessment in EI/ECSE is uniquely applied to the population of young children with special needs. The term *young children with special needs,* as it is used in this text, refers to children who have an identified disability or delay in development or who have a condition that puts them at risk of developing a disability or a delay. The focus of this text will be children from birth through age 5. As the field of EI/ECSE has grown, the unique aspects of the population of young children with special needs has become apparent (McLean & Odom, 1993). At the same time, the settings in which assessment and intervention are provided for these children have become less specialized and separate as the philosophy of serving all children in natural environments has become prevalent.

This textbook is designed to provide information needed by professionals who will be responsible for the assessment of infants, toddlers, and preschoolers with special needs. This chapter provides an overview of the legal basis for assessment, the various functions of assessment, and the special challenges presented in assessing young children with special needs. The chapter also introduces the reader to the unique characteristics of assessment that have evolved over the past two decades to meet those challenges.

THE LEGAL BASIS FOR ASSESSMENT PROCEDURES

As indicated earlier, the field of Early Intervention/Early Childhood Special Education is relatively new. Laws that govern the assessment of young children with special needs have been passed fairly recently. As shown in Figure 1.1, P.L. 94-142, passed in 1975 and called the Education for All Handicapped Children Act, mandated services for all school-age children with disabilities and facilitated the provision of services for preschool children with disabilities in some states. Under this law, states were allowed to choose whether or not to serve preschool children. P.L. 94-142 and its regulations provided guidelines for the assessment of children receiving special education services from state departments of education.

In 1986, Public Law 99-457 was passed, amending P.L. 94-142 and requiring the states to provide a free and appropriate public education to children with disabilities from age 3 through age 5. The regulations that governed school-age children were then made applicable to the assessment of preschool children. In addition, a new part (Part H) was added to the law, establishing incentives for serving infants and toddlers with special needs. Wording in this law and its subsequent regulations provides a legal basis for the assessment of infants and toddlers.

Later legislation has reauthorized and made some changes in the original legislation govern-

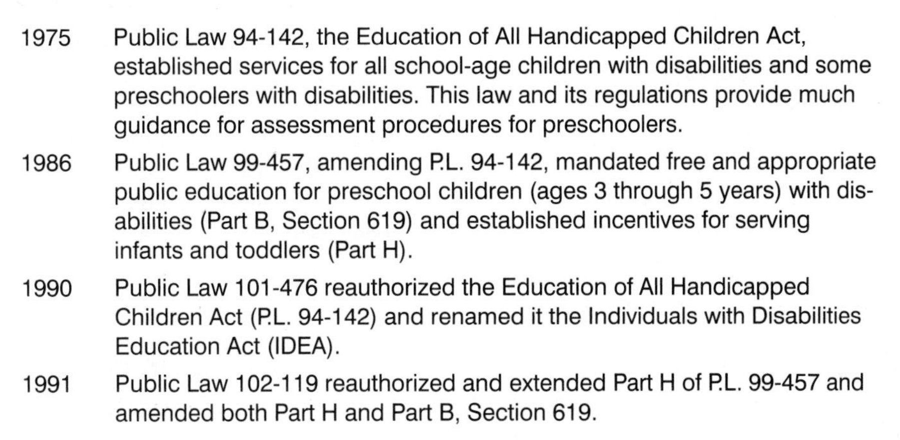

1975 Public Law 94-142, the Education of All Handicapped Children Act, established services for all school-age children with disabilities and some preschoolers with disabilities. This law and its regulations provide much guidance for assessment procedures for preschoolers.

1986 Public Law 99-457, amending P.L. 94-142, mandated free and appropriate public education for preschool children (ages 3 through 5 years) with disabilities (Part B, Section 619) and established incentives for serving infants and toddlers (Part H).

1990 Public Law 101-476 reauthorized the Education of All Handicapped Children Act (P.L. 94-142) and renamed it the Individuals with Disabilities Education Act (IDEA).

1991 Public Law 102-119 reauthorized and extended Part H of P.L. 99-457 and amended both Part H and Part B, Section 619.

FIGURE 1.1
Legislation affecting assessment in EI/ECSE

ing infant/toddler and preschool programs. In 1990, P.L. 101-476 changed the name of the Education of All Handicapped Children Act to the Individuals with Disabilities Education Act (IDEA), emphasizing "people first" terminology and using the term *disability* rather than *handicap*. In 1991, P.L. 102-119 reauthorized and amended both Part H (infant/toddler) and Part B (preschool) legislation.

As indicated, the legislation and regulations that govern the assessment of infants and toddlers are somewhat different from those that govern the assessment of preschoolers. Specifically, Part H of IDEA and the corresponding regulations developed by the U.S. Office of Education specify procedures to be followed with children under the age of 3. Part B, Section 619 of IDEA and the corresponding regulations specify procedures for children from 3 years to 6 years. In many states, the state agencies responsible for these two programs and, therefore, the state regulations to be followed, are also different. Realization of the confusion caused when families make the transition from infant/toddler services to preschool services led to a call for a "seamless" system, and efforts to legislate this system were included in P.L. 102-119. However, in many states the differences between services under Part B, Section 619 and Part H are still quite apparent.

Although Part H and Part B are similar in intent and serve populations with similar needs, there are substantial differences between the two. Part H does not view children as service recipients apart from their families and, therefore, serves birth through 2-year-old children through a family-centered approach. Part B, Section 619 programs for preschool children are, for the most part, an extension of school-age programs downward to include children from 3 through 5 years of age. These programs are administered by departments of education in each state and territory and, therefore, tend to be administered and regulated in a manner similar to school-age programs of special education. The approach tends to be more child-centered, based on the identification of the child's need for uniquely designed instruction. As indicated above, there have been attempts to reduce the discrepancy between infant/toddler and preschool programs; for example, P.L. 102-119 allows the use of an Individualized

Family Service Plan rather than an Individualized Educational Program for preschool children. However, major differences in the legislation and in regulations still exist. Differences also occur from state to state.

Definitions of Eligibility

Federal law provides a general definition of which children are eligible for EI/ECSE services, but each state and territory is responsible for the exact definition of eligibility as well as designation of diagnostic instruments or procedures to be used. EI/ECSE professionals must be thoroughly familiar with both the federal law and regulations and state guidelines relative to determination of eligibility to serve as a member of an eligibility team. It is not uncommon for there to be frequent changes in federal law and regulations and in state guidelines. The federal law must be reauthorized every five years and is subject to change during each reauthorization. State guidelines can change even more frequently. Professionals, therefore, must remain current in their knowledge of federal and state laws and regulations.

Figure 1.2 presents the wording from IDEA, Part H, relative to the determination of eligibility for early intervention services for children from birth through 2 years of age. As can be seen, three groups of children may be eligible for services:

1. Children who have a measurable developmental delay in one or more of five areas: cognitive development, physical development, communication development, social or emotional development, or adaptive development.
2. Children who have a diagnosed condition that probably will result in developmental delay (even if a delay is not currently present).
3. Children who are at risk of having a delay if early intervention is not provided. This group will be served only if a state chooses to do so. As of October 1992, only 13 states were serving a group of children in this third category, and the definitions of

(1) The term "infants and toddlers with disabilities" means individuals from birth to age 2, inclusive, who need early intervention services because they—

(A) are experiencing developmental delays, as measured by appropriate diagnostic instruments and procedures in one or more of the following areas: cognitive development, physical development, language and speech development (hereafter...referred to as "communication development"), psychosocial development (hereafter...referred to as "social or emotional development"), or self-help skills (hereafter...referred to as "adaptive development"), or

(B) have a diagnosed physical or mental condition which has a high probability of resulting in developmental delay.

(C) Such term may also include, at a State's discretion, individuals from birth to age 2, inclusive, who are at risk of having substantial developmental delays if early intervention services are not provided.

FIGURE 1.2
Statutory language pertaining to eligibility definitions—IDEA, Part H
Source: From IDEA Section 672(1); 34CFR 303.16.

at risk varied greatly among these states (Shackelford, 1992). Information on children considered to be at risk is presented in Chapter 5 of this text.

Each state or territory has established criteria for determining whether a measurable developmental delay (category 1 in previous list) exists. According to Shackelford (1992), some states use a quantitative measure of developmental delay, for instance two standard deviations below the mean (a standard deviation is a measure of the degree to which a score deviates from the mean) or a 25% delay in a developmental area. However, the specific criteria vary considerably among states in terms of the type of measure used and also in terms of the level of delay required. Shackelford found at least three different types of quantitative definitions in use:

1. The difference between chronological age and actual performance level (as determined through an age-equivalent measure of performance in the specified developmental domains). Example: Iowa—25% delay in one or more areas. A child who is 12 months old and has an age-equivalent score of 9 months or less in the area of motor development, for example, has a 25% delay in physical development.
2. Delay expressed as performance at a certain number of months below chronological age. Example: Texas—A child 2 to 12 months old must have a 2-month delay; a child 13 to 24 months old must have a 3-month delay; a child 25 to 36 months old must have a 4-month delay.
3. Delay indicated by standard deviation below the mean (requires a standardized instrument). Example: Colorado—1.5 standard deviations below the mean in one or more areas. A child must have a standard score (Z score, t score, deviation quotient, or other standard score) that is at least 1.5 standard deviations below the mean. Standard scores are discussed in Chapter 2.

In addition, some states use a qualitative definition. For example, in Hawaii, a multidisciplinary team consensus is required. No level of standard deviation or percentage delay is specified. This type of eligibility does not require a quantitative measure. Using traditional assessments that yield standard scores or age-equivalent scores has been problematic due to the paucity of reliable and valid instruments for this age group (Neisworth & Bagnato, 1992; Shonkoff & Meisels, 1991). Some states, then, have chosen to rely on professional judgment rather than on test scores in determining eligibility.

Figure 1.3 presents the wording from IDEA, Part B, relative to the determination of eligibility for services for preschool children with special needs. As can be seen, children who are 3, 4, or 5 years of age must be eligible according to the categories of disability used with school-age children. The federal definitions of the categories of disability are provided in Figure 1.4. Modifications may be made in a category so that it is a better fit for preschool children.

Since the passage of P.L. 102-119, the state may also develop a special category just for preschool children defined by a delay in one or more of five developmental areas. The preschool-specific category may be called whatever the state decides to call it. *Developmental delay* is used by some states. Other terms have also been used; *preschool delayed* and *preprimary impaired* are two examples. The possibility of using a preschool-specific category is optional for states.

Danaher (1992) reviewed preschool eligibility definitions in the 50 states and the District of Columbia and found four types of definitions:

1. Part B (school-age) disability categories only
2. Part B categories plus use of a special preschool category
3. Some (but not all) Part B categories plus a special preschool category
4. No Part B categories used (either noncategorical for all ages or only the special preschool category is used).

(A) The term "children with disabilities" means children—

(i) with mental retardation, hearing impairments including deafness, speech or language impairments, visual impairments including blindness, serious emotional disturbance, orthopedic impairments, autism, traumatic brain injury, other health impairments, or specific learning disabilities; and

(ii) who, by reason thereof, need special education and related services.

(B) The term "children with disabilities" for children aged 3 to 5, inclusive, may, at a State's discretion, include children—

(i) experiencing developmental delays, as defined by the State and as measured by appropriate diagnostic instruments and procedures, in one or more of the following areas: physical development, cognitive development, communication development, social or emotional development, or adaptive development; and

(ii) who, by reason thereof, need special education and related services.

FIGURE 1.3
Eligibility for preschool children under IDEA, Part B
Source: IDEA section 602a(1); 34CFR 300.7.

As might be expected, among the states using a special preschool category, the definition of the category differs greatly. Most common is the designation of delay in standard deviations or delay expressed as a percentage of the chronological age. Some states also allow the use of risk factors or medically diagnosed conditions. Thirteen states allow the use of qualitative criteria usually referred to as "professional judgment" or "informed clinical opinion." The state of Minnesota has titled its preschool-specific category "Eligible for early childhood special education," and defines it as a delay of 1.5 standard deviations in two areas or a medically diagnosed condition or professional judgment.

Interestingly, a comparison of data collected from the 50 states and the District of Columbia as of April 1, 1992 (Danaher, 1992) with data collected as of May 19, 1994 (Danaher, 1994) shows increased use of the preschool-specific category among states. In 1992, 15 states were using only Part B disability categories with preschoolers whereas in 1994, only eight states were. The number of states using some or all Part B categories plus a preschool-specific category increased from 27 to 34. The number of states not using any Part B categories for preschoolers remained at nine for both years.

Part H Regulations Pertaining to Assessment

Part H regulations that govern services for infants and toddlers make a distinction between evaluation and assessment of the child and also include requirements relating to the assessment of the family's concerns, resources, and priorities. Specifically, the following definitions are provided:

> *Evaluation* means the procedures used by appropriate qualified personnel to determine a child's initial and continuing eligibility under this part consistent with the definition of "infants and toddlers with disabilities," including determining the status of the child in each of the developmental areas: cognitive development, physical development (including vision and hearing), communication development, social or emotional development, adaptive development.
>
> *Assessment* means the ongoing procedures used by appropriate qualified personnel

> throughout the period of a child's eligibility under this part to identify (i) the child's unique strengths and needs and the services appropriate to meet those needs; and (ii) the resources, priorities, and concerns of the family and the supports and services necessary to enhance the family's capacity to meet the developmental needs of their infant or toddler with a disability. (34 CFR 303.322, Federal Register, July 30, 1993)

Under Part H regulations, *evaluation* refers to the procedures used to determine eligibility; *assessment* refers to the procedures that lead to the development and periodic review of the Individualized Family Service Plan (IFSP). The IFSP, which is a written plan for providing early intervention services, must include the following:

1. Information about the child's status, including a statement of the child's present level of physical development (motor, vision, hearing, and health status), cognitive development, communication development, social or emotional development, and adaptive development.
2. A statement of the family's resources, priorities, and concerns related to enhancing the development of the child. This information is optional and gathered only with parental consent.
3. A statement of the major outcomes expected for the child and the family, and the criteria, procedures, and timelines used to determine the degree to which progress is being made and whether modifications or revisions are needed.
4. A statement of the specific services needed to achieve the outcomes identified.
5. A statement of the natural environments in which services will be provided.
6. A description of the medical and other services the child needs and the funding sources to be used to pay for those services.
7. The projected dates for initiation of the services to be provided and the anticipated duration of the services.
8. The name of the service coordinator who will be responsible for the implementation of the plan and coordination with other agencies.
9. The steps to be taken to support the transition of the child to preschool services under Part B or to other services that might be appropriate.

The IFSP must be reviewed at 6-month intervals or more frequently if needed. Every 12 months the child must be re-evaluated.

Under Part H regulations, the evaluation and assessment of a child (including the assessment of family resources, priorities, and concerns) must be completed and the IFSP meeting with the family must be held within 45 days after the referral is received by the responsible agency. In addition, evaluation and assessment must be based on "informed clinical opinion" and should not be limited to the use of test scores. See Chapter 3 for further discussion of informed clinical opinion. Part H regulations also specify procedures for conducting the assessment of family resources, priorities, and concerns. These procedures are presented in Chapter 8 of this text.

Each agency responsible for administering the Part H program must ensure that nondiscriminatory procedures are followed in evaluation and assessment. Specifically, each agency must ensure that:

1. Tests and other evaluation materials and procedures are administered in the native language of the parents or other mode of communication unless it is clearly not feasible to do so.
2. Any assessment and evaluation procedures and materials that are used are selected and administered so as not to be racially or culturally discriminatory.
3. No single procedure is used as the sole criterion for determining a child's eligibility.
4. Evaluations and assessments are conducted by qualified personnel.

Autism means a developmental disability significantly affecting verbal and nonverbal communication and social interaction, generally evident before age 3, that adversely affects educational performance. Other characteristics often associated with autism are engagement in repetitive activities and stereotyped movements, resistance to environmental change or change in daily routines, and unusual responses to sensory experiences. The term does not apply if a child's educational performance is adversely affected primarily because the child has a serious emotional disturbance, as defined below.

Deafness means a hearing impairment which is so severe that the child is impaired in processing linguistic information through hearing, with or without amplification, that adversely affects educational performance.

Deaf-blindness means concomitant hearing and visual impairments, the combination of which causes such severe communication and other developmental and educational problems that they cannot be accommodated in special education programs solely for children with deafness or children with blindness.

Hearing impairment means an impairment in hearing, whether permanent or fluctuating, which adversely affects a child's educational performance but that is not included under the definition of "deafness" in this section.

Mental retardation means significantly subaverage general intellectual functioning existing concurrently with deficits in adaptive behavior and manifested during the developmental period that adversely affects a child's educational performance.

Multiple disabilities means concomitant impairments (such as mental retardation-blindness, mental retardation-orthopedic impairment, etc.), the combination of which causes such severe educational problems that they cannot be accommodated in special education programs solely for one of the impairments. The term does not include deaf-blindness.

Orthopedic impairment means a severe orthopedic impairment which adversely affects a child's educational performance. The term includes impairments caused by congenital anomaly (e.g., clubfoot, absence of some member, etc.), impairments caused by disease (e.g., poliomyelitis, bone tuberculosis, etc.), and impairments from other causes (e.g., cerebral palsy, amputations, and fractures or burns which cause contractures).

Other health impairments means having limited strength, vitality, or alertness due to chronic or acute health problems such as a heart condition, tuberculosis, rheumatic fever, nephritis, asthma, sickle cell anemia, hemophilia, epilepsy, lead poisoning, leukemia, or diabetes that adversely affects a child's educational performance.

FIGURE 1.4
IDEA definitions of disabilities (Part B)
Source: IDEA section 121a(5b); 34CFR 300.7.

Serious emotional disturbance is a term that means a condition exhibiting one or more of the following characteristics over a long period of time and to a marked degree that adversely affects educational performance:

- an inability to learn which cannot be explained by intellectual, sensory, or health factors;
- an inability to build or maintain satisfactory interpersonal relationships with peers and teachers;
- inappropriate types of behavior or feelings under normal circumstances;
- a general pervasive mood of unhappiness or depression; or
- a tendency to develop physical symptoms or fears associated with personal or school problems.

The term includes schizophrenia. The term does not apply to children who are socially maladjusted, unless it is determined that they have a serious emotional disturbance.

Specific learning disability means a disorder in one or more of the basic psychological processes involved in understanding or in using language, spoken or written, that may manifest itself in an imperfect ability to listen, think, speak, read, write, spell, or do mathematical calculations. The term includes such conditions as perceptual disabilities, brain injury, minimal brain dysfunction, dyslexia, and developmental aphasia. The term does not apply to children who have learning problems that are primarily the result of visual, hearing, or motor disabilities, of mental retardation, or emotional disturbance, or of environmental, cultural, or economic disadvantage.

Speech or language impairment means a communication disorder such as stuttering, impaired articulation, a language impairment or a voice impairment that adversely affects a child's educational performance.

Traumatic brain injury means an acquired injury to the brain caused by an external physical force, resulting in total or partial functional disability or psychosocial impairment, or both, that adversely affects a child's educational performance. The term applies to open or closed head injuries resulting in impairments in one or more areas, such as cognition; language; memory; attention; reasoning; abstract thinking; judgment; problem-solving; sensory, perceptual, and motor abilities; psychosocial behavior; physical function; information processing; and speech. The term does not apply to brain injuries that are congenital or degenerative, or brain injuries induced by birth trauma.

Visual impairment including blindness means an impairment in vision that, even with correction, adversely affects a child's educational performance. The term includes both partial sight and blindness.

FIGURE 1.4
Continued

Part B Regulations Pertaining to Assessment

The regulations for preschool children are those that apply to school-age children as well. Assessment procedures for preschool children lead to the determination of eligibility and to the development of the Individual Education Plan (IEP), which must contain the following:

1. A description of the child's present level of performance.
2. A statement of annual goals for the child, including short-term instructional objectives for each goal.
3. A statement of services needed by the child.
4. Projected dates when services will begin and the anticipated duration of the services.
5. Objective criteria and evaluation procedures for determining whether short-term instructional objectives are being achieved.

The IEP must be completed within 30 days of the time the child is determined to be eligible for services. A review of the IEP must occur annually, and a complete re-evaluation of the child must occur every 3 years.

Nondiscriminatory procedures for Part B are specified in Section 300.532, which states that state educational agencies must ensure that:

1. Tests and other evaluation materials are provided and administered in the child's native language or other mode of communication unless it is clearly not feasible to do so.
2. Tests have been validated for the specific purpose for which they are used.
3. Tests are administered by trained personnel in conformance with the instructions provided by their producer.
4. Tests are selected and administered so as to ensure that when a test is administered to a child with impaired sensory, manual, or speaking skills, the results accurately reflect the child's aptitude or achievement level or whatever other factors the test purports to measure rather than reflecting the child's impaired sensory, manual, or speaking skills (except where those skills are the factors that the test purports to measure).
5. No single procedure is used as the sole criterion for determining an appropriate educational program for a child. The assessment is made by a multidisciplinary team or group of persons, including at least one teacher or other specialist with knowledge in the area of the suspected disability. The child is assessed in all areas related to the suspected disability, including, if appropriate, health, vision, hearing, social and emotional status, general intelligence, academic performance, communicative status, and motor abilities.

Additional Legislation

In addition to the Individuals with Disabilities Education Act, there are at least three other federal laws that are important to the field of Early Intervention/Early Childhood Special Education. Professionals need to be aware of each of these laws and how they might impact young children with special needs.

Head Start Head Start is a federally funded early education program designed for children from low-income families. In 1972, P.L. 92-424 (the Economic Opportunity Amendments) mandated that Head Start programs also serve children with disabilities. No fewer than 10% of the children enrolled in Head Start must be children with disabilities. Since the passage of 99-457, there has been a good deal of confusion about how Head Start services and services through the public schools for preschool children with disabilities would interface. On January 21, 1993, 45 CFR Part 1308 was published in the Federal Register. This regulation, which provided specific performance standards, including eligibility criteria, for serving children with disabilities in Head Start, clarifies the relationship between Head Start and IDEA, Part B and identifies steps that local Head Start programs must take to provide a collaborative relationship with local public school programs. A discussion of the content of this regulation is unfortunately beyond the scope of this chapter. The reader is referred to a document published by the Division for Early Childhood of the Council for Exceptional Children, *New Opportunities for Collaboration,* for further information.

ADA The Americans with Disabilities Act (ADA), which was signed into law by President Bush on July 26, 1990, guarantees equal opportunity for individuals with disabilities in public accommodations, employment, transportation, state and local government services, and telecommunications. Title III of the ADA prohibits discrimination against individuals with disabilities in public accommodations, which includes child-care facilities. Under this law, child-care providers cannot legally deny services to a child with a disability unless it is determined that serving the child will result in an undue burden or hardship. While the ADA does not provide guidelines or requirements for assessment for early intervention, it certainly will have an impact on how services will be provided. According to Craig and Haggart (1994), as a result of the ADA, the goal of early intervention will shift toward functional independence in natural environments instead of performance within the normal range as measured by an assessment instrument. This shift will require assessment of environments as well as assessment of child performance. In addition, it will require increased collaboration between child-care professionals and early intervention personnel. Assessment of environments is discussed in Chapter 9 of this book; collaboration is discussed in Chapter 3. Craig and Haggart (1994) suggest that early intervention personnel need to be proactive to facilitate the inclusion of young children with disabilities and their families into community environments.

> The ADA needs to be celebrated as a means of returning to the larger community the gifts and resources of persons previously segregated, rather than limiting the ADA to what the community "has to do" to avoid punishment. Early intervention therapists are in a powerful position to promote this vision of reciprocity by working with child-care professionals to facilitate the inclusion and participation of children with disabilities in family and center-based programs. (Craig & Haggart, 1994, p. 19)

Section 504 of the Rehabilitation Act

Section 504 of the Rehabilitation Act became law in 1973. Since its passage, it has been enforced primarily in relation to employment for individuals with handicaps. Recently, however, the Office of Civil Rights (OCR), which enforces Section 504, has increasingly focused its requirements on the public education system. Section 504 prohibits discrimination against students with handicaps. The population of children who are considered to be handicapped under Section 504 overlaps with but is not the same as the population of students who are considered to be disabled under IDEA. All children who are identified as being disabled under IDEA are also protected under Section 504, and by fulfilling responsibilities under IDEA, school districts are also meeting the requirements of Section 504. However, there are some students who are *not* eligible for IDEA services who are considered handicapped under Section 504. Handicapped students under Section 504 are defined as those having any physical or mental impairment that substantially limits one or more major life activities including learning. For example, a student with Attention Deficit Hyperactivity Disorder (ADHD) may not meet the criteria for IDEA but would qualify under Section 504. Similarly, a student with arthritis may not be in need of special education services under IDEA but may be considered handicapped under Section 504. If a school district believes that a student is handicapped according to Section 504 and needs special accommodations or services in the regular educational setting, the student must be evaluated to determine eligibility. If the student is deemed eligible, a plan for the delivery of all needed services must be developed.

Section 504 clearly applies to children who are in kindergarten or the elementary grades; however, the relationship of 504 to preschool children is not as clear. Most states do not provide a publicly supported educational program to preschool children. When no public education is provided to any children, it is difficult to substantiate discrimination against children who are handicapped. Therefore, unless a state does provide publicly supported preschool services, Section 504 will probably not apply to preschoolers.

THE FUNCTIONS OF ASSESSMENT

Assessment is a generic term that refers to the process of gathering information for the purpose of making decisions. Several different types of decisions need to be made in working with young children with special needs. The purpose of any assessment endeavor must be clear to all involved because it will determine the questions that are asked and the instruments and procedures that are used. This textbook addresses four distinct functions of assessment: identification (including screening), diagnosis and determination of eligibility, assessment for program planning and service delivery, and monitoring of child progress during intervention. Each of these is described in Table 1.1. *Assessment,* as a general term, may refer to any of these functions and will be used generically throughout this text.

Screening is a procedure used to identify infants and preschoolers who may be in need of a more comprehensive evaluation. Screening is typically completed in a brief period of time. It usually does not provide comprehensive quantitative information relative to the child's developmental status, but rather indicates whether or not further evaluation is necessary; it facilitates the identification of infants and young children who need intervention so that services may begin as early as possible. In many states, it is part of the process of Child Find, which is mandated by federal legislation and requires states to develop and implement programs for finding and identifying young children with special needs. By kindergarten or first grade, most children are enrolled in a school program from which referral for special services will be possible. However, because the population of children under age 5 is not typically as accessible, programs designed to identify young children who need early intervention must be established. Additional information on Child Find and screening is presented in Chapter 5.

Assessment for *diagnosis and determination of eligibility* is employed to determine the presence of conditions that may qualify a child for early intervention services. Generally, medical conditions, general developmental functioning, sensory and motor functioning, and adaptive behavior in the child's typical environment are addressed. The outcome of these procedures may lead to a definitive diagnosis, such as cerebral palsy, a sensory impairment, or an identified syndrome. In many cases, however, identifying a specific condition that is the cause of the presenting problems may not be possible. In such cases, the identification of a delay in development or factors that put the child at risk of delay in development may be the outcome. The assessment team must also determine whether the child qualifies for EI/ECSE services according to the eligibility criteria followed by their particular state. As was discussed earlier, eligibility criteria differ from state to state. A child who does not qualify for EI/ECSE services in a state may qualify for other types of state or federal programs. The result of diagnostic assessment, therefore, should not only be determination of eligibility for EI/ECSE services, but should also include recommendations for other services that may facilitate the child's development. Results should also provide a solid foundation of information to assist in assessment for program planning.

Assessment for *program planning* refers to those procedures used by the assessment team to develop the IFSP or IEP and to revise these plans as necessary. The outcome of assessment for program planning is the identification of special services needed by the child and the family, the service delivery format that will be used (including location of services), and the delineation of intervention objectives as specified in the IFSP or IEP. Guidelines for conducting assessments for instructional planning are described throughout this text. In addition, Chapter 17 describes procedures and models for using assessment results to plan and implement individualized intervention plans.

Assessment continues to be an important activity for early intervention professionals after the IEP or IFSP is completed. The child's progress toward meeting the specified objectives must be *monitored* on a regular basis. Information collected on an ongoing basis allows the team to determine to what extent progress is being made toward goals and objectives and, as a result, to identify changes that should be made in intervention strategies or objectives. When such data is aggregated across all of the children in a program, it may be possible to measure overall program impact. Methods for monitoring child progress and for evaluating program impact are discussed in Chapters 16 and 2 respectively.

ASSESSMENT CHALLENGES IN EI/ECSE

All of the assessment functions delineated above pose challenges for professionals in early intervention—challenges related to the nature of young children with disabilities, the current status of assessment instruments, and the current status of professional preparation.

The Nature of Young Children with Disabilities

As the field of early intervention has grown over the past two decades, it has become increasingly apparent that effective procedures for assessing young children with disabilities differ considerably from what might be described as traditional assessment approaches. Professionals working with young children, whether a disability is present or not, become very aware of characteristics that make young children poor candidates for assessments that are conducted by unfamiliar adults in unfamiliar settings and that require children to do what the adults ask them to do. Infants and toddlers have limited verbal abilities and limited attention spans; in addition, they may show considerable anxiety when interacting with unfamiliar adults. Preschool children may have more verbal ability and a bit longer attention spans, but may not yet understand the need to follow adults' directions and also may be uncomfortable interacting with unfamiliar adults. Those charged with the assessment of young children, therefore, must determine how to assess them in ways that yield a true picture of their abilities.

A procedural error made frequently in the past, which unfortunately continues to occur, is reliance on procedures utilized with older children (Neisworth & Bagnato, in press). The resulting scenario was aptly described by Linder (1990) as she asks the reader to imagine himself or herself as a 3-year-old child who is being evaluated because of suspected developmental delays. Experiencing traditional assessment procedures as a 3-year-old emphasizes the problems inherent in using traditional approaches with young children.

> After a necessary potty break and a few tears, the lady lets you see your Mommy and Daddy. But not for long. Here comes another lady to take you to another little room with another table and chairs and different pictures on the wall. This lady doesn't talk much. She just

TABLE 1.1
Assessment for Decision Making

Decision	Assessment Type	Relevant Questions	Measurement Practices
Determine whether to refer the child for additional assessment	Screening	Does developmental screening indicate potential for developmental delay or disability?	Use of norm-referenced, developmental screening measures that address multiple domains, are implemented reliably, have concurrent validity with in-depth measures, and are nondiscriminatory.
		Does hearing or visual screening indicate potential sensory impairments or losses?	Use of screening measures that have specific criteria for audiological/visual examinations.
		Does health screening and physical examination indicate need for medical attention?	Conducted by nurse, pediatrician, or other health professional.
Determine whether the child has a developmental delay or disability	Diagnostic	Does a developmental delay or disability exist? If so, what is the nature and extent of the delay or disability?	Measures and procedures depend on the suspected delay or disability but frequently involve standardized measures conducted by professionals who are specifically trained to use them. Frequently are comprehensive and conducted in clinical settings.
Determine whether the child is eligible for special services	Eligibility	Does the child meet the criteria specified by the state to receive specialized services?	Frequently synonymous with diagnostic assessments because children are made eligible for services based on established diagnosis; however, may also include other requirements.

Determine what the child should be taught	Instructional program planning assessment	What is the child's current level of developmental functioning?	Curriculum-based assessment measures that address multiple developmental domains are used and supplemented with direct observation of children in multiple natural situations, informal testing, and interviews with others, including parents. Frequently conducted by teachers and relevant therapists.
		What does the child need to be independent in the classroom, home, and community?	Direct observation in these settings and interviews with family members.
		What are the effects of adaptations and assistance on child performance?	Direct observation, informal assessment with various levels and types of assistance in natural settings.
		What usual patterns of responding and what relationships with environmental variables appear to influence child performance?	Direct observation, informal assessment, interviews with others, reinforcement preference assessment, trial use of various instructional procedures, and clinical judgment.

TABLE 1.1
Continued

Decision	Assessment Type	Relevant Questions	Measurement Practices
Determine where the child should receive services and what services are needed	Service delivery	What does the child need?	This question is answered by the results of the instructional program planning assessment.
		Which of the possible placement options could best meet the child's needs?	Direct observation, rating scales, and interviews are used to determine the characteristics and potential of each possible placement, and parents are interviewed concerning their preferences.
		Does the child need specialized services, such as speech/language therapy, physical therapy, occupational therapy, or dietary supervision?	Based on assessments conducted by registered or licensed therapists in these various disciplines; sometimes norm-referenced measures are used and are supplemented by observation and clinical judgment.
Determine whether the child is making adequate progress in learning important skills	Monitoring of instructional program	What is the child's usual performance of important skills?	Data collected from unstructured and structured observations of the child in natural contexts; data collected from periodic probes of the child's performance.
		Is the child using important skills outside the classroom?	Reports by family members of the child's application of important skills.

Source: From "Reaching Potentials of Children with Special Needs" by M. Wolery, P. Strain, and D. Bailey, in S. Bredekamp and T. Rosegrant (Eds.), *Reaching Potentials: Appropriate Curriculum and Assessment for Young Children,* 1992, Washington, DC: National Association for the Education of Young Children. Copyright 1992 by NAEYC. Reprinted by permission.

keeps putting pictures in front of you and asking you what they are. Many of the pictures are things that you have seen, but you just don't know what to call them. So you look down at the floor and up at the pictures on the wall. You pull on your shirt and wiggle a lot. You wish this lady would quit with the pictures. You've seen more than enough pictures. Then the lady gets another suitcase, only it's a different color. She pulls out a couple of toys at a time and tells you what she wants you to do with them. Some of these are neat toys and you'd really like to play with them. Every time you start to do something other than what the lady told you to do, however, she takes the toys away. This lady sure is stingy. You are getting tired, so you put your head down on the table. The lady makes you sit up. Finally, she is through. She takes you back to your Mommy and Daddy and tells them that you were "somewhat resistant." (Linder, 1990, pp. 9-10)

The presence of a disability can greatly complicate the task of assessment. The existence of a sensory or motor impairment, for example, requires a method of interacting with the young child that incorporates adaptations into the assessment. The child with a hearing impairment may utilize an alternative method of communication, such as total communication or cued speech, which requires particular skill on the part of the examiner. The child with a visual impairment may also need to use an alternative sensory modality (touch) in exploring assessment materials. The child with a physical impairment may have verbal and motor abilities so limited that it becomes very difficult to find a modality that will allow observation of his or her abilities.

The challenge of assessment, however, is not limited to just finding alternative methods of communication for children with disabilities. The developmental impact of the disability must also be taken into consideration. The child with the hearing impairment has missed out on the verbal environment so critical to language development. The child with the visual impairment has missed out on the visual experiences that form the basis of many concepts. The child with the physical impairment may have been unable to impact his or her environment in any consistent way and therefore may have become rather passive. These are examples of secondary effects of disabilities that may affect the development of a young child.

The assessment of young children with disabilities can be likened to the task that faces a detective. There may be little or no previous information on the children. Certainly, there will be gaps in our information. Sometimes it is only through close observation that we become alerted to the presence of less obvious disabilities or delays. Therefore the process is very much one of observing, forming hypotheses, and testing those hypotheses through more observation. In fact, assessment is a never ending, ongoing process throughout the infant, toddler, and preschool years of early intervention as we gain more and more information on the impact of biological and environmental factors on a child's development.

Measurement Challenges

A major challenge to those responsible for the assessment of young children with special needs is the small number of appropriate instruments for use with this population. A handful of instruments have traditionally been used in assessing young children; their relatively small number has resulted in their use even when they are not appropriate. For example, the Denver II (Frankenburg et al., 1990), formerly the Denver Developmental Screening Test, an instrument that has been available for quite a few years, is a developmental screening tool and is not intended for use in determining eligibility or in developing intervention plans. However, it has been used for both of these purposes. The Bayley Scales of Infant Development (Bayley, 1969, 1993) also has been available for a number of years. The first edition of the Bayley was designed for use with children up to the age of 30 months. However, because few instruments were available that included items for this young population, the Bayley was used (misused) in assessing children who were older than 30 months but who functioned developmentally younger than 30 months. The Developmental Activities Screening Inventory (Fewell & Langley, 1984) is a screening tool, but because it yields developmental age scores, it has also been used for eligibility and program planning. As indicated earlier, laws governing both infant/toddler and preschool services state that a test must be validated for the purpose for which it is used (Federal Register, 1992, Section 300.532). It is incumbent upon the individual who is administering a test to be sure its use is valid for the child being assessed and for the designated purpose of assessment.

Some instruments used in EI/ECSE have been developed for use in early intervention programs but have not undergone rigorous evaluation procedures. Therefore, no information is available on their reliability or validity. Furthermore, some of them allow the generation of developmental age scores when, in fact, they have never been normed on a representative sample of children (Meisels, 1991). In other words, there is no normative population from which to derive a developmental age score. Frequently these instruments rely on developmental milestones identified by other instruments or research studies to be used as norms. Clearly, the challenges presented in the assessment of young children with special needs requires professionals who have solid clinical skills in assessment and a knowledge base that allows them to judge the quality of assessment instruments critically. Chapter 2 includes information on test construction, reliability, and validity that will help the reader evaluate assessment instruments.

A major challenge in measurement in EI/ECSE has been the problems associated with the use of intelligence testing with infants and young children with disabilities (Neisworth & Bagnato, 1992). Research has shown that intelligence tests are poor at predicting future cognitive abilities of infants and young children (Honzik, 1976; Maistro & German, 1986; McCall, 1979). Although we have known this for some time, intelligence tests continue to be used. Recently, however, there has been increasing objection to their use in EI/ECSE. Neisworth and Bagnato (1992), in fact, have suggested that early intelligence testing "must be indicted, tried and convicted for malpractice" (p. 1).

It is interesting to speculate why intelligence tests continue to be used in spite of their shortcomings. Most certainly, their use is supported in some states by eligibility requirements, as discussed previously (Danaher, 1992, 1994; Meisels, 1991). A recent survey of psychologists by Bagnato and Neisworth (1994) found that psychologists continue to use intelligence tests with young children although their use is recognized to be problematic. The psychologists surveyed indicated that administrators require the use of intelligence tests and that they had received insufficient training on alternative assessment techniques. A more detailed discussion of issues and procedures for assessing cognitive skills is presented in Chapter 10. Alternative methods for assessment other than standardized tests are discussed in Chapter 3.

The Challenge of Professional Preparation

The field of early intervention has faced severe shortages of qualified personnel from its inception. The passage of P.L. 99-457 in 1986 intensified the need for qualified personnel in Early Intervention/Early Childhood Special Education and related disciplines all across the country. Almost a decade after the passage of this law, the shortage is still being felt.

A study by Johnson and Beauchamp (1987) reported rather disturbing results relative to existing personnel competence in early intervention settings. Of 105 early childhood special education teachers who were surveyed, 50% indicated that they were using a particular instrument because it was the only one they knew of or because it was the one that had always been used in the intervention program. These teachers were clearly not matching assessment instruments or strategies to the needs of children. Even more disturbing was the finding that 20% of the teachers reported using screening tests to develop instructional programs. Another example of the lack of adequate skill in the area of assessment was reported by Bailey, Vandiviere, Dellinger, and Munn (1987), who found that teachers of young children with disabilities made many errors in scoring a standardized assessment tool. Of 79 teachers who administered the Battelle Developmental Inventory (Newborg, Stock, Wnek, Guidubaldi, & Svinicki, 1984) to 247 children, only 11 teachers (14.5%) and 50 protocols (20.2%) were free of scoring errors. Most errors were simple math miscalculations, failure to establish a basal, or errors in crediting the child for points below the basal.

Beyond the basic skills and knowledge needed for selecting and administering assessment instruments, there are other areas of competence that are needed by EI/ECSE personnel but are frequently lacking in professionals who serve young children with special needs. Perhaps the most glaring need here is the ability to work collaboratively with other professionals and parents. Since the passage of P.L. 99-457, it has been evident that early intervention personnel need to develop skills in working collaboratively with families and other professionals (McCollum & Thorp, 1988; McCollum, McLean, McCartan, & Kaiser, 1989). What has also become evident is that most early intervention professionals have primarily been trained to work with children and have received little training in collaboration with others (Bailey, Simeonsson, Yoder, & Huntington, 1990; Bailey, Palsha, & Simeonsson, 1991). Clearly much work remains to be done in developing and implementing preservice and inservice training programs that effectively address this need. The issue of collaboration is addressed throughout this textbook and is highlighted in Chapter 3.

EMERGING TRENDS

Assessment procedures for young children with special needs have historically been most strongly influenced by the traditions and legislation governing assessment in special education. A strong psychometric tradition has prevailed in special education, and this tradition has also been relatively strong in Early Intervention/Early Childhood Special Education. However, in recent years, several emerging trends have served to change the procedures recommended for assessment of young children with special needs (Neisworth & Bagnato, in press). These trends are a direct result of years of clinical experience with infants and young children and will be evident throughout the chapters of this book.

One trend is the very high priority now placed on family-centered assessment and intervention. Chapter 3 includes a discussion of the importance now placed on family participation in the assessment process. Chapter 8 is devoted to strategies for the assessment of family resources, priorities, and concerns as legislated by P.L. 99-457 and P.L. 102-119.

A second trend is the emerging emphasis on assessment in the natural environment, or ecologically sound assessment practices (Barnett, Macmann, & Carey, 1992). Originally driven by years of clinical experience and research that demonstrated the shortcomings of formal standardized assessment, this movement has been augmented by a relatively recent move toward closer collaboration with early childhood education, a discipline strongly in support of assessment of children's behavior in familiar environments and under typical circumstances (NAEYC, 1986, 1988; NAEYC & NAECS/SDE, 1991). Chapter 3 includes a discussion of the variety of strategies that have evolved as a result of efforts to ensure that assessment is ecologically valid. Each chapter of the text that addresses a particular domain also includes strategies for assessment in the natural environment.

A third trend is the importance that has been placed on interdisciplinary assessment strategies, which have been derived from the realization that development cannot realistically be separated into isolated and separate domains; in the infant and young child, developmental domains are interdependent. There are distinct advantages to assessment that is conducted by a team of professionals representing various disciplines who work closely together rather than independently. Team assessment strategies are discussed in Chapter 3. It should be pointed out that this text does present information on assessment separated into chapters by developmental domains. It is recognized that assessing specific areas of development is an artificial undertaking due to the interrelatedness of the developmental areas. However, collecting information in this manner and then reintegrating it through a team effort allows insight into an individual child's development that can facilitate the assessment process.

The purpose of this book is to provide information needed by professionals to engage in assessment activities for identification, eligibility determination, program planning, and program evaluation relative to serving young children with special needs. We believe it represents best practice at this point in time. However, work should continue in refining and improving assessment strategies. Certainly what is considered best practice now will change as new information is gained.

SUMMARY OF KEY CONCEPTS

- Assessment is an important and ongoing responsibility of professionals who work with young children. Assessment activities are necessary in order to locate and identify children who need early intervention services, plan appropriate intervention strategies, and monitor the effectiveness of services provided.
- Federal law provides a general definition of eligibility for services as well as general guidelines for the assessment process for both infant/toddler programs and preschool programs. Each state and territory then is responsible for developing the exact criteria and procedures that will be followed.
- Assessment of young children with special needs can be challenging due to the nature of young children, limitations of the assessment instruments currently available, and limitations in the area of professional preparation.
- A strong psychometric tradition has been prevalent in the assessment of children with disabilities. This tradition has been affected, however, by current trends toward family-centered assessment, utilizing natural environments, and a collaborative approach by all team members.

REFERENCES

Bagnato, S., & Neisworth, J. (1994). A national study of the social and treatment "invalidity" of intelligence testing for early intervention. *The School Psychology Quarterly, 9*(2), 81–102.

Bailey, D. B., Palsha, S., & Simeonsson, R. J. (1991). Professional skills, concerns and perceived importance of work with families in early intervention. *Exceptional Children, 58*(2), 156–165.

Bailey, D. B., Simeonsson, R. J., Yoder, D., & Huntington, G. S. (1990). Preparing professionals to serve infants and toddlers with handicaps and their families: An integrative analysis across eight disciplines. *Exceptional Children, 57*(1), 26–35.

Bailey, D. B., Vandiviere, P., Dellinger, J., & Munn, D. (1987). The Battelle Developmental Inventory: Teacher perceptions and implementation data. *Journal of Psychoeducational Assessment, 3,* 217–226.

Barnett, D. W., Macmann, G. M., & Carey, K. T. (1992). Early intervention and the assessment of developmental skills: Challenges and directions. *Topics in Early Childhood Special Education, 12*(1), 21–43.

Bayley, N. (1969). *Bayley Scales of Infant Development.* New York: Psychological Corporation.

Bayley, N. (1993). *Bayley Scales of Infant Development-II.* San Antonio, TX: Psychological Corporation.

Craig, S. E., & Haggart, A. G. (1994). Including all children: The ADA's challenge to early intervention. *Infants and Young Children, 7*(2), 15–19.

Danaher, J. (1992, November). Preschool special education eligibility classifications and criteria. *NEC-TAS Notes, 6.*

Danaher, J. (1994). *Four types of preschool special education eligibility classifications in the states and the District of Columbia.* Chapel Hill, NC: National Early Childhood Technical Assistance System.

Division for Early Childhood. (1994). *New opportunities for collaboration: A policy and implementation resource and training manual for the Head Start regulations for children with disabilities.* Reston, VA: Council for Exceptional Children.

Fewell, R., & Langley, M. B. (1984). *DASI-II: Developmental Activities Screening Inventory.* Austin, TX: PRO-ED.

Frankenburg, W. K., Dodds, J., Archer, P., Bresnick, B., Mashka, P., Edelman, N., & Shapiro, H. (1990). *Denver II.* Denver, CO: Denver Developmental Materials, Inc.

Honzik, M. P. (1976). Value and limitations of infant tests: An overview. In M. Lewis (Ed.), *Origins of intelligence* (pp. 59–95). New York: Plenum Press.

Johnson, L. J., & Beauchamp, K. (1987). Preschool assessment measures: What are teachers using? *Journal of the Division for Early Childhood, 12,* 70–76.

Linder, T. W. (1990). *Transdisciplinary play-based assessment: A functional approach to working with young children.* Baltimore, MD: Paul H. Brookes.

Maistro, A., & German, M. (1986). Reliability, predictive validity, and interrelationships of early assessment indices used with developmentally delayed infants and children. *Journal of Clinical Psychology, 15,* 327–332.

McCall, R. B. (1979). The development of intellectual functioning in infancy and the prediction of later IQ. In S. D. Osofsky (Ed.), *The handbook of infant development* (pp. 707–741). New York: Wiley.

McCollum, J., McLean, M., McCartan, K., & Kaiser, C. (1989). Recommendations for certification of early childhood special educators. *Journal of Early Intervention, 13*(3), 195–211.

McCollum, J., & Thorp, E. (1988). Training of infant specialists: A look to the future. *Infants and Young Children, 1*(2), 55–65.

McLean, M., & Odom, S. (1993). Practices for young children with and without disabilities: A comparison of DEC and NAEYC identified practices. *Topics in Early Childhood Special Education, 13*(3), 274–292.

Meisels, S. (1991). Dimensions of early identification. *Journal of Early Intervention, 15*(1), 26–35.

National Association for the Education of Young Children (NAEYC). (1986). Position statement on developmentally appropriate practice in early childhood programs serving children from birth through age 8. *Young Children, 41*(6), 4–29.

National Association for the Education of Young Children (NAEYC). (1988). Position statement on standardized testing of young children 3 through 8 years of age. *Young Children, 46*(3), 21–38.

National Association for the Education of Young Children and the National Association of Early Childhood Specialists in State Departments of Education (NAEYC & NAECS/SDE). (1991). Guidelines for appropriate curriculum content and assessment in programs serving children ages 3 through 8. *Young Children, 46*(3), 21–38.

Neisworth, J. T., & Bagnato, S. J. (in press). Assessment for early intervention: Emerging themes and practices. In S. Odom & M. McLean (Eds.), *Recommended practices in early intervention.* Austin, TX: PRO-ED.

Neisworth, J. G., & Bagnato, S. J. (1992). The case against intelligence testing in early intervention. *Topics in Early Childhood Special Education, 12*(1), 1–20.

Newborg, J., Stock, J. R., Wnek, L., Guidubaldi, J., & Svinicki, J. (1984). *The Battelle Developmental Inventory.* Allen, TX: DLM/Teaching Resources.

Shackelford, J. (1992, October). State/jurisdiction eligibility definitions for Part H. *NECTAS Notes, 5.*

Shonkoff, J., & Meisels, S. (1991). Defining eligibility for services under Public Law 99-457. *Journal of Early Intervention, 15*(1), 21–25.

Wolery, M., Strain, P., & Bailey, D. (1992). Reaching potentials of children with special needs. In S. Bredekamp & T. Rosegrant (Eds.), *Reaching potentials: Appropriate curriculum and assessment for young children* (Vol. 1). Washington, DC: National Association for the Education of Young Children.

CHAPTER

2

Tests and Test Development

Donald B. Bailey Jr.
Laura A. Nabors
University of North Carolina at Chapel Hill

Child assessment is traditionally associated with the administration of tests, although testing is but one of several strategies for gathering information about children. When properly used and interpreted, however, tests perform important functions. This chapter describes the process of test construction, procedures for summarizing test performance, and considerations in evaluating assessment tools. This information is important for at least three reasons. First, early childhood special educators and other professionals should be able to evaluate and select appropriate measures, and they will need to be able to read and understand the technical manual that accompanies most measures. Second, professionals should be aware of the limitations of existing measures so that results may be interpreted accordingly. Finally, all professionals should be able to understand test scores as reported by other members of the interdisciplinary team, to recognize the limitations of the scores, and to explain the scores to parents.

TEST STANDARDIZATION

A test is a set of standardized tasks presented to a child. The purpose of testing is to determine how well a child performs on the tasks presented. Standardization includes several components: standard materials, administrative procedures, scoring procedures, and score interpretation. The purpose of standardization is to ensure that all children taking the test receive essentially the same experience, perform the same tasks with the same set of materials, receive the same amount of assistance from the evaluator, and are evaluated according to a standard set of criteria. If the same materials, procedures, or scoring criteria are not used for all children, the results will have limited comparability among children.

For example, assume that an item on a test says "Puts together a three-piece puzzle." If no further instructions were provided, it would be up to each evaluator to decide how to administer and score this item. Some might use a simple snowman puzzle, consisting of three circles of different sizes, whereas others might choose an interlocking puzzle. Some would show the child the puzzle as it should look, disassemble it, and ask the child to put it back together, whereas others would simply place the three pieces in front of the child and ask the child to "Put the puzzle together." Some would impose a 1-minute time limit; others would give the child unlimited time. Obviously, such variations in administrative procedures will influence a child's success with this task.

Standardized procedures are essential if test performance is to be compared across children. In testing a child with disabilities, however, rigid application of standardized procedures may result in erroneous conclusions about that child. For example, a test of cognitive skills may require the child to perform many motor or verbal tasks. A child with cerebral palsy may not be able to perform the motor or verbal components of those tasks, in spite of having the cognitive skills needed to do so. In addition, standardized procedures often are difficult to apply to very young children who are easily distracted and sometimes reluctant to participate in a testing session. Teachers and other professionals who assess young children with disabilities *for instructional purposes* should modify items so that the result is an accurate picture of a child's abilities and the supports he or she needs in order to accomplish a task.

TEST CONTENT

A test consists of a set of tasks to which children must respond. How is the content of an assessment tool determined? In part, this is decided by the purpose of the assessment. A screening measure might have different content than would a diagnostic measure. A test of communication skills certainly would differ from a test of self-help skills. At least two approaches may be followed in determining test content: conceptual and statistical. Usually both are incorporated in any item selection process; however, some instruments may weigh one criteria over another, and, in some cases, only one dimension is considered.

Conceptual Criteria

The primary consideration in determining test content is the domain to be tested. For example, if a test developer wanted to create a measure of fine motor skills, several questions would need to be addressed. First, the broad domain of "fine motor" skills would be defined to determine which skills are representative of the domain. For example, *fine motor* might be defined as "any skill involving the use of small muscles." However, this definition might be too broad, since behaviors such as blinking or toe-wiggling all might fit this category. For educational purposes, *fine motor* may be defined as "skills requiring use of the hands or fingers." Regardless of how the domain is conceptualized, it must be defined so that initial decisions can be made regarding the appropriateness of item inclusion.

Second, the developer must consider the major subdomains of the domain to be assessed. For example, fine motor skills would probably include grasping and releasing objects, stacking objects, and using tools such as pencils, scissors, or a spoon. Third, important developmental milestones within each subdomain must be identified. For example, there is a well-defined sequence of milestones in grasping small objects. Finally, the developer may want to attend to functionally important skills within the domain to be assessed. This type of content analysis would focus on fine motor skills likely to be important to the success in home or school environments.

Varying degrees of sophistication and rigor could be applied in the identification of test content. For example, one strategy would be for the developer to include items he or she believed to be important in the domain to be assessed. At a more advanced level, other professionals could be consulted to determine professional consensus as to whether the item was conceptually consistent with the domain under consideration. For example, "experts" in fine motor development could rate a set of items or tasks according to their "fit" within a given domain or subdomain. Other strategies are described in the reliability and validity sections of this chapter.

Statistical Criteria

Once a large pool of potential items has been identified, how are individual items selected? For a criterion-referenced test (one in which a child's performance is compared relative to a body of information), items are selected based on the adequacy with which the items assess the skills in question. A norm-referenced test (one in which a child's performance is compared with that of other children), on the other hand, uses statistical criteria for item inclusion.

For an item to be selected based on statistical criteria, it must develop in a predictable sequence and within a relatively well-defined time frame. Egan and Brown (1986), for example, studied several performance tasks to determine if a predictable developmental sequence emerged. Their data supported use of tasks such as building a tower with 1-inch cubes, copying cube models, copying geometric shapes, and drawing a person in the developmental assessment of children between 18 and 54 months of age. For developmental scales, or those in which a child's age is taken into consideration when deciding where to place items, the most commonly used statistical criteria is to select items passed by 50% of the children at a given age level. In the test construction literature this is referred to as "item difficulty level," and often is reported as $p = .5$, which means that the probability of an individual child of a certain age passing the item is 50%. For example, if approximately half of all children walk by 12 months of age, walking would be an item assigned to the 12-month age level.

Statistical criteria are essential in developing tests to describe a child's developmental status relative to typically developing children. For example, the Bayley Scales of Infant Development (Bayley, 1969) were originally developed to evaluate "a child's developmental status in the first two and one-half years of life" (Bayley, 1969, p. 3). Items initially were selected to "take into account recent theoretical contributions dealing with the nature of early childhood development" (Bayley, 1969, p. 1). Items actually used in the final test were arranged in order of age placement and assigned an age level based on the age at which 50% of sample children passed the item.

In the revised Bayley Scales of Infant Development (Bayley, 1993) the purpose is similar, to assess "the current developmental functioning of infants and children" (p. 1). However, another goal of the BSID-II is to assess children's abilities in order to detect abnormal development and therefore provide information about the "source of the child's delay" (p. 17). Thus, new items are added, administered to a normative group, and statistically analyzed to estimate the developmental status of children with disabilities relative to typically developing children.

Integrating Conceptual and Statistical Criteria

Conceptual and statistical criteria may be used independently or in concert with each other. In an example of combined use, an item pool might be developed based on conceptual criteria and professional validation, and specific items selected from the pool on the basis of statistical criteria. Sometimes items are chosen merely on the basis of statistical criteria with only minor attention to conceptual criteria. For a developer interested only in screening for overall developmental delay, the most important question may be which items best identify children who should be referred for more extensive testing. On the other hand, other test constructors may not be interested in statistical criteria at all in selecting items. For example, if the purpose of an assessment tool is to determine a child's ability to complete certain tasks necessary for success in preschool, then certain items will be included regardless of how they discriminate among children.

Problems in Procedures for Developing Test Content

In evaluating a particular measure, professionals working with children with disabilities should carefully examine the content of the test to determine (a) how the items were derived and (b) whether the content is consistent with programmatic goals for assessment. This information will be critical in deciding whether a particular test will be appropriate for a given purpose. Many instruments currently used by early childhood special educators for instructional purposes provide little in the way of data or description to support the inclusion of items in the measure (Bailey, Jens, & Johnson, 1983).

Professionals should ask questions such as: Who were the specialists who determined test content? What criteria were employed to decide whether an item was important for inclusion? What evidence is given in support of the usefulness of this set of items?

The Battelle Developmental Inventory (Newborg, Stock, Wnek, Guidubaldi, & Svinicki, 1984) incorporated both conceptual and statistical criteria in item selection. Four conceptual criteria were used in the selection of items: "(1) the importance of the behavior in the child's development toward normal functioning in life, (2) the degree of support among professionals and in the literature for identifying the behavior as a milestone in early development,

(3) the acceptance of the skill or behavior among educational practitioners as a critical one for the child to possess or acquire, and (4) the degree to which the behavior is amenable to educational intervention" (Newborg et al., 1984, p. 9). No data are presented, however, to demonstrate how these decisions were made. Bailey, Vandiviere, Dellinger, and Munn (1987) asked 79 teachers who had used the instrument to estimate the percentage of items they considered to be skills that had the potential of being useful now or in the future or were prerequisites for important skills. Overall, the teachers indicated that they considered only about 68% of the items to be good instructional targets. Thus, just because a test developer says the instrument's content is useful for a given purpose does not mean that consumers necessarily agree.

A unique feature of the Battelle Developmental Inventory is the procedure used to select final items. From the pool of items meeting the aforementioned criteria, final items were selected and assigned an age based on statistical criteria. On this particular instrument, the age at which 75% of the children passed an item was the criterion used. Thus it cannot be assumed that every measure will incorporate the 50% criterion.

The point of this section is to encourage professionals to examine closely the procedures used to determine the items included on a particular measure. It is tempting to assume that since the items are part of a published measure, somehow they must be important. However, the items may or may not be consistent with the aims of a local program.

SUMMARIZING TEST PERFORMANCE: NORM-REFERENCED MEASURES

When a test is administered, the child's performance on each item is recorded and assigned a value, referred to as the *item score*. On some tests, the item is simply scored as passed or failed; other tests may allow a range of scores that captures partial or assisted performance. Once an assessment is completed, a *raw score* is derived by summing the item scores. A raw score can usually be computed for subtests as well as for the entire instrument. Although a child's performance on individual items provides important information about specific skills and deficits, raw scores alone are meaningless, except for providing the number of points a child has earned or the number of items passed. For this reason, raw scores are usually converted into some other type of score. The score summary used depends on whether the instrument is a norm-referenced or criterion-referenced measure.

When a single child's performance is compared with a representative sample of children, the result is a *norm-referenced test*. Such instruments are usually developed by administering the measure to a sample of children who are representative of the population to be tested. Examinee's scores can then be compared with the norm group's, allowing an understanding of where the child's performance falls relative to other children his or her age.

The Normative Group

When evaluating the usefulness of a norm-referenced measure, professionals should examine carefully the basis from which norm-referenced scores are derived. Some measures, such as the Learning Accomplishment Profile (Glover, Preminger, & Sanford, 1978; Sanford & Zelman, 1981), the Hawaii Early Learning Profile (Furuno, O'Reilly, Hosaka, Inatsuka, Allman, & Zelsloft, 1979), and the Early Intervention Developmental Profile (Rogers, D'Eugenio, Brown, Donovan, & Lynch, 1981) provide developmental age scores, but the instrument itself was never normed. A developmental age is assigned to each item based on other sources. As Bailey et al. (1987) suggest, this approach can be problematic:

> Since the norms for these measures were gathered in different years and on different populations, their equivalence is uncertain. Furthermore, even if individual item ages may be generally accurate, the summation of individual item scores to obtain a developmental age is more suspect, since total score analyses were never conducted on the particular reconfiguration of items. (p. 2)

If the test developers administered the instrument to a normative sample, several aspects of that process should be evaluated. First, the year that testing was done should be noted. As society advances, expectations for children change and so too does their typical performance. The older a set of norms, the less likely it is to be representative of children today. To compare a child's performance today with the average 4-year-old of 25 years ago would be misleading. Hanson and Smith (1987), for example, compared current administrations of the Griffiths Scales of Mental Development (Extension) (Griffiths, 1970) with the average scores of children in the normative group that was assessed in 1960 and found that the current sample scored more than 11 points higher than the children in the original standardization sample.

McLean, McCormick, and Baird (1991) suggested that the age equivalents obtained on the Griffiths Scale often overestimate developmental levels for infants. They also reported that "the tendency for Griffiths' scores to be inflated could result in some children not qualifying for services when in fact those services should be made available" (p. 343). Therefore, children with disabilities might not receive necessary services if the Griffiths Scales are used for classifying children as having developmental delays. McLean et al. proposed that the Griffiths Scales should be restandardized for American infants to increase their usefulness in diagnosing children with developmental delays for early intervention.

In addition to the year of testing, characteristics of the normative sample should be inspected. Ideally, the sample should be stratified, with proportionate representation of various cultures, geographic regions, gender, income levels, and urban-rural distribution. If the normative group failed to consider one or more of these variables, its representativeness must be questioned. For example, the Developmental Profile II (Alpern, Boll, & Shearer, 1980) collected normative data primarily in Indiana and Washington, raising concerns about its general applicability across the United States. Mardell-Czudnowski and Goldenberg (1984) describe the standardization procedures employed with the DIAL-R, a preschool screening test. The original norming population was located only in Illinois and consisted of only 320 children. The restandardization involved 2,447 children, including approximately equal numbers of boys and girls, and data were gathered proportionately from the four major geographic regions in the United States based on 1980 data from the United States Bureau of the Census. Of the total sample, 44.5% was included from diverse cultures in order to create a large and representative subsample.

It should be noted that children with disabilities are rarely included in any normative group. The rationale is that norms should provide an indication of normal developmental sequences and milestones. It is assumed that the purpose of testing is to determine the nature and extent of deviation from the norm. However, there are some valid arguments suggesting that there is some degree of unfairness inherent in comparing the development of a child with a hearing impairment, for example, with that of hearing children.

Norm-Referenced Scores

At least four types of scores can be used to compare a child's performance with that of a normative group: developmental age scores, developmental quotients, standard scores, and percentile ranks.

Developmental age scores A *developmental age score* tells the average age at which 50% of the normative sample achieved a particular raw score. For example, on a given test, 50% of the normative sample may have achieved a raw score of 75 by 36 months of age. Any child with a raw score of 75 could then be said to be functioning at a 36-month developmental level. A developmental age score may be reported for an entire measure or for individual subscales. A primary advantage of developmental age scores is that they are easily interpretable by parents and professionals. To say that a child is functioning at a 24-month level has a certain degree of simplicity and face validity. A second advantage of developmental age scores is that they usually do reflect positive change or growth in children (Fewell & Sandall, 1986). If a child has a higher raw score total in the spring than he or she did in the fall, the result will be a higher developmental age. Improvements in raw score performance may not necessarily be reflected by improvements in other types of scores. For parents of children with disabilities who are often informed of their child's slow progress, information provided by developmental age scores may confirm developmental gains where other measures may not.

Salvia and Ysseldyke (1985), however, identified four potential problems when using and interpreting developmental age scores. First, two children with the same developmental age score may have performed completely differently. Since the developmental age score depends solely on the raw score and is a global summary of performance, patterns of performance are obscured. For example, the performance of two children on a set of items from the Battelle Developmental Inventory is displayed in Table 2.1. Both children earned the same number of raw score points and thus would receive the same developmental age score. However, they clearly possess different skills.

A second problem is that most developmental ages are extrapolated scores. This means that children of a particular age may not actually have been tested as part of the normative process. The test developer instead used a statistical procedure to extrapolate such scores. Since development often is uneven (Keogh &

TABLE 2.1
Example of How Two Children with Different Profiles Can Receive the Same Raw Score

Child A		Child B	
Item Number	Raw Score	Item Number	Raw Score
1	2	1	2
2	2	2	2
3	2	3	1
4	1	4	0
5	2	5	1
6	0	6	2
7	2	7	1
8	0	8	1
9	0	9	1
10	0	10	0
11	0	11	0
12	0	12	0
Score:	11	Score:	11

Sheehan, 1981), this poses a potential problem. Third, as with all summary scores, to state that a child functions like an average 3-year-old is misleading, since 3-year-olds are quite variable in their abilities. In addition, it must be remembered that by definition, 50% of the population will score below the identified age level and 50% above. Very few children actually perform precisely at the targeted age level. A developmental age is best interpreted as an estimate within a range of performance. Finally, the differences between developmental ages are not necessarily equal. Consequently, clinicians should be cautious when using developmental age to classify children with disabilities as at-risk or delayed because the unequal intervals between different developmental ages may result in misclassification (Banerji, 1992a). At younger ages, a one-year delay may be more significant than at older ages, when one year is not as great a proportion of the child's total age.

Developmental quotient scores A *developmental quotient,* or ratio, *score* is computed by dividing a child's developmental age by his or her chronological age and multiplying the result by 100. The average child who is progressing at an average rate would receive a DQ score of 100, as illustrated below:

$$\frac{\text{37 months (developmental age)}}{\text{37 months (chronological age)}} \times 100 = 100$$

Because a developmental quotient is a ratio of developmental to chronological age, taking into account the child's age at the time of the test, it is usually a relatively stable score. For this reason, developmental quotients are seen by some as a more desirable unit of measurement than developmental age scores in assessing the effects of intervention (Snyder-McLean, 1987).

A primary limitation of the developmental quotient is that as children get older, equal increases in developmental age represent smaller proportions of chronological age and thus result in smaller DQ changes. Furthermore, calculating the developmental quotient tells us nothing about the range and standard deviation of scores. Because of this problem, ratio scores are rarely used, since a developmental quotient of 85 at one age is not directly comparable to a DQ of 85 obtained at another age (Bailey & Rosenthal, 1987). However, they are quite common in the early intervention field.

Standard scores To compensate for problems associated with developmental quotients, most standardized tests now use standard scores for interpreting child performance. A *standard score* is a score that has been transformed to fit a normal curve, with a mean and standard deviation that remain the same across ages. Understanding standard scores first requires an understanding of the normal curve and the standard deviation.

The normal curve is a theoretical distribution of scores that is the model against which actual performance is interpreted. As displayed in Figure 2.1, the normal curve is bell-shaped. It assumes that on any given variable, most individuals will score at or near the mean. As scores deviate from the mean (either greater than or less than), fewer instances of those scores will be observed. A *standard deviation* is a number that helps in interpreting where any particular score falls within a larger distribution of scores by describing how far a score is from the mean. Within the normal curve model, it is assumed that one standard deviation on either side of the mean encompasses approximately 34% of the individuals in a group, whereas two standard deviations on either side of the mean would encompass 48% of the individuals in a group. A standard deviation is always reported as being above or below the mean. Thus to say that a child's score was one standard deviation below the mean would be interpreted to mean that the child's performance was better than

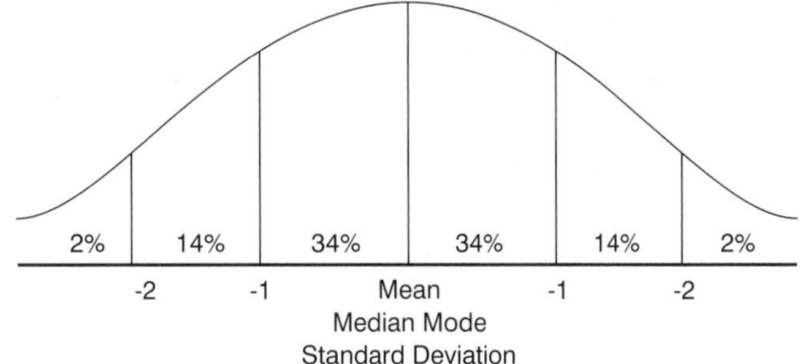

FIGURE 2.1
The normal curve, with percentages of the population expected within standard deviation units

16% of the total population. A score of one standard deviation above the mean would be interpreted to mean the child's performance was better than 84% of the population. This type of information is not available when using developmental quotient scores.

For any given test, the mean and standard deviation of standard scores will be defined by the publisher and developed according to specified criteria. Probably the best-known version of the standard score or deviation score has a mean of 100 and a standard deviation of 15, as found in the Bayley Scales of Infant Development and the Battelle Developmental Inventory. Using this scoring system, a child with a score of 85 would be said to have a score that was one standard deviation below the mean (100 – 15). Other instruments, such as the McCarthy Scales of Children's Abilities and the Stanford-Binet Intelligence Test, have a mean of 100 and a standard deviation of 16. Thus from a population perspective, a score of 70 on the Battelle would be interpreted similarly to a score of 68 on the Stanford-Binet, since both scores are two standard deviations below the mean.

Occasionally a test may report other versions of standard scores, the most common being a z score or a T score. These scores are interpreted in exactly the same fashion as any other standard score, the only difference being in the defined parameters of the score. A *z score* is a standard score distribution with a mean of zero and a standard deviation of one; a *T score* is a standard score distribution with a mean of 50 and a standard deviation of 10. Using the above examples, then, a deviation score of 115, a z score of +1, and a T score of 60 all mean that performance was one standard deviation above the mean.

Percentile ranks A *percentile rank* is another score that provides information regarding an individual's performance relative to the rest of the population. Specifically, percentile ranks tell what percentage of the population performed at or below a given score. Thus, a percentile rank of 50 would be in the average range and is interpreted to mean that the individual's performance exceeded that of 50% of the normative sample.

When the group is divided into fourths, each percentile group is called a *quartile;* when a group is divided into tenths, percentile ranks are called *deciles.* These terms are usually used in a general descriptive fashion, such as "Juan's performance was in the top decile," which means he ranks in the top 10%.

The major limitation of percentile ranks is that they are not on an equal interval scale. The difference between percentile ranks at the extremes is more significant than the difference between percentile ranks closer to the mean, as illustrated by Bailey and Rosenthal (1987). For this reason, percentile ranks should never be used to determine the success of an intervention, nor should they be submitted to any type of data analysis without first converting them to some type of standard score (Sattler, 1982).

Using Extrapolated Scores

When calculating scores for children with disabilities, the examiner often finds the child's raw scores to be too low for the range of scores covered by the specific test. In such cases, two options are available. One is simply to report the child's performance as below the lowest obtainable score on the instrument. For example, a child cannot receive a deviation score below 50 on the Bayley Scales, so many reports would simply state "below 50" as the child's obtained score. A second alternative is to *extrapolate* a score by performing additional calculations. For example, Naglieri (1981) published a table for extrapolating scores on the Bayley Scales down to 28. The Battelle Developmental Inventory provides a formula by which extreme scores may be calculated. The examiner finds the mean and standard deviation for the age level and domain of interest, subtracts the mean from the obtained raw score, and divides the resulting figure by the standard deviation, resulting in a z score. To obtain a deviation score, the z score is multiplied by 15 and then added to 100.

The use of extrapolated scores may be necessary when testing children with disabilities, particularly those with severe disabilities. However, caution should be exercised in interpreting extrapolated scores because they literally are estimates of performance. No children scoring that low were included in the normative sample, and thus the accuracy of extrapolated scores is uncertain. Additionally, extrapolated scores should only be used when a minimum level or score is earned. Wechsler (1974), for example, warned against calculating IQ scores on the Wechsler Intelligence Scale for Children—Revised when the raw scores are not above zero on three verbal and three performance subtests. Bailey et al. (1987) found that when extrapolation procedures were used for children with disabilities assessed with the Battelle Developmental Inventory, 28% of the children in their sample who required score extrapolation received negative deviation quotients, an impossible score. When writing test reports, the examiner should always indicate when scores included in the report were obtained through extrapolation procedures.

Using Norm-Referenced Scores for Evaluating Progress

Professionals in early intervention programs need to be aware that almost all procedures for summarizing child performance have limitations with respect to their use for demonstrating program or intervention effectiveness. While a developmental age score may document improvement, it is difficult to determine what proportion of that improvement is due to maturation. Although developmental quotients may be used to account for the proportion of variance due to maturation, they may not show statistically significant differences between pretest and posttest scores, particularly with older children, because the number of months or years gained becomes a smaller percentage of a child's overall chronological age as he or she gets older. This problem is illustrated in Figure 2.2, which demonstrates how a gain of 6 months in developmental age influences change in the developmental quotient of a child whose developmental age at 12 months was 6 months. As may be seen, as the child gets older, the 6-month gains result in smaller changes in the DQ. Thus two children who gained exactly the same skills and demonstrated the same amount of gain in developmental age would show very different levels of change in DQ scores if they were of different ages.

An example of how different scores can present different pictures of children is evident in a

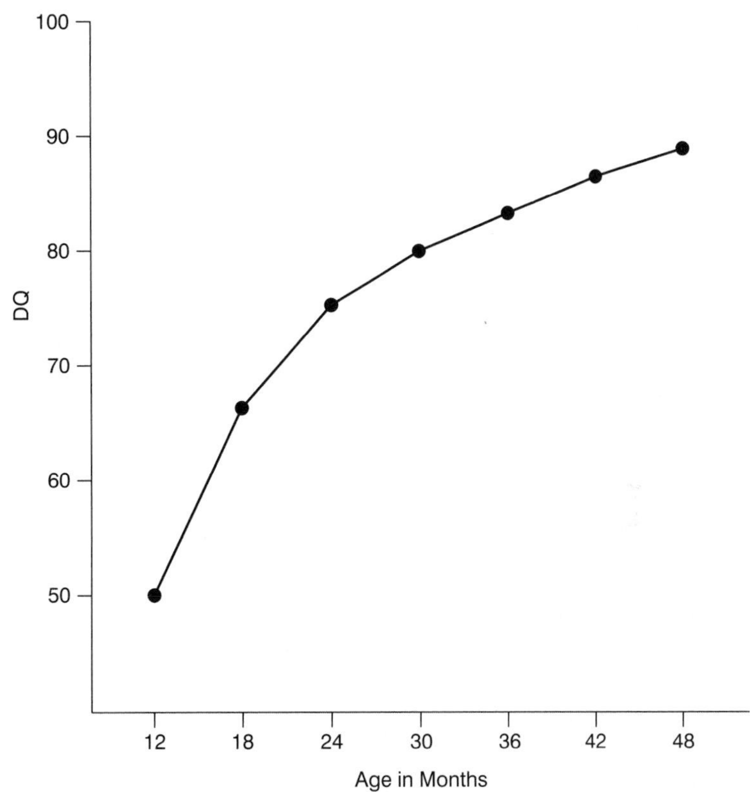

FIGURE 2.2
Effect of a 6-month increase in developmental age scores on the developmental quotient at various ages of a child who at 12 months received an age-equivalent score of 6 months

sample of 129 preschoolers with disabilities who were assessed three times (at 4-month intervals) using the Battelle Developmental Inventory. The results of the assessments when developmental quotient scores and developmental age scores were used are displayed in Figure 2.3 and Figure 2.4. As may be seen, developmental age scores displayed a steady growth or increase in total and domain scores across the 8-month period. Deviation scores showed more fluctuation across assessments, but actually remained relatively stable from Time 1 to Time 3 assessments. These data may be interpreted to mean that children in the sample were not changing their status relative to other children, although they were increasing their ability to perform developmental skills.

SUMMARIZING TEST PERFORMANCE: CRITERION- AND CURRICULUM-REFERENCED MEASURES

Criterion-referenced measures are tests that measure success or failure to meet some previously determined objective. They are made up of items selected because of their importance to school performance or daily living. Because of their importance, items that are missed typically become teaching targets. Criterion-referenced tests do not provide information about where a child's performance falls relative to his or her peers. Rather, they indicate ability with respect to specific skills.

Criterion-referenced tests attempt to determine the child's strengths and weaknesses

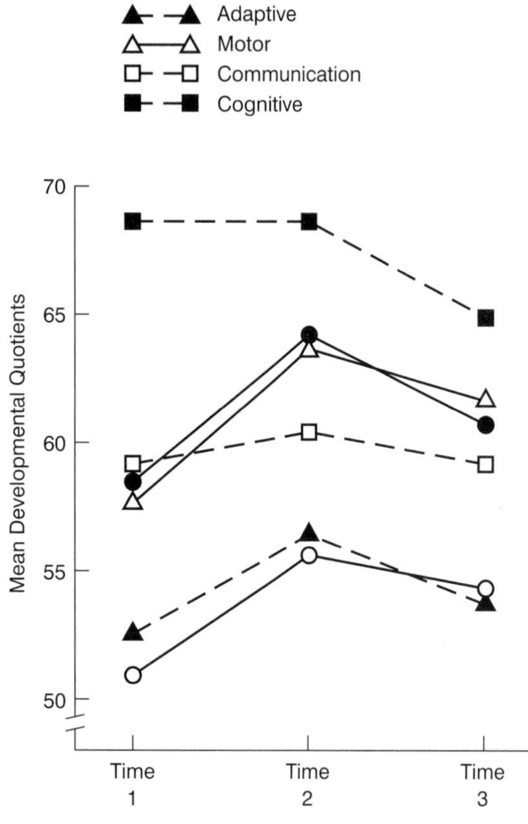

FIGURE 2.3
Change in developmental quotient scores of 129 preschoolers with disabilities at 4-month intervals

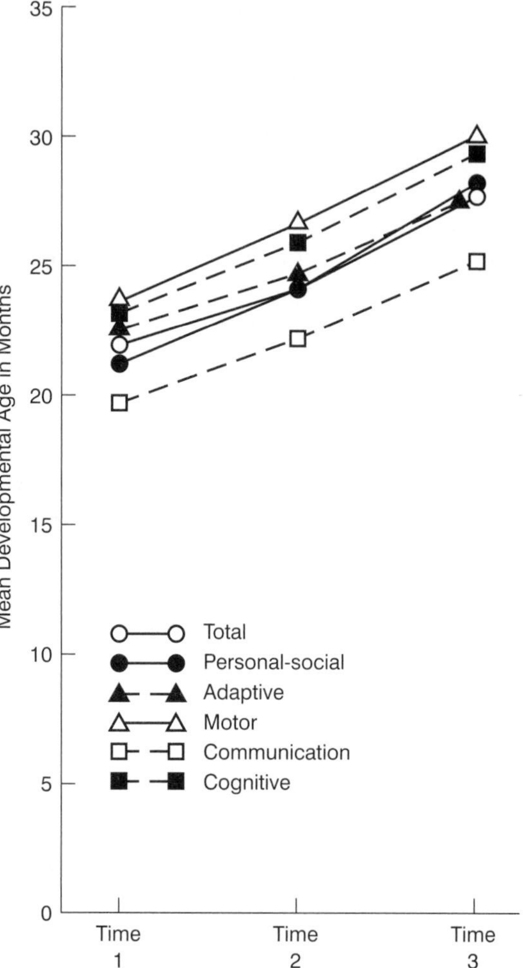

FIGURE 2.4
Change in developmental age scores of 129 preschoolers with disabilities at 4-month intervals

without comparing him or her with others and are appropriate whenever a norm-referenced score is not needed. For example, if a preschool teacher is trying to measure progress toward objectives in a center-based program, the criterion-referenced approach offers behavioral, concrete information.

Usually criterion-referenced tests cannot be used alone to make decisions regarding placement or eligibility for services, since those decisions often are based on the nature and extent of the child's developmental delay. However, criterion-referenced tests aid in the understanding of a child's abilities and needs and should be used in placement decisions to complement findings from norm-referenced measures. When determining placement, the primary question should be "Which placement option will best meet a child's needs?" rather than "Which placement option does the child qualify for according to test scores?" Criterion-referenced measures frequently do a better job of identifying functional needs than do norm-referenced tests. Also, reporting results from criterion-referenced tests often is more desired by parents, since such results can focus on specific strengths and needs rather than emphasizing the child's delay.

A special form of criterion-referenced tests, referred to as *curriculum-referenced testing* or curriculum-based assessment (Neisworth & Bagnato, 1986), involves the assessment of a child's abilities in the context of a predetermined sequence of curriculum objectives. Assessment covers the same materials presented during instruction. Curriculum-referenced tests are, in reality, criterion-referenced tests; however, they differ from other forms of criterion-referenced testing in that a predetermined criterion is not necessarily set and the test is always related to what was taught in the classroom. While the goal of norm-referenced testing is to compare a child with a norm or standard group, and the goal of criterion-referenced testing is to ascertain whether or not a child has acquired a predetermined set of skills, the goal of curriculum-referenced testing is to assess the percentage of material mastered in a given curriculum. Thus, curriculum-referenced tests compare a child's performance with the curriculum.

Curriculum-referenced assessment is a commonly used approach in infant and preschool settings (Bailey, Jens, & Johnson, 1983). Its utility lies in the fact that there is a direct correspondence between assessment procedures and intervention goals. Missed items in the curriculum become subsequent instructional objectives. The primary limitations relate to potential overreliance on the existing curriculum and overly specific interpretation of individual items. Children with disabilities are extraordinarily variable in their individual needs. Early intervention professionals will need to expand upon preset curricula to tailor assessment demands for individual children. In addition, teachers and other professionals must realize that individual curricula items are representative of complex, broad skills. For example, an item such as "puts together a three-piece puzzle" includes cognitive, visual, and motor skills. Instructional activities should not focus merely on putting together a puzzle, but also on relevant functional tasks requiring similar skills.

Criterion-Referenced Scoring

Criterion-referenced and curriculum-referenced tests are scored by first counting the number of items passed. The number itself, equivalent to a raw score, may be the score summary, as in the case of the Evaluation and Programming System for Infants and Young Children (Bailey & Bricker, 1986). The same limitations as described with raw scores for norm-referenced tests, however, pertain to criterion-referenced measures, since the raw score alone is difficult to interpret. The raw score often is converted into a percentage value computed by dividing the raw score by the total possible raw score obtainable. The resulting score is an indication of the percentage of items passed.

With school-age children, performance standards often are set on criterion-referenced tests. A *performance standard* is a specified criterion of performance, such as 8 out of 10 items or 85% of items.

Using Criterion-Referenced Scores to Evaluate Progress

Progress on criterion-referenced and curriculum-referenced tests may be described in terms of change in either raw scores or percentage scores. When interpreting criterion-referenced scores, however, professionals should be cautioned that such scores probably are only ordinal in nature, not equal interval. An equal-interval scale is one in which the difficulty level of each item is equivalent; thus, each item requires approximately the same amount of effort to achieve. Equality of item difficulty is rarely documented in criterion-referenced tests, unfortunately, making it difficult to interpret change. For example, one child could achieve several relatively easy items during a period of intervention and demonstrate a sizeable increase in percentage of items passed, whereas another child may only achieve one very difficult item and demonstrate only a small increase in percentage of items passed.

TEST RELIABILITY

In evaluating a particular assessment tool, one concern is the *reliability* of the instrument—the consistency of test performance. If several children were administered the same test and each received a different score, how much of that variability would be attributable to true differences in the children's abilities and how much would be due to what is referred to as "error variance"? If a child took a test over and over again, and no practice effect occurred, what would be the variability in the child's performance? The less error variance in the answer to either of these questions, the greater the test's reliability. Professionals in early intervention should understand the concept of reliability, recognize sources of error in measurement, and be able to read, interpret, and evaluate reliability data.

Sources of Error in Measurement

Measurement error may stem from several sources. The most common are characteristics of the test itself, variation in administrative conditions and child characteristics, and aspects of the examiner.

Test characteristics A major source of variability is the test itself, which is often the focus of reliability studies. Items on a test should be clear in regard to the materials required and to administrative procedures. If they are not, one examiner might administer an item in one way, and another might use different administrative procedures. In addition, a test should have clear scoring procedures. If not, one examiner might give a child credit for a particular response; another might credit a failure for precisely the same response. Finally, test reliability can be affected by test length; extremely short or extremely long tests are likely to be less reliable.

Administrative and subject conditions A second major source of error variance is associated with aspects of the subjects taking the test and the conditions under which the test is administered. Stanley (1971) describes several characteristics of the individual child that might result in score variance on a particular test, including general ability to comprehend instructions, test-taking skills, health, fatigue, motivation, emotional strain, or fluctuations in attention. Performance may also vary by chance associated with "lucky" responses to items. For example, a child may be asked to point to the red block. A child who does not know colors still has a 25% chance of being correct if there are four blocks from which to choose.

Aspects of a particular test administration may also affect a child's performance and result in score variability. For example, the room may be too hot, poorly lit, or stuffy. The child may not interact well with the particular adult administering the test due to unfamiliarity or characteristics of the adult such as personality style, culture, or gender.

The examiner Finally, the skill of the examiner in administering and scoring the test influences the reliability of administration. A test may have perfectly clear and precise administrative and scoring procedures, but an individual examiner may not have read them all or may have forgotten one or more guidelines. Furthermore, mistakes can be made in score calculations and transformations. The more complex the scoring procedure required and the more calculations that are necessary, the greater the likelihood of error.

Assessing Test Reliability

When examining the reliability of a given test, the professional generally has two sources for information. First, the administrative manual of the particular instrument should provide detailed reliability data. Second, reliability studies of particular measures often are published in the professional literature. This body of information, however, is generally much less accessible to most practicing professionals working with young children with disabilities.

As Stanley (1971) suggests, "there is no single, universal, and absolute reliability for a test" (p. 363). There are many ways to document test reliability, including procedural and scoring reliability, test-retest reliability, alternate forms reliability, the Standard Error of Measurement, and internal consistency reliability. The reliability measure used varies according to the question of interest.

Procedural and scoring reliability *Procedural reliability* refers to the extent to which the examiner follows the administrative procedures required by a particular test; scoring reliability refers to the extent to which the score calculations and score summaries are accurate. Both must be assessed by having another individual check the examiner. Procedural reliability could be assessed by having one person observe another administer a test. For each item, the observer notes whether the examiner used the proper materials, placed them in the proper positions, gave the proper directions, and in general followed the test protocol accurately. In this case the reliability measure would be the percentage of items administered correctly. *Scoring reliability* consists of two major aspects. First, did the examiner give the proper credit for the child's response? Generally this will require observation and simultaneous scoring, since testing young children does not generally result in a permanent product such as a written word. Second, did the examiner correctly calculate the child's total score? This question does not require observation. Rather, two individuals must independently score a test. The reliability measure is the extent to which the individuals agree on the final score calculation.

One example of observer reliability was provided by Bailey and Bricker (1986). Two observers independently observed a child participating in routine classroom activities and scored items on the Evaluation and Programming System. A correlation coefficient was used to determine the extent of interobserver agreement. (A correlation coefficient is a statistical measure of how two variables relate to each other. It ranges from −1 to +1, with coefficients near −1 or +1 considered high correlations and coefficients near zero considered low correlations. Generally in reliability studies, one would expect that correlations should be high and positive.) The results of the study indicated that the two observers were much more likely to agree on some domains than on others. For example, the correlations for the Gross Motor (.95), Communication (.85), and Social (.85) domains were much higher than those for the Fine Motor (.64) and Cognitive (.23) domains.

An example of assessing the reliability of score calculations was provided by Bailey et al. (1987). Seventy-nine teachers of 247 preschoolers with disabilities administered the Battelle Development Inventory and sent the results to the authors. Graduate research assistants subsequently checked each protocol for accuracy in score calculation and summaries. Only 11 teachers (14.5%) and 50 protocols (20.2%) had no scoring errors. The most common problems included simple math errors, failure to establish a basal, and errors in crediting the child for points below the basal.

Test-retest reliability A second form of reliability, *test-retest reliability,* requires administering the same test to a group of children on two different occasions and assessing the extent to which their scores are stable over time. For example, Bailey and Bricker (1986), after assessing 28 children, observed and assessed those children again 1 or 2 weeks after the initial testing period. The correlation between total test scores in first and second administration was .84. Test-retest reliability for individual subdomains ranged from .46 to .93.

Alternate forms reliability Some instrument developers will develop alternate forms of the same measure. *Alternate,* or parallel, *forms reliability* assesses the extent to which a child's performance on one measure is consistent with his or her performance on the other. It requires that the same child be administered both forms of the test. For example, Boehm (1971) developed two forms of the Boehm Test of Basic Concepts. A median alternate form reliability coefficient of .76 is reported in the administrative manual of the instrument. In a sample tryout of the measure, the mean scores on Form A (42.4) and Form B (42.9) were almost equivalent.

Internal consistency A fourth form of test reliability seeks to determine whether a child's responses on a given administration of a test are *internally consistent.* In other words, was there variability in performance across items or was the child's performance relatively consistent? This type of question can only be asked if an instrument is assumed to assess a single construct; a child's performance across very different domains (e.g., communication and motor) might be expected to vary.

Internal consistency may be assessed using several procedures. One of the simplest is referred to as split-half reliability, a procedure in which the test essentially is divided into two parts (usually odd versus even items). The reliability measure then is the correlation between the two parts. At a more complex level, formulas such as the Kuder-Richardson procedure or Cronbach's Alpha could be used, in which all possible splits are assessed. For example, McLean, McCormick, Bruder, and Burdg (1987) assessed the internal consistency of the Battelle Developmental Inventory using Cronbach's Alpha with data collected on 40 children with disabilities under 30 months of age. Internal consistency was high in all five domains of the measure, ranging from .887 to .963. Similarly, McLean, McCormick, and Baird (1991) analyzed the internal consistency of the Griffiths Scales using Cronbach's Alpha and found high values, ranging from .959 to .97, indicating the performance was consistent across children for each of the scales.

Standard Error of Measurement A final measure of test reliability, the Standard Error of Measurement, seeks to answer the hypothetical question of how stable a child's performance on a test would be if he or she could take the test over and over again. Assume that this was done, resulting in a large number of scores for the same child on the same test. That set of scores would have mean and a standard deviation. The Standard Error of Measurement is the standard deviation of that hypothetical distribution and is thus an estimate of that variability. It is reported in units of the test score itself. For example, the administrative manual of the Battelle Development Inventory reports that the Standard Error of Measurement for the Total BDI score for children in the 6- to 11-month age range is 3.28. This is interpreted to mean that 68% of the time (since, as displayed in Figure 2.1, one standard deviation above and below the mean encompasses 68% of a normal distribution) a child's total raw score would fall within a range of plus or minus 3.28 points.

Summary comments regarding reliability Clearly, test reliability is an important concern in selecting a measure. Although no one score is the "right" reliability, professionals should examine the evidence available for any given measure. Instruments should be selected that have reliability coefficients greater than .80 and preferably greater than .90, and for which there is a small Standard Error of Measurement. Examiners using the test should be familiar with all aspects of test administration and scoring, and periodic checks of both administrative and scoring procedures should be conducted. If a test is known to have low reliability but is still used by a program, results should be interpreted cautiously. For unclear items, a program should adopt local standards for those items and ask each staff person to adhere to them. However, when reports of such administrations are shared with other agencies, any such standards should be fully explained.

TEST VALIDITY

In addition to test reliability, professionals using tests must also be concerned about test *validity,* which refers to the extent to which a test performs the functions for which it was intended. At least four types of validity should be considered: content, instructional, criterion, and construct.

Content Validity

Content validity refers to how well the content of the test represents the domain tested. For example, a test of cognitive skills should cover the major cognitive attainments of young children and should reflect current theories of cognitive development. According to the Standards for Educational and Psychological Tests (American Psychological Association, 1985), "to demonstrate the content validity of a set of test scores, one must show that the behaviors demonstrated in testing constitute a representative sample of behaviors to be exhibited in a desired performance domain. . . . An investigation of content validity requires that the test developer or test user specify his objectives and carefully define the performance domain in light of those objectives" (p. 28).

In evaluating the content validity of a given test, professionals should examine the rationale for item selection as described in the test's technical manual. An initial test of content validity would be the extent to which the test developer convinces you that a thorough and systematic process has occurred in the selection of test content. This should include a discussion of the theoretical basis for item selection, the source of items, and any data to support the extent to which test content reflects the domain assessed. Data supporting content validity typically would consist of the judgment of experts as to the appropriateness of the content. Essentially, content validity is assessed through a logical analysis of the item development process and of the actual items.

Instructional Utility

A second type of validity, one that is closely related to content validity, is *instructional utility.* Here the user would determine the extent to which an instrument provides useful information for planning intervention programs for young children with disabilities.

One way to assess instructional utility is to ask test users to rate the appropriateness of the items for instruction. As described earlier, Bailey et al. (1987) asked teachers to rate the instructional utility of the Battelle Developmental Inventory. They also asked teachers to rate the extent to which standardized adaptations for children with sensory or motor impairments allowed an individual child to demonstrate his or her optimal skills. Bailey and Bricker (1986) asked staff members using the EPS-I to fill out a form regarding the usefulness and appropriateness of items for designing instructional programs. Such information, particularly when provided at the item level, can be useful in revising instruments as well as in evaluating their overall utility.

Criterion Validity

Criterion validity assesses the extent to which a test corresponds to some other independent measure. Two types of criterion validity have been described. Concurrent validity refers to the extent to which a test correlates with another measure administered close in time to the first; predictive validity refers to the extent to which a test relates to some future measure of performance. An example of concurrent validity was provided by Bruder (1984), who compared infants' scores on the communication section of the Revised Gesell Schedules of Infant Development with the same infants' scores on the Snyder Imperative Tasks to determine the extent to which the two instruments correlated. An example of predictive validity was provided by Diamond (1987), who conducted a 4-year follow-up of the Denver Developmental Screening Test to determine the extent to which it identified children who later displayed severe learning problems in school.

Concurrent and predictive validity are particularly important for screening tests. Screening tests that lack concurrent validity are likely to result in children being referred for assessment who will not be diagnosed as delayed. Concurrent validity is also critical in tests used for diagnosis.

Construct Validity

A *construct* is a hypothetical attribute, such as intelligence or creativity, that is designed to account for variability in behavior. The following statements summarize the essence of construct validity:

> Evidence of construct validity is not found in a single study; rather, judgments of construct validity are based upon an accumulation of research results. In obtaining the information needed to establish construct validity, the investigator begins by formulating hypotheses about the characteristics of those who have high scores on the test in contrast to those who have low scores. Taken together, such hypotheses form at least a tentative theory about the nature of the construct the test is believed to be measuring. In a full investigation, the test may be the dependent variable in some studies and the independent variable in others. Some hypotheses may be "counter-hypotheses" suggested by competing interpretations or theories. (American Psychological Association, 1985, p. 30)

A test's construct validity is often assessed by determining its *convergent* and *discriminant* validity. A test that has good convergent validity has high positive correlations with other tests measuring the same construct. In contrast, a test that has good discriminant validity has low correlations with tests that measure different constructs. A sample construct validity question would be to ask whether a particular instrument is, in fact, a measure of intelligence. Mahoney (1984) provided an example of testing the construct validity of the Receptive-Expressive Emergent Language Scale with children with mental retardation. In this study, he demonstrated that the instrument provided a developmental sequence of data about children's communicative behavior and that it correlated well with another measure designed to assess the same construct (convergent validity). However, a thorough documentation of construct validity should also show that the measure in question has a low correlation with measures from other domains (discriminant validity). For example, a communication measure should correlate highly with established communication measures and have lower correlations with social and cognitive measures. Although these skills are interrelated, the question is whether the instrument successfully isolates and differentiates those abilities or skills. In test development, the internal consistency of a test is calculated by using a statistical test to evaluate the test's interitem consistency. If the items of a test are positively correlated, then the items are measuring the same construct and the test is thought to have high internal (interitem) consistency. If, however, only clusters of items are correlated with each other, the items are often divided into subtests assessing different constructs. Similar items are often grouped into clusters by experts who have judged the content of the group of items as similar.

Once items have been grouped into subtests, an intercorrelation matrix allows investigation of the relationship among the subtests. When subtests show significant positive correlations with each other they are said to be intercorrelated and therefore measure the same construct. On the other hand, if the intercorrelation matrix shows that subtests are not significantly correlated, each subtest is probably assessing a different construct. An intercorrelation matrix, correlating domains and subdomains (subtests) of the Battelle Developmental Inventory (Newborg et al., 1984), was used when this test was developed to see if the domains and subdomains were significantly intercorrelated. There were high positive correlations among subtests, providing construct validity for the idea that skills on one subtest serve as a basis for predicting similar levels of development on other subtests for typically developing children.

Another statistical method for analyzing a test's construct validity is factor analysis, which is a method for analyzing all the test items to determine which clusters of items are significantly correlated. The results from a factor analysis provide information about whether the content of the items reflects the theory or constructs underlying the test's development. A test's factorial validity is determined in two ways. One method is to correlate scores on the test with scores on other tests that are supposed to measure the same construct(s). The second method is to correlate the scores for all the subtests on a single test, in order to determine what common constructs are measured among the subtests. The latter method is typically used when the test is initially developed.

When a factor analysis is used to assess the relationship between clusters of test items, this method yields a factor matrix, which shows the correlation between factors, representing a cluster of items measuring the same construct and each subtest. If there are high correlations between the subtests and the factors, and if the factors reflect the theoretical constructs that the test is supposed to measure, the test is said to have high construct validity. The researcher is responsible for naming the factors in the factor matrix, based on his or her knowledge of the theoretical constructs assessed by each cluster of items. This type of decision making, in which subjective judgment determines the factors, has been one cause for the criticism of factor analysis.

Banerji (1992b) conducted a factor analysis to determine the factor structure of the Gesell School Readiness Screening Test (Ilg & Ames, 1972; Ilg, Ames, Haines, & Gillespie, 1978), a screening test for children ages 2 to 6 that is often used to determine school readiness. The Gesell has eight subtests assessing skills such as writing, copying shapes, and naming animals. In this factor analysis, the factorial validity of the Gesell was assessed by correlating the eight subtests to see which ones were highly correlated. Results indicated that all the subtests of the Gesell were highly intercorrelated; hence, Banerji concluded that the factor structure of the Gesell could be described by one general factor. Banerji found, however, that it was easier to explain the constructs measured by the Gesell by referring to two factors, visual-motor and language and cognition tasks (Meisels, 1983), even though the test could be described using one general factor. This is an example of how judgment is used to name and choose factors from a factor analysis.

Another problem with factor analysis is that different constructs may describe a child's performance on a test at different ages. For instance, one factor (sensorimotor) may describe a toddler's performance, while several factors (verbal, visual-spatial, cognitive, and motor) may describe a preschooler's performance on the test. Different factor groupings may reflect differences in children's cognitive development at different ages. This may make the age level constructs from factor analyses presented in test manuals inappropriate for children with developmental delays, because their developmental level differs from that of the typically developing children whose scores were used in the original analyses. Therefore, additional factor analyses for groups of children with different types of developmental disabilities may be necessary to determine what constructs the test measures for children with special needs.

For instance, Snyder and associates (Snyder, Lawson, Thompson, Stricklin, & Sexton, 1993) used factor analysis to evaluate the constructs measured by the Battelle (Newborg et al., 1984) for a sample of children with severe developmental disabilities. The factor matrix indicated that the Battelle measured only three factors for children with severe developmental disabilities. In contrast, the factor matrix for typically developing children presented in the Battelle test manual suggests that this test assesses five factors (called domains). Thus, developmental tests may assess different constructs in children with disabilities, and, if the performance of children with disabilities is interpreted based on factors developed from analyses of the test scores of typically developing children, the clinician will probably draw inaccurate conclusions about the performance of children with disabilities. This error is magnified if the same test is used with a child with a disability over time, because children with disabilities may mature in a way that is qualitatively and quantitatively different from that of their typically developing peers (Snyder et al., 1993).

The factor analysis conducted by Snyder et al. (1993) was a confirmatory factor analysis, which determined whether the factors found for one sample, typically developing children, would be the same for another sample, children with severe developmental disabilities. Bailey, Blasco, and Simeonsson (1992) also conducted a confirmatory factor analysis for mothers' and fathers' responses on the Family Needs Survey to determine whether the needs expressed by mothers and fathers of young children with disabilities were similar. The first factor matrix for a sample of mothers of children with disabilities indicated six factors representing the following needs: family and social support, information, financial, explaining to others, child care, and professional support. The second factor matrix for fathers indicated the Family Needs Survey assessed some similar factors for fathers, but fathers' needs were clustered into a smaller number of factors. Also, the group of test items forming the cluster representing the family and social support factor was different for fathers and mothers. This study provides further support for conducting factor analyses to assess the construct validity for the test for any new group taking a test, because the test may assess different factors for different groups.

Comments About Validity

Questions about validity are of ultimate importance for early childhood special educators and related service personnel because they ask whether an instrument fulfills the function for which it was intended. Validity is both separate from and tied to reliability. Although conceptually they ask very different questions, it is a well-accepted axiom in test development that test validity can be no higher than the test's reliability, and usually is considerably lower. This makes sense, for how could an unreliable or inconsistent measure have any accuracy? However, the fact that a test is reliable does not mean that it has any validity for certain purposes. For example, a screening test may be perfectly reliable but be of no use in planning instructional programs.

Finally, it must be noted that the vast majority of validity studies conducted on norm-referenced measures have failed to examine the validity of these instruments for use with individuals with disabilities (Fuchs, Fuchs, Benowitz, & Barringer, 1987).

SUMMARY OF KEY CONCEPTS

- Testing is the assessment of children's abilities through the presentation of standardized tasks and application of standardized procedures for interpreting children's performance. It is probably the most widely used, and widely misused, form of assessment, and thus an understanding of the process underlying testing is essential.
- Standardized administration and scoring of tests is important when test scores are used. Standardized procedures may penalize some children with disabilities, however, and results from standardized testing should be interpreted with caution.
- Teachers and other professionals should examine how test content was derived to ensure that content is adequate for the intended purpose.
- Norm-referenced tests compare a child's performance with that of other children, using developmental age scores, developmental quotients, standard scores, or percentile ranks. Each score has advantages and disadvantages. Clinicians should examine the norm group from which these scores were derived, be able to interpret each, and recognize the limitations of each.
- Criterion-referenced measures document children's attainment of predetermined objectives or curriculum items, and generally are more useful than norm-referenced measures for instructional purposes.
- *Reliability* refers to the consistency of test performance. Several factors can influence test reliability.
- *Validity* refers to the extent to which a test performs the functions for which it was intended.

REFERENCES

Alpern, G. D., Boll, T. J., & Shearer, M. S. (1980). *Developmental Profile II.* Aspen, CO: Psychological Development Publications.

American Psychological Association. (1985). *Standards for educational and psychological tests.* Washington, DC: APA.

Bailey, D. B., Blasco, P. M., & Simeonsson, R. J. (1992). Needs expressed by mothers and fathers of young children with disabilities. *American Journal on Mental Retardation, 97*(1), 1–10.

Bailey, D. B., Jens, K. G., & Johnson, N. (1983). Curricula for handicapped infants. In S. G. Garwood & R. R. Fewell (Eds.), *Educating handicapped infants* (pp. 387–415). Rockville, MD: Aspen.

Bailey, D. B., & Rosenthal, S. L. (1987). Basic principles of measurement and test development. In W. H. Berdine & S. A. Meyer (Eds.), *Assessment in special education.* Boston: Little, Brown.

Bailey, D. B., Vandiviere, P., Dellinger, J., & Munn, D. (1987). The Battelle Developmental Inventory:

Teacher perceptions and implementation data. *Journal of Psychoeducational Assessment, 3,* 217–226.

Bailey, E. J., & Bricker, D. (1986). A psychometric study of a criterion-referenced assessment instrument designed for infants and young children. *Journal of the Division for Early Childhood, 10,* 124–134.

Banerji, M. (1992a). An integrated study of the predictive properties of the Gesell School Readiness Screening Test. *Journal of Psychoeducational Assessment, 10,* 240–256.

Banerji, M. (1992b). Factor structure of the Gesell School Readiness Screening Test. *Journal of Psychoeducational Assessment, 10,* 342–354.

Bayley, N. (1969). *Bayley Scales of Infant Development.* New York: The Psychological Corp.

Bayley, N. (1993). *Bayley Scales of Infant Development: Second Edition.* New York: The Psychological Corp.

Boehm, A. E. (1971). *Boehm Test of Basic Concepts.* New York: The Psychological Corp.

Bruder, M. B. (1984). The validation of a scale to measure early social-communicative behavior. *Journal of the Division for Early Childhood, 9,* 67–75.

Diamond, K. E. (1987). Predicting school problems from preschool developmental screening: A four-year follow-up of the revised Denver Developmental Screening Test and the role of parent report. *Journal of the Division for Early Childhood, 11,* 247–253.

Egan, D. F., & Brown, R. (1986). Developmental assessment: 18 months to 4½ years. Performance test. *Child: Care, Health, and Development, 12,* 339–349.

Fewell, R. R., & Sandall, S. R. (1986). Developmental testing of handicapped infants: A measurement dilemma. *Topics in Early Childhood Special Education, 6,* 86–99.

Fuchs, D., Fuchs, L. S., Benowitz, S., & Barringer, K. (1987). Norm-referenced tests: Are they valid for use with handicapped students? *Exceptional Children, 54,* 263–271.

Furuno, S., O'Reilly, A., Hosaka, C. M., Inatsuka, T. T., Allman, T. L., & Zelsloft, B. (1979). *The Hawaii Early Learning Profile.* Palo Alto, CA: VORT.

Glover, M. E., Preminger, J. L., & Sanford, A. R. (1978). *The Early Learning Accomplishment Profile.* Winston-Salem, NC: Kaplan.

Griffiths, R. (1970). *The abilities of young children.* High Wycombe, Great Britain: Cournswood House.

Hanson, R., & Smith, J. A. (1987). Achievements of young children on items of the Griffiths Scales: 1980 compared to 1960. *Child: Care, Health, and Development, 13*(3), 181–195.

Ilg, F. L., & Ames, L. B. (1972). *School readiness.* New York: Harper & Row.

Ilg, F. L., Ames, L. B., Haines, J., & Gillespie, C. (1978). *School readiness.* New York: Harper & Row.

Keogh, B. K., & Sheehan, R. (1981). The use of developmental test data for documenting handicapped children's progress: Problems and recommendations. *Journal of the Division for Early Childhood, 3,* 42–47.

Mahoney, G. (1984). The validity of the Receptive-Expressive Emergent Language Scale with mentally retarded children. *Journal of the Division for Early Childhood, 9,* 86–94.

Mardell-Czudnowski, C., & Goldenberg, D. (1984). Revision and restandardization of a preschool screening test: DIAL becomes DIAL-R. *Journal of the Division for Early Childhood, 8,* 149–156.

McLean, M. E., McCormick, K., & Baird, S. M. (1991). Concurrent validity of the Griffiths Mental Development Scales with a population of children under 24 months. *Journal of Early Intervention, 15*(4), 338–344.

McLean, M., McCormick, K., Bruder, M. B., & Burdg, N. B. (1987). An investigation of the validity and reliability of the Battelle Developmental Inventory with a population of children younger than 30 months with identified handicapping conditions. *Journal of the Division for Early Childhood, 11,* 238–246.

Meisels, S. J. (1983). *Developmental screening in early childhood: A guide.* Washington: NAEYC.

Naglieri, J. A. (1981). Extrapolated developmental indices for the Bayley Scales of Infant Development. *American Journal of Mental Deficiency, 85,* 548–550.

Neisworth, J. T., & Bagnato, S. J. (1986). Curriculum-based developmental assessment: Congruence of testing and teaching. *School Psychology Review, 15,* 180–199.

Newborg, J., Stock, J. R., Wnek, L., Guidubaldi, J., & Svinicki, J. (1984). *The Battelle Developmental Inventory.* Allen, TX: DLM/Teaching Resources.

Rogers, S. J., D'Eugenio, D. B., Brown, S. L., Donovan, C. M., & Lynch, E. W. (1981). *Early intervention developmental profile.* Ann Arbor, MI: University of Michigan Press.

Salvia, J. & Ysseldyke, J. E. (1985). *Assessment in special and remedial education.* Boston: Houghton Mifflin.

Sanford, A. R., & Zelman, J. G. (1981). *The learning accomplishment profile.* Winston-Salem, NC: Kaplan.

Sattler, J. (1982). *Assessment of children's intelligence and special abilities.* Boston: Allyn & Bacon.

Snyder, P., Lawson, S., Thompson, B., Stricklin, S., & Sexton, D. (1993). Evaluating the psychometric integrity of instruments used in early intervention research: The Battelle Developmental Inventory. *Topics in Early Childhood Special Education, 13*(2), 216–232.

Snyder-McLean, L. (1987). Reporting norm-referenced program evaluation data: Some considerations. *Journal of the Division for Early Childhood, 11,* 254–264.

Stanley, J. C. (1971). Reliability. In R. L. Thorndike (Ed.), *Educational measurement* (2nd ed.) (pp. 356–442). Washington, DC: American Council on Education.

Wechsler, D. (1974). *Manual for Wechsler Intelligence Scale for Children—Revised.* New York: Psychological Corp.

CHAPTER

3

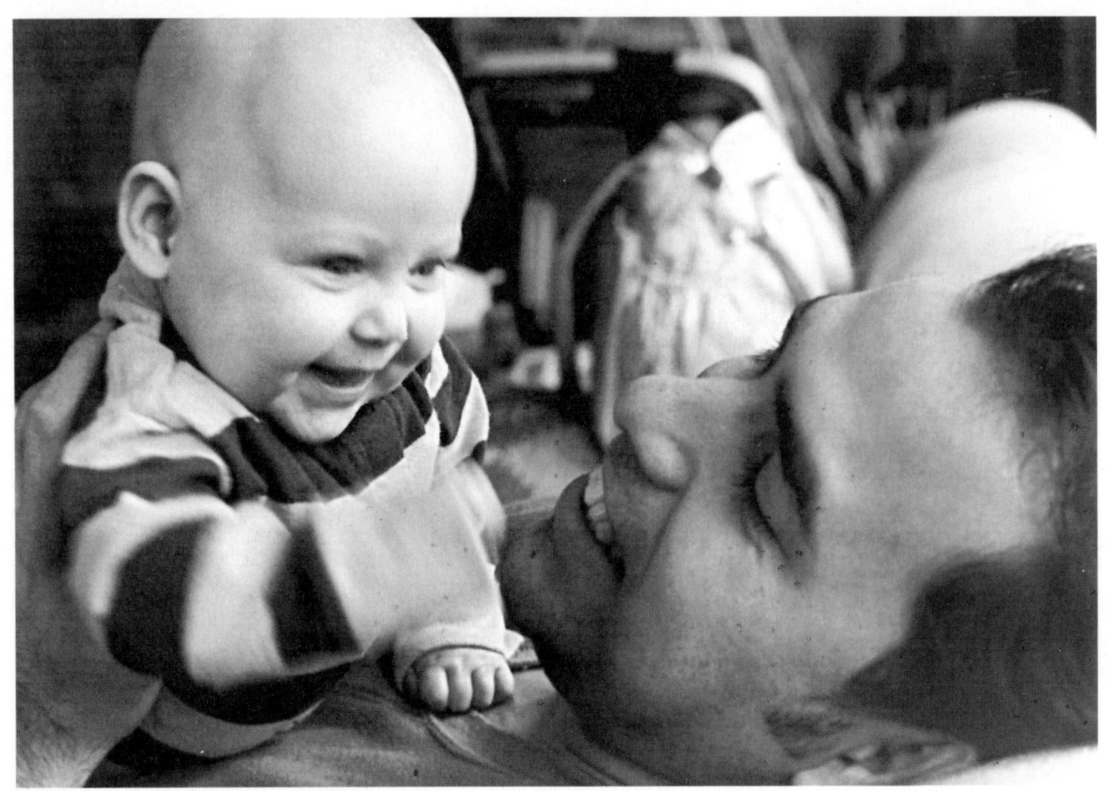

Procedural Considerations in Assessing Infants and Preschoolers with Disabilities

Mary McLean
Cardinal Stritch College
Elizabeth R. Crais
University of North Carolina at Chapel Hill

Over the past two decades, some consensus has developed in the field as to the assessment procedures that are most effective with children from birth through age 5 with disabilities (DEC Task Force on Recommended Practices, 1993; Bagnato & Neisworth, 1991; Wolery, Strain, & Bailey, 1992). This chapter describes the procedures that are recommended for use with these children, organized within discussions of the importance of family participation in assessment, the importance of cross-disciplinary collaboration, and the importance of assessment in the natural environment.

IMPORTANCE OF FAMILY/ CAREGIVER PARTICIPATION IN ASSESSMENT ACTIVITIES

In recent years, when focusing on the assessment of young children, many professionals have stressed the need to involve family members and other caregivers in assessment (Bailey, McWilliam, Winton, & Simeonsson, 1992; Crais, 1992, 1993; Gibbs & Teti, 1990; Gradel, Thompson, & Sheehan, 1981; Sheehan, 1988). Traditionally, this involvement included asking case history and developmental questions and, on occasion, having the family complete a family report instrument. In response to legislative and theoretical trends, a number of professionals have attempted additional techniques to encourage family members to take part in assessment. For example, families have been asked to administer certain test items, demonstrate typical interactions with their child, or be physically present during the assessment. Although these efforts may provide professionals with increased information and encourage family members to be more active in the testing sessions, they alone may not facilitate the development of truly collaborative relationships with families in the assessment process. In addition, the many people who are involved in caring for a very young child throughout the day may be important members of the assessment and intervention team. When possible and when desired by the family, all the child's family members or caregivers may be included in the assessment and intervention planning so as to promote shared knowledge and experiences regarding the child and the early intervention process. For brevity, the authors have chosen to use the term *family* to represent the legal and other primary caregivers (e.g., relatives, child-care workers) who spend time with the child and who are responsible for the care of the child.

As suggested by Crais (1993), collaborative relationships in early intervention are recognized by several characteristics, including equality in the status of each partner, respect for each other's opinions and contributions, and a developing trust. If professionals and families seek to be collaborators, they may describe themselves using synonyms commonly substituted for the word *collaborator,* such as *colleague, coworker, copartner,* or *ally.* Some professionals suggest that if full collaboration is to be achieved within assessment, families must have the opportunity to be active participants throughout the entire process rather than just during the actual testing (Crais, 1993; Kjerland & Kovach, 1990; McGonigel, Kaufmann, & Johnson, 1991; McLean & McCormick, 1993). Through collaborative efforts, families are provided decision-making opportunities about all aspects of the assessment process from the first decision to the last. This would include planning the assessment activities, gathering information, determining whether the gathered information is a fair reflection of a child's abilities and needs, and making decisions based on the results of assessment.

Reasons for Building Collaborative Relationships in Assessment

Before entering the discussion of strategies to facilitate collaborative efforts by families and professionals, it is necessary to understand why interaction may be beneficial and desirable. The reasons center around the rights of the family and family members and the increased family satisfaction and empowerment that are made possible by collaborative efforts in assessment.

First, from both theoretical and legislative perspectives, the family is viewed as holding a central position in the child's life and development. If this position is to be maintained, early interventionists must ensure that the family has choices about the roles they play in assessment. One way to ensure that they have such choices is to support and encourage their right to be part of all discussions and activities related to the child. When family members are present and feel supported, they may be more likely to take advantage of opportunities to be a part of and shape the entire assessment process.

Because of the family's central position in the child's life, family members have unique knowledge about the child that is unavailable to professionals. As suggested by McLean and McCormick (1993), "Parents know their child better than any other member of the assessment team" (p. 65). Indeed, families' concerns about their child's developmental status have been well correlated with the outcome of developmental screening tests (Glascoe, MacLean, & Stone, 1991). Professionals must, therefore, recognize the importance of tapping into the family's knowledge base and gaining the family's input in the assessment process. Assessment activities must evolve out of the family's concerns and priorities and be responsive to what the family hopes to gain through assessment.

Families have also been shown to be reliable in performing activities such as completing screening tools or developmental checklists of their child's behaviors. Their participation in direct assessment has led to their increased sensitivity to the development of the child (Bricker & Squires, 1989) and increased contributions by families in intervention planning and decision making (Brinckerhoff & Vincent, 1987). In addition to evaluating their own child, family participation in identifying areas, contexts, and techniques for assessment can be efficient ways to use families' knowledge of the child and can improve the ecological validity of assessments. Moreover, identification of families' priorities for intervention (e.g., whether to intervene, when, where, and in what way) can only be accomplished through collaboration.

Finally, collaborative relationships in assessment are desirable because assessment has a significant impact on current and subsequent feelings and behaviors of both professionals and families. Most families enter the early intervention system by taking part in some type of evaluation of their child, and this experience may set the tone for the interactions that will follow. If a professional takes a directive role during assessment, family members may be prompted to take more passive roles. Much has been written in recent years regarding the empowerment of families within early intervention (Dunst, Trivette, & Deal, 1988), but families may not *feel* empowered in the assessment process. As suggested by Dunst and his colleagues, families who do not feel empowered are less likely to take an active role or to follow through on actions that are recommended for their children. Professionals may therefore develop incomplete pictures of families and may make faulty assumptions based on information gained in less than optimal conditions. As suggested by Bricker and Squires (1989), providing opportunities for family participation in assessing the child conveys to families that they are important to the assessment process.

Another issue related to the impact of assessment is the level of satisfaction felt by families during and following an evaluation. Through the years there have been numerous reports of family dissatisfaction with evaluation services (Olson, 1988; Poyadue, 1988; Tarran, 1991). In examining this issue, Dunst et al.

(1988) suggest that the primary reason for dissatisfaction is the failure of professionals to gain consensus with family members on three critical points: (a) the nature of the presenting concern, (b) the need for treatment, and (c) the course of action. They argue that if professionals would focus on gaining consensus on these points, their relationships with families would improve, as would the families' satisfaction.

In sum, collaborative relationships not only recognize the rights of families, they may also improve the efficiency and validity of assessment activities and, ultimately, the satisfaction felt by families. In an attempt to help professionals develop collaborative relationships with families, the next section provides an overview of suggested strategies.

Strategies for Building Collaborative Relationships in Assessment

Three primary strategies for developing collaborative relationships within assessment activities include (a) preassessment planning, (b) active participation in assessment, and (c) mutual sharing of assessment results. The focus in all activities is on providing opportunities for family input and decision making and respecting the family's choices and actions.

Preassessment planning The purpose of assessment planning is to develop a plan for assessment that will be tailored to the individual child and family and will guide the selection of instruments and procedures to be used as well as the schedule of assessment activities (Kjerland & Kovach, 1990; McGonigel et al., 1991).

The evaluation/assessment plan cannot be developed by one individual. It must be a collaborative effort involving the family and professionals. Input must be obtained from persons who, because of their expertise and because of their relationship to the child, can observe, gather data, and evaluate the child's functioning.

The steps involved in planning include:

1. Obtaining background information
2. Determining family goals and participation in the process
3. Formulating a plan

There are a variety of formats for planning, including face-to-face meetings, forms sent to families, telephone discussions, or a combination of formats. In some programs, a service coordinator or family facilitator may meet with the family prior to the assessment to discuss the available options and relay this information to other professionals involved. In other instances, the family may meet with the entire team prior to assessment. Useful forms for preassessment planning appear in McGonigel et al. (1991) and typically include questions such as "What questions or concerns do you have about your child?" "How can we be of service to you?" and "What would you like to gain from your interactions with us?" In identifying first the family's concerns about the child and what the family wants or needs from professionals, the collaborators have in essence outlined the direction that the assessment will take. The questions the family has about the child will shape the assessment activities and professionals can be more responsive to what the family wants from assessment.

For gaining information about family concerns, priorities, and resources, various instruments are available, including the Family Information Preference Inventory (Turnbull & Turnbull, 1986), the Family Needs Survey (Bailey & Simeonsson, 1990), and the Family Resource Scale (Leet & Dunst, 1988). These instruments are typically completed by family members, thereby facilitating self-identification of the concerns, priorities, and resources that are most important to them. In recent work by Bailey and Blasco (1990), the majority of families reported that instruments such as these were helpful to them; however, they also stressed their strong preference that they be given the option to complete the instruments. In addition, families differed as to whether they preferred the use of a written survey versus more informal and open-ended discussions. Thus, professionals are wise to offer alternatives and to respect families' preferences as to how information is gathered about these issues. In addition to stand-alone instruments for gaining information on family concerns, interests, or priorities, a few child assessment tools now include some of these areas in their family questionnaire. Representative tools include the Family Interest Survey of the Assessment, Evaluation, and Programming System (AEPS) (Bricker, 1993) and the Parent Questionnaire of the Infant-Toddler Language Scale (Rossetti, 1990). Helpful ideas for gathering this type of information with families in face-to-face discussions can be found in Winton (1988) and Winton and Bailey (1993). Chapter 8 of this text presents a comprehensive discussion of assessing family concerns, resources, and priorities.

A further issue in preassessment is determining the context for assessment—both the location and the way in which assessment will take place. Useful questions include "When or where would you like the assessment to take place?" "What are some of the activities you feel are important for letting us see what's typical for your child?" and "Who would you like to be included in the assessment?" A sample preassessment planning form developed by Project Dakota (Kjerland & Kovach, 1990) is included in Figure 3.1.

Using a form such as that in Figure 3.1, professionals can gather information about the settings (e.g., home versus daycare), types of activities (e.g., observing the child at play, watching as a family member feeds the child), and persons (e.g., families, family members) that the family believes may show the child's strengths and needs. In response to identified areas of concern, the professional can also suggest a variety of activities that family members may choose to take part in with the child (e.g., completing a developmental checklist, helping administer some test items, engaging the child in social routines). Through this process the professional and the family begin to identify activities that will be representative of the child's strengths and needs and to identify the desired level of participation by family members in each activity.

Active participation by family members in assessment Traditionally, family participation in child assessment was primarily limited to the provision of background information about the child (e.g., birth history, developmental milestones) and brief descriptions of the child's current difficulties. As noted, efforts to involve families currently encompass a wider variety of activities, including eliciting particular behaviors from the child, performing some test items, or confirming that the testing was representative of the child. One assessment activity that is increasingly being encouraged by professionals is that of families evaluating their own children. The move toward greater utilization of families as evaluators has been fueled by several factors related to assessment. A primary factor has been the increased recognition that families can be reliable judges of their children's behavior, even in areas in which they were traditionally thought to be unreliable (e.g., developmental level, communication skills). For example, good reliability by families has been seen in determining (a) the child's current level of development (Bricker & Squires, 1989; Gradel et al., 1981); (b) whether the child needs referral for testing (Bricker & Squires, 1989); and (c) the child's current vocabulary and syntax levels (Dale, 1991; Dale, Bates, Reznick, & Morisset, 1989).

Increased reports of family-professional agreement may be partially due to changes in the way children are currently assessed. The use of observational and informal methods to

1. Questions or concerns others have (e.g., babysitter, clinic, preschool) about my child:

2. Other places you can observe my child:

Place:	Place:
Contact person:	Contact person:
What to observe:	What to observe:

3. I want others to see what my child does when:

4. I prefer the assessment take place:

   _____at home   _____at another location   _____at the center

5. A time when my child is alert and when working parents can be present is:

   _____morning   _____afternoon   ______early afternoon

6. People whom I would like to be there other than parents and early intervention staff:

7. My child's favorite toys or activities to help her/him become focused, motivated, and comfortable:

8. During the assessment, I prefer to:

   _____a. Sit beside my child
   _____b. Help with activities to explore her/his abilities
   _____c. Offer comfort and support to my child
   _____d. Exchange ideas with the facilitator
   _____e. Carry out activities to explore my child's abilities
   _____f. Permit facilitator to handle and carry out activities
   _____g. Other:

FIGURE 3.1

Preassessment planning: The setting (Project Dakota)

Source: From "Family-Staff Collaboration for Tailored Infant Assessment" by L. Kjerland & J. Kovach, in E. Gibbs & D. Teti (Eds.) *Interdisciplinary Assessment of Infants: A Guide for Early Intervention Professionals,* 1990, Baltimore, MD: Paul H. Brookes. Reprinted by permission.

assess children within naturalistic settings has led professionals to do more of what families typically do, namely, to watch children at play and in daily routines. The use of less formal methods may provide increased opportunities for families and professionals to see the child's typical behaviors and come to similar conclusions. In addition, when using more formal methods, families and professionals have often disagreed on "ceiling" levels or those indicating emerging behaviors (Gradel et al., 1981). However, because families have multiple opportunities to observe their child and because the child is more comfortable with family members, families are probably more likely to see emerging behaviors. Moreover, when observing the child, families often take into account the child's difficulties and can interpret what the child may be able to do with support. As suggested by Gradel and her colleagues (1981), rather than family reliability improving, it may be more a matter of professionals coming closer to what families see and thereby improving their own reliability.

Another factor that may have an impact here is the format of the tools families are asked to use to evaluate their child's behavior. For most people, performance improves with the use of recognition versus recall questions. As the work of Dale and his colleagues (Dale, 1991; Dale et al., 1989) and Bricker and Squires (1989) has shown, families can be quite reliable when asked to indicate whether their child currently has a particular skill (e.g., uses a pincer grasp, says the word *cookie).* Even mothers who themselves were at risk (e.g., had physically abused or neglected their child, had a history of substance abuse, had not completed high school) have been shown to be reliable in completing developmental questionnaires on their infants (Squires & Bricker, 1991). In addition, the work of Bloch and Seitz (1989) has indicated that families who wish to complete developmental assessments of their children can be taught to do so with a small amount of professional help.

In regard to tools that utilize family report, there are a variety available that encourage differing levels of family participation. Traditionally, these instruments fall into two categories, those that rely solely on family report and those that utilize family report along with elicitation and observation of child behavior. Example instruments specifically designed to be completed from family report alone include the Vineland Adaptive Behavior Scales (Sparrow, Balla, & Cicchetti, 1984) and the Receptive-Expressive Emergent Language Scale-2 (Bzoch & League, 1991). Instruments that combine family report with other information sources include the Battelle Developmental Inventory (Newborg, Stock, Wnek, Guidubaldi, & Svinicki, 1988), the Sequenced Inventory of Communication Development (Hedrick, Prather, & Tobin, 1984), and more recently the Infant-Toddler Language Scale (Rossetti, 1990). With all of these instruments, information is typically gathered by the professional interviewing the family and/or asking about specific behaviors.

In recent years, in response to the challenge to include families more directly in assessment and the need to gain greater efficiency and ecological validity, several tools have been designed for completion by families themselves; an example is the Ages and Stages Questionnaires (Bricker et al., 1995), formerly the Infant/Child Monitoring Questionnaires (Squires, Bricker, & Potter, 1993). The Ages and Stages Questionnaires are a multidomain developmental measure used to monitor at-risk children. Two recently developed family-completed measures of communication skills are the MacArthur Communicative Development Inventories (Fenson et al., 1990) and the Language Development Survey (Rescorla, 1989). All three of these tools utilize a recognition format in which families indicate whether their child currently has a particular skill. Other tools created for use by nonspecialists (e.g., teachers, aides) have also been utilized for completion by families; examples include the Denver Articulation Screening Exam (Drumwright, Van Natta,

Camp, Frankenburg, & Drexler, 1973), used by families to screen their preschool children's articulation skills (Dopheide & Dallinger, 1976), and the Learning Accomplishment Profile (Sanford & Zelman, 1981). In addition, some standardized assessment tools have recently been utilized by families who wish to evaluate their children. Gradel et al. (1981) and Sheehan (1988) have noted the successful completion by families of the Developmental Profile II (Alpern, Boll, & Shearer, 1980) and with modifications (e.g., use of an interview format, simpler vocabulary, and a demonstration of each item), the Bayley Scales of Infant Development (Bayley, 1993) and the McCarthy Scales of Children's Abilities (McCarthy, 1972). To further highlight the collaborative relationship possible between families and professionals, a few instruments have been developed specifically to encourage evaluation by families and professionals. Example tools are the Family Report instrument from the AEPS (Bricker, 1993) and the Parent/Professional Preschool Performance Profile (Bloch, 1987). Both instruments encourage separate evaluation of a child's behaviors by families and professionals and discussion as to what behaviors were seen in one setting (e.g., home, school, clinic) versus another.

In sum, offering families the option to participate in evaluating their child has many advantages. It is an efficient use of family and professional time, provides information not available to professionals, and could improve the ecological validity of the assessment process. Yet, as Sheehan (1988) has suggested regarding family involvement throughout early intervention, "parental involvement is not a universal good for all parents, for all children, or for all schools. Rather it is an activity that has benefits for some parents, many children, and most schools" (p. 85). Therefore, professionals must be careful not to judge families who do not choose to evaluate their own children. Indeed, there are numerous other roles that family members may choose that facilitate their participation in assessment. The important issue is not whether families choose to participate in evaluating their child, but whether they are given the opportunity.

To offer a wider range of roles for families in assessment, professionals are increasingly using a variety of new and older assessment instruments. Adapting the work of Bailey, McWilliam, Winton, and Simeonsson (1992), the following section highlights some of the roles possible and provides examples of instruments that may facilitate them. A role that uses families as experts on their children is that of *interpreter* of the child's behaviors. This may be done informally or in an organized manner. Cardone and Gilkerson (1989) have developed a set of activities to elicit families' interpretations of their child's behavior based on the Neonatal Behavioral Assessment Scale (Brazelton, 1973).

Another role that recognizes the family's unique relationship with the child is that of *participant.* The recent popularity of arena assessment models, which typically include family members as part of the assessment team, is testimony that professionals believe that caregivers are essential to the assessment process. During an arena assessment, a family member may be asked to demonstrate certain skills of the child (e.g., motor or feeding skills) or to administer some test items. Asking families to elicit familiar social routines (e.g., Peek-a-Boo, This Little Piggie) is one means of facilitating a participant role by families. One example procedure for examining family-elicited social routines is described by Platt and Coggins (1990). Through this procedure, families can be asked to elicit favorite routines, then families and professionals can look at Platt and Coggins's hierarchical list of expected behaviors, which can help to sort what behaviors are typical at each level and what behaviors are expected at the next level. A standardized tool that encourages families to be participants in assessment is the Communication and Symbolic Behavior Scale (CSBS) (Wetherby & Prizant, 1993). In the administration of the CSBS, the family member is seated on one side of the child, and the examiner is seated on the other. If the child prefers to interact with the family member, the examiner guides the family member through the administration of the tasks. Family members who choose a participant role can provide comfort to and information about the child and can also be actively engaged in interacting with the child.

Another role that family members may be encouraged to take is that of *validator* of the assessment activities. This role may be utilized first as family members help plan the activities and later as they reflect on their child's behavior relative to the activities and the results gained. Asking families to validate both the assessment activities and their results can provide additional validity and reliability to the entire assessment process. One instrument that formally includes postassessment validation by families is the Communication and Symbolic Behavior Scale (CSBS) by Wetherby and Prizant (1993) noted previously. Following the administration of this instrument, families are asked to use the "Caregiver Perception Rating" form from the CSBS to rate their child's behavior during the assessment (e.g., less than usual, typical, greater than usual) on several components such as alertness, comfort level, and overall communication.

Finally, in response to identified areas of concern, professionals can offer various levels of participation to families in assessment. Professionals can first describe possible assessment activities and the typical role that may be associated with an activity (e.g., use of vocabulary checklist, family completes checklist at home). They can then ask families to indicate both the type of activities and the role they prefer. As suggested by Crais (1993), the activities and family roles selected will depend on (a) the family's priorities regarding the type of information they seek (e.g., developmental levels, ideas for intervention); (b) the system requirements for assessment (e.g., eligibility requirements); (c) the family's ideas and preferences for how information is gathered about the child; and (d) the type of tools or activities that will provide the information desired. As suggested by Sheehan (1988), there may also be a minimum level of interest and skill exhibited by families that may influence their participation in assessment. However, as noted by Diamond and Squires (1993), this hypothesized minimum level may vary with the content of the questions and the way information is gathered (e.g., interview format versus having the family complete a form). Therefore, in seeking family participation in assessment, professionals may wish to offer a variety of available activities and roles and encourage each family to choose the ones they prefer.

Mutual sharing of assessment results

A final strategy for building collaborative relationships between professionals and families in assessment is to focus on the sharing of assessment results and to determine ways that families may actively participate. Traditionally, assessment results have been shared at the end of the process and professionals have often taken the lead and played the largest role. In recent years, professionals have begun to develop alternative strategies such as beginning the discussion by (a) asking family members to give their impressions of the assessment; (b) addressing the family's major concerns first in the sharing session; and (c) asking family members what they currently view as their child's strengths or needs. In addition, a number of professionals have suggested ways that families can not only take part in the sharing meeting, but can also play a prominent role.

One important idea in helping families take a greater part in sharing meetings is to recognize that generally, the more active families are during the assessment planning and assessing, the more likely they are to take an active part during the sharing of the results and the intervention planning. Brinckerhoff and Vincent (1987) demonstrated this principle by asking several families before their child's IEP meetings to complete a family profile and a developmental assessment of their child, to provide an overview of their daily routines, and to meet with a liaison person to prepare for the meeting. The families in the control group were contacted in the usual way about the meetings, but were not asked to perform any special activities prior to the meeting. Brinckerhoff and Vincent reported significant differences between the two groups of families in their participation in the IEP meetings. The families who had been more active in the process before the meeting made more contributions, generated more goals, and made more programming decisions during the meeting. In addition, the professionals in the meetings made more home programming suggestions for the families in the experimental group and made more decisions for the control group. Brinckerhoff and Vincent (1987) also noted that the premeeting activities helped the families in the experimental group match their information on the child with the school personnel's information and helped them pinpoint their child's abilities and needs.

Whether or not family members participate directly in assessment, they may be offered additional options that could help them prepare for the sharing session. For example, they may be encouraged to think about or write down characteristics of the child, their observations of when and under what conditions the child performs best, what they would like the child to achieve in the next month or year, and what possible ways they see to help the child achieve in these areas. In addition, when there is time between the assessment and the discussion of results (even several minutes), some professionals suggest providing families with a list of questions they may want to consider before the discussion. Useful questions could include: "What were your overall impressions of the assessment today?" "What were the activities that your child seemed to do well?" "What were the activities that seemed difficult for your child?" and "What area would you like to discuss first?"

Another successful strategy that may facilitate family/professional collaboration is the sharing of assessment information in an ongoing manner. Rather than save all the assessment results until the end, some professionals and families have found it useful to discuss the information at discrete points throughout the assessment. For example, as each task, tool, or series of tasks is completed, the families and professional(s) may relate their observations and/or findings. In addition, this ongoing sharing may lead families and professionals to work together throughout the assessment to develop and try various modifications or interventions. By discussing the assessment information in an ongoing way, professionals and families can reduce the amount of information to be shared at any one time and can integrate intervention planning in earlier phases of the assessment.

Whether information is shared during or after the assessment, it is important that the sharing be performed in a way that is useful to families in decision making, that promotes feelings of competence and self-worth, and that facilitates ownership of the decisions by family members. It is often useful at the end of the assessment process for professionals to ask families if their concerns were addressed and what, if anything, they still need from professionals. Reviewing any preassessment or information-gathering forms that were utilized earlier may help to identify new or continuing concerns and the need for support or further information. After the sharing meeting, some families may also appreciate the option of having a follow-up meeting to review the information with others important to the child's development. In addition, some professionals find it helpful to offer families the option of reviewing a draft of the follow-up report in case they wish to add or change information before the report is finalized. In these ways, professionals ensure that families are receiving the services and information that are most useful to them.

In summary, it is clear that assessment activities are extremely important in setting the tone and expectations for subsequent interactions. When families and professionals are partners in assessment, they work together to achieve commonly agreed on goals and outcomes, they develop a relationship built on trust and respect, and they seek to strengthen the child's and the family's feelings of self-worth. As families and professionals determine together the assessment content, activities, and results, they are shaping the future for what will happen for the child and the family.

IMPORTANCE OF CROSS-DISCIPLINARY COLLABORATION

The need for building collaborative relationships in assessment is not limited to the relationship between families and professionals. Collaborative relationships must also be forged among the various disciplines and agencies involved. Both Part B and Part H require that assessment be a multidisciplinary effort. According to the law, *multidisciplinary* means "the involvement of two or more disciplines or professions in the provision of integrated and coordinated services, including evaluation and assessment activities" [34 CFR Sec. 303.17]. The disciplines that may be involved in assessing young children with special needs include early childhood education, early childhood special education, medicine, nursing, nutrition, occupational therapy, physical therapy, psychology, social work, and speech/language pathology. Not all of these disciplines will necessarily be involved in the assessment of a particular child, although the family should always be central to the assessment team, as discussed above. The manner in which the various individuals involved in assessment organize themselves and relate to one another is critical in the assessment of young children. The importance of collaborative relationships extends, of course, to intervention as well and includes not only individuals but also agencies (Bruder & Bologna, 1993).

Models of Team Functioning

Typically, three models of team organization are described in relation to assessment: multidisciplinary, interdisciplinary, and transdisciplinary (Foley, 1990; McGonigel, Woodruff, & Roszmann-Millican, 1994; Woodruff & McGonigel, 1988). A diagram representing each of these team organizations is presented in Figure 3.2.

Members of a *multidisciplinary team* work independently, using instruments or procedures representative of their disciplines. Assessment results are reported separately to the family, who must then try to mesh the information and suggestions given them by different professionals. According to Bagnato and Neisworth (1991), it is not accurate to refer to this approach as a model of team functioning, since the professionals involved do not in fact operate as a team but rather as individuals. This approach is often not family-friendly and can create a burden and confusion for the family.

As Figure 3.2 demonstrates, in the *interdisciplinary team,* a premium is placed on communication among team members so that the outcome of assessment and program planning is more unified. In this model, professionals may work individually during the assessment or may work together in subgroups, but there is a definite attempt to communicate. However, McGonigel et al. (1994) point out that communication problems frequently remain within an interdisciplinary model, since team members may not fully understand the training and expertise of their teammates. In addition, team members working separately may find discrepancies in their assessment results. The reader will notice that the family is considered to be a part of the team in this model.

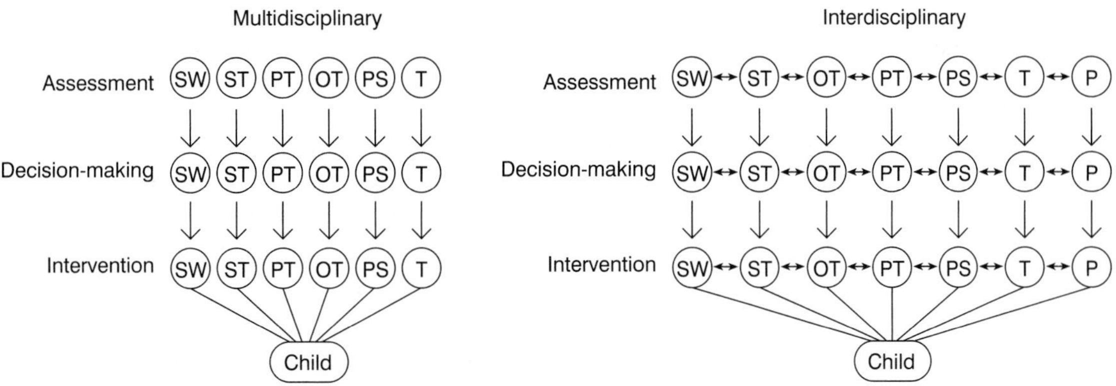

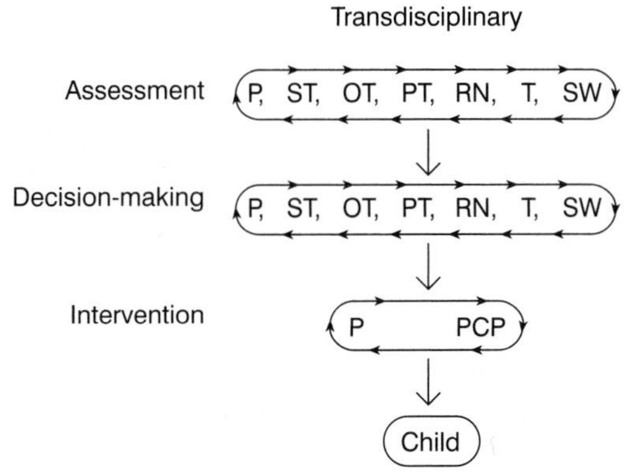

Key: P = Parent
ST = Speech Therapist
OT = Occupational Therapist
PT = Physical Therapist
RN = Registered Nurse
T = Teacher
SW = Social Worker
PCP = Primary Care Provider

FIGURE 3.2
Models of assessment team organization
Source: From *Project KAI Training Packet* by G. Woodruff and C. Hanson (1987). Unpublished manuscript. Reprinted by permission.

The *transdisciplinary team model* is an attempt to maximize communication and collaboration among team members by crossing disciplinary boundaries. According to Bruder and Bologna (1993), the family is also more central on transdisciplinary teams than in the interdisciplinary model. Families are involved to whatever extent they choose in assessment and program planning, and family choices predominate. All team members share responsibility for assessment and development of the intervention plan, but the plan will be carried out by the family and one team member who serves as the primary service provider (McGonigel et al., 1994). The transdisciplinary approach has been identified as being especially appropriate for Part H programs due to its emphasis on the family and on cross-disciplinary work. However, it has also been applied in school-age settings (Rainforth, York, & MacDonald, 1992) and in serving preschool children with disabilities in typical early childhood settings (Bruder, 1994).

McGonigel et al. (1994) suggest that these three models of team functioning are not mutually exclusive, but that they actually represent points on a continuum moving from less to more interaction among the disciplines. Developing a transdisciplinary team approach may not be possible for every assessment team. Central to becoming transdisciplinary is the process of *role release,* which allows individual team members to carry out activities that would normally be the responsibility of another discipline. McGonigel et al. (1994) provide a description of the components of this process and warn that successful role release requires continuous attention to team building and team maintenance, which will require staff training, time, and support from administrators.

One component of the transdisciplinary team approach that has been adopted by many assessment teams is the arena approach. *Arena assessment* is the simultaneous evaluation of the child by multiple professionals of differing disciplines (Foley, 1990; Linder, 1993; McGonigel et al., 1994). Instead of each professional working with the child separately, the team of professionals works together with the child, allowing a common sample of behavior and immediate sharing of expertise and information. The rationale for arena assessment is based on the relative difficulty of separating physical, cognitive, and sensory domains of development in the young child. When implemented correctly, the advantages of this approach extend to everyone involved—the child, the family, and the professionals. Since all professionals are working together, the amount of actual time spent in assessment by the child and the family is reduced. Family members can provide information once rather than being asked the same questions by each professional in turn. Professionals have the advantage of immediate access to the skills and knowledge of their teammates. In addition, consensus building is facilitated since a common sampling of behavior has been the basis of evaluation for all team members. Figure 3.3 presents a sequence of events that might be followed during an arena assessment as described by Foley (1990).

The organization of an arena assessment is based on the concept of a primary facilitator. One member of the team is designated to serve as primary facilitator by interacting with the parent and child and eliciting the main sample of structured behavior. This does not mean that other team members are forbidden to interact with the child; for example, the physical therapist may need to lay hands on the child to assess muscle tone even though another team member is the primary facilitator. It does mean, however, that if there is an instrument or instruments that serve as the more structured part of the evaluation, all team members may need to become proficient at administration. The primary facilitator may be designated as such because the needs of the child best match his or her discipline, because of a relationship established with the child or the family, or because of other considerations that may arise. A family facilitator may also be designated to record family members' input and answer their questions throughout the evaluation (Linder, 1993). Some teams also choose one member to be the coach for the arena assessment. The coach serves as a resource to the facilitator by observing the process and reminding the facilitator of planned assessment strategies or items that may be overlooked as the assessment proceeds. Figure 3.4 is a drawing that depicts an arena assessment.

The arena assessment incorporates preassessment planning (described earlier) as an important component of the assessment process. The family may be a part of the plan-

Greeting and Warm-Up
(Family and team members visit, child is allowed to explore and get to know team members.)

Formal Task-Centered Sequence
(The main assessment instrument is administered by the primary facilitator. Other team members observe and may score discipline-specific instruments or make clinical notes.)

Snack Break and Refueling
(Snack and bathroom break provides an opportunity to observe self-help skills and parent-child interaction.)

Story Time or Teaching Samples
(A story-time format may be used to expand the language sample, or a brief teaching sequence might be used to observe how the child processes new information and generalizes learning to new materials.)

Free Play
(The child's spontaneous movement and interaction with toys will be observed. With older children, bringing in a peer at this point may allow observation of social interaction skills as well.)

Brief Staffing and Feedback
(The team members take a minute to formulate impressions while the parent facilitator collects the parents' comments about the session. Parents and other team members will then come together to share initial impressions so the parents have some closure and do not go away with undue anxiety. A formal staffing of the evaluation will be held at a later time.)

FIGURE 3.3
Possible sequence for an arena evaluation
Source: From "Portrait of the Arena Evaluation: Assessment in the Transdisciplinary Approach" by G. M. Foley, in E. Gibbs & D. Teti (Eds.) *Interdisciplinary Assessment of Infants: A Guide for Early Intervention,* 1990, Baltimore, MD: Paul H. Brookes. Adapted by permission.

ning meeting if they choose; they are also present or invited to be present at all meetings in which assessment results are discussed. As noted in Figure 3.3, assessment results may be shared with the family, at least informally, immediately after the assessment.

McGonigel et al. (1994) describe a meeting of the team for the purpose of team maintenance that takes place after the arena assessment and does not include the family. The purpose of this meeting is to evaluate the team process and how it went during the assessment. Even though an additional meeting could be costly in terms of the professionals' time, McGonigel and her colleagues stress the importance of this procedure for team functioning.

The arena format has been identified as especially appropriate for the assessment of young children (Foley, 1990; Linder, 1993; McGonigel et al., 1994). However, McGonigel and her colleagues caution that it will not be best for all children and all families. Therefore, assessment teams must be willing to change their methods of assessing young children to fit the needs of individual children and families.

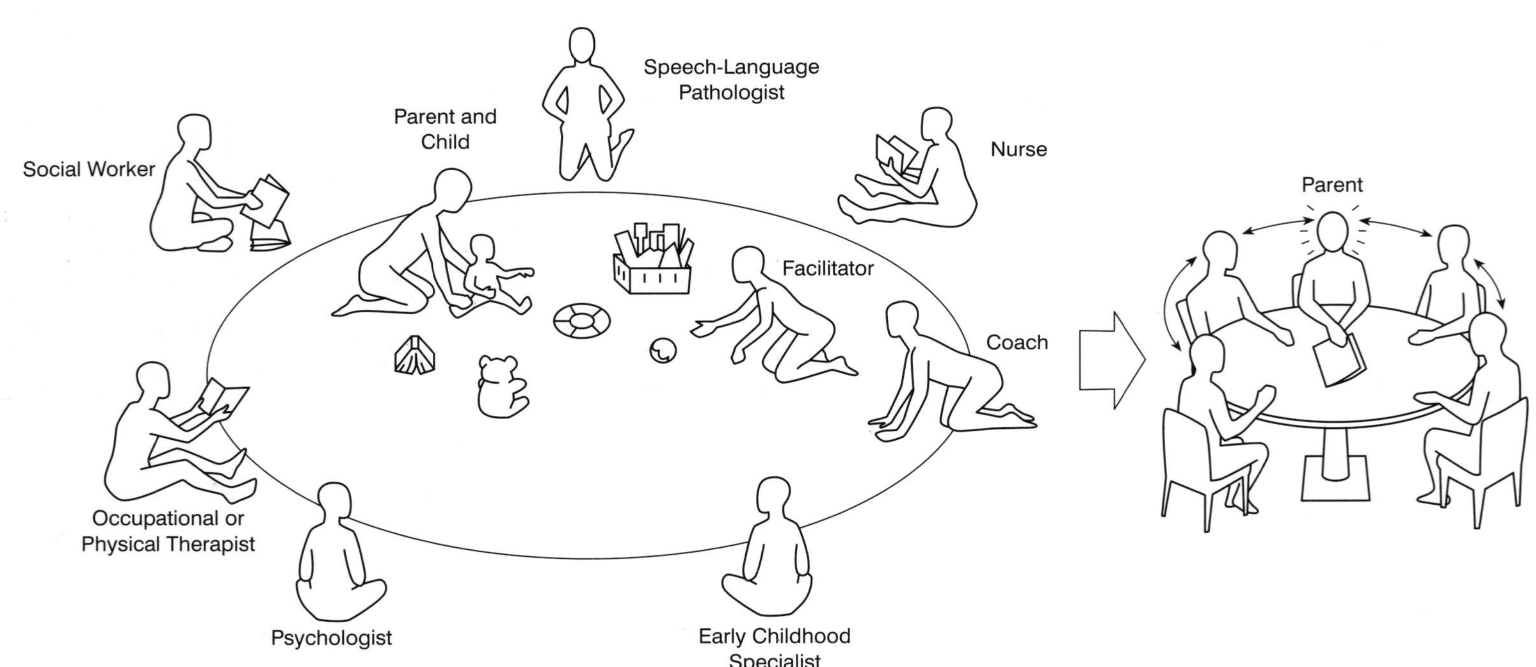

FIGURE 3.4

Example of an arena assessment

Source: From "The Transdisciplinary Team: A Model for Family-Centered Early Intervention" by M. J. McGonigel, G. Woodruff, & M. Roszmann-Millican, in L. J. Johnson, R. J. Gallagher, M. J. LaMontagne, J. B. Jordan, J. J. Gallagher, P. L. Hutinger, & M. B. Karnes (Eds.) *Meeting Early Intervention Challenges, Issues from Birth to Three* (2nd ed.), 1994, Baltimore, MD: Paul H. Brookes. Copyright 1994 by Child Development Resources. Reprinted by permission.

Collaborative Decision Making

Inherent in the transdisciplinary team model described above is attention to team building and team maintenance activities that will facilitate the process of decision making by team members. The EI/ECSE professional may work consistently with the same group of people in doing assessments, but it is more likely that he or she will work with at least several if not many different groups. A group of individuals will not necessarily work together as a team without some conscious effort being put toward team building. Maddux (1988) has identified differences between groups and teams. According to Maddux, a group of people become a team when they are working from a common philosophy with shared goals. In addition, team members need to develop the skills necessary to maintain open and honest communication and to resolve conflicts that may arise as part of the decision-making process. Unfortunately, preservice training programs for professionals who will be serving young children frequently do not include preparation in the skills needed to become an effective team member (Bailey, Palsha, & Huntington, 1990).

The System to Plan Early Childhood Services (SPECS) (Bagnato & Neisworth, 1990), a team decision-making format that links cross-disciplinary assessment, was derived to facilitate the process of decision making by teams of professionals representing various disciplines (Bagnato & Neisworth, 1991). It uses structured clinical judgment ratings to evaluate the competencies of children from 24 to 72 months of age in six domains. SPECS is composed of three components: Developmental Specs, Team Specs, and Program Specs. Developmental Specs uses five-point Likert rating scales to record the judgments of the family and professional team members about the child's developmental and behavioral capabilities and needs. Team Specs enables the team to determine a consensus rating of each developmental area, which is then cross-referenced with ten therapy options (physical therapy, speech/language therapy, etc.). Program Specs assists the team in making decisions about the content and strategies to be designated in the intervention plan (Bagnato & Neisworth, 1991).

Members of early childhood assessment teams must be aware of the extent to which their group is actually functioning as a team in carrying out the responsibilities of assessment and decision making. Requests for support in the form of inservice training on team building or additional time that may be necessary for team maintenance should be made to administrators as needed. Collaborative decision making is central to quality assessment of young children. It will not, however, automatically occur but must be nurtured.

IMPORTANCE OF ASSESSMENT IN THE NATURAL ENVIRONMENT

A quote from Urie Bronfenbrenner (1977) about developmental psychology has recently been applied to describe the assessment of young children: "The science of the strange behavior of children in strange situations with strange adults for the briefest possible period of time" (p. 513). This quote communicates our seemingly increasing dissatisfaction with traditional assessment strategies that perhaps rely too much on highly structured practices and unfamiliar settings. The danger is that test scores that result from such practices will be used to make eligibility and programmatic decisions without adequate consideration of whether such results adequately characterize the child's typical behavior.

According to Bracken (1991), "test behavior should never be interpreted unconditionally as representative of a child's typical behavior in any other setting" (p. 42). It is customary to end an assessment session by asking the family whether their child's behavior was representative of his or her typical behavior. Even a positive response to this question, however, should not result in reliance on the outcome of direct testing as the sole basis upon which eligibility or program planning decisions are made.

The infant/toddler program has a built-in safeguard against evaluation and assessment decisions that are made on the basis of test scores only. Under Part H regulations, such decisions must be based on "informed clinical opinion" [34 CFR Sec. 303.322(c)(2)]. According to Biro, Daulton, and Szanton (1991), informed clinical opinion emerges from the knowledge and skill of the team, including the family, and may be based on the integration of information obtained from interviews with family, evaluation of the child at play, observation of family-child interaction, and information obtained from the teacher or child-care provider. Information from these sources can then be used by the team to explain variable performance on assessment instruments, to support the validity or invalidity of test scores, and to develop hypotheses about the child's current functioning and need for intervention. As indicated in Chapter 1, in some states, test scores are not needed; only the informed clinical opinion of the assessment team is required.

While tests or assessment instruments certainly may be a part of the assessment process, particularly if state regulations do require a quantitative score for determining eligibility, it is also fair to say that the assessment of young children does not need to be test-based or limited to the use of tests (Bagnato & Neisworth, 1991; Wolery, 1994). In other words, in addition to traditional assessment instruments or tests, the assessment team has a variety of assessment strategies available that will allow the team to sample behavior in a way that is representative of the child's typical functioning.

As indicated earlier, one function of the pre-assessment planning process will be to identify the questions that will guide the assessment, the strategies and instruments to be used, and the times and places for carrying out the planned strategies. This procedure will allow the team to plan assessment strategies that will gather information in a way that is most reflective of the child's typical behavior.

A variety of assessment formats can be used in assessing young children. Norm-referenced, criterion-referenced, and curriculum-referenced instruments have traditionally been part of assessment and are discussed in Chapter 2. A *norm-referenced* instrument compares a measure of the child's development to norms derived from a population of children. Norm-referenced instruments commonly utilize rather structured procedures for assessment; however, some, for example the Battelle Developmental Inventory (Newborg et al., 1988) also allow the use of observation and family report. If a quantitative score is required as an outcome of assessment, the team will probably decide to utilize a norm-referenced instrument that then can be supplemented with other procedures that require less structure. *Criterion-referenced* instruments measure success or failure in meeting some previously determined objectives. Items are selected for inclusion on a criterion-referenced instrument because of their importance to the child's daily functioning. *Curriculum-referenced* instruments, which compare a child's developmental attainments with a pre-existing curriculum, facilitate the process of program planning, since intervention targets might then be suggested by the curriculum. Norm-referenced, criterion-referenced, and curriculum-referenced instruments are certainly important tools for determining eligibility for services and program planning and can also be used to monitor child progress. There are, however, additional formats that might be used by the team to ensure that assessment results are representative of the child's typical behavior. These include judgment-based assessment, systematic observation, anecdotal recording, play-based assessment, ecological assessment, interactive assessment, and authentic assessment.

Judgment-based instruments ask professionals or caregivers to record their perceptions of the child's functioning. Usually in the form of a checklist or a rating scale, these instruments provide information from family members, caregivers, and/or professionals based on their observation of the child. This can be done through in situ observation, meaning that the rater observes the child for a period of time and then records his or her impressions, or it can be done based on impressions over time. The newly developed Behavior Rating Scale, which is part of the revised Bayley Scales of Infant Development (Bayley, 1993), uses judgment-based assessment by asking the examiner to judge the child's behavior following administration of the Bayley. The System to Plan Early Childhood Services (SPECS) (Bagnato & Neisworth, 1990), which was discussed earlier, uses judgment-based assessment to facilitate team decision making regarding program eligibility and the level and scope of intervention services needed. Judgment-based assessment provides a mechanism for getting input from a variety of individuals who are familiar with the child.

Systematic observation can be carried out in the home or in preschool settings, allowing measurement of behavior occurring in any environment. It involves structured observation and recording of child behavior and yields quantifiable data. It has been utilized traditionally in applied behavior analysis research. As indicated above, observation can be carried out in natural settings (in vivo) or through a staged or structured situation in order to elicit particular behaviors (Neisworth & Bagnato, 1988). Systematic observation differs from judgment-based assessment in that it is designed to yield an objective reporting of observed behavior rather than a judgment or an impression of behavior. As described in Chapter 13, systematic observation typically includes the use of time-sampling and interval-recording procedures to record observed behavior.

Anecdotal recording is a written description of a child's behavior in a particular situation. Anecdotal records can be kept by caregivers, teachers, and therapists as part of initial assessment or to monitor child progress. In making an anecdotal record, the individual attempts to describe the behavior as completely as possible. Anecdotal recording may be objective (facts) or may include impressions or judgments as long as this is clearly indicated. Frequently, circumstances or events in the environment that preceded or followed the child's behavior will also be recorded. A running record is a form of anecdotal recording that typically is planned in advance and continues for a longer period of time. The communication-sampling strategy that is described in Chapter 11 is an example of a running record.

It is common for early childhood professionals to keep a record of children's behavior in a log or journal. Sometimes the adult will record anecdotally while observing the child; at other times, information or observations may be recorded at the end of the day or during a period of free time (Bentzen, 1985; Cohen, Stern, & Balaban, 1983). Such logs or journals can be very helpful in adding information from the natural environment to the assessment of a child with special needs.

Play-based assessment utilizes play as the medium for observing child behavior. Since this type of assessment is done rather informally in a play setting, the behavior observed is considered to be more typical of the child's behavior in the natural environment than in a structured assessment. The work of Linder (1993) has been instrumental in demonstrating how play can be used as the basis for assessment. A typical assessment using Linder's system includes free-play and also semistructured play, during which the facilitator attempts to elicit particular behaviors from the child. It includes an opportunity for observation of parent-child interaction and also of the child's interaction with peers. Linder's system utilizes a transdisciplinary team approach, as described earlier, and covers all areas of development. The work of Bricker and her colleagues on the Assessment, Evaluation, and Programming System (Bricker, 1993) also utilizes play as a medium for curriculum-based assessment and, in addition, describes strategies for setting up play centers within a classroom to facilitate the assessment process.

Ecological assessment provides information on the physical and social features of the child's typical environments, both at home and in child-care or preschool settings. Ecological assessment is exemplified by instruments such as the Early Childhood Environment Rating Scale (Harms & Clifford, 1980), which is designed to give an overall picture of surroundings for children and adults in preschool settings. Ecological assessment has also been applied to the preparation of children for other environments through the use of the ecological inventory (Noonan & McCormick, 1993), which evaluates the skills required in other current or future environments as a basis for program planning. See Chapter 9 for further information on this subject.

Interactive assessment is actually a component of ecological assessment that focuses on the social interactions that take place between children and family members or between children and peers. Interactive measures may take the form of rating scales, checklists, or coded observation of interactions. For example, the Parent Behavior Progression (Bromwich, 1981) is a checklist that measures the initial status and subsequent changes in parenting behavior. It is the result of observation of parent-child interactions and is completed as part of an infant intervention program that focuses on the parent-child dyad. Another measure of parent-child interaction that is accomplished through systematic observation is the Infant-Parent Social Interaction Code (Baird, Haas, McCormick, Carruth, & Turner, 1992), which utilizes a videotaped sample of parent-child interaction as a basis for coding various infant and parent behaviors.

Authentic assessment refers to assessment based on student efforts in actual performance situations rather than on the results of group tests such as achievement tests. One approach to authentic assessment is the collection in a *portfolio* of examples of a child's work that illustrates efforts, progress, and achievements over time. A child's portfolio is typically composed of work samples that might include the child's writing, drawings, pages of journals, photos of the child's constructions, tape recordings, or video recordings (Meisels & Steele, 1991). Portfolios are designed to demonstrate the child's emerging abilities over a period of time; they provide an opportunity for the child to be involved in selecting and judging his or her own work. The Work Sampling System (Meisels, 1992) is an example of an authentic assessment system; it includes developmental checklists, portfolios, and summary reports. It is designed for children from age 3 to grade 3.

For young children who do not yet write or draw, the use of photographs and audio- or videotapes might be the most feasible way to demonstrate progress in developmental areas. Anecdotal notes and running records such as a language sample might also be included. Family members might also want to contribute to their child's portfolio.

The assessment team has many options for gathering information for the purpose of making decisions about young children with special needs. To obtain a truly representative picture of child functioning, the team must strive to obtain information from multiple sources and multiple settings.

SUMMARY OF KEY CONCEPTS

- Recommended practices for assessing infants and preschoolers include providing the opportunity for family participation, cross-disciplinary collaboration, and assessment in the natural environment.
- Establishing a truly collaborative relationship with families during assessment means providing them the opportunity to be active participants throughout the entire process, including planning the assessment, gathering information, and making decisions as a result of the assessment.
- A plan for assessment can be developed by the family/professional team that will determine the goals for assessment and the strategies/instruments to be used.
- Families can be offered the opportunity to participate in the assessment in a variety of roles, including interpreters of their child's behavior, participants in the assessment, and validators of the assessment activities.
- Typical models of team functioning include the multidisciplinary, interdisciplinary, and transdisciplinary approaches. Arena assessment, the simultaneous assessment of the child by multiple professionals, is one component of the transdisciplinary team model.
- Assessment of infants and preschoolers does not need to be limited to the use of tests. Other strategies that allow the gathering of information from natural environments include judgment-based assessment, systematic observation, narrative descriptions, play-based assessment, ecological inventories, interactive assessment, and authentic assessment.

REFERENCES

Alpern, G., Boll, T., & Shearer, M. (1980). *Developmental Profile II.* Aspen, CO: Psychological Development Publications.

Bagnato, S. J., & Neisworth, J. T. (1991). *Assessment for early intervention: Best practices for professionals.* New York: Guilford Press.

Bagnato, S. J., & Neisworth, J. T. (1990). *System to plan early childhood services.* Circle Pines, MN: American Guidance Service.

Bailey, D., & Blasco, P. (1990). Parents' perspectives on a written survey of family needs. *Journal of Early Intervention, 14*(3), 196–203.

Bailey, D., McWilliam, P., Winton, P., & Simeonsson, R. (1992). *Implementing family-centered services in early intervention: A team-based model for change.* Cambridge, MA: Brookline Books.

Bailey, D., Palsha, S., & Huntington, G. (1990). Preservice preparation of special educators to serve infants with handicaps and their families: Current status and training needs. *Journal of Early Intervention, 14*(1), 43–54.

Bailey, D., & Simeonsson, R. (1990). *Family Needs Survey Revised.* Chapel Hill, NC: Frank Porter Graham Child Development Center.

Baird, S. M., Haas, L. M., McCormick, K., Carruth, C., & Turner, K. (1992). Approaching an objective system for observation and measurement: Infant-parent social interaction code. *Topics in Early Childhood Special Education, 12*(4), 544–571.

Bayley, N. (1993). *Bayley Scales of Infant Development—Second Edition.* San Antonio, TX: The Psychological Corp.

Bentzen, W. R. (1985). *Seeing young children: A guide to observing and recording behavior.* Albany, NY: Delmar Publishers.

Biro, P., Daulton, D., & Szanton, E. (1991). Informed clinical opinion. *NEC*TAS Notes, 4,* 1-4.

Bloch, J. (1987). *Parent/Professional Preschool Performance Profile.* Syosset, NY: Variety Pre-Schoolers' Workshop.

Bloch, J., & Seitz, M. (1989). Parents as assessors of children: A collaborative approach to helping. *Social Work in Education, 11*(4), 226–244.

Bracken, B. (1991). The clinical observation of preschool assessment behavior. In B. Bracken (Ed.), *The psychoeducational assessment of preschool children* (2nd ed.) (pp. 40–52). Boston: Allyn and Bacon.

Brazelton, T. (1973). *Neonatal Behavioral Assessment Scale.* Philadelphia, PA: J. B. Lippincott.

Bricker, D. (1993). *Assessment, evaluation, and programming system for children: AEPS measurement for birth to three years* (Vol. 1). Baltimore, MD: Paul H. Brookes.

Bricker, D., & Squires, J. (1989). The effectiveness of parental screening of at-risk infants: The infant monitoring questionnaires. *Topics in Early Childhood Special Education, 9,* 67–85.

Bricker, D., Squires, J., Mounts, L., Potter, L., Nickel, B., & Farrell, J. (1995). *Ages and Stages Questionnaires.* Baltimore, MD: Paul H. Brookes.

Brinckerhoff, J., & Vincent, L. (1987). Increasing parental decision making at the individualized educational program meeting. *Journal of the Division for Early Childhood, 11,* 46–48.

Bromwich, R. (1981). *Working with parents and infants.* Baltimore, MD: University Park Press.

Bronfenbrenner, U. (1977). Toward an experimental ecology of human development. *American Psychologist, 32*(7), 513–531.

Bruder, M. B. (1994). Working with members of other disciplines: Collaboration for success. In M. Wolery & J. S. Wilbers (Eds.), *Including children with special needs in early childhood programs* (pp. 45–70). Washington, DC: National Association for the Education of Young Children.

Bruder, M. B., & Bologna, T. (1993). Collaboration and service coordination for effective early intervention. In W. Brown, S. K. Thurman, & L. F. Pearl (Eds.), *Family-centered early intervention with infants and toddlers* (pp. 103–128). Baltimore, MD: Paul H. Brookes.

Bzoch, K., & League, R. (1991). *Receptive-Expressive Emergent Language Scale—2.* Austin, TX: PRO-ED.

Cardone, I., & Gilkerson, L. (1989). Family administered neonatal activities: An innovative component of family-centered care. *Zero to Three, 10*(1), 23–28.

Cohen, D., Stern, V., & Balaban, N. (1983). *Observing and recording the behavior of young children* (3rd ed.). New York: Teachers College Press.

Crais, E. (1992). "Best practices" with preschoolers: Assessing within the context of a family-centered approach. *Best Practices in School Speech-Language Pathology, 2,* 33–42.

Crais, E. (1993). Families and professionals as collaborators in assessment. *Topics in Language Disorders, 14*(1), 29–40.

Dale, P. (1991). The validity of a parent report measure of vocabulary and syntax at 24 months. *Journal of Speech and Hearing Research, 34,* 565–571.

Dale, P., Bates, E., Reznick, S., & Morisset, C. (1989). The validity of a parent report instrument on child language at twenty months. *Journal of Child Language, 16,* 239–249.

Diamond, K., & Squires, J. (1993). The role of parental report in the screening and assessment of young children. *Journal of Early Intervention, 17*(2), 107–115.

DEC Task Force on Recommended Practices (1993). *DEC recommended practices: Indicators of quality in programs for infants and young children with special needs and their families.* Reston, VA: Council for Exceptional Children.

Dopheide, W., & Dallinger, J. (1976). Preschool articulation screening by parents. *Language, Speech, and Hearing in the Schools, 7,* 124–127.

Drumwright, A., Van Natta, P., Camp, B., Frankenburg, W., & Drexler, H. (1973). The Denver Articulation Screening Exam. *Journal of Speech and Hearing Disorders, 38,* 3–14.

Dunst, C., Trivette, C., & Deal, A. (1988). *Enabling and empowering families.* Cambridge, MA: Brookline Books.

Fenson, L., Dale, P., Reznick, S., Thal, D., Bates, E., Hartung, J., Pethick, S., & Reilly, J. (1990). *MacArthur Communicative Development Inventories.* San Diego, CA: Center for Research in Language.

Foley, G. M. (1990). Portrait of the arena evaluation: Assessment in the transdisciplinary approach. In E. Gibbs & D. Teti (Eds.), *Interdisciplinary assessment of infants: A guide for early intervention* (pp. 271–286). Baltimore, MD: Paul H. Brookes.

Gibbs, E., & Teti, C. D. (1990). Issues and future directions in infant and family assessment. In E.

Gibbs & D. Teti (Eds.), *Interdisciplinary assessment of infants: A guide for early intervention professionals* (pp. 77–90). Baltimore, MD: Paul H. Brookes.

Glascoe, F., MacLean, W., & Stone, W. (1991). The importance of parents' concerns about their child's behavior. *Clinical Pediatrics, 30,* 8–11.

Grace, C., & Shores, E. F. (1994). *The portfolio and its use: Developmentally appropriate assessment of young children* (3rd ed.). Little Rock, AR: Southern Early Childhood Association.

Gradel, K., Thompson, M., & Sheehan, R. (1981). Parental and professional agreement in early childhood assessment. *Topics in Early Childhood Special Education, 1,* 31–39.

Harms, T., & Clifford, R. M. (1980). *Early Childhood Environment Rating Scale.* New York: Teachers College Press.

Hedrick, D., Prather, E., & Tobin, A. (1984). *Sequenced Inventory of Communication Development—Revised.* Seattle, WA: University of Washington Press.

Kjerland, L., & Kovach, J. (1990). Family-staff collaboration for tailored infant assessment. In E. Gibbs & D. Teti (Eds.), *Interdisciplinary assessment of infants: A guide for early intervention professionals* (pp. 287–298). Baltimore, MD: Paul H. Brookes.

Leet, H., & Dunst, C. (1988). *Family Resource Scale.* In C. Dunst, C. Trivette, & A. Deal, *Enabling and empowering families* (p. 141). Cambridge, MA: Brookline Books.

Linder, T. (1993). *Transdisciplinary play-based assessment: A functional approach to working with young children* (rev. ed.). Baltimore, MD: Paul H. Brookes.

Maddux, R. E. (1988). *Team building: An exercise in leadership.* Los Altos, CA: Crisp Publications.

McCarthy, D. (1972). *McCarthy Scales of Children's Abilities.* New York: The Psychological Corp.

McGonigel, M., Kaufmann, R., & Johnson, B. (1991). *Guidelines and Recommended Practices for the Individualized Family Service Plan* (2nd ed.). Bethesda, MD: Association for the Care of Children's Health.

McGonigel, M. J., Woodruff, G., & Roszmann-Millican, M. (1994). The transdisciplinary team: A model for family-centered early intervention. In L. J. Johnson, R. J. Gallagher, M. J. LaMontagne, J. B. Jordan, J. J. Gallagher, P. L. Hutinger, & M. B. Karnes (Eds.), *Meeting early intervention challenges* (pp. 95–131). Baltimore, MD: Paul H. Brookes.

McLean, M., & McCormick, K. (1993). Assessment and evaluation in early intervention. In W. Brown, S. Thurman, & L. Pearl (Eds.), *Family-centered early intervention with infants and toddlers* (pp. 43–79). Baltimore, MD: Paul H. Brookes.

Meisels, S. (1992). *The work sampling system: An overview.* Ann Arbor, MI: University of Michigan.

Meisels, S., & Steele, D. (1991). *The early childhood portfolio collection process.* Ann Arbor, MI: University of Michigan Center for Human Growth and Development.

Neisworth, J. T., & Bagnato, S. J. (1988). Assessment in early childhood special education: A typology of dependent measures. In S. L. Odom & M. L. Karnes (Eds.), *Early intervention for infants and children with handicaps* (pp. 23–44). Baltimore, MD: Paul H. Brookes.

Newborg, J., Stock, J. R., Wnek, L., Guidubaldi, J., & Svinicki, J. (1988). *The Battelle Developmental Inventory.* Dallas, TX: DLM Teaching Resources.

Noonan, M. J., & McCormick, L. (1993). *Early intervention in natural environments: Methods and procedures.* Pacific Grove, CA: Brooks/Cole Publishing Company.

Olson, J. (1988). *Delivering sensitive information to families of handicapped infants and young children.* Unpublished manuscript, University of Idaho, Special Education Department, Moscow, ID.

Platt, J., & Coggins, T. (1990). Comprehension of social-action routines in prelinguistic children: Levels of participation and effect of adult structure. *Journal of Speech and Hearing Disorders, 55,* 315–326.

Poyadue, F. (1988). In my opinion: Parents as teachers of health care professionals. *Child Health Care, 17*(2), 82–84.

Rainforth, B., York, J., & MacDonald, C. (1992). *Collaborative teams for students with severe disabilities: Integrating therapy and educational services.* Baltimore, MD: Paul H. Brookes.

Rescorla, L. (1989). The language development survey: A screening tool for delayed language in toddlers. *Journal of Speech and Hearing Disorders, 54,* 587–599.

Rossetti, L. (1990). *Infant-Toddler Language Scale.* East Moline, IL: Linguisystems.

Sanford, A., & Zelman, J. (1981). *The Learning Accomplishment Profile.* Winston-Salem, NC: Kaplan.

Sheehan, R. (1988). Involvement of parents in early childhood assessment. In R. Sheehan & T. Wachs (Eds.), *Assessment of young developmentally disabled children* (pp. 75–90). New York: Plenum.

Sparrow, S., Balla, D., & Cicchetti, D. (1984). *Vineland Adaptive Behavior Scales.* Circle Pines, MN: American Guidance Service.

Squires, J., & Bricker, D. (1991). Impact of completing infant developmental questionnaires on at-risk mothers. *Journal of Early Intervention, 15,* 162–172.

Squires J., Bricker, D., & Potter, L. (1993). *Infant/child monitoring questionnaires: Procedures manual.* Eugene, OR: University of Oregon Center on Human Development.

Tarran, E. (1991). Parents' view of medical and social-work services for families with cerebral palsied children. *Developmental Medicine and Child Neurology, 23,* 173–182.

Turnbull, A., & Turnbull, H. (1986). *Family Information Preference Inventory.* In A. Turnbull & H. Turnbull (Eds.), *Families, professionals, and exceptionality: A special partnership* (pp. 368–373). Englewood Cliffs, NJ: Merrill/Prentice Hall.

Wetherby, A., & Prizant, B. (1993). *Communication and Symbolic Behavior Scale* (1st ed.). Chicago, IL: Riverside Publishing Company.

Winton, P. (1988). Effective communication between parents and professionals. In D. Bailey & R. Simeonsson (Eds.), *Family assessment in early intervention* (pp. 207–208). Englewood Cliffs, NJ: Merrill/Prentice Hall.

Winton, P., & Bailey, D. (1993). Communicating with families: Examining practices and facilitating change. In J. Paul & R. Simeonsson (Eds.), *Children with special needs: Family, culture and society* (pp. 210–230). Orlando, FL: Harcourt Brace Jovanovich.

Wolery, M. (1994). Assessing children with special needs. In M. Wolery & J. S. Wilbers (Eds.), *Including children with special needs in early childhood programs* (pp. 71–96). Washington, DC: National Association for the Education of Young Children.

Wolery, M., Strain, P. S., & Bailey, D. B. (1992). Reaching potentials of children with special needs. In S. Bredekamp & T. Rosegrant (Eds.), *Reaching potentials: Appropriate curriculum and assessment for young children* (pp. 92–111). Washington, DC: National Association for the Education of Young Children.

Woodruff, G., & Hanson, C. (1987). *Project KAI training packet.* Unpublished manuscript.

Woodruff, G., & McGonigel, M. J. (1988). Early intervention team approaches: The transdisciplinary model. In J. B. Jordan, J. J. Gallagher, P. L. Hutinger, & M. B. Karnes (Eds.), *Early childhood special education: Birth to three* (pp. 164–181). Reston, VA: The Council for Exceptional Children.

CHAPTER

4

Ensuring Cultural Competence in Assessment

Eleanor W. Lynch
San Diego State University
Marci J. Hanson
San Francisco State University

There never were, in the world, two opinions alike, no more than two hairs, or two grains; the most universal quality is diversity.

Montaigne, *Essays* (1580-88)

Families, like the fingerprints of the individuals who comprise them, are all different. Opinions, values, goals, resources, languages, styles, and modes of communication vary from family to family, just as they do for individuals. Service providers who work closely with young children and their families are required to provide consistent standard procedures through their service delivery agency, while at the same time delivering these services in a manner that is responsive and sensitive to the diverse characteristics of the families served.

For many years service providers in the educational, social, and health fields have grappled with issues surrounding the provision of "appropriate," culturally nonbiased, multidisciplinary assessments of young children. As this and other volumes attest, assessment in early childhood remains a rather elusive topic; no one method or instrument is identified as capable of detecting and/or predicting all the children in need of intervention or evaluating the effects of the intervention regimen. The introduction and implementation of the Individualized Family Service Plan (IFSP) through Public Law 99-457 in 1986 (now retitled the Individuals with Disabilities Education Act, or IDEA, Public Law 102-119 of 1991) has provided a further challenge of devising methods to assess and evaluate family strengths and needs appropriately and to ensure family input and participation in the IFSP process. As Colarusso and Kana (1991) cautioned:

> Differences in variables, such as socioeconomic status, marital status, cultural background, geographic location, family values, attitudes, interests, desires, and coping strategies for dealing with this potentially stressful situation, leave policy makers the potential to design rules applicable and appropriate for some families and not others. (p. 9)

These challenges highlight the need for an examination of the methods used in assessing child and family concerns, priorities, and resources. The impact of cultural and family diversity on developing and implementing child and family assessment techniques is explored in this chapter. Considerations regarding the influence of varying family characteristics on gathering information and planning and developing assessment and intervention strategies for young children and their families are raised in light of the changing demographics in the United States. This is followed by a discussion of the importance of developing cross-cultural competence in the assessment process and a review of methods or strategies for achieving effective assessment techniques. Finally, each component of the assessment process is examined and analyzed with regard to implementation through culturally competent practices and procedures.

RATIONALE FOR EXAMINATION OF SERVICE MODELS

The service models for young children and their families have evolved over the past 25 years. However, the changes in demographics, family constellation, and overall diversity have outpaced the changes in the models. As a result, it is time to examine what we do and how we do it in relation to the families who are being served.

Implications of Diversity on the Child and Family Assessment Process

Almost daily a story of a potential cultural clash emerges in the communities in which the authors live. One recent example involved an activity implemented through the local and statewide effort to plan for services to infants and toddlers with disabilities and risk conditions and their families (through participation in the Part H, P.L. 99-457 planning phase). A representative of the local interagency coordinating council was hired to conduct a family needs assessment. Knowing the importance of sampling from a wide range of parents in this culturally diverse community, she contacted all early intervention programs and arranged to interview designated families who were representative of the many groups in the community. In these interviews, she asked family members questions regarding their satisfaction with the services they had received for their children with disabilities/risk conditions and requested that they identify any other services that would have been helpful. During one interview a mother from an Asian background became uncomfortable and finally, through her translator, indicated how bad she felt. To her, being singled out to discuss this issue of her child with a disability brought shame to her and her family. The interviewer had the best intentions in gathering this information; the mother was very helpful by agreeing to be interviewed. However, the process was unsuccessful and culturally insensitive. Such situations highlight the need for a range of information-gathering options that truly reflect the diversity of family preferences and backgrounds.

Examples of cultural clashes in family service delivery settings, however well intentioned, could fill this volume. Obvious difficulties may arise from differences between service providers and the children and families with whom they work with respect to primary language used. Apart from these potential difficulties are examples that range from cases of inappropriate referral for child abuse when "bruises" found on children were really birthmarks or had been created by native medical/health practices, to failure of families to participate in services due to misunderstanding of terms and procedures. Dale and Hoshino (1984) describe misunderstandings that led to communication barriers and relate examples of confusion and difficulties with terminology. For example, the word *surgery* translates to "butchery" in the Hmong language. Another example of a cultural clash between a service provider and a family is provided by Joe and Malach (1992). A Native American family traveled from the reservation to meet with an early interventionist. She suggested that they eat lunch at the local Owl Cafe. The suggestion was inappropriate because in the family's culture, owls are considered a bad omen. As these illustrations point out, merely translating terms or discussing procedures with families is not enough.

Other illustrations of difficulties in the assessment process focus on the materials or methods used. As one parent from an upper-middle-class background recently observed, her young child did not know what an ironing board was because she had so rarely seen one! Other less humorous examples of evaluating children's developmental knowledge and skills abound. For instance, children may be unable to identify or manipulate items in a standard testing kit because they have never had the opportunity in their homes to see these items (most of which are based on materials available in middle-class, Anglo-European households). Repeatedly, we are reminded that assessment and intervention services for young children and their families must be delivered in a culturally competent way by individuals sensitive to, respectful of, and knowledgeable about the families' cultural practices, values, and folkways.

Changing Demographics in the United States

As suggested in the previous section, the great variability among children and families can present enormous challenges in developing and implementing services. In this section, some of the ways in which families may vary are discussed. The reader is asked to examine each variance in light of potential issues that may arise in the assessment process.

Ethnic and cultural diversity The United States is no longer considered a melting-pot nation comprised of individuals from a wide range of cultural and ethnic backgrounds who share a common cultural value system. Today the nation reflects a wide range of groups who retain a primary identification with their native heritage. While most members do participate and share in aspects of the dominant culture orientation of the United States, terms such as *cultural diversity, cultural pluralism,* and *multiculturalism* more clearly define the society as it exists today.

The 1990 census data showed a total United States population of 248,709,873 persons; of that number, 60,581,577 were Hispanic or people of color. The term *minority population* has become increasingly meaningless in many communities; today many localities have no one group that represents 50% or more of the population.

The trend toward an increasingly diverse population is likely to continue. Estimates made by the Children's Defense Fund show that by the year 2000 it is expected that there will be "2.4 million more [than in 1985] Hispanic children; 1.7 million more African-American children; 483,000 more children of other races; and 66,000 more white, non-Hispanic children" (Children's Defense Fund, 1989, p. 166). By the year 2030, the projections as compared with 1985 figures indicate that "there will be 5.5 million more Hispanic children; 2.6 million more African-American children; 1.5 million more children of other races; and 6.32 million fewer white, non-Hispanic children" (Children's Defense Fund, 1989, p. 166). It is projected that 41% of the nation's children will be Latino and children of color by the year 2030 (Hanson, Lynch, & Wayman, 1990).

Socioeconomic status and effects of poverty The family's socioeconomic status is likely to exercise a profound effect on the family's resources and ability to muster resources. The Children's Defense Fund (1991) reported that in 1989 more than 19.6% of the children in the United States lived below the poverty line as defined by family size and income. In that study the following 1990 figures were used to define poverty: $8,420 or less for families of two; $10,500 or less for families of three; and $12,700 or less for families of four (Children's Defense Fund, 1991). These figures are particularly alarming in that in 1989, 41% of children of poverty lived in families whose incomes were below *half* of the poverty line (Children's Defense Fund, 1991).

According to the Children's Defense Fund (1991), "Every 35 seconds an infant is born into poverty" (p. 5). It is estimated that over 20% of children were living in poverty by the end of the 1980s and also that the distribution of impoverished children varied by race and ethnicity with 15.4% of white children, 38.2% of Hispanic children, and 43.8% of African-American children identified as living in poverty (The Center for the Study of Social Policy, 1991).

Families living in poverty may be deeply and negatively affected by their socioeconomic situation, and situations created by poverty may create or interact with other risk factors. For example, studies have revealed a strong relationship between poverty and outcomes such as poor health, high infant mortality, lack of child care, homelessness, poor educational outcomes, and crime (reviewed in Hanson & Lynch, 1992). It is unrealistic to expect families who are grappling with the effects of poverty and struggling to survive to wholeheartedly and willingly embrace and participate in early assessment and educational services for their youngsters.

Family structure The makeup and appearance of families of today is very different from what it was 20 to 30 years ago. Data from the National Health Interview Survey showed that in 1960 almost 75% of all of the children in the United States lived with both of their biological parents, each of whom had been married only once (Dawson, 1991). Subsequent figures from the Joint Center for Urban Studies for the period between 1960 and 1975 indicated that the proportion fell to slightly over 65%; by 1990 the proportion was projected to fall to approximately 28% (Masnick & Bane, 1980).

Families of today are characterized by great variation in terms of size and composition and include those with two parents, a single parent, teen parents, gay/lesbian parents; divorced, blended, extended, adoptive, and foster families; and couples without children. The terms *traditional family* and *nuclear family* have become meaningless.

Family characteristics Just as dramatic changes have occurred in recent decades in the structure of families, other characteristics of families, such as the age of childbearing, also reflect change and great variability. Demographic trends show increases at both ends of the childbearing age spectrum (Levitan, Belous, & Gallo, 1988; Rosenbaum, Layton, & Liu, 1991).

Of greatest concern is the number of children born to teenage mothers. One study reported that 12.5% of births in the United States in 1988 were to women under age 20 and that the number of births to teens (ages 15 to 19) increased between 1987 and 1988 with a birth rate of 43.7 per 1,000 for white women and 105.9 births per 1,000 for African-American women (Rosenbaum et al., 1991). Further, childbearing in the teenage years is strongly associated with long-term poverty (Rosenbaum et al., 1991). In addition, there is a strong, positive relationship between teen parenting and single parenting, as indicated by the Children's Defense Fund (1991), "Every 31 seconds an infant is born to an unmarried mother. Every 64 seconds an infant is born to a teenage mother" (p. 5).

Another family characteristic reflecting demographic shifts is that of family size. In general, families are smaller today. Average national figures on family size have shown a decline in size. However, fertility rates differ across ethnic and cultural groups and some groups live in larger extended family groups than do others (Wayman, Lynch, & Hanson, 1990). Groups define *family* differently; some include only members with blood or legal ties, other groups include a wider range of members.

Religion Because of our national perspective on separating issues of church and state, defining families in terms of religious orientation is often not addressed in discussions of assessment and intervention. However, families' religious beliefs and practices may greatly influence their choices, preferences, goals, and resources. The population of the United States varies greatly with respect to religious beliefs. It was recently reported that 86.5% of people in the United States are Christians who belong to a number of different Christian denominations (largest groups: 26% Roman Catholic, 19% Baptist, 8% Methodist, 5% Lutheran). Approximately 2% of the population is Jewish; Muslims represent .5% of the population ("Religion Coats U.S.," 1991). These data, from a study commissioned by the Graduate School of the City University of New York, indicated that more than 9 out of every 10 Americans in the United States identify with a religion. Although a family's religious or spiritual orientation may not initially seem to be important to the assessment process, it may influence their goals for their child, the way in which they describe their family's priorities, and the extent to which they choose to become involved in intervention programs and services.

Summary

These factors represent a few of the many dimensions on which families vary. An examination of population trends indicates increasing diversity in the years to come and also serves to identify some areas of concern in population shifts (e.g., poverty, teenage parenting).

A review of the changing demographics highlights the need for service providers to develop flexibility, openness, respect, sensitivity, new knowledge, and an appreciation of the many facets that make up family life. Because this may be complicated by the fact that many of the current service providers are from ethnic and cultural groups that differ from the family groups with whom they work, there will be important needs in the areas of personnel training and in the recruitment, hiring, and retention of individuals from groups that have previously been underrepresented in the population of service providers (Lynch & Hanson, 1993).

DEVELOPING COMPETENCE IN WORKING ACROSS CULTURES

As the previous review suggests, our society has become increasingly culturally diverse. This fact underscores the need for those assessing and intervening with young children and their families to implement services in a manner that is effective across cultures. The remainder of this chapter will focus on the issue of developing cross-cultural competence and on implementing these practices in the assessment process.

Cross-Cultural Competence

Ethnic competence is defined by Green (1982) as the ability "to conduct one's professional work in a way that is congruent with the behavior and expectations that members of a distinctive culture recognize as appropriate among themselves" (p. 52). It is important to remember that an individual's culture is not a prescribed script for behavior. However, it does represent a cultural framework that "must be viewed as a set of tendencies or possibilities from which to choose" (Anderson & Fenichel, 1989, p. 8). The cultural identification that children and their families hold most likely exercises a profound influence on all aspects of their lifeways.

The ability to work with children and families who identify with cultural practices that differ from one's own perspective requires a commitment to gaining new information and becoming aware of the ways in which one thinks and behaves. Green (1982) describes the personal attributes of individual service providers and the types of support that should be provided by their organizations if one is to demonstrate ethnic competence, including (1) awareness of one's own cultural limitations; (2) openness to cultural differences; (3) adoption of a learning style that is client-oriented, interactive, and flexible; (4) ability to help someone recognize and use resources; and (5) recognition of the integrity of all cultures. These characteristics provide the undergirding for the development of cultural competence.

Attaining Cross-Cultural Competence

The topic of attaining cultural competence is not new (Lynch & Hanson, 1993). Business and government organizations have long recognized the need for training their workers employed overseas. A number of training models have been used and most share some common characteristics. Lynch and Hanson (1993) suggest that these characteristics can be applied to personnel preparation for individuals employed in the service professions in the United States who may be called upon to work with families from a variety of ethnic, cultural, and linguistic backgrounds, and they outline three training components that are essential in the quest to attain cross-cultural competence. These components are (1) clarifying one's own values, (2) gaining cultural-specific information, and (3) applying and practicing the methods and information acquired through self-examination and information gathering.

First, culture is a part of all of us. We may or may not be aware of how our beliefs and values affect the ways in which we conduct our lives. It is not until we are aware of this influence and are clear about our own cultural perspectives that we can truly recognize and appreciate the cultural perspectives of others. Without this clarification and appreciation of differences in ways of conducting daily living, the potential for cultural clashes exists between service providers and children and families participating in the services. (For additional information on this topic see Harry, 1992, *Topics in Early Childhood Special Education, 12*[3].)

Second, cross-cultural competence is facilitated by the acquisition of culture-specific information, which can be acquired through reading (both fiction and nonfiction), the arts (movies, paintings, etc.), cultural festivals, travel, sampling foods from other cultures, and so on. Perhaps the best way to acquire this information is through personal and professional contacts with individuals who bridge cultures, in other words, individuals who understand and are able to operate in several cultures. These cultural guides to a perspective that may be new and unfamiliar are invaluable in the process of designing and implementing appropriate services. Such guides can be located through participation in community events, personal contacts, suggestions from client families, and state and local professional networks and organizations designed for this purpose.

The third component in attaining cross-cultural competence involves applying the knowledge and information in service delivery practices (Lynch & Hanson, 1993). The application of this new knowledge may require organizational change and certainly support for efforts to make service systems more responsive to a wide range of children and families. It also requires the efforts of individuals to seek coaches and guides in the process. Methods for obtaining feedback and continually updating knowledge are essential as well. In addition to developing sensitivity to and appreciation for differences in families' values on such issues as child independence, early education and treatment, family participation, and health care, practitioners must acquire and apply skills related to effective communication. Communication styles may vary radically from child to child and family to family. For some, informal contacts may be the norm; for others, highly formalized interactions may be appropriate. Some may benefit from the use of a direct communication approach, but in other cases a more indirect method of communicating may be warranted. Attaining cross-cultural competence requires a tremendous openness, sensitivity, and commitment to learning about and respecting the lifeways of groups whose values may be different from one's own.

Strategies for Working Effectively with Interpreters and Translators

Given the tremendous diversity in terms of ethnicity, culture, and languages spoken in families served through educational, social, and health-care agencies, special attention must be given to the issue of interpretation or translation. Typically, a cultural or linguistic match between the orientation of the family and the service provider does not exist given the shortages in professionally trained personnel and the lack of attention in the past to issues of culture in personnel preparation. Therefore, most practitioners will be called upon to work extensively with translators and interpreters. As the following section points out, speaking the language is not enough. The person providing the translation, as well as the professional practitioner, must be familiar with the family's culture and the meaning of terms and actions in that culture. The discussion that follows draws heavily from work in Lynch (1992, pp. 52–56) contributed by Sam Chan, Ph.D.

Skills of the interpreter To be effective, interpreters should be proficient in the family's language and dialect as well as the language of the interventionist. However, language proficiency is not enough. Interpreters must also be aware of the cultural rules that are governing each person's interactions and be able to interpret subtle nuances with tact and sensitivity. According to Randall-David (1989), "These interpreters are ideal because they not only translate the interaction but also bridge the culture gap" (p. 31).

Interpreters should also be trained in the dynamics and principles of interpretation and understand their role. Training in the specific field in which they are doing the interpretation is equally important, because interpreting in a court of law requires different skills and vocabulary from interpreting in a program for young children with disabilities and their families. At the least, interpreters should have a basic understanding of the content areas in which they will be interpreting so that they can convey information accurately. Although context rather than literal, word-for-word translations is the goal, interpreters should not gloss over information, insert their own opinion and advice, or omit, add, or paraphrase in ways that alter the intent or content of the information (Tinloy, Tan, & Leung, 1986).

Interpreters should facilitate the communication by helping the interventionist establish a comfortable pace and watching for cues that reflect the family's acceptance and understanding of the information being presented. Like all professionals, they should respect the rules of confidentiality, maintain neutrality, and present themselves in manner and dress in ways that convey respect to the family.

Friends and family members as interpreters Because the demand for fully qualified interpreters is typically greater than the supply, interventionists often find themselves relying on family friends or family members to translate and interpret. Although this may seem to be the only alternative, it is often unsatisfactory. The relationships of family members and friends often interfere with accurate interpretation. To save the family from difficult news, a friend serving as an interpreter may soften the message in ways that are not accurate and do not convey the essential information. Families may also feel that the confidentiality of the information is compromised when friends become interpreters, especially if the friend is known to gossip. In some instances, families may feel that the information that is being exchanged is extremely personal and should not be shared outside the family.

Using family members as interpreters is also fraught with difficulty. Because the older children of recent immigrants are often more skilled in English than their parents, it often falls to them to interpret for the parents and grandparents. Because such a role reversal can lead to mutual resentment, discomfort for all family members, and a manipulation of information that is detrimental to family functioning, using children or teens to interpret should be avoided.

The right to privacy and using an interpreter Families have both legal and moral rights to privacy. Adding a third party to the interactions makes it even more important to constantly monitor these rights and ensure that they are being respected. Anyone acting as an interpreter should be trained in confidentiality issues, and families should be given choices for interpretation. For example, families and interpreters who share the same language but not the same cultural background or country of origin may not be an appropriate match. Differences in social class, recency of arrival, gender, and educational level may also contribute to a family's trust and level of comfort with an interpreter. And, like everyone else, interpreters will bring to the situation different communication styles and levels of interpersonal skills, credibility, and competence that can enhance or be a barrier to family/professional relationships.

The needs of the interpreter From the preceding paragraphs it is evident that the role of the interpreter is complicated. It requires a wide range of cross-cultural, language, content, and interpersonal skills. It is not surprising therefore that interpreting can be stressful. Because of the shortage of qualified interpreters, those who are well trained are often overused and overworked. They may contribute to their own exhaustion because they see themselves as the family's "life raft" and the only person who can help the family negotiate the system. The emotional demands brought about by the content of the information may also cause stress. As interpreters watch families struggle with difficult information and limited options, they may overidentify with the family and take on some of the burden that they assume the family is feeling.

Professionals who work with interpreters may add to the stress. They too are often overworked and have little time for preparing the interpreter for the next interaction. Some of their frustration may result in impatience, which makes it more difficult for the interpreter to do his or her job well. In some instances bilingual staff in agencies are asked to serve as interpreters without compensation or without relief from their other day-to-day responsibilities (Benhamida, 1988). This dual role and the guilt associated with not doing either job as they would like adds further pressure to the lives of many interpreters.

Although interpreting will always be demanding, those who work with interpreters can help to reduce the most stressful aspects. Planning ahead, allowing adequate time, and regarding the interpreter as an essential member of the team will benefit families, interpreters, and interventionists.

Preparing for interpreted interactions Interpreters and interventionists need time together to prepare for interactions with families. The interpreter should be made aware of the purpose of the meeting, the content that is of greatest importance, issues that may be sensitive, and any technical words or terms that may be used. If written documents are to be shared, the interpreter should be given the opportunity to review them prior to the interaction. The interpreter may also want to meet with the family prior to the three-way interaction to establish rapport and to learn their patterns of communication and language sophistication.

Guidelines for working with an interpreter Several authors, including Hagen (1989), Randall-David (1989), Schilling and Brannon (1986), and Chan (as cited in Lynch, 1992), have suggested guidelines for working more effectively with interpreters. Strategies include learning some words and phrases in the family's language; addressing all words and remarks to the family, not the interpreter; avoiding verbal and nonverbal language that could be culturally offensive to the family; speaking somewhat more slowly and clearly but not more loudly; and limiting the amount of information communicated to a few sentences before translation. For a more complete list of suggestions, see Lynch (1992, pp. 55, 56).

The importance of skilled interpreters cannot be underestimated in human service agencies where many professionals do not share the language or the culture of the families whom they serve. Training, supporting, and incorporating interpreters on the team is becoming a prerequisite to effective service in many areas of the country.

Guidelines and Cultural Considerations in Data Gathering

Cultural considerations may play a significant role in family views of children and childrearing practices, family roles and structures, disability and causation, health and healing practices, and views toward change and intervention, as well as in communication styles and methods (Hanson et al., 1990). For the practitioner involved in the assessment of young children and their families, these considerations can be overwhelming. Wayman et al. (1990) suggest a series of thought-provoking questions that are designed to provide guidance to the assessor or interventionist who is called on to work with families from various cultures. The questions are not meant to be used as an assessment of the families or as a checklist for evaluating families; they merely highlight issues that may be encountered in the process of working closely with families of young children in gathering information (see Figure 4.1).

Influence of Other Dimensions of Family Life

As noted earlier, cultural orientation is only one dimension on which children and families may vary. It is essential that practitioners make no assumptions about needs and goals based on the families' ethnic and/or cultural perspective. First, family members may differ both across cultural groups and within cultural groups (even within the family itself) in terms of the degree to which they identify with a given cultural perspective or practice. Some individuals wholly adopt their native perspective and customs, some pick and choose from their primary or native perspective as well as from that of the culture in which they now live. Life circumstances and historical events may even affect this degree of identification—which in turn will affect the interventionists' behavior and style during assessments.

Other factors also interact with or override the influence of culture at any given time. For example, a family living in poverty or in homeless conditions may have very different needs and motivation to seek assessment and intervention services from those of another family from the same cultural group who has adequate income and a roof over their heads. Issues of socioeconomic status, wellness/sickness, education, job opportunities, immigration circumstances, age, gender, and language proficiency, for instance, all may exert a profound influence over families' concerns, priorities, and resources.

Summary

As Lynch and Hanson (1993) stated: "Many of the early intervention programs of today and all of the early intervention programs of tomorrow require staff members who are able to work respectfully and effectively with families whose values, beliefs, behaviors, and language differ from their own" (p. 54). These abilities are of particular importance in the assessment process. The remainder of this chapter outlines strategies and steps toward becoming culturally competent in each phase or component of the assessment process.

CULTURAL COMPETENCE AND THE ASSESSMENT PROCESS

Part H of Public Law 99-457 of 1986 (now retitled the Individuals with Disabilities Education Act, or IDEA, Public Law 102-119 of 1991) affirms the importance of family diversity in the assessment process (McGonigel, 1991). Part H regulations require that assessments be nondiscriminatory, that they be conducted in the family's native language or other preferred mode of communication unless it is clearly not feasible, and that procedures and materials used in the assessment do not discriminate based on culture or race (Early Intervention Program for Infants and Toddlers with Handicaps: Final Regulations, 1989). The same is true in the assessment of preschoolers under Part B of IDEA. These regulations are intended to implement the spirit and intent of the law, but broadly stated regulations must be transformed into strategies that can be implemented at the programmatic level to ensure that the regulations are put into practice. The remaining sections of this chapter highlight some of the issues that assessors encounter when working with families from diverse cultural, ethnic, linguistic, and socioeconomic backgrounds and suggest some strategies to make assessment more responsive to diversity. Although the issues focus on child assessment, many can also be applied to gathering information about families' concerns, priorities, and resources.

As the previous sections of this chapter have described, ensuring that assessment is culturally competent begins long before assessing a child or gathering information about the family's concerns, priorities, and resources. It begins with the philosophy and approach of the program or service system, the interpretation of administrative requirements related to assessment practices, and the individual values, beliefs, and biases of each staff member. In other words, the stage for culturally competent assessment is set before members of the assessment team ever meet the family. The remainder of this chapter assumes that the stage has been well set and focuses on practical issues and strategies for achieving cultural competence in assessment.

The multiple steps within the assessment process (McLoughlin & Lewis, 1990) may be described in different terms by different people, but the assessment process in early childhood typically includes identification and screening, assessment planning, direct assessment, interpretation of assessment findings, and decision making regarding intervention. In the sections that follow, each of these steps is described briefly, the issues related to cultural competence are presented, and guidelines are recommended for addressing the issues.

Identification and Screening

Identification and screening procedures are typically designed to determine which children require more formalized assessment. Assessments used for screening purposes are always designed with balance in mind—balance between overidentifying and underidentifying children who may need further assessment and services. Overidentification results in referring too many children without developmental problems for costly and potentially anxiety-producing assessments. Underidentification results in missing some children with developmental difficulties who need more comprehensive assessments that lead to recommendations for services. However, when identification and screening programs are designed to include children from diverse cultural, ethnic, socioeconomic, and linguistic backgrounds, achieving the balance between overidentification and underidentification is more complex. The complexity arises because of differences in experience, language, and childrearing practices that may influence a child's performance as well as from the paucity of adequate measures and the inherent problems of measuring the skills and abilities of very young children.

Screening procedures for infants, toddlers, and preschoolers typically include multiple measures such as measures of developmental status, general health, sensory system functioning, and behavioral characteristics (Bailey & Wolery, 1989). Past practice has tended to consider the child's performance in these areas to be directly related to innate characteristics. However, as the literature on risk factors versus opportunity factors grows, it is becoming clear that all of the variables that provide the context

Part I—Family Structure and Childrearing Practices

- **Family Structure**
  - **Family Composition**
    - Who are the members of the family system?
    - Who are the key decision makers?
    - Is decision making related to specific situations?
    - Is decision making individual or group-oriented?
    - Do family members all live in the same household?
    - What is the relationship of friends to the family system?
    - What is the hierarchy within the family? Is status related to gender and/or age?
  - **Primary Caregiver(s)**
    - Who is the primary caregiver?
    - Who else participates in the caregiving?
    - What is the amount of care given by mother vs. others?
    - How much time does the infant spend away from the primary caregiver?
    - Is there conflict between (among) caregivers regarding appropriate practices?
    - What ecological/environmental issues impinge upon general care-giving (i.e., housing, jobs, etc.)?
- **Childrearing Practices**
  - **Family Feeding Practices**
    - What are the family feeding practices?
    - What are the beliefs regarding breast-feeding and weaning?
    - What are the beliefs regarding bottle feeding?
    - What are the family practices when transitioning to solid food?
    - Which family member(s) prepare food?
    - Is food purchased or homemade?
    - Which family member(s) feed the child?
    - What is the configuration of the family mealtime?
    - What are the family's views on independent feeding?
    - Is there a discrepancy among family members regarding the beliefs and practices related to feeding the infant/toddler?
  - **Family Sleeping Patterns**
    - Does the infant sleep in the same room/bed as the parents?
    - At what age is the infant moved away from close proximity to the mother?
    - Is there an established bedtime?
    - What is the family response to an infant when he/she awakes at night?
    - What practices surround daytime napping?

FIGURE 4.1
Guidelines for the home visitor
Source: From "Home-Based Early Childhood Services: Cultural Sensitivity in a Family Systems Approach" by K. I. Wayman, E. W. Lynch, & M. J. Hanson, 1990, *Topics in Early Childhood Special Education, 10,* pp. 65-66. Copyright 1990 by PRO-ED, Inc. Reprinted by permission.

- **Family's Response to Disobedience and Aggression**
  - What are the parameters of acceptable child behavior?
  - What form does the discipline take?
  - Who metes out the disciplinary action?
- **Family's Response to a Crying Infant**
  - Temporal qualities—How long before the caregiver picks up a crying infant?
  - How does the caregiver calm an upset infant?

Part II—Family Perceptions and Attitudes

- **Family Perception of Child's Disability**
  - Are there cultural or religious factors that would shape family perceptions?
  - To what/where/whom does the family assign responsibility for their child's disability?
  - How does the family view the role of fate in their lives?
  - How does the family view their role in intervening with their child? Do they feel they can make a difference or do they consider it hopeless?
- **Family's Perception of Health and Healing**
  - **What is the family's approach to medical needs?**
    - Do they rely solely on Western medical services?
    - Do they rely solely on holistic approaches?
    - Do they utilize a combination of these approaches?
  - **Who is the primary medical provider or conveyer of medical information?**
    - Family members? Elders? Friends? Folk healers? Family doctor? Medical specialists?
  - **Do all members of the family agree on approaches to medical needs?**
- **Family's Perception of Help-Seeking and Intervention**
  - Who does the family seek help from—family members or outside agencies/individuals?
  - Does the family seek help directly or indirectly?
  - What are the general feelings of family when seeking assistance—ashamed, angry, demand as a right, view as unnecessary?
  - With which community systems does the family interact? (educational/medical/social)?
  - How are these interactions completed (face to face, telephone, letter)?
  - Which family member interacts with other systems?
  - Does that family member feel comfortable when interacting with other systems?

FIGURE 4.1
Continued

Part III: Language and Communication Styles

- **Language**
  - **To what degree:**
    - Is the home visitor proficient in the family's native language?
    - Is the family proficient in English?
  - **If an interpreter is used:**
    - With which culture is the interpreter primarily affiliated?
    - Is the interpreter familiar with the colloquialisms of the family members' country/region of origin?
    - Is the family member comfortable with the interpreter? (Would the family member feel more comfortable with an interpreter of the same sex?)
  - **If written materials are used, are they in the family's native language?**
- **Interaction Styles**
  - Does the family communicate with each other in a direct or indirect way?
  - Do family members share feelings when discussing emotional issues?
  - Does the family ask you direct questions?
  - Does the family value a lengthy social time at each home visit unrelated to the early childhood services program goals?
  - Is it important for the family to know about the home visitor's extended family? Is the home visitor comfortable sharing that information?

FIGURE 4.1
Continued

for the life of the child and family contribute to the child's performance (Dunst, 1993; Rhodes & Brown, 1991). Culture and language are certainly contextual variables, as are length of time in the United States, socioeconomic status, and cultural affiliation that may influence a child's performance on screening measures; these factors may also determine whether or not a family participates in screening activities. Factors related to diversity interact with procedures that are used for screening and identification. Therefore, as practices and procedures are developed, the following issues may arise. Each issue is presented with a short description, an example that might be encountered in practice, and guidelines for assessors.

Issue: Family participation Encouraging families from diverse cultural and language groups to participate in screening opportunities is one of the first issues that assessors may encounter. There are multiple opportunities in the United States for families to have their young children screened. Neighborhood clinics, health fairs at hospitals and shopping centers, and screening clinics sponsored by health and education agencies are frequent occurrences in most communities. Typically they are free and are held at places that are thought to be easily accessible to families. However, not all families choose to participate. Consider these examples.[1]

[1]The examples used throughout the narrative are hypothetical, although many draw upon actual events and experiences or composites of actual events and experiences.

The Estrella family has recently come to Florida from El Salvador. Although they are fully documented, they have temporarily moved in with relatives who fled El Salvador in fear of political reprisals. These relatives were originally given political asylum in the U.S., but they no longer are eligible for that status. Although Mr. and Mrs. Estrella are concerned about their daughter Oralia, they are afraid to get involved with any organization that might ask questions that would expose their undocumented relatives.

The Woo family has lived in San Francisco's Chinatown for several generations. Despite their long-time residence in the U.S., they have maintained many of the traditional practices that their ancestors brought from Mainland China. For health care they use a wide range of herbal medicines. Except for the immunizations and vaccinations that are required to enter their children in school, they have never become involved in Western medicine. Recently they have noticed that their youngest son is developing very slowly compared with his older brothers and sisters. Although they have seen posters advertising a community health fair that includes developmental screening, it is not something that they have considered. Such a public event using Western medicine is not a part of their experience nor is the idea that one should "look for trouble."

These are just two examples of families who may choose not to participate in screening and identification efforts. Other families may not because they do not understand the language in which the events are publicized, because they do not have transportation to get to screening programs, or because they are not familiar with the reasons for screening.

Guidelines for encouraging families to utilize identification and screening programs To encourage families to participate, screening efforts should be embedded in the natural events and activities of the community. The best way to learn about what is natural for the community is to ask cultural guides or mediators who live in or are familiar with the community and its residents (Chan, 1990; Lynch & Hanson, 1992a; Yonemitsu & Cleveland, 1992). If particular holidays or celebrations, political activities, or religious ceremonies traditionally bring people together, they may be the venue for screening efforts and may also provide opportunities for community leaders to talk with families about the importance of screening and early intervention. The importance of anything is related to its value to each individual; therefore, the Anglo-European view of the importance of finding problems and working to resolve them early may be quite contrary to the position that problems and their resolution are God's will (Lynch & Hanson, 1992a). The value of services for children who have developmental difficulties may best be explained from the perspective of another member of the same cultural or ethnic group who can work from the same frame of reference to personalize the discussion (Harry, 1992a).

Even families who are eager to participate cannot become involved if the information advertising the screening or the information that they are given as a result of screening is not presented in a language that they can understand. Communicating with families requires that printed materials be available in the family's language, that there be nonprint methods available for sharing information with those who have limited literacy, and that trained personnel be available who are both bilingual and bicultural.

Procedures that are designed to look for problems are threatening by nature. Most individuals are anxious when they are being evaluated. Families who are not familiar with screening and assessment and who are not from cultures or families in which evaluation is commonplace may feel considerable discomfort with the idea of screening and the procedures that are used. Linking screening to events and activities that are accepted by individuals within the community and devising procedures that emphasize strengths and include incentives such as free diapers, a gift certificate at a neighborhood store, or a toy for the child may encourage families to participate.

Issue: Selecting appropriate screening procedures Procedures used in the screening and identification of young children typically compare the child's performance with the performance of others of the same chronological age. Although the achievement of developmental milestones is often thought to be universal, different families, and sometimes different cultures, place different emphases on various behaviors and developmental milestones (Lynch & Hanson, 1992b). Just as different families have different expectations for their children, so too may families from diverse cultures. The following example illustrates such differences.

▪ ▪ ▪ ▪ ▪ ▪ ▪ ▪

When the mobile screening van came into their neighborhood, her parents eagerly took 3-year-old Sharma. They were surprised when the assessors expressed concerns about toilet training, her limited use of expressive language, and her willingness to interact so comfortably with strangers. Now Sharma's parents are confused and worried. Toilet training is not a family priority; Sharma's six older brothers and sisters are very attentive to her, and she never has to ask for anything. Sharma is also part of a large, extended family that includes grandparents, aunts, uncles, and cousins. She has become used to lots of people who play with and care for her. Why do the assessors think she should be toilet trained so early, talking more, and unfriendly to people? Is Sharma really behind?

▪ ▪ ▪ ▪ ▪ ▪ ▪ ▪

Family priorities, opportunities to practice, and culture influence when children reach developmental milestones. In cultures in which individuation and independence are considered less important than interdependence, young children may demonstrate different developmental patterns. For example, in many Middle Eastern and Latino families, the emphasis is upon attachment and parent-child bonding (Sharifzadeh, 1992; Zuniga, 1992); toddlers and preschoolers may not be pushed toward independence in eating, dressing, sleeping, or toilet training. As a result, screening instruments that rely on norms for Anglo-European children from middle-income homes may over-identify children from other cultural or economic groups.

Children who come from homes in which English is not spoken or homes in which more than one language is spoken may also be over-identified in screening programs (Gollnick & Chinn, 1990). Although children from families who speak languages other than English often learn one or more languages, their initial vocabularies may be smaller in each language; they may mix grammar and syntax in their early years of language learning. In a screening assessment, these children's language may differ from the norm.

Guidelines for selecting appropriate screening measures There are several strategies that assessors can use to help ensure that screening instruments do not overselect or underselect children from various cultural groups. The first is to have professionals and parents from the cultural community review the instruments prior to selection. They may find that specific items are not appropriate or occur at different times for children in their community. For example, young children who are learning to use chopsticks rather than a knife and fork might fail some self-help items simply because they have not had opportunities to practice. Likewise, young children who are carried all the time and not allowed to play on the floor may appear to be somewhat behind their age peers in motor development. By having professionals and family members from the groups to be screened examine the screening instruments and procedures prior to their use, a great deal of misunderstanding can be avoided.

Some communities may decide that norms on the existing screening instruments are not appropriate for them. One option is to develop community-based norms that compare children with others of the same background in the same area. However, community-based norms can be a double-edged sword. Although they do not overidentify, they can provide a false sense of well-being and cause later inequities when children within a particular community have limited opportunities to learn the behaviors and skills that are expected in school. For example, young children with and without disabilities in affluent homes are typically exposed to lots of books, toys, and the kinds of communicative patterns that are used in preschool and school environments. Young children in less affluent settings may not have the same opportunities to interact with materials and language, and their skills in these areas may be less well developed when they enter preschool or school. Because community-based norms would not identify children if they were not different from others within their immediate community, young children who might profit from added opportunities would not be identified.

A final strategy for selecting appropriate screening procedures is to integrally involve parents or other knowledgeable family members in the screening process. Several open-ended questions that ask parents or primary caregivers what they see as the child's strengths or whether or not they have any concerns can contribute significantly to accurate screening. The accuracy of parents' perceptions is being increasingly confirmed by the literature (Hayes, 1990; Sexton, Thompson, Perez, & Rheams, 1990).

Assessment Planning

When a child has been referred for more comprehensive assessment, the first step in the process is planning. Family-centered planning is a joint effort between professionals, family members, and any other individuals whom the family selects (Dunst, Trivette, & Deal, 1988; McGonigel, Kaufman, & Hurth, 1991; Stevens-Dominguez, Beam, & Thomas, 1989). For families who do not speak English well or who have had little exposure to special education practices in the United States, participating in the assessment planning process may be especially difficult. They may be unfamiliar with the assessment process, have different expectations and beliefs about parental and professional roles, and be unable to communicate in the language of the assessors.

Issue: Collaborating with families who view professionals as experts

In many cultural groups, teachers and others related to education are viewed as experts. Getting families to share information, express their concerns, or even to make eye contact with professionals may be difficult. To speak out may be considered rude or offensive. The example that follows illustrates one family's thoughts as they were encouraged to participate in planning the assessment for their child.

• • • • • • • •

Tuyet's parents are recent immigrants from Vietnam. They were brought up to respect teachers, and in their village teachers held positions of high esteem. Tuyet has Down syndrome, and their physician suggested that they contact the local early intervention program. After much discussion within the family and assistance from an agency that works with new immigrants, they made the contact. The early intervention team asked to assess Tuyet and invited her parents to pose questions, provide information, and be involved in all aspects of the planning process. Tuyet's parents were very confused. To ask a question of a teacher or other person who is highly respected would be an insult. It would mean that the person had not explained things well enough. To point that out by questioning would cause that person to lose face. Tuyet's parents certainly wouldn't want to be responsible for all of those professionals losing face. And besides, what did they know? Professionals are supposed to know what to do. Why were they asking them, her parents? Could it be that they really don't know how to do their job? If that is so, then they don't want them working with Tuyet.

▪ ▪ ▪ ▪ ▪ ▪ ▪ ▪

Regardless of the professionals' desire and eager attempts to get Tuyet's family to express their concerns and priorities, the family felt confused and constrained. The assessment team members were working with a cultural perception that was different from their own.

Guidelines for encouraging family participation in assessment planning Longstanding beliefs are not changed overnight. Some families may need extended periods of time in the system before they openly express their concerns or question professionals; others may elect to adapt to the ways of the new systems that they encounter fairly quickly. Still others may never comfortably exchange information with professionals. Regardless of where the family is on this continuum, family-centered services make it imperative for professionals to determine the family's level of comfort with involvement and work to incorporate their input.

As in many of the transactions that occur between interventionists and families whose culture, ethnicity, language, or socioeconomic status differ, a bilingual/bicultural mediator can play an important role in gathering information about the family's concerns, priorities, and resources. In less formal conversations, mediators can talk with appropriate family members and learn about the child and the family context. With the family's permission, this information can be shared with the team. When members of the assessment team meet with the family, the mediator may be the family's voice describing the child's strengths, the family's major concerns, and the best way to approach the child.

Some families who are not comfortable talking about their child's problems may be willing to complete short checklists that pinpoint the child's development or list areas in which families typically have concerns. If written forms are used, it is, of course, equally important to provide them in the family's preferred language and to determine whether or not family members are literate. Other families, such as many newly arrived Hmong, Laotians, Cambodians, and Vietnamese, may not choose to respond to written materials (personal communication, J. O. Cleveland, October 1, 1993). For them, the bilingual/bicultural guide may be especially important.

In some instances, families may elect not to participate in the assessment planning process. If this occurs, interventionists need not feel that they have failed; however, they may want to continue to invite family participation in the process and continually review their practices to ensure that families are truly welcomed.

Issue: Selection of assessment instruments and strategies Determining what instruments and strategies are to be used is an issue in any assessment; however, selecting those that are culturally and linguistically appropriate adds another dimension that assessors must consider. The first concern is language. Is the instrument available in the family's/child's preferred language? If it is, are there norms that are appropriate for comparisons or has the instrument simply been translated? Although assessors may decide that a translated instrument will provide more information than they can gather in any other way, it is important to view the results with caution. Finally, if the instrument is available in the child's and family's language and determined to be appropriate for the child, is there a trained assessor who can administer the test? In situations in which these conditions cannot be met, assessors may find that observation, play assessments, and family interviews conducted by a trained translator may provide more useful information than any formal assessment instrument. The example that follows provides an illustration of the difficulties that can occur when instruments are not culturally and linguistically appropriate.

....

The da Silva family just moved to the U.S. from Brazil, and they have come to the local school district to inquire about special education support services for their son Jarvis, who has muscular dystrophy. Jarvis's parents are fluent in both Portuguese and English, but Jarvis's only language is Portuguese. Unsure about how to proceed, one assessor suggested that an instrument available in Spanish be used for the assessment, assuming that everyone in South America speaks Spanish. Another assessor suggested that Jarvis's parents be asked to translate the questions from a standardized instrument used to measure general information into Portuguese to get Jarvis's response. But as the test went on, it became clear that many of the items dealt with information specific to growing up in the U.S., such as the names and values of various coins. After a frustrating experience for everyone involved, it was obvious that the team needed another strategy.

....

Another aspect of instrument and strategy selection relates to the child's experiences and opportunities. Children who have been carried for their first year of life and never been put on the floor to play or explore may be less motorically competent than their age peers who have been encouraged to move around their environments. Children who have not had toys to play with or other objects to manipulate may not show the same interest in or competence with objects. They may, however, show considerable interest in people and interpersonal interactions. Children whose families put considerable emphasis on nurturing and do not push for early independence may lack some of the self-help skills displayed by their age peers. Children who have been very ill or malnourished, or those who have had very limited or uneven nurturing may show deficits in cognitive abilities as well as in social interactions. Delays in any of these areas are important to determine, but the child's experiential base must be considered before the information is used for diagnosis or intervention planning.

Guidelines for selecting appropriate assessment instruments and strategies

Before selecting any standardized assessment strategy or procedure, members of the assessment team may wish to consider alternative ways to gather the same information. For children whose cultures and languages are not represented in the test repertoire, nonstandardized measures may be preferable. If a child has severe multiple disabilities, observation and family report typically yield the most useful information regardless of culture and language.

Even for children with less severe disabilities, observation and report are preferred to results of a standardized instrument that may be invalid and unreliable.

It is not uncommon for cultural taboos to arise during an assessment. For example, shaking a rattle found in the home of a Native American infant to check hearing is not considered appropriate. The way in which a child is handled during an assessment is equally important in some cultures. Patting a Moslem child on the head is incorrect. Washing off pollen or dyes on Native American or East Indian children is not appropriate; offering enthusiastic compliments and praise may cause Latino families to fear that attention has been unduly called to the child, putting him or her in danger (Lynch, 1993). When selecting assessment strategies, check with a cultural mediator who can provide insight into beliefs that the family may have that could lead to discomfort or embarrassment in an assessment.

Assessors typically try to determine when and where the assessment should take place in order to interact with the child in optimal circumstances. In addition to the considerations that are a part of that decision for any child, it may be important to ensure that the time meets the family's cultural preferences. For example, some families may depend upon astrologers to determine auspicious times for important life events. Although one day may be like any other to the professional members of the assessment team, for the family, one may be associated with better luck than another. An additional consideration has to do with various holidays and religious celebrations that may be important to the family but unfamiliar to the assessors. Learning more about each of the cultures, religions, and practices in one's own community can prevent discomfort caused by conflicts in families' and professionals' priorities.

Finally, part of the planning process is determining what is needed during the assessment. Translator or interpreter services may need to be arranged. Materials that are familiar to the child may need to be gathered; instruments in other languages may need to be reviewed and evaluated for their relevance.

Conducting the Assessment

When the time for the assessment has been determined, family members and assessors need to feel as comfortable as possible with one another. Assessment is not easy for any family, but when everything in the setting is unfamiliar, it is even more difficult. Thinking through the procedures and the process and considering the setting from the family's perspective may help increase everyone's comfort. The following issues may need to be considered to make the assessment go smoothly.

Issue: Supporting communication and understanding Exemplary child assessment requires a set of highly technical skills as well as the ability to be flexible and attend to the responses and reactions of family members. Many of the tasks that are a part of traditional, standardized assessments have little face validity for parents. All of the skills and behaviors that assessors look for when a child is being assessed are not intuitively obvious. For example, for someone unfamiliar with what can be learned from a specific task, putting forms in a formboard does not appear to provide much information about the child's performance or ability. However, the assessor may use formboards to assess the child's grasp, reach, motor planning skills, problem solving strategies, and attention and to screen for tremors. Although a wealth of information can be gained by observing children perform specific tasks for which the demands are well known, what is being observed and learned needs to be made explicit.

▪ ▪ ▪ ▪ ▪ ▪ ▪ ▪

Jennifer's parents were concerned about her development, so they requested that she be assessed by the school district's transdisciplinary team. The team members requested that they conduct the assessment in the family's home. When they arrived, one person, who had brought a bag of toys, played with Jennifer, another talked to her parents, and the third observed and listened. Jennifer's parents thought that Jennifer was going to be assessed. Why were the professionals just playing and asking questions? Why didn't they do something?

▪ ▪ ▪ ▪ ▪ ▪ ▪ ▪

Standardized assessments are not the only types of assessment about which families may have questions. As play-based assessment becomes more common (Linder, 1990), parents may have questions about what assessors are learning from play.

Guidelines for supporting communication and understanding When assessors explain what they are observing and why it is important, assessment tasks make sense. One way assessors can support communication and understanding is by describing what they will be doing in an assessment, how they will be doing it, and why it is important. When assessment is demystified, it can increase everyone's comfort in the situation.

Another way to support communication and understanding is to ask for the parents' or family members' perspectives on the child's performance in the assessment situation. Assessments conducted outside of the child's natural environment by an unfamiliar assessor may not yield results that accurately reflect the child's skills and abilities. If an assessment must occur in such a situation, parents should be asked to comment on how they judged the performance. Was it similar to or different from the child's typical responses? Were any materials used that are unfamiliar to the child? How did they think the child responded to the assessor?

Issue: Creating a nonthreatening environment For both the child and the family, a nonthreatening assessment environment is optimal. All individuals have settings and situations in which they are comfortable and those in which they are not. For many people, assessments and evaluations—whether they relate to one's health, financial status, or job performance—are situations that create anxiety. This anxiety is heightened when the assessment involves your own child or someone who is very close to you, especially if the assessment might result in bad news. Creating an assessment environment that is as comfortable as possible for all involved will ease some of this anxiety. Consider the following scenario.

▪ ▪ ▪ ▪ ▪ ▪ ▪ ▪

Latanya was born in her mother's seventh month of pregnancy. At birth she weighed under 1500 grams, and she spent the first three months of her life in the neonatal intensive care unit. At 15 months of age, she was scheduled to be assessed at a follow-up clinic connected to the NICU where she was born. Latanya's mother, Myrene, dreaded this assessment, but she knew that it was important to learn more about how Latanya was doing. When she arrived at the clinic, she was told that the assessors were running a little late and that she would have to wait for about 45 minutes before they would see her and Latanya. As they waited, Latanya became tired and fussy. When it was finally their turn, Myrene explained to the assessors that Latanya was not at her best. They brushed off her comments, took Latanya from her, and proceeded with the assessment. Several times Myrene tried to tell them that Latanya wasn't doing things for them that she did at home, but they didn't seem to be listening. Following the assessment, they said that they had some concerns but didn't share what they were. They told Myrene that they'd have to go write their report and that they'd ask her to come back in a couple of weeks. Before she had time to ask any questions, they were gone. Myrene left the clinic full of fear. What were their concerns? Why didn't they talk with her about them? Was there something so seriously wrong that they were afraid to tell her? How could she possibly wait two weeks to know what they were thinking?

It may seem that Myrene's experience is too bad to be true, but things like that do happen. Instead of making assessment less threatening, some settings actually raise anxiety. Although it is not possible to eliminate all concerns, the guidelines that follow suggest ways in which thoughtful planning can reduce the threat of assessment.

Guidelines for creating a nonthreatening environment Prior contact with the parents and family is one way to reduce the threat of assessment. Knowing who will be working with the child and what they will be doing enables parents to feel more comfortable with the process.

Conducting the assessment in surroundings that are familiar to the child and the family may also help to reduce anxiety. Most children and families are more comfortable in their own homes than in a clinic. When assessments are conducted in the home, families from some cultural groups may serve food to their guests. Sharing food and drink is an important custom that demonstrates the family's generosity and signifies respect for the visitors. The guests' acceptance and enjoyment of what is offered is an important part of the ritual.

For those who prefer not to have the assessment take place in their home, making the assessment setting as comfortable as possible is important. One way to do this may be to create a setting that is professional yet friendly in appearance by providing, for example, chairs that are comfortable for adults; toys for children; extra diapers; attractive pictures, posters, or children's art; and juice, tea, coffee, soft drinks, and snacks for adults and children. The point is not that the setting has to be expensively decorated or extensively furnished, but it should be a welcoming environment that invites families in.

Even more important than the message that the physical space sends is the message that the assessors communicate, which should be one of respect, equality, support, and expertise. Although families come to professionals to seek their expertise, the professionals should not assume that they are the only experts. Each family brings a wealth of knowledge about their child's temperament, behavior, likes, dislikes, skills, and abilities. Knowledge of such factors informs the assessment and is extremely valuable for adequately assessing the child's needs and the family's concerns, priorities, resources, and preferences.

Knowledge of family and culture-specific information may assist assessors to reduce the threat in assessment settings. Some families may prefer a very direct approach; others may want to spend time talking with the assessor and socializing before the assessment is conducted. Some will want to begin over a cup of tea and seemingly unrelated conversation; others will want to maximize the child's time with the assessor. No family wants to feel rushed or pushed or that the assessors are not doing a thorough job.

Exchanging information about the assessment findings immediately after its conclusion can help to allay fears. Instead of sending families away to wait for results, discussing what was observed and how the child performed can mitigate concerns. Of equal importance is getting the family members' perceptions of how the child performed. Was it a good day for the child or a bad day? Was the performance typical or atypical? Ensuring that families know that assessment is an ongoing process and that there will be other opportunities to gather information can also make the situation less threatening. Finally, allowing time for questions and explanations and making it clear that families can contact the team member with whom they are most familiar if they have questions also reduces the threat of assessment.

Interpreting and Presenting Assessment Findings

Assessment is technical. It requires considerable training in measurement, the areas being assessed, specific instruments and strategies, and typical and atypical child development. Information gathered in assessments is often associated with technical language or jargon. One of the responsibilities of the assessment team is to make the information clear to those who have not been technically trained. Making assessment information clear is even more difficult when family members and assessors do not share the same language and must work through interpreters and translators.

Issue: Sharing information clearly and caringly In addition to making information clear, assessors are responsible for making it as acceptable as possible. Because assessments do not always result in findings that families are hoping to hear, it is important to consider how the information will be received and to use strategies that make it as easy as possible to hear.

. . . .

Gavin's parents felt that he should be assessed prior to entry into a neighborhood preschool because of their concerns over his behavior. He spoke very little, spent hours spinning toys, and had tantrums whenever his routine was changed. After a comprehensive assessment, the team members sat down with Gavin's parents to discuss their findings. Several read their reports, which were full of acronyms, columns of standard scores, and paragraphs that detailed his difficult behavior during the assessments. After each of the assessors had presented this information, the chair of the group said, "Well, Mr. and Mrs. Carson, it seems clear that Gavin is autistic." Gavin is now 23 years old, and his parents still describe that experience as one of the worst of their lives.

. . . .

There is no good way to deliver bad news, but some ways are kinder and more caring than others. The treatment of Gavin's parents was neither kind nor caring.

Guidelines for sharing information clearly and caringly Perhaps the most important guideline for making information clear is to present it in the language the family uses. If this involves an interpreter or a translator, the guidelines presented earlier in this chapter can be used to increase the likelihood that families and professionals will have a positive experience. One of the most critical factors when working in translation is to allow enough time for the interaction to take place. Translating doubles the usual time needed, and it is a process that cannot be rushed.

For families who share the same primary language as the assessors, there may still be communication problems because of technical terms. The goal is for the family to understand exactly what is being said, not to impress them with fancy language. A rule of thumb is to present information as if you were presenting it to a friend who is bright but knows nothing about assessment, child development, or disability.

In addition to language considerations, some families from diverse cultural groups may have different understandings of the words that are used in relation to children with special needs (Harry, 1992b). To avoid confusion, a cultural guide is particularly important to help the assessment team and family members reach a common understanding of what each is saying.

A final guideline applies across all cultures and languages. Because no parents want to hear that their child is having problems with learning, behavior, or development, it is important to find the most sensitive way to present the information. Emphasizing the child's strengths while being realistic about weaknesses; allowing time for family members to process the information; letting silences occur; listening; supporting; accepting parents' anger; and demonstrating one's own care and concern for the child and the family make the process more humane. These practices are more natural and sincere if the bearer of bad news has taken time to establish relationships with the family during the assessment process.

Family-Professional Decision Making

A final step in the assessment process is making decisions about programs, services, and placement. The best decisions are those that are made collaboratively by family members and professionals, with each bringing his or her expertise to the table. However, it is not always easy. Professionals have to view family members as having knowledge and preferences that are important to the decision. Likewise, family members must view themselves as having expertise that is important to the decision-making process. Reaching this understanding is sometimes complicated by differences in language, communication style, and culture.

Issue: Determining what families want When languages, culturally determined expectations, and styles of communication differ, it is especially challenging to engage in joint decision making. The following example illustrates one of the problems that can occur.

▪ ▪ ▪ ▪ ▪ ▪ ▪ ▪

Depak was assessed six months ago and it was jointly decided by his parents and the professionals on the assessment team that he should be enrolled in a preschool program where the staff would receive support and consultation from one of the preschool resource teachers. In addition, Depak's parents, who had recently arrived from India, would receive home visits to help them understand more about Depak's development and the range of community services that would be available to them. At the time, the parents seemed quite pleased with the decisions that were made at the meeting. They nodded in apparent agreement and signed all of the forms. However, Depak has attended the preschool program only a few days over the past six months, and his parents have never been available when the home visitor arrives at the time they have scheduled for the visit. The resource teacher and the home visitor are provoked about the family's lack of follow-through, and they have begun to question how much they care about helping Depak. On the other hand, Depak's parents can't believe that the teachers wanted to enroll Depak in a regular preschool program where there would be children without disabilities. They also can't imagine having someone come into their home to discuss community services for Depak's needs. Don't these professionals realize how ashamed they are of having a child with a disability? Why do they insist on calling attention to it? Of course they agreed to what was suggested and signed the papers, but they were just being polite.

▪ ▪ ▪ ▪ ▪ ▪ ▪ ▪

It is often difficult for professionals to determine what families want. Different values, beliefs, experiences, and styles of communicating result in clashes even when both parties are trying to understand and work with each other.

Guidelines for determining what families want Perhaps the best way to determine what any family wants is to listen to what they say. Even small interchanges can provide valuable information that will enable professionals to make suggestions that are consistent with family concerns, priorities, and preferences. In addition, a cultural guide who understands the cultural implications of various decisions can be a valuable resource in the decision-making process.

Professionals should be aware of culture- and family-specific information that will help them determine who the real decision makers are. In some families, grandparents may play that role. In others, elders or chiefs may need to be involved in all decisions related to the family's welfare. In some cultures, decisions are not made by the mother and father, but are brought to others because of their wisdom or role in the larger community.

A final caveat relates to differences in communication patterns and styles that may interfere with understanding. When families from diverse cultures nod in apparent agreement, sign the forms, or smile as decisions are being made, it does not necessarily mean that they are in agreement with what is occurring or that they intend to act on the decisions that are being made. Instead, they are showing their politeness and deference to presumed authority. When families do not do what professionals expect, it is often because professionals had inaccurate expectations.

SUMMARY OF KEY CONCEPTS

- Families and children who are served by early intervention and early childhood special education programs are characterized by their diversity in culture, ethnicity, language, family structure, composition, values, and socioeconomic status. Because this diversity among families is often greater than the diversity among service providers, it is important to examine professional and program practices to ensure that they are sensitive to families' preferences and backgrounds.
- Family diversity requires that professionals develop cross-cultural competence, which includes three components: clarifying one's own values, gaining culture-specific information, and applying the information acquired through self-examination and information gathering and practicing appropriate methods.
- Working with and through interpreters and translators requires time and skill. All interactions that are mediated by translation require thoughtful planning, additional time to conduct, and debriefing of all concerned.
- Culture influences childrearing practices, and these influences must be considered when gathering data. Developmental milestones are not universal and may differ, depending on the family's views of infancy and early childhood.
- Cultural, ethnic, and socioeconomic diversity affect every aspect of the assessment process. Assessors can work with families and cultural mediators to develop guidelines for culturally competent assessment practices that respect families' backgrounds and preferences and ensure that the information gathered is accurate and useful.

REFERENCES

Anderson, P. P., & Fenichel, E. S. (1989). *Serving culturally diverse families of infants and toddlers with disabilities.* Washington, DC: NCCIP.

Bailey, D. B., Jr., & Wolery, M. (1989). *Assessing infants and preschoolers with handicaps.* Englewood Cliffs, NJ: Merrill/Prentice Hall.

Benhamida, L. (1988). *Interpreting in mental health settings for refugees and others: A guide for the professional interpreter.* Minneapolis, MN: University of Minnesota Refugee Assistance Program, Mental Health Technical Assistance Center.

The Center for the Study of Social Policy. (1991). *Kids count data book: State profiles of child well-being.* Washington, DC: Author.

Chan, S. (1990). Early intervention with culturally diverse families of infants and toddlers with disabilities. *Infants and Young Children, 3*(2), 78–87.

Children's Defense Fund. (1989). *A vision for America's future.* Washington, DC: Author.

Children's Defense Fund. (1991). *The state of America's children 1991.* Washington, DC: Author.

Colarusso, R. P., & Kana, T. G. (1991). Public Law 99-457, Part H, infant and toddler programs: Status and implications. *Focus on Exceptional Children, 23*(8), 1–12.

Dale, M. L., & Hoshino, L. B. (1984). Belief systems of Hispanic and pan-Asian populations in California: Implications for the delivery of care in the neonatal intensive care unit. *Journal of the California Perinatal Association, 4*(2), 21–25.

Dawson, D. A. (1991). Family structure and children's health and well-being: Data from the 1988 national health interview survey on child health. *Journal of Marriage and the Family, 53,* 573–584.

Dunst, C. J. (1993). Implications of risk and opportunity factors for assessment and intervention practices. *Topics in Early Childhood Special Education, 13,* 143–153.

Dunst, C. J., Trivette, C., & Deal, A. (1988). *Enabling and empowering families: Principles and guidelines for practice.* Cambridge, MA: Brookline Books.

Early Intervention Program for Infants and Toddlers with Handicaps: Final Regulations, 34 CFR 303. (1989, June 22). *Federal Register, 54*(119), 26306–26348.

Gollnick, D. M., & Chinn, P. C. (1990). *Multicultural education in a pluralistic society.* Englewood Cliffs, NJ: Merrill/Prentice Hall.

Green, J. W. (1982). *Cultural awareness in the human services.* Englewood Cliffs, NJ: Prentice Hall.

Hagen, E. (1989). *Communicating effectively with Southeast Asian patients.* Los Angeles: Immaculate Heart College Center.

Hanson, M. J., & Lynch, E. W. (1992). Family diversity: Implications for policy and practice. *Topics in Early Childhood Special Education, 12*(3), 283–306.

Hanson, M. J., Lynch, E. W., & Wayman, K. I. (1990). Honoring the cultural diversity of families when gathering data. *Topics in Early Childhood Special Education, 10*(1), 112–131.

Harry, B. (1992a). Restructuring the participation of African-American parents in special education. *Exceptional Children, 59,* 123–131.

Harry, B. (1992b). *Cultural diversity, families, and the special education system: Communication and empowerment.* New York: Teachers College Press.

Hayes, A. (1990). The context and future of judgment-based assessment. *Topics in Early Childhood Special Education, 10*(3), 1–12.

Joe, J. R., & Malach, R. S. (1992). Families with Native American roots. In E. W. Lynch & M. J. Hanson (Eds.), *Developing cross-cultural competence: A guide for working with young children and their families* (pp. 89–119). Baltimore, MD: Paul H. Brookes.

Levitan, S. A., Belous, R. S., & Gallo, F. (1988). *What's happening to the American family? Tensions, hopes, and realities* (rev. ed.). Baltimore, MD: The Johns Hopkins University Press.

Linder, T. W. (1990). *Transdisciplinary play-based assessment.* Baltimore, MD: Paul H. Brookes.

Lynch, E. W. (1992). Developing cross-cultural competence. In E. W. Lynch & M. J. Hanson (Eds.), *Developing cross-cultural competence: A guide for working with young children and their families* (pp. 35–59). Baltimore, MD: Paul H. Brookes.

Lynch, E. W. (1993, June). *Cross-cultural competence: From surprise to sensitivity to success.* Paper presented at the 28th Annual Meeting of the Association for the Care of Children's Health, Chicago, IL.

Lynch, E. W., & Hanson, M. J. (Eds.). (1992a). *Developing cross-cultural competence: A guide for working with young children and their families.* Baltimore, MD: Paul H. Brookes.

Lynch, E. W., & Hanson, M. J. (1992b). Steps in the right direction: Implications for interventionists. In E. W. Lynch & M. J. Hanson (Eds.), *Developing cross-cultural competence: A guide for working with young children and their families* (pp. 355–370). Baltimore, MD: Paul H. Brookes.

Lynch, E. W., & Hanson, M. J. (1993). Changing demographics: Implications for training in early intervention. *Infants and Young Children, 6*(1), 50–55.

Masnick, G., & Bane, M. J. (1980). *The nation's families: 1960–1990.* Boston: Auburn House.

McGonigel, M. J. (1991). Philosophy and conceptual framework. In M. J. McGonigel, R. K. Kaufman, & B. H. Johnson (Eds.), *Guidelines and recommended practices for the individualized family service plan* (2nd ed.) (pp. 7-14). Washington, DC: Association for the Care of Children's Health.

McGonigel, M. J., Kaufman, R. K., & Hurth, J. L. (1991). The IFSP sequence. In M. J. McGonigel, R. K. Kaufman, & B. H. Johnson (Eds.), *Guidelines and recommended practices for the individualized family service plan* (2nd ed.) (pp. 15–28). Washington, DC: Association for the Care of Children's Health.

McLoughlin, J. A., & Lewis, R. B. (1990). *Assessing special students* (3rd ed.). Englewood Cliffs, NJ: Merrill/Prentice Hall.

Randall-David, E. (1989). *Strategies for working with culturally diverse communities and clients.* Washington, DC: The Association for the Care of Children's Health.

Religion coats U.S. with many colors. (1991, April 10). *San Jose Mercury News,* pp. 1, 12.

Rhodes, W., & Brown, W. (Eds.). (1991). *Why some children succeed despite the odds.* New York: Praeger.

Rosenbaum, S., Layton, C., & Liu, J. (1991). *The health of America's children.* Washington, DC: Children's Defense Fund.

Schilling, B., & Brannon, E. (1986). *Cross-cultural counseling: A guide for nutrition and health counselors.* Washington, DC: U.S. Department of Agriculture/Department of Health and Human Services.

Sexton, D., Thompson, B., Perez, J., & Rheams, T. (1990). Maternal versus professional estimates of developmental status for young children with handicaps: An ecological approach. *Topics in Early Childhood Special Education, 10*(3), 80–95.

Sharifzadeh, V-S. (1992). Families with Middle Eastern roots. In E. W. Lynch & M. J. Hanson (Eds.), *Developing cross-cultural competence: A guide for working with young children and their families* (pp. 319–351). Baltimore, MD: Paul H. Brookes.

StevensDominguez, M., Beam, G., & Thomas, P. (1989). *Guide for family-centered services.* Albuquerque, NM: University of New Mexico.

Tinloy, M. T., Tan, A., & Leung, B. (1986). *Assessment of Chinese speaking limited English proficient students with special needs.* Sacramento, CA: Special Education Resource Network, Resource Service Center.

Wayman, K. I., Lynch, E. W., & Hanson, M. J. (1990). Home-based early childhood services: Cultural sensitivity in a family systems approach. *Topics in Early Childhood Special Education, 10*(4), 56–75.

Yonemitsu, D. M., & Cleveland, J. O. (1992). *Culturally competent service delivery: A training manual for bilingual/bicultural casemanagers.* (Available from Southeast Asian Developmental Disabilities Project of the San Diego Imperial Counties Developmental Services, Inc., 4355 Ruffin Road, San Diego, CA 92123.)

Zuniga, M. E. (1992). Families with Latino roots. In E. W. Lynch & M. J. Hanson (Eds.). *Developing cross-cultural competence: A guide for working with young children and their families* (pp. 151–179). Baltimore, MD: Paul H. Brookes.

CHAPTER

5

Child Find, Tracking, and Screening

Mary McLean
Cardinal Stritch College

Finding those children who are in need of early intervention services is part of the assessment process in early intervention. Unlike school-age children, infants, toddlers, and preschoolers in most states are not required to participate in publicly supported educational programs. Having a program available for young children with special needs does not ensure that the children who need such services will find their way to the program. Similarly, parents frequently report that it takes much time and effort to discover how to access assessment and intervention services for a child with special needs. To address these problems, Child Find programs have been established in each state and territory. This chapter will present information relative to Child Find programs and to tracking and screening, which are used to assist in the child identification process.

DEFINITIONS AND RATIONALE

Child Find is a systematic process of identifying infants and young children who are eligible or potentially eligible for enrollment in intervention programs. Child Find efforts are designed to inform the general public, both professionals and nonprofessionals, about typical and atypical child development as well as referral procedures if assessment or intervention is thought to be necessary for a particular child. According to Scott and Hogan (1982), finding the children who need services requires identification of three different groups: children with diagnosed disabilities, children with "hidden" disabilities (when caregivers or others may suspect that something is wrong, but no diagnosis has been made), and children who are at risk (nothing seems to be wrong, but biological or environmental conditions suggest that the child may demonstrate developmental problems in the future). Children with readily identified and diagnosed disabilities are typically the easiest for medical, educational, or social service professionals to identify. Child Find activities for this group consist of ensuring appropriate referral as soon as the disability is suspected or diagnosed. For the latter two groups of children, children with hidden disabilities and children at risk of developing a disability, tracking or screening programs can help to identify the need for services as early as possible.

Screening is an assessment process, the purpose of which is to identify children who may need further evaluation in order to determine whether early intervention should be provided (Meisels & Provence, 1989). Screening tests are generally quickly administered and inexpensive and yield only a determination of whether or not further evaluation is needed. Screening a child's hearing and vision, general development, and health is standard practice, although recently there has been increased emphasis on screening environmental factors as well as the child's health and development (Kochanek, Kabacoff, & Lipsitt, 1990; Meisels & Wasik, 1990).

Tracking is a system for providing continuous monitoring of the developmental progress of children who are thought to be at risk of manifesting developmental difficulties (Blackman, 1986). Sometimes referred to as a "high-risk registry" or "follow-up services," a tracking system can also provide data that are useful to agencies for program planning purposes.

The rationale for establishing a system of child identification and referral is based on the importance of intervening as early as possible, the need to support families of young children with special needs, and the legal mandates for child identification with which states must comply. Without such a system, many young children will go without needed services until they are of school age. It has been well established that intervening early can lessen or prevent the need for special education services at a later age and, therefore, can result in a financial savings for states (McNulty, Smith, & Soper, 1983; Schweinhart & Weikart, 1980; Wood,

1981). To the extent that children are not identified early, services in the future may be more costly.

Another reason for establishing a system of child identification is to assist families in their initial search for assistance with their child. At a time when the family is dealing with the difficulties inherent in learning about their child's disability, the resulting stress can be lessened if access to information about services is readily available to them. Unfortunately, many families have stories about the frustration they faced in finding out what services might be available for their child. Professionals in education, medicine, social services, and child care can help by being knowledgeable about early intervention services in their state and community.

Finally, there are legal mandates for child identification with which states must comply. Both Part B and Part H of IDEA require Child Find procedures, as do other programs serving young children. The legal basis for Child Find is described below.

CHILD FIND

Legal Basis of Child Find

P.L. 94-142 required the establishment of a Child Find program in each state for children from birth through age 21. Part H of P.L. 99-457, which established the infant/toddler program, also requires a comprehensive Child Find system. Part H specifies that the lead agency for infant/toddler services in each state, with the assistance of the governor-appointed Interagency Coordinating Council, must ensure coordination of the Child Find system with all other state efforts to identify children for various education, health, and social service programs, including (a) Part B of the Individuals with Disabilities Education Act (IDEA), (b) Maternal and Child Health programs under Title V of the Social Security Act, (c) the Early and Periodic Screening, Diagnosis, and Treatment (EPSDT) program under Title XIX of the Social Security Act, (d) programs under the Developmental Disabilities Act, (e) Head Start, and (f) the Supplemental Security Income program under Title XVI of the Social Security Act (34 CFR 303.321). Coordination with these programs must ensure that there will not be duplication of efforts and that the Child Find system will be implemented effectively within the state by making use of existing resources of the state. In many states, the Interagency Coordinating Council established under Part H serves in an advisory capacity for infant, toddler, and preschool programs in the state, thus helping to coordinate Child Find efforts for children from birth through age 5.

Under Part H, the Child Find system that is developed within a state must also include procedures to be used by primary referral sources when referring a child for evaluation and assessment or for intervention. Primary referral sources are specified as hospitals, physicians, parents, daycare programs, local education agencies, public health facilities, social service agencies, and other health-care providers. Specifically, for infants and toddlers, the system must ensure that referrals for evaluation and assessment or intervention are made no more than two working days after a child has been identified by a referral source.

Components of Child Find Programs

Bourland and Harbin (1987) suggested that Child Find should be broadly defined and should include at least ten components, which are described in Table 5.1. In any state, and even in a particular community, responsibility for these components may certainly cut across agencies and service programs. Coordination is essential so that duplication of efforts can be reduced and gaps in services can be identified. Formalized interagency agreements have been developed in many states to assist in the coordination of child identification

TABLE 5.1
Components of Comprehensive Child Find Programs

Component	Description
Definition of target population	The population to be identified must be defined and described.
Coordination	Coordination of Child Find activities across agencies must occur to ensure efficient use of resources.
Financial resources	The limited financial resources available for child services must be reviewed to ensure efficient use.
Public awareness	Information about services and how to access them is described through the mass media and other communication mechanisms.
Referrals	A mechanism must exist for different agencies and professionals to be informed about making appropriate referrals to other agencies.
Screening and prescreening	Procedures should exist for informal screening information being disseminated to the public (e.g., listing of developmental skills on a brochure) and formal screening available to individuals and groups.
Data management, registries, and tracking systems	A means of tracking children, ensuring follow-up, and maintaining records must be established.
Case management	Some person or agency must be responsible for maintaining contact with identified children and ensuring that they obtain necessary services.
Diagnostic assessment	Services must be available for conducting diagnostic assessments and for identifying the intervention services needed.
Trained personnel	Personnel must be trained to implement the Child Find program.

Source: Based on information from *START Resource Packet: Child Find* by B. Bourland and G. Harbin, 1987, Chapel Hill, NC: Frank Porter Graham Child Development Center, University of North Carolina.

efforts. The realization that every community is unique also has prompted many states to establish local coordinating groups and even formalized local agreements to assist in coordination.

Public Awareness Program

Part H of P.L. 99-457, as amended by P.L. 102-119, also specifies that each state must implement a public awareness program focusing on the early identification of children who are eligible for services. The lead agency for Part H must make available to all primary referral sources (specified above) information to be given to parents on the availability of early intervention services. In addition, the public must be informed about the state's early intervention program, the Child Find system (including how to make referrals and how to gain access to evaluation and intervention services), and the state central directory, which includes information on early intervention services, resources, and experts available in the state. The law suggests that methods used to inform the public might include television, radio, and newspaper releases, pamphlets and posters in locations such as hospitals and doctors' offices, and the use of a toll-free telephone service (34 CFR 303.320).

TRACKING

As part of the Child Find program, many states have implemented a system for following or tracking infants and young children who are considered to be at risk due to identified biological or environmental factors. By monitoring the development of these children frequently throughout infancy and the preschool years, a tracking program can help to ensure that children who are in need of early intervention will receive services as soon as possible. Under Part H, states are required to have a system for compiling data on the number of eligible infants and toddlers who are in need of early intervention services, the number actually served, and the types of services provided. The development of a tracking program can ensure compliance with this requirement of Part H as well and can thus also serve an important planning function for states and communities. The potential for tracking programs to serve a role in the prevention of disability has also become apparent. In order to understand these potential benefits of a tracking system, it is important to first understand the concepts of *prevention* and *at risk* as they relate to early intervention.

Prevention

Prevention efforts, as discussed in the public health literature, are frequently identified as occurring at three levels (Sameroff & Fiese, 1990; Simeonsson, 1991). *Primary prevention* is practiced prior to the onset of the disease (or disability) and has the effect of reducing or removing factors that contribute to the condition, thereby preventing the occurrence of the condition. *Secondary prevention* is practiced after the condition has been identified but before it has caused disability, thereby reducing the occurrence of disability. *Tertiary prevention* occurs after the disability has been experienced with the goal of reducing other problems that might occur directly or indirectly as a result of the disability.

Providing early intervention services to children who are at risk is a form of primary prevention. The definition of *at risk* will be discussed further in the following section. Intervention in this case is provided before symptoms (problems or delays in development) are apparent. Under Part H, states may choose whether to provide intervention services to infants and toddlers who are at risk. Currently, 12 states provide early intervention to children under age 3 who are considered to be at risk (Harbin, Danaher, & Derrick, 1994). In some states, children who are at risk but do not qualify for early intervention services are provided with a tracking service, which is a form of secondary prevention (Berman, Biro, & Fenichel, 1989; Graham & Scott, 1988). A tracking system facilitates the early identification of problems and thereby provides the opportunity to intervene early and reduce or eliminate the problem in development. An example of this would be an infant with chronic ear infections. Monitoring this child's development through a tracking program would allow the early identification of hearing problems or a speech and language delay. The earliest intervention might then prevent the need for special education services for this child at a later time.

Meisels (1991) suggests that the Child Find and public awareness requirements of Part H may, in fact, lead to primary prevention activities. For example, if, as a result of public awareness activities, a woman abstains from drinking alcohol during her pregnancy, public awareness efforts have served a primary prevention role.

Determination of eligibility for special education services has traditionally followed a treatment approach in which eligibility is contingent on some predetermined criterion, usually the identification of a disability (Simeonsson, 1991). Only after a condition has become manifest is treatment offered. This is an example of tertiary prevention in that intervention here might reduce other problems that directly or indirectly occur as a result of the disability. For example, intervention services for a child with cerebral palsy can prevent the development of muscle contractures (shortened muscles) and thus also may prevent the occurrence of joint deformities. The child will still have cerebral palsy but may have increased capacity to move in his environment as a result of early intervention.

Viewing intervention from a primary, secondary, and tertiary prevention perspective may result in a more inclusionary and thus more effective approach to reducing the incidence of developmental delay and disability in the population of infants and young children. As indicated earlier, Part H allows the provision of services to children who are at risk before a disability or delay is evident. States that do not choose to provide intervention services to this group may decide to provide tracking services so that problems can be identified as soon as possible, and the impact on the child can be minimized through early intervention. It has been argued that Part H of P.L. 99-457 in fact moves special education from a treatment-only perspective to the realm of prevention (Graham & Scott, 1988).

Determination of Risk

As explained above and in Chapter 1, according to the federal definition of eligibility for services under Part H (see Figure 5.1), there is a category of children designated as at risk who may receive early intervention services at a state's discretion (in other words, the state is not required to serve these children but may use federal money to do so). Dunst (1993) defines *at risk* as "the probability or chance that a poor or detrimental outcome might occur" (p. 143). Discussions of risk factors in children have traditionally been based on three categories, identified by Tjossem (1976) as the following:

Established risk: diagnosed medical disorders of known etiology bearing relatively well-known expectancies for developmental outcome within specified ranges of developmental delay (p. 5).

Biological risk: a history of prenatal, perinatal, neonatal, and early development events suggestive of biological insult(s) to the developing central nervous system and which, either singly or collectively, increase the probability of later appearing aberrant development (p. 5).

Environmental risk: biologically sound infants for whom early life experiences including maternal and family care, health care, opportunities for expression of adaptive behaviors, and patterns of physical and social stimulation are sufficiently limiting to the extent that, without corrective intervention, they impart high probability for delayed development (p. 5).

Established risk corresponds to the second category of eligibility listed in Figure 5.1, children with a diagnosed condition that has a high probability of resulting in developmental delay. As defined in the law, examples of conditions that fit into this category include:

> chromosomal abnormalities; genetic or congenital disorders; severe sensory impairments, including hearing and vision; inborn errors of metabolism; disorders reflecting disturbance of the development of the nervous system; congenital infections; disorders secondary to exposure to toxic substances, including fetal alcohol syndrome; and severe attachment disorders. (Note 1, 34 CFR 303.16)

Children in this category are automatically eligible for services under Part H. There are, however, differences among the states concerning which conditions qualify a child for services. Unless a state's definition of this category is very clear, there also may be differences in eligibility practices among early intervention programs within a state.

The category of *at risk* in the federal law (see Figure 5.1) pertains primarily to biological and environmental risk as defined above. As indicated earlier, a state may decide to provide early intervention services to children who are at risk, but it is not required to do so. According to Harbin, Danaher, and Derrick (1994), 27 states originally indicated an intent to serve children who are at risk. As of 1994, however,

The term "infants and toddlers with disabilities" means individuals from birth to age 2, inclusive, who need early intervention services because they—

(1) are experiencing developmental delays, as measured by appropriate diagnostic instruments and procedures in one or more of the following areas: cognitive development, physical development, language and speech development (hereafter...referred to as "communication development"), psychosocial development (hereafter...referred to as "social or emotional development"), or self-help skills (hereafter... referred to as "adaptive development"), or

(2) have a diagnosed physical or mental condition which has a high probability of resulting in developmental delay.

(3) Such term may also include, at a State's discretion, individuals from birth to age 2, inclusive, who are at risk of having substantial developmental delays if early intervention services are not provided.

FIGURE 5.1
Statutory language pertaining to eligibility definitions—IDEA, Part H
Source: IDEA section 672(i); 34 CFR 303.16.

only 12 states actually did provide intervention services to such children. A state that decides to serve this group must develop guidelines for determining which children will be eligible for services under this category; these guidelines vary considerably. When Harbin, Gallagher, and Terry (1990) studied the risk factors listed by the 27 states originally indicating intent to serve children at risk, they found that 69 different biological criteria were listed; only four factors were selected in common by five or more states. Twenty-three of the states identified 39 different criteria for environmental risk; again only four factors were listed in common by more than five states.

There is a considerable amount of evidence that the presence of multiple risk factors, specifically three or more, is related to a higher probability of difficulties in child development and therefore a greater need for intervention (Dunst, 1993; Sameroff, Seifer, Barocas, Zax, & Greenspan, 1987; Greenbaum & Auerbach, 1992). Harbin, Gallagher, and Terry (1990) recommend that states who opt to provide services to children at risk should require the presence of at least three risk factors. However, Simeonsson (1991) suggests that simply counting the number of factors demonstrated by a child may not be most predictive since it may be the interaction between factors that is most important. At this time, there is not universal agreement on which factors or combinations of factors are most predictive of developmental delay or disability. States that offer tracking services to children who do not qualify for intervention services must also decide what risk factors will qualify a child for tracking. Typically a single risk factor, either biological or environmental, serves as a qualification; however, much remains to be learned about which factors or combination of factors should qualify a child.

Dunst (1993) suggests that early interventionists also consider how risk factors interfere with opportunities that might enhance development. Dunst reviewed the literature on opportunity factors and concludes that multiple opportunity factors are related to increased positive outcomes for child development. Opportunity factors may compensate for risk factors and prevent their potentially negative effect on development. The presence of opportunity factors may explain why some children at risk do not develop a disability or delay. Although consideration of opportunity factors is currently not included in child identification and assessment procedures, this is an area that holds great promise for the future; however, much research remains to be done. Table 5.2 presents a proposed list of risk and opportunity factors that influence human development, as summarized from the literature by Dunst (1993).

Tracking Systems

Many states have developed tracking systems to follow children who are at risk for developmental delay or disability but do not qualify for early intervention services. A document developed by the National Center for Clinical Infant Programs provides an overview of 15 state tracking programs (Berman et al., 1989).

Typically, referral for tracking can be made by medical, social service, or education professionals, or by parents or family members. In some states, a system of registry is tied to the birth certificate process. Under a *birth review* system, information about the newborn's birth can make the child eligible for tracking. The parents then are offered tracking services if they desire. In North Dakota, for example, a birthweight of less than 5.5 pounds is one of 14 factors that make a child eligible for services from the North Dakota Early Childhood Tracking System. The parents receive a letter informing them of the condition that puts their child at risk and are also provided information about the potential effect on their child's development as well as resources available in the state.

Tracking programs monitor the development of children on a regular basis. In some states, monitoring instruments are sent to parents, who fill them out and return them by mail. In other states, professionals administer an instrument either through home visits or at a clinic. Sensitivity to cultural variations and differences among families is critical for a successful tracking program whether services are home-based or provided at a distance. Chapter 4 provides information on cultural competence. As in the provision of early intervention services, it may be necessary to provide several options for participation in a tracking program to best meet families' diverse needs.

In most states the tracking program is an interagency effort even if administratively it is housed with one agency. Some states provide tracking services for infants and toddlers only; others extend tracking up to the point of entry into kindergarten. Some states specify eligibility requirements for tracking services. The state of Hawaii offers home visits by public health nurses to all families of newborns who wish to participate.

Example of a Monitoring Instrument

An instrument that was developed specifically for monitoring child development at a distance is the Ages and Stages Questionnaires (ASQ) (Bricker, Squires, Mounts, Potter, Nickel, & Farrell, 1995), formerly called the Infant/Child Monitoring Questionnaire (ICMQ). The ASQ includes 11 questionnaires to be given when the child is 4, 6, 8, 12, 16, 18, 20, 24, 30, 36, and 48 months of age. The questionnaires are mailed to the family one week before the child reaches each designated age.

Each questionnaire contains 30 questions divided into five sections: gross motor, fine motor, communication, personal-social, and adaptive development. Many of the items include small illustrations to assist the parents in evaluating their child's behavior. An example from the 8th-month questionnaire is provided in Figure 5.2. The parents are instructed to try each item with their child before scoring it. Scoring is done by checking the appropriate box: "yes," "sometimes," or "not yet."

TABLE 5.2
A Proposed List of Risk and Opportunity Factors Influencing Human Development and Functioning

Variables	Risk Factors	Opportunity Factors
Mother's age	Younger or older than normal childbearing years	Within optimal childbearing years
Parent education	Low educational attainment	High educational attainment
Income	Inadequate income	Adequate income
Occupation status	Low occupation status for head of household	High occupation status for head of household
Socioeconomic status (SES)	Low SES	High SES
Job stability	Repeated job changes or unemployment	Stable job
Pregnancy	Unplanned	Planned
Number of siblings	More than four children	One or two children
Residential stability	Repeated relocations	None or few relocations
Marital status	Absence of spouse or partner	Supportive spouse or partner present
Marital relationship	Conflictive	Harmonious
Marital stability	Repeated changes in a conjugal relationship	Stable conjugal relationship
Child temperament	Avoidant, difficult	Warm, responsive
Infant separation	Prolonged separation in first year	Limited separation in first year
Parental health	Poor physical health	Excellent physical health
Parental mental health	Repeated ocurrences of mental health-related problems	Stable emotional well-being
Parental self-esteem	Low self-esteem	High self-esteem
Parental locus of control	External	Internal
Parental social skills	Poor	Good
Coping strategies	Reactive	Proactive
Quality of primary caregiver/child interaction	Controlling and emotionally unavailable	Stimulating and warm
Parenting style	Authoritarian/directive	Responsive/facilitative
Toxic substances	High exposure	No exposure
Nutritional intake	Inadequate	Adequate
Accidents	Frequent	Infrequent
Infections/illnesses	Frequent	Infrequent
Alternative caregivers	None	One or more
Presence of extended family	None or few available	Many and supportive
Extrafamily support	Poor/unsupportive	Good/supportive
Life events	Negative life events	Positive life events

Source: From "Issues Related to 'At-Risk': Implications of Risk and Opportunity for Assessment and Intervention Practice" by C. J. Dunst, 1993, *Topics in Early Childhood Special Education, 13*(2), 143–153.

The returned questionnaire is scored by staff by assigning a value of 1 to "yes" answers, .5 to "sometimes" answers, and 0 to "not yet" answers. The ratio for each domain is then computed and compared with cutoff scores in the manual. If the child's score falls at or below the cutoff score in any area, arrangements are made to refer him or her for further evaluation. The cutoff score can be set at 1.0, 1.5, or 2.0 standard deviations below the mean. Of course, using the 1.0 or 1.5 standard deviation cutoff scores will increase the number of children who are referred.

The Ages and Stages Questionnaires can also be used as an interview tool with families either in person or over the telephone as long as the parent has a copy of the instrument to refer to during the interview. It is available in English and in Spanish. The ASQ user's guide (Squires, Bricker, & Potter, 1995) includes procedures to be used by a program in establishing a monitoring system, for example, establishing children's files and implementing a "tickler" system to prompt the mailing of questionnaires to families at appropriate times.

SCREENING

Definition and Rationale

Screening, which is generally considered to be part of Child Find efforts, is defined by Meisels and Provence (1989) as

> a brief assessment procedure designed to identify children who should receive more intensive diagnosis or assessment. Screening is designed to help children who are at risk for health and developmental problems, handicapping conditions, and/or school failure to receive ameliorative intervention services as early as possible. (p. 58)

Screening large numbers of children for possible biological or developmental problems should allow the early detection of such problems. Early intervention may then serve to prevent the development of a disability or at least may lessen the impact on child development. This in turn may serve to reduce the need for special services as the child grows older.

It should be possible to do screening quickly and economically. It can be cost effective in that it may reduce the need for complete evaluations of some children if the outcome of screening suggests that further evaluation is not needed. Similarly, screening can reduce the long-term cost of special education if it leads to earlier intervention than otherwise would have been provided.

It should be remembered that not all children will need to be screened. There are children who will be clearly eligible for early intervention services as a result of a diagnosed condition or a substantial developmental delay. These children can proceed directly to the evaluation process and do not need to be screened.

Recommended Guidelines for the Screening Process

A document published by the National Center for Clinical Infant Programs (Meisels & Provence, 1989) lists recommended guidelines for screening and assessment, which are listed in Figure 5.3.

The following discussion will focus on several aspects of the screening process: the use of multiple sources of information, the provision of family-centered services, and evaluation of screening programs.

Multivariate screening A comprehensive screening program should include information from a variety of sources. According to Meisels and Wasik (1990), "early identification requires that data be obtained from multiple sources; that it combine caregiving and environmental information with data about the child's biological status" (p. 624). It has been standard practice in the past for screening efforts to include

III. Fine Motor *(Be sure to try each activity with your child.)*

	Yes	Sometimes	Not Yet	
1. Does your baby reach for a crumb or Cheerio and touch it with her finger or hand? (If she already picks up a small object, check "yes" for this item.)	☐	☐	☐	____
2. Does your baby pick up a small toy, holding it in the center of her hand with her fingers around it?	☐	☐	☐	____
3. Does your baby ***try*** to pick up a crumb or Cheerio by using her thumb and all her fingers in a raking motion, even if she isn't able to pick it up? (If she already picks up a crumb or Cheerio, check "yes" for this item.)	☐	☐	☐	____
4. Does your baby usually pick up a small toy with only one hand?	☐	☐	☐	____
5. Does your baby ***successfully*** pick up a crumb or Cheerio by using her thumb and all her fingers in a raking motion? (If she already picks up a crumb or Cheerio, check "yes" for this item.)	☐	☐	☐	____
6. Does your baby pick up a small toy, with the ***tips*** of her thumb and fingers? You should see a space between the toy and her palm.	☐	☐	☐	____

FIGURE 5.2

Sample of items from the 8th-month Ages and Stages Questionnaire

Source: From *Ages and Stages Questionnaires: A Parent-Completed Child Monitoring System* by D. Bricker, J. Squires, L. Mounts, L. Potter, B. Nickel, and J. Farrell, 1995, Baltimore, MD: Paul H. Brookes, P.O. Box 10624, Baltimore, MD 21285-0624. Reprinted by permission.

1. Screening and assessment should be viewed as services—as part of the intervention process—and not only as means of identification and measurement.
2. Processes, procedures, and instruments intended for screening and assessment should only be used for their specified purposes.
3. Multiple sources of information should be included in screening and assessment.
4. Developmental screening should take place on a recurrent or periodic basis. It is inappropriate to screen young children only once during their early years. Similarly, provisions should be made for reevaluation or reassessment after services have been initiated.
5. Developmental screening should be viewed as only one path to more in-depth assessment. Failure to qualify for services based on a single source of screening information should not become a barrier to further evaluation for intervention services if other risk factors (e.g., environmental, medical, familial) are present.
6. Screening and assessment procedures should be reliable and valid.
7. Family members should be an integral part of the screening and assessment process. Information provided by family members is critically important for determining whether or not to initiate more in-depth assessment and for designing appropriate intervention strategies. Parents should be accorded complete informed consent at all stages of the screening and assessment process.
8. During screening or assessment of developmental strengths and problems, the more relevant and familiar the tasks and setting are to the child and the child's family, the more likely it is that the results will be valid.
9. All tests, procedures, and processes intended for screening or assessment must be culturally sensitive.
10. Extensive and comprehensive training is needed by those who screen and assess very young children.

FIGURE 5.3
Guidelines for screening and assessment
Source: From *Screening and Assessment: Guidelines for Identifying Young Disabled and Developmentally Vulnerable Children and Their Families* by S. Meisels and S. Provence, 1989, Arlington, VA: *Zero to Three.* Reprinted by permission.

developmental and sensory screening as well as screening of health factors. However, as the knowledge base increases relative to the factors that best predict the later occurrence of developmental delay or disability, there is increased emphasis on screening environmental and caregiving factors as well. Henderson and Meisels (1994) combined results from a parent questionnaire with results from an individually administered developmental screener and found increased accuracy in determining which children did not need further evaluation. In a study of adolescents both with and without disabilities, Kochanek et al. (1990) found that characteristics of the family, such as maternal education, were more predictive of child status at adolescence than characteristics of the child from birth to age 3. Based on this research, the authors suggest that family factors, not just attributes of the child, must be considered in any determination of the need or potential need for early intervention services.

Kochanek (1988) described a multivariate screening model developed for the state of Rhode Island. This model incorporates a two-tiered approach to screening that reflects different levels of specificity at each level. The first level identifies a relatively large number of children (approximately 30% of the population) as risk positive. The second level is completed in the home environment and selects out a smaller percentage of the population (approximately 15%) as risk positive. This smaller group is then evaluated for eligibility for early intervention. It is estimated that 5% of the population will emerge from the evaluation process as eligible for intervention services. This two-tiered process combines information on child characteristics, parental traits, and maternal/child interaction rather than focusing only on child characteristics. Kochanek suggests that the factors that are used as a basis for screening in this model are precursors not only to developmental disabilities, but also to infant and child mortality, child abuse and neglect, and psychiatric hospitalization. Such a model leads logically to collaborative efforts among the various state agencies and programs involved with infant and early childhood problems in the population.

Family-centered screening procedures

In Chapter 3, a rationale for the provision of family-centered evaluation and assessment services is provided. A family-centered philosophy should also be the basis for screening programs, and several of the recommendations for screening and assessment listed in Figure 5.3 relate to such a theory. To be consistent, screening should be viewed as part of intervention. Meisels and Provence (1989) remind us that screening is often the family's first experience with the educational or human service system and is "potentially a short-term therapeutic experience in itself" (p. 23).

The seventh recommendation listed in Figure 5.3 is that family members should be an integral part of the screening process. Chapter 3 provides a strong rationale for the inclusion of information from family members in the screening process. Furthermore, parents and caregivers should be informed about the entire process in advance; they should be told about the purpose and the potential outcomes, the procedures to be followed, and the qualifications of the professionals involved. The parents should be given the option to participate in the screening process where possible. Perhaps most important, the parents should receive the results of the screening immediately and in jargon-free terminology.

Evaluation of screening programs

Because screening programs should be evaluated on a regular basis to ensure effectiveness, several types of data will need to be collected and analyzed. The following evaluation questions might guide evaluation efforts:

- Are there children who passed the screening and later are found to need special education services?
- Are there children referred for evaluation who are found to not be eligible for services?
- Are the families who participate in screening satisfied with the experience?
- Is evaluation being completed in a timely fashion for those children who are referred for evaluation as a result of screening?

The first two questions can be answered by completing a follow-up of the children who have been screened and comparing these data with the children who eventually are identified as needing special services. There may be children identified as needing special education during the elementary years who were never screened during their early years. Follow-up can assist in determining if this is happening and why, so that steps can be taken to correct the problem. Ideally, a screening program would identify for evaluation only those children who are later found to be eligible for early intervention or special education services. Because children either are or are not in need of special services (as determined by the eligibility criteria that guide admission into early intervention or special education programs), and children either are or are not referred for evaluation to determine this eligibility as a result of the screening program, four potential outcomes are possible, as indicated in Figure 5.4.

A *false positive* refers to a situation in which a child is referred for evaluation based on the results of a screening, but is not found to be in need of special services. In other words, the screening incorrectly identifies the child as being in need of special services. A *false negative* refers to a situation in which a child passes the screening and is not referred for evaluation, but later is identified as being in need of special services. Both false positives and false negatives indicate situations in which an error has been made. False positives can unnecessarily cause anxiety in families and can be costly in terms of evaluation expenses. False negatives, however, create even more serious consequences for the children who may have benefitted from early intervention but did not receive it due to errors in the screening process. Generally, it is preferable to err on the side of false positives than to fail to identify children who are in need of services.

Families should be given the opportunity to evaluate their experience with the screening program. This can be done by survey either immediately following the screening, through a mailed questionnaire, or by telephone contact. A follow-up of each child who is screened can also determine how quickly evaluation is completed after screening so that time lags can be identified and corrected if possible.

In addition to these areas of evaluation, the reliability and validity of the screening instruments used should be considered. The following section includes information on reliability and validity.

Selection of Screening Instruments

According to Meisels and Wasik (1990), developmental screening instruments should be "brief, norm-referenced, inexpensive, standardized in administration, objectively scored, broadly focused across all areas of development, reliable and valid" (p. 613). Meisels and Wasik add to this that screeners should be "sensitive to the sample of children who are developmentally at risk and specific to the portion of the screening population that is not at risk" (p. 613).

Reliability of screening tools and procedures Reliability, as described in Chapter 2, is a critical dimension of tests and other measurement activities. It refers to the consistency and stability of measurement. Screening measures are usually norm-referenced tests for

FIGURE 5.4
Potential outcomes for screening

	Referred for Evaluation	Not Referred for Evaluation
Eligible for Special Services		False Negative
Not Eligible for Special Services	False Positive	

which reliability estimates can be obtained. When establishing a screening program, interventionists should read the test manual carefully and review research articles that have assessed the reliability of the measure in question. However, the presence of acceptable reliability estimates and studies by the test author or other researchers is only the beginning in ensuring that screening procedures are reliably implemented. Procedural reliability and scoring reliability, as described in Chapter 2, are also critical in screening. To ensure that instruments are appropriately administered and scored, all members of the screening team should be fully trained in test administration and scoring. Periodically conducting procedural and scoring reliability checks as described in Chapter 2 can also serve to ensure reliability in screening.

Validity of screening tools and procedures As also noted in Chapter 2, validity is a critical dimension of tests and deals with the extent to which measures can be used for specific purposes. Two types of criterion validity are important for screening measures: concurrent validity and predictive validity. *Concurrent validity,* as it relates to screening measures, refers to the extent to which the screening test agrees with more thorough measures (usually diagnostic tests) at about the same point in time. Because the focus of screening frequently is development, the screening tests should have high agreement with more thorough developmental measures that would be administered within a few days. *Predictive validity,* as it relates to screening measures, refers to the extent to which the screening test agrees with children's performance on outcome measures later in time. For example, predictive validity is seen when a screening measure given to 4-year-old children accurately predicts performance on an instrument administered in first grade. The validity of commonly used screening tests is addressed later in this chapter.

To be valid, screening measures should also be free from bias due to age, sex, geographic factors, economic background, and racial or ethnic status. Interventionists should carefully evaluate the test manuals and the research that has been conducted on various measures to determine whether the standardization population included children from the ages to be screened, an equal distribution of males and females, children of different racial and ethnic groups, and families from a variety of economic backgrounds, and that it sampled geographic regions similar to those for which the measures are being considered.

Sensitivity and specificity Of particular importance in selecting a screening instrument is the degree of sensitivity and specificity reported (Lichtenstein & Ireton, 1991). *Sensitivity* refers to the ability of the test to identify a high proportion of the children who are indeed developmentally delayed or have a disability. *Specificity* refers to the ability of the test to not identify children who do not have a disability or developmental delays. In other words, the test should sort those who should and should not be referred to evaluation for eligibility. Evaluating sensitivity and specificity is important in determining the cutoff score for making referrals. Screening programs can adjust the cutoff score for screening instruments in order to increase the sensitivity and specificity of the instrument in relation to the community of children with whom it is being used. For example, the Battelle Developmental Inventory Screening Test (Newborg, Stock, Wnek, Guidubaldi, & Svinicki, 1988) allows the examiner to choose a cutoff score that is equivalent to 1.0, 1.5, or 2.0 standard deviations below the mean. The Denver II (Frankenburg & Dodds, 1990) can also be adjusted by referring children whose outcome is abnormal or questionable instead of only those whose outcome is abnormal. The Brigance Screener (Brigance, 1985) allows the examiner to determine what cutoff score will be used based on data collected at the screening site. The DIAL–R (Mardell-Czudnowski & Goldenberg, 1990) test results can be interpreted using a cutoff score at 1.0, 1.5, or 2.0 standard deviations below the mean or at the 5th or 10th percentile. In addition, DIAL–R users can also choose the norm sample that best fits the composition of their community. Any of the DIAL–R cutoffs can be applied to norms for a "Caucasian" sample, a "Minority" sample or a "Census" sample (the Caucasian and Minority samples combined), which reflects the 1990 U.S. census.

Information on Selected Screening Instruments

The following section provides information on seven currently used screening instruments. The information is summarized in Table 5.3.

AGS Early Screening Profiles

The AGS Early Screening Profiles (Harrison et al., 1990), published by the American Guidance Service (AGS), is norm-referenced and consists of seven parts: Cognitive/Language Profile, Motor Profile, Self-Help/Social Profile, Articulation Survey, Home Survey, Health History Survey, and Behavior Survey. Each component can be used independently or in combination with other components. The Cognitive/Language Profile was developed by the authors of the Kaufman Assessment Battery for Children (Kaufman & Kaufman, 1983); the Motor Profile was developed by the author of the Bruininks-Oseretsky Test of Motor Proficiency (Bruininks, 1978); the Self-Help/Social Profile was developed by two of the authors of the Vineland Adaptive Behavior Scales (Sparrow, Balla, & Cicchetti, 1984).

The AGS Early Screening Profiles is an individually administered screening instrument for children from 2 years 0 months through 6 years 11 months. Development is screened in multiple domains (cognitive/language, motor, self-help/social) and includes information obtained from multiple sources—parents, teachers or day-care providers, and examiners. The Cognitive/Language Profile consists of four subtests—verbal concepts, visual discrimination, logical relations, and basic school skills. The Motor Profile includes a gross motor subtest and a fine motor subtest; the Self-Help/Social Profile includes both parent and teacher reports on communication, daily living skills, and socialization and motor skills domains. The Articulation Survey uses direct testing to measure articulation of single words and intelligibility during continuous speech. The Home Survey and Health History Survey are 12-item questionnaires to be completed by the parents. The Behavior Survey is completed by the examiner following administration of the Cognitive/Language and Motor Profiles.

The Early Screening Profiles can be administered to large numbers of children using a station format, where children move from place to place. The authors suggest that a screening coordinator be responsible for developing and implementing the screening program and training other examiners. Administration time for the three profiles is estimated to be between 15 and 40 minutes, and time estimated for completion of the surveys is 15 minutes.

The AGS Early Screening Profiles provide a choice of two levels of scoring. Level I scores yield Screening Indexes, which can be obtained quickly. They range from 1 to 6; 1 and 2 are below average performance and 5 and 6 are above average. Screening Indexes can be obtained for the Cognitive/Language Profile, the Motor Profile, the Self-Help/Social Profile: Parent, and the Self-Help/Social Profile: Teacher. In addition, a Total Screening Index can be obtained and the Cognitive/Language Profile can yield a Cognitive Index and a Language Index.

Level II scoring yields standard scores, normal curve equivalents, percentiles, stanines,

TABLE 5.3
Selected Screening Instruments

Instrument	Publisher	Age Range	Domains	Outcomes	Norms
AGS Early Screening Instrument (Harrison et al., 1990)	American Guidance Service, Inc., Circle Pines, MN	2 years to 6 years, 11 months	Profiles: Cognitive/Language Motor Self-Help/Social Surveys: Articulation Home Survey Health History Survey Behavior Survey	Level I: Above Average Average Below Average Level II Profiles: Standard scores Normal curve equivalents Percentile scores Stanines Age equivalents	1,149 children stratified by age, geographic region, race, gender, parent education, and size of school district
Battelle Developmental Screening Test (Newborg, Stock, Wnek, Guidubaldi & Svinicki, 1988)	Riverside Publishing Company, Chicago, IL	Birth to 8 years	Personal/Social Adaptive Motor Communication Cognition	Pass/Fail based on -1.0, -1.5, or -2.0 cut-off; age equivalents	800 children stratified by age, race, and gender
Brigance Preschool Screen (Brigance, 1985) Brigance Early Preschool Screen (Brigance, 1990)	Curriculum Associates, North Billerica, MA	2 years, 9 months to 5 years; 21–36 months	Not divided into domains	Referral for further evaluation or no referral	None reported
Denver II (Frankenburg & Dodds, 1990)	Denver Developmental Materials, Denver, CO	Birth to 6 years	Personal/Social Fine Motor/Adaptive Language Gross Motor	Normal Abnormal Questionable Untestable	2,096 children stratified by age, maternal education, ethnicity, and urban or rural residence

Developmental Activities Screening Inventory–II (Fewell & Langley, 1984)	Pro-Ed Publishing Company, Austin, TX	1 month to 60 months	Not divided into domains	Developmental age scores	None reported
Developmental Indicators for the Assessment of Learning–Revised (DIAL–R) (Mardell-Czudnowski & Goldenberg, 1990)	American Guidance Service, Circle Pines, MN	2 years to 5 years, 11 months	Motor Concepts Language Social-Emotional Checklist	Potential Problem; OK; Potential Advanced; based on +/–1.0, +/–1.5, or +/–2.0 cutoff	1983 standardization reanalyzed; 2,227 children stratified by age, geographic region, sex, size of community, and race; Caucasian sample, Minority sample, or Census sample may be chosen
FirstSTEP (Miller, 1993)	Psychological Corporation, San Antonio, TX	2 years, 9 months to 6 years, 2 months	Cognition Communication Motor Social/Emotional Adaptive Parent/Teacher Scale	Scaled scores; normal, borderline, delayed outcomes	1,433 children stratified by age, sex, geographic region, race/ethnicity, and parent education

and age equivalents for the three profiles and the Total Screening score. For the surveys, Level II provides a descriptive outcome: above average, average, and below average.

The AGS Early Screening Profiles were standardized on 1,149 children. The population was stratified according to the 1990 census estimates on sex, race/ethnic group, region of the U.S., size of school district, and parental level of education.

The manual for the AGS Early Screening Profiles includes a good deal of information on reliability and validity. Internal consistency reliability is reported to range from .41 to .95 for each component. Test-retest reliability ranged from .66 to .91. Interrater reliability was measured for the Motor Profile and ranged from .83 to .99.

The manual also includes considerable evidence of concurrent validity measured as comparisons with numerous other instruments. Short-term (two years) evidence of predictive validity is also provided. The authors addressed construct validity by demonstrating that the profiles effectively identified both at-risk and gifted children.

Battelle Developmental Inventory Screening Test The Battelle Developmental Screening Test (Newborg et al., 1988) consists of 96 items taken from the 341 items of the Battelle Developmental Inventory (BDI), which is described in Chapter 10. The BDI Screening Test is a norm-referenced, individually administered screener that covers the five domains assessed with the full BDI: personal-social, adaptive, motor, communication, and cognition. The same age range is covered: birth to age 8. Administration and item scoring procedures for the BDI screener are the same as for the full BDI. Three different procedures may be used: direct testing, observation, and interview. Cutoff scores may be chosen from three probability levels that correspond to 1.0, 1.5, or 2.0 standard deviations below the mean.

The BDI was standardized on a sample of 800 children selected on the basis of geographical region, race, gender, and urban or rural residence. The manual reports administration to a "clinical" sample that included children with disabilities, but little information is provided about this group. The original manual, which was published in 1984, included norms that were inaccurate. A new manual with "recalibrated" norms was published in 1988.

The BDI manual provides no information on reliability of the screener, but reports that it correlates highly with the full BDI. McLean, McCormick, Baird, and Mayfield (1987) found the correlations to be less than those reported by the manual. Perhaps more importantly, however, this study also found that the specificity of the BDI was poor. Use of this instrument with a population of 30 children resulted in considerable overreferral.

Brigance Preschool Screen and Early Preschool Screen Two preschool screening instruments have been developed by Albert Brigance: the Brigance Early Preschool Screen (Brigance, 1990) and the Brigance Preschool Screen (Brigance, 1985). The Early Preschool Screen has a section for 2-year-old children (ages 21 to 30 months) and a section for 2-and-a-half-year-old children (27 to 36 months). The Preschool Screen has a section for 3-year-olds (2 years, 9 months to 4 years) and a section for 4-year-olds (3 years, 9 months to 5 years).

The Brigance instruments are individually administered and can be administered by one examiner or by a team. Fine motor, gross motor, receptive and expressive language, and cognitive items are included in each age group, although only one overall score is yielded. Materials needed beyond the testing manual are minimal (colored blocks, a pencil or crayons, a line on the floor).

Points are awarded based on the child's response to individual items, with 100 points possible. The manual does not specify what the cutoff score should be for referral for further evaluation. It is recommended that a child who scores 60 or below be referred; however, it is also recommended that each community should develop its own cutoff scores based on analysis of the scores of children in the community.

The Brigance instruments are not norm-referenced. The manual states that the items were developed through a literature search and then field tested (reviewed) by professionals. One potentially confusing aspect of these instruments is the overlap in ages between them. For example, a child of 3 years, 11 months could be tested with either the 3-year-old screen or the 4-year-old screen. No data on reliability or validity are reported in the manual.

Denver II The Denver II (Frankenburg & Dodds, 1990) is the latest revision of the Denver Developmental Screening Test, which was originally published in 1975. It is norm-referenced and is individually administered. The Denver II can be administered to children between birth and 6 years of age and covers four domains of child development: personal-social, fine motor-adaptive, language, and gross motor. Figure 5.5 illustrates the protocol for the Denver II. The materials needed for administration are provided in a test kit that is small and very portable.

The Denver II includes 125 items across the four domains. However, only the items that lie closest to the age line that is drawn on the protocol are typically administered (see Figure 5.5). Items that run through and to the left of the age line are administered to determine whether the child needs further assessment for possible developmental delay. If time permits, items to the right of the age line may be administered to determine relative strengths of the child. The latest version of the Denver has added five ratings of the child's behavior during testing, which are recorded in the bottom left-hand corner of the protocol.

Four possible scores may be recorded for the items: pass, fail, no opportunity, and refusal. Based on the position of failed or refused items relative to the age line, the overall outcome for the screener may be interpreted as normal, abnormal, questionable, and untestable. An abnormal outcome warrants referral for further assessment; questionable and untestable outcomes warrant rescreening. The choice of terms for outcomes on this screener is unfortunate: an outcome of abnormal clearly does not mean that the *child* is abnormal, only that the outcome of this screening is abnormal and further evaluation is recommended.

The Denver II provides printed training materials in the manual, and a training videotape is available. The manual also provides a proficiency test that can be self-administered and scored in order to determine readiness for administration of the instrument. A technical manual is available that includes information about the standardization process and studies involving the Denver.

The Denver II was standardized on 2,096 children in Colorado, stratified according to maternal education, ethnic group, and rural or urban residence. Marking and shading on each item on the protocol provides information on the average age at which 25%, 50%, 75%, and 90% of the population passed each item. This information is also in table form in the manual.

Reliability information on a very small sample of children is reported for both interrater reliability (.99) and test-retest reliability (.90). The only validity discussion provided by the authors refers to the qualifications of the professionals who developed the new items and the test's acceptance as a widely used (internationally used) screener.

Developmental Activities Screening Inventory-II (DASI-II) The Developmental Activities Screening Inventory-II (DASI-II) (Fewell & Langley, 1984), which is the second edition of the original DASI, covers the age range from

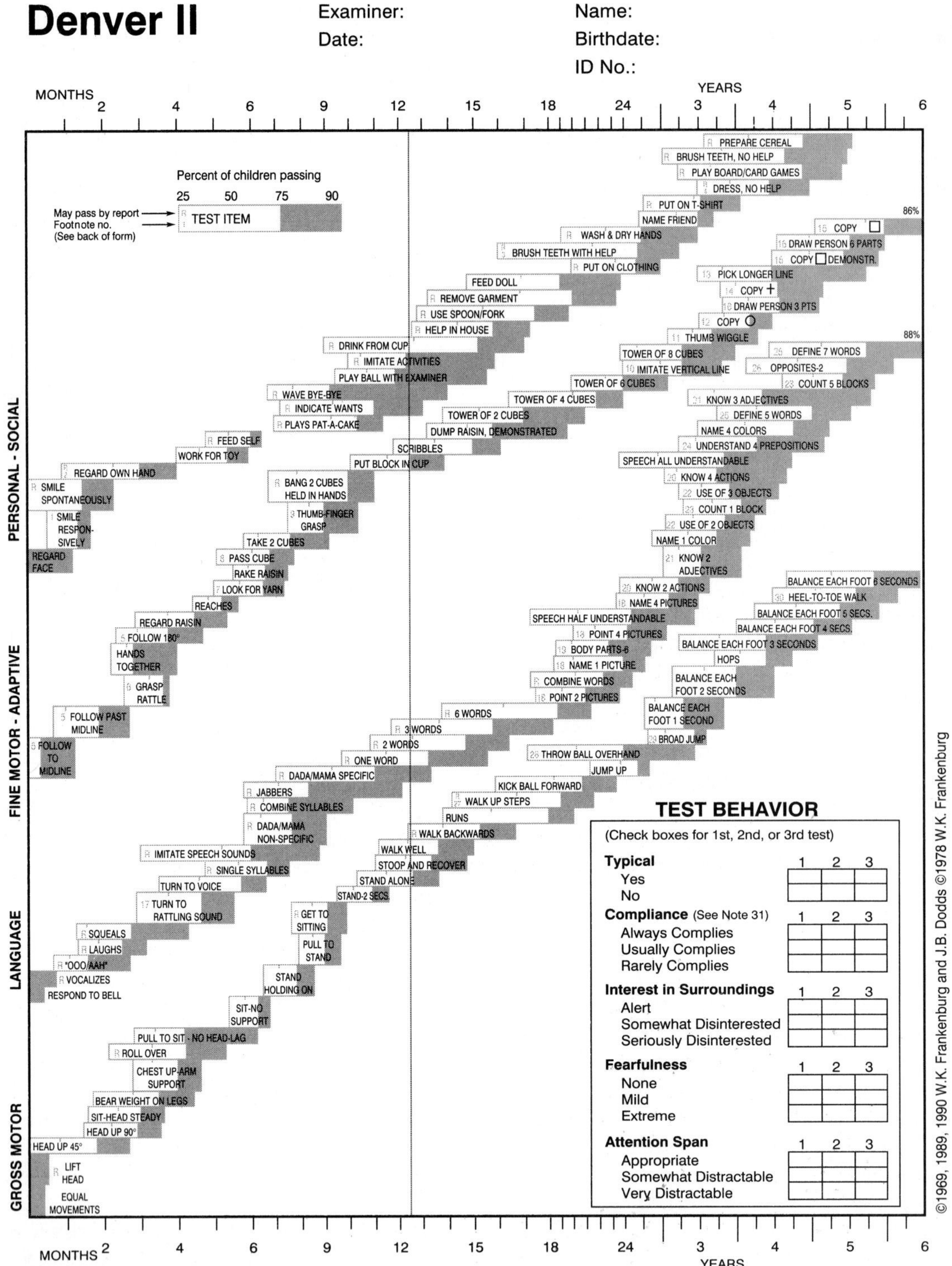

FIGURE 5.5
Protocol for the Denver II with age line drawn at 12 months, 15 days
Source: From *Denver II Screening Manual* by W. K. Frankenburg and J. B. Dodds, 1990, Denver, CO: Denver Developmental Materials. Reprinted by permission.

1 to 60 months. It is individually administered, but is not norm-referenced. This instrument is unique among screening tests in that it is a nonverbal test designed to be useful for children with sensory or language impairments. Since the test is nonverbal, it does not penalize children who have hearing problems or language disorders. Adaptations are specified for children with visual impairments so that they are not penalized. This test is also unique in that the authors have included instructional suggestions for children based on items that were not passed in the screening. The authors suggest that it is unfortunately very common for a good deal of time to pass between a screening and the follow-up evaluation. These suggestions, then, might help the parent, preschool teacher, or daycare provider in teaching the child during this time. The instructional suggestions might also be helpful to parents and child-care providers for children who are not referred for further evaluation.

The DASI-II kit includes picture and symbol cards; other necessary materials can be obtained from a typical preschool classroom. The test is administered by the examiner working directly with the child rather than through observation or interview. Instructions for administering and scoring each item are provided in the manual. Administration time is approximately 25 to 30 minutes.

Each item on the DASI-II is scored as plus or minus. The raw score is then converted to a developmental age through the use of a table in the manual. The test yields one overall developmental age and does not provide domain scores, but an analysis of each item according to primary perceptual or conceptual component is provided in the manual. It is important to remember, however, that because the DASI-II was designed for screening purposes, it is not appropriate for eligibility determination even though developmental age scores can be determined. Cutoff points for passing or failing the screening are not provided but will need to be determined by those administering this instrument.

The DASI-II has not been standardized, and no reliability information is provided in the manual. Concurrent validity studies on the original instrument are reported; they compared the DASI with other cognitive measures and also with other developmental screeners.

Developmental Indicators for the Assessment of Learning–Revised (DIAL–R) Developmental Indicators for the Assessment of Learning (Mardell & Goldenberg, 1975) was published in 1975. The first DIAL–R was published in 1983; the current edition (Mardell-Czudnowski & Goldenberg, 1990) has been modified considerably from the first two editions and includes, among other changes, reanalyzed norms. The DIAL–R has also changed publishers and is currently available from the American Guidance Service. The DIAL–R is a norm-referenced instrument that includes three screening areas—motor, concepts, and language. Each area includes a checklist of social-emotional behaviors that are to be observed during screening. Children between the ages of 2 years and 5 years, 9 months can be screened with the DIAL–R, and the estimated time of administration is 20 to 30 minutes.

Most of the materials needed for testing are available in the DIAL–R materials kit. The test uses a station format with children rotating through the stations. Three adults are the operators who administer the items in the motor, concept, and language areas, and one adult serves as the coordinator for the overall process. Volunteers may also be used to play with children who are waiting or to accompany some children through the stations. Six to nine children can be screened in an hour. Figure 5.6 presents a possible floor plan for a screening.

The DIAL–R also includes training materials and a supplementary training video to prepare adults to administer the test; a Parent

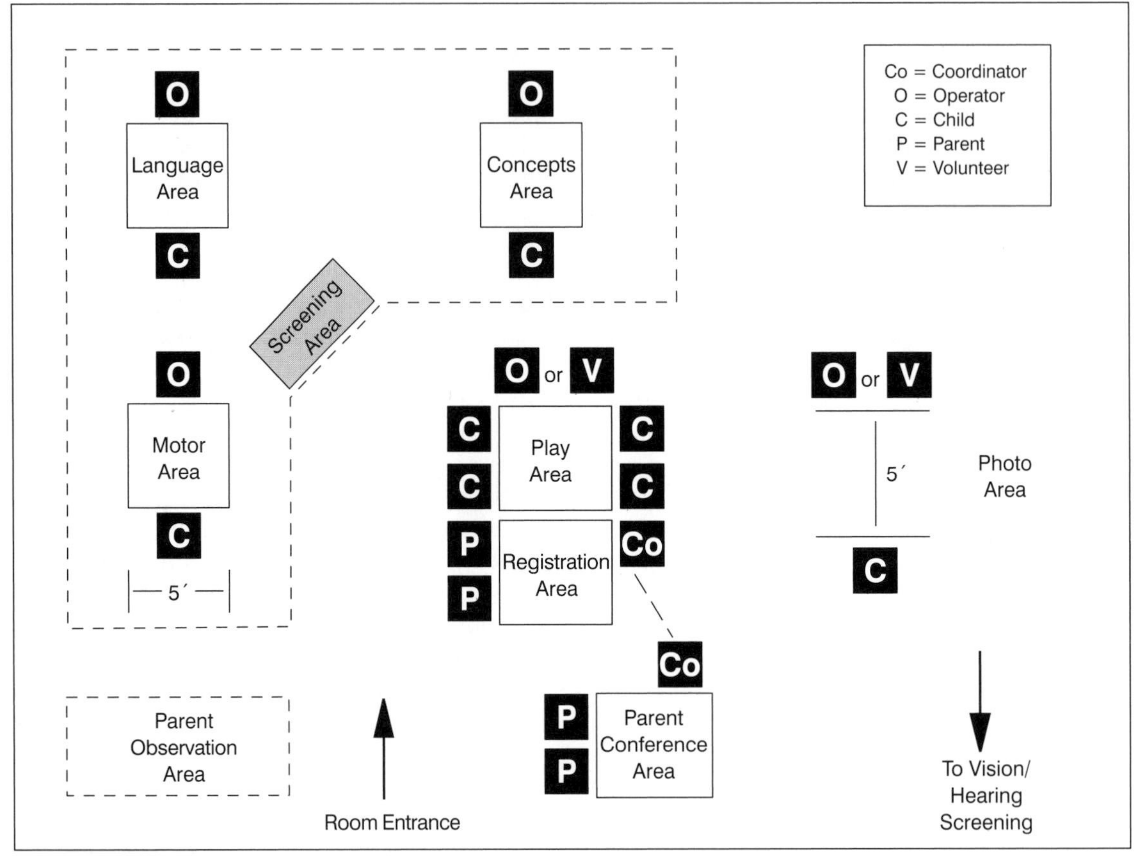

FIGURE 5.6
Suggested floor plan for DIAL–R screening
Source: From *Developmental Indicators for the Assessment of Learning–Revised* by C. Mardell-Czudnowski and D. Goldenberg, 1990, Circle Pines, MN: American Guidance Service. Reproduced with permission of the publisher. All rights reserved.

Information Form to assist the screening team in collecting information on the child's health and environment; and Parent-Child Activity Forms that suggest activities that can be used by parents to facilitate their child's development in each of the three areas of the screener.

Three results are possible from the composite score of the DIAL–R: potential problem, OK, and potential advanced. As indicated earlier, the cutoff scores for these three outcomes can be adjusted for increased sensitivity or specificity in relation to a particular community. Scores can be reported to parents immediately, before they leave the screening site.

The norms that are used in the current DIAL–R were obtained from a standardization process that took place between 1981 and 1983. The sample was stratified according to age, sex, geographic region, size of community, and race based on the 1981 census. The norms were reanalyzed in 1990 for 2,227 children based on the 1990 census.

The DIAL–R manual reports test-retest and internal consistency reliabilities. The test-retest reliabilities range from .13 to .98. Internal consistency reliabilities for the three area scores range from .70 to .87. The manual also addresses content, concurrent, predictive, and construct validity. The reliability, concurrent, and predictive validity studies were completed on the 1983 edition of the DIAL–R, and the authors suggest caution in drawing conclusions based on these studies.

FirstSTEP: Screening Test for Evaluating Preschoolers FirstSTEP (Miller, 1993) is an individually administered, norm-referenced screening test for children from 2 years, 9 months to 6 years, 2 months. It is designed to be a companion to the Miller Assessment for Preschoolers (MAP) (Miller, 1988). FirstSTEP covers the five developmental domains specified by IDEA: cognition, communication, motor, social-emotional, and adaptive behavior.

FirstSTEP includes 12 subtests in game format; they are divided into cognitive, communication, and motor domains (four subtests in each of the three domains). The results on these three domains make up the Composite Score for the test. In addition, a Social-Emotional Scale and an Adaptive Behavior Checklist cover the two additional domains specified by IDEA. A third and optional scale, The Parent/Teacher Scale, has also been developed to add information about the child's typical behavior at home or at school in addition to the behavior observed during the screening.

The item pool for FirstSTEP was developed from examination of the tryout edition items from the Miller Assessment for Preschoolers. Two pilot editions and a tryout edition were tested and reviewed by subject matter experts prior to standardization of the instrument. The standardization population consisted of 1,433 children across seven age groups. Approximately equal numbers of boys and girls were included. The sample was spread across nine geographic regions of the United States and paralleled the 1988 census data in terms of geographical location and race/ethnicity. The sample included the same proportion of whites, African Americans, Hispanics, Asian Americans, and Native Americans as delineated in the 1988 census. In addition, parent education was also a stratification variable.

Each domain has a mean of 10 and a standard deviation of 3. The composite score has a mean of 50 and a standard deviation of 10. Within each domain, a scaled score of 7 or 13 represents 1 standard deviation below or above the mean. Scaled scores of 4 or 16 represent 2 standard deviations below or above the mean. A color-coded system is used to indicate whether the child's score is in the normal or delayed range; green indicates that the score is within acceptable limits, red indicates performance is below acceptable limits and further testing is necessary. A score in the yellow area can be considered borderline, and clinical judgment plus information from the developmental history and parent/teacher input should be used to determine whether to refer the child for evaluation.

The FirstSTEP manual presents split-half reliability coefficients for the domain scores and internal consistency scores (using coefficient alpha) for the adaptive behavior checklist, social-emotional scale, and parent/teacher scale. Standard Errors of Measurement are also provided. Reliability coefficients ranged from .65 to .95. Test-retest reliability was also assessed for a group of 86 children randomly selected from the standardization group. Decision consistency as assessed for this group ranged from .85 to .93. Stability coefficients of the domain and composite scores ranged from .82 to .93. Interrater agreement also was assessed on 43 cases from the standardization group. The correlation coefficients obtained from the resulting scaled scores of two raters ranged from .77 to .96.

The FirstSTEP manual presents the results of a number of concurrent validity studies, including correlations with the Miller Assessment for

Preschoolers, the Wechsler Preschool and Primary Scale of Intelligence—Revised, the Bruininks-Oseretsky Test of Motor Proficiency, the Test of Language Development Primary—Second Edition, the Walker Problem Behavior Identification Checklist—Revised, and the Vineland Scale of Adaptive Behavior. Evidence of both convergent validity (high correlations between scales that measure the same thing) and discriminant validity (lower correlations with measures of different constructs) is provided.

SUMMARY OF KEY CONCEPTS

- Child Find is a systematic process of identifying infants and preschoolers who are potentially eligible for early intervention services. Each state is required to establish a system of Child Find for children from birth to age 21.
- Screening is an assessment process designed to identify children who may need further evaluation in order to determine whether early intervention should be provided.
- Tracking is a system for providing continuous monitoring of the developmental progress of children who are thought to be at risk for developmental problems.
- Prevention efforts can be described as primary, secondary, or tertiary prevention. Tracking is an example of secondary prevention.
- Risk factors in children have been described as established risk, biological risk, and environmental risk.
- Screening programs for young children should include information from a variety of sources, should include family members in the screening process, and should be evaluated on a regular basis to determine effectiveness.
- In selecting screening instruments, early intervention personnel should consider reliability, validity, sensitivity, and specificity.

REFERENCES

Berman, C., Biro, P., & Fenichel, E. S. (1989). *Keeping track: Tracking systems for high risk infants and young children.* Washington, DC: National Center for Clinical Infant Programs.

Blackman, J. A. (1986). *Warning signals: Basic criteria for tracking at-risk infants and toddlers.* Washington, DC: National Center for Clinical Infant Programs.

Bourland, B., & Harbin, G. (1987). *START resource packet: Child Find.* Chapel Hill, NC: Frank Porter Graham Child Development Center, University of North Carolina.

Bricker, D., Squires, J., Mounts, L., Potter, L., Nickel, B., & Farrell, J. (1995). *Ages and Stages Questionnaires.* Baltimore, MD: Paul H. Brookes.

Brigance, A. H. (1985). *Brigance Preschool Screen for Three- and Four-Year-Old Children.* North Billerica, MA: Curriculum Associates.

Brigance, A. H. (1990). *Brigance Early Preschool Screen for Two-Year-Old and Two-and-One-Half-Year-Old Children.* North Billerica, MA: Curriculum Associates.

Bruininks, R. H. (1978). *Bruininks-Oseretsky Test of Motor Proficiency.* Circle Pines, MN: American Guidance Service.

Dunst, C. J. (1993). Issues related to "at risk": Implications of risk and opportunity for assessment and intervention practice. *Topics in Early Childhood Special Education, 13*(2), 143–153.

Fewell, R. R., & Langley, M. B. (1984). *Developmental Activities Screening Inventory-II.* Austin, TX: PRO-ED Publishing Co.

Frankenburg, W. K., & Dodds, J. B. (1990). *Denver II screening manual.* Denver, CO: Denver Developmental Materials.

Graham, M. A., & Scott, K. G. (1988). The impact of definitions of high risk on services to infants and toddlers. *Topics in Early Childhood Special Education, 8*(3), 23–38.

Greenbaum, C., & Auerbach, J. (Eds.). (1992). *Longitudinal studies of children at psychological risk: Cross national perspectives.* Norwood, NJ: Ablex.

Harbin, G., Danaher, J., & Derrick, T. (1994). Comparison of eligibility policies for infant/toddler programs and preschool special education programs. *Topics in Early Childhood Special Education, 14*(4), 455–471.

Harbin, G., Gallagher, J., & Terry, D. (1990). Defining the eligible population: Policy issues and challenges. *Journal of Early Intervention, 15*(1), 13–20.

Harrison, P. L., Kaufman, A. S., Kaufman, N. L., Bruininks, P. H., Rynders, J., Ilmer, S., Sparrow, S. S., & Cicchetti, D. V. (1990). *AGS Early Screening Profiles.* Circle Pines, MN: American Guidance Service.

Henderson, L. W., & Meisels, S. (1994). Parental involvement in the developmental screening of their young children: A multiple-source perspective. *Journal of Early Intervention, 18*(2), 141–154.

Kaufman, A. S., & Kaufman, N. L. (1983). *Kaufman Assessment Battery for Children.* Circle Pines, MN: American Guidance Service.

Kochanek, T. T. (1988). Conceptualizing screening models for developmentally disabled high risk children and their families. *Zero to Three, 9*(2), 16–20.

Kochanek, T. K., Kabacoff, R. I., & Lipsitt, L. P. (1990). Early identification of developmentally disabled and at-risk preschool children. *Exceptional Children, 56*(6), 528–538.

Lichtenstein, R., & Ireton, H. (1991). Preschool screening for developmental and educational problems. In B. A. Bracken (Ed.), *The psychoeducational assessment of preschool children* (pp. 486–513). Boston: Allyn & Bacon.

Mardell, C., & Goldenberg, D. (1975). *Developmental Indicators for the Assessment of Learning.* Edison, NJ: Childcraft Education Corporation.

Mardell-Czudnowski, C., & Goldenberg, D. (1990). *Developmental Indicators for the Assessment of Learning–Revised.* Circle Pines, MN: American Guidance Service.

McLean, M., McCormick, K., Baird, S., & Mayfield, P. (1987). A study of the concurrent validity of the Battelle Developmental Inventory Screening Test. *Diagnostique, 13*(1), 10–20.

McNulty, B., Smith, D. B., & Soper, E. W. (1983). *Effectiveness of early special education for handicapped children.* Denver, CO: Colorado Department of Education.

Meisels, S. (1991). Dimensions of early identification. *Journal of Early Intervention, 15*(1), 26–35.

Meisels, S. J., & Provence, S. (1989). *Screening and assessment: Guidelines for identifying young disabled and developmentally vulnerable children and their families.* Washington, DC: National Center for Clinical Infant Programs.

Meisels, S. J., & Wasik, B. A. (1990). Who should be served? Identifying children in need of early intervention. In S. J. Meisels & J. P. Shonkoff (Eds.), *Handbook of early childhood intervention* (pp. 605–632). New York: Cambridge University Press.

Miller, L. J. (1988). *Miller Assessment for Preschoolers (MAP).* San Antonio, TX: The Psychological Corp.

Miller, L. J. (1993). *FirstSTEP Screening Test for Evaluating Preschoolers.* San Antonio, TX: The Psychological Corp.

Newborg, J., Stock, J. R., Wnek, L., Guidubaldi, J., & Svinicki, J. (1988). *Battelle Developmental Inventory.* Allen, TX: Developmental Learning Materials.

Sameroff, A. J., & Fiese, B. H. (1990). Transactional regulation and early intervention. In S. J. Meisels & J. P. Shonkoff (Eds.), *Handbook of early childhood intervention* (pp. 119–149). New York: Cambridge University Press.

Sameroff, A. J., Seifer, R., Barocas, R. M., Zax, M., & Greenspan, S. (1987). Intelligence quotient scores of 4 year old children: Social-emotional risk factors. *Pediatrics, 79,* 343–350.

Schweinhart, L. J., & Weikart, D. P. (1980). *Young children grow up: The effects of the Perry Preschool Program on youths through age 19.*

Ypsilanti, MI: High/Scope Educational Research Foundation.

Scott, K. G., & Hogan, A. E. (1982). Methods for the identification of high-risk and handicapped infants. In C. T. Ramey & P. L. Trohanis (Eds.), *Finding and educating high risk and handicapped infants.* Baltimore, MD: University Park Press.

Simeonsson, R. (1991). Primary, secondary and tertiary prevention in early intervention. *Journal of Early Intervention, 15*(2), 124–134.

Sparrow, S. S., Balla, D. A., & Cicchetti, D. V. (1984). *Vineland Adaptive Behavior Scale.* Circle Pines, MN: American Guidance Service.

Squires, J., Bricker, D., & Potter, L. (1995). *Ages and Stages Questionnaires user's guide.* Baltimore, MD: Paul H. Brookes.

Tjossem, T. D. (1976). Early intervention: Issues and approaches. In T. D. Tjossem (Ed.), *Intervention strategies for high risk infants and young children* (pp. 3–33). Baltimore, MD: University Park Press.

Wood, M. E. (1981). Costs of intervention programs. In C. Garland et al. (Eds.), *Early intervention for children with special needs and their families: Findings and recommendations.* Westar Series Paper No. 11. Seattle, WA: University of Washington. (ERIC Document Reproduction Service No. 207 278)

CHAPTER

6

Screening and Assessment of Sensory Functions

M. Beth Langley, M.S.
Prekindergarten Handicapped Assessment Team, Pinellas County Schools, Largo, FL

Increased survival rates of preterm infants have contributed to a significant rise in major disabling conditions among those infants, with approximately 20% of premature infants manifesting cerebral palsy, mental retardation, hydrocephalus, or visual and/or hearing impairments. Many of these infants may also manifest immature, disorganized, and/or dysfunctional proximal sensory systems that interfere with the perception, integration, and application of sensory information from the auditory and visual channels. Prior to the initiation of a developmental assessment of cognitive, communicative, motoric, or social abilities, the auditory and visual systems must be screened to ensure normal function and to rule out the possibility that developmental delays are the result of an impairment in one or more sensory modalities. If a child has been identified as having a significant deficit in one of the major sensory channels, an assessment of residual functional ability of the impaired system as well as of the functional application of other sensory systems will yield information regarding potential compensatory mechanisms that will facilitate adaptation to the environment and developmental demands. Whether assessing auditory, visual, tactile, proprioceptive, or vestibular function, the clinician must keep in mind the child's general developmental level, behavioral state, and attentional and motivational factors when selecting assessment strategies, eliciting stimuli, and anticipating response topographies. Regardless of age, the child's ability to attend to, receive, process, and respond to incoming sensory experiences will be governed by the integrity and organizational capacity of his or her central nervous system.

In this chapter, issues related to hearing impairments and assessment of auditory functioning; visual impairment and assessment of visual functioning; and vestibular, tactile, and proprioceptive dysfunction and assessment are described.

Grateful appreciation is extended to Paula Ciely-Siegel, Pediatric Audiologist with Pinellas County Schools, for her time and expertise shared during the development of portions of this chapter.

SCREENING AND ASSESSMENT OF AUDITORY FUNCTIONING

Incidence of Hearing Impairment Among Young Children with Disabilities

Moore, Thompson, and Folsom (1992) reported that hearing loss associated with prematurity ranges between 1.5% and 3.4%, although estimates as high as 17.5% have also been recorded. Roush (1990) estimated that 1 of every 750 healthy infants is born with a bilateral sensorineural hearing loss of some degree and that this incidence increases to 1 in every 25 to 50 for high-risk (NICU) infants. Madell (1988) suggested that between 32% and 78% of children with developmental disabilities manifest some degree of hearing impairment and that children with Down syndrome have a high incidence of otitis media. Siegenthaler (1987) reported a high incidence of hearing impairment in children with cerebral palsy, with a higher frequency of loss occurring in children with athetosis. Additionally, Siegenthaler noted that many children with cerebral palsy demonstrate functional hearing for low-frequency sounds but experience a rapid drop-off for mid- and high-frequency sounds.

Initial Identification of Hearing Impairment

Evidence suggests that early onset of even a mild hearing loss places a child at risk for delayed and diminished speech and language development and for academic failure as well (Auslander, Lewis, Schulte, & Stelmachowicz, 1991; Madell, 1988; Roush, 1990). While profound hearing losses are typically identified between 9 and 12 months, 20% of moderate to severe losses are detected after 18 months of age, and often not until 2½ years of age (Clarkson, Vohr, Blackwell, & White, 1994). Kramer and Williams (1993) expressed frustration that even though early identification technology is available, the average toddler with a hearing impairment does not receive intervention until 18 to 30 months of age. Unilateral losses may not be identified until 5 or 6 years of age (Auslander et al., 1991). Unilateral loss may go undetected in infants and toddlers, since most hearing screenings at this age are conducted in sound fields and an interaural loss may not be found. The high incidence of hearing loss among premature infants prompted the Joint Committee on Infant Hearing (JCIH) of the American Speech-Language-Hearing Association (ASHA) (1991) to endorse early identification programs and auditory brainstem response (ABR) evaluations in the newborn period for all infants at risk for hearing loss, preferably prior to their discharge from the hospital. The JCIH high-risk criteria for identifying neonates and infants at risk for hearing loss is presented in Figure 6.1. Northern and Downs (1991) simplified the identification of risk factors for hearing loss through the development of a mnemonic, the ABC's of high-risk deafness:

> **A**sphyxia,
> **B**acterial meningitis,
> **C**ongenital perinatal infections,
> **D**efects of head and neck,
> **E**levated bilirubin,
> **F**amily history, and
> **G**ram birthweight less than 1500.
> (pp. 246–252)

Parents are typically the first to notice that something is wrong with their infant's hearing if the loss is significant; when the child fails to develop speech and language skills commensurate with peers, a hearing loss is often the suspected etiology for delayed speech. Signs that a physical problem with the ear or an associated hearing loss may exist include the following:

- Discharges from the ear canal
- Mouth breathing
- The child tugs or pulls at his or her ears
- Decreased or abnormal quality of vocalization
- Failure to respond to sudden, loud sounds
- Failure to orient to parents' voices
- Heightened visual awareness during play and social interactions
- A look of surprise and/or smiling as the parent picks up the child even though the parent has been engaged in conversation with the child at near distances
- Musical or other auditory toys are held against a preferred ear
- The child tends to orient his or her head so that the better ear is toward sound sources
- The child omits voiceless sounds when speaking
- The child has difficulty discriminating similar sounds (e.g., *tongue–thumb; goat–coat; gum–done)*

Nature of Hearing Impairment

Hearing impairments may be conductive, sensorineural, mixed, or central in nature depending on the site of the dysfunction or impairment (see Figure 6.2). A *conductive* hearing loss occurs when there is any interference in the conduction of sound between the external auditory canal and the inner ear due to damage to the external or the middle ear. While conductive losses may affect hearing across all ranges, the lower frequencies may be more impaired (Stangler, Huber, & Routh, 1980), and the child loses sensitivity but hears speech clearly when it is sufficiently loud. Conductive hearing losses are frequently associated with middle ear effusion (fluid) subsequent to repeated otitis media (middle ear infections). Generally, such losses are managed through a regimen of antibiotics and decongestants to open the eustachian tube. However, chronic fluid in the middle ear may require the

Risk Criteria for Hearing Loss in Neonates (birth to 28 days)

- Family history of childhood hearing loss
- Infections during pregnancy or at birth of child such as rubella, cytomegalovirus, toxoplasmosis, herpes, or syphilis
- Birthweight less than 1500 grams (3 lbs, 5 oz.)
- Unusual ear, eye, head, or neck development, including cleft lip or palate, absent philtrum, low hairline, ear tags or pits, etc.
- Severe jaundice requiring an exchange blood transfusion
- Presence of bacterial meningitis
- APGAR score of 3 or less at 5 minutes after birth; failure to initiate spontaneous respiration by 10 minutes, or hypotonia persisting to 2 hours of age
- Need for prolonged mechanical ventilation of 10 or more days' duration
- Presence of syndromal characteristics associated with hearing loss
- Certain ototoxic drugs or medications including, but not limited to, aminoglycosides used for more than 5 days

Risk Criteria for Hearing Loss in Infants (29 days to 2 years)

- Presence of any of criteria listed for neonates at risk
- Parents/caregivers have concern regarding hearing, speech, language, and/or developmental delay
- Presence of neonatal risk factors associated with progressive sensorineural hearing loss
- History of head trauma
- Presence of neurodegenerative disorders
- History of childhood infectious diseases associated with sensorineural hearing loss (mumps, measles)

FIGURE 6.1
Joint Committee on Infant Hearing (JCIH): Factors that may place neonates and infants at risk for hearing loss
Source: From the Joint Committee on Infant Hearing High-Risk Registers. Reprinted by permission of the American Academy of Audiology.

placement of pressure equalizing (PE) tubes through an outpatient surgical procedure referred to as a myringotomy, in which a small incision is made in the tympanic membrane. Small polyethylene PE tubes are then inserted to equalize the pressure between the middle ear and the ear canal, enabling fluid to drain. Normally, the tube works its way out of the eardrum over several months and the eardrum closes over the incision. Conductive losses are common in children with Down syndrome, whose ear canals are often narrow, and among children with cranial-facial anomalies such as cleft palate, who may also manifest a sensorineural loss.

When hearing is impaired as the result of damage to either the sensory end organs (cochlear hair cells), the cochlea (the organ within the ear that converts vibrations into nerve impulses), the auditory nerve, or the

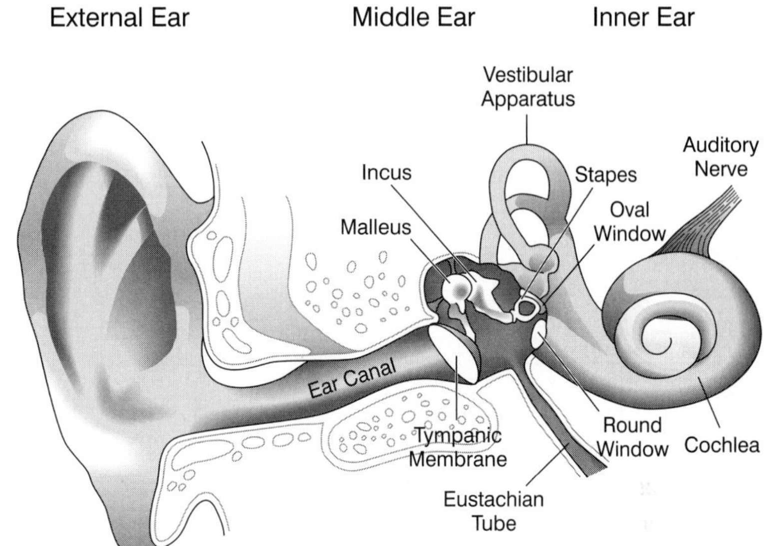

FIGURE 6.2
Structure of the ear. The middle ear is composed of the tympanic membrane (eardrum), and the three ear bones, the malleus, the incus, and the stapes. The stapes lies next to the oval window (opening to the inner ear). The inner ear contains the cochlea and the vestibular organs (labyrinths).
Source: From *Children with Handicaps: A Medical Primer* (2nd ed.) (p. 225), by M. L. Batshaw and Y. M. Perret, 1986, Baltimore, MD: Paul H. Brookes. Copyright 1986 by M. L. Batshaw, M.D. Reprinted with permission.

brain, the resulting hearing loss is referred to as a sensorineural impairment. Sensorineural losses primarily involve the higher frequencies; clarity of auditory perceptions is diminished even after speech is made sufficiently loud. Sensorineural losses are often associated with prenatal infections such as rubella, cytomegalovirus (CMV), and toxoplasmosis, and with central nervous system dysfunction such as cerebral palsy; they are common among children with athetosis (Siegenthaler, 1987). Meningitis is also a frequent cause of sensorineural loss during infancy and early childhood due to damage to the auditory nerve. Premature infants are susceptible to sensorineural losses resulting from kernicterus, a severe form of jaundice. Losses of this nature often are irreversible although the effects of such a loss can be managed through amplification or through cochlear implants if the loss is bilateral and profound or total and amplification is not beneficial. However, children with cognitive delays and additional handicapping conditions are typically not considered good candidates for a cochlear implant (Madell, 1988).

A mixed hearing loss occurs when both a conductive and a sensorineural component are present. Such a loss is detected on the audiogram when there is a significant gap (space) between the threshold levels obtained by air conduction and by bone conduction. In a mixed loss, the sensorineural component is the more severe and the hearing will improve only as much as the conductive loss can be ameliorated.

A central auditory disorder is commonly associated with developmentally delayed children, particularly those with severe neurological impairment and with autism. Children diagnosed with central deafness perceive sound but have difficulty responding on a cortical level (processing and interpreting the incoming sound). They demonstrate inconsistent responses to speech, sudden sounds, and simultaneous noises and may not localize to sound although the peripheral auditory system is intact. Although hearing sensitivity may be normal, the child often functions as if he or she were deaf. Audiograms depicting each of the primary hearing losses are presented in Figure 6.3.

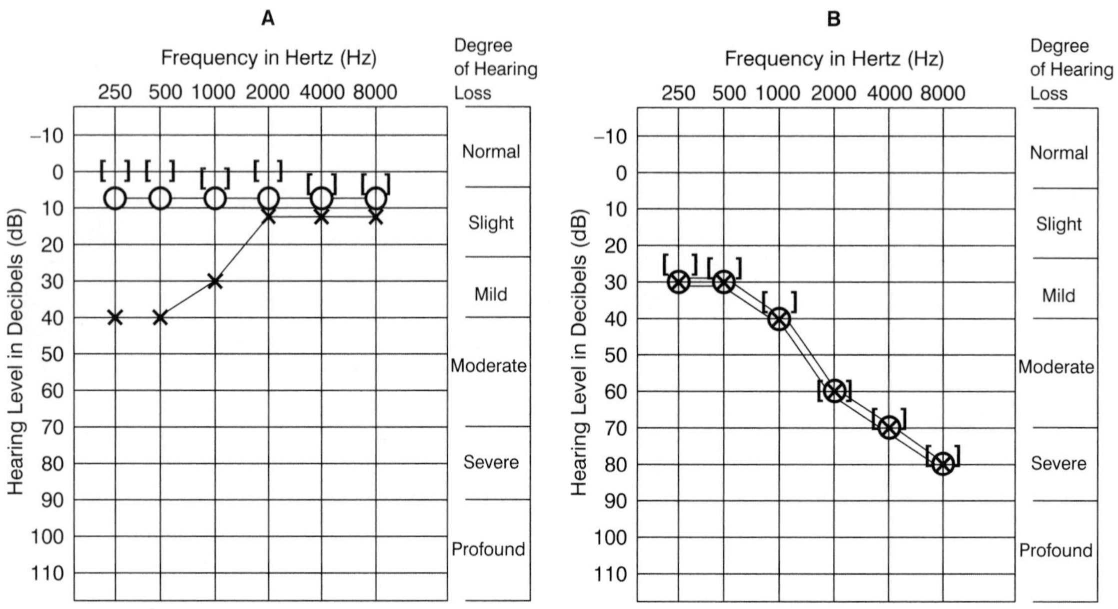

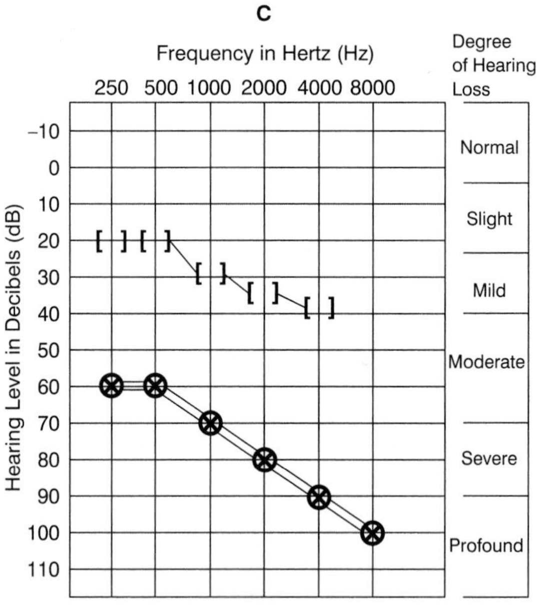

Key: [= R ear, bone conduction
] = L ear, bone conduction
O = R ear, air conduction
X = L ear, air conduction

FIGURE 6.3
Sample audiograms depicting three types of hearing loss. (A) depicts a unilateral conductive loss in the left ear; (B) represents a bilateral sensorineural loss; and (C) indicates a mixed hearing loss.

Classification of Hearing Loss

Hearing level (HL) threshold is assessed by determining the minimal intensity (loudness) of sound the child perceives 50% of the time across a range of frequencies (pitch). Hearing in children is considered normal when hearing level thresholds fall between 15 and 20 dB HL. Frequency is measured in cycles per second or hertz (Hz) from 125 to 8000 Hz. Low-frequency sounds are considered to be below 500 Hz; sounds above 2000 Hz are high-frequency sounds. The child's performance at ranges between 500 and 2000 Hz is particularly important because these frequencies are critical to speech (Orelove & Sobsey, 1987). Intensity is assessed by sound pressure or decibels (dB) from 0 to 110. A whisper is estimated to be 30 dB, conversational level speech 45 to 50 dB, and loud music 100 dB. Threshold sensitivity is plotted on an audiogram with the right ear represented with an *O* and the left ear with an *X*. It is common practice to use the average audiometric air conduction threshold across the middle three frequencies (500, 1000, and 2000 Hz) to classify level of acuity.

Hearing loss is defined by the location of the impairment, the degree of severity of loss, and whether the loss is unilateral or bilateral. Northern and Downs (1991) proposed that 15 dB HL be considered the lower limit of normal hearing for children, since many of the unvoiced consonants fall below normal hearing thresholds. Thus, hearing that falls below 15 dB HL would be considered impaired. However, these authors suggested that for screening the hearing of children with cognitive impairments through behavioral observation, awareness or localization at 45 dB HL constitutes a passing response.

Audiological Screening

The primary functions of a hearing screen are to determine whether hearing is within the normal range and if a subsequent referral to a pediatric audiologist is warranted. Audiological screening may be conducted by speech and language therapists, early childhood specialists, special education teachers, nurses, and even well-trained volunteers. When a screening indicates that hearing is at risk or that a loss is present, a thorough audiometric evaluation should be performed by a pediatric audiologist. Typically, hearing screens are conducted through the use of an audiometer, a machine calibrated to ensure the accuracy of pure tones issued through headphones. Pure-tone screening is most reliable with children functioning at a developmental level of 3 years and older. It is helpful to tell the child to listen for a "little bird" and then present tones of 50 to 60 dB through the headphones prior to placing them on the child. This demonstration alerts the child to the nature of the sound for which he or she will be listening. During a screening, the frequencies of 500, 1000, 2000, and 4000 Hz are swept through at an intensity level of 20 dB HL and the child is instructed to raise a hand when he or she hears the tone. If the ambient noise of the screening setting is too great, a level of 25 dB is used and/or the frequency of 500 Hz omitted. Martin and Gravel (1989) found that 70% of audiologists questioned indicated that the criteria for failure that they used was the lack of a response to the specified screening level at any one frequency in either ear.

Audiological Assessment

An audiological assessment should provide information regarding both the physiological level of hearing sensitivity, or threshold (the softest sound detected 50% of the time), at various frequencies and the functional application of hearing in day-to-day situations. Additionally, the assessment should include a visual inspection of the outer ear for any malformations or signs indicative of a possible hearing loss. An otoscopic exam of the ear canal can ascertain the health status of the middle ear and detect indications of an infection. Drainage from the ear or excess cerumen may preclude objective testing such as impedance audiometry. An accurate and reliable assessment of hearing in young children is best obtained when the procedures selected accommodate the child's developmental level and response capability (Batshaw & Perret, 1986; Hodgson, 1985; Thompson & Folsom, 1981).

When an audiometer cannot be used to obtain traditional pure-tone hearing thresholds, an estimate of hearing sensitivity may be obtained through behavioral audiometric procedures. Behavioral observations are based on the infant's or child's responses to auditory input in structured conditions, referred to as *behavioral observation audiometry (BOA)*. Techniques that use reinforcement to develop reliable responses to auditory input, known as *visual reinforcement audiometry (VRA), tangible reinforcement operant conditioning audiometry (TROCA),* and *play audiometry* are also in the realm of behavioral observation. Auditory responses are elicited in a soundproofed room with stimuli administered either directly or through speakers. The primary problem associated with behavioral audiometric procedures that utilize a sound field milieu is that a hearing loss in at least one ear cannot be ruled out as both ears are tested simultaneously. The more critical aspect of behavioral testing, however, is the expertise of the audiologist in accurately interpreting responses and his or her knowledge of the range and quality of normal auditory responses characteristic of each developmental stage in the sequence of hearing maturation. Madell (1988) advised that BOA and VRA procedures may not elicit optimal hearing thresholds but that with developmental progress and experience, children become more responsive to auditory stimuli and may raise their hearing thresholds by 10 dB.

Behavioral observation testing Prior to a developmental age of 6 months, behavioral observation audiometry (BOA) is used to detect a hearing loss and is often the procedure of choice for children with multiple disabilities. BOA provides a quick, simple, and inexpensive means of estimating hearing sensitivity, facilitates decisions regarding which formal test procedures may be most effective, and suggests the level and quality of responses that can be expected. Although sound field audiometry (indicated on the audiogram with an *S*) by BOA does not yield a specific threshold but rather the child's overt responses to sound, it is a valid and effective procedure for identifying hearing loss in children with profound handicapping conditions (Flexor & Gans, 1985; Gans, 1987; Hayes, 1986; Wilson & Thompson, 1984). Flexor and Gans (1985) suggest that the auditory responses of the multiply handicapped child be judged in relation to their developmental level. Cox (1988) warned that informal BOA will typically identify only severe to profound hearing loss and additionally cautioned against its use with neonates due to poor reliability agreement with ABR procedures at that level.

During BOA, the infant may be held in the parent's lap or secured in an infant carrier or seat and given or shown a quiet, but not too attractive, toy both to hold his or her attention between presentation of sound stimuli and to distract him or her from watching the presentation of noisemakers. The best responses are elicited prior to feeding and when the child is in a quiet or light sleep state. A variety of acoustically defined toys are presented in a soundproofed area once the child is stabilized and positioned comfortably. Typical stimuli used to elicit responses include squeak toys, bells, rattles, whistles, and calibrated input such as audiometric warbled tones, white noise, voice, and music (Madell, 1988). All noisemakers used should be measured for signal intensity output at some specific distance that will be typical in the testing situation (Northern & Downs, 1991). Noisemakers are presented several inches from the infant's ears and out of his or her visual field. It is important to ensure that the infant does not see the noisemakers or feel the air expressed as they are activated, that his or her attention is maintained, and that he or she is allowed sufficient time to process the stimuli. The quality of the signals will vary with the force with which they are activated, their distance from the child, and the surface against which they are struck. Stangler, Huber, and Routh (1980) advised that noisemakers will be most effective if they are activated with equal force at a maintained equal distance from the child's ear each time they are used. Northern and Downs (1991) recommend that the softest noisemakers be administered first, followed sequentially by the louder ones, ending with the loudest signal, which will elicit the startle response. Indicators of sound awareness include both reflexive and attentive behaviors, which are delineated in Table 6.1.

A child's failure to attend to noisemakers may be attributed to factors other than hearing loss. The sound signal may not be motivating to the child; he or she may habituate quickly and fail to respond to subsequent presentations of sound stimuli; physical impairment may interfere with the readability of the child's response; or medication or recent seizure activity may negatively affect auditory responsiveness. Auditory responses of children with cognitive impairments are more in line with their mental age than with their chronological age. Hyvarinen (1988) reported that localization responses are often delayed in blind and severely visually impaired infants. Several authors report that in infants from 6 to 12 months, attention is most difficult to manage with warble tones and easiest with speech (Auslander et al., 1991; Thompson, Thompson, & McCall, 1992). The child's minimal response level to each calibrated tone or noise stimuli is plotted on a sound field audiogram. The audiogram, however, represents only overall overt responses to sound from the child's better hearing ear, because individual ears cannot be tested under this condition. While most clinicians have selected their own set of noisemakers for screening hearing through behavioral observation techniques, a commercial set of noisemakers, the HEAR-Kit (Downs, 1979) is available and consists of preselected and premeasured toys to use in the screening of infants and young children. Kukla and Connolly (1978) measured the dB level of a wide variety

TABLE 6.1
Examples of Responses Observed During Behavioral Observation Audiometry

Reflexive Responses	Attentive Responses
Startle responses	Decrease or increase in ongoing activity
Auropalpebral reflex	Breath holding and changes in respiration patterns
Limb jerks	Sudden stopping of vocalizations or crying
Slow limb movements	Eye widening, searching, and localization of the sound source
Changes in sucking behavior	Smiling and changes in facial expression
Eye-blinks	Furrowing of eyebrows
Facial twitches	Shriek of surprise

Source: From *Hearing in Children, Fourth Edition* by J. L. Northern and M. P. Downs, 1991, Baltimore, MD: Williams & Wilkins. Copyright 1991 by Williams & Wilkins. Adapted by permission.

of commercially available toys and of common environmental sounds and listed them in checklist form.

Visual reinforcement audiometry

Visual reinforcement audiometry (VRA) is an effective and reliable means of gathering audiological information on children between 6 and 24 to 30 months, but it is not considered an acceptable technique below a developmental level of 5 to 6 months. Based on their investigation of the auditory responsiveness of premature infants, Moore, Thompson, and Folsom (1992) recommended that preterm infants should demonstrate a mental age of 6 to 7 months and/or have a corrected age of 8 to 9 months before routine follow-up VRA hearing screens can be effective and reliable.

In visual reinforcement audiometry the child may be supported by a parent or second observer, placed in a high chair, or seated or positioned adaptively in a sound field environment between speakers positioned 45 degrees to the right and left of the child as he or she faces forward. Auditory stimuli can be presented through the speakers or through earphones, by bone conduction transducers, or through hearing aids, although speakers are most often used with children with disabilities. Initially, activation of a mechanical toy, flashing lights, or a combination of both is paired with an auditory signal to elicit visual orientation to the sound source. Once reliable responses are obtained, the toys or lights are used to reward correct localization responses rather than to elicit them. Goetz, Utley, Gee, Baldwin, and Sailor (no date) designed specific strategies for shaping VRA responses in severely handicapped deaf-blind students.

A primary limitation with VRA is that children often quickly habituate to the stimuli and cease to respond. Thompson, Thompson, and McCall (1992) reported that introduction of novel reinforcement procedures after a habituation or a brief break from testing facilitated the acquisition of additional responses in 1- and 2-year-olds. The effectiveness of VRA is dependent on the nature and extent of the visual reinforcement strategies employed as well as the developmental abilities of the child being assessed. Moore, Thompson, and Thompson (1975) demonstrated that complex visual reinforcement such as a mechanical toy that moved in place when activated was the most effective condition for recruiting localization responses.

Localization behavior is among the most common responses elicited in the auditory assessment of infants between 6 months and 2 years of age. Moore, Thompson, and Folsom (1992) indicated that newborns will demonstrate reflexive eye movements toward very brief sounds, turn to sound at birth and during the 1st month, respond inconsistently to sound during the 2nd and 3rd months, and then localize well at 4 months. The decline in responsiveness during the 2nd and 3rd months is felt to represent a developmental shift from an innate, reflexive reaction to the organization of sensory and motor schemes and intentional behavior. Localization abilities will be influenced by both the child's developmental level and the nature of the stimulus, particularly its appropriateness to the child's developmental level. By 18 months, most toddlers can respond to speech stimuli to look for specific objects in the testing area, to point to body parts, or to respond to familiar phrases such as "go bye-bye?" or "where's mom?" A summary of the developmental sequence of localization behavior is depicted in Figure 6.4.

Reinforcement with tangible rewards for responses to sound stimuli, TROCA, requires the child to press a button or lever at the presentation of auditory stimuli in order to receive edibles such as Fruit Loops™ or small trinkets. TROCA procedures may be used either in sound field or under earphones. Figure 6.5 portrays the use of TROCA with a visually impaired child.

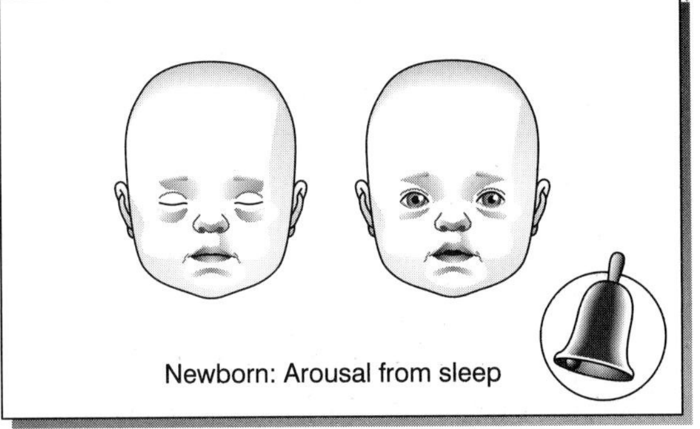

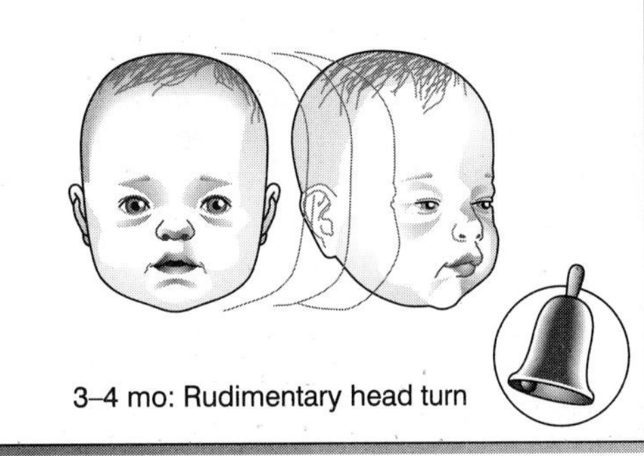

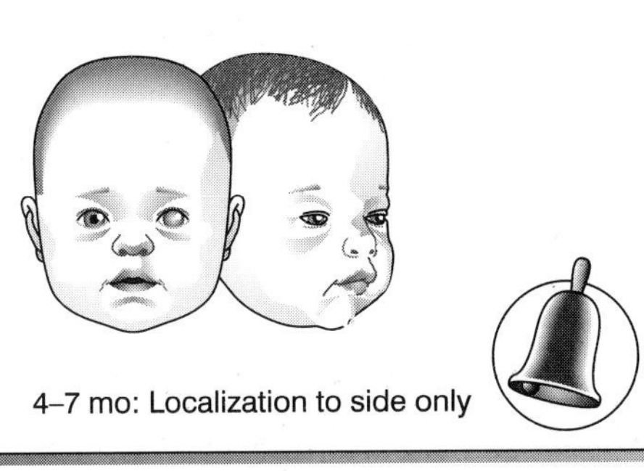

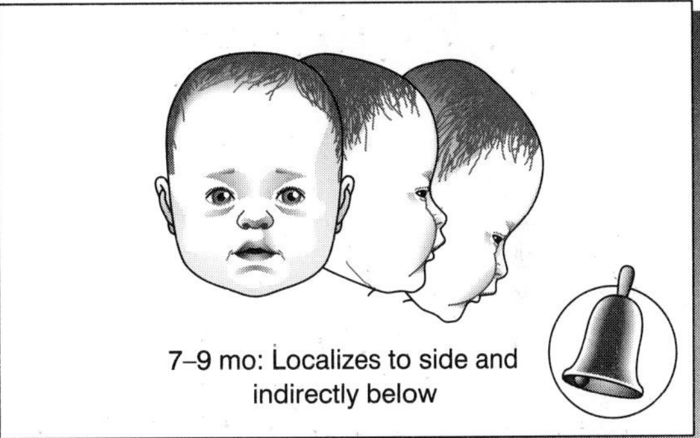

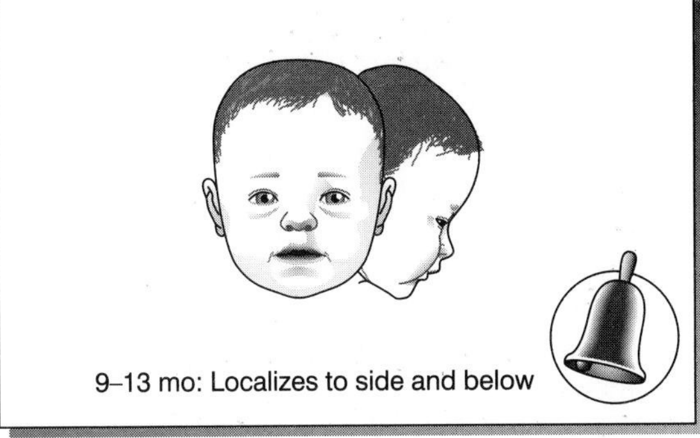

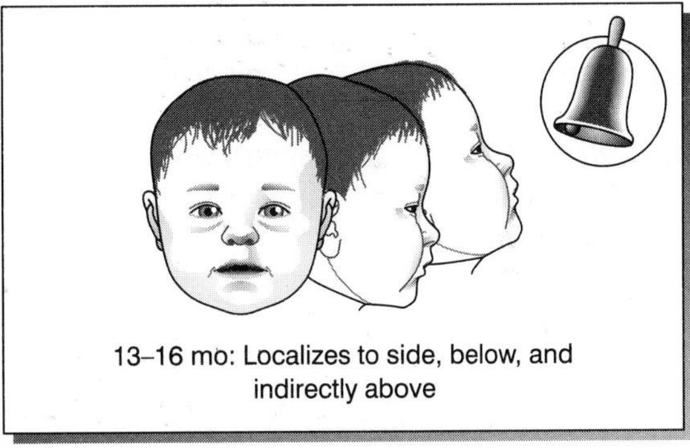

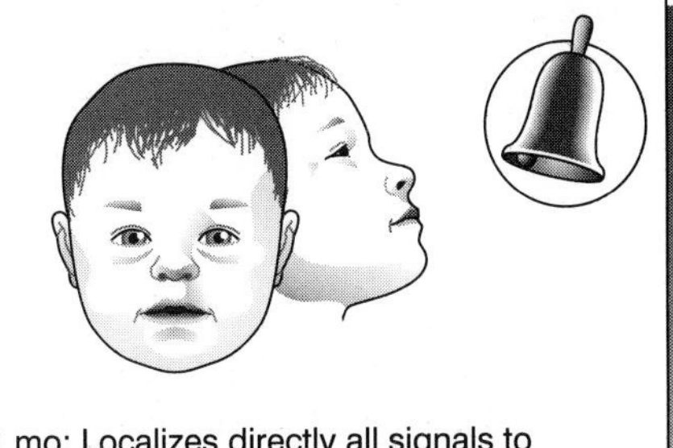

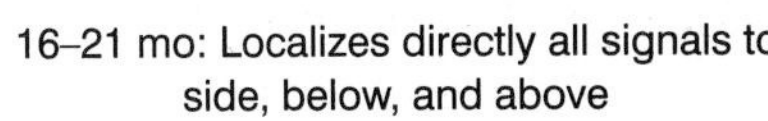

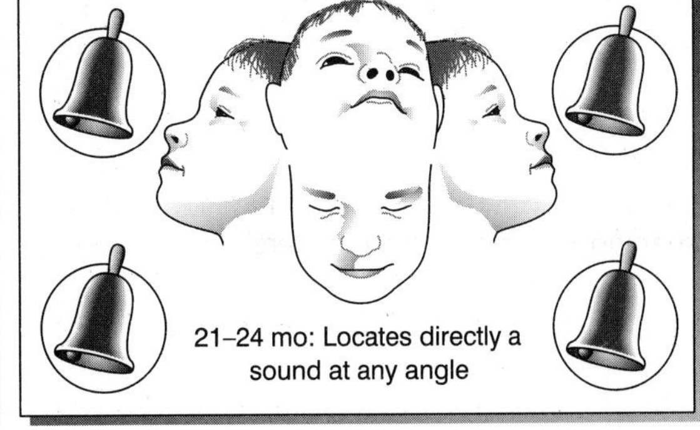

FIGURE 6.4

Developmental progression of auditory localization behaviors

Source: From *Hearing in Children, Fourth Edition* (p. 254), by J. L. Northern and M. P. Downs, 1991, Baltimore, MD: Williams & Wilkins. Copyright 1991 by Williams & Wilkins. Reprinted with permission.

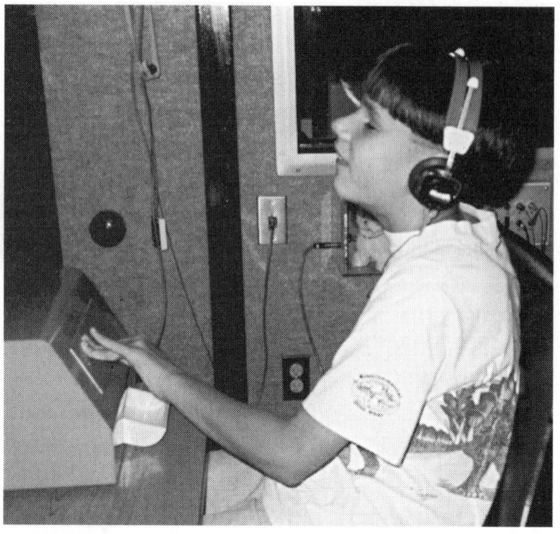

FIGURE 6.5
Tangible reinforcement operant conditioning audiometry (TROCA) being used with a child with multiple impairments. Each time the child presses the touch pad in response to an auditory signal, he is rewarded with cereal delivered through the tray of the reinforcement unit.

Play audiometry Children as young as 18 months may be conditioned to respond through play audiometry to pure-tone auditory signals produced either in a sound field or through earphones. Typically, pure-tone audiometric testing is more appropriate for children older than 3 years of age, and most young children with cognitive delays are not ready for this technique until 4 or 5 years of age. Traditionally, the child is conditioned to place a ring on a stacking cone, remove or place a peg in a pegboard, or release a block or other small toy into a container when the signal is perceived. It is helpful for the child to hold the manipulative item, such as the stacking ring or the peg, next to the earphone on the same side of the body as the ear being tested while waiting for the signal. This strategy structures the child and provides a clear beginning and end to each stimulus. The child is guided through the procedure of releasing an item into a container when he is presented with a 50 dB signal at 1000 Hz produced through the earphone prior to having the earphones placed on his ears so that he knows what to expect. The audiologist may tell the child to listen for the little bird to help the child identify the sound. Gradually, the tone signals are decreased as the central frequencies (between 500 dB and 2000 to 4000 dB) are swept through at 20 dB. Northern and Downs (1991) recommend that the criteria for referral for further audiometric testing be failure to respond to a 20 dB signal at any frequency during pure-tone screening.

Speech Reception Thresholds

Speech reception thresholds (SRT) may be established in many 2- and 3-year-old children in sound field conditions and in 3- and 4-year-old children under earphones. Typically, toys or pictures, depending on the age and developmental level of the child, are selected to represent spondees (words that are pronounced with equal stress on each syllable). Traditional spondaic toys and pictures include items such as an airplane, baseball, toothbrush, hot dog, cowboy, fire truck, and so forth. The child is presented with an appropriate number of toys and asked to select the one designated in the sound field or through the earphones. The words are presented in gradually decreasing intensity increments until a *speech reception threshold (SRT)* is established. Speech discrimination tests include the Sound Effects Recognition Test (SERT) (Finitzo-Hieber, Gerling, & Matkin, 1980), the Audio Numbers Test (ANT) (Erber, 1980), the Northwestern University Children's Perception of Speech (Nu-CHIPS) (Elliott & Katz, 1980), and the Pediatric Speech Intelligibility (PSI) (Jerger, Lewis, & Hawkins, 1980). See Jerger (l984) for a thorough review of these instruments.

Regardless of the strategies employed during an audiological assessment, Northern and Downs (1991) emphasized that behavioral observation testing should be cross-checked with impedance audiometry, tympanometry, and acoustic reflex measurement, but they cautioned that while these physiological tests may yield an index of auditory sensitivity, they are not true measures of hearing and should never be used as a substitute for behavioral audiometry.

Impedance Audiometry

The most widely used procedure for assessing the integrity and function of peripheral (outer or middle ear) auditory abilities in infants and young children is *impedance* (also referred to as immittance) *audiometry.* Acoustic impedance measurements are especially valuable for young children with special needs, and Northern (1978, 1980) has provided extensive insight into the use of impedance audiometry with special populations. An objective measure of the integrity and function of the peripheral auditory system, impedance audiometry determines "existing middle ear pressure, tympanic membrane (eardrum) mobility, eustachian tube function, continuity and mobility of the middle ear ossicles (bones), acoustic reflex thresholds, and nonorganic hearing loss" (Northern & Downs, 1991, p. 190). Although an impedance test battery consists of four components: (1) tympanometry, (2) static impedance, (3) ear canal physical volume, and (4) acoustic reflex threshold, the two most frequently applied components are the tympanometry and the acoustic reflex measurements, especially in children under 6 years of age (Northern & Downs, 1991). The principle disadvantage associated with impedance testing is that the test battery cannot be completed during vocalizations, crying, or yelling, and any movement will influence the accuracy of the acoustic reflex.

Impedance measurements are obtained through the use of a small probe that is "sealed" into the external ear canal while constant sound pressure is issued through the probe. The ability of the eardrum to reflect the sound pressure yields an estimate of its mobility and predicts the presence of middle ear dysfunction (Hayes, 1986). Figure 6.6 demonstrates the use of impedance with an infant as he is held by his mother.

Impedance audiometry yields a *tympanogram,* a graph of the compliance (mobility) of the eardrum, which is classified according to three primary degrees of curve obtained during testing. Type A tympanograms resemble a bell-shaped curve and reflect normal middle ear pressure, with the peak of compliance occurring approximately at 0 degrees of pressure, although changes in degree of compliance of the eardrum relative to the mobility of the normal eardrum may be indicated. A Type B curve depicts little or no change in compliance of the eardrum in the presence of air pressure and is associated with patent (open) PE tubes, an ear canal blocked by excess wax, a perforation of the tympanic membrane, or the presence of serous otitis media. A Type C curve reveals a definite peak but at significant degrees of negative pressure (ranging from -150 to -250 mm H_2O) and implies that the eardrum is intact and compliant but only with significant amounts of air pressure; persistence of this type of curve infers poor eustachian tube function (Northern & Downs, 1991). Examples of tympanograms are depicted in Figure 6.7.

Auditory Brain-Stem Evoked Responses (ABR)

An ABR is an objective electrophysiological measurement of hearing that yields information regarding auditory functioning and the identification of lesions in the auditory brain-stem pathways. Kramer and Williams (1993) believe

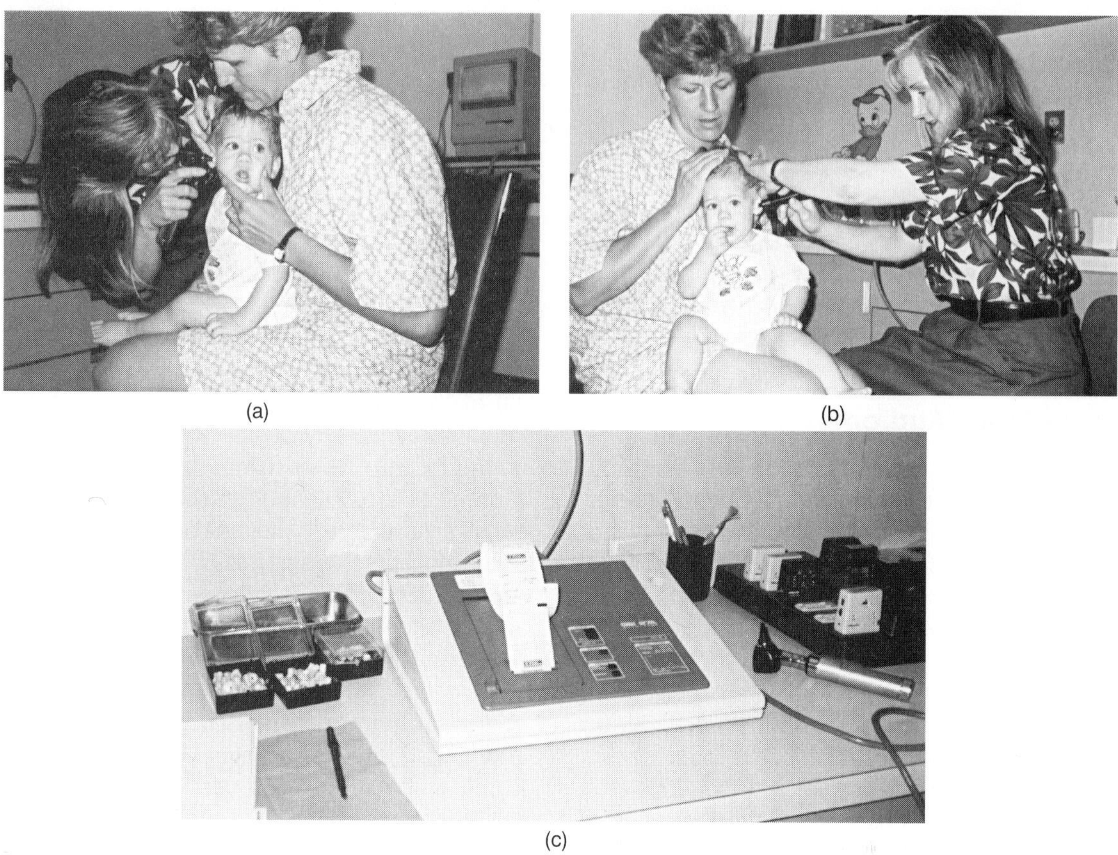

(a) (b) (c)

FIGURE 6.6

Figure 6.6(a) shows a pediatric audiologist inspecting the ear canal of an infant prior to conducting impedance (or immittance) audiometry. In Figure 6.6(b), an infant's middle ear functioning is assessed with impedance audiometry. Figure 6.6(c) depicts the impedance unit with the printout of the tympanogram.

that the ABR is the most reliable objective audiological tool for use with infants younger than 6 months as well as for difficult-to-test, multiply handicapped children. An ABR is obtained through the use of three electrodes that are attached to the child's forehead and behind each ear and evoked with repetitive click stimuli at specific intervals. A computer averages the neural activity produced in response to the clicks and graphs the results. The ABR can estimate hearing thresholds in the 2000 to 4000 Hz region of the pure-tone audiogram when broad spectrum clicks are used. Passing criteria consist of responses from both ears at intensity levels of 30 to 40 dB HL within the frequency band for speech recognition (Kramer & Williams, 1993). However, because the ABR gives accurate reading of hearing only in the high-frequency ranges, it is possible that low-frequency losses go undetected until a pure-tone audiogram can be obtained. The primary disadvantages of the ABR are the expense of the procedure and the fact that most children between 6 months and 4 years of age must be sedated for the duration of the procedure. In addition, an ABR cannot provide information regarding the functional application of existing hearing. Northern and Downs (1991) also warn

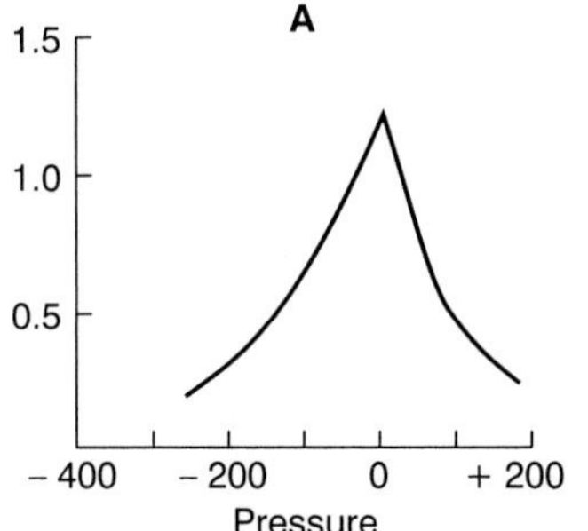

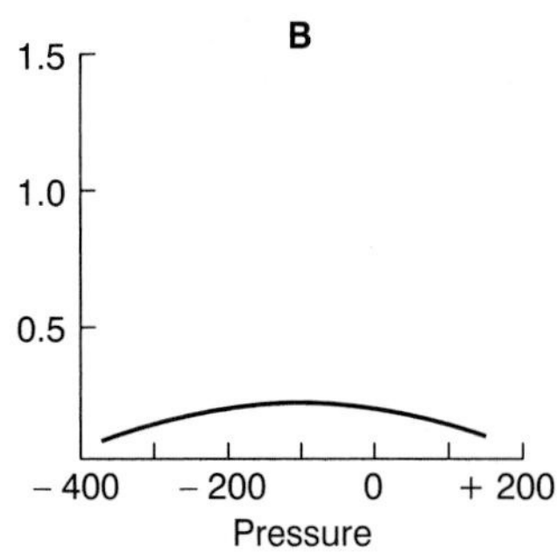

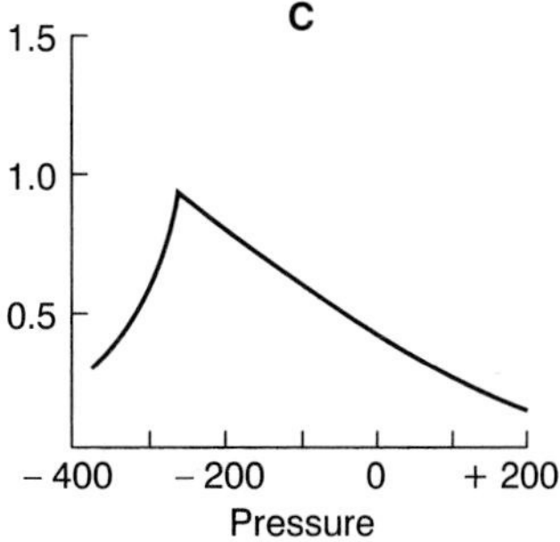

FIGURE 6.7
The three major types of tympanograms. Type A shows normal functioning; Type B shows fluid in the middle ear or an open pressure equalizing tube; Type C shows negative middle ear pressure.

that ABRs may not yield valid data on children with severe neurological impairments, since such damage interferes with registration of the signal at the brain level and, consequently, recorded responses may be more a reflection of the central nervous system impairment than of the perception of sound.

The *Crib-O-Gram* is a microprocessor-based system attached to a motion sensitive transducer that is placed under the mattress of a crib and records the infant's responses to an auditory stimulus and related stimulus-produced motor activity (Cox, 1988). A loudspeaker delivers a series of one-second 3000 Hz bursts of noise at 92 dB SPL. The microprocessor unit both delivers the stimulus and records the infant's response to the stimulus. The Crib-O-Gram is most reliable with full-term and older babies, is cost effective, and detects severe to profound hearing losses. However, the Crib-O-Gram has been reported to yield a high false-positive referral rate, to agree poorly with other audiological procedures, and to fail to detect mild, moderate, or unilateral losses of any magnitude (Cox, 1988).

Informal Auditory Assessment Techniques

Items used both during play and in formal testing can be scanned by a sound level meter to ascertain the dB level produced at specific distances. Stimuli that have proven effective include activation of squeak toys and bells of various frequencies and intensities, crickets, small wooden beads in a plastic box, wooden blocks in a cardboard box, and small wind-up toys. Other strategies encompass crumpling tissue paper, rattling a plastic and/or a metal spoon against a plastic cup, and jingling keys in a pocket. Once estimates of the intensity of these items are made, the stimuli are listed on a simple form on which the child's reactions to each are recorded. Unexpected and silly sounds often attract the child's attention when more familiar sounds are ignored. An effective strategy with children developmentally as young as 6 to 8 months entails engaging the child in play momentarily with a squeak toy or a sealed stacking ring filled with bells, beans, and/or rice. While the child is still interested in the item, it is gently extracted and replaced with a duplicate that has had the auditory component removed. Typically, the child initially exhibits surprise in response to the absence of sound and attempts to elicit the noise again through activation of the toy. The original toy should then be returned to the child and his reactions observed. Children with significant hearing losses will show no indication that anything is different when given the silent toy. A simple strategy for eliciting responses to softer sounds entails allowing the child to remove several pieces of cereal, small crackers, cookies, or chips from a plastic container after rattling the container in the child's view to attract his or her attention. The empty container is put away and several minutes later, the refilled container is again rattled out of the child's view. Most children turn immediately in search of more edibles. If this method is used, a caregiver should be consulted to ensure the child is permitted the treats and that he or she is not allergic to the edibles used. Haeussermann (1958) subtly activated a comb by running her fingers across its teeth while holding it under the table on which the child was working. Additional items from formal developmental instruments that have been designed to assess hearing have been compiled in chart form by Langley (1986).

The Role of Early Childhood Personnel in the Assessment of Auditory Functioning

Instructional personnel who work with the child on a daily basis may be the first to detect the possibility of a hearing loss and to make the initial referrals for remediation or amplification. Audiological assessments conducted in unfamiliar settings may not provide an accurate account of how the child uses hearing in day-to-day situations. Early childhood personnel are able to observe the child's reactions to common environmental sounds such as garbage trucks, emergency vehicles, and telephones. Attention to the types of noisemakers the child chooses during music time and to the nature of his or her responses and attention during group instructional settings often yields valuable data regarding both frequencies and intensities of sound that influence the child's hearing during routine activities and in familiar settings. The child with a hearing loss may fail to respond to directions or to the announcement of exciting or preferred activities if he or she is not looking at the teacher. During group activities, the child may be inattentive or may fail to monitor his or her loudness during quiet activities such as watching a movie or during story or nap time. Frequent requests for repeated directions or responses of "huh?" even when the child is looking may indicate a hearing loss. The teacher should pay particular attention to the auditory attentiveness and articulation patterns of children who sustain frequent ear infections.

In conclusion, whether a hearing impairment is detected through informal observation, through formal screening measures, or through sophisticated procedures and instruments, the earlier a child with a hearing impairment is referred and the exact nature of the hearing impairment identified, the better the developmental, educational, communicative, and social prognosis for the child. When the parameters that facilitate use of hearing are delineated, the child can be encouraged to use his or her hearing optimally to adapt to all environments.

SCREENING AND ASSESSMENT OF VISUAL FUNCTIONING

The first three months of a child's life are the most critical to the development of the visual system; even a few days of monocular deprivation during this time can permanently alter the visual system. The presence of a visual impairment affects every aspect of development and has a particularly profound effect on early relationships and communicative functions (Fraiberg, 1977; Holt & Reynell, 1967). Because it has been estimated that 80% of all learning is visual, Morse, Trief, and Joseph (1987) stressed the importance of early identification and treatment of children with visual deficits to maximize their potential, both visually and developmentally (Langley, 1980, in press; Morse & Trief, 1985; Sheridan, 1960).

Prevalence of Visual Impairment in Children with Disabilities

Jan, Skyanda, and Groenveld (1990) reported that congenital legal blindness occurs with the frequency of 4 per 10,000 births and that acquired visual impairment during childhood is approximately one fifth as prevalent. Deitz and Ferrell (1993) reported that approximately one infant per 3,000 live births is born with a visual disability, although only approximately 25% of visually impaired children are totally blind. The most common cause of blindness in infants is retinopathy of prematurity (ROP), occurring at a rate of 75% in infants weighing less than 1,000 grams at birth but affecting only 4% (the majority of active ROP cases resolve spontaneously with few sequelae) (Glass, 1993). Other visual problems associated with prematurity include congenital cataracts, high myopia, strabismus, and amblyopia (Trief & Morse, 1987). Glass (1993) also reports that cortical visual impairment occurs with extreme prematurity and is most often associated with severe central nervous system damage. The most common cause of visual loss (1% to 2%) in children under 6 is amblyopia, while strabismus has been documented in 2% to 5% of the pediatric population (Morse & Trief, 1985). Hyvarinen and Lindstedt (1981) estimate that strabismus occurs in children with cognitive impairments 5 to 10 times more frequently than in their nonhandicapped peers. There is a higher percentage of hyperopia and strabismus in children with neurological disorders; approximately 50% of children with cerebral palsy have some form of strabismus. It has been estimated that 40% to 66% of visually impaired infants are multiply handicapped (Deitz & Ferrell, 1993). Jan et al. (1990) found visual impairment in approximately 23% of children with mental retardation, 8% of children with hearing impairment, 13% of children with a seizure disorder, and 14% of children with heart defects. Down syndrome children have a high incidence of strabismus, hyperopia, and cataracts (Pagon & Disteche, 1989); glaucoma and corneal defects have also been associated with Down syndrome (Kivlin, 1989).

Classification of Visual Impairment

Vision is assessed in terms of acuity, the sharpness of an image one can detect at a specified distance, and, in regard to visual fields, the entire area of physical space visible to the eye without shifting gaze. A visual acuity of 20/20 represents normal vision. The numerator indicates the distance at which acuity is measured; the denominator imparts the size of the visual stimulus correctly and consistently identified. An individual whose visual acuity is 20/70 or worse in the better eye with best correction is considered *partially sighted.* One is considered *legally blind* when the acuity is 20/200 or worse in the better eye with best correction. Children who incur significant visual impairment after birth are considered *adventitiously blind.* These definitions of visual impairment are often confusing and misleading to parents and other caregivers because the numbers, especially in young children, often are not accurate reflections of how the child uses existing residual vision. Deitz and Ferrell (1993) argued that the current definition of visual impairment does not consider fluctuating visual abilities as seen in cortically visually impaired children, environmental factors that affect vision in specific situations, or deteriorating visual loss. Regardless of the level of acuity, personal factors such as neuromotor integrity, cognitive functioning, attention and organizational behaviors, and experience will influence how and what a child actually sees. Romano (1990) posited that an acuity of 20/200 was sufficient and adequate visual ability for the tasks and activities expected of preschool children. A child with an acuity of 20/200 can identify and discriminate details in 2-inch pictures when held close to the eyes and can typically visualize simple, colorful 5- to 7-inch pictures at 3 to 5 feet. Sonksen (1983) and Sonksen, Petrie, and Drew (1991) pointed out the distinction between minimal *observance* and minimal *discrimination* or *separableness* of a stimulus. The minimal observable distance represents the point at which a stimulus can be seen (observed) but not necessarily recognized in terms of finite detail or characteristics. Sonksen et al. (1991) further clarified that the definition of visual acuity requires spatial resolution of two points while identification of three-dimensional objects measures only resolution of single points. Minimal discriminatory distance is typically measured by standard acuity measures, and a clear distinction and recognition must be made of figures of specific ototype (Snellen-type) notation. The acuity measurement of young children and difficult-to-test populations most often represents an estimate of minimal observance acuity.

The normal visual field in a newborn is comprised of 28 degrees to either side horizontally, 11 degrees superiorly, and 16 degrees inferiorly; the upper visual field is near adult level by one year of age. Hyvarinen (1988) stated that at 3 months a child reacts to objects only in the central 60 degrees of the visual field, although by 6 months he or she responds quickly to peripheral information, indicating that the full 180-degree visual field is intact. The visual field of an adult when looking straight ahead is approximately 65 degrees nasally (toward the nose), 95 degrees temporally (toward the temples or ears), 65 degrees inferiorly (downward toward the mouth), and 45 degrees superiorly (upward toward the forehead) (Duckman, 1987; Vaughan, Asbury, & Tabbara, 1989). An individual whose visual field is 20 degrees or less, regardless of acuity, is considered legally blind. A common field deficit in children with severe neurological impairment is hemianopsia, in which half of the visual field in each eye is impaired.

The classification of vision problems in children with disabilities may be organized by their effects on the visual system. Common childhood visual defects can be grouped according to (1) structural abnormality or disease of the visual system, such as conjunctivitis, aniridia, and cataracts; (2) impaired visual acuity, such as nearsightedness or farsightedness (myopia and hyperopia); (3) impaired ocular movements, such as nystagmus, strabismus, and paresis; and (4) impaired visual awareness due to constricted visual fields or cortical impairment (Jan, Skyanda, Groenveld, & Hoyt, 1987). The most common cause of visual loss in preschool children is amblyopia (France, l989).

Amblyopia is the reduction of acuity in one eye when no apparent pathological aberration exists in either the eye or the visual pathways. It is commonly agreed that the primary etiology of amblyopia is visual confusion that occurs with the loss of equal binocular input and the presence of dissimilar visual images at the retinal level. In an attempt to resolve the visual confusion, the child subconsciously "turns off" the vision in the weaker eye and the stronger eye becomes dominant. Conditions that place children at risk for amblyopia include strabismus, ptosis (drooping of the upper eyelid), congenital nystagmus, optic nerve hypoplasia, convergence insufficiency, and progressive vision loss disorders (Cibis & Fitzgerald, 1993). Amblyopia is easily treatable if it is the primary cause of low vision and is diagnosed prior to 4 years of age (France, 1989). Success in restoring complete vision, however, diminishes between 4 and 9 years of age. Patching is the first line of defense in the remediation of amblyopia. The patch is placed over the good or stronger eye in an effort to force the child to use, and subsequently improve the vision in, the weaker eye. The regime of patching depends on the age of the child, the severity of the amblyopia, and the time of initial detection of the loss of vision. Romano (1990) urged the detection and remediation of amblyopia as early as possible, since the general rule of thumb is one month of treatment for each year of age at the time of diagnosis.

When one eye deviates in any direction from its normal alignment, *strabismus* is the resulting sequelae. Strabismus is found in 5% of preschool children and can result from impaired motor function, impaired sensory functioning, and refractive errors. Infants often give the appearance of strabismus because of prominent epicanthal folds and reduced interpupillary distance although the eyes are straight. This condition is referred to as pseudostrabismus and resolves with growth. Esotropia (turning in or adduction of eyes from the midline) and exotropia (turning out or abduction of eyes from the midline) are forms of strabismus. While normal neonates often exhibit exotropia, a constant esotropia observed during the neonatal phase is abnormal and referred to as congenital esotropia. Archer and Helveston (1989) noted that congenital esotropia is the most common pathological strabismus diagnosed in infancy. Depending on the nature of the strabismus and the age of onset, it is managed either surgically or through the prescription of corrective lenses. Strabismus is often associated with neurological impairments such as hydrocephalus and cerebral palsy and with interuterine infections, especially toxoplasmosis and cytomegalic inclusion disease, as well as with prematurity. Additional visual defects common to young children with disabilities and associated visual effects are described in Figure 6.8.

Screening for Visual Impairment

Crouch and Kennedy (1993) advised that vision screening is essential to the detection of strabismus, amblyopia, ocular disease, and refractive errors. The American Academy of Pediatrics (1986) recommends that children be screened for eye problems in four stages: in the newborn nursery, and at 6 months, 3½ years, and 5 years of age. Young children should be screened at any time either by an eye-care professional or by the pediatrician if there are physical or behavioral signs that alert caregivers that something may be wrong with the child's visual system. Sheridan (1969) and Stangler, Huber, and Routh (1980, p. 221) delineated a number of factors that place a child at risk for visual disability:

- prenatal infections such as toxoplasmosis, maternal rubella, and cytomegalic inclusion disease (CMV)
- chromosomal conditions
- trauma during the birth process
- structural abnormalities of the eye
- family history of vision problems
- complications of retinopathy of prematurity

Behavioral and functional indices suggestive of a visual disorder may include the following:

- lack of orientation to light sources, visual inspection of hands, and visual regard of the caregiver's face at expected ages in the absence of other developmental problems
- lack of visual curiosity
- constant tilt or rotation of the head to one side in the absence of a motor impairment such as torticollis
- widely roving eye movements
- subtle, "oscillating" eye movements
- regard of objects held very near the face
- closing of one eye when viewing objects and pictures
- avoidance of tasks requiring near visual attention

Albinism	congenital absence of eye pigment caused by an enzyme insufficiency	acuity of 20⁄200 or better; photophobia, refractive errors, loss of central vision, nystagmus; poor depth
Cataracts	opacity of any size or degree in the crystalline lens	acuity of 20⁄50 to 20⁄200; possible photophobia; if the lens is removed, accommodative power is lost; strabismus may develop
Congenital Amaurosis of Leber (CAL)	congenital tapetoretinal degeneration beginning in utero	profound visual loss at birth, nystagmus, poorly reactive pupils, extinguished ERG, light perception may be present, high incidence of hyperopia
Color Blindness	congenital dysfunction of the cones, nerves of retina	blue/yellow vision lost initially with retinal diseases; red/green loss first associated with optic nerve lesions
Congenital Glaucoma	congenital condition caused by an increase in intraocular pressure	photophobia, bulging or hazy cornea, excess tearing, optic nerve damage, with early onset blindness may be present; later developing glaucoma may reduce acuity to 20⁄50; amblyopia
Cortical Visual Impairment	a lack of visual attention and awareness in the absence of nystagmus and normal ocular evaluation	aware of flashing lights, movement, and bright colors, peripheral fields most functional; tactile exploration substituted for visual, reaches with face turned to the side, use of vision fluctuates

FIGURE 6.8
Common childhood visual conditions
Source: From *Decision Making in Pediatric Ophthalmology* by G. W. Cibis, A. C. Tongue, and M. L. Stass-Isern (Eds.), 1993, St. Louis, MO: Mosby–Year Book, Inc.; *The Eye in Infancy* by S. J. Isenberg (Ed.), 1989, Chicago, IL: Year Book Medical Publisher; "Pediatric Neuro-ophthalmology" by L. J. Martyn, 1983, *The Pediatric Clinics of North America, 42*(8), 103–1121.

- excessive blinking, rubbing of eyes, and squinting
- poking of the eyes or pressing of eyes with the back of the hand
- side-to-side rhythmic movements of the head without fixation of the eyes in steady gaze
- sensitivity to direct lighting or sunlight
- excessive light gazing

Observation of any of these symptoms warrants evaluation by a professional eye-care specialist. Parents typically are the first to notice visual differences in the young child, especially if they are subtle or inconsistent. Even the pediatrician may be unaware of visual problems that are not significant or constant because he or she sees the child for such a brief period of time during routine checkups or when the child is ill and the focus of the exam is the diagnosis of the presenting problem. Friendly (1989) and Romano (1990) stressed the importance of listening to parents' concerns regarding their child's vision. Romano insightfully advised,

Nystagmus	a congenital or acquired condition that results in rhythmic eye oscillations that are either equal in amplitude or greater in one direction	acuity may be diminished, compensatory head turn may evolve
Optic Atrophy	degeneration of the optic nerve that can be either congenital or acquired and may result from post-inflammatory infection or compressed optic nerve or may be part of a multisystem disorder affecting the CNS	depending on the form, acuity 20/30 to 20/200; sluggish pupillary response, visual field deficits, color vision loss, nystagmus
Optic Nerve Hypoplasia	nonprogressive, congenital disorder of the optic nerve; diminished number of optic nerve fibers in the optic nerve	minimal vision impairment to total blindness; bitemporal field defects; diminished pupillary reaction; associated with midline defects and growth hormone deficiency
Retinopathy of Prematurity (ROP)	congenital condition of the retinal vascular system associated with prematurity in which there is extraretinal vascular proliferation which may lead to tractional retinal detachment	depending on the progress of the fibrovascular process, minimal to no effects in Grade I to high myopia, loss of central vision, glaucoma and strabismus in Grade III to total retinal detachment and blindness in Plus disease
Strabismus	a deviation in the alignment of the eyes either inward (esotropia) or outward (exotropia)	loss of fusion, depth; if uncorrected amblyopia may occur; child may adopt a compensatory head posture

FIGURE 6.8
Continued

"parents are rarely wrong when they think that there is a problem with their child's eyes or vision" (p. 361).

Dimensions of an Assessment of Visual Capacity

A thorough eye examination by a medical eyecare specialist, either an ophthalmologist or an optometrist, consists of assessment of the structural integrity of the external eye, the pupillary reflexes, range of the extraocular movements, ocular alignment and binocularity, acuity, visual fields, depth perception, and color perception, if possible. Examination of the health status of both the anterior and the posterior segments of the eye are essential to the diagnosis of anomalies that threaten the child's visual health and/or place the child at risk for vision loss.

Observation of the cornea, lens, iris, and anterior vitreous humor comprise an assessment of the anterior chamber. Miller (1993) suggested that parents detect anterior segment

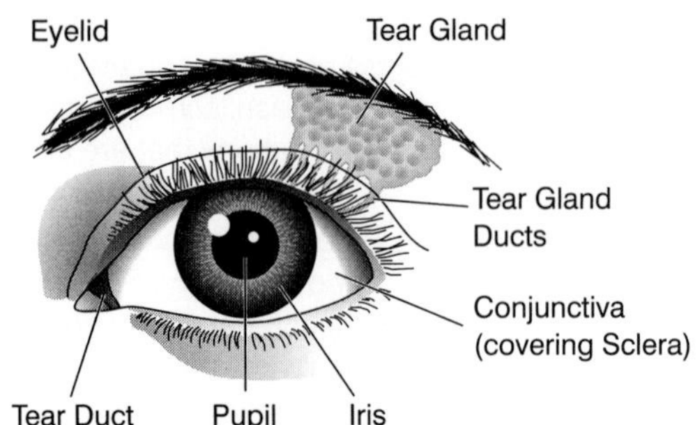

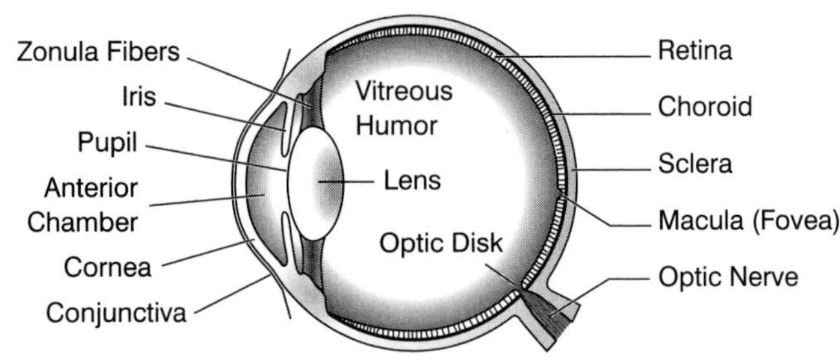

FIGURE 6.9
Diagrams of the external surface of the eye and its surrounding structures (top) and of a lateral view of the posterior segment of the eye and the optic nerve (bottom). The posterior segment of the eye and any related anomalies may be viewed only through indirect ophthalmoscopy whereas the superficial structures of the eye can be observed with the naked eye.
Source: From *Children with Handicaps: A Medical Primer, Second Edition* (p. 201), by M. L. Batshaw and Y. M. Perret, 1986, Baltimore, MD: Paul H. Brookes. Copyright 1986 by M. L. Batshaw, M.D. Adapted with permission.

pathology early because problems associated with anterior structures, such as glaucoma, strabismus, cataracts, and nystagmus, are obvious on inspection. Figure 6.9 depicts the general anatomy of the healthy eye.

Indirect ophthalmoscopy allows the physician to examine the posterior chamber of the eye including the macula, the optic disc, the choroid, and the retina. The Brueckner method, the preferred subjective approach with nonverbal and difficult-to-test children for estimating acuity and detecting amblyopia, is conducted with the ophthalmoscope. In the Brueckner test, simultaneous observations of the corneal reflex and the red fundus reflex reflected from the back of the eye permit observation of fixation and alignment from which a gross estimate of acuity can be determined. Additionally, the ophthalmoscope can identify misalignment of the eye, media opacities, and high refractive errors (Cibis, 1993; Romano, 1990).

The cornerstone of a vision assessment of a young child is the evaluation of visual acuity (Isenberg, 1989), which represents the smallest retinal image (finest detail) that the eye can distinguish (Crouch & Kennedy, 1993). When appropriate and possible, both near-point acuity (vision within 16 inches [40 cm] from the face) and far-point acuity (vision at and beyond 10 feet [3 meters]) should be measured. Estimation of acuity in infants and young children is dependent on fixation and following abilities, under both monocular and binocular conditions. The eye-care specialist uses a variety of moving or illuminated toys, finger puppets, wiggle pictures on the end of tongue depressors or penlights, and hand-held lights as targets to elicit fixation and accommodation. The notation CSM indicates that fixation under monocular conditions is central, both fixation and following are steady, and, when the occluder is removed, fixation and following are maintained. If this condition is met by both eyes, Isenberg (1989) suggests that vision is normal in the absence of strabismus. Patterson (1980), however, implied that fixation may be central and steady even with acuity levels up to 20/200.

The acuity of preschool, preverbal children can be estimated by a variety of instruments. *Optokinetic nystagmus* (OKN) can be induced with stripes of graded degrees printed on either a rotating drum or a cloth flag. When the stripes are moved across the visual field, involuntary oscillations of the eyes, referred to as nystagmus, are elicited. Acuity is determined by the smallest width of stripe that triggers the nystagmus.

Grating acuity is used in *preferential looking* (PL) and forced-choice preferential looking (FPL) techniques, the Teller Acuity Cards (Teller, 1979) (see Figure 6.10) being the most widely used procedure. Based on the child's visual fixation to varying widths of alternating black and white stripes, acuities are estimated. This procedure is most effective with infants under 6 to 8 months of age; it is difficult to hold the attention of older infants. Several clinicians have adapted the procedure for office use, and preferential looking techniques have been used effectively to determine acuity levels in neurologically impaired and cortically visually impaired children (Adams & Courage, 1990; Birch & Bane, 1991; Cibis, 1993). Greenwald (1983) warns, however, that grating acuity may not correlate with other measures of acuity and may underestimate the severity of a visual deficit.

A disturbance of the visual pathway in the brain is assessed by *visual evoked responses* (VER), also called visual evoked potentials (VEP). Electrodes are positioned over the occipital cortex to record electrical potentials that have been extracted from the background EEG by signal averaging (Creel, 1993). The VEP quantifies the degree of vision present and can determine whether a visual problem is due to a

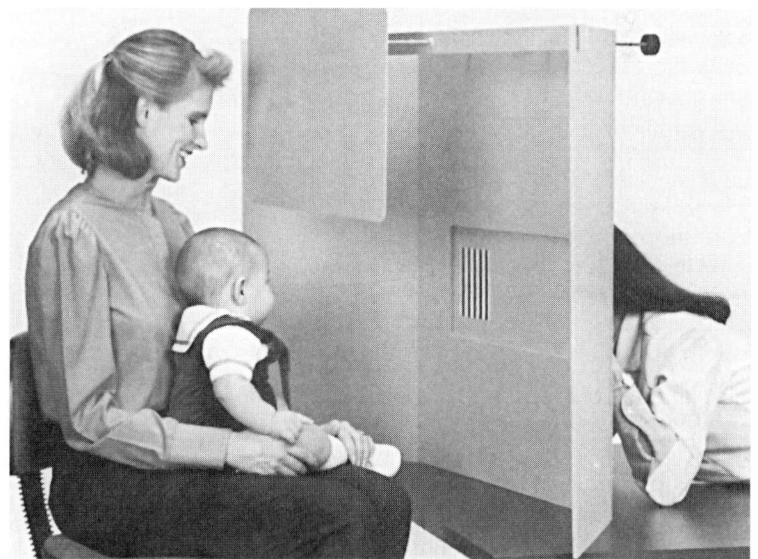

FIGURE 6.10
Preferential Looking (PL) assessment with the Teller Acuity Cards
Source: Reprinted with permission from Vistech Consultants, Inc., Manufacturer of the Teller Acuity Card Testing System.

retinal or more central visual dysfunction. The quality of the VER is dependent on the nature of the stimulus selected. The child is seated in front of a television screen with a checkerboard pattern, which is reversed during the testing. This stimulus is effective for children with acuities of 20/200 or better who do not have nystagmus. Pattern onset in which a pattern appears and then disappears on a television screen is preferred for children whose acuities fall between 20/200 and 20/400 and/or who have nystagmus. When acuity is worse than 20/400 and the child is uncooperative or sedated, a strobe flash or light-emitting diodes are used (Creel, 1993). Generally, the better the VEP, the better the prognosis that vision is normal; however, it has not been a reliable tool in children with delayed visual maturation. Fulton (1989) remarked that whether acuity is measured by VEP or by preferential looking (PL) procedures, the acuities of developmentally delayed children with normal eyes demonstrate poorer acuity results than do those of normally developing children.

Video vision development assessment (VVDA) uses a Super VHS video camera with a specially modified light source to capture the dynamic aspects of fixation, accommodation, and foveation (focusing light rays on the fovea, the center of the macula). A video printer produces a hard copy of the process for analysis. Although the video viewer detects amblyopic factors such as misalignment of the eyes, a difference in refractive error between the two eyes (anisometropia), high refractive errors, and media opacities, this process does not test depth, fusion, or binocularity. VVDA can also perform photorefraction (described below) and is reportedly more accurate than a photograph (Cibis & Luke, 1993). The advantage of VVDA over photorefraction is that VVDA can discriminate whether the patient is truly fixating the light source rather than simply looking at it.

Eccentric photorefraction operates on the principle that a sufficiently large refractive error will be indicated by reflected light from the patient's fundus (the inferior part of the eye, including the retina, the optic disc, and the macula) spilling into the optical aperture of the viewing instrument. This spillage is seen as a crescent within the aperture of the child's eye. Crescent size is a factor of pupil size, patient to light source distance, and degree of light eccentricity (distance light source is from the center of camera lens). The refractive power of the eye can be calculated when all these factors are known. The disadvantages of the photorefraction are that small refractive errors may be missed, the child must be actively focusing on the light, and children who are cortically visually impaired may test as having normal vision. Photoscreening is estimated to be 85% to 94% accurate and identifies twice as many children with amblyopia than do procedures intended to assess acuity and binocularity. However, Romano (1990) cautioned that photoscreening is reliable only if the child accurately fixates on the camera lens center or visual target long enough for the picture to be taken and that this method of screening has not proven effective with developmentally delayed young children.

Ototype Acuity Measures

When a child is able to match or label, more traditional ototype acuity measures such as the Tumbling E, the Allen Cards (Allen, 1957), the New York Flashcard Test of Vision (New York Flashcards) (Faye, 1968), the HOTV (Lippmann, 1969), the Panda Tests (Sheridan, 1973) or the more recent LH Symbols (Hyvarinen, 1992) may be administered. The Snellen E Charts and the Allen Cards (Preschool Vision Test) have not been effective with preschool children with disabilities because of their perceptual demands for discrimination of spatial orientation and visual closure. Although the Panda Test, a component of the STYCAR battery (Sheridan, 1973), the New York Flashcards (also referred to as the Lighthouse Test), and the LH Symbols have all been developed for use with preschool children with disabilities, the New York Flashcards are the most effective with lower-functioning children who are able to respond to symbol tests. The New York Flashcards are comprised of three symbols, an apple, a house, and an umbrella. A single symbol is printed on each card, representing Snellen acuities from $^{10}/_{15}$ to $^{20}/_{200}$. The child may be given the $^{20}/_{200}$ symbols and asked to point to the one that matches the stimulus flashcard. If the child is severely physically limited, two symbols may be presented simultaneously at distance and the child asked to look at the one specified by the examiner. The LH Symbols consist of a house, an apple, a ball (circle), and a block (square) and offer several advantages over the New York Flashcard Test. The LH Symbols are available in several test configurations so that they may be adapted for use at different developmental levels. All LH symbols are equally sensitive to blur and equally difficult to distinguish; a chart is available for assessing contrast sensitivity. The LH system provides training cards and three-dimensional symbols in puzzle form to familiarize the child with the task. However, the LH Single Symbol Book consists of several symbols on the same page, and it is confusing for lower-functioning children to have to search for the symbol in a different place each time on the same page. Since the symbol is always in the same location on the New York Flashcards, the cards represent a cognitively easier task than the LH Symbols. Greenwald (1983) observed that even when children are apparently old enough to perform on more standard acuity measurements, their level of visual competence is governed more by their ability to handle the conceptual rather than the visual demands of the tasks.

When formal acuity measures are not feasible, the general level of acuity may be estimated by enticing the child to pick up or point to small items such as bits of crackers, threads, tiny toys and candies, and cake decorating beads (Langley, 1980; Nelson, Rubin, Wagner, & Breton, 1984; Sonksen, 1983). While clinical measures of visual acuity are quite imperfect (Friendly, 1989), they are essential when attempting to estimate the quality and quantity of vision in children who cannot perform on formal acuity measures. Assessment of acuity in infants and preschoolers should yield some estimate of both the smallest item detected and the optimal size and distance of stimuli that consistently evoke visual attention. Orelove and Sobsey (1987) suggested that a child with $^{20}/_{20}$ vision can detect an object $^{1}/_{8}$ of an inch long with detail up to $^{1}/_{16}$ of an inch at 20-foot distances and the child with an acuity of $^{20}/_{200}$ can see an object 3.5 inches long with details of $^{13}/_{16}$ of an inch. Bailey and Hall (1983) have devised an ingenious acuity measurement that assesses the amount of detail discriminated by the child through the use of small cereals.

Functional Vision Assessment

The most important data for a parent, a teacher, other caregivers, and service providers to have is knowledge of what the child can see and predictions of how he may respond to items encountered in different environments. Jose, Smith, and Shane (l980) emphasized that "the numbers attached to a diagnosis are not as important as the information that the child can see a half-inch block at three feet" (p. 4). Additionally, individual children with the same acuity level will function quite differently as a function of neurological, cognitive, and experiential influences. A pioneer in the field of visual learning and assessment, Barraga (1976) coined the term *visual efficiency* to refer to each child's unique ability to use his vision functionally to process, accommodate, and adapt to his visual environment. Sonksen et al. (1991) included in an assessment of functional vision the child's visual reactions in natural context, such as visual awareness of silent objects of different sizes, color, and luminance available at various distances and in different fields of vision. A valid and reliable assessment of vision is dependent on the clinician's knowledge of the components of visual function, on an appreciation of the type and quality of responses expected at different developmental levels, and on the nature of stimuli critical to eliciting specific visual behaviors. Observations of how the child spontaneously uses his vision in his natural environment will yield information valuable to an assessment of functional vision. Any assessment of functional vision must address acuity, visual fields, and ocular motility (Vaughan et al., 1989). Specific visual components typically addressed in a functional vision evaluation are delineated in Figure 6.11. Qualitative aspects of the child's visual abilities should also be documented and may include the following:

1. the general health status and structural integrity of the child's eyes,
2. the child's head posture and visual behavior when looking at both near and far stimuli,
3. the child's responses to various lighting conditions,
4. where the child positions objects and pictures when examining them,
5. the range of sizes and distances and types of visual stimuli to which the child responds,
6. the general level of the child's visual attention and fatigue, and
7. the range and quality of visual perceptual abilities including
   - depth and color perception,
   - discrimination and identification of detail,
   - ability to resolve figure-ground contrasts,
   - ability to identify visual stimuli when only a small portion is visible,
   - ability to perform visual cognitive tasks such as recalling, associating, and sequencing details such as size, color, form, and temporal and spatial relationships.

The precise measurement of visual fields, depth, and color is often difficult if not impossible in young children with delays. An estimate of the child's visual fields may be achieved with the use of two equally attractive mechanical, illuminated, or motion toys. The child's attention is held at the midline with one of the toys while the second toy is moved systematically around the face of an imaginary clock approximately 18 inches away from the child. With the child's attention held at midline, the second toy is activated at each clock position and observations of the positions that elicit the child's gaze shift are recorded. Positions in which the child failed to orient may be reassessed to determine whether the lack of orientation was due to lack of attention or to a true absence of vision in that field. Flashing a light on and off at various positions in a dimly lit room also is effective in obtaining an idea of visual fields. Color perception may be assessed by having the child match various shades of primary and secondary colors through commercially available toy sets, pegs, blocks, and crayons, or through paint or wallpaper samples. It is important to have the child discriminate among combinations of reds, browns, and greens simultaneously and among blues and yellows, to rule out the two primary color deficiencies. The child's ability to perceive depth may be noted as he or she moves across various textures, descends or ascends different levels of height, and reaches into deep containers to obtain chips or cookies. Offering the child a tall potato chip can containing a small edible at the bottom and observing whether he or she detects the edible without verbal cues is a simple and effective technique for assessing depth. The child who overreaches or underreaches when taking items off surfaces or placing items in small holes, on stacking posts, or in containers and who avoids stairs, curbs, and crossing from the tile to the carpet may have some form of depth perception impairment. Langley (in press) described the outcomes anticipated from an assessment of functional vision:

Components of a Functional Vision Assessment

1. Structural Integrity
   - Size, shape, clarity, and symmetry of eyes/pupils/iris
   - Pupillary reflexes
   - Alignment (binocularity) of eyes
2. Oculomotor Abilities
   - Extent and quality of fixation
   - Extent and quality of tracking (pursuit)
   - Extent and quality of gaze shift (saccadic)
   - Extent and quality of eye mobility (left and right)
   - Extent and quality of convergence
   - Extent and quality of accommodation to shift gaze between near and mid space
3. Visual Fields
   - Central fields
   - Peripheral fields
4. Visual Acuity
   - Formal measures of near and far point
   - Informal, clinical measures of near and far point

Distance from child	Size and nature of stimulus
Near (within 16 inches)	
Far (10 feet and farther)	

5. Visual Perceptual Skills
   Discrimination
   Closure
   Figure-ground
   Spatial orientation
   Memory and association
   Depth
   Color
6. Visual Function During Movement
   Self-imposed
   In response to postural shifts by others
   During movement on riding toy, with walker, or in wheelchair

FIGURE 6.11
Aspects of vision addressed within an assessment of functional vision

1. a description of how, what, and where the child sees,
2. a description of visual compensations used to maximize visual capacities,
3. a description of the stimulus variables that maximize visual functioning such as:
   - stimulus quality (i.e., dynamic motion, illuminated toys, or fluorescent colors)
   - stimulus size
   - stimulus distance
   - stimulus position/orientation
   - foreground and background lighting conditions
   - environmental conditions
   - optimal positioning, equipment, and handling techniques needed for best visual functioning
4. a description of child variables influencing optimal use of vision, such as:
   - pacing and interaction styles of assessor
   - child endurance level
   - optimal attending time
   - optimal response time
   - behavioral cues and prompts needed to facilitate vision
   - rate of change during assessment of visual potential
5. a description of how the child uses residual vision during play, social interaction, learning experiences, and adapting to environmental demands

Several commercial assessments are available for assessing the functional vision of young children with disabilities. Among the most innovative, creative, and practical are the Screening Tests for Young Children and Retardates (STYCAR) (Sheridan, 1973). Despite its unfortunate title, the STYCAR is an easily administered, comprehensive assessment, using miniature toys and graduated sizes of styrofoam balls to estimate acuity, visual fields, and visual processing abilities. Children from the age of 6 months are easily motivated to participate in this assessment because of the nature of the manipulatives. Sonksen has enriched the field of functional vision assessment by providing several critical articles that detail both the assessment of and programming for visual development in young children with visual impairments and multiple disabilities (Sonksen, 1983; Sonksen & Macrae, 1987; Sonksen, Petrie, & Drew, 1991). Langley (1980, in press), Langley and Dubose (1976), and Smith and Cote (1982) developed comprehensive assessment and intervention manuals that offered specific strategies and techniques for delineating the quantity and quality of visual responses of children with severe and multiple handicapping conditions.

The most recent contribution to the field, the Individualized, Systematic Assessment of Visual Efficiency (ISAVE) provides both a detailed assessment process and a screening instrument for the assessment of visual behaviors in children with severe disabilities functioning within the birth to 5 years developmental range (Langley, in press). Although the ISAVE provides strategies for assessing all of the components in Figure 6.12, it is designed to allow the evaluator to select the components of the instrument that are most relevant to the needs of the child being assessed. Unique features of the ISAVE include (1) an ecological assessment of visual behaviors, (2) a component that addresses critical postural, movement, and transitional behaviors that support and contribute to the development of specific visual skills, (3) a component that ascertains whether the child displays the hallmark characteristics associated with cortical visual impairment, and (4) the development of an Individualized Functional Vision Service Plan (IFVSP) based on the results obtained from administration of the ISAVE. An additional component, the Baby Screen, screens eight areas of visual functioning in infants from prematurity through 12 months of age. Figure 6.12 presents three of the eight scales from the Baby Screen. In addition to Response to Light, Fixation, and Following, the other five domains encompass the assessment of Visual Acuity, Visual Fields, Binocularity, Social Gaze, and Visual Perception.

Response to Light		
P		Pupils respond slowly
P		Pupil size very small
P		Incubated infant may not turn toward light
B–6wk		Turns to diffuse light
B–6wk		Minimal pupil response
B–6wk		Eyes orient light source
6wk–4mos		Brisk response to light
8–12mos		Creeps toward light
8–12mos		Uncovers light
Comments		
P Passed F Failed		

Fixation		
P		Eyes open, no fixation
P		Fixation fleeting
B–6wk		Brief fixation light
B–6wk		Regards colorful object
6w–4mo		Sustained fixation
6w–4mo		Shift: Stuck one object
6w–4mo		Preoccupied human face
4–8mos		Attends object 5–10 sec
4–8mos		Fixates image in mirror
4–8mos		Fixates object in room
Comments		
P Passed F Failed		

Following		
B–6wk		Unstable, brief
B–6wk		Head/eyes together
B–6wk		Jerky: direction of moving target
B–6wk		Follows object to mid-line, <90 degrees
B–6wk		Central pursuit 90
6w–4mo		Follows upward 30
6w–4mo		Follows downward
6w–4mo		Central pursuit 180
6w–4mo		Eyes follow all planes of gaze
6w–4mo		Eyes more mobile
Comments		
P Passed F Failed		

FIGURE 6.12
Three scales of visual functioning
Source: From *Individualized, Systematic Assessment of Visual Efficiency: Baby Screen* by M. B. Langley (in press), Louisville, KY: American Printing House for the Blind. Copyright held by American Printing House for the Blind. Reprinted with permission from the author.

Examples of strategies for screening the vision of infants and toddlers and of children with multiple disabilities are demonstrated in Figure 6.13.

The Role of Early Childhood Personnel in the Assessment of Visual Functioning

Early childhood personnel may be the first to engage the toddler and young child in activities requiring focusing at near point for varying amounts of time. Initial play activities consist of general gross motor exploration and play with large, colorful toys; the child does not need to use refined visual abilities. Once in an instructional setting, however, the need for closer investigation and visual monitoring of activities may reveal visual difficulties. The instructor may notice that the child consistently moves closer to see books and pictures or that the child's eyes are red and watery after prolonged attention to art work, picture books, and fine motor activities. The child may be observed to tilt his or her head when focusing on something in the distance or when trying to string beads or cut. The child may be observed consistently to label items according to their general configuration rather than to more specific details (e.g., labeling a shovel a spoon). During play in various activity centers, the child may be noted to consistently ignore items on one side of his or her body or, when engaged in matching or Lotto games, fail to scan the same general area each time. The instructor should be particularly concerned about the child who may be extremely sensitive to changes in lighting or who may lack awareness of surface changes when moving from one area to another. Children who are drawn to light, who prefer to light gaze rather than play with toys or to flick their fingers before their eyes but in the direction of a light source, or children who appear suddenly to lack awareness of objects around them or have difficulty distinguishing details and complain of headaches should be referred immediately to an eye specialist for formal vision screening or assessment.

In an intervention setting, the primary goals of the early interventionist working with a visually impaired infant or preschooler are (1) to arrange the instructional environment and the child's posture so as to facilitate optimal use of residual vision in contingent learning situations, (2) to monitor and adjust illumination and working distances to minimize fatigue factors, and (3) to select, design, and modify learning materials to enhance the child's visual attention and organizational processes.

In summary, regardless of the specific instrument or process selected for the screening and assessment of visual behaviors, the child's characteristic visual performance, potential for improvement or expansion of existing visual behaviors, and the qualities of stimuli and specific conditions that will facilitate optimal use of vision for the functional adaptation to environmental demands must be addressed. Although hearing and vision are addressed in most well-baby clinics and in early childhood screening programs, tactile, vestibular, and proprioceptive sensory systems are typically not screened unless an insightful pediatrician or parent suspects problems in these areas. However, because of the importance of these underlying sensory modalities in the development of compensatory behaviors in hearing impaired and visually impaired children, knowledge of their intactness and integration with other sensory channels is essential. In addition, young children who demonstrate significant difficulty organizing themselves and responding appropriately to social interactions and sensory information from the environment may be manifesting some degree of sensory integration dysfunction.

FIGURE 6.13
The assessment of (a) fixation, (b) tracking, and (c) peripheral visual fields in an infant with visual disabilities

SCREENING AND ASSESSMENT OF VESTIBULAR, TACTILE, AND PROPRIOCEPTIVE MODALITIES

While the senses of vision and hearing are considered distal sensory modalities, the vestibular, tactile, and proprioceptive sensory receptors comprise the cluster of proximal sensory modalities. Integration of these basic sensory processes forms the foundation for emotional stability and organized learning behaviors. Whenever a deficit occurs in one sensory modality, the quality of input to the central nervous system from other sensory channels is compromised. Proximal sensory dysfunction and disturbances are prevalent in several groups of children and affect development, learning, and behavior in a number of different ways, depending on the etiology, type, and degree of impairment. Sensory deficits may result either in a lack of sufficient information for processing incoming stimuli or in disorganization and defensive behaviors.

Children at Risk for Proximal Sensory Dysfunction

The very premature child is significantly at risk for both proximal and distal sensory disorders and disorganization (Anderson, 1986). The premature child may be either hyporesponsive to sensory information or hyperaroused and easily overwhelmed by sensory stimuli. Visually impaired infants often manifest proximal sensory deficits in the forms of tactile defensiveness, gravitational insecurity, and poor feeding behaviors. Hearing impaired children with a sensorineural loss may experience poor balance and coordination due to the damage to the vestibular nerve. Poor tactile-kinesthetic awareness and bilateral integration may interfere with the planning, organization, and formation of manual signs. Children who exhibit self-injurious behaviors or cravings for intense forms of sensory input from one or all of the proximal sensory receptors are often found to have seriously disturbed, disorganized, or poorly integrated sensory systems. Children with movement disorders such as cerebral palsy and spinal cord damage experience a vast array of sensory perception difficulties and the quality of their movement is often a direct reflection of their ability to perceive incoming sensory information critical to body schema and awareness of position in space. All of these developmental problems depict dysfunction in vestibular, tactile, or proprioceptive sensory modalities.

Children with *sensory integration dysfunction* exhibit attentional, emotional, organizational, and motor delays in addition to tactile defensiveness, distractibility, and poor language and visual-spatial skills (DeGangi & Greenspan, 1989; Sears, 1994). The ability to tolerate sensory information is inherently related to the child's ability to regulate arousal states. DeGangi and Greenspan (1989) noted that infants unable to process sensory experiences normally might not avail themselves of the spectrum of sensory experiences critical for responding to and assimilating new learning opportunities. At greater risk for being able to organize themselves in order to attend to, process, and learn from experiences are children labeled as *regulatory disordered*. DeGangi (1991) explained that a regulatory disorder is "defined by persistent symptoms that interfere with adaptive functioning" (p. 3). Regulatory disordered infants have been found to be at high risk for later perceptual, language, sensory integrative, and behavioral difficulties during the preschool years (DeGangi, 1991). DeGangi detailed the primary identifying characteristics of a child with regulatory disorders:

- sleep disorders that result from high states of arousal that inhibit the ability to sleep;
- extreme difficulties self-consoling and severe temper tantrums;
- significant feeding problems;

- hyperarousal that leads to disorganization during transitions from one activity to the next, distractibility, attention to extraneous details in the environment, and easy sensory overloading; and
- "fussiness, irritability, an unhappy mood state, and a tendency to quickly escalate from contentment to distress." (p.4)

Dimensions of an Assessment of Proximal Sensory Systems

An assessment of vestibular, proprioceptive, and tactile systems should ascertain the level of intactness of each modality and identify which modalities are preferred for or support learning from other sensory channels. The optimal quality and intensity of stimuli that facilitate processing by each modality should be identified so that the child will be able to respond adaptively to learning opportunities. The child's ability to integrate sensory modalities, including the ability to filter out extraneous information and to attend to relevant sensory data, should be analyzed. In an assessment of sensory functions, the child's general developmental level must be considered in determining the appropriateness of behavioral responses. Additionally, responses should be assessed relative to the nature, purpose, and level of novelty of the task being presented. If during an assessment of specific sensory behaviors, the child becomes disorganized, the efficiency with which he regroups and organizes himself will add valuable information regarding the integrity of the proximal sensory systems. The assessment should include observations of the child's typical behaviors and responses in day-to-day situations as noted by his primary caregivers, as well as notations of environments and conditions that appear to calm the child and those that exacerbate his sensory dysfunction.

Assessment of vestibular function should include observations regarding the child's quality of postural tone and postural reactions, her ability to assume and maintain supine flexion and prone extension patterns, her reactions to imposed movement and to antigravity movement, and observations of behaviors such as self-imposed spinning, spinning of objects, stereotypic rocking behaviors, and excessive and disorganized movement (i.e., hyperactivity). The presence and length of nystagmus in response to controlled spinning or of nystagmus in the absence of visual impairment will provide insight regarding the integrity of the vestibular system. Figure 6.14 suggests behavioral characteristics associated with vestibular, tactile, and proprioceptive dysfunction.

The *tactile system* is responsible for perception of touch, pressure, temperature, and pain. The sense of touch or tactile sensation is comprised of an early protective system that becomes integrated into a more mature discriminative system that interprets tactile input for cognitive functions. Children who tend to be tactilely defensive have failed to fully integrate the early protective touch system. Sears (1994) explained that dysfunction in the tactile system may result in aversive responses such as pain, fear, and discomfort. There is evidence that tactile defensiveness is a neurologically based impairment and is only a component of a larger constellation of aversive reactions in response stimulation across one or more sensory modalities that results in irrational-appearing behaviors (Sears, 1994). Determining whether a tactile response is indicative of a defensive system or whether the response is a reaction to novelty and unfamiliarity will depend on the context in which the response is elicited and on how quickly the child adapts to the stimuli. A child's resistance to imposed demands may mistakenly be perceived as tactile defensiveness. Observing the child as he explores a set of novel materials will facilitate decisions regarding the integrity of the tactile system. If he willingly explores items such as slinkies,

Characteristics of Vestibular Dysfunction

- Fearful of movement; hesitant to participate in movement activities
- Righting and equilibrium reactions delayed
- Avoids movement; prefers to remain curled up with head resting on surface
- Unsure of where he is in space; has difficulty identifying or localizing body parts
- Strives to maintain upright postures by relying heavily on visual and proprioceptive feedback; fixes gaze on floor rather than on where he is going
- Bumps into objects because of distorted sense of movement in space
- Difficulty walking in dark or on uneven surfaces
- Exhibits rigid posture; moves only in straight planes
- Easily overcome with motion sickness
- Spontaneously engages in repetitive spinning motions; seeks out swings and merry-go-rounds: plays on them for extensive time
- Spends hours rocking or shaking head and/or hands

Characteristics of Tactile Dysfunction

- Walks on toes or creeps by bearing weight only on fingertips and knees; fists hands during weightbearing to avoid touch to palms
- Resists handling during bathing, dressing, and other self-care routines
- Prefers body surfaces covered with long-legged pants/long-sleeved shirts or prefers to be free of clothing altogether
- Prefers and is insistent about wearing only certain textures
- Sensitive to light intermittent touch (nuzzling); may resist cuddling
- Strives to remain in control of who touches him and of when he is touched
- Oral area remains hypersensitive to tactile input and textures; rejects foods that are not bland or smooth; smells food prior to eating
- Avoids common childhood textures such as sand, playdough, paint
- Avoids contact with other children
- May seek intensive tactile input such as flipping objects against mouth or teeth, scratching fingers against carpet or other textures, or rubbing ropes, strings, or similar objects between fingers or hands

FIGURE 6.14
Behavioral characteristics associated with proximal sensory dysfunction

Koosh™ balls, stuffed animals, and playdough but refuses to cooperate when directed specifically to play with an item that may be above his competency level, tactile defensiveness may be ruled out. The child's awareness of both light and firm touch should be explored in addition to requiring him to identify or match objects placed in his hand without the assistance of his vision. This ability to discriminate tactile properties of objects is referred to as stereognosis. The

Characteristics of Proprioceptive Dysfunction

- Sleeps with head against wall or headboard; seeks corners, places self under furniture to play or rest
- Experiences difficulty in motor planning; may assume awkward postures
- Experiences difficulty timing and differentiating movements
- Needs to visually monitor movements to know how and where his body is moving; has difficulty learning self-care tasks
- Has difficulty localizing facial parts; may use two hands
- Has poor alignment of extremities during weightbearing activities
- Cannot sustain postures against gravity
- Cannot grade control of postures during movement transitions
- Has limited ability to imitate body, facial, or extremity postures
- Cannot reach or position extremities accurately for support
- Adjusts grasp only after contact is made with object
- Lacks awareness of when mouth is full during eating; continues to stuff food
- Craves spicy foods and crunchy textures of food
- Constantly mouths objects or must be chewing something
- Plays too roughly with others or with animals without intending to
- Momentarily extends and stiffens extremities against gravity
- Manifests high sensory threshold; responses to pain are dampened; appears unaffected by severe injuries
- Craves firm, deep pressure; headbangs, bites self and others, pinches self and others, picks at scabs, hits self; constantly tapping or kicking hard, firm surfaces in repetitive manner
- Seeks vibration from washing machine, stereo speakers, wind-up toys, electric typewriters

FIGURE 6.14
Continued

child's responsiveness to texture and temperature as well as his ability to localize and discriminate single and dual touch points (two-point discrimination) should also be assessed. Royeen (1986, 1987) developed strategies for assessing the tactile ability of young children and for determining the presence of tactile defensive behaviors.

Receptors within the joints, tendons, and muscles that govern awareness of the position of body parts, of the body's position in space, both at rest and during movement, are referred to as the *proprioceptive system. Kinesthesia* is the conscious awareness of joint motion. *Somatosensory perception* is the integration of vestibular, tactile, and proprioceptive modalities and is critical for development of body scheme and for the organization, planning, and initiation of movement. Tasks traditionally administered to assess proprioceptive awareness and function include identification and localization of body parts, imitation of postures, and maintenance of imposed postures, both with and without vision (vision occluded). Although children with developmental disabilities may experience difficulty in complying with tasks designed to assess proprioceptive function, postural and movement behaviors and reactions to firm or deep pressure indicate level of intactness. Porter (1984) suggests that proprioceptive dysfunction may be suspected if an extremity lags behind during movement transitions or if the child fails to appropriately position extremities during transitions, weight bearing, or resting postures. Observing the child's reactions to vibration, traction, and approximation of joints, her ability to grade strength and rhythm of movement, and her ability to accommodate to size, shape, and weight of objects will also provide some indication of proprioceptive function.

Assessment Procedures

Traditionally, the assessment of sensorimotor functions is addressed by occupational and physical therapists; however, developmental specialists, early intervention specialists, teachers of the visually impaired and hearing impaired, and nurses are often responsible for assessment of basic sensory processes. Assessment procedures consist of both formal instruments designed to assess sensorimotor functions and of individual items that address specific sensory processes and are incorporated into developmental scales.

The Miller Assessment for Preschoolers (MAP) (Miller, 1982) is a standardized screening tool designed to identify children with "moderate preacademic problems" (manual, p. 1) that place a child developmentally at risk. The MAP consists of 27 items that address critical skills in the areas of Sensory and Motor, Cognitive, and Combined Abilities. The Sensory Motor section is divided into a Foundations Index and a Coordination Index. The Foundations Index includes items that address sensory integrative and neurodevelopmental parameters of sensory functioning such as (1) sense of position and movement, (2) sense of touch, and (3) basic components of movement. A Supplemental Observations section provides subjective but qualitative information regarding a child's performance. Miller explains that "certain children, although scoring within acceptable limits on these items, must use *unusual compensatory* methods to do so. It might be suspected that if increasingly complex demands were made of these children, these unusual methods, requiring increased effort, would no longer be adequate to compensate for the underlying problems" (p. 175).

A criterion-referenced test of sensory processing and reactivity in infants from 4 to 18 months, the Test of Sensory Function in Infants (TSFI) (DeGangi & Greenspan, 1989), assesses 24 items across five subdomains, which include reactivity to tactile deep pressure, adaptive motor functions, visual tactile integration, ocular motor control, and reactivity to vestibular stimulation. Individual items were selected based on their ability to indicate sensory integrative dysfunction in children and to identify children at risk for learning disability. DeGangi and Greenspan (1989) suggested that the TSFI should be used in conjunction with other standardized assessment measures.

Developmental scales that address tactile, vestibular, and/or proprioceptive functions include the Hawaii Early Learning Profile for Special Preschoolers (Furuno, O'Reilly, Hosaka, Inatsuka, Zeisloft-Falbey, & Allman, 1988), the Preschool Developmental Profile (Brown, D'Eugenio, Drews, Haskin, Whiteside-Lynch,

Moersch, & Rogers, 1981), the Psychoeducational Profile (Schopler, Reichler, Bashford, Lansing, & Marcus, 1990), the Carolina Curriculum for Infants and Toddlers with Special Needs (Johnson-Martin, Jens, Attermeier, & Hacker, 1991), and the Vulpé Assessment Battery (Vulpé, 1979). In addition, the second edition of the Bayley Scales of Infant Development (Bayley, 1993) incorporated specific items to assist in the diagnosis of children with sensory integration dysfunction.

The Role of Early Intervention Personnel in the Assessment of Sensory Perception and Integration

When an infant or toddler is difficult to console, irritable, and easily disorganized, even in the context of routine and familiarity, early childhood personnel should suspect a regulatory disorder or dysfunctional sensory integration processes. The caregiver may note that the child avoids direct gaze, prefers not to be held and cuddled, and may persist in rocking behaviors and head banging behaviors beyond the expected time frame or engage in these behaviors to an excessive degree and to the exclusion of other, adaptive behaviors. This infant may crave firm, deep pressure and seek out vibratory sources such as stereo speakers and the washing machine.

Behaviors in the classroom that may be indicative of sensory integration dysfunction encompass difficulties in changing response modes and in performing simultaneous actions—such as listening to a story and stringing beads—and a desire to play away from other children and in enclosed spaces. The instructor may notice that the child frequently leaves a group setting for a short period of time but returns spontaneously, appearing calmer and more organized. In contrast, he or she may lack appropriate strategies for social interaction, aggressing toward children by pushing and grabbing rather than seeking attention or requesting toys in more socially acceptable ways. He or she may avoid specific art activities, food textures, and the dress-up center. During sensory activities, he or she may not be able to identify objects held in the hand when vision is occluded and may be overly sensitive to smells. During group activities, the child does not want to be touched or held. Patting him or her on the back during rest time may result in explosive tantrums. The early interventionist should also be concerned when a child sustains a severe injury but reacts with minimal awareness or pain. A child with spina bifida should be checked frequently for abrasions and monitored carefully for deficiencies in perception because injuries may be exacerbated due to a lack of sensitivity and subsequent lack of awareness. When observations and impressions of reactions to various types of sensory experiences culminate in a profile of abnormal behaviors and responses such as those mentioned above, early childhood personnel should refer the child for a comprehensive assessment by a pediatric occupational therapist.

The integration of sensory processes is essential to the development of adaptive cognitive and motoric abilities. Determining specific sensory processing strengths, weaknesses, and needs will identify a child's primary learning channels as well as critical compensatory strategies needed to support optimal developmental functioning in a range of environments. An understanding of the child's unique sensory abilities and needs will also facilitate selection of appropriate learning materials, instructional pacing, and specific handling techniques that will enable the child to function comfortably and efficiently in response to daily demands.

SUMMARY OF KEY CONCEPTS

- Vision and hearing screenings must precede assessment of other developmental areas to ensure normal functioning and to rule out the possibility that delays may exist as a result of impaired sensory systems.
- There is a high incidence of hearing loss, visual impairment, and regulatory disorders associated with prematurity; the earlier they are detected and managed, the less at risk the child may be for developmental delays associated with the specific impairment.
- Parents are often the first to detect that something is wrong with their infant's hearing, vision, or regulatory systems.
- Accurate and efficient assessments of vision and hearing in young children are obtained when the procedures selected match the child's developmental level and response topography.
- Classification of hearing loss is based on the location of the impairment, the degree or severity of loss, and whether the loss is bilateral or unilateral. Hearing in children is considered normal when sounds are detected between 15 and 20 dB HL.
- Audiological assessments of very young children are typically obtained through observations of behaviors in response to auditory input in structured situations, referred to as behavioral observation audiometry (BOA). Assessment of middle ear function through impedence audiometry usually accompanies BOA testing.
- It has been estimated that 80% of all learning is acquired through the visual system.
- The most prevalent cause of visual loss in early childhood is amblyopia.
- Vision loss is classified based on levels of acuity, degree of visual fields, and whether the visual impairment is progressive. Normal vision in a preschool child ranges from 20/20 to 20/40 ototypes.
- The proximal sensory systems include vestibular, tactile, and proprioceptive modalities and serve as the foundation for emotional stability and organized learning behaviors.
- Children who display difficulty with the integration of information from several sensory systems, who are easily disorganized, and who have difficulty regulating or modulating their behavior may have a sensory integration disorder.

REFERENCES

Adams, R. J., & Courage, M. L. (1990). Assessment of visual acuity in children with severe neurological impairments. *Journal of Pediatric Ophthalmology & Strabismus, 27,* 57–62.

Allen, H. F. (1957). Testing visual acuity in preschool children: Norms, variables, and a new picture test. *Pediatrics, 19,* 1093–1100.

American Academy of Pediatrics Committee on Practice and Ambulatory Medicine. (1986). Vision screening and eye examination in children. *Pediatrics, 77,* 918.

Anderson, J. (1986). Sensory intervention with the preterm infant in the neonatal intensive care unit. *American Journal of Occupational Therapy, 40,* 19–26.

Archer, S. M., & Helveston, E. M. (1989). Strabismus and eye movement disorders. In S. J. Isenberg (Ed.), *The eye in infancy* (pp. 215–237). Chicago, IL: Year Book Medical Publisher.

Auslander, M. C., Lewis, D. E., Schulte, L., & Stelmachowicz, P. G. (1991). Localization ability in infants with simulated unilateral hearing loss. *Ear and Hearing, 12*(6), 371–376.

Bailey, I. L., & Hall, A. (1983). *Bailey-Hall Cereal Test for the Measurement of Acuity in Children.* Berkeley, CA: Multimedia Center, School of Optometry, University of California.

Barraga, N. C. (1976). *Visual handicaps and learning: A developmental approach.* Belmont, CA: Wadsworth.

Batshaw, M. L., & Perret, Y. M. (1986). *Children with handicaps: A medical primer.* Baltimore, MD: Paul H. Brookes.

Bayley, N. (1993). *Bayley Scales of Infant Development* (2nd ed.). San Antonio: The Psychological Corp.

Birch, E. E., & Bane, M. C. (1991). Forced-choice preferential looking acuity of children with cortical visual impairment. *Developmental Medicine and Child Neurology, 33,* 722–729.

Brown, S. L., D'Eugenio, D. B., Drews, J. E., Haskin, B. S., Whiteside-Lynch, E., Moersch, M. S., & Rogers, S. J. (1981). *Preschool Developmental Profile.* Ann Arbor, MI: University of Michigan Press.

Cibis, G. W. (1993). Vision testing in infants and children. In G. W. Cibis, A. C. Tongue, & M. L. Stass-Isern (Eds.), *Decision making in pediatric ophthalmology* (pp. 304–305). St. Louis, MO: Mosby–Year Book.

Cibis, G. W., & Fitzgerald, K. (1993). Electrophysiologic acuity testing. In G. W. Cibis, A. C. Tongue, & M. L. Stass-Isern (Eds.), *Decision making in pediatric ophthalmology* (pp. 298–299). St. Louis, MO: Mosby–Year Book.

Cibis, G. W., & Luke, T. P. (1993). Video vision development assessment. In G. W. Cibis, A. C. Tongue, & M. L. Stass-Isern (Eds.), *Decision making in pediatric ophthalmology* (pp. 202–203). St. Louis, MO: Mosby–Year Book.

Cibis, G. W., Tongue, A. C., & Stass-Isern, M. L. (Eds.). (1993). *Decision making in pediatric ophthalmology.* St. Louis, MO: Mosby–Year Book.

Clarkson, R. L., Vohr, B. R., Blackwell, P. M., & White, K. R. (1994). Universal infant hearing screening and intervention: The Rhode Island program. *Infants and Young Children: An Interdisciplinary Journal of Special Care Practices, 6*(3), 65–74.

Cox, L. C. (1988). Screening the high-risk newborn for hearing loss: The Crib-O-Gram v. auditory brainstem response. *Infants and Young Children: An Interdisciplinary Journal of Special Care Practices, 1*(1), 71–81.

Creel, D. J. (1993). Visual evoked response. In G. W. Cibis, A. C. Tongue, & M. L. Stass-Isern (Eds.). *Decision making in pediatric ophthalmology* (pp. 296–297). St. Louis, MO: Mosby–Year Book.

Crouch, E. R., & Kennedy, R. A. (1993). Vision screening guidelines. In G. W. Cibis, A. C. Tongue, & M. L. Stass-Isern (Eds.), *Decision making in pediatric ophthalmology* (pp. 196–197). St. Louis, MO: Mosby–Year Book.

DeGangi, G. A. (1991). Assessment of sensory, emotional, and attentional problems in regulatory disordered infants: Part 1. *Infants and Young Children: An Interdisciplinary Journal of Special Care Practices, 3*(3), 1–8.

DeGangi, G. A., & Greenspan, S. I. (1989). *Test of Sensory Function in Infants.* Los Angeles, CA: Western Psychological Services.

Deitz, S. J., & Ferrell, K. A. (1993). Early services for young children with visual impairment: From diagnosis to comprehensive services. *Infants and Young Children: An Interdisciplinary Journal of Special Care Practices, 6*(1), 68–76.

Downs, M. (1979). *The HEAR-Kit.* Denver, CO: BAM World Markets, Inc.

Duckman, R. H. (1987). Visual problems. In E. T. McDonald (Ed.), *Treating cerebral palsy: For clinicians by clinicians* (pp. 105–131). Austin, TX: PRO-ED, Inc.

Elliott, L., & Katz, D. (1980). *Development of a new children's test of speech discrimination.* St. Louis, MO: Auditec.

Erber, N. P. (1980). Use of the auditory numbers test to evaluate speech perception abilities of hearing-impaired children. *Journal of Speech and Hearing Disorders, 45,* 527–531.

Faye, E. E. (1968). An acuity test for preschool children with subnormal vision. *Journal of Pediatric Ophthalmology, 5,* 210–212.

Finitzo-Hieber, T., Gerling, I. J., & Matkin, N. D. (1980). A sound effects recognition test for the pediatric audiologic evaluation. *Ear and Hearing, 1,* 271–275.

Flexor, C., & Gans, D. P. (1985). Comparative evaluation of the auditory responsiveness of normal infants and profoundly multihandicapped children. *Journal of Speech and Hearing Research, 28,* 163–168.

Fraiberg, S. (1977). *Insights from the blind.* New York: Basic Books.

France, T. D. (1989). Amblyopia. In S. J. Isenberg (Ed.), *The eye in infancy* (pp. 100–109). Chicago, IL: Year Book Medical Publisher.

Friendly, D. S. (1989). Visual acuity assessment of the preverbal patient. In S. J. Isenberg (Ed.), *The eye in infancy* (pp. 48–56). Chicago, IL: Year Book Medical Publisher.

Fulton, A. B. (1989). Testing of the possibly blind child. In S. J. Isenberg (Ed.), *The eye in infancy* (pp. 485–491). Chicago, IL: Year Book Medical Publisher.

Furuno, S., O'Reilly, K. A., Hosaka, C. M., Inatsuka, T. T., Zeisloft-Falbey, B., & Allman, T. (1988). *Hawaii Early Learning Profile (HELP).* Palo Alto, CA: VORT Corp.

Gans, D. P. (1987). Improving behavioral observation audiometry testing and scoring problems. *Ear and Hearing, 8,* 92–99.

Glass, P. (1993). Development of visual function in preterm infants: Implications for early intervention. *Infants and Young Children: An Interdisciplinary Journal of Special Care Practices,* 6(1), 11–20.

Goetz, L., Utley, B., Gee, K., Baldwin, M., & Sailor, W. (no date). *Auditory assessment and program manual for severely handicapped deaf-blind students.* Parsons, KS: Words & Pictures Corporation.

Greenwald, M. J. (1983). Visual development in infancy and childhood. *The Pediatric Clinics of North America, 30,* 977–993.

Haeussermann, E. (1958). *Developmental potential of preschool children.* New York: Grune and Stratton.

Hayes, D. (1986). Audiological assessment. In D. L. Wodrich and J. E. Joy (Eds.), *Multidisciplinary assessment of children with learning disabilities and mental retardation* (pp. 109–131). Baltimore, MD: Paul H. Brookes.

Hodgson, W. R. (1985). Testing infants and young children. In J. Katz (Ed.), *Handbook of clinical audiology* (3rd ed.) (pp. 650–656). Baltimore, MD: Williams and Wilkins.

Holt, K. S., & Reynell, J. K. (1967). *Assessment of cerebral palsy* (Vol. II). London: Lloyd Duke, Ltd.

Hyvarinen, L . (1988). *Vision in children: Normal and abnormal.* Meaford, Ontario, Canada: Canadian Deaf-Blind & Rubella Association.

Hyvarinen, L . (1992). *The L. H. Symbol Tests: A system for vision testing in children.* Long Island City, NY: The Lighthouse, Inc.

Hyvarinen, L., & Lindstedt, E. (1981). *Assessment of vision in children.* Stockholm: SRF Tal & Punkt.

Isenberg, S. J. (1989). Examination methods. In S. J. Isenberg (Ed.), *The eye in infancy* (pp. 57–68). Chicago, IL: Year Book Medical Publisher.

Jan, J. E., Skyanda, A., & Groenveld, M. (1990). Habilitation and rehabilitation of visually impaired and blind children. *Pediatrician, 17,* 202–207.

Jan, J. E., Skyanda, A., Groenveld, M., & Hoyt, C. S. (1987). Behavioural characteristics of children with permanent cortical visual impairment. *Developmental Medicine and Child Neurology, 29,* 571–576.

Jerger, J. (Ed.). (1984). *Pediatric audiology.* San Diego, CA: College Hill Press.

Jerger, S., Lewis, S., & Hawkins, J. (1980). Pediatric speech intelligibility test: I. Generation of test materials. *International Journal of Pediatric Otorhinolaryngology, 2,* 217–230.

Joint Committee on Infant Hearing (1991). 1990 position statement. *ASHA, 33,* 3–6.

Johnson-Martin, N., Jens, K. G., Attermeier, S. M., & Hacker, B. J. (1991). *The Carolina Curriculum for Infants and Toddlers with Special Needs* (2nd ed.). Baltimore, MD: Paul H. Brookes.

Jose, R. T., Smith, A. J., & Shane, K. G. (1980). Evaluating and stimulating vision in the multiply impaired. *Journal of Visual Impairment and Blindness, 74,* 2–8.

Kivlin, J. D. (1989). Systemic disorders and the eye. In S. J. Isenberg (Ed.), *The eye in infancy* (pp. 459–484). Chicago, IL: Year Book Medical Publisher.

Kramer, S. J., & Williams, D. R. (1993). The hearing-impaired infant and toddler: Identification, assessment, and intervention. *Infants and Young Children: An Interdisciplinary Journal of Special Care Practices,* 6(1), 35–49.

Kukla, D., & Connolly, T. T. (1978). *Assessment of auditory functioning of deaf-blind multihandicapped children.* Dallas, TX: South Central Regional Center for Services to Deaf-Blind Children.

Langley, M. B. (1980). *Functional vision inventory for the multiply and severely handicapped.* Chicago, IL: Stoelting.

Langley, M. B. (1986). Psychoeducational assessment of visually impaired students with additional handicaps. In D. Ellis (Ed.), *Sensory handicaps in mentally handicapped people* (pp. 253–296). London, England: Croom Helm, Ltd.

Langley, M. B. (in press). *Individualized, systematic assessment of visual efficiency (ISAVE).* Louisville, KY: American Printing House for the Blind.

Langley, M. B., & Dubose, R. (1976). Functional vision screening for the severely handicapped. *New Outlook for the Blind, 70,* 346–350.

Lippmann, O. (1969). Vision of young children. *Archives of Ophthalmology, 81,* 763–775.

Madell, J. R. (1988). Identification and treatment of very young children with hearing loss. *Infants and Young Children: An Interdisciplinary Journal of Special Care Practices, 1*(2), 20–30.

Martin, F. N., & Gravel, K. L. (1989). Pediatric audiologic practices in the United States. *The Hearing Journal, 42*(8), 33–48.

Miller, K. M. (1993). Poor vision in childhood. In G. W. Cibis, A. C. Tongue, & M. L. Stass-Isern (Eds.), *Decision making in pediatric ophthalmology* (pp. 178–179). St. Louis, MO: Mosby–Year Book.

Miller, L. J. (1982). *Miller Assessment for Preschoolers.* Littleton, CO: Foundation for Knowledge in Development.

Moore, J. M., Thompson, G., & Folsom, R. C. (1992). Auditory responsiveness of premature infants utilizing visual reinforcement audiometry (VRA). *Ear and Hearing, 13*(3), 187–193.

Moore, J. M., Thompson, G., & Thompson, M. (1975). Auditory localization of infants as a function of reinforcement conditions. *Journal of Speech and Hearing Disorders, 40,* 29–34.

Morse, A. R., & Trief, E. (1985). Diagnosis and evaluation of visual dysfunction in premature infants with low birth weight. *Journal of Visual Impairment and Blindness, 79,* 248–251.

Morse, A. R., Trief, E., & Joseph, J. (1987). Vision screening: A study of 297 Head Start children. *Journal of Visual Impairment and Blindness, 81,* 200–203.

Nelson, L. B., Rubin, S. E., Wagner, R. S., & Breton, M. E. (1984). Developmental aspects in the assessment of visual function in young children. *Pediatrics, 73,* 375–380.

Northern, J. L. (1978). Impedance screening in special populations: State of the art. In E. R. Harford, F. H. Bess, C. D. Bluestone, (Eds.), *Impedance Screening for Middle Ear Disease in Children.* New York: Grune and Stratton.

Northern, J. L. (1980). Acoustic impedance measures in the Down's population. *Seminars in Speech, Language, and Hearing, 1,* 81–86.

Northern, J. L., & Downs, M. P. (1991). *Hearing in children* (4th ed.). Baltimore, MD: Williams and Wilkins.

Orelove, F. P., & Sobsey, D. (1987). *Educating children with multiple disabilities: A transdisciplinary approach.* Baltimore, MD: Paul H. Brookes.

Pagon, R. A., & Disteche, A. (1989). Chromosome abnormalities. In S. J. Isenberg (Ed.), *The eye in infancy* (pp. 127–143). Chicago, IL: Year Book Medical Publisher.

Patterson, J. H. (1980). *Vision screening techniques.* Anchorage, AK: The Print Shop.

Porter, R. (1984). Sensory considerations in handling techniques. In B. H. Connolly & P. C. Montgomery (Eds.), *Therapeutic exercise in developmental disabilities* (pp. 43–53). Chattanooga, TN: Chattanooga Corporation.

Romano, P. E. (1990). Vision/eye screening: Test twice and refer once. *Pediatric Annals, 19,* 359–367.

Roush, J. (1990). Acoustic amplification for hearing-impaired infants and young children. *Infants and Young Children: An Interdisciplinary Journal of Special Care Practices, 2*(4), 59–71.

Royeen, C. B. (1986). Development of a touch scale for measuring tactile defensiveness in children. *American Journal of Occupational Therapy, 40*(6), 414–419.

Royeen, C. B. (1987). TIP—Touch inventory for preschoolers: A pilot study. *Physical and Occupational Therapy in Pediatrics, 7*(1), 29–41.

Schopler, E., Reichler, R. J., Bashford, A., Lansing, M. D., & Marcus, L. M. (1990). *Psychoeducational Profile—Revised (PEP-R).* Austin, TX: PRO-ED.

Sears, C. J. (1994). Recognizing and coping with tactile defensiveness in young children. *Infants and Young Children: An Interdisciplinary Journal of Special Care Practices, 6,* 47–53.

Sheridan, M. (1960). Vision screening of very young or handicapped children. *British Medical Journal, 51,* 453–456.

Sheridan, M. (1969). The development of vision, hearing, and communication in babies and young children. *Procedures of the Royal Society of Medicine, 62,* 999–1004.

Sheridan, M. (1973). *The STYCAR Test of Vision.* Windsor, Berks, England: NFER Publishing Co., Ltd.

Siegenthaler, B. M. (1987). Auditory problems. In E. T. McDonald (Ed.), *Treating cerebral palsy: For clinicians by clinicians* (pp. 85–103). Austin, TX: PRO-ED.

Smith, A., & Cote, K. S. (1982). *Look at me: A resource manual for the development of resid-*

ual vision in multiply impaired children. Philadelphia, PA: Pennsylvania College of Optometry Press.

Sonksen, P. (1983). The assessment of vision for development in severely visually handicapped babies. *Acta Ophthalmologica* (Copenhagen) *157,* 82–90.

Sonksen, P. M., & Macrae, A. J. (1987). Vision for colored pictures at different acuities: The Sonksen picture guide to visual function. *Developmental Medicine and Child Neurology, 29,* 337–347.

Sonksen, P. M., Petrie, A., & Drew, K. J. (1991). Promotion of visual development of severely visually impaired babies: Evaluation of a developmentally based programme. *Developmental Medicine and Child Neurology, 33,* 320–335.

Stangler, S. R., Huber, C. J., & Routh, D. K. (1980). *Screening growth and development of preschool children: A guide for test selection* (pp. 213–268). New York: McGraw-Hill.

Teller, D. Y. (1979). The forced choice preferential looking procedure: A psychophysical technique for use with human infants. *Infant Behavior and Development, 2,* 135–153.

Thompson, G., & Folsom, R. (1981). Hearing assessment of at-risk infants. *Clinical Pediatrics, 20*(4), 257–261.

Thompson, G., Thompson, M., & McCall, A. (1992). Strategies for increasing response behavior of 1- and 2-year-old children during visual reinforcement audiometry (VRA). *Ear and Hearing, 13*(4), 236–240.

Trief, E., & Morse, A. R. (1987). An overview of preschool vision screening. *Journal of Visual Impairment and Blindness, 81,* 197–199.

Vaughan, D., Asbury, T., & Tabbara, K. F. (1989). *General ophthalmology* (12th ed.). East Norwalk, CT: Lange Medical Publications.

Vulpé, S. G. (1979). *Vulpé Assessment Battery.* Toronto, Ontario: National Institute on Mental Retardation.

Wilson, W, R., & Thompson, G. (1984). Behavioral audiometry. In J. Jerger (Ed.), *Pediatric audiometry* (pp. 1–44). San Diego, CA: College Hill Press.

CHAPTER

7

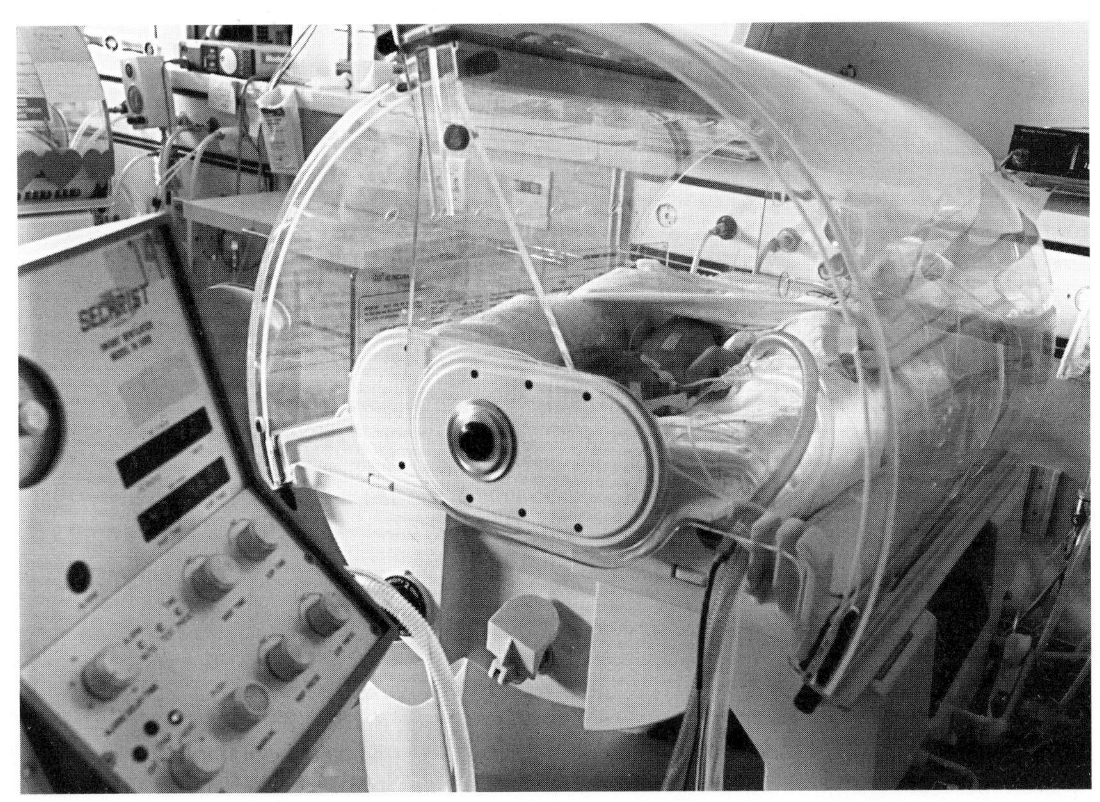

Neurobehavioral Assessment of the Newborn Infant

Karen J. O'Donnell
Duke University Medical Center

The neurobehavioral assessment of the newborn infant was introduced to the field of child development over two decades ago. The developmental examination of the newborn is now nearly ubiquitous in training programs and in the practice of early intervention. Although the major constructs used in newborn neurobehavioral assessment have their roots in developmental neurology and pediatrics, their understanding is critical to the conduct of early intervention. Newborn assessment is important in early childhood research, establishing models for intervention, and evaluating the effectiveness of intervention approaches.

This chapter describes the history and the current status of the behavioral assessment of the human neonate. It is written for early intervention personnel who are consumers of test information on neonates and for those who are interested in obtaining further training in neonatal settings. The chapter serves primarily as a broad introduction to the major constructs and strategies involved in assessing a newborn; a secondary goal is to place neonatal assessment in its historical and contemporary context. Newborn assessment is presented as a highly specialized area and not a downward extension of preschool and school-age educational testing. For that reason, some attention is given to the medical and psychological origins of the exams, suggesting that only with the integration of the developmental behavior of the young infant with medical and psychological information is very early intervention feasible and responsible.

The chapter is organized into six sections. A rationale for and various approaches to evaluating the newborn are introduced, and the historical roots of current assessment strategies are reviewed. Dimensions important in evaluating newborns are described: the infant's status and aspects of the physical and social environment. Procedural guidelines for good clinical practice in the assessment of the newborn infant are identified, including the needed prerequisites of training and experiences with newborn infants. Descriptions of several commonly used newborn assessments are included. Briefly, approaches to translating assessment data into interventions for the infant and family are noted.

RATIONALE

Consider the following infants for whom *neurobehavioral assessment* could provide an important contribution to their care.

....

Baby Boy Brown is in an isolette in the neonatal intensive care unit (NICU) of the hospital. At present, he is at 37 weeks postconception, having been born at 32 weeks of gestation. The infant is recovering from the respiratory illness that often occurs in premature infants. He is doing well, feeding from a nipple, and not receiving supplemental oxygen. After 2 days of adjusting to an open crib in the nursery, discharge to home is planned. As a developmental specialist in the nursery, you are asked to evaluate Baby Brown and to provide information about him to his physicians, his parents, and to the community early intervention program. Primary questions for the assessment include his current behavioral and developmental status, needs for follow-up assessments, and specific needs for caregiver interventions that support further recovery and an optimal developmental outcome. How would you go about this? Or, if you were the educational specialist in the early intervention program, how would you utilize the assessment information provided by the developmental specialist from the nursery?

....

Baby Girl Lucas, on the other hand, is the full-term newborn daughter of a young girl in the alternative high school program for teenage parents. Baby Lucas and her mother are preparing to go home from the hospital, to the mother's parents' home. The mother's teachers have been concerned about her interest in the infant and about her hints that she is afraid to care for the baby. The mother and infant have been referred to your early intervention program, and you would like to use newborn assessment techniques as an intervention to demonstrate to the mother her infant's behavioral capabilities. Your goal is to help the mother see her daughter as a unique person and to facilitate her awareness of the infant's needs and her ability to respond to them. What are some of the dimensions of the infant's behavior that can be observed and used in the intervention?

▪ ▪ ▪ ▪ ▪ ▪ ▪ ▪

Baby Boy Mitchell is also in the NICU. At 30 weeks postconception, he still requires supplemental oxygen delivered by mechanical ventilation. His medical caregivers are concerned because he is so restless and irritable that adequate mechanical ventilation is very difficult. As a clinician trained in the behavioral assessment of the newborn, you are in a position to evaluate this infant to assist his nurses and physicians with strategies for calming him and for providing environmental support for improved respiratory functioning. What can you observe about this infant's behavior that provides information about his responses to stress and what he needs from caregivers for support? How can you accomplish this support without additional handling (and irritation) of this fragile infant?

▪ ▪ ▪ ▪ ▪ ▪ ▪ ▪

Baby Girl Curtis is a one-day-old infant in the Newborn Nursery about whom the nurses are concerned because of maternal HIV (Human Immunodeficiency Virus) infection and the infant's prenatal exposure to her mother's illicit drug use. The newborn's blood has been drawn for HIV viral culture testing to determine her infection status. Her medical providers are asking you for any neurodevelopmental indicators of central nervous system (CNS) injury that could be consistent with HIV infection. In addition, the newborn is described by the nurses as hard to calm and difficult to feed. The staff wants to know if her behavioral disorganization is secondary to drug withdrawal or developmental injury from drug exposure. Developmental interventions for the nursing staff and for the mother and family are requested.

▪ ▪ ▪ ▪ ▪ ▪ ▪ ▪

These infants represent four opportunities for the evaluation of a newborn infant or the use of information from a behavioral assessment for intervention. The four assessments likely will have much in common; they will address the infants' neurological integrity, behavioral organization and needs, and individual personalities or temperament. The assessments also will differ. The infants are at different chronological (postconception) ages with different medical conditions creating their developmental risk.

As is implied in the examples, particularly Baby Lucas, the newborn infant can be assessed to describe the individuality of the infant and his or her contribution to the critical beginnings of relationships with caregivers. The assessment can provide the basis for intervention with the caregiving system before patterns of behavior, expectations, and attributions are well established. In this way, the assessment can be used to enhance the parents' understanding of the infant as an individual and to underline their mutual influences.

As with Babies Brown and Curtis, neonatal assessment also is used to provide an index of neurological integrity and developmental status. It can be used to determine needs for follow-up assessments or intervention programs and to provide a baseline from which to assess behavioral recovery from a biomedical event or condition (e.g., birth asphyxia, very low birthweight). For Baby Curtis, the neurodevelopmental assessment can also contribute an important piece of information for HIV diagnosis. Although ultimately the diagnosis is based on viral cultures or on a technique of identifying the presence of the HIV genome, a finding of neurodevelopmental abnormalities in the newborn can be suggestive of the encephalopathy secondary to HIV injury in the central nervous system.

Baby Mitchell's newborn assessment can result in strategies to determine his needs for physiological support from the environment (e.g., "How, when, how much to touch fragile preterm infants" [Gorski, 1984]), to design a physical and social environment supportive of his fragile and developing respiratory and central nervous systems. Newborn infants also are systematically evaluated to research the effects of a specific biomedical event or process on behavioral organization and development or to evaluate the effects of medical or environmental intervention strategies on the infant. In other words, there is a wide range of reasons to assess a newborn infant and more than one approach to doing so.

The professional's understanding of the historical context of neonatal assessment is important to the use and application of contemporary methodologies, particularly given that neonatal assessment did not develop from an educational tradition. For this reason, the origins of specific components of contemporary methods of neonatal assessment are reviewed. Figure 7.1 depicits a preterm infant being assessed in an isolette in an NICU setting.

HISTORICAL PERSPECTIVE

The assessment of the newborn infant is often associated with the Neonatal Behavioral Assessment Scale (NBAS) (Brazelton, 1973, 1984). In fact, the introduction of the NBAS marked a wave of interest in the behavioral status of the newborn for clinicians and researchers concerned with early development. Its popularization heightened awareness of the newborn's behavioral capabilities and individual differences, including but extending beyond the traditional focus on neurological reflexes. This heightened awareness led the way to a burgeoning of literature on early infant development, focusing on the importance of and strategies for assessment.

Trends in current assessment techniques, such as the NBAS, are apparent in the works of various clinicians and researchers throughout the 20th century. It is difficult to identify a single clinical or research tradition that led to the current state of newborn assessment, however. As pointed out in St. Clair's (1978) review of neonatal assessment, newborns have been tested from different perspectives by different disciplines, often attempting to measure different basic constructs seen as important in the behavior of the newborn. Indeed, it can be said that the currently popular assessments of the newborn (e.g., Brazelton, 1984; Als, Lester, Tronick, & Brazelton, 1982; Dubowitz & Dubowitz, 1981) involve the logical integration of disparate historical traditions. Three of these traditions are described below with emphasis on their relevance to current assessment approaches: developmental neurology, behavioral pediatrics, and developmental psychology.

Contributions from Developmental Neurology

One major component of the behavioral assessment of the newborn infant is rooted in the tradition of neurological assessment, with emphasis on evaluating reflexes. The first identified reflex, the papillary reflex, is credited to Magitat in 1903 (St. Clair, 1978); Moro described the well-known startle reflex in 1918 (St. Clair, 1978). There was no comprehensive

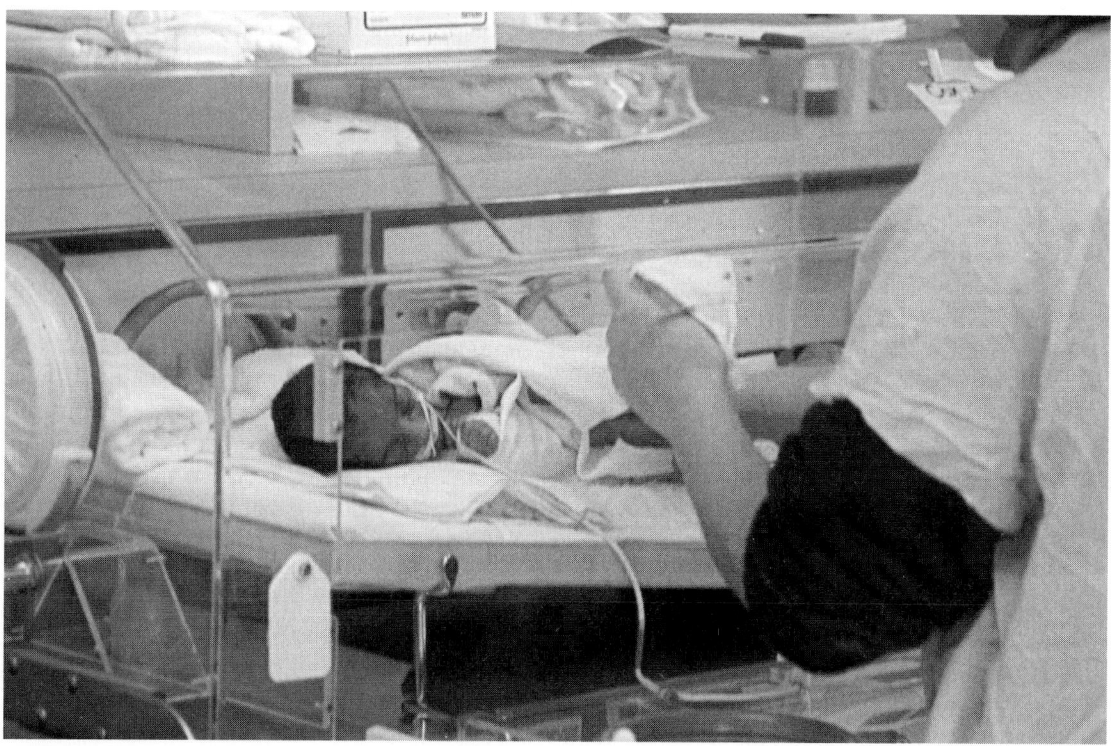

FIGURE 7.1
Preterm infant being examined in an isolette
Source: Used with permission of James M. Helm.

description of infant reflexes until the late 1920s, however.

The works of several European developmental neurologists, in particular, mark the evolution of hypotheses about infant neurological development and about strategies for examining the developmental level or integrity of the newborn's CNS by observing and eliciting reflex behavior. In a review of the contributions of four of these individuals (Peiper, André-Thomas, Saint Anne-Dargassies, and Prechtl), Parmelee (1962) outlined developmental neurology's early contributions to neonatal behavioral assessment.

Albrecht Peiper (1928) provided the first comprehensive description of reflex behavior in the human infant. This German neurologist drew substantially from the work of Magnus (e.g., 1924), a neurologist in Holland who documented the persistent asymmetric tonic neck reflex (ATNR) as well as other obligatory movement patterns in adults with brain injuries. Magnus hypothesized that the same reflexes are present in the human newborn and disappear with the development of higher brain centers.

Peiper, then, studied the reflex behavior of the human newborn and young infant as an index of brain development. He devised a scheme for observing the newborn's control of posture and movement, demonstrating that innate newborn postural responses disappear as the CNS matures. Peiper did not develop a systematic assessment for diagnosing neurological difficulties in the newborn, and he made no attempt to correlate his observations about stages of neurobehavioral development with chronological age. With Isbert (Peiper & Isbert, 1927), he did provide a model for changes in infant posture and movement over development.

In France, André-Thomas and his colleagues also were studying newborn movement patterns as an index of development and as it related to the integrity of the CNS. This group is given credit for the first systematic neurological examination for the neonate (André-Thomas, Chesni, & Saint Anne-Dargassies, 1960; Saint Anne-Dargassies, 1960). André-Thomas's major interest was in the primary reflexes, not the postural responses that had intrigued Magnus and Peiper. They studied the Moro reflex (the startle), the rooting reflex, automatic walking, incurvation of the spine, and the grasp reflex. They hypothesized that the primary reflexes would decrease in intensity over the first 3 months of life and become integrated into voluntary movement patterns.

Several of André-Thomas's contributions can be found in contemporary strategies used for newborn assessment. He approached the assessment of the newborn by observing spontaneous movement, eliciting reflexes, and assessing the extent to which developmentally less mature reactions were still present in movement. He compared different parts of the body in terms of movement patterns and muscle tone, introducing the concepts of active (in spontaneous movement) versus passive (when manipulated by an examiner) muscle tone and "extensibility" (i.e., degree of increased muscle tone; spasticity) versus "flaccidity" (i.e., low muscle tone; hypotonia). André-Thomas's observations extended beyond posture and movement; he suggested that even newborn infant behavior is "governed by affect" (André-Thomas, 1959) and that the full-term newborn's behavior is well organized. With his student Saint Anne-Dargassies, he published two texts on neonatal neurology and assessment (André-Thomas & Saint Anne-Dargassies, 1952; André-Thomas, Chesni, & Saint Anne-Dargassies, 1960).

Saint Anne-Dargassies made several of her own contributions to the neurobehavioral assessment of the newborn. She studied the prognostic value of André-Thomas's assessment techniques and found fairly successful prediction of abnormal development at 2 years (1965). She also examined neurobehavioral differences between preterm and full-term infants and found that the behavior of preterm infants came closer to that of full-term infants as they approached 40 weeks postconceptional age (Saint Anne-Dargassies, 1955, 1957). She proposed a developmental scale for evaluating the preterm infant prior to term age; the exam focuses on muscle tone, primary reflexes, and the infant's general adaptive ability.

Saint Anne-Dargassies's assessment of the newborn begins with the close observation of the undisturbed infant's behavior, attending to the infant's *autonomic stability* (e.g., respiratory regularity, temperature control), *motor status* (movement and posture), and *state organization* (i.e., control over level of arousal). Examiner manipulations include testing visual responses, muscle tone, and primary reflexes. Repeated exams and the importance of the persistence of abnormal responses in indicating neurological dysfunction are emphasized. Dargassies's exam was designed specifically to differentiate brain-injured infants from non-brain-injured infants by the presence or absence of expected or abnormal responses.

Heinz Prechtl was born and trained medically in Austria and did most of his work in the Netherlands. His aim was to develop an evaluation of the newborn to use in studying the effects of various obstetric conditions. Prechtl also trained in ethology with Konrad Lorenz, and his approach emphasizes more subtle aspects of movement than its predecessors, such as close attention to the symmetry of motor responses. Prechtl's exam (1977; Prechtl & Beintema, 1964) was first in this tradition to be well conceptualized and well standardized and to have well-defined scoring. He emphasized the importance of the physical environment and the infant's posture and state to responses to test items.

The Prechtl and Beintema exam (1964) has two parts. The examiner first observes the infant's state of arousal, posture, movements, skin color, and respiratory regularity. Then the exam moves to the elicitation of reflexes and to other examiner maneuvers. Behavioral state is seen as very important to the infant's responses and, therefore, to the timing of examiner maneuvers. Brazelton (1973) utilized this organizing concept of state in the development of the NBAS. In 1977, a 10-minute screening version of the Prechtl exam was developed for use in clinical practice. No well-designed, specific studies of the exam's reliability and validity are reported, but examples of use of the assessment with infants with prenatal or perinatal complications versus normal infants can be found elsewhere (e.g., Prechtl, 1965).

Paine (1960, 1961) was one of the first American physicians to develop a neurological examination for infants and young children. The exam includes tests of neuromotor behavior (e.g., muscle tone, primitive reflexes, deep tendon reflexes), sensory abilities, the cranial nerves, and speech and mental state. Relevant to current neonatal assessment strategies, Paine described several methods for assessing muscle tone, including resistance to movement (similar to Brazelton's passive movement items) and muscle palpation (examining by touch).

Other neurological exams for the newborn and young infant, most notably that of Amiel-Tison and Grenier (1983), have emerged. Multidisciplinary approaches to the clinical care of infants has resulted in the inclusion of more behavioral test items, such as the assessment of responses to visual and auditory stimuli. These neurologically based exams have in common the view that infant behavior is an index of neurological status and that the maturation of the CNS results in behavioral change (DiLeo, 1967).

The historical focus of developmental neurologists, by and large, was the identification of gross brain dysfunction by the assessment of movement and reflexes. Few studies tested which reflexes or responses individually or in combination were most predictive of brain damage. In many cases, the meaning of the presence or absence of a particular response is not clear; many authors have indicated that the neurological examination does not, by itself, capture the sum of infant behavioral organization. Although there are hints of interest in the newborn's sensory capabilities and overall organizational competence, the exams are not focused in this way. No substantive attempts have been made to assess behavioral capabilities and individual differences in infant attention and responses to social stimuli. The neurological examination, by itself, does not reflect a model of development that includes the contribution of the caregiving context to infant behavior and development.

Contributions from Behavioral Pediatrics

In his text, *The Development of the Infant and Young Child,* Illingworth (1960) credits Charles Darwin with the first major attempt to document the sequence of development in a child. Darwin described in detail the developmental milestones of 1 of his 10 children, perhaps marking the beginning of significant public and scientific interest in the nature of growth and change in early childhood.

More known for his pioneering work in this area is Arnold Gesell. His work, first published in 1925, represents his several decades of observing and documenting developmental milestones for the first 5 years of life and developing a system for the diagnosis of developmental delay. Gesell's group focused initially on the first year of life (see Gesell & Thompson, 1938). Subsequently, they provided developmental schedules over the preschool years (Gesell, 1940). Gesell's view of early development is a maturational one: "The environment inflects preliminary patterns; it determines the occasion, the intensity, and the correlation of many aspects of behavior; but it does not engender the basic progressions of behavior development. These are determined by inherent, maturational mechanisms" (p. 13). His focus, then, was the age-related sequence of developmental change across infants.

Gesell's contribution to newborn assessment lies largely in the developmental norms, established on a large group of children seen monthly, beginning at 4 weeks of age. The work was expanded by his colleagues (e.g., Knobloch, Stevens, & Malone, 1980) and others (e.g., Bayley, 1969, 1993) to include markers of development status in newborn behavior. In the most recent revision of the Gesell scales (Knobloch et al., 1980) newborn assessment includes observations of posture and movement (e.g., the ATNR, hands being predominantly fisted versus open, right head-turning preference), visual responses to a red ring, and responses to animate (the examiner's voice) and inanimate (a rattle) auditory stimuli. The revision includes normative data on many more subjects than did the original; these authors view the work as less maturation-based than did Gesell, stressing the social context in which developmental change occurs.

The most widely used developmental assessment and screening tools today draw heavily on the Gesell schedules, in particular the Bayley Scales of Infant Development (Bayley, 1969, 1993) and the Denver Developmental Screening Test (DDST) (Frankenburg & Dodds, 1967; Frankenburg et al., 1990). Current strategies for newborn assessment include, to a limited extent, the developmental norm approach, especially in the examination of visual and auditory responses to animate and inanimate stimuli.

The Contribution of Developmental Psychology

Contemporary approaches to newborn assessment are seen as more complex than the mere addition of age-normed milestones to neurological assessment. Recent approaches reflect evolving models for understanding human development found primarily in the fields of psychology and education. In several of her papers, Als (e.g., Als et al., 1982) traces the theoretical underpinnings of behavioral assessment from developmental psychology; her work is a substantial attempt to reconcile notions about developmental processes with the manner in which development and behavior are assessed. Theoretical assumptions about human development are complex in terms of both determinants and mechanisms. The importance of the caregiving context and the transactional nature of the infant and context relationship are emphasized (Sameroff & Chandler, 1975). Principles of development derived from current models are summarized here; they are seen as central to understanding newborn behavior and being able to attach meaning to assessment findings. The three principles are (1) development is hierarchical; (2) development is dialectical; and (3) development is teleological.

Development is hierarchical Development has order, steps, or stages; there is mutual dependence from one step or stage to the others. Each step or developmental task is seen as more complex than the preceding one because it incorporates the preceding one. The hierarchical notion is well known in developmental psychology from Piaget's (see Ginsburg & Opper, 1969) descriptions of stages in cognitive development.

Relevant to the newborn, Als and colleagues (1982), for example, define the infant's development as a hierarchy of tasks or as developing *behavioral subsystems* of overall organization. The developing subsystems are identified, in order, as physiological stability and autonomic control; freedom and control in movement; differentiation of and control over states of arousal; social interactive competence through attention and response to social stimuli; and *self-regulation,* that is, the ability to manage complex environmental demands with minimal expense to lower subsystems.

For an infant like Baby Brown, overall developmental status is assessed not only by indicators of individual subsystems but also by the way in which each subsystem affects the others. He may, for example, have achieved physiological stability but still be struggling to control movements in his arms and legs when he is placed on his back. Incomplete development in the motor area, then, may compromise the development of well-defined states of arousal and responses to social stimuli.

Development is dialectical Sameroff (1983) offers one of the best descriptions of the dialectic in development. In brief, this principle assumes that at each developmental step or stage and with each developmental task, the achievement and its integration into overall functioning is subject to the relationship between the infant and the context or environment in which development occurs. Descriptions of the dialectic in development can be found at the level of the cell (e.g., Palay, 1979; cf. Als et al., 1982) and at the level of the family or community (e.g., O'Donnell, 1986). The assumption involves more than a simple interaction; the infant and the physical and social context are seen in mutual, ongoing transactions, each contributing to change in the other and in itself through the transaction.

This view of development suggests a different meaning for the assessment of the newborn than did that of Gesell, for example, who viewed test responses as reflecting maturation or the interruption of maturation by brain damage. In contrast, Als's *synactive model* (e.g., Als, 1986) incorporates the assumption of a hierarchy of subsystem development with the notion that the subsystems develop through transactions with one another and with the environment. In other words, newborns bring behavior patterns to their experiences, affecting those experiences, which in turn influence infants' behavior patterns.

Baby Lucas and her mother offer a good example of the dialectic principle, that is, that the behavior of each is shaped by the other in an ongoing manner. If the infant should begin her life as active and difficult to console, the mother's low self-confidence might be reinforced. If she then feels helpless in calming her infant and withdraws, the infant is deprived of the environmental support that would help her increase overall behavioral organization. The infant may become more disorganized and unresponsive, further exacerbating the young mother's despair and withdrawal.

Development is teleological Teleology is the view that developmental changes are pushed not only by the mechanical forces of maturation but by movement toward certain goals. It is suggested that the view of the human infant as developing in a hierarchical and dialectical manner carries with it the notion of direction. Infant development is seen as progressing from diffuse, general functioning to the differentiation of specialized components of behavior to an organization of these components into a system that functions as a whole. Teleological assumptions are not new to newborn development and assessment. Werner (1957), for example, indicated that all development moves from globality to increased differentiation and hierarchical integration. The principle is particularly helpful in newborn assessment, however, in developing a model for the infant's current status and needs for future developmental progress.

Baby Mitchell, the very young sick infant in the previous examples, may be so vulnerable to the stimulation in the nursery because of his "all or nothing" responses to touch, light, or sound. In other words, stress for this infant may result in decreased physiological stability, motor disorganization, and irritability. As he recovers and matures, with the help of a supportive caregiving environment, we expect that these subsystems of behavior will become increasingly differentiated and subsequently will provide the foundation for organized behavioral responses.

In summary, these three assumptions underpin many of the current techniques for the assessment of the newborn. Assessment is seen as an opportunity for the examiner and the infant to act out the dialectic between the infant and the caregiving context. Tests are constructed, using many items from traditional age-norm and neurological approaches, to elicit from the infant indicators of current functioning and individual responses to and needs from the environment. The meaning of the assessment lies in the ability to generalize beyond the assessment itself to the infant's current status and needs and in anticipation of future development.

DIMENSIONS OF ASSESSMENT

The domain of neonatal assessment is infant behavior. Neonatal testing makes the assumption that infant behavior is meaningful and that it is organized. The question of how behavior is organized has been answered in different ways; tests have been constructed to reflect different models. In newborn neurological examinations, behavior is seen as having meaning for the integrity of the CNS; the presence or absence of specific reflexes and reactions indicates the presence or absence of brain damage. Therefore, test evaluation studies focus on the neurological examination's prediction of a subsequent normal versus abnormal diagnosis. Similarly, assessment of the newborn and young infant on a developmental schedule is based on the assumption that behavior has meaning for the child's maturity, for whether or not the child is delayed or comparable to same-aged children in the normative group.

Contemporary approaches to the assessment of the newborn combine test items from the neurological and age-norm approaches, but they define meaning in the infant's behavior in a very different way. The infant's behavior is seen as having meaning not only about the infant but also about the physical and social context and the transactions between infant and context. Contemporary developmental theories suggest, then, that assessment should address the child, the environment, and transactions between child and the caregiving context. Clinicians and researchers using infant assessments struggle with these complexities in the assessment task, especially with test evaluation concepts like reliability and validity.

Several commonly used instruments focus primarily on the infant's status. The theoretical perspective may include the importance of the context, but the assessment is directed to the infant and his or her behavior at a single point in time. There also are well-known examinations of the newborn that attempt to capture the dialectic between infant behavior and context. These authors emphasize that the infant's response is subject to his or her biologic status, behavior organizational agenda, and support or disruption from the context. Finally, there are assessment strategies designed to evaluate the developmental context primarily. Several dimensions of the physical and social context have been explored with the goal of identifying more or less optimal environments for an individual infant.

Dimensions of Infant Behavior

Neonatal assessment can be seen as addressing three broad dimensions of infant behavior: neurological integrity, behavioral organization, and individual differences or temperament. These are seen as major constructs of concern to the clinician or researcher; assessment is the task of identifying qualitative and quantitative indicators of the abstract constructs.

One of the early uses of neonatal assessment was for the identification of the brain-damaged infant. This focus is still a major area of concern, with the infant's behavior providing information about CNS functioning. Indicators of neurological integrity include reflexes and postural responses, skill achievement on a developmental schedule, and behavioral organization congruent with gestational age. Unfortunately, the infant's performance on any of these areas can be difficult to interpret. Poor performance can represent a transient process in the brain (e.g., recovery from swelling); good performance could mask an insult not yet evident in behavior. For this reason, it is generally recommended that there be repeated assessments and identification of a pattern of an infant's performance over time (Brazelton, 1973). For example, neurobehavioral changes in an asphyxiated (i.e., lack of oxygen at birth) newborn over the first 7 to 14 days of life likely provide more information about subsequent prognosis than any single exam. For an infant being followed for the possibility of developing hydrocephalus (i.e., enlarged ventricles due to poor drainage of cerebrospinal fluid), changes in behavior can support other indicators of a nonoptimal process. Neurobehavioral status is only one indicator of brain injury, and these data are best combined with information about neurostructural change using brain imaging techniques (e.g., brain CT scans, magnetic resonance imaging) and assessments of neurological functioning (e.g., EEG, brain-stem-evoked potential testing).

Beyond the concern of brain injury versus no brain injury are more complex questions about the behavioral organization of the newborn infant. The full-term, healthy newborn is seen as a competent individual with the abilities to attend and respond in social interactions as well as to influence those interactions (Brazelton, 1973, 1984). This level of competence is based on well-organized and coordinated behavioral subsystems (Als et al., 1982). That is, for a newborn infant to attend to his mother's voice and reinforce her interactions with him, he must be able to maintain alertness, control arm and leg movements, continue to breathe, control his body temperature and skin color, and so on. The notion here is that difficulty on any level will affect the other levels; trouble controlling his movements may interfere with his ability to stay alert and attentive.

The third area of concern identified for newborn assessment is temperament. The NBAS, for example, is based on a model of the full-term newborn as a well-organized social partner. Relative strengths and weaknesses in subsystem organization may underpin behavioral differences; an original intent of the assessment was to identify individual constitutional differences (Brazelton, 1973, 1984) and to appraise the way these differences influence caregivers. One goal of assessing individual differences in newborns as social partners is to facilitate intervention with caregivers and infants before dysfunctional patterns of interaction become established. The assessment can be used to describe the newborn's individuality to a parent and to emphasize their mutual effects. Neurobehavioral assessment, in particular the NBAS, has often been used as an intervention with parents to support the developing relationship. Baby Lucas's mother could learn that she did not cause her infant's irritability and that she can help her baby become calm.

Dimensions of the Infant's Caregiving Context

If newborn assessment strategies are to reflect the theoretical notions about the dialectic between the infant and the caregiving context, an important area of concern is the nature of that context and how it affects and is affected by the infant. Two dimensions of the context relevant to the assessment and understanding of newborn behavior are the physical environment and the social environment. Assessment strategies for the hospital environment, the home, and the parent-infant relationship are beyond the scope of the chapter. Chapter 9 provides an overview of environmental assessment, and the assessment of family functioning is addressed in Chapter 8. Several comments about the effects of aspects of the infant's environment are warranted, however.

Literature on infant development for the past two decades has included in its scope the effects of nonoptimal physical environments. Various studies have demonstrated the full-term and preterm infant's vulnerability to differences in environmental input; behavioral organization appears to be dependent on support from the outside as well as maturation from the inside. A major focus of research on the effects of the physical environment is the NICU, and it is well accepted that components of the environment experienced by sick and immature infants can affect their behavioral functioning and, perhaps, their subsequent developmental outcome. The nature of environmental effects is still argued, however. The NICU has been seen as sensorily deprived (Rice, 1977; Scarr-Salapatek & Williams, 1973) and as providing excessive stimulation (Cornell & Gottfried, 1976). Some investigators claim that there is an inappropriate pattern of stimulation rather than an inadequate amount (Gottfried, Wallace-Lande, Sherman-Brown, King, & Coen, 1981; Lawson, Daum, & Turkewitz, 1977).

In studies of environmental stress and support, some findings are compelling and argue for inclusion in neonatal assessment approaches. For example, excessive lighting in the NICU has been associated with increased incidence of visual deficits in premature infants (Glass et al., 1985). While a single study does not suffice to indict excessive lighting, many neonatal units have included better control over lighting in structural revisions. Certainly, excessive lighting interferes with an infant's ability to open his eyes, look at his caregivers, and explore the environment. In addition, numerous studies have documented excessive noise in the NICU (Kellman, 1982; Bess, Peck, & Chapman, 1979; Gottfried et al., 1981) and its association with negative effects on the infant's physiological stability, such as decreased oxygen levels in the blood (Long, Lucey, & Philip, 1980; Martin, Herrell, Rubin, & Fanaroff, 1979). Medical procedures that are necessary in a critical care setting also can be physiologically expensive for sick infants; infants often show distress for up to 5 minutes after a 1-minute procedure (Gorski, 1983).

Many clinicians and researchers conclude that not enough is known about the physiological and sensory needs and thresholds of infants or about the effects of various levels or durations of stimulation to make substantial environmental changes with confidence. Others disagree; many neonatal settings have made environment changes consistent with findings in this research area. For more information about the NICU environment, the reader is referred to Gottfried and Gaiter (1985). *Infant Stress Under Intensive Care* is an edited volume that includes studies of the nursery setting and its effects on infants, parents, and medical caregivers. These authors contend that there currently is enough evidence about the effects of the NICU environment on newborn recovery and stability to make close assessment of an infant and her responses to perturbations in the environment a necessary dimension of newborn behavioral assessment.

PROCEDURAL GUIDELINES

The assessment of a newborn infant is very different from testing an older child or an adult. Previous training in the standardized and informal testing of older children will apply to testing strategies in general, but testing a newborn infant in a newborn setting presents several new demands. Guidelines for good practice in testing newborns are discussed for the examiner's training and experience, for the infant's status in testing, and for the testing environment.

The Examiner

Educators and other developmental specialists are generally well trained in the close observation of behavior, and this is the essence of newborn assessment. The examiner also needs to be knowledgeable in several other areas. Training programs in infancy and infant assessment usually include rather extensive material on brain-behavior relationships, motor development, and biomedical risk factors for the premature or ill newborn. The infant's behavior is seen as having meaning about the functioning of the CNS, so newborn assessment requires some understanding of neonatal neurology and neuropathology. The clinician is referred to several excellent texts on neonatology or neonatal nursing (e.g., Volpé, 1981; Avery, 1987; Fanaroff and Martin, 1987; Oehler, 1981); chapters on the CNS and neurologic problems in the newborn are excellent introductions to this area.

The second area of knowledge needed for newborn assessment is motor development and the assessment of movement. In addition to course work and direct supervision, it is recommended that training include observations of infant-trained physical or occupational therapists in performing newborn assessments. Qualitative aspects of and subtle components of movement are important in newborn assessment and cannot be learned from a textbook only.

Similarly, if you will be doing assessments in a newborn nursery, particularly an NICU, you will find that you need to become comfortable in that setting and knowledgeable about equipment and procedures. In most nursery settings, there are very important rules about behavior: When to wash? What can you touch? The nursery may have a procedure manual for you to review. At first, your ignorance may feel embarrassing and overwhelming. You likely will find that nursery personnel would rather educate you than be uncomfortable with you in their setting.

The Infant

The theoretical basis of neurobehavioral assessment presumes close attention to the responses, thresholds, and needs of the infant being tested. In particular, most exams ask for close monitoring of behavioral state; many map the order of items by the infant's minute-to-minute level of arousal. Some exams are to be given at specified times (e.g., halfway between feedings) as an attempt to minimize variability in states of arousal at the beginning of the exam.

This attention to state is an excellent example of one of the basic differences between newborn and older child assessment; that is, what you do in the assessment is determined by what the infant does. You want to experience a range of the infant's responses, so you attempt to elicit the best responses as well as observe the modal ones. The examiner does what is necessary to elicit these responses. For example, if an infant's motor disorganization is interfering with visual tracking, the examiner likely will stop, swaddle, hold the infant in a contained position, and try again. The approach requires a thorough knowledge of the exam and much experience in handling infants.

Sick and premature infants require even more flexible procedures. A good newborn examiner will derive as much data from observations of the undisturbed infant as possible and as much from observing necessary procedures as possible. It is known that handling can negatively affect sick and premature infants' physiological status (e.g., heart rate, respiratory regularity, oxygen saturation). Minimizing aversive input is one goal of assessment; it should also be the method of good assessment. When handling is required, close attention to the infant's responses is necessary. Stress responses are respected; recovery time and support are given. Testing is terminated if the infant indicates continued stress. The goal is to obtain information about an individual infant's thresholds, not to take the infant beyond them.

In general, the method of assessment is determined by the infant's status. A full-term, healthy newborn may readily engage with an examiner for an NBAS assessment in the infant's home. A growing preterm infant may require the tempered, well-modulated assessment described by Als (e.g., 1986). A sick newborn, still being mechanically ventilated, might benefit from an assessment of her responses to environmental stimuli but will require a minimally intrusive measure, such as the *naturalistic observation* system provided by Als (1984).

The Physical Environment

Newborn environments, nurseries and homes, usually are the settings for assessment. Most test developers recommend an environment with reduced external stimuli. You may get very different responses to an NBAS or Dubowitz exam administered in the center of a noisy, brightly lit nursery from those elicited in a quiet, nearly dark room with a rocking chair and a place for the examiner to prop his feet. Developmental clinicians have gotten very clever at finding corners, closets, or rooms adjacent to nurseries for their assessments.

Another issue to consider about the context of testing is the presence or absence of the parent. With the parent present, the assessment is an intervention. The assessment provides an opportunity for the parent to get to know and understand the individuality of the child and the meaning in his or her behavior. Testing with the parent can be distracting for the examiner, however. There are many reasons to examine an infant with parents present or without; the goal and results of the testing will differ. You also can choose to do two exams or to see the infant alone and report, in detail, your findings to the parent.

REPRESENTATIVE METHODS

Representative newborn assessment strategies are divided into two categories: those focused primarily on the infant and those that, to some extent, consider the mutual influences of infant and caregiving context. Each exam is described in terms of its theoretical perspective, the major constructs of concern, indicators of the major constructs, specific procedures for administration and scoring, research and evaluation information, and general comments.

Assessment of Newborn Status

The Apgar score and the assessment of *gestational age* are systems for describing the infant's status at birth. They usually are done by physicians or nurses, but the information is useful for developmental specialists.

The Apgar Scoring System (Apgar, 1953) The Apgar score was devised as an index of the effects of obstetrical procedures, such as medication for the mother during labor and delivery or resuscitation efforts. The score also is used as a measure of the infant's immediate need for assistance with cardiopulmonary adaptation (Oehler, 1981). For this reason, the score is seen as an index of birth asphyxia. To obtain the Apgar score, the infant's physiologic stability is observed in five areas: heart rate, respiratory effort, reflex irritability, muscle tone, and color. Scoring criteria are shown in Table 7.1.

The physician or nurse in the delivery room observes the infant in the five areas, assigning a score of 2, 1, or 0 in each for a maximum total score of 10, which is seen as representing

TABLE 7.1
The Apgar Scoring Criteria

Sign	0	1	2
Heart rate	Absent	Slow (below 100)	Over 100
Respiratory effort	Absent	Weak cry, hypoventilation	Good, strong cry
Muscle tone	Limp	Some flexion of extremities	Well-flexed
Reflex response			
1. response to catheter in nostril (tested after oropharynx is clear)	No response	Grimace	Cough or sneeze
2. tangential foot slap	No response	Grimace	Cry and withdrawal of foot
Color	Blue, pale	Body pink, extremities blue	Completely pink

Source: Based on "A Proposal for a New Method of Evaluation of the Newborn Infant" by V. Apgar, 1953, *Current Researches in Anesthesia and Analgesia, 32,* pp. 250–267.

optimal physiological status. A total score is assigned at 1 minute after birth and again at 5 minutes. Sometimes, especially in instances of low initial scores, the infant is assessed at 10 and 20 minutes as well.

No studies of interrater reliability for the Apgar score are available. Test-retest reliability is, of course, not an applicable construct; change in infant status from one observation to the next is anticipated and desirable. The criteria used for scoring represent the content validity of the system.

It is important to point out that predictive validity studies of the Apgar score often test the effectiveness of the exam for purposes for which it was not designed. The majority of studies reported in the literature address the relationship between the Apgar score and subsequent infant mortality and morbidity. The results are relevant to the care and planning for the high-risk infant. They are not true validity tests, however; the Apgar was designed to document the newborn's immediate status and needs, not to predict the future.

Studies of the prediction of mortality in the neonate from the Apgar score are fairly consistent. For example, Apgar, Holaday, James, Weisbrot, and Berrien (1958) found a mortality of 0.13% with an initial Apgar score of 10 versus 15% for an initial score of 0, 1, 2, or 3. A low Apgar score, then, does not predict mortality well, but it predicts it better than a high score.

In contrast, findings about the Apgar and morbidity are very inconsistent; results seem related to which outcome measures are used at what age and to the variation in scores for the groups studied. For example, Serunian and Broman (1975) were able to discriminate high (7–10) versus low (0–3) Apgar-scoring children on the Bayley Scales of Infant Development (1969) at 8 months of age. However, Shipe, Vandenberg, and Williams (1968) found no relationship between neonatal Apgar scores and scores on the Stanford-Binet Intelligence Scale at 3 years of age.

Some investigators contend that if the Apgar is to be used as a predictor of developmental outcome, the scores assigned later (e.g., at 5 or

10 minutes) are better. Illingworth (1960) argues that if a measure of asphyxia is needed, the length of time until the onset of regular respiration is at least as adequate as the Apgar score.

The Apgar score can be an important source of information for the developmental clinician. An indicator of a stressful labor and delivery often is enough to consider an infant to be at developmental risk, to warrant careful attention to the infant's subsequent adaptation and organization, and to assist the caregiving environment in optimizing recovery and developmental outcome.

Gestational Age Assessment (Dubowitz, Dubowitz, & Goldberg, 1970)

The goal of this exam is to provide a reliable method of determining the gestational age of the newborn infant. It is recognized that weight alone is not a sufficient indicator of age; an infant can be larger than average for gestational age or small for gestational age. Distinguishing between prematurity and growth retardation has implications for medical care and developmental follow-up (Oehler, 1981). There is some evidence that for the preterm infant the Apgar score does not reflect physiological well-being, but developmental maturity (Catlin et al., 1986). Therefore, knowing the infant's gestational age or maturity is important in interpreting other behavioral assessments as well as in anticipating developmental needs.

The exam has two parts: neurological criteria and an assessment of external criteria. The external characteristics are adapted from Farr, Mitchell, Neligan, and Parkin (1966) and include skin texture, skin color, skin opacity, edema (swelling), lanugo (body hair), ear form, ear firmness, genital appearance, breast size, nipple formation, and plantar skin creases.

The neurological criteria include 10 items, scored from 1 to 5, from less mature to more mature. The 11 external criteria items are scored from 1 to 4, also from less mature to more mature. Scores from both parts of the exam are summed, then combined for determining a gestational age estimate.

The Dubowitz gestational age assessment claims as its roots the neurological assessment strategies of André-Thomas and Saint Anne-Dargassies. The content of the neurological criteria on the gestational age exam was selected from a pilot study of items derived from various neurological exams (e.g., Amiel-Tison & Grenier, 1983; Robinson, 1966). Items were chosen to be easily definable, reliable among observers, and least affected by the infant's state of arousal or the presence of neurological abnormalities. Interobserver agreement of the final items was found to be 89% in a study of 167 infants. For the external criteria, the Dubowitz group adapted the work by Farr and colleagues (1966), who obtained gestational age norms from 280 infants of mothers who were certain of their pregnancy dates. In the Dubowitz reliability work, with 167 infant subjects, interrater agreement on external criteria was 91%. In this particular study, infant weight did not seem to affect scoring.

In an attempt to examine validity for the gestational age assessment, the group (Dubowitz et al., 1970) examined 150 infants, 87 of whom had very reliable obstetric dates. Scores from external characteristics were more highly correlated with known gestation than the neurological criteria; however, the highest correlation was obtained between age and the total score of external and neurological characteristics.

Research from other groups indicates some of the possible problems with the use of the exam for determining gestational age. One study demonstrated that the examiner's knowledge of the obstetrician's estimated gestational age introduced bias in the Dubowitz exam (Gagliardi, Brambilla, Bruno, Martinelli, & Console, 1993). At least two investigators (Robillard, DeCaunes, Alexander, & Sergent,

1992; Sanders et al., 1991) present findings that indicate that the exam overestimates gestational age in premature and low-birthweight infants.

For child development personnel working in developing countries, the Dubowitz exam may provide invaluable information, especially when information about the mother's last menstrual cycle is not known. The gestational age assessment can be used to identify newborns who are poorly grown for their gestational age and require special nutritional and other health and developmental intervention. Simplified methods of the gestational age exam have been developed for clinical use in health settings where there is little prenatal information and/or a poor level of health services makes a longer exam prohibitive (Eregie & Muogbo, 1991).

Administration of the gestational age assessment requires rather extensive experience observing and handling newborn infants. Individual exam items are listed on the test form from less disturbing to the infant to more disturbing, but no recommendations about the optimal behavioral state for the exam are made. The gestational age of an infant is so important that one measure often is not adequate; the "best guess" about gestational age comes from combining information about dates, from the gestational age exam, and (if available) from prenatal ultrasound findings. Also, examinations of lens vascularity (Hittner, Hirsch, & Rudolph, 1977) and modified head ultrasound assessments of cerebral sulcal development (Huang & Yeh, 1991) have been used to estimate gestational age, particularly for infants younger than 28 weeks.

Assessment of Newborns and Context

The following six assessments represent the most commonly used tests of neurobehavioral status in the newborn. Each lends itself to some extent to interpretation of the relationship between infant behavior and the social and physical context.

The Graham Rosenblith Behavior Test for Neonates (Rosenblith, 1961a)

Graham's (1956) exam was initially developed to distinguish brain-injured from normal newborns. Rosenblith's revision of the original scales was intended to identify high-risk infants—those who warrant medical and psychological attention and follow-up—and to make selecting a group of low-risk infants possible for use in adoption cases (Rosenblith, 1974). Both exams incorporated age-normed items, measures of muscle tone, and behavioral responses to stimuli.

There were five discrete areas in the original Graham exam. A pain threshold test involved a mild electrical stimulus applied to just below the infant's knee; intensity varied to elicit movement of the limb. Impaired sensory functioning was considered one indicator of brain damage. The maturation scale included nine items drawn from various developmental schedules (e.g., Gesell & Amatruda, 1941). A variety of stimuli or conditions were included, such as observations of posture, auditory responses, reactions to aversive stimuli, and strength of grasp. The vision scale examined eye movements, fixation, and tracking with scoring adapted from Gesell and Ilg (1949). The muscle tension rating was designed to quantify deviations in muscle tone. An irritability rating was derived from the infant's sensitivity to stimuli during the exam as a whole. The Rosenblith revision of the Graham Scales (1961b) eliminated the pain threshold test. The new scales yield two scores (motor and tactile-adaptive) and two ratings (muscle tone and irritability).

Administration of the Graham Rosenblith Behavior Test requires 30 minutes to 1 hour. Infant state is not controlled but is noted. No special training is said to be required for administration; but, again, familiarity with newborns and close observation of behavior and movement patterns is essential. It is interesting to note that Rosenblith, in the 1961 manual of the revised scales, suggested that the infant's best performance, not modal performance, be used for scoring. Brazelton (1973) followed this lead in developing the NBAS.

The Graham Rosenblith exam is not now frequently used; for that reason, its psychometric properties are not emphasized here. Its major importance is that it marks the beginning of a behavioral or neurobehavioral approach to newborn testing. As noted, many threads found in more contemporary assessments were first defined by Graham's and Rosenblith's work.

The Neurological Assessment of the Preterm and Full-Term Newborn Infant (Dubowitz & Dubowitz, 1981) This exam also has its roots in the neurological tradition. The intent of the exam is to measure the functional neurological status of the newborn, to document abnormal behavior, and to provide a means for comparing full-term and preterm infants.

There are four major areas of concern in the assessment. They include habituation (the ability to manage environmental input), assessment of muscle tone and movement patterns, testing of reflexes (primitive reflexes and tendon reflexes), and several neurobehavioral items. Habituation is tested to a repetitive flashlight-and-rattle stimulus and can be administered in the infant's drowsy or sleep states. Sixteen items measure muscle tone and movement patterns; they include assessment of posture, resistance to movement, head control, posture in prone and ventral suspension, spontaneous movement, tremors, and startles. Deep tendon reflexes and four primitive reflexes are tested, including palmar grasp (hand grasp) and the Moro reflex. Neurobehavioral items are very similar to the state organization and orientation items on the NBAS. State of arousal and asymmetry of responses are seen as important in interpreting results, and they are documented for each item.

The exam was designed specifically not to require extensive training, to be brief (15 minutes or less), and to be easy to administer. The exam can be done in an isolette if necessary (Dubowitz, Dubowitz, Palmer, & Verhote, 1980). Optimal timing for the infant, for consistency in state of arousal, is seen as two thirds of the way between feedings. Materials are simple: a light, a rattle, and a red yarn ball. Test items are grouped on two pages with diagrams and brief scoring instructions. Most items are scored on a 5-point scale, 1 to 5 for minimal to maximal response. No summary scores are derived. The test manual suggests and provides examples for interpretation of various response patterns.

Dubowitz and Dubowitz constructed their exam with items from Saint Anne-Dargassies (1965), Prechtl (1977), and Parmelee and Michaelis (1971), as well as items adapted from the NBAS (Brazelton, 1973). Items were piloted over a two-year period and with over 500 infants, and the test underwent several revisions. No reliability data is provided in the manual. Two studies of observer agreement with an earlier version of the exam were reported, however (Dubowitz et al., 1980). In the first, 11 infants were seen by two observers; for the 352 items scored, there was one 3-point discrepancy, two 2-point differences, and twenty-four 1-point disagreements. Higher disagreement rates were found in the second study with 12 infants, 2 raters, and 340 items: ten 3-point differences, twelve 2-point differences, and eighty-two 1-point differences.

Concurrent criterion-related validity was examined by the same group (Dubowitz et al., 1980). The criterion was an ultrasound assessment of the presence or absence of intraventricular hemorrhage (IVH) in the 32- to 35-weeks postconception infant. The Dubowitz exam was able to discriminate between the two groups of infants: IVH versus no-IVH.

Twenty-four of 31 infants with IVH had three or more abnormal signs on the exam; only 2 of 37 infants without IVH had three or more abnormal signs. Signs most frequently associated with IVH were decreased muscle tone, decreased motility, and increased tightness in the popliteal angle.

Predictive criterion-related validity was examined by comparing the newborn assessment with normal versus abnormal diagnoses based on the Griffiths's Test (Griffiths, 1954) (a test of developmental milestone achievement) and a neurological assessment at one year. Ninety-one percent of infants who were normal at one year were assessed as normal at term gestational age. Only 35% of the normal one-year-olds had tested abnormal at term age.

In another approach to the validity question, however, the Dubowitz exam failed to discriminate infants (born <32 weeks, 40 weeks postconception at exam) with and without chronic lung disease and with and without documented central nervous system abnormalities (Byrne, Piper, & Darrah, 1989). It may be that the test, as well as many newborn assessments, is not sensitive to the subtle behavioral differences between acute illness and developmental abnormalities. It is important to exercise caution in interpreting the meaning of suspect or abnormal developmental findings in a very sick infant.

On the other hand, an exam like the Dubowitz may be very helpful in assessing the short-term behavioral organization effects of specific interventions. In a study by Clark, Cordero, Goss, and Manos (1989), the exam successfully documented gains in muscle tone, movement motility, orientation, alertness, and defensive maneuvers in preterm infants who received a rocking intervention versus a control group.

This exam is quick and easy to administer and score. The claim that no special training is needed is misleading; in fact, rather extensive experience with reflex testing and handling newborn infants is essential. This assessment often is compared, favorably and unfavorably, with the NBAS. The two exams have many overlapping test items but use different scoring systems. Interpretations of exam findings in terms of environmental effects on the infant and the influence of the infant on caregivers is not stressed.

The Neonatal Behavioral Assessment Scale (Brazelton, 1973, 1984) The NBAS was designed to measure "interactive behavior," "the infant's available responses to his environment, and so, indirectly, his effect on the environment" (Brazelton, 1973, p. 4). The focus of the exam is individual differences in the behavioral organization of full-term newborn infants. The newborn is seen as active, interactive, and capable of shaping social interactions. The theoretical perspective is an organismic view of infant development and of the infant assessment: "It is obvious that a baby's responses should not be seen as static but that each one will lead to and become the background for the next one—and, as a result, the processes through which infants go as we interact with them become the best measure of their potential" (Brazelton, 1973, p. 4).

A major concept in the NBAS is the importance of the infant's behavioral state to his or her responses to the examiner's handling and to test stimuli. Brazelton uses behavioral state as defined by Prechtl and Beintema (1964) to direct the examiner in the timing of item administration. State organization is also assessed by measures of the infant's lability and control of state. Brazelton emphasizes the infant's capacity to manage input, to close it out (habituation), and to attend (orientation). This concept is similar to descriptions of infant temperament, and Brazelton acknowledges the assessment of temperamental differences to be one of the goals of the exam.

From the theoretical perspective of the NBAS, the infant is seen as an active, not passive, contributor to her own caregiving through her individual differences in behavioral organization. Areas in which individual differences are found include autonomic control, neurological or motor maturity, state organization, and orientation and habituation capacities. Items seen as indicators of each area comprise the exam.

The NBAS is recommended for the full-term newborn or the preterm infant 37 weeks post-conception and in a stable medical condition. Desired environmental conditions include quiet, comfort, and dim lights. Test equipment is a flashlight, a rattle, a bell, a red ball, and a sterile stick (for habituation to mild pain to the heel). A sequence for item administration is presented in the manual, and is designed to elicit a range of states from sleep to alertness, gradually, with perturbations from less to more intense and stimuli presented in a distal to proximal manner. The examiner is counseled, however, to attend to the infant's state and to shift the administration sequence as needed to elicit optimal performance from the infant.

The Brazelton group emphasizes the importance of examiners being reliable with one another in administration and scoring. Training involves extensive practice handling newborn infants, observing trained examiners, and doing supervised exams. All examiners using the test for research purposes are required to obtain the formal reliability training available at the Child Development Unit at Children's Hospital, Harvard Medical Center, Boston.

To administer the NBAS, the examiner and the infant engage in a 30-minute interaction (approximately); scoring occurs after the exam. Scoring includes 28 behavioral items, each rated on a 9-point scale; 18 elicited responses from the reflex profile of Prechtl and Beintema (1964) are scored on a 3-point scale. Many clinicians and researchers use a 5-point scale instead for the reflex assessment as suggested by Sostek and Anders (1977). The NBAS scoring sheet is shown in Figure 7.2.

There are several ways to condense NBAS data. Initially, Als, Tronick, Lester, and Brazelton (1977) presented a system of a priori clusters for items. Optimal versus worrisome scores for Interactive Processes, Motoric Processes, Organizational Processes: State Control, and Organizational Processes: Response to Stress can be derived. Several factor analytic studies have emerged; the most commonly used factor analytically determined clusters are those by Als et al. (1982): Range of State, Regulation of State, Motor Status, Autonomic Stability, Orientation, and Habituation.

There have been two significant modifications of the NBAS since its 1973 introduction. The NBAS with Kansas Supplements (NBAS-K) was published in 1978. The authors (Horowitz, Sullivan, & Linn, 1978) argue that the infant's typical behavior is as important as his optimal behavior (emphasized on the original NBAS). They added modal scores for Orientation, Consolability, and Defensive Movement items. The Kansas group also contributed several items that address qualitative aspects of the examiner-newborn interaction: Overall General Irritability, Overall Quality of Infant Responsiveness, Persistence of the Examiner Needed, and the Reinforcement Value of the Infant's Behavior. Finally, they added tests of the infant's responses to inanimate auditory and visual stimuli to complete that sequence in the NBAS.

The Kansas group assessed the NBAS-K with 221 normal newborns (Lancioni, Horowitz, & Sullivan, 1980), finding that (similar to the NBAS) individual items showed low to moderate stability over the first 3 days of life, at 2 weeks, and at 1 month. The use of modal scores did not result in more consistent data over time. Although disappointed with these results, the authors argue that the changes are intuitively attractive and that efforts to demonstrate their utility in understanding the stability and change in newborn behavior should continue.

Brazelton also considered many of the Kansas supplemental items intuitively attractive and included them in his 1984 revision of the

NBAS. The second edition of the NBAS includes nine additional "supplementary items" modeled after the Kansas items. Again, the new assessments reflect the infant's stability and fragility across subsystems as she is able to engage with the examiner and the exam. The supplementary items are scored on a 1 to 9 scale, generally from less to more optimal: Quality of Alert Responsiveness, Cost of Attention, Examiner Persistence, General Irritability, Robustness and Endurance, Regulatory Capacity, State Regulation, Balance of Motor Tone, and Reinforcement Value of the Infant's Behavior (Brazelton, 1984).

The NBAS is the most studied of neurobehavioral exams for the newborn infant. Several reviews or annotated bibliographies, such as the one by Sostek (1978) are available. Several studies can be cited that are representative of this large area of research. In terms of reliability, the Brazelton group found that interrater reliability (after training) was greater than 90% if within one point was considered to be an agreement (Als et al., 1977). This level of reliability is intended to hold up for 2 years, but no studies of interobserver agreement several months after training were found. In general, test-retest reliability studies found low to moderate correlations between scores. Brazelton would contend (e.g., 1978) that a significant amount of the variability is in the infant, not in the test. He suggests that the continuities in behavior likely would be found between the infant and the caregiving system, not in the infant over time.

One group (Sameroff, Krafchuk, & Bakow, 1978) compared 35 infants 24 hours apart to assess short-term stability for individual items, factors, and a priori clusters. The best stability was in scores for muscle tone and motor maturity ($r = .57$, $r = .78$, respectively). Only the initial habituation task was stable, that is, the light versus rattle, bell, and pin prick ($r = .46$ versus $r = .05$, $r = .05$, and $r = .07$). Irritability measures were unstable. Factor scores showed better stability than cluster scores; however, the motor cluster scores correlated .56 with one another. Asch, Gleser, and Steichen (1986) examined the sources of variance for repeated measures of the NBAS, concluding that measurement error is too high for one exam on one occasion with one examiner to have meaning for the individual infant. For clinical prediction, this group agrees with several other authors that at least two test occasions and possibly two raters are necessary.

Validity questions for the NBAS generally are approached by predictive criterion-related tests. The best predictive success has been with recovery curves, or repeated exams, at 40, 42, and 44 weeks postconception when compared with the 18-month scores on the Bayley Scales of Infant Development (Lester, 1984). In this particular study, recovery curve scores were significantly related to mental and motor performance on the Bayley Scales of Infant Development (1969) for both term and preterm infants; from 42% to 63% of the variance on 18-month scores was predicted by the NBAS scores.

Sostek and Anders (1977) examined concurrent and predictive validity with the NBAS. The exam was accomplished between 5 and 12 days of life with an interrater reliability of .85 on the a priori clusters. Simultaneously, nurses completed an adaptation of the Carey (1970) measure of infant temperament; that is, they used 35 items out of the original 70 that were seen as appropriate for the newborn. The temperament factor, distractibility, was significantly associated with the a priori motor score and total score on the NBAS. At 4 months of age, NBAS scores did not predict performance (motor) scale scores on the Bayley Scales of Infant Development (1969). Rather, mental scale scores were associated with the NBAS state organization and overall score. These findings underline not only the complex issues involved in infant assessment but also the complexity of models of early infant development.

Behavioral and Neurological Assessment Scale

Infant's name		Date	Hour
Sex	Age	Born	
Mother's age	Father's age	Father's S.E.S.	
Examiner(s)		Apparent race	
Conditions of examination:		Place of examination	
Birthweight		Date of examination	
Time examined		Length	
Time last fed		Head circ.	
Type of delivery		Type of feeding	
Length of labor		Apgar	
Type, amount, and timing of medication given mother		Birth order	
		Anesthesia?	
		Abnormalities of labor	

Initial state: observe 2 minutes

1	2	3	4	5	6
deep	light	drowsy	alert	active	crying

Predominant states (mark two)

1	2	3	4	5	6

Elicited Responses

		O*	L	M	H	A†
Plantar grasp			1	2	3	
Hand grasp			1	2	3	
Ankle clonus			1	2	3	
Babinski			1	2	3	
Standing			1	2	3	
Automatic walking			1	2	3	
Placing			1	2	3	
Incurvation			1	2	3	
Crawling			1	2	3	
Glabella			1	2	3	
Tonic deviation of head and eyes			1	2	3	
Nystagmus			1	2	3	
Tonic neck reflex			1	2	3	
Moro			1	2	3	
Rooting (intensity)			1	2	3	
Sucking (intensity)			1	2	3	
Passive movement			1	2	3	
Arms	R		1	2	3	
	L		1	2	3	
Legs	R		1	2	3	
	L		1	2	3	

O* = response not elicited (omitted), A† = asymmetry

Descriptive paragraph (optional)

Attractive	0	1	2	3
Interfering variables	0	1	2	3
Need for stimulation	0	1	2	3

What activity does he use to quiet self?

hand to mouth

sucking with nothing in mouth

locking onto visual or auditory stimuli

postural changes

state change for no observable reason

COMMENTS:

FIGURE 7.2

NBAS scoring sheet

Source: From *Neonatal Behavioral Assessment Scale* (2nd ed.) by T. B. Brazelton, 1984, Philadelphia: J. B. Lippincott. Copyright 1984 by J. B. Lippincott.

Behavior Scoring Sheet

Initial state ____________________

Predominant state ____________________

Scale (Note State)	1	2	3	4	5	6	7	8	9
1. Response decrement to light (1,2)									
2. Response decrement to rattle (1,2)									
3. Response decrement to bell (1,2)									
4. Response decrement to tactile stimulation of foot (1,2)									
5. Orientation—inanimate visual (4,5)									
6. Orientation—inanimate auditory (4,5)									
7. Orientation—inanimate visual and auditory (4,5)									
8. Orientation—animate visual (4,5)									
9. Orientation—animate auditory (4,5)									
10. Orientation—animate visual and auditory (4,5)									
11. Alertness (4 only)									
12. General tonus (4,5)									
13. Motor maturity (4,5)									
14. Pull-to-sit (4,5)									
15. Cuddliness (4,5)									
16. Defensive movements (3,4,5)									
17. Consolability (6 to 5,4,3,2)									
18. Peak of excitement (all states)									
19. Rapidity of build-up (from 1,2 to 6)									
20. Irritability (all awake states)									
21. Activity (3,4,5)									
22. Tremulousness (all states)									
23. Startle (3,4,5,6)									
24. Lability of skin color (from 1 to 6)									
25. Lability of states (all states)									
26. Self-quieting activity (6,5 to 4,3,2,1)									
27. Hand-to-mouth facility (all states)									
28. Smiles (all states)									
29. Alert responsiveness (4 only)									
30. Cost of attention (3,4,5)									
31. Examiner persistence (all states)									
32. General irritability (5,6)									
33. Robustness and endurance (all states)									
34. Regulatory capacity (all states)									
35. State regulation (all states)									
36. Balance of motor tone (all states)									
37. Reinforcement value of infant's behavior (all states)									

Although the NBAS has become a very popular approach to newborn assessment, the exam has been judged negatively for its low to moderate stability and mixed predictive findings. In his review of the use of the NBAS over the first 15 years, Brazelton (1990) argues that the exam is not primarily a predictive instrument and that long-term studies of continuities and discontinuities in development are still inadequate. He suggests that there is stability in an infant's coping abilities and that there should be continuity in how an individual handles stress that could be discernible in the newborn period. Brazelton recommends that NBAS examiners focus on the infant's profile of scores, not the total score, and that the infant's "cost of achievement" (p. 1666) be considered an important marker of impairment. He emphasizes that newborn assessment findings represent only one aspect of the child's social context. The stress of socioeconomic deprivation, for example, likely plays a major role in continuing or interrupting the pattern of coping behavior evident in the newborn's behavior (e.g., Parker, Greer, & Zuckerman, 1988).

The use of the NBAS over the past two decades has addressed important developmental questions other than the prediction of future development from newborn neurobehavioral scores. The exam is used to mark the acute effects of biomedical events and processes as well as to evaluate the effects of developmental and environmental interventions. In many studies, the NBAS has successfully documented the effects of in utero drug exposure on the neonate, even when traditional tests of drug withdrawal fail to demonstrate the sometimes subtle manifestations of behavioral disorganization (see review by Gingras, Weese-Mayer, Hume, & O'Donnell, 1992; also Chasnoff, Burns, Burns, & Schnoll, 1986). Similar studies using the NBAS have demonstrated the effects of prenatal alcohol exposure on newborn behavior (e.g., Coles, Smith, Fernhoff, & Falek, 1985). Other studies that control for some of the methodological difficulties inherent in studies of drug- and alcohol-using women and their children do not demonstrate these significant differences with the NBAS (Coles, Platzman, Smith, James, & Falek, 1992). However, the variability among studies may be less a function of the test than a demonstration of the wide variability in the behavioral status of drug- and alcohol-exposed infants. It is possible that neurobehavioral assessments of the newborn could be more useful with questions about acute effects than about predictive ones.

The NBAS approach is used successfully as a conceptual model for early intervention with high-risk infants and their parents (Rauh, Nurcombe, Achebach, & Howell, 1990) and as an intervention strategy with mothers and fathers. One study with fathers, in particular, involved a demonstration of the NBAS with first-time fathers on the infants' second or third day of life (Beal, 1989). At 8 weeks postpartum, there was a positive effect on qualitative aspects of caregiving compared with control fathers. Although the long-term implications of the intervention are not known, the experience of intimacy with the newborn mediated by an exam like the NBAS seems to have a general positive effect on parents.

In its two-decade history, the NBAS has been used extensively, studied, modified, praised, and criticized. The exam continues to contribute to both research and the clinical care of young infants. Hopefully, scientific investigations about its meaning for newborn status, its developmental outcome, and its usefulness in studies similar to the one described above will continue. Compared with its predecessors, the NBAS provides an organized view of the newborn infant's behavioral competence and the infant's possible effects on caregivers. The exam does emphasize individual differences, as intended; in addition, it is seen as an effective mode for intervention with parents. When assessments are used over time, there also seems to be some continuity between newborn behavior and developmental progress, at least during the first 4 months.

The Assessment of Preterm Infant Behavior (APIB) (Als et al., 1982) Als's original intent for the APIB was for the exam to be an extension of the NBAS for use with preterm and ill newborn infants. Als combined the NBAS framework with her synactive model of development, and the primary goal of the APIB is to examine the infant's behavioral organization within each evolving subsystem in the model's hierarchy. Table 7.2 describes these subsystems and the indicators used to assess the infant's status in each.

The "synactive" model for the development of the newborn specifies a "continuous intra-organizational subsystem interaction seen in continuous interaction with the environment" (Als, 1986, p. 17). Key features of the model are the hierarchy of behavioral subsystems, the teleology of behavioral organization, and the assumption of the infant's continuous interactions with the environment. As Als (1986) states, the assessment is directed at "the way the individual infant appears to handle his experience of the world around him, rather than on the assessments of skills per se" (p. 18).

The APIB is designed so that the examiner provides systematic sensory and handling input to the infant in order to assess each behavioral subsystem. The intervention with the infant is by "packages," or graded maneuvers. Like the NBAS, items are planned to move from distal to proximal and provide less to more intense stimulation; the general sequence of the exam is very similar to the NBAS. With the exception of the Attention/Interaction maneuvers, all packages contribute items to all subsystems. Scores that reflect the subsystem scheme are derived.

The APIB exam takes approximately 30 minutes, but administration time can be quite variable. With the premature infant, the examiner often must stop and offer time-out, or support for stress reactions. At the beginning of the exam, the infant is to be asleep and midway between feedings. The examiner moves through the sequence of packages, observing the infant's responses to the stimuli, the infant's coping with stressful stimuli, and the infant's need for and use of external support. Scoring the exam takes approximately 1 hour.

Administering the APIB requires the examiner to be very skilled in handling premature newborn infants and experienced in examining in an isolette if necessary. Extensive training is recommended to be able to observe infant responses at this subtle and detailed level as the examiner is required to modulate input, minute by minute, to the infant's thresholds. Training with Dr. Als is available at the Child Development Unit at Children's Hospital in Boston and is seen as necessary for valid administration of the APIB.

Little research, except from the authors themselves, is available on the APIB. Als (1985a) found good stability in APIB scores in both full-term and preterm infants examined

TABLE 7.2
Behavioral Subsystems and Their Indicators
Source: Adapted from "Toward a Research Instrument for the Assessment of Preterm Infants' Behavior (APIB)" by H. Als, B. M. Lester, E. Z. Tronick, and T. B. Brazelton, in H. Fitzgerald, B. M. Lester, and M. W. Yogman (Eds.) *Theory and Research in Behavioral Pediatrics* Vol. 1, 1982, New York: Plenum.

Behavioral Subsystem	Examples of Indicators
Autonomic stability	Heart rate, lability of color, respiratory regularity, visceral signs
Motor status	Posture, tone, movements
State organization	Definition and range of states, control of states
Attention and orientation	Attention, quality of responsiveness
Self-regulation	Maintenance and recovery of behavioral organization

2 weeks after their expected due dates. Validity studies come from two directions of research. First, concurrent criterion-related validity was established with brain electrophysiological correlates of patterns of behavioral organization (Duffy, 1985). Second, predictive validity of patterns of behavior to 9 months and to 5 years (Als, 1985a, 1985b) were found. Specifically, overall disorganized, easily distressed newborn behavior was predictive of disorganized behavior in the older child.

The APIB is a complex exam. It is not easy to administer; the examiner must be constantly alert to the infant's subtle responses and be able to modulate stimulation and handling accordingly. Scoring is very time consuming. Whether the results of the exam are worth the expense to the infant, clinician, or researcher should be determined by the specific clinical or research question. One important use of the exam is in evaluating improved stability and recovery in premature infants related to changes in the NICU environment; environmental changes may result in subtle behavioral outcomes only discernible on this comprehensive and detailed exam.

Newborn assessment consumers need more information about the meaning of the APIB assessment and its possible contribution to various clinical and research tasks. The model it provides for viewing newborn behavior and the approach to assessment by participation in the infant and context dialectic are very attractive. Observations of infant stress, self-regulation, and response to support appear to lend themselves directly to intervention strategies for improved medical care and psychological outcome (Als et al., 1986).

Neurobehavioral Maturity Assessment (NB-MAP) (Korner et al., 1987) The NB-MAP, like the APIB, was designed to assess the preterm infant. The theoretical perspective reflects the several years of experience clinicians and researchers have had with the NBAS and the growing awareness that newborns manifest change over time (maturation) as well as stability (individual differences), making reliability and validity assessments difficult. The primary goal of the NB-MAP is the assessment of the maturity of the preterm infant from 32 weeks to term age. The exam was developed accordingly with a priori attention to the psychometric soundness of items and their patterns of change with time.

The Korner group selected test items for their perceived clinical relevance, most of which overlap with those on other newborn neurobehavioral exams. The resulting test is unique in several ways, however. In order to develop the exam, a cohort of infants was identified and tested weekly for at least 3 weeks. Items were chosen for inclusion by their demonstrated psychometric properties; specifically, an item was required to be reliable by two observers on two consecutive days when the infant was 34 weeks postconception.

In addition, nine a priori conceptual clusters of items were tested statistically, also on the 34-week data. Cluster test-retest reliability was examined and subjected to a criterion agreement of at least .6. Tests for redundancy were conducted, and of clusters that correlated .6 or more, only one was kept. The resulting exam consists of 28 items, each of which is scored quantitatively from least to more mature performance; the items form eight conceptual clusters.

The validity of the NB-MAP approach was examined during test development by mathematical modeling of cluster scores by age over time. Clusters that did not demonstrate developmental change over time were dropped from the exam. In this way, the authors demonstrated the ability of the exam to index developmental progression from birth to 40 weeks postconception. Finally, interobserver reliability was tested during development and with a subsequent study; the mean agreement was .77 with a range from .35 to .97.

It is apparent, then, that an important contribution of the NB-MAP is that the psychometric soundness was established from its development. This is very different from the approach of other exams, that is, to develop a test that appeared to have clinical relevance and then test its test-retest reliability, interobserver reliability, and validity using external criteria.

The Korner approach profited from the experience of previous newborn test developers in other ways as well. Noting that the clinical administration of the NBAS or APIB requires the examiner to move between items depending on the behavioral state of the neonate, the Korner group suggested that some of the variability from one performance to another or one infant to another is that the exams themselves are different. The NB-MAP has an invariant sequence, so that each infant receives the same exam. The authors do not ignore the need to optimize the infant's state, however; they have designed the sequence of the exam so that items are likely to be administered in appropriate states of arousal. For example, aversive items from other exams are excluded. Arousing items are followed by soothing ones for all infants.

The NB-MAP is a model of newborn neurobehavioral exam development: the attention to its psychometric properties, the standardized administration, and its consistency with the theoretical perspective of infant developmental change and stability. In one study (Korner et al., 1989), the group was able to identify domains that improve with chronological age (e.g., motor maturity and orientation) as well as those that manifest stability over time, the infants' individual differences. They concluded that common developmental trends are greater than individual ones. They ask for further studies of whether developmental trends continue into childhood and of the biological and environmental influences of stability and change.

The NB-MAP requires the same experience and training handling fragile newborn infants as the APIB. The standardized procedures also require on-site training with Dr. Korner, who provides a training manual and tapes.

Naturalistic Observation of the Preterm Neonate (Als, 1984) This behavioral observation method was designed to document observations of preterm newborn infants' responses to stress and support from the environment. Observations are based on the conceptual framework for the APIB; in this assessment, however, the observer is able to assess the infant's well-being in each behavioral subsystem without actually handling the infant.

Major areas of concern are the infants' responses to and recovery from stress in the neonatal setting, such as sound, lighting changes, procedures, and attempts to recover from aversive stimuli. Stress and defense behaviors (from the APIB, 1982) are identified and observed; they include autonomic and visceral stress signals, motoric stress signals, and state-related stress signals. Indicators of autonomic and visceral stress signals, for example, include sighing, yawning, hiccuping, sneezing, coughing, and color changes.

The method for this system involves observing the infant in 2-minute epochs, scoring heart rate and oxygen levels from the monitor, respiratory rate by counting respirations, the infant's posture and position, and the stress and defense behaviors in the areas described above. The infant is observed for a period of time before a procedure (e.g., feeding, the assessment of vital signs), during the procedure, and during recovery from the procedure. A sample score sheet is presented in Figure 7.3.

There is no quantitative scoring. Results are reported in written descriptions of the infant stress and defense reactions and recommendations for interventions that support increased overall stability and organization.

The major research done with the naturalistic observation system was not designed to test reliability and validity per se. Als et al. (1986)

OBSERVATION SHEET Name: ______________ Date: ________ Sheet Number ______

	Time:	0-2	3-4	5-6	7-8	9-10
Resp:	Regular					
	Irregular					
	Slow					
	Fast					
	Pause					
Color:	Jaundice					
	Pink					
	Pale					
	Webb					
	Red					
	Dusky					
	Blue					
	Tremor					
	Startle					
	Twitch Face					
	Twitch Body					
	Twitch Extremities					
Visceral/ Resp:	Spit up					
	Gag					
	Burp					
	Hiccough					
	BM Grunt					
	Sounds					
	Sigh					
	Gasp					
Motor:	Flaccid Arm(s)					
	Flaccid Leg(s)					
	Flexed/ Tucked Arms Act.					
	Pas.					
	Flexed/ Tucked Legs Act.					
	Pas.					
	Extend Arms Act.					
	Pas.					
	Extend Legs Act.					
	Pas.					
	Smooth Mvmt. Arms					
	Smooth Mvmt. Legs					
	Smooth Mvmt. Trunk					
	Stretch/Drown					
	Diffuse Squirm					
	Arch					
	Tuck Trunk					
	Leg Brace					
Face:	Tongue Extension					
	Hand on Face					
	Gape Face					
	Grimace					
	Smile					

	Time:	0-2	3-4	5-6	7-8	9-10
State:	1A					
	1B					
	2A					
	2B					
	3A					
	3B					
	4A					
	4B					
	5A					
	5B					
	6A					
	6B					
	AA					
Face (cont.):	Mouthing					
	Suck Search					
	Sucking					
Extrem.:	Finger Splay					
	Airplane					
	Salute					
	Sitting on Air					
	Hand Clasp					
	Foot Clasp					
	Hand to Mouth					
	Grasping					
	Holding on					
	Fisting					
Attention:	Fuss					
	Yawn					
	Sneeze					
	Face Open					
	Eye Floating					
	Avert					
	Frown					
	Ooh Face					
	Locking					
	Cooing					
	Speech Mvmt.					
Posture:	(Prone, Supine, Side)					
Head:	(Right, Left, Middle)					
Location:	(Crib, Isolette, Held)					
Manipulation:						
	Heart Rate					
	Respiration Rate					
	$TcPO_2$					

FIGURE 7.3

A behavioral score sheet

Source: From "Individualized Behavioral and Environmental Care for the Very Low Birth Weight Preterm Infant at High Risk for Bronchopulmonary Dysplasia: Neonatal Intensive Care Unit and Developmental Outcome" by H. Als, G. Lawhon, E. Brown, R. Gibes, F. Duffy, G. McAnulty, and J. Blickman, 1986, *Pediatrics, 78*(6), 1123–1132.

used the system to design individual care plans for very low birthweight infants. The observations were completed on infants in the study with a greater than 85% agreement between two observers. Then the infant's care and physical environment were modified according to an individual plan derived from the observations and shared with the nursing staff and the parents. Study outcome measures are seen as reflecting the individualized care that resulted from the observations. In general, findings indicated significant differences with individualized care in time required for recovery from respiratory illness and in developmental assessment results. These findings were confirmed by another study, one that employed an experimental design using two cohorts of preterm infants; the group receiving individualized developmental care showed relatively better performances on the APIB (Mouradian & Als, 1994).

TRANSLATING ASSESSMENT DATA INTO INTERVENTION

Various assessment strategies for the newborn infant are seen as addressing one or more dimensions of behavior: neurological integrity, individual differences and needs in behavioral organization, and the infant in relationships with caregivers. Whether or not these are the important dimensions of infant behavior to assess and whether or not existing test strategies measure them well are still widely discussed. There is much to learn about the meaning in newborn behavior and how to measure important dimensions of it.

Even within the current state of knowledge, however, newborn assessment can be seen as offering information about intervention needs and approaches. Is this child at high risk for mental retardation and/or central nervous system dysfunction? If so, how can we plan for the child and the family? How is this individual infant developing on the hierarchy of developmental tasks? What in the caregiving context supports or interferes with optimal development? What would it be like to care for this infant?

Assessment of Neurological Integrity

This is perhaps the oldest reason to test newborn infants behaviorally; it may also be the least effective one for an individual infant. However, combined information about the infant's biological risk status (possible insults to the CNS) and neurobehavioral status in the neonatal period can be helpful in planning for the infant and the family. For an infant like Baby Boy Brown, behavioral information can support recommendations for immediate intervention (e.g., demonstrating his attentional abilities to his mother), long-term intervention (e.g., if there are consistent concerns about muscle tone and asymmetry in movement, a referral to physical therapy may be considered), and long-term follow-up of developmental and behavioral functioning.

Assessment of Behavioral Organization

Models from which we assess an infant's individual differences in behavioral organization (e.g., Als et al., 1982) are predicated on the notion of developmental intervention. That is, examining indicators of an infant's functioning on a hierarchy of behavioral subsystems tells us specifically about the infant's status. Interventions in the physical and social context can be mapped to his needs in each area. The major focus of this approach to intervention is the individualization of the physical environment and social interactions for the infant with the goal of increased behavioral organization, which is seen as facilitating physical recovery as well.

The approach to intervention from this perspective follows the hierarchical scheme provided by Als and colleagues (e.g., 1982). The assessment provides the framework for defining sources of stress and support for the infant and determining priorities for intervention strategies. Figure 7.4 provides an overview of the hierarchy of behavioral subsystems with a focus for intervention for each.

It is important to differentiate this developmental approach to intervention from an earlier infant stimulation model. The latter approach to preterm infants, in particular, was based on the notion that the NICU environment was sensorily deprived and/or that input for the infant was to be modeled from the physical and social environment of the full-term, healthy newborn. Further studies of the NICU environment and the development of the fetal neonate do not support that approach (e.g., Gottfried & Gaiter, 1985). Developmental or individualized intervention strategies have been validated to a limited degree; they remain vulnerable to further research (Harris, 1986).

Baby Boy Mitchell, if assessed from a developmental model using the naturalistic observation scheme described above, would be described in this way:

▪ ▪ ▪ ▪ ▪ ▪ ▪ ▪

The infant's pulmonary pathology along with immaturity makes him very vulnerable to environmental stimulation. His autonomic instability is manifested by mild color changes, oxygen desaturation, decreased heart rate, and tachypnea during tactile stimulation and conversation around his isolette. In terms of motor status, he maintained a flexed position in both upper and lower extremities. Arching and diffuse squirming were observed with tactile and/or auditory stimulation. His attempts to move away from the stimulation and "tuck" himself in were hampered by the physical restraints used. Fairly rapid shifts in states of arousal from sleep to high activity with stimulation were noted, resulting in an "all or nothing" response to being perturbed. No alert or drowsy states were observed; there was no cry.

▪ ▪ ▪ ▪ ▪ ▪ ▪ ▪

Given the observation that stimulation is, in fact, very threatening to Baby Mitchell's overall stability, intervention recommendations likely would focus on protecting the infant from overwhelming input. It may be suggested, for example, that conversation that is not directed at the infant should take place away from the bedside. Oxygen levels should be allowed to return to baseline between procedures, allowing time for recovery between manipulations. Grouping procedures, as feasible, to every 3 or

FIGURE 7.4
Hierarchy of developmental tasks for the high-risk newborn
Source: From "Toward a Research Instrument for the Assessment of Preterm Infants' Behavior (APIB)" by H. Als, B. M. Lester, E. Z. Tronick, and T. B. Brazelton, in H. Fitzgerald, B. M. Lester, and M. W. Yogman (Eds.) *Theory and Research in Behavioral Pediatrics,* Vol. 1, 1982, New York: Plenum.

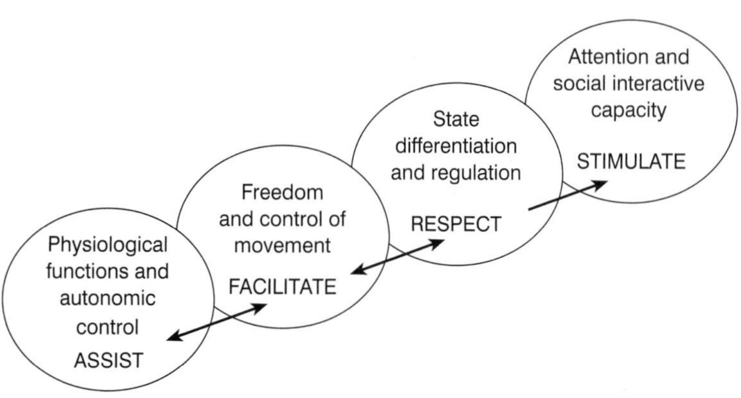

4 hours can be recommended to support more quiet sleep. Positioning in sidelying allows the infant to get his hands to his mouth and provides at least one avenue for self-consoling. Foot rolls, lambskin, and other bedding arrangements can be made for "nesting." Light and environmental noise can be reduced somewhat by covering the top of the isolette. Many of these recommendations can be found in the paper by Als and her colleagues (1986); training in the assessment and intervention is available from this group.

The research in this area is compelling but not conclusive. There is evidence that overstimulating a medically fragile infant can have negative physiological and developmental effects. There also is evidence that individualizing the environment to the infant's specific needs and competencies will promote improved immediate outcomes and possibly longer-term ones. What is not known is *which* infant can benefit from *which* intervention. It is not known which interventions may be harmful to which infant. It is essential that the developmental clinician be armed with information about intervention studies as well as some reasonable skepticism about current models for positively influencing the future of a developing person.

Assessment of Newborn Infant Temperament and Relationships with Caregivers

Since its development, the NBAS has been extensively used and studied as an intervention with caregivers. The behavioral exam is seen as an opportunity for the clinician to join with caregivers in observing, discovering, and discussing the newborn's individuality—in particular, the infant's competencies and characteristic responses to caregiver behavior. Indeed, this type of intervention has substantial face validity: Any relationship requires two individuals, each responding to and perceiving a response from the other. A parent's becoming acquainted with the infant's needs and responses could facilitate a view of the infant as separate, as having individual characteristics, and as influencing and being influenced by the parent. At least in theory, the intervention could support a more optimal beginning relationship for vulnerable infants and caregivers.

Several studies support this notion. Outcome measures of qualities of the developing parent-child relationship such as sensitivity, involvement, responsiveness, and reciprocity have been associated with the NBAS being used as an intervention. Worobey (1984) has provided a comprehensive review of these studies. One study in particular is relevant to the concerns about Baby Girl Lucas and her mother. Widmayer and Field (1981) demonstrated the NBAS to a group of teenage mothers from lower socioeconomic groups. The intervention seemed to be associated with higher infant performance at one year on the Mental Scales of the Bayley Scales of Infant Development (1969).

The manner in which effects like those from the Widmayer and Field study are mediated is not clear and probably is quite complex. One scenario might be that Baby Lucas's mother does not appear interested in the infant because of her own low self-esteem and lack of confidence that she can care for her baby. In addition, the infant's temperament may be predominantly quiet, not intense, and not demanding. The couple may be the kind of "fit" that could produce neglect, increase infant lethargy, and increase maternal withdrawal. The experience of the infant as having needs and as positively responding to her caregiving could provide a foundation for a long-term relationship of mutual awareness, need, and response.

Several works are available to guide the clinician for using neurobehavioral assessment to identify individual differences and to intervene with families. Nugent (1985) has provided an excellent text that includes descriptions of individual test items from the NBAS, interpretations that can be used with caregivers, and implications for caregiving.

SUMMARY OF KEY CONCEPTS

- The constructs of concern and assessment strategies for newborn behavioral assessment have their origins in developmental neurology, behavioral pediatrics, and developmental psychology.
- One major component of the behavioral assessment of the newborn is rooted in the tradition of neurological assessment with emphasis on evaluating reflexes.
- A pioneer in the field of behavioral pediatrics, Arnold Gesell, observed and documented developmental milestones for the first 5 years of life. Aspects of this normative approach can be found in current strategies for newborn assessment.
- Recent approaches to newborn assessment reflect the evolving models for child development, emphasizing not only the infant's behavior but also the infant's physical and social context and transactions between the infant and context.
- Contemporary views of newborn behavior and development are summarized by three principles: development is seen as hierarchical, dialectical, and teleological.
- Newborn assessment is predicated on the notion that behavior has meaning and is organized. Different models for newborn behavioral organization have fostered different assessment approaches: the neurological exam, an assessment of development milestone achievement, and approaches that integrate both with a view of the infant in an ongoing dynamic relationship with the caregiving context.
- Testing a newborn is highly specialized and requires training in brain-behavior relationships, motor development, and biomedical risk conditions as well as extensive experience handling full-term and preterm delivered infants.
- Newborn infants, especially sick and immature ones, require flexible test procedures. The good examiner derives as much data from observations of the unperturbed infant as possible. When handling the infant, close attention to and respect for the infant's stress signals are necessary.
- With the parent present, newborn assessment provides the opportunity for intervention—for the parent to get to know and understand the individuality of the child and to attach meaning to the infant's behavior.
- The assessment of gestational age and the Apgar score are systems for describing the infant's status at birth; they are usually done by physicians and nurses.
- The Graham Rosenblith exam marked the beginning of a behavioral approach to newborn assessment. Many of the strategies from this exam are found in current popular approaches.
- The Dubowitz neurobehavioral assessment addresses four areas: habitation, muscle tone and movement, reflexes, and behavioral responses to stimuli.
- In an assessment with the NBAS, the infant is seen as an active contributor to his own caregiving through individual differences in behavioral organization. In particular, behavioral state is seen as the mediator of the infant's responses in the areas of autonomic control, motor maturity, state organization, and orientation and habitation.
- The APIB systematically examines the preterm delivered infant's behavioral organization within each evolving subsystem in the synactive model's hierarchy of developing tasks.
- The Neurobehavioral Maturity Assessment (NP-MAP) was designed to assess the preterm delivered infant's developmental

maturity. This exam was developed with a priori attention to the psychometric properties and the standardized administration of test items.

- The strategy of Naturalistic Observation of the Preterm Neonate is a behavioral observation methodology designed to document the preterm delivered infant's responses to stress and support from the environment. The infant's status in each behavioral subsystem from the APIB is assessed without the examiner actually handling the infant. This approach is useful for developing environmental strategies for supporting infant recovery in the neonatal intensive care setting.

REFERENCES

Als, H. (1986). Assessing the neurobehavioral development of the premature infant and the environment of the neonatal intensive care unit: A synactive model of neonatal behavioral organization. *Physical and Occupational Therapy in Pediatrics, 6,* 3–53.

Als, H. (1985a). *Newborn behavior in preterms and full terms.* (Presented at the biannual meeting of the Society for Research in Child Development, Toronto.)

Als, H. (1985b). Patterns of infant behavior: Analogs of later organizational difficulties? In F. H. Duffy & N. Geschwind (Eds.), *Dyslexia: Current status and future directions* (pp. 67–92). Boston: Little, Brown.

Als, H. (1984). *Manual for the naturalistic observation of newborn behavior (preterm and full term).* Unpublished manuscript, Child Development Unit, Children's Hospital Medical Center, Boston, MA.

Als, H., Lawhon, G., Brown, E., Gibes, R., Duffy, F., McAnulty, G., & Blickman, J. (1986). Individualized behavioral and environmental care for the very low birth weight preterm infant at high risk for bronchopulmonary dysplasia: Neonatal intensive care unit and developmental outcome. *Pediatrics, 78*(6), 1123–1132.

Als, H., Lester, B. M., Tronick, E. Z., & Brazelton, T. B. (1982). Toward a research instrument for the assessment of preterm infants' behavior (APIB). In H. Fitzgerald, B. M. Lester, & M. W. Yogman (Eds.), *Theory and research in behavioral pediatrics* (Vol. 1) (pp. 35-132). New York: Plenum.

Als, H., Tronick, E., Lester, B. M., & Brazelton, T. B. (1977). Specific neonatal measures: The Brazelton neonatal behavioral assessment scale. In J. Osofsky (Ed.), *Handbook of infant development* (pp. 185-215). New York: John Wiley & Sons.

Amiel-Tison, C., & Grenier, A. (1983). *Neurologic evaluation of the newborn and the infant.* New York: Masson.

André-Thomas, J., Chesni, Y., & Saint Anne-Dargassies, S. (1960). *The neurological examination of the infant.* London: Medical Advisory Committee of the National Spastics Society.

André-Thomas, J. (1959). Integration in the infant. *Cerebral Palsy Bulletin, 1,* 3–12.

André-Thomas, J., & Saint Anne-Dargassies, S. (1952). *Etudes neurologiques sur le nouveau-né et le jeune nourrission.* Paris: Masson.

Apgar, V. (1953). A proposal for a new method of evaluation of the newborn infant. *Current Researches in Anesthesia and Analgesia, 32,* 260–267.

Apgar, V., Holaday, D., James, L., Weisbrot, I., & Berrien, C. (1958). Evaluation of the newborn infant: Second report. *Journal of the American Review Medical Association, 168,* 1985–1988.

Asch, P., Gleser, G., & Steichen, J. J. (1986). Dependability of Brazelton neonatal behavioral assessment cluster scales. *Infant Behavior and Development, 9,* 291–306.

Avery, G. B. (Ed.). (1987). *Neonatology: Pathophysiology and management of the newborn* (3rd ed.). Philadelphia: Lippincott.

Bayley, N. (1969). *The Bayley scales of infant development.* New York: The Psychological Corp.

Bayley, N. (1993). *The Bayley scales of infant development* (2nd ed.). New York: The Psychological Corp.

Beal, J. A. (1989). The effect on father-infant interaction of demonstrating the neonatal behavioral assessment scale. *Birth, 16,* 1.

Bess, F. H., Peck, B. F., & Chapman, J. J. (1979). Further observations on noise levels in infant incubators. *Pediatrics, 63,* 100–106.

Brazelton, T. B. (1973). *Neonatal behavioral assessment scale.* (Clinics in Developmental Medicine No. 50). Philadelphia: Lippincott.

Brazelton, T. B. (1978). Introduction. In A. Sameroff (Ed.), Organization and stability of newborn behavior: The Brazelton neonatal behavioral assessment scale. *Monographs of the Society for Research in Child Development, 43*(5–6), 1–14.

Brazelton, T. B. (1984). *Neonatal behavioral assessment scale* (2nd ed.). (Clinics in Developmental Medicine No. 88). Philadelphia: Lippincott.

Brazelton, T. B. (1990). Saving the bathwater. *Child Development, 61,* 1661–1671.

Byrne, P. J., Piper, M. C., & Darrah, J. (1989). Motor development at term of very low birthweight infants with bronchopulmonary dysplasia. *Journal of Perinatology, 9*(3), 301–306.

Carey, W. B. (1970). A simplified method for measuring infant temperament. *Journal of Pediatrics, 77,* 188–194.

Catlin, E. A., Carpenter, M. W., Brann, B. A., Mayfield, S. R., Shaul, P. W., Goldstein, M., & Oh, W. (1986). The Apgar score revisited: Influence of gestational age. *Journal of Pediatrics, 109,* 865–868.

Chasnoff, I. J., Burns, K. A., Burns, W. J., Schnoll, S. H. (1986). Prenatal drug exposure: Effects on neonatal and infant growth and development. *Neurotoxicology and Teratology, 8,* 357–362.

Clark, D. L., Cordero, L., Goss, K. C., Manos, D. (1989). Effects of rocking on neuromuscular development in the premature. *Biology of the Neonate, 56*(6), 306–314.

Coles, C. D., Smith, I., Fernhoff, P. M., Falek, A. (1985). Neonatal neurobehavioral characteristics as correlates of maternal alcohol use during gestation. *Alcoholism, 9,* 1–7.

Coles, C. D., Platzman, K. A., Smith, I., James, M. D., & Falek, A. (1992). Effects of cocaine and alcohol use in pregnancy on neonatal growth and neurobehavioral status. *Neurotoxicology and Teratology, 14,* 23–33.

Cornell, E. H., & Gottfried, A. W. (1976). Intervention with premature human infants. *Child Development, 47,* 32–39.

DiLeo, J. (1967). Developmental evaluation of very young infants. In J. Hellmuth (Ed.), *Exceptional infant* (Vol. 1) (pp. 121–142). New York: Brunner/Mazel.

Dubowitz, L., & Dubowitz, V. (1981). *The neurological assessment of the preterm and full term newborn infant.* (Clinics in Developmental Medicine No. 79). London: Heinemann.

Dubowitz, L. M. S., Dubowitz, V., Palmer, P., & Verhote, M. (1980). A new approach to the neurological assessment of the preterm and full term newborn infant. *Brain Development, 2,* 3–14.

Dubowitz, V., Dubowitz, L., & Goldberg, S. (1970). Clinical assessment of gestational age. *Journal of Pediatrics, 77,* 1–10.

Duffy, F. H. (1985). *Evidence for hemispheric differences between full terms and preterms by electrophysiological measures.* Paper presented at the biannual meeting of the Society for Research in Child Development, Toronto.

Eregie, C. O., & Muogbo, D. C. (1991). A simplified method of estimating gestational age in an African population. *Developmental Medicine & Child Neurology, 33*(2), 146–152.

Fanaroff, A. A., & Martin, R. S. (1987). *Neonatal-prenatal medicine.* St. Louis: C. V. Mosby.

Farr, V., Kerridege, D. F., and Mitchell, R. G. (1966). The value of some external characteristics in the assessment of gestational age at birth. *Developmental Medicine and Child Neurology, 8,* 657.

Farr, V., Mitchell, R. G., Neligan, G. A., and Parkin, J. M. (1966). The definition of some external characteristics used in the assessment of gestational age in the newborn infant. *Developmental Medicine and Child Neurology, 8,* 507.

Frankenburg, W. K., Dodds, J., Archer, P., Bresnick, B., Maschka, P., Edelman, N., & Shapiro, H. (1990). *Denver-II: Technical manual.* Denver, CO: Denver Developmental Materials.

Frankenburg, W., & Dodds, J. (1967). The Denver developmental screening test. *Journal of Pediatrics, 71*(2), 181–191.

Gagliardi, L., Brambilla, C., Bruno, R., Martinelli, S., & Console, V. (1993). Biased assessment of gestational age at birth when obstetric gestation is known. *Archives of Disease in Childhood, 68*(1), 32–34.

Gesell, A. (1925). *The mental growth of the preschool child: A psychological outline of normal development from birth to the sixth year, including a system of developmental diagnosis.* New York: Macmillan.

Gesell, A. (1940). *The first five years of life: A guide to the study of the preschool child.* New York: Harper & Brothers.

Gesell, A., & Amatruda, C. (1941). *Developmental diagnosis.* New York: Hoeber.

Gesell, A. L., & Ilg, F. L. (1949). *Child development: An introduction to a study of human growth.* New York: Harper.

Gesell, A., & Thompson, H. (1938). *The psychology of early growth.* New York: Macmillan.

Gingras, J., Weese-Mayer, D., Hume, R., & O'Donnell, K. (1992). Cocaine and development: Mechanisms of fetal toxicity and neonatal consequences of prenatal drug exposure. *Early Human Development, 31,* 1–24.

Ginsburg, H., & Opper, S. (1969). *Piaget's theory of intellectual development.* Englewood Cliffs, NJ: Prentice-Hall.

Glass, P., Avery, G., Kolinjavadi, N., Subramanian, S., Keys, M., Sostek, A., & Friendly, D. (1985). Effect of bright light in the hospital nursery on the incidence of retinopathy of prematurity. *The New England Journal of Medicine, 313*(7), 401–404.

Gorski, P. (1984). Caring for immature infants—a touchy subject. In C. C. Brown (Ed.), *The many facets of touch* (pp. 84–91). Skillman, NJ: Johnson and Johnson.

Gorski, P. A. (1983). Premature infant behavioral and physiological responses to caregiving interventions in the intensive care nursery. In J. Call, E. Galenson, & R. Tyson (Eds.), *Frontiers of infant psychiatry.* New York: Basic Books.

Gottfried, A., & Gaiter, J. (Eds.). (1985). *Infant stress under intense care.* Baltimore, MD: University Park Press.

Gottfried, A. W., Wallace-Lande, P., Sherman-Brown, S., King, J., & Coen, C. (1981). Physical and social environment of newborn infants in special care units. *Science, 214,* 637–675.

Graham, F. K. (1956). Behavioral differences between normal and traumatized newborns: I. The test procedures. *Psychological Monographs, 70*(20, Whole No. 427).

Griffiths, R. (1954). *The abilities of babies.* London: University of London Press.

Harris, M. (1986). Stimulation of premature infants: The boundary between believing and knowing. *Infant Mental Health Journal, 7*(3), 171–188.

Hittner, H. M., Hirsch, J. J., & Rudolph, A. J. (1977). Assessment of gestational age by examination of the anterior vascular capsule of the lens. *Journal of Pediatrics, 91,* 455–458.

Horowitz, F. D., Sullivan, J., & Linn, P. (1978). Stability and instability in the newborn infant: The quest for elusive threads. In A. J. Sameroff (Ed.), Organization & stability of newborn behavior: A commentary on the Brazelton Neonatal Behavioral Assessment Scale. *Monographs of the Society for Research in Child Development, 43,* 29–45.

Huang, C. C., & Yeh, T. F. (1991). Assessment of gestational age in newborns by neurosonography. *Early Human Development 25*(3), 209–220.

Illingworth, R. S. (1960). *The development of the infant and young child: Normal and abnormal.* New York: Churchill Livingstone.

Kellman, N. (1982). Noise in the intensive care nursery. *Neonatal Network, 1,* 81–87.

Knobloch, H., Stevens, F., & Malone, A. F. (1980). *Manual of developmental diagnosis: The administration and interpretation of the revised Gesell and Amatruda developmental and neurologic examination.* Hagerstown, MD: Harper & Row.

Korner, A. F., Brown, W. B., Dimiceli, S., Forrest, T., Stevenson, D. K., Lane, N. M., Constantinou, J., & Thom, V. A. (1989). Stable individual differences in developmentally changing preterm infants: A replicated study. *Child Development, 60,* 502–513.

Korner, A. F., Kraemer, H. C., Reade, E. P., Forest, T., Dimiceli, S., and Thom, V. (1987). A methodological approach to developing procedures for testing the neurobehavioral maturity of preterm infants. *Child Development, 58,* 1479–1487.

Lancioni, G. E., Horowitz, F. D., & Sullivan, J. W. (1980). The NBAS-K: I. A study of its stability and

Individualizing Services

Early intervention professionals spend hundreds of hours every year assessing children and interpreting the results of that process. Although some assessments are conducted to determine eligibility for services, the majority of assessment activities are designed to determine each child's abilities and needs so that an individualized program of services can be provided. A fundamental tenet of all special education endeavors is that each child is unique. Because no one curriculum can meet the diverse needs of children with disabilities, the operational definition of *appropriate education* rests heavily on the extent to which the particular goals established and services provided meet the needs of the individual child. The vehicle by which a child's goals and services are determined is the assessment process.

This reasoning can be extended quite logically to the provision of services for families. Families differ widely in many respects, including the meaning they attach to their child's disability, the way the family is organized, the goals they have for their children, their views of service providers and public systems of family assistance, and the ways in which they want to be involved in making decisions and providing services for their child. Making assumptions about any of these dimensions for a particular family could easily result in faulty conclusions and the provision of a service plan that is not consistent with an individual family's needs and priorities. Thus a second rationale for family assessment is to ensure that family services are individualized.

Building Relationships

An early intervention endeavor is rarely accomplished in a neutral and distant fashion. Most of the time it rests on a relationship or set of relationships that families establish with professionals. There is often a close bond between parent and professional, but the relationship may become strained or even adversarial. A third goal of family assessment is to promote positive relationships between parents and professionals by communicating, in a positive fashion, that professionals generally are aware that raising a child with a disability imposes unique challenges for a family, are interested in listening to the family's concerns and priorities, and are willing, given the resources that are available, to individualize child and family services accordingly.

It should be noted that while family assessment has the potential for achieving this goal, it also has the potential for standing in the way of positive relationships, especially if families view the process as intrusive or not relevant to their child's needs. Thus caution must be exercised in the way family assessment is conceptualized and implemented.

Theoretical Rationale

The rationale for family assessment also has an important theoretical basis. Several decades ago, the prevailing view was that the relationship between parent and child, especially between parent and infant, was unidirectional. That is, most effort was expended in understanding how the parent influenced the child. Bell (1968) argued that, in fact, this relationship is bidirectional; although the parent certainly influences the child, it is clear that parental behavior is in turn altered by the child's behavior. Sameroff and his colleagues (Sameroff & Chandler, 1975; Sameroff & Fiese, 1990) have expanded this concept to a transactional model, arguing that not only is the interaction bidirectional, but also, children and caregivers continue to influence each other in repeated transactions over time. Bronfenbrenner (1977) proposed an ecological model that expands the sphere of influence beyond parent and child to include broader neighborhood and community systems. Although our field continues to discuss alternative models, it is widely agreed that some sort of general systems model is needed to understand families and how they function (Campbell & Draper, 1985). According to systems theory, families function as organizational units—they struggle to achieve balance, they become increasingly complex over time, and family members continually affect and are influenced by each other (Steinglass, 1984).

These theories have helped us realize several important facts (Bailey & Simeonsson, 1988b). First, a child with a disability inevitably has an effect on a family—usually a range of effects, some positive and some challenging. Thus family support becomes an important goal of early intervention. Second, any intervention with the child almost certainly will have an influence on the family. Furthermore, any intervention or support with one family member is likely to affect the child with a disability as well as other family members. Finally, families live in a broader community that includes their culture, neighborhoods, extended family members, friends, and religious organizations. Family assessment ought to help professionals understand and appreciate the complex ecology in which families live so that services can be provided in a way that builds on natural ecological supports and fits with what Bernheimer, Gallimore, and Weisner (1990) refer to as the family's "ecological niche." They argue that each family constructs a view of itself that is consistent with their culture and circumstances. Family assessment can help professionals understand both the objective aspects of this ecology (e.g., family living conditions) as well as how family members perceive their ecology.

Evaluating Quality of Services

Early intervention programs are accountable to the children and families they serve, to the local community, and to the state and federal agencies that provide much of the funding for early intervention services. Historically this accountability has rested almost exclusively on the quality of services for children with disabilities. Today, however, early intervention programs must also be accountable for services to families. This poses significant challenges to any evaluator. Although it is relatively easy to document child changes in basic areas of development (e.g., cognitive, language, motor), behavioral and social skills, and engagement, the effects of programs on families can be more difficult to document. This does not reduce the importance of this concept, however, and thus a final reason for engaging in family assessment activities is to document whether the program has been responsive to family needs and the decision to be involved.

DIMENSIONS OF FAMILY ASSESSMENT

Although family assessment is a relatively recent phenomenon in early intervention, the process of gathering information about families has a much more extensive history. Understanding the historical context and roots is important as we seek to construct a framework for assessment that is meaningful in the context of early intervention. This framework then provides the basis for determining the various dimensions of family assessment.

Traditions in Family Assessment

Professionals from a variety of disciplines have engaged in family assessment for years. These efforts have yielded a large number of instruments and procedures. Which of them have relevance for early intervention? This question is best answered by examining the measures in the context of three related but distinct historical traditions: research, clinical, and support (Bailey & Henderson, 1993). In the research tradition, investigators have used assessment instruments in order to understand the general nature of families, how they function, and how they develop. As described by Simeonsson (1988), researchers have focused on structural aspects of the family (who is in the family and how they interact with each other), developmental aspects (how the family grows and changes over time), and functional aspects (what tasks the family needs to accomplish, what stresses they experience, and what strategies they use to meet demands and adapt to stressful events). In the clinical tradition, assessment instruments have been developed to help family therapists, psychologists, and social workers counsel families who are experiencing problems in some aspect of family relationships. A variety of assessment techniques have been developed to pinpoint specific areas of difficulty, and some are used to classify families into typologies (e.g., Beavers & Voeller, 1983; McCubbin & Thompson, 1987b).

The research and clinical traditions differ in a number of ways. In the research tradition the goal is to develop a generalized understanding about the nature of families, whereas the goal of clinical assessment is to gain a better understanding of a particular family. Scientists who gather data in the research tradition rarely meet the families they study; clinicians often know the most intimate and personal details about a particular family. Assessments in the research tradition do not usually benefit families directly; clinical assessment is designed to aid directly through the process of therapeutic counseling.

These frameworks are presented in order to emphasize that a fundamental criterion for evaluating the appropriateness of a given family assessment procedure is whether its purpose and format are consistent with the goals of the context in which it is being used. Although many of the instruments developed in the research and clinical traditions have excellent psychometric properties and have yielded important information about families, this does not necessarily mean that the measures will be especially useful in the context of early intervention, which is neither necessarily clinically nor research-based in its orientation.

Family assessment strategies for early intervention have emerged out of a third tradition, the support tradition (Bailey & Henderson, 1993). Zigler and Black (1989) have suggested that family support programs have as their ultimate goal enabling families to be independent by promoting their own informal support network. The support tradition differs from the clinical tradition in that it does not assume that there is something inherently wrong or problematic within the family. Rather it starts with the assumption that each family is competent and like any other family, the primary difference being that this family happens to have a child with a disability. In recognition of the difficulties that often arise in raising a child with a disability, the support tradition attempts to provide services to alleviate any perceived caregiving burden, make available to families an array of resources and services, and facilitate easy access to these services, hopefully helping families feel competent to deal with present and future challenges. Family assessment strategies evolving from the support tradition are designed to determine a family's resources and supports and how the family perceives those resources relative to their concerns and priorities. The overall goal is to gather sufficient information so that the early intervention professional can provide an array of supportive services that are consistent with each family's values and concerns.

Recognizing that family assessment in early intervention emanates from the support tradition has direct implications for early intervention professionals. For example, an assessment of marital satisfaction would be highly consistent with the research on clinical traditions (depending on the particular problem under study or treatment). However, it is highly unlikely that such a measure would be used in the support tradition. Although perceived support by a spouse has been shown to be important for many individuals (e.g., McKinney & Peterson, 1987), improving marital relations is not likely to be an early intervention goal; furthermore, asking questions about marital relations is likely to be viewed as intrusive by many families and thus prevent the development of a trusting and collaborative relationship between parents and professionals. On the other hand, family members who express concern about marital relationships should be supported in finding services to address that concern.

Domains of Family Assessment

What, then, are the domains of family assessment? This would be a relatively easy question to answer if we were talking about children; most professionals would identify such critical areas of development as motor, communication, cognitive, adaptive, and social skills. But in the case of family assessment, the answer is not so clear. A review of the existing literature reveals many potential domains that could be assessed: stress, coping styles, teaching skills, parent-child interaction, the home environment, locus of control, support systems, and stages of grief, to name but a few. However, the discussion of traditions in family assessment suggests that most of these domains are not likely to be appropriate for family assessment conducted for the purpose of providing support.

According to federal legislation, the appropriate domains for assessment are family resources, priorities, and concerns related to the care of the child with a disability. This means that family assessments ought to be designed to determine the family's perception of the child, of his or her needs, and of the family's desires for services or other kinds of support from professionals. This still is very general, however. In order to provide a more functional framework for family assessment, it might be useful to organize the assessment model around key questions, the answers to which would help professionals provide services in a more family-centered fashion (Bailey & Henderson, 1993). Three questions are likely to be essential in this process: (1) What roles does the family want to play in the process of making decisions about their child and in providing educational or therapeutic interventions? (2) What does this family want from the service system? (3) How do family members perceive the service system and what constitutes an acceptable relationship between parents and service providers? Each of these questions likely will result in a series of related questions that provide important supplementary information.

How does this family want to be involved in planning and providing services? Families vary considerably in the extent to which they want to be involved in assessment, team meetings, decision making, and service delivery. Some families want to play a major leadership role in determining the assessment information to be gathered, participating in the team meeting, and making decisions about goals and services for the child and the family. At the other end of the continuum, some families would prefer that professionals take the leadership in these roles. In fact, the range of possible roles family members could fill is very wide. Four considerations are important in the context of this domain.

First, a family-centered approach does not force families to be at any particular point in the continuum of involvement in planning. Turning over the leadership of a team meeting, for example, might be very positive and supportive for some families, but might be quite threatening for others. Because such wide variability exists in desired parental roles, an individualized assessment of these preferences is essential.

Second, it should be recognized that family preferences for involvement may vary depending on the nature of the activity. For example, there are many domains in which parents could potentially be involved: decisions about the goals and nature of the child assessment process, the extent to which they want to be involved in child assessment, participation in team meetings and decision making, involvement in the child's intervention activities, and participation in case management activities. One parent may want to participate actively in the team meeting but would prefer that professionals make all decisions related to the child's assessment. A second parent may prefer a professional case manager but want to be actively involved in her child's treatment. A third parent may want to play leadership roles in all areas. Therefore, any assessment of the parents' wishes to be involved in the process of making decisions and providing services should not be a general assessment, but rather should seek to ascertain preferred roles in a variety of different contexts.

Third, it is also important to recognize that family preferences could easily change over time. For example, one parent might initially feel insecure and very uncomfortable in trying to play a leadership role when surrounded by a team of highly trained professionals. But after almost a year of early intervention services and frequent interactions with professionals, he feels more comfortable and confident in his own opinions and skills and gradually begins to exert more influence and play more extensive roles. Another parent, however, may initially not trust professionals and therefore play a very active role in the initial processes. After a year of participating in early intervention, however, she gradually relinquishes some of those roles as she takes on her own professional responsibilities and feels more comfortable with allowing the professionals to make decisions without her constant input. These two examples demonstrate the changes in role preference that quite likely will occur during the period of time a professional has the opportunity to provide services to a child and family. Thus it becomes important for professionals not to assume continuity of role preferences and to provide regular opportunities for parents to express their desired roles.

Finally, professionals should also realize that some families may want or need assistance so that they can participate fully in various program activities. For example, Brinckerhoff and Vincent (1986), prior to the IEP meeting, gave parents a brief assessment inventory for them to describe their child's typical skills at home and then met with the parents individually to help them anticipate what would happen in the team meeting. They found that parents who participated in these activities were more likely to make comments and suggestions during the actual team meeting. Likewise, Goldstein and Turnbull (1982) found that an informal individual meeting with parents served to increase active parent participation in the subsequent IEP meeting. These data suggest that for some parents lack of participation reflects an insecurity about the process or a perceived lack of skills. Thus it would be a good idea to make options available for parents on an ongoing basis that recognize the concerns parents might have and provide opportunities for building both confidence and skills.

What does this family want from the service system? The second major focus of family assessment is determining family goals and desires for services. Historically, of course, the primary service most parents want is therapeutic and specialized educational interventions for their child with a disability, and this remains true today. As professionals, we would never have the chance to interact with a particular family if that family did not have a child with a disability, and it is the disability itself that is likely to be of concern to most parents. Thus one essential aspect of family assessment is determining the goals families have for their children, the settings in which they would like their child to spend time, and the services they feel would best help their child achieve his or her goals.

For some families, a focus on the child's needs is sufficient. However, many families have additional concerns, sometimes temporary and sometimes long-term, with which early intervention professionals could be of help. Many early intervention programs have made assumptions about the kind of support services families would like, offering such activities as parent support groups, parent training sessions, or sibling support groups. However, we have come to realize that a standard program of services is likely to meet the needs of only some families. Thus an assessment of individual priorities and concerns is important.

A primary consideration in this aspect of family assessment is recognizing that the likely range of concerns families might have is considerable. One of the needs most frequently expressed by parents is for more information about their child and his or her disability, suggestions for teaching the child or handling behavior problems, and information regarding services available for their child both now and in the future (Bailey, Blasco, & Simeonsson, 1992; Cooper & Allred, 1992). Other families may have needs related to family and social support (e.g., someone to talk with about concerns), finances (ranging from basic expenses to the costs of special equipment), ideas for explaining their child's condition to other people or helping nuclear or extended family members cope with the disability, child care (e.g., babysitters, respite care providers, daycare), professional and community support (e.g., a counselor, an understanding physician, or a parents' support group), or case management services to help locate and gain access to a variety of community resources and coordinate efforts across agencies. This short list provides some indication of the expanded roles now expected of early intervention programs and professionals. Obviously, early intervention and preschool programs will not be able to provide all of these services directly; however, professionals should be aware of other community resources that could be helpful and provide support and assistance for families. For example, if a family wants their child placed in a regular daycare center near the office where one of the parents is employed, an early intervention professional might work with the staff of the child-care program so that they can appropriately support the child's learning and therapeutic goals.

It should also be recognized that family needs and concerns are likely to change over time. Families may have more needs for support when they are experiencing or anticipating an event of some significance (Wikler, 1981). Some of these events are directly related to the child with a disability. For example, when parents are first told about their child's disability or when they gain new and unexpected information at a later time (e.g., a preschooler begins to experience mild seizures), they may want repeated opportunities to speak with a professional to discuss the meaning or implications of this information (Cunningham, Morgan, & McGucken, 1984). A transition from one program to another is also a stressful event. During the early childhood period, at least four such transitions are potentially challenging: (1) from the hospital to home (especially if the hospital is where the initial diagnosis occurred or if the stay in the hospital was extended due to complications, illness, or surgery); (2) first-time entry into the early intervention service delivery systems; (3) the transition into some type of center-based program with other children; and (4) entry into kindergarten. Prior to these transitions, parents may want information and support in making decisions regarding the transition placement decision, the child may need to be prepared for the transition in some way, and an early intervention professional may need to be available during the transition period to ensure that things go smoothly. Often this involves significant parent involvement, several meetings, and interagency cooperation (Noonan & Kilgo, 1987; Rosenkoetter, Hains, & Fowler, 1994). In recognition of the special challenges associated with changes in programs and agencies, Public Law 99-457 even requires that a formal transition plan be developed prior to the child's third birthday to ensure a smooth transition from infant to preschool programs.

How do family members perceive the service system? A third domain of family assessment is determining each family's perception of the service system. Such information is important as professionals seek to establish and build relationships with families. It is also an important part of any program evaluation effort.

At the outset it must be recognized that family perceptions of the service system are often deeply rooted in cultural or family group values about what constitutes an appropriate relationship between families and professionals. In some cultures going to a professional or public agency for services and support is a completely logical and acceptable course of action. In other cultures, professionals and persons who are not members of the cultural group may be viewed with distrust, or dealing with such professionals may simply be viewed as an inappropriate thing to do (see Chapter 4). Even within cultures there is likely to be great variability in families' willingness to seek outside help. Thus an important goal of family assessment, especially when professionals are just getting to know a family, is to ascertain the family's view of service providers. Such information is critical in determining how fast to move with a family and will be essential in formulating an approach that is sensitive to the family's expectations for appropriate behavior.

A related goal in this domain is the documentation of parent satisfaction with services and the interactions they have had with professionals. Assessment of satisfaction should be multifaceted rather than generic, because families may be satisfied with some aspects of the program but not others. Simeonsson (1988) recommends that the assessment of satisfaction should cover communication patterns between parents and professionals, the quality of service provided to both child and family, and the extent to which parents consider the early intervention team to be competent, sensitive, and empathetic.

GENERAL PROCEDURAL CONSIDERATIONS IN FAMILY ASSESSMENT

Family assessment, when conducted appropriately, can expand traditional child-focused assessment models and help early intervention programs be consistent with a family-centered approach to services. Many professionals and parents, however, experience a negative reaction when they hear the term *family assessment,* probably because they associate it with more formal testing with its standardized procedures and scores that are often interpreted in comparison with some normative sample. Because of the potentially sensitive nature of family assessment for both parent and professional, this section draws heavily on two previous publications (Bailey, 1991; Bailey & Henderson, 1993) to discuss six considerations: multimethod approaches, assessment as intervention, timing of assessment, whose job family assessment is, variations in family and professional perceptions, and evaluation of family assessment instruments and procedures.

Multimethod Approaches

At the beginning of this chapter family assessment was defined as the process of gathering information in order to determine family priorities for goals and services. From this framework, one could view every interaction a professional has with a family as a form of family assessment. It is well known from the family therapy literature that an effective therapist takes the opportunity to learn about a family or a family member in the context of all interactions. This requires starting out with a set of questions (e.g., How do these parents want to participate in the decision-making process?), gathering information related to those questions, forming and reformulating hypotheses over the context of repeated interactions with families, and maintaining an open and noncritical stance throughout this process (Selvini, Boscolo, Cecchin, & Prata, 1980). Early intervention professionals should take advantage of the information that is inherent in phone calls, notes, and informal exchanges during arrival and departure in order to learn about family resources, priorities, and concerns. Typically this information is available from the verbal and nonverbal exchanges that occur between parents and professionals.

In addition to using effective communication skills in informal contexts, at least three other general strategies are available. The focused interview (Winton, 1988b; Winton & Bailey, 1988) is a somewhat more structured interaction in which the professional identifies in advance topics to be discussed and plans a series of questions likely to develop a positive relationship with the family members participating in the interview and elicit the desired information. Paper-and-pencil measures primarily exist in the form of questionnaires and rating scales. Some families prefer paper-and-pencil strategies for sharing information, either because it is a more comfortable format for them or because the items on the survey (e.g., a list of possible family needs or program services) provide a set of definite options from which to choose as compared with an open-ended interview (Bailey & Blasco, 1990). Finally, direct observation procedures can be used to describe such dimensions as parent-child interactions or the home environment.

Each of the procedures will be described in greater detail later in this chapter. The message in this section is that family assessment can involve an array of strategies, all of which should be taken advantage of as professionals seek to ascertain family perceptions and desires.

Assessment as Intervention

A second general point is that the assessment process itself is rarely a neutral event, and in fact may have the effect of an intervention, sometimes with intended effects but perhaps more often resulting in unintended consequences. Tomm (1987), speaking from the context of family therapy, suggests that anything a therapist does is possibly significant because it might either affirm or challenge something the family or an individual family member says or does. This is likely to be true in early intervention as well. Despite all of our efforts to enable and empower families so that they feel competent as caregivers and as decision makers (Dunst, Trivette, & Deal, 1988), most parents view professionals as having a great deal of valuable expertise as well as being in control of resources. Because parents often want access to both information and services, professionals are seen as authority figures and gatekeepers, providing or denying access to services. Professional views of both the child and the family are thus of great importance to families and, as Tomm (1987) suggests, all professional activities may take on great meaning for many families.

Given this possibility, professionals should recognize that the very act of conducting family assessment is likely to affect the relationship between parents and professionals as well as the parents' views of themselves. The nature of this influence will vary depending on the assessment activity and the parents' perception of it. For example, informally asking how a sibling reacted to recent surgery for a brother or sister with Down syndrome might be viewed as prying by some families and as caring by others. Providing families with the opportunity to complete a survey of family needs might be viewed as meaningless paperwork by some fathers and as a good vehicle for identifying needed support services by others.

An assessment of the quality of parent-child interactions might be viewed as a helpful attempt to deal with behavior problems by one mother and as a judgmental effort to determine adequacy of parenting styles by another. These examples show that it is important for professionals to recognize that family assessment activities ought to improve the relationships between families and professionals and should help identify needs for services. However, sometimes the assessment process can have negative effects and thus great care must be taken to ensure that the extent, nature, and methodology of family assessment is consistent with each individual family's preferences and views.

Timing of Family Assessments

When in the process of becoming acquainted with families should assessments be conducted? Some professionals argue that assessment is too personal to do when one is just beginning to know a family. Others have argued that an early assessment of family resources, priorities, and concerns is essential to good planning. Consistent with earlier points in this chapter, two guidelines are important. First, if one takes the broad definition of family assessment as any activity in which the professional gains new information about the family's perception of resources, priorities, and concerns, then the question is meaningless. A professional engages in family assessment from the first interaction. Thus the question becomes not one of if and when family assessments are done, but rather one of the nature and formality of the assessment activities. Second, regardless of the nature and timing of the assessment, it is important that the professional communicate, very early in the acquaintance process, a willingness to listen to family concerns and to respond to an array of family requests for services. How this is done will vary from family to family, but the family support component of early intervention should not be viewed as something that is put off until the professional has had a chance to focus on the child's needs and the family has had time to develop a relationship with professionals. It is in the context of those very processes that the most important family assessment activities are conducted.

Assigning Responsibility for Family Assessment

Whose job is it to conduct family assessments? The regulations accompanying federal early intervention legislation state that such assessments must be conducted by individuals who have received appropriate training. What does this mean? One interpretation is that only social workers, nurses, or psychologists should conduct family assessments, since they are the professionals most likely to have received extensive training in working with families (Bailey, Simeonsson, Yoder, & Huntington, 1990). If one takes the definition of family assessment offered in this chapter, however, it is every professional's responsibility to engage in assessment activities. Every professional who interacts with a family and their child has the opportunity to learn more about the nature and extent of family preferences for services, roles, and relationships with professionals, by paying attention to the questions, comments, and behavioral responses observed in the context of those interactions.

This diffuse responsibility does not reduce the need for specialized training, however. Research has documented that professionals in special education and the allied health professions often receive only minimal training in working with families (Bailey et al., 1990). Furthermore, they report that their family skills and the extent to which they value family roles are less than that reported by social workers and nurses (Bailey, Palsha, & Simeonsson, 1991). These data, coupled with findings across multiple settings indicating discrepancies between typical and desired practices in working with families (Bailey, Buysse, Edmondson, & Smith, 1992; Brown & Ritchie, 1990; Mahoney & O'Sullivan, 1990; Rushton, 1990), suggest that more training is needed so the professionals who interact most frequently with children and families have the skills needed to assess family resources, priorities, and concerns. Probably the most important of these skills is the ability to communicate effectively with families and to establish a trusting and collaborative relationship. Beyond that, specific training is certainly needed for particular assessment procedures, especially those such as measures of parent-child interaction that require reliable observational techniques.

Professional versus Family Perceptions

A frequently raised concern among early intervention professionals is the discrepancy that is sometimes observed between parent and professional perceptions of needs for the child and the family (Bailey, 1991). This concern gets to a more basic issue in the context of assessment, namely the difference between objective and subjective perceptions of reality. Historically, child assessment procedures have had the goal of obtaining an objective view of the child, one that is not biased by the tester's own values or experiences, a view that is applied and interpreted in similar ways across all children tested. Thus children are presented a standard set of materials, in a standard format, with standard directions, and standard criteria for scoring responses. Each item has an agreed-upon correct answer, and the quality of the child's performance is evaluated against this standard.

In family assessment, however, it is the subjective and personal view of families that is essential. Research across a number of fields of inquiry has documented that perception of events is a powerful determinant of the way in which an individual or a family responds to that event (McCubbin & Patterson, 1983). Families and professionals are quite likely to disagree on several perceptual dimensions. For example, when discussing the cause and meaning of disability, professionals are likely to focus on biomedical, genetic, and experiential aspects of causation. Although families are interested in these aspects, they are also likely to address questions of meaning: Why did this happen to me or my child, and what is the meaning of this event? Research indicates that culture is a powerful determinant of a family's interpretive frameworks, resulting in a continuum of beliefs ranging from biomedical to folk to religious. Perceived needs of the child and the family constitute a second arena in which the perceptions of parents may be different from that of professionals. For example, the physical therapist may feel strongly that the most important service for a child relates to positioning and adaptive equipment, but a parent might feel that integration with typically developing children is of utmost importance. A third area of possible disagreement is one's perception of the need for and usefulness of particular services. For example, a professional may feel that a parent support group would be very helpful for a father, but the father is not at all interested in participating in such an activity.

These examples are presented to support the argument that subjective views of family resources, priorities, and concerns constitute the primary basis of family assessment. This point of view is reflected in federal legislation, which states that the results of family assessment must be based on the family's own description of its resources, priorities, and concerns. Rarely will there be a "correct" answer in family assessment that is comparable to the "correct" answer in child assessment. Professionals must, for the most part, accept the family's view as the legitimate assessment at a particular point in time. This ensures that the resulting information is useful in designing services that meet individual family perceptions of needs. Of what use is a program of services that by professional standards is outstanding but is not perceived by family members as useful or responsive?

Evaluating Assessment Methods and Procedures

Throughout this text we have discussed the importance of evaluating the reliability and validity of instruments for assessing children's behavior and development. In some instances, these same standards apply to family assessment procedures. This is especially true for measures that have norms and standardized scoring procedures such as the Parenting Stress Index (Abidin, 1990) or observational measures requiring precise coding of parent or child behaviors, such as the Nursing Child Assessment Feeding Scale (Barnard, 1978a). McGrew, Gilman, and Johnson (1992) reviewed a variety of scales designed to assess family needs and rated them on various dimensions of reliability and validity. Many of the measures fell short of the usual expectations for such information, and the authors called for more research to document psychometric properties of family assessment measures.

However, in many cases traditional measures of the quality of an instrument may not be sufficient for family assessment procedures (Henderson, Aydlett, & Bailey, 1993). Consider, for example, an interview with a father, the purpose of which is to discuss his feelings about his child's transition from preschool to kindergarten. No score emerges from this process and the father's responses are not compared with some norm group. His feelings may be time-limited, changing with home circumstances and in accordance with his perceptions of the quality of program for his child. Or take the example of a written survey of family needs. Should this measure have internal consistency or test-retest reliability? What is the criterion against which such responses should be validated? Furthermore, what if one argues that the only way to get a comprehensive view of family resources, priorities, and concerns is to use multiple methods for assessment? If this is the case, does it make sense to evaluate one piece of the assessment process as an isolated measure, or should the evaluation address the overall process? In many ways, this is not too different from assessments conducted to establish goals for children. For example, in identifying the factors that are related to high levels of children's engagement, direct observation with a reliable and valid code may be helpful; however, informal observations, anecdotal records, and the general perceptions of caregivers may be used to obtain rich information about the toys, activities, and contexts that excite, motivate, and captivate children's attention and interaction. To ignore such "subjective" measures would mean that critical information would be lost.

Clearly, family assessment strategies should be evaluated rigorously with regard to their effects and usefulness. When appropriate, the traditional standards of reliability and validity should be applied, and the measurement procedures judged accordingly. However, as Henderson et al. (1993) suggest, two criteria are of fundamental importance. Does the assessment procedure result in useful information? Is the process acceptable to families? With regard to the first criterion, professionals should ask whether the process is helpful in developing an IEP or IFSP that is functional for the child or the family. Too often, assessments are conducted and the results are filed away with little attempt to use the data in a meaningful way for intervention purposes. Families naturally feel frustrated when asked to provide information that is not subsequently used to individualize services (Bailey & Blasco, 1990). The likelihood of this happening is reduced if the process provides information that is truly helpful and of direct relevance for planning purposes. With regard to the second criterion, it may be helpful to ask families to provide feedback on the extent to which they believe certain assessment procedures would provide them appropriate and acceptable avenues for conveying information about resources, priorities, and concerns. Examples of gathering information about family perceptions of the acceptability of different procedures have been provided by Bailey and Blasco (1990), Sexton, Snyder, Rheams, Barron-Sharp, and Perez (1991), and Summers et al. (1990). In general, this research shows that families have definite opinions about the content, timing, and format of family assessment procedures. Their opinions vary, however, and while it may be useful to get group information, an individualized approach will be needed. For example, Bailey and Blasco (1990) asked parents if they would prefer sharing information in a written format or through face-to-face discussions with a professional. About 60% of the mothers preferred personal discussions, but 40% preferred a written survey. The opposite findings were obtained from fathers. Clearly, different parents have different preferences. A family-centered approach to assessment not only allows families to decide whether or not they want to participate in family assessment activities, but also provides reasonable alternatives for strategies for sharing this information.

REPRESENTATIVE METHODS AND PROCEDURES

As we have already discussed, family assessment can take many forms, ranging from informal to very structured. In this section we review and discuss four types of family assessment strategies: informal communication, semistructured interviews, surveys and rating scales, and direct observation procedures.

Informal Communication

Probably the most frequently used form of family assessment (although often not recognized as family assessment) is the informal communication that occurs in the context of daily routines and interactions between families and professionals. Telephone calls, arrival and departure times, notes, and chance interactions that occur in the community all provide occasions for learning more about family resources, priorities, and concerns. The key strategy is for professionals to take advantage of these opportunities and to use the information gained to help answer three ongoing questions: (1) How does this family want to be involved in decision making and service provision? (2) What does this family want from the service system? and (3) How do family members perceive the service system and our relationship with them?

Of fundamental importance in informal contexts is the professional's use of good communication skills. Winton (1988a), in a synthesis of research findings, suggests that there are four critical communication skills: listening, asking questions, responding, and integrating.

Listening One of the most frequent complaints of parents is that professionals have not heard what parents are trying to say to them (Turnbull & Turnbull, 1990). Being a good listener sounds easy, but in fact it is a skill that must be developed and used in an active rather than a passive fashion. According to Winton (1988a), listening requires the professional to show interest in what the parent has to say by attending and responding in both verbal (e.g., responding to comments) and nonverbal (e.g., nodding, appropriate eye contact) ways. A good listener hears what the parent is saying and also pays attention to the nonverbal cues that parents send. Maintaining an accepting attitude is important; judgmental comments, too much suggestion-giving, and preaching are sure ways to cut a communicative interchange short. Among the most frequently observed errors in communicating are interrupting, making irrelevant responses, and using communication styles that seem awkward or unnatural (Matarazzo, Phillips, Wiens, & Saslow, 1965). A good listener allows the communicative partner time to speak, pays attention to the verbal and nonverbal components of communication, and responds in a relevant and noncritical fashion. A good listener also recognizes individual variation in communication styles and preferences, which are likely to vary as a function of culture, education, personality, and experience and comfort in interacting with professionals.

Asking questions A second key communication skill is the ability to ask questions in an appropriate fashion. Asking questions is one way of showing interest in the person with whom you are communicating and is an important way to elicit information that might not otherwise be provided. However, questions can create problems if they are viewed as intrusive or prying or if they are asked in a way that limits responses or communicates judgment. Professionals need to be aware of various ways in which questions can be asked and the advantages and disadvantages of each.

Winton and Bailey (1993) compare and contrast three dimensions of question asking. The first dimension addresses the focus and specificity of questions, with a distinction usually being drawn between closed-ended and open-ended questions. A closed-ended question is one that has a specific answer, either a yes/no response or a specific fact. Examples of closed-ended questions include "How old is Yolanda?" and "Does Marcus have a regular bedtime?" Closed-ended questions are very appropriate if facts are essential. However, it should be recognized that closed-ended questions usually result in short conversations and provide only the information asked for. Open-ended questions are asked in such a way as to allow for a range of responses. For example, instead of asking whether or not Marcus has a regular bedtime, one could ask "What are bedtimes like with Marcus?" This question gives the respondent an opportunity to share a range of things about bedtime and to describe feelings about that experience as well. More importantly, it allows the respondent to focus on what is of importance to him or her rather than on what is of importance to the person asking the question.

A second dimension of question asking is the nature of the question being asked and the message it sends. Some questions appear investigatory in nature and may send a message of blaming the respondent. For example, on a Friday morning drop-off at the child-care center a parent may comment to the therapist that she had not been able to do much with her daughter's physical therapy activities this week. A follow-up question to this comment could be asked in two different ways: "These activities are really important for Maria; why didn't you do them?" or "I know you have other children at home and you are really busy. Is there anything else going on that I should know about that could be of help to us?" The first question places blame on the parent and conveys judgment about the parent's decision not to do therapy. The second conveys a sensitivity to the complicated demands of family life.

A third dimension of questioning addresses the extent to which a question should offer explicit suggestions for solving a problem, and a distinction has been drawn in the literature between strategic and reflexive questions (Tomm, 1987). The suggestion emanating from this literature is that professionals should ask questions in ways that help families develop solutions on their own rather than making specific suggestions. For example, a father might call to let the social worker know that he and his wife will not be attending a parent meeting because they cannot find a babysitter. A strategic question like "Why don't you call the local respite care program?" suggests a specific strategy and either places the parent in a position of having to justify why this was not done or perhaps makes them feel incompetent (Why didn't I think of that?). An alternative question would be "Can you think of ways in the future that you could participate in the meeting and still feel comfortable with child care?"—a reflexive question that prompts the father to think about the situation and reflect on alternative solutions. This is not to suggest that strategic questions should never be used, but rather that alternatives should be considered whenever possible to help families feel competent as decision makers and problem solvers.

Responding A third communication skill is the ability to respond appropriately to parents' comments and questions, and two considerations are important here. First, responses should be related to both the content and the feelings expressed by parents (Winton, 1988a). A conversation is an interaction between two or more individuals in which there is a logic to the flow and in which each participant responds to the messages sent by the other. Messages usually have information about both objective and subjective reality, providing facts as well as telling how the participant feels about the situation. One way to be an effective communicator is to acknowledge and reflect on what you think are both the content ("So you're saying that you would like Diane to be placed in the Tiny Tots Daycare Center") and the feelings contained in a particular message ("So you're saying that although you are worried about whether Diane will have access to all of the special services you need, placement in her sister's daycare center is more important to you at this time"). This conveys an interest in what the communicator says, states what you have heard or felt, and allows the communicator to verify or alter your interpretation of the messages.

Second, responses should attempt to be neutral as opposed to overly supportive or critical (Selvini et al., 1980). The reason for this suggestion relates back to the whole concept of enabling and empowering parents and supporting them in their decision making. The professional's criticism or praise of a parent's decision can create an artificial level of permission and support that may not be helpful for some families. Ultimately, the criteria for evaluating a decision should be whether it accomplishes the goals established and whether parents are satisfied. Although it is certainly acceptable and sometimes an ethical imperative for professionals to give feedback on choices that parents make, it is important to recognize that too much dependency on professional opinion is probably not a good situation.

Integrating Finally, a good communicator is able to conduct a communicative interchange in as natural a fashion as possible and to integrate the information received in that context with other knowledge in order to gain from this assessment opportunity. It is important that parents feel that they have engaged in a conversation with a caring professional, not that they have just seen a therapist who was using professional therapeutic tactics to uncover hidden concerns or meanings. These conversations occur in the context of normal daily routines and as such should feel comfortable and helpful for parents. This increases the likelihood that they will use the opportunities again in the future to share information and feelings. After such interchanges, professionals should reflect on the three fundamental questions described earlier regarding the domains of family assessment and ask whether the interaction changed the nature of the information available regarding family resources, priorities, and concerns.

Semistructured Interviews/Discussions

A second family assessment procedure is the use of semistructured interviews or discussions. These procedures rely heavily on the use of the communication skills described in the preceding section; in fact, face-to-face verbal communication is the essence of both contexts. In contrast to informal communication exchanges, however, which are rarely planned, semistructured interviews or discussions are usually planned and conducted in order to achieve one or more goals. The goal may be very specific, such as determining family preferences for their child's placement next year, or very global, such as discussing hopes and aspirations for the child and the family. These interactions may be initiated by either the parent or the professional.

Given the goal-oriented nature of these interviews and discussions, a structure is needed to ensure that the intended goals are achieved. It is important, however, for this structure to be flexible enough that the interview or discussion is comfortable for both parents and professionals and that it can adjust itself according to the interactions that occur rather than strictly following a preset agenda. Winton (1988b) and Winton and Bailey (1988) suggest that five phases be considered in these interactions: preliminary preparations, introduction, inventory, summarizing, and closure.

Preliminary preparation The first step is to prepare for the meeting. Typically this would involve clarifying the goals of the meeting and gathering any data that would facilitate the discussion and decision making. For example, if the discussion were to focus on placements for next year, it would be helpful to have information about essential characteristics of the placement options that exist. If the purpose of the meeting is more global, it may sometimes be helpful to have families complete or at least look at a survey of family needs (described in the next section) or a list of potential program services so that they have an idea of what is possible for the program to provide. In any case, the professional should take time prior to the meeting to review any existing information, gather pertinent new information, and anticipate possible concerns or requests that might emerge in the meeting.

Introduction One of the first things that should be done at the beginning of the interview is to review the purpose of the meeting. This could be done either by the parent or by the professional, but it is important that each participant has an understanding of what is intended to be accomplished. This does not mean that other goals might not emerge; in fact, they often will. But it sets out an agreed-upon expectation that at least provides a beginning point for discussion. This time can also be used to confirm the time allotted for the meeting, to reaffirm confidentiality, and to assess whether the initial goals are indeed the ones the parents want to address or if other more pressing concerns have emerged.

Inventory This phase essentially is a review of the facts and feelings as perceived by all relevant parties so that an informed decision can be made. Of essential importance is to assess the family's perceptions. For example, in the context of placement decisions, the professional may have the facts about different options, but the parents will have preferences that are influenced by their perceptions of their child's needs and abilities, proximity to home, ease of access, perceived fit, cost, and other factors that would be impossible for the professional to know. This phase is important because full disclosure and discussion of all relevant information is essential for effective decision making.

Summarizing When all of the information has been discussed, it should be reviewed and the costs and benefits of various options weighed. The professional can play an important role in summarizing this information and reflecting both the content of the information and the feelings shared by parents or other caregivers. Parents then need to have the opportunity to make decisions that are consistent with their resources, priorities, and concerns. These can often be elicited through effective use of the reflexive questioning strategies as described above; additional examples of these strategies are provided by Winton and Bailey (1993). Included in this discussion must be the feasibility of the goals and the extent to which the services desired can be provided by the early intervention program or if they must be sought through other agencies and programs. Supportive case management from the early intervention program can help families gain access to these additional services and is thus an important early intervention service in and of itself.

Closure The final phase of the interview or discussion is a summary of the events that have transpired, an expression of appreciation on the part of the professional for the family's time and willingness to share, and a final opportunity to make changes or reflect on the process itself. It is important for the meeting to have some closure to it and ideally it should not be ended until everyone, but especially the family members, feels that the goals originally established have been met or at least addressed in a satisfactory fashion.

Caregiver-Completed Surveys and Rating Scales

A third type of family assessment procedure is the use of surveys and rating scales that are completed by the caregiver. Typically these measures fall into two categories. The first consists of nonstandardized instruments designed primarily to give parents an opportunity to indicate perceived needs for services that could be provided by the early intervention program or that the early intervention program could help access. The second consists of standardized measures designed to assess a variety of domains such as parenting stress, child temperament, or parental locus of control.

Nonstandardized surveys/rating scales

Since the mid-1980s several nonstandardized surveys or rating scales have been developed to assist caregivers and early intervention professionals in identifying family needs for services. Some characteristics of four such measures are displayed in Table 8.1, and a copy of one such instrument is displayed in Figure 8.1. Each consists of a list of needs commonly expressed by families of young children with disabilities. Some are needs for services that might be provided directly by the early intervention program, such as information about their child's disability or more time to talk with their child's teacher or therapist. Others are needs that could best be provided by other agencies, but for which the early intervention program could be helpful in terms of identifying relevant agencies, facilitating initial contacts, and providing supportive coordination of services. Although the surveys differ to some extent in terms of content, there is considerable overlap and it is probably safe to say that each provides a relatively comprehensive listing of reasonable needs and services. Each also has a way for parents or other caregivers to indicate the extent to which they perceive each item to be a need or the extent to which they would like services. However, the nature of these response formats varies considerably. For example, the Family Needs Scale (Dunst, Cooper, Weeldreyer, Snyder, & Chase, 1988) asks parents to rate the frequency of each need on a scale from 1 (almost never) to 5 (almost always), whereas the Family Needs Survey (Bailey & Simeonsson, 1990), simply asks parents to indicate if this is a topic they would like to discuss further with a staff member. A final characteristic of these instruments is that they were designed primarily as practical aids for professionals and family members as they seek to develop individualized family support programs. Thus the use of summary scores or the comparison of responses to a norm group are not characteristic of these instruments. Although some have been used for research purposes, with summary scores used for various analyses (e.g., Bailey et al., 1992), their primary use is a straightforward interpretation of responses to individual items.

TABLE 8.1
Characteristics of Some Commonly Used Surveys of Family Needs

Instrument	Number of Items	Domains	Response Format	Sample Item
Family Needs Survey (Bailey & Simeonsson, 1990)	35	Information Family and Social Support Financial Explaining to Others Child Care Professional Support Community Services	Would you like to discuss this topic with a staff person from our program? No Not sure Yes	Locating a day-care program or preschool for my child
Family Needs Scale (Dunst et al., 1988)	41	Items not grouped by domain	To what extent do you feel the need for any of the following types of help or assistance? NA Not applicable 1 Almost never 2 Seldom 3 Sometimes 4 Often 5 Almost always	Having medical and dental care for my child
Parent Needs Survey (Seligman & Darling, 1989)	26	Items are not grouped by domain	Please check the space that best describes your need or desire for help in each area _____ I really need some help in this area. _____ I would like some help, but my need is not that great. _____ I don't need any help in this area.	More information about how I can help my child
How Can We Help? (Child Development Resources, 1989)	39	Information Child Care Community Services Medical and Dental Care Talking About Our Child Planning for the Future	_____ We have enough. _____ We would like more. _____ Not sure.	Determining the best setting for our child

Research in recent years has provided important information about the nature and usefulness of these measures. First, both parents and professionals have reported that measures such as these are potentially useful ways for parents to share perspectives with professionals. For example, Bailey and Blasco (1990) found that most mothers and fathers in a multistate study rated the Family Needs Survey as likely to be helpful for them and for professionals and stated that they would feel comfortable in sharing this information. Sexton et al. (1991) found that although mothers made some distinctions among measures, they rated three different measures as positive and helpful. Interestingly, mothers' ratings of the potential usefulness of the surveys was higher than the ratings of professionals. Both the Bailey and Blasco study and the Sexton et al. study found that, if given a choice, nearly half of the mothers actually preferred sharing this information through written rather than verbal means. Both studies also showed that parent ratings did not vary as a function of ethnic background or family income.

A second finding that has emerged from the research literature is that if asked, families will indeed express needs for support in a variety of areas. A consistent finding across several studies is the high frequency of expressed needs for information (Bailey et al., 1992; Bailey & Simeonsson, 1988a; Cooper & Allred, 1992; Garshelis & McConnell, 1993). Beyond informational needs, quite a bit of variability has been observed, but it is safe to say that in every study published thus far, all items are endorsed by at least some families. This suggests that families of young children with disabilities are highly individualized in their needs and are willing to express their individual needs in a survey format. Of course, this has implications for early intervention programs because it shows that programs must be prepared to respond to a wide variety of needs.

A third finding is that although the surveys include a wide array of family concerns, it is clear that a professionally generated list is insufficient to capture all of the concerns a family may want to express. Open-ended questions on the survey (Bailey & Simeonsson, 1988a) and follow-up interviews (Winton & Bailey, 1988) have both been shown to be important additions for comprehensive information gathering and clarification of survey responses.

Fourth, professionals need to realize that families are very sensitive about both the wording and the format of material that is sent to them. For example, Bailey and Blasco (1990) found that parents did not like the original wording of a response for the Family Needs Survey *(Definitely need help)* because it made it seem that they were desperate and really had a problem. If a written survey is used, it would probably be a good idea to ask some parents to review it to determine its acceptability and perceived usefulness and to make changes if necessary.

Finally, asking parents to complete a survey sends an explicit message that the program is willing to tailor services in accordance with caregiver responses. Families are understandably frustrated when they are asked to complete forms that they perceive as meaningless or that they perceive as meaningful but for which there is no follow-up. Professionals should be aware of the expectations such a survey establishes and be prepared to either provide services or help families locate services in accordance with expressions for desired assistance.

It should be noted that other measures have been developed in the past five years that tap areas in addition to family needs for services. Dunst and his colleagues have developed a number of these; they are described in Dunst, Trivette, and Deal (1988). Perhaps the most frequently used of the Dunst measures is

Child's Name: ____________________ Person Completing Survey: ____________________

Date Completed: ___/___/___ Relationship to Child: ________________________

Dear Parent:

Many families of young children have needs for information or support. If you wish, our staff are very willing to discuss these needs with you and work with you to identify resources that might be helpful.

Listed below are some needs commonly expressed by families. It would be helpful to us if you would check in the columns on the right any topics you would like to discuss. At the end there is a place for you to describe other topics not included in the list.

If you choose to complete this form, the information you provide will be kept confidential. If you would prefer not to complete the survey at this time, you may keep it for your records.

	Would you like to discuss this topic with a staff person from our program?		
TOPICS	**No**	**Not Sure**	**Yes**
Information			
1. How children grow and develop			
2. How to play or talk with my child			
3. How to teach my child			
4. How to handle my child's behavior			
5. Information about any condition or disability my child might have			
6. Information about services that are presently available for my child			
7. Information about the services my child might receive in the future			
Family & Social Support			
1. Talking with someone in my family about concerns			
2. Having friends to talk to			
3. Finding more time for myself			
4. Helping my spouse accept any condition our child might have			
5. Helping our family discuss problems and reach solutions			
6. Helping our family support each other during difficult times			
7. Deciding who will do household chores, child care, and other family tasks			
8. Deciding on and doing family recreational activities			
Financial			
1. Paying for expenses such as food, housing, medical care, clothing, or transportation			
2. Getting any special equipment my child needs			
3. Paying for therapy, day care, or other services my child needs			
4. Counseling or help in getting a job			
5. Paying for babysitting or respite care			
6. Paying for toys that my child needs			

FIGURE 8.1

Family Needs Survey (Revised 1990)

Source: The Family Needs Survey was developed by Don Bailey, Ph.D., and Rune Simeonsson, Ph.D. For further information, write the authors at the Frank Porter Graham Development Center, CB#8180, University of North Carolina, Chapel Hill, NC 27599.

TOPICS	Would you like to discuss this topic with a staff person from our program? No	Not Sure	Yes
Explaining to Others			
1. Explaining my child's condition to my parents or my spouse's parents			
2. Explaining my child's condition to his or her siblings			
3. Knowing how to respond when friends, neighbors, or strangers ask questions about my child			
4. Explaining my child's condition to other children			
5. Finding reading material about other families who have a child like mine			
Child Care			
1. Locating babysitters or respite care providers who are willing and able to care for my child			
2. Locating a daycare program or preschool for my child			
3. Getting appropriate care for my child in a church or synagogue during religious services			
Professional Support			
1. Meeting with a minister, priest, or rabbi			
2. Meeting with a counselor (psychologist, social worker, psychiatrist)			
3. More time to talk to my child's teacher or therapist			
Community Services			
1. Meeting and talking with other parents who have a child like mine			
2. Locating a doctor who understands me and my child's needs			
3. Locating a dentist who will see my child			

Other: Please list other topics or provide any other information that you feel would be helpful to discuss.

____

____

____

Is there a particular person with whom you would prefer to meet?

____

____

____

Thank you for your time.

We hope this form will be helpful to you in identifying the services that you feel are important.

FIGURE 8.1
Continued

the Family Support Scale (Dunst, Jenkins, & Trivette, 1988), which consists of a list of 18 people and groups that families may use as sources of support. Respondents are asked to rate on a scale from 1 (not at all helpful) to 5 (extremely helpful) how helpful the sources have been to their family over the past 3 to 6 months. Research with this measure (e.g., Dunst, 1985) as well as research in other contexts provides clear evidence that perceived support is critical to family coping and adaptation. Knowledge of family resources is a key aspect of family assessment, and scales such as the Family Support Scale, used in conjunction with interviews and informal discussions with parents, can provide information that would be useful in working with families to identify areas in which additional support is needed or areas of special strength (e.g., an extended family that lives nearby) that could be drawn on to meet particular needs (e.g., child care during parent meetings).

Standardized parent-completed measures The types of scales mentioned in the previous section were developed by researchers and practitioners working with early intervention programs in need of a practical means to identify family concerns. Other measures have been developed using more traditional instrument development procedures and have been recommended for different purposes. In general, such measures are not likely to be used globally with all families in the context of a program's family assessment efforts, but only occasionally depending on the assessment needs of a particular context. They are similar to the measures described in the previous section in that they rely almost exclusively on the parent's or other caregiver's response to a particular item. The major differences have to do with the way data are summarized and interpreted. Measures in this category typically result in scores that are interpreted in reference to a normative group or relative to a cut-off score that indicates that an individual or a family is at risk for some type of problem.

Stress measures constitute one such assessment. One of the original stress measures that has been widely used in the research literature and clinical practice is the Questionnaire on Resources and Stress (QRS) (Holroyd, 1974, 1986). The instrument consists of 285 items grouped into three scales: Personal Problems, Family Problems, and Problems of Index Case (limitations and needs of the family member with a disability). Each item consists of a problem statement (e.g., "As the time passes I think it will take more and more to care for ____," which the respondent marks as true or false. A 66-item short form was developed by the author and a 52-item short version was empirically developed and reported by Friedrich, Greenberg, and Crnic (1983). Another example of a stress measure is the Parenting Stress Index (PSI) (Abidin, 1990). Whereas the QRS is designed for all ages, the PSI focuses on families with children up to 12 years of age. The PSI has 101 items organized into two domains (child domain and parent domain) and 16 scales. Each item consists of a statement (e.g., "Since having this child I have been unable to do new and different things"). The respondents use a scale from 1 (strongly agree) to 5 (strongly disagree) to indicate the extent to which the statement is true for them. Both the PSI and the QRS can be interpreted relative to normative groups and have cut-off scores that suggest the need for referral to specialized services. Thus the measures might best be used as a screening procedure for subsequent referral.

Literally hundreds of studies have used these two measures and generally have found them to be useful indicators of stress and predictive of families in need of additional support. For example, research on the PSI has shown that stress can vary as a function of child characteristics (e.g. Bendell, Stone, Field, & Goldstein,

1989) and that the scale can be used to evaluate the impact of a family support program (Telleen, Herzog, & Kilbane, 1989) or predict maternal responsiveness (Wilfong, Saylor, & Elksnin, 1991).

Other measures have been developed for documenting other aspects of family functioning in a normative fashion. For example, McCubbin and Thompson (1987a) describe a wide variety of measures developed by the Family Stress Coping and Health Project. Among the most well known of these are the Family Inventory of Life Events and Changes (McCubbin, Patterson, & Wilson, 1983) (an indicator of life events likely to cause stress in families), the Family Inventory of Resources for Management (McCubbin, Comeau, & Harkins, 1981) (a documentation of the resources families feel they have available to them in everyday life), and the Family Crisis Oriented Personal Evaluation Scales (McCubbin, Olson, & Larsen, 1981) (a measure of problem-solving strategies used by families). As with the PSI and the QRS, all of these measures emanate from a strong research tradition, and their usefulness in the context of research and clinical work has been well documented.

Despite this considerable research and the well-documented usefulness of these measures, early intervention professionals should exercise caution in using them. Recalling our discussion at the beginning of this chapter, these measures come from the research and clinical traditions and usually do not have direct relevance for early intervention professionals. They were designed primarily for use by psychologists and family therapists; most early intervention professionals do not have the training needed to interpret the results accurately or to follow up except through referral (Slentz & Bricker, 1992). In addition, some families may view use of measures such as these as an intrusion on their personal lives, especially if they have not approached the early intervention professional with concerns in these areas.

Standardized Measures and Rating Scales Completed by Professionals

A final category of family assessment procedures is the use of standardized measures and rating scales completed by professionals. As in the previous two categories, these measures can be relatively informal, with a straightforward interpretation resting primarily on responses to each item, or normative, with interpretation based on external norms or criteria. The primary differentiating feature is that these instruments are completed by professionals rather than by parents, and thus constitute a situation in which a person who is not a family member is making a judgment about some aspects of the family. Although such information can be useful, early intervention professionals should be aware that some families may find such ratings judgmental and, if done improperly, offensive. Thus care should be exercised in the use of these measures. Professionals should discuss them with parents and make sure that the assessment is consistent with the family's view of what they want from the early intervention services system.

One set of measures that fall in this category consists of instruments to assess the amount and quality of the interaction between parents and children. The use of parent-child interaction measures is typically justified for two reasons. The first reason is the well-documented finding that the quality of parent-child interactions significantly shapes the child's language, cognitive, social, and emotional development (e.g., Hart & Risley, 1992). Early intervention professionals see children with disabilities for only a short time. Parents spend much more time with their children and thus it is argued that by helping the family improve the amount and quality of parent-child interactions the professional extends the benefits of early intervention in a powerful and enduring fashion. The second reason is that there have been a large number of studies that have documented inadequacies in one or more aspects of the interactions between parents and their children with disabilities (e.g., McGhee & Eckerman, 1983; Yoder, 1987). In part this has been attributed to characteristics of the child with a disability (e.g., being difficult to "read") and in part to what some have described as an overcompensation on the part of the parent to ensure that their child succeeds and learns. Thus the literature argues that parent-child interaction is critical to a child's development and provides some evidence that the quality of interactions between parents and children with disabilities sometimes appears to be inadequate. Parent-child interaction measures are designed to help professionals document whether or not there is a problem and, if so, to describe its nature and the context in which it occurs.

A number of parent-child interaction measures are described by Comfort (1988) and Grotevant and Carlson (1989). Two of the better-known measures are in the Nursing Child Assessment Satellite Training (NCAST) tools: the Nursing Child Assessment Feeding Scale (NCAFS) (Barnard, 1978a) and the Nursing Child Assessment Teaching Scale (NCATS) (Barnard, 1978b), both of which are used to rate the extent to which parents and children interact in a mutually effective and synchronous fashion. The NCAFS, used during the first year of life, employs 76 items in four domains (sensitivity to cues, response to distress, social-emotional growth fostering, and cognitive growth fostering) rated as yes or no in the context of a feeding experience. The NCATS, used from birth to 3 years, uses 73 items to rate the same four domains when the parent is asked to try to teach the child something. Huber (1991) summarizes the research on the NCAST scales and finds them to have adequate reliability and validity. They are efficient, requiring only a short administration time, and can provide useful clinical information about the quality of interaction. Another example of a parent-child interaction scale is the Maternal Behavior Rating Scale (Mahoney, Finger, & Powell, 1985). This scale uses a 10-minute sample of free-play between parent and child to assess parent's expressiveness, warmth, sensitivity to child state, achievement orientation, social stimulation, effectiveness, directiveness, child's activity level, attention span, enjoyment, and expressiveness. Other measures, such as the Social Interaction Assessment/Intervention measure (McCollum & Stayton, 1985), the Parent Behavior Progression (Bromwich, 1981), and the Teaching Skills Inventory (Rosenberg, Robinson, & Beckman, 1984), have different formats but assess similarly overlapping dimensions of parent-child interaction.

In addition to measures of parent-child interaction, another example of a professionally completed measure is a rating of the child's home environment. By far the best known of these measures is the Home Observation for the Measurement of the Environment (HOME) (Caldwell, 1972). Two versions of this instrument exist, one for infants from birth to 3 years and one for preschoolers ages 3 to 6 years. The measures are divided into subscales such as emotional and verbal responsivity of the mother, avoidance of restriction and punishment, organization of physical and temporal environment, provision of appropriate play materials, maternal involvement with the child, and opportunities for variety in daily stimulation. Each item is rated true or false by the professionals after a home visit. Research has clearly documented relationships between the HOME ratings and children's language and cognitive development (e.g., Piper & Ramsay, 1980).

Measures of parent-child interaction and the home environment share similar assumptions. They both assume that the home environment and the quality of parent-child interactions are critical to the child's development. However, they constitute a professional judgment about the competence of a parent or the quality of a home, two dimensions of family life that are fundamental to a family's identity and pride and represent dimensions of family life that may differ across cultures. Because most measures of the quality of parent-child interactions and the home environment are based on a white, middle-class conception of quality, professionals should be aware of two essential aspects of this type of assessment. First, the process of conducting such assessments can be threatening to parents because it addresses the very heart of parent competence. Second, the process may incorporate criteria for quality with which some families do not agree. Professionals need to be very careful in the ways such measures are used. Ideally their use should grow out of parents' initiatives and concerns so that the professional is not put in the role of critic or evaluator, but rather the role of consultant and supporter.

STRATEGIES FOR TRANSLATING FAMILY ASSESSMENT INFORMATION INTO GOALS AND SERVICES

The family assessment process has as its ultimate goal the identification of family resources, priorities, and concerns so that early intervention and preschool programs can be tailored to individual family needs and desires for services. In striving to achieve this goal, the strategies by which family assessment information is gathered ought to foster a trusting relationship between parents and professionals and help families feel confident in their roles as team members and parents. Ample research suggests that programs are not providing the full array of family services, that parents want such services (DeGangi, Royeen, & Wietlisbach, 1992; Mahoney, O'Sullivan, & Dennebaum, 1990), and that parents are frustrated when services are provided in a way that ignores the other demands of family life or fails to consider how intervention efforts fit into family routines and environments (Brotherson & Goldstein, 1992). Family assessment can identify the kinds of services or resources parents want so that programs can become more responsive.

This chapter concludes with several recommendations about the assessment process and the translation of assessment information into goals and services. These recommendations address the collaborative nature of this process, the values and perspectives of each team member, and the identification of goals and services.

The Collaborative Process

Virtually every publication that addresses the process of family assessment and goal planning emphasizes the importance of making this a collaborative process (e.g., Turnbull & Turnbull, 1990). The variability across families and across cultures and the goal of promoting the role of families as full team members necessitate a collaborative endeavor (Lynch & Hanson, 1992). Duwa, Wells, and Lalinde (1993) suggest that a family-centered approach to the identification of concerns, priorities, and resources ought to encompass the following characteristics: (1) all concerns evolve from the family based on their culture, values, and lifestyle; (2) concerns encompass the entire family unit and their lifestyle, culture, values, etc.; (3) priorities are based on what the family wishes to focus their energy on; (4) formal and/or informal resources will be utilized as selected by the family; (5) families identify what resources are acceptable from a complete list of what is available; (6) families are encouraged to visualize needs and assess family strengths and weaknesses themselves; and (7) families use their emotions to sort out their strengths, weaknesses, concerns, priorities, and resources (pp. 108-109).

These recommendations are consistent with those offered by other groups (e.g., McGonigel, Kaufmann, & Johnson, 1991), emphasizing the nature of this process as a collaborative one that involves open and ongoing communication between parents and professionals, a recognition of family diversity, and a heavy reliance on family priorities for services and the ways in which this process occurs.

Throughout this process, professionals must work hard to promote family participation and family choice. Kaiser and Hemmeter (1989) argue that many decisions involved in early intervention reflect value-grounded assumptions about what is best for a child or a family. As Bailey (1987) has shown, in many cases the values of professionals and the values of parents differ. Garshelis and McConnell (1993), in a comparison of professional and parent perceptions of family needs, found that only 47% of the professionals' responses matched those of families. These findings emphasize that the perspective of families must form the basis for determining goals and deciding on services as a result of family assessment activities.

Identifying Family Goals and Responding to Expressed Needs

What goals are likely to emerge from this process? For many families, the goals on the IFSP or the IEP will address only the child's needs. If family assessment is conducted properly, part of its focus is on the family's goals and aspirations for their child. Since the child is the reason that professionals have a chance to interact with families, it is entirely appropriate that a child-focused plan be the result of this process for many families. Professionals should not feel disappointed if family assessment does not result in goals other than child goals. The key is for families to be involved in the assessment and planning process, and for them to feel that their opinions have been valued and their concerns heard.

For other families, the goals that emerge from this process may address a variety of other areas in addition to developmental or behavioral goals for the child. As suggested by Bailey, Winton, Rouse, and Turnbull (1990) and Beckman and Bristol (1991), family goals range on a continuum from child proximal to child distal. Child proximal goals are family goals that relate directly to the child with a disability and often involve activities such as home-based instruction by parents or the search for more information about their child's disability. Child distal goals are family goals related to broader family needs, some of which are related to their child's disability (e.g., family support or participation in community services beyond those provided by the school or early intervention program, such as community recreational programs) and some of which relate to the family's ability to access basic resources such as transportation, food stamps, or housing.

Research suggests that in most cases IFSPs are far more likely to address child goals or child proximal goals. For example, Mahoney et al. (1990) found that families received services in a wide variety of areas, but they were more likely to receive services related to information about their child, engagement with the service system (e.g., laws, advocacy, transition planning, etc.), and family instructional activities (e.g., teaching the family how to perform a teaching or therapeutic activity with the child), and were less likely to receive services related to personal and family assistance (e.g., counseling, stress management, parent support groups) or resource assistance (e.g., transportation, community services). All areas of support were rated by families as highly desired, with the exception of personal and family assistance, which was endorsed by only one third of the families. These data suggest that, despite the concerns of some professionals that family assessments will result in massive changes in the types of services provided, most families request support in areas that are directly related to their child or access to community services. They also suggest, however, that professionals may find it easier to write child goals; when family goals are written, they are most likely to focus on family implementation of therapy and instruction, a finding also reported by Bailey et al. (1990). An exception to this finding is a study by Espe-Sherwindt (1991), who examined a number of IFSPs written with parents with mental retardation or other special needs. She found that the majority of outcome statements could be categorized as basic family needs, family enrichment, and support or counseling services. This finding most likely reflects the unique needs of this group of parents; however, it may also reflect the author's systematic use of strategies for promoting problem-solving opportunities for parents with mental retardation (Espe-Sherwindt & Crable, 1993). Regardless, it is clear that the nature and content of the IFSP can (and should) vary depending on the individual family.

Ample research (e.g., Bailey et al., 1992; Garshelis & McConnell, 1993) demonstrates that if asked, many families will express a wide variety of needs, some of which are related to the child and some to broader family support. Thus early interventionists should be prepared to expand the nature and format of services offered or to refer parents to other agencies and professionals when requested services are not directly available through the early intervention program. Raab, Davis, and Trepanier (1993) argue that planning goals in the area of family support should focus away from the provision of services (assistance drawn from existing services offered in a relatively inflexible fashion) and toward the provision of resources (assistance in the form of a range of supports that can be drawn on and adapted in a flexible fashion). This suggestion is consistent with the broader goals of the family assessment process, and emphasizes the need for a flexible support system that is driven by the needs and desires of the family rather than by the extent to which a particular service is currently in existence.

Writing goals and developing a service or resource plan for family support may be different from the process of writing specific objectives for children. Perhaps instead of talking about objectives it may be more useful to refer to goals or outcomes. Drawing on a series of ethnographic interviews with families, Able-Boone, Sandall, Loughry, and Frederick (1990) found that families preferred that IFSP outcomes be stated in the form of suggestions rather than in the usual objective format. Thus the emphasis should be on stating the goal or outcome using the family's terms and then developing a resource implementation plan that is consistent with the way they would like the need to be met.

SUMMARY OF KEY CONCEPTS

- Family assessment is a process by which information is gathered to determine family priorities for goals and services.
- Family assessment is justified because of legislative requirements to individualize services, to establish positive relationships, for theoretical reasons, and to evaluate the quality of services.
- Family assessment is best conducted in an informal fashion, using a variety of procedures over time.
- Family assessment should be designed to determine (a) the family's goals for their child, (b) the family's desires for family support, and (c) the family's view of the service system and service providers.
- When conducting assessments with families, professionals should (a) use multimethod approaches, (b) recognize that assessment activities are potential interventions, (c) consider carefully the timing of assessment activities, (d) define with the family their

roles in assessment, (e) seek families' perceptions, and (f) evaluate the measures and procedures that are used.

- Potential assessment strategies include informal communication, semistructured interviews, surveys and rating scales, and direct observations.
- When translating assessment information into goals and services, professionals should engage in a collaborative process with families, recognize the values and perspectives of each team member, and develop supportive and individualized goals and services.

REFERENCES

Abidin, R. R. (1990). *Parenting Stress Index* (3rd ed.). Charlottesville, VA: Pediatric Psychology Press.

Able-Boone, H., Sandall, S. R., Loughry, A., & Frederick, L. L. (1990). An informed, family-centered approach to Public Law 99-457: Parental views. *Topics in Early Childhood Special Education, 10*(1), 100–111.

Bailey, D. B. (1987). Collaborative goal-setting with families: Resolving differences in values and priorities for services. *Topics in Early Childhood Special Education, 7*(2), 59–71.

Bailey, D. B. (1991). Issues and perspectives on family assessment. *Infants and Young Children, 4*(1), 26–34.

Bailey, D. B., & Blasco, P. M. (1990). Parents' perspectives on a written survey of family needs. *Journal of Early Intervention, 14,* 196–203.

Bailey, D. B., Blasco, P. M., & Simeonsson, R. J. (1992). Needs expressed by mothers and fathers of young children with disabilities. *American Journal on Mental Retardation, 97,* 1–10.

Bailey, D. B., Buysse, V., Edmondson, R., & Smith, T. M. (1992). Creating family-centered services in early intervention: Perceptions of professionals in four states. *Exceptional Children, 58,* 298–309.

Bailey, D. B., & Henderson, L. (1993). Traditions in family assessment: Toward a reflective, inquiry-oriented approach. In D. M. Bryant & M. Graham (Eds.), *Implementing early intervention: From research to best practice* (pp. 124–147). New York: Guilford Press.

Bailey, D. B., Palsha, S. A., & Simeonsson, R. J. (1991). Professional concerns, skills, and perceived importance of work with families in early intervention. *Exceptional Children, 58,* 156–165.

Bailey, D. B., & Simeonsson, R. J. (1988a). Assessing needs of families with handicapped infants. *Journal of Special Education, 22,* 117–127.

Bailey, D. B., & Simeonsson, R. J. (Eds.) (1988b). *Family assessment in early intervention.* Englewood Cliffs, NJ: Merrill/Prentice Hall.

Bailey, D. B., & Simeonsson, R. J. (1990). *Family needs survey.* Chapel Hill, NC: Frank Porter Graham Child Development Center, University of North Carolina.

Bailey, D. B., Simeonsson, R. J., Yoder, D. E., & Huntington, G. S. (1990). Preparing professionals to serve infants and toddlers with handicaps and their families: An integrative analysis across eight disciplines. *Exceptional Children, 57,* 26–35.

Bailey, D. B., Winton, P. J., Rouse, L., & Turnbull, A. P. (1990). Family goals in infant intervention: Analysis and issues. *Journal of Early Intervention, 14,* 15–26.

Barnard, K. E. (1978a). *Nursing Child Assessment Feeding Scale.* Seattle: University of Washington.

Barnard, K. E. (1978b). *Nursing Child Assessment Teaching Scale.* Seattle: University of Washington.

Beavers, W. R., & Voeller, M. N. (1983). Family models: Comparing and contrasting the Olson model with the Beavers systems model. *Family Process, 22,* 85–98.

Beckman, P. J., & Bristol, M. M. (1991). Issues in developing the IFSP: A framework for establishing family outcomes. *Topics in Early Childhood Special Education, 11*(3), 19–31.

Bell, R. Q. (1968). A reinterpretation of the direction of effects in studies of socialization. *Psychological Review, 75,* 81–95.

Bendell, R. D., Stone, W. L., Field, T. M., & Goldstein, S. (1989). Children's effects on parenting stress in a low income, minority population. *Topics in Early Childhood Special Education, 8,* 58–71.

Bernheimer, L. P., Gallimore, R., & Weisner, T. S. (1990). Ecocultural theory as a context for the Individual Family Service Plan. *Journal of Early Intervention, 14,* 219–233.

Brinckerhoff, J. L., & Vincent, L. J. (1986). Increasing parental decision-making at the Individualized Educational Program meeting. *Journal of the Division for Early Childhood, 11,* 46–58.

Bromwich, R. (1981). *Working with parents and infants: An interactional approach.* Baltimore, MD: University Park Press.

Bronfenbrenner, U. (1977). Toward an experimental ecology of human development. *American Psychologist, 32,* 513–531.

Brotherson, M. J., & Goldstein, B. L. (1992). Time as a resource and constraint for parents of young children with disabilities: Implications for early intervention services. *Topics in Early Childhood Special Education, 12,* 508–527.

Brown, J., & Ritchie, J. A. (1990). Nurses' perceptions of parent and nurse roles in caring for hospitalized children. *Children's Health Care, 19,* 28–36.

Caldwell, B. (1972). *HOME Inventory.* Little Rock, AR: University of Arkansas.

Campbell, D., & Draper, R. (1985). *Applications of systematic family therapy.* London: Grune & Stratton.

Child Development Resources. (1989). *How Can We Help?* Lightfoot, VA: Child Development Resources.

Comfort, M. (1988). Assessing parent-child interaction. In D. Bailey & R. Simeonsson (Eds.), *Family assessment in early intervention* (pp. 65–94). Englewood Cliffs, NJ: Merrill/Prentice Hall.

Cooper, C. S., & Allred, K. W. (1992). A comparison of mothers' versus fathers' needs for support in caring for a young child with special needs. *Infant-Toddler Intervention, 2*(3), 205–221.

Cunningham, C. C., Morgan, P. A., & McGucken, R. B. (1984). Down's syndrome: Is dissatisfaction with disclosure of diagnosis inevitable? *Developmental Medicine and Child Neurology, 26,* 33–39.

DeGangi, C., Royeen, C. B., & Wietlisbach, S. (1992). How to examine the individualized family service planning process: Preliminary findings and a procedural guide. *Infants and Young Children, 5*(2), 42–56.

Dunst, C. J. (1985). Rethinking early intervention. *Analysis and Intervention in Developmental Disabilities, 5,* 165–201.

Dunst, C. J., Cooper, C. S., Weeldreyer, J. C., Snyder, K. D., & Chase, J. H. (1988). Family needs scale. In C. J. Dunst, C. M. Trivette, & A. G. Deal (Eds.), *Enabling and empowering families: Principles and guidelines for practice* (p. 151). Cambridge, MA: Brookline Books.

Dunst, C. J., Jenkins, V., & Trivette, C. (1988). Family support scale. In C. J. Dunst, C. M. Trivette, & A. G. Deal, *Enabling and empowering families: Principles and guidelines for practice.* Cambridge, MA: Brookline Books.

Dunst, C. J., Trivette, C. M., & Deal, A. G. (1988). *Enabling and empowering families: Principles and guidelines for practice.* Cambridge, MA: Brookline Books.

Duwa, S. M., Wells, C., & Lalinde, P. (1993). Creating family centered programs and policies. In D. M. Bryant & M. A. Graham (Eds.), *Implementing early intervention: From research to effective practices* (pp. 92–123). New York: Guilford Press.

Espe-Sherwindt, M. (1991). The IFSP and parents with special needs/mental retardation. *Topics in Early Childhood Special Education, 11*(3), 107–120.

Espe-Sherwindt, M., & Crable, S. (1993). Parents with mental retardation: Moving beyond the myths. *Topics in Early Childhood Special Education, 13,* 154–174.

Friedrich, W. N., Greenberg, M. T., & Crnic, K. (1983). A short form of the questionnaire on resources and stress. *American Journal of Mental Deficiency, 88,* 41–48.

Garshelis, J. A., & McConnell, S. R. (1993). Comparison of family needs assessed by mothers, individual professionals, and interdisciplinary teams. *Journal of Early Intervention, 16,* 36–49.

Goldstein, S., & Turnbull, A. P. (1982). The use of two strategies to increase parent participation in IEP conferences. *Exceptional Children, 48,* 360–361.

Grotevant, H. D., & Carlson, C. I. (1989). *Family assessment: A guide to methods and measures.* New York: Guilford Press.

Hart, B., & Risley, T. R. (1992). American parenting of language learning children: Persisting differences in family-child interactions observed in natural home environments. *Developmental Psychology, 28,* 1096–1105.

Henderson, L. W., Aydlett, L. A., & Bailey, D. B. (1993). Evaluating family needs surveys: Do standard measures of reliability and validity tell us what we want to know? *Journal of Psychoeducational Assessment, 11,* 208–219.

Holroyd, J. (1974). The questionnaire on resources and stress: An instrument to measure family response to a handicapped member. *Journal of Community Psychology, 2,* 92–94.

Holroyd, J. (1986). *Questionnaire on resources and stress for families with a chronically ill or handicapped member: Manual.* Brandon, VT: Clinical Psychology Publishing.

Huber, C. J. (1991). Documenting quality of parent-child interaction: Use of the NCAST Scales. *Infants and Young Children, 4*(2), 63–75.

Kaiser, A. P., & Hemmeter, M. L. (1989). Value-based approaches to early intervention. *Topics in Early Childhood Special Education, 8*(4), 72–86.

Lynch, E. W., & Hanson, M. J. (Eds.) (1992). *Developing cross-cultural competence.* Baltimore, MD: Paul H. Brookes.

Mahoney, G., Finger, I., & Powell, A. (1985). Relationship of maternal behavioral style to the development of organically impaired mentally retarded infants. *American Journal of Mental Deficiency, 90,* 296–302.

Mahoney, G., & O'Sullivan, P. (1990). Early intervention practices with families of children with handicaps. *Mental Retardation, 28,* 169–176.

Mahoney, G., O'Sullivan, P., & Dennebaum, J. (1990). A national study of mothers' perceptions of family-focused intervention. *Journal of Early Intervention, 14,* 133–146.

Matarazzo, R., Phillips, J., Wiens, A., & Saslow, G. (1965). Learning the art of interviewing: A study of what beginning students do and their patterns of change. *Psychotherapy: Theory, Research and Practice, 2,* 49–60.

McCollum, J. A., & Stayton, V. D. (1985). Infant/parent interaction: Studies and intervention guidelines based on the SIAI model. *Journal of the Division for Early Childhood, 9*(2), 125–135.

McCubbin, H. I., Comeau, J. K., & Harkins, J. A. (1981). *Family Inventory of Resources for Management.* Madison, WI: Family Stress Coping and Health Project.

McCubbin, H. L., Olson, D. H., & Larsen, A. S. (1981). *Family Crisis Oriented Personal Scales.* Madison, WI: Family Stress Coping and Health Project.

McCubbin, H. I., & Patterson, J. M. (1983). Family transitions: Adaptation to stress. In H. McCubbin & C. Figley (Eds.), *Stress and the family: Vol. 1. Coping with normative transitions* (pp. 5–25). New York: Brunner/Mazel.

McCubbin, H. I., Patterson, J. M., & Wilson, L. R. (1983). *Family Inventory of Life Events and Changes.* Madison, WI: Family Stress Coping and Health Project.

McCubbin, H. I., & Thompson, A. I. (1987a). *Family assessment inventories for research and practice.* Madison, WI: University of Wisconsin-Madison.

McCubbin, H. I., & Thompson, A. I. (1987b). Family typologies and family assessment. In H. I. McCubbin & A. I. Thompson (Eds.), *Family assessment inventories for research and practice* (pp. 35–62). Madison, WI: University of Wisconsin.

McGhee, L. J., & Eckerman, C. O. (1983). The preterm infant as a social partner: Responsive but not readable. *Infant Behavior and Development, 6,* 461–470.

McGonigel, M. J., Kaufmann, R. K., & Johnson, B. H. (Eds.). (1991). *Guidelines and recommended practices for the Individualized Family Service Plan* (2nd ed.). Bethesda, MD: Association for the Care of Children's Health.

McGrew, K. S., Gilman, C. J., & Johnson, S. (1992). A review of scales to assess family needs. *Journal of Psychoeducational Assessment, 10,* 4–25.

McKinney, B., & Peterson, R. A. (1987). Predictors of stress in parents of developmentally disabled children. *Journal of Pediatric Psychology, 12,* 133–150.

Noonan, M. J., & Kilgo, J. L. (1987). Transition services for early age individuals with severe mental retardation. In R. N. Ianacone & R. A. Stodder (Eds.), *Transition issues and directions* (pp. 25–37). Reston, VA: Council for Exceptional Children.

Piper, M. C., & Ramsay, M. K. (1980). Effects of early home environment on the mental development of Down syndrome infants. *American Journal of Mental Deficiency, 85,* 39–44.

Raab, M. M., Davis, M. S., & Trepanier, A. M. (1993). Resources vs. services: Changing the focus of intervention for infants and young children. *Infants and Young Children, 5*(3), 1–11.

Rosenberg, S., Robinson, C., & Beckman, P. (1984). Teaching skills inventory: A measure of parent performance. *Journal of the Division for Early Childhood, 8,* 107–113.

Rosenkoetter, S. E., Hains, A. H., & Fowler, S. A. (1994). *Bridging early services for children with special needs and their families: A practical guide for transition planning.* Baltimore, MD: Paul H. Brookes.

Rushton, C. H. (1990). Family-centered care in the critical care setting: Myth or reality? *Children's Health Care, 19*(2), 68–77.

Sameroff, A. J., & Chandler, M. J. (1975). Reproductive risk and the continuum of care-taking casualty. In F. D. Horowitz, M. Hetherington, S. Scarr-Salapatek, & G. Siegel (Eds.), *Review of child development research* (Vol. 4) (pp. 187–244). Chicago: University of Chicago Press.

Sameroff, A. J., & Fiese, B. (1990). Transactional regulations and early intervention. In S. J. Meisels & J. P. Shonkoff (Eds.), *Handbook of early childhood intervention* (pp. 119–149). Cambridge: Cambridge University Press.

Seligman, M., & Darling, R. B. (1989). *Ordinary families, special children: A systems approach to childhood disability.* New York: Guilford.

Selvini, M. P., Boscolo, L., Cecchin, G., & Prata, G. (1980). Hypothesizing—circularity—neutrality: Three guidelines for the conductor of the session. *Family Process, 19,* 3–12.

Sexton, D., Snyder, P., Rheams, T., Barron-Sharp, B., & Perez, J. (1991). Considerations in using written surveys to identify family strengths and needs during the IFSP process. *Topics in Early Childhood Special Education, 11,* 81–91.

Simeonsson, R. J. (1988). Unique characteristics of families with young handicapped children. In D. B. Bailey & R. J. Simeonsson (Eds.), *Family assessment in early intervention* (pp. 27–43). Englewood Cliffs, NJ: Merrill/Prentice Hall.

Slentz, K. L., & Bricker, D. (1992). Family-guided assessment for IFSP development: Jumping off the family assessment bandwagon. *Journal of Early Intervention, 16,* 11–19.

Steinglass, P. (1984). Family systems theory and therapy: A clinical application of general systems theory. *Psychiatric Annals, 14*(8), 582–586.

Summers, J. A., Dell'Oliver, C., Turnbull, A. P., Benson, H. A., Santelli, E., Campbell, M., & Siegel-Causey, E. (1990). Examining the Individualized Family Service Plan process: What are family and practitioner preferences? *Topics in Early Childhood Special Education, 10,* 78–99.

Telleen, S., Herzog, A., & Kilbane, T. L. (1989). Impact of a family support program on mothers' social support and parenting stress. *American Journal of Orthopsychiatry, 59,* 410–419.

Tomm, K. (1987). Interventive interviewing: Part 1. Strategizing as a fourth guideline for the therapist. *Family Process, 26,* 3–13.

Turnbull, A. P., & Turnbull, H. R. (1990). *Families, professionals, and exceptionality: A special partnership* (2nd ed.). Englewood Cliffs, NJ: Merrill/Prentice Hall.

Wikler, L. (1981). Chronic stresses of families of mentally retarded children. *Family Relations, 30,* 281–288.

Wilfong, E. W., Saylor, C., & Elksnin, N. (1991). Influences on responsiveness: Interactions between mothers and their premature infants. *Infant Mental Health Journal, 12,* 31–39.

Winton, P. J. (1988a). Effective communication between parents and professionals. In D. Bailey & R. Simeonsson (Eds.), *Family assessment in early intervention* (pp. 207–228). Englewood Cliffs, NJ: Merrill/Prentice Hall.

Winton, P. J. (1988b). The family-focused interview: An assessment measure and goal-setting mechanism. In D. B. Bailey & R. J. Simeonsson (Eds.), *Family assessment in early intervention* (pp. 185–206). Englewood Cliffs, NJ: Merrill/Prentice Hall.

Winton, P. J., & Bailey, D. B. (1988). The family-focused interview: A mechanism for collaborative goal-setting with families. *Journal of the Division for Early Childhood, 12,* 195–207.

Winton, P. J., & Bailey, D. B. (1993). Communicating with families: Examining practices and facilitating change. In J. Paul & R. J. Simeonsson (Eds.), *Children with special needs: Family, culture, and society* (pp. 210–230). Orlando, FL: Harcourt Brace Jovanovich.

Yoder, P. (1987). Relationship between degree of infant handicap and clarity of infant cues. *American Journal of Mental Deficiency, 91,* 639–641.

Zigler, E., & Black, K. (1989). America's family support movement: Strengths and limitations. *American Journal of Orthopsychiatry, 59,* 6–19.

CHAPTER

9

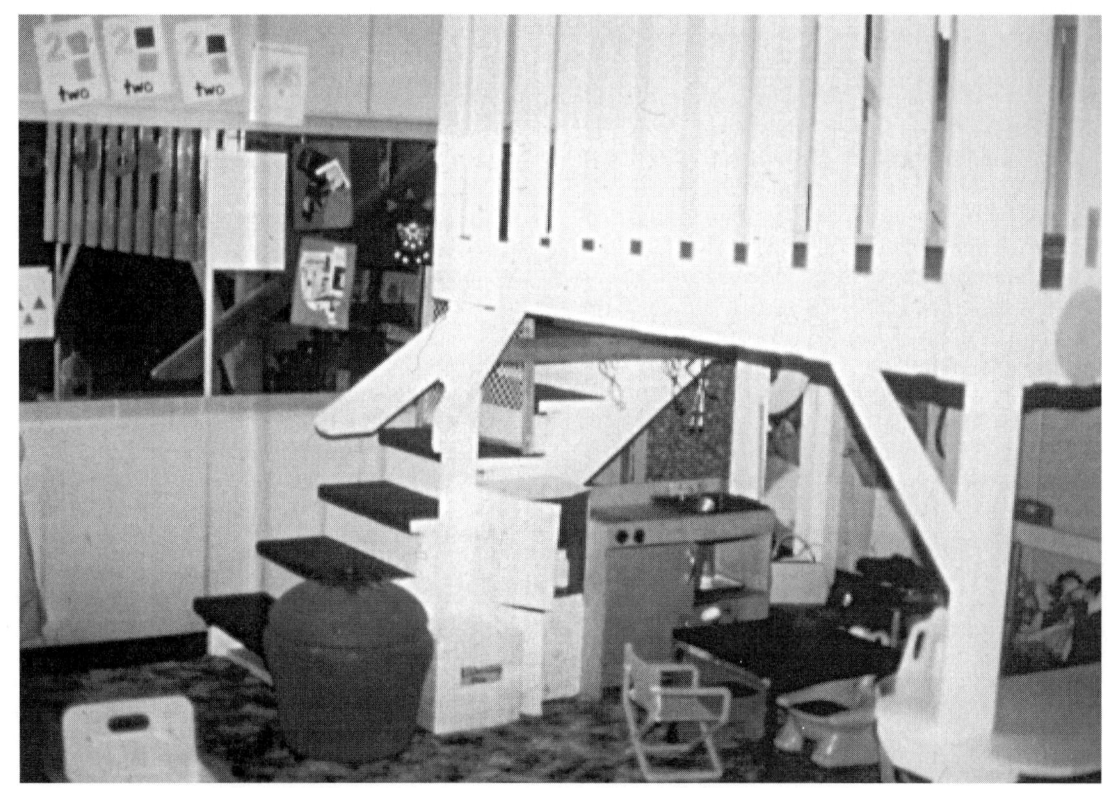

Assessing Environments

Joan M. Karp
University of Minnesota–Duluth

. . . .

An environment is a living, changing system. More than the physical space, it includes the way time is structured and roles we are expected to play. It conditions how we feel, think, and behave; and it dramatically affects the quality of our lives.

Greenman, *Caring Spaces, Learning Places: Children's Environments That Work* (1988).

. . . .

As progressively more young children with disabilities are enrolled in child-care centers, family child care, kindergarten, and Head Start programs, finding a match between children's needs, interests, abilities, and disabilities and the characteristics of the setting becomes more important. This chapter provides a rationale for assessing early childhood settings. It summarizes the considerations most commonly used to describe those environments and suggests methods for assessing them. Specific instruments and ways to use such information for planning and placement decisions are included.

RATIONALE FOR ASSESSING ENVIRONMENTS

Studies of the effects of the environment on development in young children have found positive changes in the development of very low birthweight and premature infants who received consistent pediatric care and regularly scheduled home visits and whose mothers were provided a systematic education program (Brooks-Gunn, Klebanov, Liaw, & Spiker, 1993; Ramey et al., 1992; Spiker, Ferguson, & Brooks-Gunn, 1993). The quality of child-care environments has been shown to have effects on typically developing young children (Howes & Stewart, 1987; McCartney, 1984; Phillips, 1987; Phillips, McCartney, & Scarr, 1987; Phyfe-Perkins, 1980; Weinstein & David, 1987), on children from low-income families (Ramey, Bryant, Sparling, & Wasik, 1985), and on children with disabilities (Rogers-Warren, 1982). The quality of the home environment and its relationship to the cognitive, social, and linguistic developmental progress of typically developing children (Gottfried, 1984; MacPhee, Ramey, & Yeates, 1984) and of children with disabilities (Piper & Ramsay, 1980) is well documented.

Three primary reasons can be proposed for assessing children's environments. First, such assessments can be used to inform placement decisions. Young children with disabilities may be placed in a wide array of environments, including nursery schools, child-care centers, family child-care programs, kindergarten classes, preschool special education classes, hospitals, and home settings. When such a variety of options are available, making the correct decision about the best placement for a young child with disabilities has become an important part of the planning process. These decisions are made during initial placement of the child and later during the child's transition into the next environment. The transition from one environment to another has recently become more systematic, with judgments about the receiving environment an important step in the transition process (Bruder & Walker, 1990; Chandler, 1993; Hanline & Knowlton, 1988; Rosenkoetter, Hains, & Fowler, 1994; Sainato, 1990). Judgments about the degree to which an environment is least restrictive and normalized under Public Law 102-119 (IDEA) have become routine in placement decisions. To assess the restrictiveness of an environment for a young child with disabilities, an early childhood educator examines the availability of nondisabled peers, the accessibility of the setting, and the effectiveness of the teaching strategies (Kenowitz, Zweibel, & Edgar, 1979).

Beyond general restrictiveness, specific qualities in some environments preclude certain children from being successful. For example, a 3-year-old child with visual and physical impairments was being assessed for a preschool placement in the community. The nearest center-based early childhood program was in a new facility that was physically accessible on the exterior and provided many typically developing children as models and interactive partners. Until the staff visited, they did not realize that the interior was a series of small classrooms surrounding a circular seating area with five broad circular steps leading down into the center, where the play equipment was kept. Children from all five classrooms converged on the center area from multiple directions and with no consistent pathways. After examining the arrangement, the staff and parents decided that the child's needs for consistency and mobility would not be met by this center.

The second reason for assessment is that professionals and parents are concerned with the overall quality and safety of the environments in which children with disabilities are placed. Guidelines for determining whether and to what degree an environment is a safe, warm, comfortable, well-staffed place for the care of young children have been developed (Fowler, 1980; Greenman, 1988; Harms & Clifford, 1980; Harms, Cryer, & Clifford, 1990; National Academy of Early Childhood Programs, 1991). Studies of early childhood environments reveal a number of important characteristics that can be used to determine overall quality and safety (Clarke-Stewart, 1982; Phillips, 1987). These qualities will be described in more detail later in this chapter. Studies of center-based programs have documented developmentally supportive and nonsupportive environments for young children with disabilities (e.g., Bailey, Clifford, & Harms, 1982); there have been similar studies of hospital environments for premature and very low birthweight neonates (e.g., VandenBerg, 1982; Wolke, 1987a, 1987b; Ramey et al., 1992).

In a review of physical environment and children's development, David and Weinstein (1987) summarize this rationale for environmental assessment by asserting that all environments should fulfill certain basic functions for children. These include fostering personal identity through stable interactions within a pleasant environment, fostering the development of competence by engaging in a facilitative environment, providing opportunities for growth, fostering a sense of security and trust, and providing a balance of opportunities for social interactions and privacy. Through assessment, professionals can describe the ways in which a particular environment might meet the needs of an individual child and family while maintaining healthy development in the young child.

Third, a thorough understanding of the environment can assist teachers or caregivers in making adaptations and designing the environment for the child with special needs (Nordquist, Twardosz, & McEvoy, 1991). Fleming, Wolery, Weinzierl, Venn, and Schroeder (1991) described the variety of different roles that center-based teachers play during the course of a day. They assert that understanding the daily schedule and the teacher's usual roles should guide the types of strategies recommended for the teacher's use with the young child with disabilities. A similar process for family child-care providers has been described by Mulligan et al. (1992).

DIMENSIONS OF ENVIRONMENTS

In the broadest sense, an environment is "the totality of circumstances surrounding an organism or group of organisms, especially the combination of external physical conditions that affect and influence growth, development and survival of the organism" *(The American*

Heritage Dictionary of the English Language, 3rd ed.). Different types of environments have been found to support different types of skill development in typically developing children (Clarke-Stewart, 1987; Phillips, 1987) and children with disabilities (McEvoy, Fox, & Rosenberg, 1991). Figure 9.1 highlights environmental differences that affect children's development found in center-based child care as compared with home-based child care. For the purpose of this text, we will focus on the environmental dimensions found in centers, classrooms, homes, and hospitals.

Environmental Dimensions of Centers and Classrooms

McEvoy et al. (1991) suggest that the preschool environment for children with disabilities should be considered from two perspectives: the physical environment, which includes the layout of the classroom and encompasses the furniture, materials, and equipment, and the social/programmatic environment, which includes the daily schedule, the grouping of children, the responsibilities of the teaching staff, and the curriculum. In this section, we focus on the amount and type of space; variety, location, and type of materials; organization and scheduling; safety; peer interaction; caregiver responsiveness; promoting independence; and language stimulation in center and classroom programs.

Physical Environment

The physical space The physical space refers to the amount of space that is available and the way that space is arranged. A variety of relationships have been noted between amount of space per child and differing play patterns (see Sainato & Carta, 1992, for a review). There appears to be more rough-and-tumble play when there is more than 50 square feet per child (Smith & Connolly, 1976) and less social interaction when the space is greater than 20 square feet per child (Loo, 1972). Increases in aggression have been noted in areas that provide less than 20 feet per child (Smith & Connolly, 1976).

In a systematic study of spatial density, Brown, Fox, and Brady (1987) compared children's play and social interactions in the entire classroom (58 square feet per child) and in a restricted space (19 square feet per child). Maintaining the same toys and play material in each area and the same amount of teacher supervision, they found that more socially directed play occurred in the smaller area with no increase in aggression. The authors believe that classroom management procedures used by the teachers discouraged aggressive behavior.

Most states have regulations pertaining to the minimum amount of square footage necessary per child in any child-care program. According to the accreditation criteria and procedures of the National Academy of Early Childhood Programs (1991), a center should have at least 35 square feet of usable indoor space and 75 square feet of outdoor play space for each child in the program. These figures may need to be expanded when children with adaptive or supportive equipment, such as prone boards or wheelchairs, are enrolled.

An important aspect of the physical environment is the organization of space. Moore (1987) described three basic types of spatial arrangements. An *open-plan facility* has "unpartitioned space with few or no internal walls"; a *closed-plan facility* has "self-contained classrooms usually arranged along corridors or as in a house with several small interconnecting rooms" (p. 51). In contrast, a *modified open-plan facility* entails the "organization of space into a variety of large and small activity spaces open enough to allow children to see the play possibilities available to them while providing enough enclosure for the child to be protected from noise and visual distractions" (p. 52). In a

Differences in center-based (nursery schools and daycare centers) and home-based daycare (babysitters, child-minders, daycare homes)

- center-based programs were more likely than home-based programs to provide educational opportunities for children and to increase their social competence, maturity, and intellectual development.
- home-based care is more likely than center-based care to offer authoritative discipline, socialization training, and one-to-one adult-child interaction.
- publicly funded daycare centers and nursery schools are the most likely kinds of group or center-based programs to offer care of high quality.
- gains in children's achievement, positive attitude, intellectual development, and constructive play are most likely in programs (in homes or centers) that offer a basic diet of free choice punctuated by a moderate number of prescribed educational activities.
- sociability, cooperation, and self-motivated exploration are most likely to develop in programs that are "open" and focus their efforts on free-play and social interactions among children in a rich and varied environment.
- an environment that offers a wide variety of materials and easy accessibility of things to do is ideal.
- a daycare setting in which the child is part of a small group of children, both boys and girls, with an age range of about two years, offers more positive, cooperative, complex, and sustained interactions with both other children and the caregiver and has benefits for social interaction.
- the caregiver is the most important aspect of daycare. The caregiver ratio is not as important as the types of behaviors the caregiver exhibits. Behaviors indicative of high quality:
  - —active involvement by talking, teaching, and playing
  - —providing interesting materials
  - —responding to the child's interests, advances, and questions
  - —positive encouragement and suggestions
  - —no demands, threats, or punishments
  - —not restrictive or critical
- a caregiver in either a home or a center who thinks of herself as a professional, has been trained in child development, has five to ten years of experience, and is part of a training and support network or education-oriented center is more likely to give this involved, active, positive care and to have a positive influence on the child's development.
- the best quality child care varies according to the individual needs of the child.

FIGURE 9.1

Center-based child care compared to home-based child care

Source: Reprinted by permission from the publishers from *Daycare* by Alison Clarke-Stewart, 1982, Cambridge, Mass.: Harvard University Press, Copyright © 1982 by Kathleen Alison Clarke-Stewart; Revised edition © 1993 by Kathleen Alison Clarke-Stewart.

study of these three environments with typically developing children ages 2 to 6, Moore found that the modified open-plan centers resulted in greater use of activity settings, smaller group sizes, increased engagement in cognitively oriented behaviors, and increased child-initiated behaviors. Open-plan centers were likely to result in more "random" behavior; closed-plan facilities resulted in greater amounts of time spent in transitions from one activity or setting to another and increased observations of withdrawn behavior in children. Moore argued that the use of modified open-plan facilities is important for children's development. Professionals engaged in the assessment of environments should examine spatial arrangement.

Several authors have argued that space must be organized and well defined according to use or function (Moore, 1987; Olds, 1979). For example, Moore (1987) examined the extent to which child-care centers incorporated spatial definition (e.g., appropriateness of storage, work surfaces and display space, separation of activities, degree of area definition and enclosure) in environmental design and use and found that the degree or level of engagement in activities was higher in spaces that were well defined. Olds (1987) suggests that a well-defined activity area should have five attributes: a specific location, visible boundaries, surfaces for both work and seating, adequate space for storing and displaying materials, and a "mood" or "personality" that is achieved by the use of color and soft materials. Generally, preschool children have shown higher-level cognitive skills when the environment of a center "was safer, more orderly, and contained more varied and stimulating toys, decorations, and educational materials appropriately organized into activity areas" (Clarke-Stewart, 1987, p. 37).

An additional aspect of the physical space important to young children with disabilities is the availability of accessible space, that is, space that children can move in and make use of independently. This is particularly important for children with visual or motor impairments. An inaccessible environment is one in which the child's freedom within that environment is restricted (Kenowitz et al., 1979) or in which some portion of the environment is unattainable without teacher assistance. For example, if a room contains multiple levels separated by stairs, a child in a wheelchair will not be able to move from one level to another. Likewise, if the dramatic play center is located in a loft, it may be difficult for children with visual impairments or motor impairments to gain access to that area. Brown et al. (1987) have demonstrated that interactions are most likely to occur when children are in small areas, in close proximity to each other. Sufficient space should be provided so that children move from area to area quickly and easily during transitions (McEvoy et al., 1991). Therefore, professionals should assess the extent to which children's movements are inappropriately restricted by some dimension of the physical environment.

Equipment and materials The scale of the objects in the environment have an effect on the child's perception of self in relation to the world around him or her, creating a sense of power, independence, and competence (Greenman, 1988). The ways in which furniture, equipment, and toys are sized and the way the environment looks from a child's level create a sense of welcome and empowerment to the young child. Center-based programs for toddlers may have particular problems in providing materials that are at the proper scale for a toddler's hands and body and that provide the safety needed. A mixture of child-scaled and adult-scaled equipment, shelving, furniture, and materials are most ideal (Greenman, 1988). For children who have limited capacity to lift their bodies from the floor, the provision and accessibility of toys within their visual field and reach are important.

An environment should contain sufficient materials for the number of children who will use the setting. The materials should be colorful and appealing, appropriate for children's developmental levels, and developmentally facilitative. They should be planned and available; different kinds of toys and materials are likely to encourage different kinds of behavior. For example, some toys, such as crayons, are more likely to promote "isolate" behavior (children playing by themselves), whereas other toys, such as games and dress-up clothes, are likely to promote social interactions between two or more children (Quiltich & Risley, 1973; Hendrickson, Strain, Tremblay, & Shores, 1981). Materials should be in good repair, and it is essential that multiples of the same toy or materials be available to prevent arguments and facilitate parallel and cooperative play activities. Having materials available that reflect gender, disability, and cultural differences among people, such as books, dolls, clothing, and musical instruments, facilitates children's questions and assists them in exploring similarities and differences among people (Derman-Sparks and the A.B.C. Task Force, 1989; Gonzalez-Mena, 1993).

Social/Programmatic Environment

Children's use of their environment is mediated by the amount and type of teacher supervision and involvement. For example, LeLaurin and Risley (1972) compared two procedures for teacher supervision of activity areas. The zone procedure, in which adults were assigned to activity areas and children were allowed to move at their own pace, resulted in higher levels of engagement than did a "man-to-man" procedure, in which teachers were assigned a group of children and the group had to stay together at all times. Burstein (1986) found that the preschoolers she observed were on task most often during small-group activities such as those at learning centers. While at the center, the children with disabilities engaged in the activities only when adults were present, otherwise they were either alone or off-task.

Teacher-child ratios and group size

Staff ratios recommended for early childhood centers by the National Academy of Early Childhood Programs (1991), which are displayed in Table 9.1, reflect the relationship between responsiveness on the part of the caregiver to the needs of the children in the group. Children in smaller groups have been found to display more positive affect (Cummings & Beagles-Ross, 1983), more social and cooperative interactions (Clarke-Stewart & Gruber, 1984), and more verbal interactions and engagement in play (Bruner, 1980; Field, 1980; Howes & Rubenstein, 1985). Caregivers with smaller groups have been shown to be more responsive and nurturing to children and less restrictive (Howes, 1983; Howes & Rubenstein, 1985; Smith & Connolly, 1981; Stith & Davis, 1984). In center-based programs, the effects of regulated features such as teacher-student ratios have not been found to predict children's development as effectively as a family's socioeconomic status, so caution must be exercised in using pupil-staff ratios to determine quality of centers (Kontos & Fiene, 1987; Goelman & Pence, 1987). Generally, smaller staff-to-children ratios, smaller group sizes, and well-educated staffs are found in higher-quality programs (Phillips, 1987; Phillips & Howes, 1987). Howes, Phillips, and Whitebook (1992) demonstrated that licensing standards influencing smaller teacher-to-child ratio, group size, and teacher training do make a difference in the quality of care provided to preschool children.

Clarke-Stewart (1987) found that the caregiver-to-child ratio is not as important as the types of behaviors that the caregiver exhibits. For example, providing interesting materials and active adult involvement (talking, teaching, and playing); responding to the child's interest, initiations, and questions; using positive encouragement and suggestions without demands, threats, or punishments; and not being restrictive or critical were caregiver behaviors associated with the most growth in preschool children and were more important

TABLE 9.1
Recommended Staff-Child Ratios Within Group Size

	Group Size*									
Age of Children	**6**	**8**	**10**	**12**	**14**	**16**	**18**	**20**	**22**	**24**
Infants (birth–12 mos.)	1:3	1:4								
Toddlers (12–24 mos.)	1:3	1:4	1:5	1:4						
2-year-olds (24–36 mos.)		1:4	1:5	1:6						
2½-year-olds (30–36 mos.)			1:5	1:6	1:7					
3-year-olds					1:7	1:8	1:9	1:10		
4-year-olds						1:8	1:9	1:10		
5-year-olds						1:8	1:9	1:10		
6- to 8-year-olds								1:10	1:11	1:12

*Smaller group sizes and lower staff-child ratios have been found to be strong predictors of compliance with indicators of quality such as positive interactions among staff and children and developmentally appropriate curriculum. Variations in group sizes and ratios are acceptable in cases where the program demonstrates a very high level of compliance with criteria for interactions (A), curriculum (B), staff qualifications (D), health and safety (H), and physical environment (G).

Source: From *Accreditation Criteria and Procedures of the National Academy of Early Childhood Programs* (rev. ed.), 1991, Washington, DC: The National Association for the Education of Young Children. Copyright 1991 by NAEYC. Reprinted by permission.

than the number of staff members. The type of language used by classroom teachers in both integrated and segregated preschools has been found to influence the improvement of language in preschool children with language delays (Pearson, Pearson, Fenrick, & Greene, 1988). Using specific language development techniques of "samples, mands, and delays," teachers increased the language of 4- and 5-year-old children to a level greater than expected.

The impact of a child with disabilities on teacher-child ratios has not been quantified; however, depending on the needs of the child, the impact on staff can be important. Preschool children who are not toilet trained when placed in settings with children who are already toilet trained take more caregiver time. Children with physical, emotional, behavioral, or sensory impairments also require additional caregiver time, so the ratios of children to staff need to be flexible to accommodate specific needs (Snart & Hillyard, 1985). In settings where children with disabilities are able to follow directions or imitate the behavior of peers, the need for additional staff may not be as great as for children without these skills (Karp & Carlson, 1993). Measures of child social and self-help skills can be found in Chapters 13, 14, and 15 of this text.

In their studies of the security of attachments between infants, toddlers, and preschool-age children and their teachers and parents, the consistency of staff had greatest positive benefits with the youngest children (Howes & Hamilton, 1992). The National Academy of Early Childhood Programs (1991) suggests that continuity of adults is very important, especially for infants and toddlers.

Scheduling of activities The use of a predictable classroom schedule has been found to assist children with disabilities in anticipating scheduled transitions, moving from one activity to another with minimal staff supervision, and increasing time on task (Anderson, 1984; Fredericksen & Fredericksen, 1977; Ostrosky, Skellenger, Odom, McConnell, & Peterson, 1994; Sainato, Strain, Lefebvre, & Rapp, 1987). Commonly accepted practice suggests that the younger the children and the shorter their attention span, the shorter the activities (McEvoy et al., 1991). Krantz and Risley (1977) found that the transition from an outdoor activity to an indoor rest time was smoother when a quiet time was included between them. Clear knowledge of the daily schedule and of the persons responsible for the children during each activity facilitates staff roles (Hart, 1982).

Peer environment The role of the teacher in facilitating peer interactions has been well documented (Odom & McEvoy, 1988). Depending on the size of the group, the way the group is organized, the way staff are deployed, the ages of the children in the group, and the level of disability among the children, the extent to which nondisabled children will be playmates of children with disabilities can vary greatly (Guralnick, 1984,1986; Karp & Carlson, 1993). Age, grouping (mixed- vs. same-age), activity structure, and disability all affect the level of engagement of the children with other children and the materials in the environment (McWilliam & Bailey, 1992). Children in smaller groups (2 to 4 children) and with familiar peers have been shown to engage in more social behavior (McWilliam & Bailey, 1992; Sainato & Carta, 1992). Children with disabilities are more solitary in same-age groups (Bailey, Burchinal, & McWilliam, 1993). Younger children are more engaged when in same-age groups; older children are more engaged when in mixed-age groups (Bailey, Burchinal, & McWilliam, 1993). Mixed-age groups have demonstrated more help-giving and assistance-seeking behaviors. Opportunities for modeling, sharing, and social interaction are highly dependent on children being in close proximity to each other, so it is important to assess the degree to which staff are willing to integrate the child with disabilities fully into the environment, organize group activities, and provide the adult supervision needed for successful integration.

Environmental Dimensions of Homes

Young children with disabilities often receive early intervention services in their own home with their parents, with in-home caregivers (babysitters or relatives), or with family child-care providers. These environments share many important characteristics that are different from the environmental dimensions found in early childhood centers:

> Child-care homes "may be licensed or unlicensed; the caregiver (daycare home provider) may be related or unrelated, trained or untrained; the number of children may range from one to six (family daycare home) or six to twelve (group daycare home). The basis for this arrangement ranges from an informal agreement about shared caregiving between friends to a highly formal, supervised network of licensed homes. Daycare homes have a number of distinct advantages as a form of care. . . . They are in a familiar neighborhood where people are likely to share the parents' values and circumstances. The mother has more control over what happens to her child than she would in a daycare center; she can give instructions to a daycare home provider that she would not be able to give a daycare center teacher. A caregiver is usually flexible about taking children of different ages and in adjusting her hours to the mother's schedule. She may accept children with special needs or handicaps who wouldn't be accepted in a center." (Clarke-Stewart, 1982, pp. 45-46)

Environmental dimensions that have been studied in homes include caregiver responsivity and involvement, variety of materials and stimuli provided (Gottfried, 1984), health and safety features, physical space, caregiver-child ratios, and group size (Clarke-Stewart, 1982).

Caregiver responsivity and involvement In a review by Barnard and Kelly (1990) of over 50 studies, the responsivity of caregivers to infant's and young children's behavior and cues has been repeatedly shown to affect the young child's development in cognitive, motor, and social interaction skills. Overly restrictive behavior on the part of the caregiver is usually related to poorer developmental outcomes. Both the child and the caregiver bring important dimensions to the interaction: The caregiver brings sensitivity to cues and behaviors and the child brings consistency in responses and clarity of cues. Once this mutuality has been developed, the adaptation of the partners (caregiver and infant) over time plays an important role in the young child's development (Brazelton, Koslowski, & Main, 1974; Kaye, 1975, 1977; Sander, 1964; Thoman, 1975). Barnard and Kelly (1990) highlight four important features of the "mutually adaptive dance": (a) each partner has a sufficient repertoire of behaviors—the child sees, hears, visually attends to the mother, smiles, adapts to holding, is soothable, regular, and predictable; the mother has the ability and willingness to read and respond to infant cues and a repertoire of behaviors to stimulate and engage the child; (b) the responses are contingent on one another; (c) there is richness of interactive content; and (d) there are adaptive patterns that change over time.

In populations of children with special needs, a child may not bring all of the usual interactive abilities to the situation. There may be wider than normal variation in the clarity, the predictability, and the readability of cues. For example, with a premature infant who shows many disorganized behaviors, it is important that caregivers learn how much stimulation the infant can tolerate (Field, 1982); he or she may startle easily or show very subtle signs of discontent such as yawning or eye aversion. An infant who comes from a neonatal intensive care unit will in all likelihood not be on a routine sleep-wake schedule and may be difficult to feed.

In comparisons of parent interactions in groups of typical children and children with disabilities, it was found that mothers of children with disabilities initiated play more often and took a more controlling role in play (Brooks-Gunn & Lewis, 1982; Jones, 1977; Eheart, 1982). Fraiberg (1974) has shown the importance of sensitizing parents to subtle cues of their infants who are blind; she teaches parents to observe cues expressed through the child's hand movements. Bromwich (1981) also points out how important it is to teach parents to observe the behavior of their young children with disabilities.

Infants with mental impairments show improved cognitive development when the caregiver is sensitive to the child's state, enjoyment, and responsiveness and uses appropriate teaching styles (Mahoney, Finger, & Powell, 1985). Maternal directiveness, control, and insensitivity to the child's interests were related to poorer Bayley Scales of Infant Development scores in these studies. The highest Bayley scores were found among mothers who let the child lead the activity and supported the initiated activities rather than leading the interaction.

Environmental Dimensions of Hospitals

The hierarchical structure, methods of intervention, and relationships among staff and children in hospitals differ greatly from home or center-based interventions. Gilkerson, Gorski, and Panitz (1990) reviewed and summarized the differences on five aspects:

> To illustrate, an average NICU, with 20 beds, admits approximately 300 infants per year. Larger units with 50 beds may care for as many as 500 babies. Staff size can vary from 30 nurses with 4 attending physicians in 20-bed units to 200 nurses with 15 physicians in large units. . . . Whereas length of stay in an NICU ranges from 1 to 2 days for observation to more than a year for comprehensive care for a small number of the smallest and sickest neonates, early intervention programs are

> available to families for the first 3 years of their child's life. NICUs have greater breadth of exposure to different families; early intervention specialists may have greater depth of contact. . . . This [early intervention] relationship may include home as well as center contacts, and may focus on the full functioning of the family in addition to the child's developmental progress. This long-term relationship provides early intervention staff with the knowledge of how families adapt over time and how they function when they are not in a state of crisis. (Gilkerson et al., 1990, pp. 446-447)

The environment of the NICU has been described as a "bombardment" of stimuli from the many different caregivers and procedures the infant encounters. There are few regular routine patterns of contact for the infant with human caregivers; often the contact is with machines (High & Gorski, 1985). The infant's sleep and wake cycles, while very irregular, are not attended to by medical and social caregivers in the NICU (High & Gorski, 1985). Gorski and Huntington (1988) found potentially life-threatening events such as heart rate deceleration following medical and social interventions. Als et al. (1986) developed individual care plans based on observations of infants' responses to stress in the NICU. It is clear that since NICUs have been consistently caring for small and sick infants, the parents of these infants also experience high levels of stress, related to the "overall sights and sounds of the unit and the large number of other acutely ill infants; changes in the expected parental role that are imposed by the environment; and staff communication and behavior patterns with parents" (Zeanah & Jones as reported by Miles, Funk, & Carlson, 1993, p. 148).

While this field has not yet yielded standardized rating scales such as those designed for rating home and center environments, several important dimensions of the NICU setting have been identified. For example, observations can be made in the following four areas.

Noise levels The level of noise in the hospital environment is usually high because of the number of people in the room at any one time, telephones ringing, equipment and alarms buzzing, and the noises of many caregivers. This high noise level is potentially problematic because it may result in sleep disturbances in infants, interrupting patterns of sleep and awake cycles. Decreases in the noise level result in fewer infants crying during regularly scheduled quiet hours and more infants in deep or light sleep (Strauch, Brandt, & Edwards-Beckett, 1993).

Light levels Light levels are usually high in the NICU, both to facilitate caregiving responsibilities and to provide treatment for some infants. Furthermore, light levels are likely to remain constant 24 hours a day. At least two problems may result from high light levels. First, they may actually damage the retinas of low birthweight infants (Glass et al., 1985). In addition, constant light levels make it almost impossible for an infant to establish any sense of a regular day/night cycle. Artificially darkening the NICU for regular periods of time by blindfolding the infants resulted in lower yet stable respiration and less activity among the blindfolded infants (Shiroiwa et al., 1986).

Handling Patterns of care can also be disruptive. The high frequency of handling sick infants, which usually occurs as a result of some procedure performed by a nurse, pediatrician, or other medical specialist, can be painful and disrupt sleep patterns. In addition, it has been demonstrated that unusually high levels of medical complications occur during or immediately after routine handling of preterm infants (Murdoch & Darlow, 1984; Gorski & Huntington, 1988).

Early learning Finally, many NICU researchers such as VandenBerg (1982), Wolke

(1987a, 1987b), and Gilkerson et al. (1990) suggest that the NICU is not usually an environment that facilitates early learning. Social interactions are brief and often precluded by necessary medical procedures. Many experiences are unpleasant, and opportunities to experience predictable, response-contingent relationships are few.

GENERAL CONSIDERATIONS IN ASSESSING ENVIRONMENTS

Assessing environments is in many ways a very different process from assessing children. In conducting environmental assessments, professionals should be aware of these unique issues and be able to design individualized assessments appropriate for a variety of environments.

Published Guidelines Can Inform Environmental Assessment

Although few assessment tools exist to measure environments, published guidelines are available that allow professionals to design and conduct their own assessments. One of the best known and visible of these guidelines is published by the National Academy of Early Childhood Programs (1991), a division of the National Association for the Education of Young Children. The guidelines were developed to facilitate a process by which early childhood programs can be accredited according to criteria established for high-quality center-based programs. These published criteria cover ten areas: interactions among staff and children, curriculum, staff/parent interaction, staff qualifications and development, administration, staffing, physical environment, health and safety, nutrition and food service, and evaluation. The criteria for the physical environment are displayed in Figure 9.2. Although primarily developed for centers serving normally developing infants, toddlers, and preschoolers, the guidelines are also appropriate for programs designed for young children with disabilities. However, additional criteria may need to be examined when evaluating environments for young children with disabilities. The guidelines developed by the Division for Early Childhood of the Council for Exceptional Children (DEC Task Force on Recommended Practices, 1993) cover 14 areas: assessment, family participation, IFSPs and IEPs, service delivery models, general curriculum and intervention strategies, interventions to promote communication skills, interventions to promote social skills and emotional development, interventions to promote adaptive behavior skills, interventions to promote motor skills, transition, personnel competence, program evaluation, and early intervention with children who are gifted. The section on service delivery models has recommended practices for home-based, center-based, clinic-based, and hospital-based environments that are especially relevant for environmental assessment for children with disabilities.

As integrated early childhood settings are used more often, many states are developing criteria for environments that take into account the specialized needs of children with disabilities and the way programs meet other published guidelines such as those described above. Massachusetts, Arizona (see Smith & Rose, 1993, for examples of the guidelines), and Ohio (Johnson, Johnson, McMillan, Rogers, & Ames, 1989) have published just such guidelines. Being aware of and using these checklists assists the assessor in making general judgments about the quality of the environment, but given the wide array of potential sites in which preschool children with disabilities may be placed, professionals will need to individualize and tailor assessments to individual programs.

1. The indoor and outdoor environments are safe, clean, attractive, and spacious. There is a minimum of 35 square feet of usable play room floor space per child and a minimum of 75 square feet of play space outdoors per child. Program staff have access to the designated space in sufficient time to prepare the environment before children arrive.
2. Activity areas are defined clearly by spatial arrangement. Space is arranged so that children can work individually, together in small groups, or in a large group. Space is arranged to provide clear pathways for children to move from one area to minimize distractions.
3. The space for older toddlers and preschool children is arranged to facilitate a variety of small-group and/or individual activities including block building, sociodramatic play, art, music, science, math, manipulative, and quiet book reading. Other activities such as sand/water play and woodworking are also available on occasion. Carpeted space as well as hard surfaces such as wood floors and ample crawling/toddling areas are provided for infants and young toddlers. Sturdy furniture is provided so nonwalkers can pull themselves up or balance themselves while walking. School-age children are provided separate space arranged to facilitate a variety of age-appropriate activities and permit sustained work on projects.
4. Age-appropriate materials and equipment of sufficient quantity, variety, and durability are readily accessible to children and arranged on low open shelves to promote independent use by children. Materials are rotated and adapted to maintain children's interest.
5. Individual spaces for children to hang their clothing and store their personal belongings are provided.
6. Private areas are available indoors and outdoors for children to have solitude.
7. The environment includes soft elements such as rugs, cushions, rocking chairs.
8. Sound-absorbing materials are used to cut down on excessive noise.
9. Outdoor areas include a variety of surfaces such as soil, sand, grass, hills, flat sections and hard areas for wheel toys. The outdoor area includes shade; open space; digging space; and a variety of equipment for riding, climbing, balancing, and individual play. The outdoor area is protected by fences or by natural barriers from access to streets or other dangers.

FIGURE 9.2

Criteria for the physical environment

Source: From *Accreditation Criteria and Procedures of the National Academy of Early Childhood Programs*, Rev. ed. (pp. 43–46) by the National Academy of Early Childhood Programs, 1991, Washington, DC: The National Association for the Education of Young Children. Copyright 1991 by NAEYC. Excerpted by permission.

Focus on the Child's and the Family's Needs and the Match with the Environmental Dimensions

When selecting the most appropriate program for a specific child, it is important to recognize that the needs of the child as they are perceived by the family and by the early childhood special education staff are usually similar, but they may have some important differences. Winton, Turnbull, and Blacher (1984) suggest that three important considerations are "the professional involvement with the education of the child so parents can relax, reasonable cost of program, and convenience" (pp. 43-44). Early childhood special education staff and administrators' first priority is most often placing the child in the setting that can meet his or her educational needs. By listening to parents' interests and concerns and matching them with observation of potential sites, the best interests of both groups can be accommodated. Fowler,

Chandler, Johnson, and Stella (1988) found that parents of young children who were making a transition between programs were very interested in actively taking part in the preparation for their child's transition. They participated in activities such as identifying what they wanted in the receiving classroom, visiting the receiving classroom, and helping identify the child's skills and needs.

The child brings special capabilities that affect the best match as well. The degree of the child's engagement with the environment, and his or her independence, aggression, social interaction, and happiness all have important relationships with environmental dimensions (Bailey, Harms, & Clifford, 1983).

Recognize the Complexity of Environmental Assessment

In their review of the research on early childhood environments, Sainato and Carta (1992) suggested that the research has primarily examined the effects of single environmental dimensions and has failed to recognize the complexity of environments and the nature of environmental influences. The effects of a given environment will depend in part upon the space and materials, but also will vary according to the individuals in the space and how they continually react to and modify the environment over time. Environmental assessments must be conducted with the realization that it is always an interactive context. This means that environmental assessment cannot be done completely in the absence of children. Walking into a room and examining the materials, equipment, and arrangement is an important first step; however, until the observer has had an opportunity to see how the environment is used and how adults and children in the environment interact, the overall picture will be incomplete. We are not always able to predict how a given child will interact with the environment, so it is important to remember that "there is no evidence that children with certain handicapping conditions or levels of disabilities make more or less good candidates for integration" (Strain, 1990, p. 293).

When observing in homes, it is important to understand and be sensitive to the cultural expectations of the family; their perceptions of a developmentally supportive environment may differ from the perspective of professionals (Vincent, Salisbury, Strain, McCormick, & Tessier, 1990).

Be Familiar With and Use a Variety of Assessment Strategies

As described in Chapter 1, effective assessment of children incorporates multiple sources and multiple measures. Likewise, a number of strategies may be used to assess environments. Measures of the environment range from specific schematic drawings of classrooms to global rating scales. A sample schematic drawing for a preschool classroom is displayed in Figure 9.3. Ideally, a schematic drawing should be proportionally accurate, with room and equipment size in proportion to reality. Using various symbols to label areas and equipment can facilitate visual analyses of the schematic.

Drawing a schematic allows the professional to analyze the classroom environment in terms of spatial arrangement and priority. Such analysis can be enhanced by using the schematic in conjunction with an observational analysis of activity patterns of children. For example, at selected intervals notations could be made as to how many children were in a given area. Several of these observations could provide an indication of which are the most popular activity areas and which are infrequently used. Also, a single child's use of the environment could be documented by simply drawing lines to represent the child's movement during a defined time period. As displayed in Figure 9.4, such an analysis could help differentiate children who wander around an environment from activity to activity from those who become seriously involved in one or two activities for extended periods of

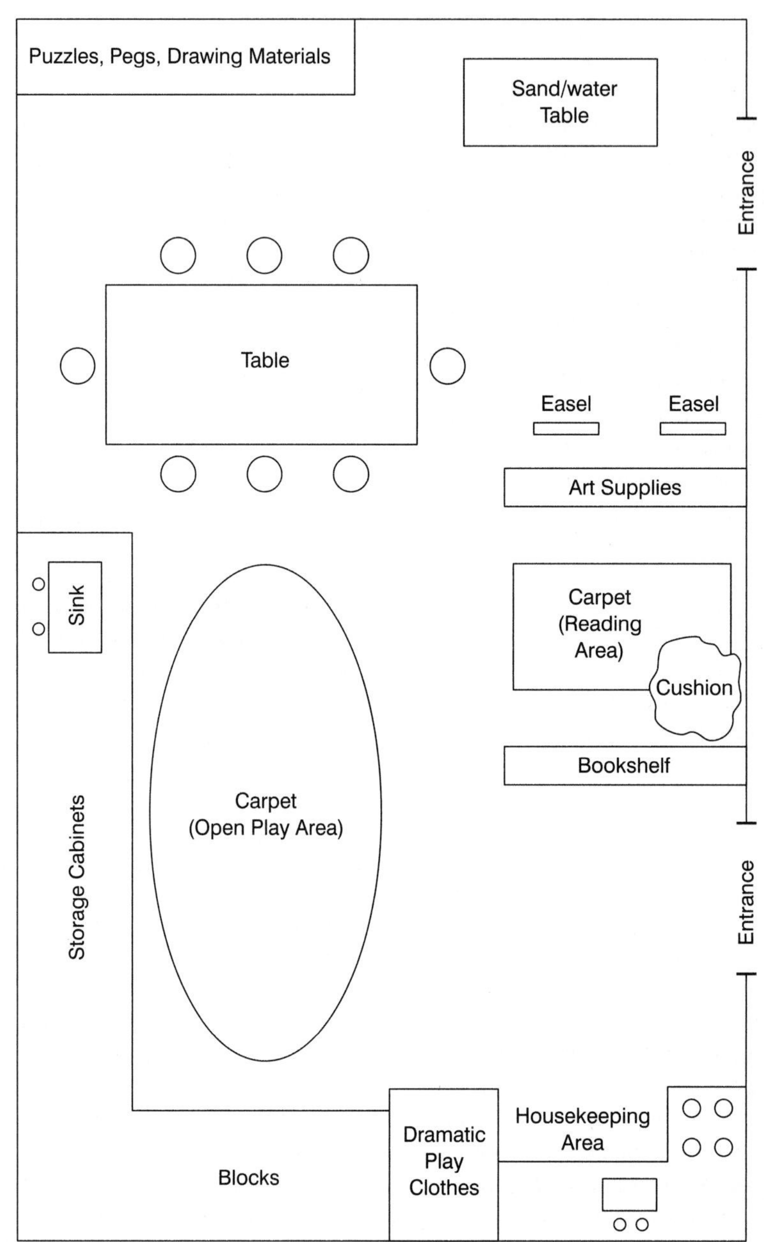

FIGURE 9.3
Schematic depicting a preschool environment

time. If few children spend a lot of time in activities, the environment probably needs modification. If more detailed information is needed, a momentary time-sampling procedure can be used to note where each child is at each observation point. This procedure will allow assessment of the proportion of time each child in the center spends in each area.

A second strategy for evaluating environments is to document environmental quality through the use of checklists. A checklist is simply a list of environmental provisions that someone considers important. By studying the environment, consulting adults who work in the environment, or observing interactional patterns, the checklist can be completed. Numerous examples of checklists for various dimensions of infant and toddler centers (e.g., nap and potty charts, activity records) have been described by Herbert-Jackson, O'Brien, Porterfield, and Risley (1977) and O'Brien, Porterfield, Herbert-Jackson, and Risley (1979). Dimensions of preschool programs have been cited in Smith and Rose (1993) and the DEC Task Force on Recommended Practices (1993).

Third, environments can be evaluated using rating scales. Probably the most common format utilized, a rating scale generally consists of a number of items organized into several dimensions of environmental provisions. The items may be scored in a binary (yes/no) fashion similar to a checklist or may use several possible values, depending on the quality of the environment observed. Ideally, a rating scale is based on substantial professional expertise and evaluation regarding scale content, with supporting data indicating the scale's validity for various purposes. Several examples of rating scales are described in subsequent sections of this chapter.

It is important for professionals to recognize the limitations of existing standardized measures of environments and to use them only as intended. For example, the HOME scale was designed as a screening measure. As indicated in Chapter 5, screening measures are not designed for planning interventions. In addition, professionals should recognize that many items on existing measures are "indicator" items that describe a specific aspect of the environment that serves as an indicator of something bigger. For example, the Purdue Home Stimulation Inventory asks whether the child is fed supper at a regular time or whenever the child seems hungry. Wachs (1979) suggests that this item reflects the broader construct of "temporal regularity in the home." A naive interventionist might set as a goal to change supper to a regular time. If the rest of the child's life is irregular, however, such an environmental modification is likely to have little influence.

Assess the Effects of Environments

Because environments are interactive, the ultimate test of an environment is how it influences the behavior of children and adults. These effects are clearly illustrated in the research on child engagement and ecobehavioral assessment. Engagement refers to "the amount of time children spend interacting with the environment at different levels of competence" (McWilliam & Bailey, 1992, p. 234). For infants, toddlers, and preschoolers, engagement is broken down into the components of attention, active engagement, mastery motivation, and competence (McWilliam & Bailey, 1992). Studies using child engagement and environmental measures have shown that children are more actively engaged in their environment when the program, materials, and instruction are organized (Dunst, McWilliam, & Holbert, 1986; Krantz & Risley, 1977). Incidental teaching, caregiver's elaboration, and goal directedness stimulate active engagement and play with materials (Dunst et al., 1986).

McWilliam and Bailey (1992) suggest behavioral descriptions of five different levels of child engagement that range from nonengagement to active involvement and sustained engagement. Before measuring a child's engagement with the environment, it is important to determine whether engagement is the desired

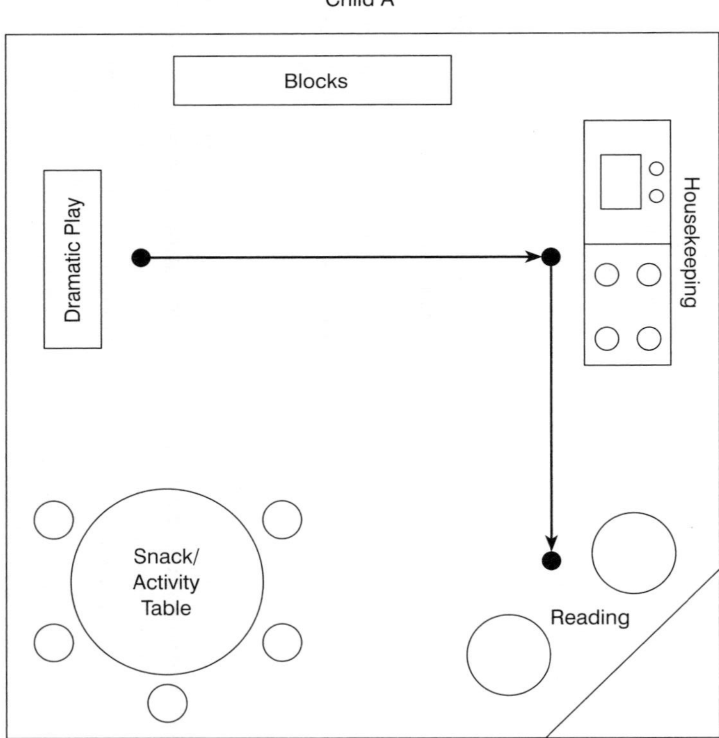

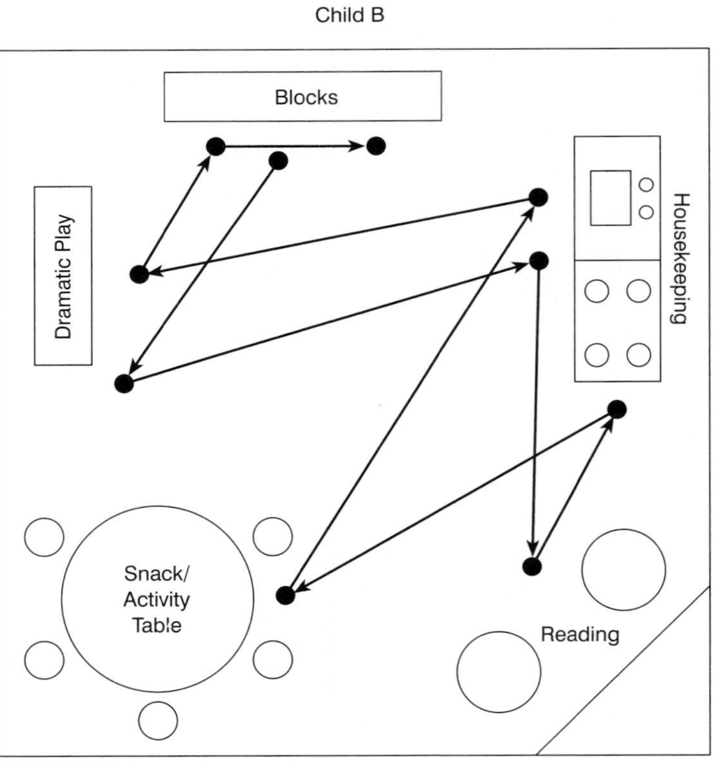

FIGURE 9.4
Schematic comparing the activity/movement patterns of two children during a 30-minute free-play period

outcome or if it is an intermediate step in the attainment of another functional or developmental skill.

Engagement is assessed by observing children and documenting the extent to which they are interacting with appropriate activities, materials, adults, and peers. Obviously the precise definition of engagement will vary according to the classroom situation and expectations for children in each activity area (Bailey et al., 1983). Instances of nonengagement include self-stimulatory behavior, nonattending, aggressive behavior, aimless wandering, or inappropriate use of materials. The first step in assessing engagement is to develop a definition of the behaviors considered on-task or appropriate for a specific child. The child is then observed, and the amount of time spent on one or more activities is recorded and charted. These figures form the baseline of engagement for that child. Specific environmental manipulations are made, the child is again observed for a specified period of time, and the amount of time engaged in the appropriate behaviors is recorded. Comparisons of the baseline and intervention times are made to determine whether or not the environmental manipulation has resulted in the desired change.

McWilliam, Trivette, and Dunst (1985) investigated the possible utility of engagement as a measure of the efficacy of early intervention. Using engagement assessments in two different types of programs, they showed that the two program types could be distinguished on the basis of measures of child engagement, with one model resulting in higher levels of engagement within certain activities than another.

A second broad strategy for assessing the interactive effects of environmental provisions has been referred to as ecobehavioral assessment, "a means of assessing program variables through systematic observation and measuring the moment-to-moment effects of an array of variables upon student behavior" (Carta & Greenwood, 1985, p. 92). In evaluating early intervention programs, these authors have focused on three levels of analysis, all based on direct observational data. Molar descriptions of programs are used to show how adults and children spend their time during the day, in general terms (e.g., engaged vs. nonengaged) or in more specific terms (e.g., direct instruction, location of play, peer interaction). Molecular descriptions of programs are determined by computing conditional probabilities. For example, given that the teacher is reading a story, what is the likelihood that a child or a group of children is listening or participating? Finally, a process-product analysis looks at the relationship between molecular relationships, molar descriptions, and children's subsequent outcomes, such as enhanced developmental progress.

To summarize this section, there are times when an overall assessment of a program's environment is needed and other times when assessing the environment's effect on a particular child is desired. To accomplish the first purpose, examining published guidelines and using checklists, rating scales, and environment floor plans are effective. Landesman-Dwyer (1985) suggests taking the following steps in documenting general environmental effects: (1) list the environmental features believed to effect the program's success, (2) ask key informants about their objective and subjective insights into the program's functioning, (3) examine how individual items on standardized measures relate to environmental variables, and (4) select "success" or "outcome" measures that are separate from description of the environment.

When placement decisions or environmental adaptations for an individual child are the prime purpose, critical considerations include focusing on the match between the child's and the family's needs and environmental dimensions, recognizing the complexity of the environment, and choosing appropriate tools such as examining engagement time.

TABLE 9.2
Two Sample Items from the Early Childhood Environment Rating Scale

	Inadequate 1	2	Minimal 3	4	Good 5	6	Excellent 7
9. Room arrangement	No interest centers defined. Room inconveniently arranged (Ex. traffic patterns interfere with activities). Materials with similar use not placed together		One or two interest centers defined, but centers not well placed in room (Ex. quiet and noisy activities near one another, water not accessible where needed). Supervision of centers difficult, or materials disorganized.		Three or more interest centers defined and conveniently equipped (Ex. water provided, shelving adequate). Quiet and noisy centers separated. Appropriate play space provided in each center (Ex. rug or table area out of flow of traffic). Easy visual supervision of centers.		Everything in 5 plus centers selected to provide a variety of learning experiences. Arrangement of centers designed to promote independent use by children (Ex. labeled open shelves, convenient drying space for art work). Additional materials organized and available to add to or change centers.

REPRESENTATIVE METHODS OF ASSESSING ENVIRONMENTS

A variety of measures and procedures have been proposed for assessing environments related to the care of children. This section describes representative methods and procedures for assessing center and classroom environments, home environments, and hospital environments. The section concludes with a discussion of the assessment skills needed for successful participation in a given environment. Such assessment is important for placement purposes as well as for instructional activities likely to facilitate successful transitions. These assessment tools can be used to determine the overall quality and safety of a preschool setting. In addition, they can be used in making adaptations for specific child needs and for designing environments in which all children can participate more successfully and more fully.

Assessing Center and Classroom Environments

Infants, toddlers, and preschool-age children are often cared for or educated in early child-care centers or family child-care programs. Early child-care centers often have multiple caregivers working with one or more groups of young children. Children cared for in family child-care programs usually have one caregiver working with several children. There are a number of instruments designed to rate the quality of these environments.

TABLE 9.2
Continued

	Inadequate 1	2	Minimal 3	4	Good 5	6	Excellent 7
33. Provisions for exceptional children Exceptional child: any child whose physical, mental, or emotional needs are not met by regular program alone. Modifications: Physical environment, Program, Schedule [Examples of each modification are provided in the manual.]	No provisions or plans for modifying the physical environment, program, schedule for exceptional children. Reluctance to admit children with special needs		Minor accommodations made to get through the day, but no long-range plans for meeting the special needs of exceptional children. No attempt to assess degree of need.		Staff assess needs of children and make modifications in environment, program, and schedule to meet the special needs of exceptional children.		Everything in 5 plus: individually planned program for exceptional children involving parents and using professionally trained person as consultant to guide assessment and planning. Referral to support services.

Source: From *Early Childhood Environment Rating Scale* (pp. 17, 35) by T. Harms and R. M. Clifford, 1980, New York: Teachers College Press. Copyright 1980 by T. Harms and R. M. Clifford. Reprinted by permission.

Early Childhood Environment Rating Scale The Early Childhood Environment Rating Scale (ECERS) (Harms & Clifford, 1980) "was designed to give an overall picture of the surroundings for children and adults in preschool settings, including the use of space, materials, and activities to enhance children's development, daily schedule, and supervision" (Harms & Clifford, 1983, p. 262). It is designed for use across environments serving typical infants and/or preschoolers. The 37 items are organized into seven categories: personal care routines, furnishings and displays for children, language-reasoning experience, fine and gross motor activities, creative activities, social development, and adult needs. Scoring the entire instrument generally requires a morning's observation and interviews with staff. Each item is scored on a scale from 1 (inadequate) to 7 (excellent), with criteria provided for ratings for 1, 3, 5, and 7. Two sample items from the ECERS are displayed in Table 9.2.

Items on the scale were developed based on an extensive literature review and input from practicing caregivers and supervisors. Their importance was validated by a panel of seven experts in early childhood education. Studies reported by the authors indicate that scores on the scale correlate well with broader ratings by experts of program quality. Interrater reliability was .88 and test/retest reliability was .96 (Harms & Clifford, 1983). Videotapes are available to train observers to use this instrument (Harms, Fleming, & Cryer, 1992).

Several studies have documented the utility of the ECERS in evaluating important dimensions of environmental quality. A series of studies have examined the relationship between

ECERS ratings and various developmental outcomes for children. McCartney, Scarr, Phillips, Grajek, and Schwarz (1982), McCartney (1984), and McCartney, Scarr, Phillips, and Grajek (1985) found significant relationships between overall ratings of environmental quality and measures of both intellectual and language development in children. Children in high-quality centers generally were rated by both parents and caregivers as more considerate and more sociable than children attending other daycare programs. Bjorkman, Poteat, and Snow (1986), however, found no clear-cut association between ECERS ratings and observed social behavior of 4-year-olds in four daycare centers, two with high ECERS scores and two with low ECERS scores.

Bailey et al. (1982) used the ECERS to compare environments in 56 classrooms for normally developing preschoolers with 25 classrooms for preschoolers with disabilities. Overall scores for classrooms with typically developing children were significantly higher than those for classrooms for preschoolers with disabilities, with 12 individual items rated higher: furnishings for relaxation and comfort, room arrangement, child-related displays, space for gross motor practice, scheduled time for gross motor activities, art, blocks, sand/water, dramatic play, space to be alone, free-play, and cultural awareness. The authors suggested that the data indicated that these preschool environments were significantly different from those usually provided for young children and apparently were less normalized. The extent to which these differences represented appropriate modifications for children with disabilities was not known.

Two additional environmental assessment instruments have been developed by Harms and Clifford: the *Family Day Care Rating Scale (FDCRS)* (Harms & Clifford, 1989) and the *Infant/Toddler Environment Rating Scale (ITERS)* (Harms et al., 1990). The FDCRS, which was designed to assess the quality of family child-care settings, is comprised of 32 items in six subscales: space and furnishings for care and learning, basic care, language and reasoning, learning activities, social development, and adult needs. A seventh category is especially designed for assessing the quality of the environment for children with disabilities. In this category, eight additional items are included in a subscale called "supplementary items: provisions for exceptional children." The format of the FDCRS is similar to that of the ECERS. The items are each rated on a 7-point scale based on observation and interviews. Reliability and validity have been established for this instrument; positive correlations with children's prosocial behavior (Howes & Stewart, 1987), language development, and caregiver language stimulation (Goelman & Pence, 1987) have been found.

The ITERS (Harms et al., 1990) was designed to provide an overall assessment of center-based care for children younger than 30 months of age. The 35 items on this scale are organized into seven subscales: furnishings and displays for children, personal care routines, listening and talking, learning activities, interaction, program structure, and adult needs. Scoring is based on the same scheme as in the ECERS and FDCRS. Reliability and validity have been established by the authors.

The Early Childhood Physical Environment Scales The Early Childhood Physical Environment Scales (Moore, 1982) were developed to describe the arrangement and atmosphere of early childhood programs. There are two scales; one rates the organization of the space of the center as a whole, the other rates the organization and character of individual rooms or areas. The whole-center scale assesses 10 dimensions: visual connection between spaces, closure of spaces, spatial separation, mixture of large and small spaces, separation of staff and children's areas, separation of age groups, circulation, visibility, and connection between indoor and outdoor spaces. Each item is rated on a 5-point scale. The scale rating individual rooms or areas also assesses 10 dimensions: spatial definition of activity centers, visual connections to other centers, size, storage and work space, concentration of same-use resources, softness, flexibility, variety of seating and working positions, amount of resources, and separation of activity centers from circulation paths.

Moore (1982) recommends that these scales be used in conjunction with other measures to gain a more complete picture of the environment. He developed two measures to assess teachers, one focusing on teacher style and the other on educational philosophy. Both are self-ratings completed by teachers. Additionally, an Environment/Behavior Observation Schedule is used to code the behavior of children and adults in early childhood settings. Before observation begins, a schematic is drawn of the environment, which is then divided into cells representing approximately 60 square feet. A time-sampling system is recommended, in which several categories of behavior are coded according to the cell in which they occurred. An example of the scale's use was reported by Moore (1986), who found that differences in engagement were related to the amount of spatial definition in a given area.

Preschool Assessment of the Classroom Environment–Revised The Preschool Assessment of the Classroom Environment Scale (PACE–R) (Raab, Dunst, Whaley, LeGrand, & Taylor, 1994) consists of 35 items organized into seven categories: program foundation and philosophy, management and training, environmental organization, staffing patterns, instructional context, instructional techniques, and program evaluation. Each item is scored on a 5-point scale that is completed after observing the classroom environment for two to four hours, interviewing staff, and reviewing written materials.

From a sample of 28 of 100 child-care programs using the PACE–R, the mean percentage of agreement of two independent observers was 92% (Raab, Dunst, & Whaley, 1994). Factor analysis of the instrument components supports the instrument's organization into the seven subscales. In a correlational study, environmental organization, staffing patterns, instructional context, and instructional techniques were moderately positively related to children's social engagement, engagement with the physical environment, social responsiveness, and cognitive style.

Assessing Home Environments

The environment in which most infants and preschoolers spend considerable time is the home. Early interventionists, particularly those working in home-based infant programs, may be interested in assessing the home environment to determine the extent to which it is safe, warm, and developmentally facilitative. A detailed description of considerations and procedures in assessing family environments is presented by Simeonsson (1988); thus assessment of the home environment is only briefly addressed here.

Home Observation for the Measurement of the Environment By far the best-known and most commonly used measure of the home environment is the Home Observation for the Measurement of the Environment (HOME) (Caldwell & Bradley, 1984), which was designed to identify home environments that pose a "risk" for children's development, evaluate programs designed to improve parenting skills, and research relationships between home environment and children's health and development. There are three versions of the HOME Inventory; Infant and Toddler, Early Childhood, and Middle Childhood (only the two scales for younger children are discussed here). Each version assesses the quantity and quality of the physical environment of the home as well as the social, emotional, and cognitive support provided children in their own homes. The infant version (for children from birth to 3 years) contains 45 items organized into six subscales: emotional and verbal responsiveness of mother, avoidance of restriction and punishment, organization of physical and temporal environment, provision of appropriate play materials, maternal involvement with child, and opportunities for variety in daily stimulation. The preschool version (for children ages 3 to 6) contains 55 items organized into eight subscales: stimulation through toys, games, and reading materials; language stimulation; physical environment; pride, affection, and warmth; stimulation of academic behavior; modeling and encouraging of social maturity; variety of stimulation; and physical punishment. Both instruments are completed on the basis of a home visit by a trained observer. Each item contains a statement about the environment (e.g., "Child has some muscle activity toys or equipment"), which is scored as either *yes* or *no* on the basis of observation and interviews with the parent. Raw scores may be generated for each subscale and for the total score. No norms or score transformations are available.

Numerous studies have examined the reliability of the HOME scales and their utility in regard to their primary purpose, which is to serve as a screening measure to identify high-risk home environments. In regard to reliability, Elardo, Bradley, and Caldwell (1977) reported high interrater agreement, and Mitchell and Gray (1981) found total scores to be consistent over time, although subscales were not. The relationship between HOME scores and subsequent testing of cognitive and language development has been documented repeatedly (Gottfried, 1984; Elardo et al., 1977). Piper and Ramsay (1980) found a relationship between the quality of the home environment as indicated by ratings on the HOME scale and changes in the developmental status of infants with Down syndrome.

Although it was designed primarily as a screening tool, Powell (1981) suggests that the HOME scale can serve as a mechanism for feedback to parents and as a teaching tool to promote high-quality interpersonal interactions between parent and child. However, the interventionist using the HOME scale in this fashion should take care to communicate a positive impression of parenting skills and to build on parent priorities for services (Bailey, 1987). In addition, because there is considerable variability in the importance of individual items, interventionists should examine the pattern of scores and not just individual items, which may reflect values that the parent does not hold or may not be sensitive to qualitative issues. For example, one item on the infant scale is "Family has a pet." Obviously, it would be quite inappropriate to suggest that owning a pet is an important goal for all families. Furthermore, some families may have a pet, but it could be inappropriate for the age of the child (e.g., a snake or an aggressive dog) and thus not fulfill the function for which it was intended.

Cultural differences in families are reflected on the HOME. For example, in a study of urban Native American families, Seideman, Haase, Primeaux, and Burns (1992) found lower scores than the norm on the Parental Involvement subscale, while other subscale scores were not significantly different from the norms. Because Native American families place high value on observation and silence in young children, they frequently use nonverbal teaching and learning strategies with their children. Since items on the Parental Involvement subscale focus on the mother's involvement with the child in activities such as talking to the child, structuring play, and providing toys to develop new skills, it is understandable that Native American parents would score lower on this subscale.

Purdue Home Stimulation Inventory

The Purdue Home Stimulation Inventory (Wachs, 1979), which was developed to assess the infant's physical environment provided in the home, consists of 30 items gathered through interviews and observations in the home environment. According to the author, the instrument was not developed with the intent of being theoretically consistent, but rather with the purpose of tapping as many relevant dimensions of the physical environment as possible. Items assess dimensions such as routines, number of adults and siblings living in the home, materials available, and activity levels. In a study of 39 normally developing infants from a range of environmental arrangements, Wachs (1979) found that children's gains in cognitive development were associated with a physically responsive environment, an adequate degree of personal space as defined by the presence of a stimulus shelter and a lack of overcrowding, the degree to which the setup of the home permitted exploration, and degree of temporal regularity. A high level of noise was related to lower levels of cognitive development.

Assessing Hospital Environments

Hospitals, particularly neonatal intensive care units (NICUs) or pediatric units, make up the third environment in which infants and preschoolers with disabilities spend time. When hospital stays are required, the primary concern is the health of the child, so medical routines and procedures generally take first priority. The importance of the child's developmental and emotional needs in such environments, however, is increasingly being recognized (see Chapter 7). Of particular concern relative to this chapter is the nature of hospital environments. VandenBerg (1982) described the rapidly changing technology in neonatal intensive care nurseries (ICNs) and its contribution to increased survival rates for low-birthweight and otherwise high-risk infants. However, she also suggested that "the same technical advances have brought with them a host of new problems. The modern ICN environment is replete with negative stimuli for infants and their caregivers" (p. 83). It is an inherently stressful environment for infants, caregivers, and parents, due to the serious nature of the infants' health status, the nature of treatment procedures used, high noise levels, frequent changes of caregivers, disruptions in the parent/child relationship, and work-related stresses for staff. She argued that the ICN should have one or more developmental specialists to provide infant care that is coordinated and responsive to infant developmental needs and ensure a "humanization" of the intensive care nursery.

Parental Stressor Scale: Neonatal Intensive Care Unit Although few standardized instruments exist for assessing the quality of care provided in hospitals, some new ones are being developed. The Parental Stressor Scale: Neonatal Intensive Care Unit (Miles et al., 1993), which was developed for nurses, also shows promise for use by early interventionists. This scale was designed to measure parental perception of stressors related to the physical and psychosocial environment of the pediatric intensive care unit. The instrument has three subscales: appearance and behavior of a premature infant, changes in the parental role that differ for parents of sick infants, and differences in the routines and environment of the NICU. Parents rate their stress on each of 26 items on a rating scale of 1 to 5. A score of 1 indicates that the item is not stressful at all; a 5 means extremely stressful. Since parents may not have experienced every situation on the scale, there are three ways to score the instrument. In the first method only those items with which a parent has had specific experience are scored and the average stress score is calculated. In the second method an overall stress level is calculated from all items combined. If a parent has not experienced a particular situation, a 1 (not stressful) is scored. These are averaged. In the third method all items in which the parent indicates "yes" on the subscales are counted, yielding a total number of PSS:NICU items the parent has experienced.

USING ENVIRONMENTAL ASSESSMENT INFORMATION

The three main purposes for assessing the environment are assisting in initial placement and transition planning, determining the overall quality of an environment, and assisting teachers and caregivers in making adaptations to environments to more effectively instruct children.

How are environmental assessments effectively integrated into the total planning and placement decision-making process? First, determining the skills that an environment requires for a child to be successful in it is an important issue at the time of initial placement of a child into a program and subsequently at transition points when the child moves from one program to another. For example, a multidisciplinary team is working with parents to identify the most appropriate placement for their 3-year-old son with Down syndrome. One option is placement in a regular preschool program for normally developing children, with periodic consultation by specialists. Will this be an appropriate learning environment, and is the child likely to succeed in it? These questions can be answered in part by using rating scales such as the ECERS or the PACE–R to determine the quality of the environment. But because such an assessment is not likely to provide complete information regarding the child's ability to be successful in that environment, a more complete transition plan may be needed. This plan includes the following steps: gathering information from the receiving program(s), using available print materials, classroom visits, and interviews; examining the child's present program to determine ways to adapt present practices to ease the transition; assessing the child's coping skills, learning-to-learn skills, and knowledge of the upcoming transition; assessing the entire class or caseload to identify practices that can facilitate future placements; and determining other community resources that can help (Rosenkoetter et al., 1994). Pretransition visits and conversations between the sending and receiving teachers can facilitate "conveying the characteristics and preferences of individual children, effective methods of teaching them, and suggestions for supporting their families" (Rosenkoetter et al., 1994, p. 120).

Some programs have developed criteria or identified formal checklists indicating the behaviors or skills expected in that environment. Preacademic skills (Rule, Innocenti, Coor, Bonem, & Stowitschek, 1989) and behaviors for successful mainstreaming in kindergarten (Beckoff & Bender, 1989; Polloway, 1987) and child care (Murphy & Vincent, 1989) have been identified. These inventories are useful as assessment tools in identifying a child's strengths and deficits relative to a placement under consideration. However, such inventories are not always available or relevant for the particular environment under consideration, and other strategies may be needed. Vincent et al. (1980) suggest four strategies for determining survival skills. These include trial placement (placing the child in the new environment for a short period of time to determine functional abilities), follow-up studies (studying children who have already made the transition to determine if they were successful), skill generation (asking teachers to identify important behaviors or skills), and direct observation (observing programs and using coding procedures to identify the range and types of skills needed and the contexts in which they are used).

It must also be recognized that while standardized measures of environments have been developed, the ultimate question is whether a particular environment is appropriate for a particular child and family; often the professional will need to rely on a combination of standardized and naturalistic observations to determine if there is a "goodness of fit" between the child's interests, needs, and abilities, the family's desires, and the environment. It is this fit that is of utmost importance, rather than the characteristics of the child, the family, or the environment in isolation from each other. Planning for initial placement and transitions now includes families as key decision makers to a much greater extent than in the past, so the family must be included in either naturalistic or systematic observations of the environmental options.

The child is not the only person to be assessed when trying to predict the future success of a child with disabilities into an integrated setting. It is important to determine the willingness of the teachers and staff to provide the accommodations that the child will need. Planning for children with disabilities takes time and collaboration among many specialists, so it is exceedingly important for planning time to be available (Karp & Carlson, 1993; Rosenkoetter et al., 1994; Schumm et al., 1995). Persons responsible for environments may not always be receptive to suggestions regarding changes, particularly if those suggestions require major changes or embrace values not held by the individual or the program personnel. There are philosophical differences among early childhood educators in terms of the intrusiveness of interventions, and some programs may be unwilling to modify the environment because the changes are viewed as too intrusive. Similarly, some suggestions to families regarding changes to the environment may reflect differences in cultural values or personal lifestyle that may create conflict between intervenors and family members. Environmental changes therefore should be thoroughly discussed among family members and intervenors, and only those changes deemed acceptable to all should be made.

Second, determining the overall quality of an environment can facilitate decisions about how well a particular program will fit with a child's needs and can also facilitate overall program improvements. In communities where many different programs are available for placement of children with disabilities, having consistent environmental ratings on them assists the team in determining which site may be the least restrictive environment for a child. For example, knowing the openness of the various environments and the gradualness with which they shift from one activity to another as measured on the PACE–R would be valuable information in placing a child who has temper tantrums at every transition and for whom constant supervision is necessary.

In cases where professionals desire to change the environment through a systematic environmental assessment, Dunst et al. (1986) suggest five steps. First, the classroom teacher or other caregiver responsible for an environment conducts a self-evaluation of environmental provisions, using an instrument with content similar to standardized rating scales. Included in the self-evaluation should be the caregiver's indication of whether assistance would be desired to change environmental dimensions. Second, an independent assessment is conducted by an outside assessor. Third, both assessments are used to discuss the existing environment and possible changes. Fourth, a systematic plan is developed that reinforces existing program strengths and builds up weak or inadequate areas. The plan should be developed recognizing that the measures used may not necessarily have been designed to plan changes in environments, and thus additional information may be needed. Finally, once plans are developed they should be considered tentative. Changes in children's behavior and functioning within environments should be monitored and evaluated to determine the effectiveness of those environmental modifications. As Bailey et al. (1983) note, such an assessment must be conducted so that the child behaviors measured, such as independence, engagement, aggression, or social play, are consistent with the goals of the environmental change. As implementation proceeds, adjustments may be needed. Further, the extent to which the plan actually is implemented should be documented.

Third, at times teachers and caregivers recognize that their environment, as it is organized, is not effective for the children or for themselves. In this case, teachers and caregivers use environmental assessment tools to describe the existing environment so that it can be examined and changed. Nordquist et al. (1991) provide a specific example of this type of environmental assessment and describe the changes that occurred in two classrooms for six autistic children as a result of an environmental assessment and change plan. After taking baseline data on the children's use of materials and compliance in the existing environment and the teacher's behavior, the physical and programmatic environments were described. Floor plans were drawn of the current physical environment and the proposed new arrangement. Descriptions of the ways the teachers and assistants were supervising children and using their time were written. In the new arrangement, the rooms were divided into small functional activities areas with clearer divisions between areas and more efficient use of space, a greater number and variety of play materials were available, and instruction and free-play occurred concurrently. The schedule was changed so short (5-minute) individual instruction periods were followed by 15-minute free-play times. The ways teachers supervised children were changed. In the reorganized classrooms, teachers and assistants increased their smiling at and use of affectionate words with the children. The children increased their use of materials in free-play and compliance.

SUMMARY OF KEY CONCEPTS

- Environmental assessment is useful when planning a placement for a young child with disabilities, when planning a transition from one program to another, and when planning an individualized intervention plan.
- Environments should be assessed to determine whether they (a) facilitate children's development; (b) are safe, warm, and comfortable places; (c) are least restrictive; (d) require particular skills; and (e) match child and family needs.
- Environmental dimensions of centers and classrooms include the physical characteristics (amount and type of space, physical layout, variety, location, and type of materials) and social/programmatic characteristics (teacher/child ratio, group size, schedule of activities, and peer interactions).
- Environmental dimensions of homes include caregiver responsivity and involvement, restriction and control, play materials, variety of materials and stimuli, and family resources and supports.
- Environmental dimensions of hospital settings and neonatal intensive care units include noise levels, light, handling/caretaking, and early learning.
- Published guidelines for environmental provisions at national, state, and local levels are useful tools for determining the overall and specific quality of environments.
- Environmental assessment strategies include observing, drawing schematics, using checklists and rating scales, recording children's level of engagement, and using ecobehavioral assessment procedures.

REFERENCES

Als, H., Lawhon, G., Brown, E., Gibes, R., Duffy, F. H., McAnulty, G., & Blickman, J. G. (1986). Individualized behavioral and environmental care for the very low birthweight preterm infant at high risk for bronchopulmonary dysplasia: Neonatal intensive care unit and developmental outcome. *Pediatrics, 78,* 1123–1132.

Anderson, L. W. (1984). *Time and school learning: Theory, research and practice.* London: Croom Helm Ltd.

Bailey, D. B. (1987). Collaborative goal-setting with families: Resolving differences in values and priorities for services. *Topics in Early Childhood Special Education 7*(2), 59–71.

Bailey, D. B., Burchinal, M. R., & McWilliam, R. A. (1993). Age of peers and early childhood development. *Child Development, 64*(3), 848–862.

Bailey, D. B., Clifford, R. M., & Harms, T. (1982). Comparison of preschool environments for handicapped and nonhandicapped children. *Topics in Early Childhood Special Education, 2*(1), 9–20.

Bailey, D. B., Harms, T., & Clifford, R. M. (1983). Matching changes in preschool environments to desired changes in child behavior. *Journal for the Division for Early Childhood, 7,* 61–68.

Barnard, K. E., & Kelly, J. F. (1990). Assessment of parent-child interaction. In S. J. Meisels & J. P. Shonkoff (Eds.), *Handbook of early childhood intervention* (pp. 278–302). Cambridge, England: Cambridge University Press.

Beckoff, A. G., & Bender, W. N. (1989). Programming for mainstream kindergarten success in preschool: Teachers' perceptions of necessary prerequisite skills. *Journal of Early Intervention, 13*(3), 269–280.

Bjorkman, S., Poteat, G. M., & Snow, C. W. (1986). Environmental ratings and children's social behavior: Implications for the assessment of day care quality. *American Journal of Orthopsychiatry, 56,* 271–277.

Brazelton, T. B., Koslowski, B., & Main, M. (1974). The origins of reciprocity: The early mother-infant interaction. In M. Lewis & L. R. Rosenblum (Eds.), *The effect of the infant on its caregiver* (pp. 49-76). New York: Wiley-Interscience.

Bromwich, R. (1981). *Working with parents and infants: An interactional approach.* Baltimore, MD: University Park Press.

Brooks-Gunn, J., Klebanov, P. K., Liaw, F., & Spiker, D. (1993). Enhancing the development of low-birthweight, premature infants: Changes in cognition and behavior over the first three years. *Child Development, 64,* 736–753.

Brooks-Gunn, J., & Lewis, M. (1982). Development of play behavior in handicapped and normal infants. *Topics in Early Childhood Special Education, 2,* 14–27.

Brown, W. H., Fox, J. J., & Brady, M. P. (1987). The effects of spatial density on the socially directed behavior of three and four year old children during freeplay: An investigation of a setting factor. *Education and Treatment of Children, 10,* 247–258.

Bruder, M. B., & Walker, L. (1990). Discharge planning: Hospital to home transitions for infants. *Topics in Early Childhood Special Education, 9*(4), 15–25.

Bruner, J. (1980). *Under five in Britain.* Ypsilanti, MI: High/Scope.

Burstein, N. D. (1986). The effects of classroom organization on mainstreamed preschool children. *Exceptional Children, 52,* 425–434.

Caldwell, B. M., & Bradley, R. H. (1984). *Home observation for the measurement of the environment (HOME).* Little Rock, AR: Center for Research on Teaching and Learning, University of Arkansas at Little Rock.

Carta, J. J., & Greenwood, C. R. (1985). Ecobehavioral assessment: A methodology for expanding the evaluation of early intervention programs. *Topics in Early Childhood Special Education, 5*(2), 88–104.

Chandler, L. K. (1993). Steps in preparing for transition: Preschool to kindergarten. *Teaching Exceptional Children, 25,* 52–55.

Clarke-Stewart, A. (1982). *Daycare.* Cambridge, MA: Harvard University Press.

Clarke-Stewart, A. (1987). Predicting child development from child care forms and features: The Chicago study. In D. Phillips (Ed.), *Quality in child* care: *What does research tell us?* (pp. 21–42). Washington, DC: National Association for the Education of Young Children.

Clarke-Stewart, A., & Gruber, C. (1984). Daycare: Forms and features. In R. C. Ainslie (Ed.), *Quality variations in daycare* (pp. 35–62). New York: Praeger.

Cummings, M., & Beagles-Ross, J. (1983). Towards a model of infant daycare: Studies of factors influencing responding to separation in daycare. In R. C. Ainslie (Ed.), *Quality variations in daycare* (pp. 159–182). New York: Praeger.

David, T. G., & Weinstein, C. S. (1987). The built environment and children's development. In C. S. Weinstein & T. G. David (Eds.), *Spaces for children: The built environment and child development* (pp. 3–20). New York: Plenum.

DEC Task Force on Recommended Practices. (1993). *DEC recommended practices: Indicators of quality in programs for infants and young children with special needs and their families.* Reston, VA: Division for Early Childhood Council for Exceptional Children.

Derman-Sparks, L., and the A.B.C. Task Force (1989). Anti-bias curriculum: Tools for empowering young children. Washington, DC: National Association for the Education of Young Children.

Dunst, C. J., McWilliam, R. A., & Holbert, K. (1986). Assessment of preschool classroom environments. *Diagnostique, 11,* 212–232.

Eheart, B. K. (1982). Mother-child interactions with nonretarded and mentally retarded preschoolers. *American Journal of Mental Deficiency, 87,* 20–25.

Elardo, R., Bradley, R., & Caldwell, B. M. (1977). A longitudinal study of the relation of infants' home environments to language development at age three. *Child Development, 48,* 595–603.

Field, T. (1980). Preschool play: Effects of teacher-child ratio and organization of classroom space. *Child Study Journal, 10,* 191–205.

Field, T. (1982). Interaction coaching for high-risk infants and their parents. *Prevention in Human Services, l,* 5–54.

Fleming, L. A., Wolery, M., Weinzierl, C., Venn, M. L., & Schroeder, C. (1991). Model for assessing and adapting teachers' roles in mainstreamed preschool settings. *Topics in Early Childhood Special Education, 11*(1), 85–98.

Fowler, W. (1980). *Curriculum and assessment guides for infant and child care.* Boston: Allyn and Bacon.

Fowler, S., Chandler, L. K., Johnson, T. E., & Stella, M. E. (1988). Individualizing family involvement in school transitions: Gathering information and choosing the next program. *Journal of the Division for Early Childhood, 12,* 208–216.

Fraiberg, S. (1974). Blind infants and their mothers: An examination of the sign system. In M. Lewis & L. A. Rosenblum (Eds.), *The effect of the infant on its caregiver.* New York: Wiley-Interscience.

Fredericksen, L. W., & Fredericksen, C. B. (1977). Experimental evaluation of classroom environments: Scheduling planned activities. *American Journal of Mental Deficiency, 81,* 421–427.

Gilkerson, L., Gorski, P., & Panitz, P. (1990). Hospital-based intervention for preterm infants and their families. In S. J. Meisels & J. P. Shonkoff (Eds.), *Handbook of early childhood intervention* (pp. 445–468). Cambridge, England: Cambridge University Press.

Glass, P., Avery, G. B., Subramaniou, K. N., Keys, M. P., Sostek, A. M., & Friendly, D. S. (1985). Effect of bright light in the hospital nursery on the incidence of retinopathy of prematurity. *New England Journal of Medicine, 313,* 401–404.

Goelman, H., & Pence, A. (1987) Effects of child care, family, and individual characteristics on children's language development: The Victoria Day Care Project. In D. A. Phillips (Ed.), *Quality in child care: What does research tell us?* (pp. 89–104). Washington, DC: National Association for the Education of Young Children.

Gonzalez-Mena, J. (1993). *Multicultural issues in child care.* Mountain View, CA: Mayfield Publishing Company.

Gorski, P. A., & Huntington, L. (1988). Physiological measures relative to tactile stimulation in hospitalized preterm infants. *Pediatric Research, 23,* 210a.

Gottfried, A. W. (Ed.). (1984). *Home environment and early cognitive development.* New York: Academic Press.

Greenman, J. (1988). *Caring spaces, learning places: Children's environments that work.* Redmond, WA: Exchange Press.

Guralnick, M. J. (1984). The peer interactions of young developmentally delayed children in specialized and integrated settings. In T. Field (Ed.), *Friendships between normally developing and handicapped children* (pp. 139–152). Chicago: Society for Research in Child Development.

Guralnick, M. J. (1986). The peer relations of young handicapped and nonhandicapped children. In P. S. Strain, M. J. Guralnick, & H. Walker (Eds.), *Children's social behavior: Development, assessment, and modification* (pp. 93–140). New York: Academic Press.

Hanline, M. F., & Knowlton, A. (1988). A collaborative model for providing support to parents during their child's transition from infant intervention to preschool special education public school programs. *Journal of the Division for Early Childhood, 12*(2), 116–125.

Harms, T., & Clifford, R. M. (1989). *Family Day Care Rating Scale.* New York: Teachers College Press.

Harms, T., & Clifford, R. M. (1980). *Early Childhood Environment Rating Scale.* New York: Teachers College Press.

Harms, T., & Clifford, R. M., (1983). Assessing preschool environments with the Early Childhood Environment Rating Scale. *Studies in Educational Evaluation, 8,* 261–269.

Harms, T., Cryer, D., & Clifford, R. M. (1990). *Infant/Toddler Environment Rating Scale.* New York: Teachers College Press.

Harms, T., Fleming, J., & Cryer, D. (1992). *Videotape for the Early Childhood Environment Rating Scale with video guide and training workbook.* New York: Teachers College Press.

Hart, B. (1982). So that teachers can teach: Assigning roles and responsibilities. *Topics in Early Childhood Special Education, 2*(1), 1–8.

Hendrickson, J. M., Strain, P. S., Tremblay, A., & Shores, R. E. (1981). Relationship between toy and material use and the occurrence of social interactive behaviors by normally developing preschool children. *Psychology in the Schools, 18,* 50–55.

Herbert-Jackson, E., O'Brien, M., Porterfield, J., & Risley, T. R. (1977). *The infant center.* Baltimore, MD: University Park Press.

High, P. C., & Gorski, P. A. (1985). Womb for improvement—A study of preterm development in an intensive care nursery. In A. W. Gottfried & J. L. Gaiter (Eds.), *Infant stress under intensive care* (pp. 131–155). Baltimore, MD: University Park Press.

Howes, C. (1983). Caregiver behavior in center and family day care. *Journal of Applied Developmental Psychology, 4,* 99–107.

Howes, C., & Hamilton, C. E. (1992). Children's relationships with child care teachers: Stability and concordance with parental attachments. *Child Development, 63,* 867–878.

Howes, C., Phillips, D. A., & Whitebook, M. (1992). Thresholds of quality: Implications for the social development of children in center-based child care. *Child Development, 63,* 448–460.

Howes C., & Rubenstein, J. (1985). Determinants of toddlers' experience in daycare: Age of entry and quality of setting. *Child Care Quarterly, 14,* 140–151.

Howes, C., & Stewart, P. (1987). Child's play with adults, toys and peers: An examination of family and child care influences. *Developmental Psychology, 23,* 423–430.

Johnson, L. G., Johnson, P. A., McMillan, R. P., Rogers, C. K., & Ames, K. (1989). *Early childhood special education program evaluation.* Columbus, OH: Ohio Department of Education.

Jones, O. H. M. (1977). Mother-child communication with pre-linguistic Down's syndrome and normal infants. In H. R. Schaffer (Ed.), *Studies in mother-infant interaction* (pp. 379–401). San Francisco: Academic Press.

Karp, J. M., & Carlson, H. C. (1993, April). *Integration in a kindergarten classroom.* Paper presented at the annual meeting of the American Educational Research Association, Atlanta, GA.

Kaye, K. (1975, September). *Toward the origin of dialogue.* Paper presented at the Loch Lomond Symposium, University of Strathclyde.

Kaye, K. (1977). Infants' effects upon their mothers' teaching strategies. In J. Glidewell (Ed.), *The social context of learning and development.* New York: Gardner Press.

Kenowitz, L., Zweibel, S., & Edgar, G. (1979). Determining the least restrictive educational opportunity. In N. B. Haring & D. D. Bricker (Eds.), *Teaching the severely handicapped* (Vol. III). Columbus, OH: Special Press.

Kontos, S., & Fiene, R. (1987). Child care quality, compliance with regulations, and children's development: The Pennsylvania study. In D. A. Phillips (Ed.), *Quality in child care: What does research tell us?* (pp. 57–80). Washington, DC: National Association for the Education of Young Children.

Krantz, P., & Risley, T. R. (1977). Behavior ecology in the classroom. In K. D. O'Leary & S. G. O'Leary (Eds.), *Classroom management: The successful use of behavior modification* (2nd ed.) (pp. 349–367). New York: Pergamon Press.

Landesman-Dywer, S. (1985). Describing and evaluating residential environments. In R. H. Bruininks & K. C. Lakin (Eds.), *Living and learning in the least restrictive environment* (pp. 185–196). Baltimore, MD: Paul H. Brookes.

LeLaurin, K., & Risley, T. R. (1972). The organization of day-care environments: "Zone" versus "man-to-man" staff assignments. *Journal of Applied Behavior Analysis, 5,* 225–232.

Loo, C. M. (1972). The effects of spatial density on the social behavior of children. *Journal of Applied Social Psychology, 2,* 372–381.

MacPhee, D., Ramey, C. T., & Yeates, K. O. (1984). Home environment and early cognitive development: Implications for intervention. In A. W. Gottfried (Ed.), *Home environment and early cognitive development* (pp. 343–369). New York: Academic Press.

Mahoney, G., Finger, I., & Powell, J. A. (1985). Relationship of maternal behavioral style to the development of organically impaired mentally retarded infants. *American Journal of Mental Deficiency, 90,* 296–302.

McCartney, K. (1984). The effect of quality of day care environment upon children's language development. *Developmental Psychology, 20,* 244–260.

McCartney, K., Scarr, S., Phillips, D., & Grajek, S. (1985). Day care as intervention: Comparisons of varying quality programs. *Journal of Applied Developmental Psychology, 6,* 247–260.

McCartney, K., Scarr, S., Phillips, D., Grajek, S., & Schwarz, J. C. (1982). Environmental differences among day care centers and their effects on children's development. In E. F. Zigler & E. W. Gordon (Eds.), *Day care: Scientific and social policy issues* (pp. 126–151). Boston: Auburn House.

McEvoy, M., Fox, J. J., & Rosenberg, M. S. (1991). Organizing preschool environments: Suggestions for enhancing the development/learning of preschool children with handicaps. *Topics in Early Childhood Special Education, 11*(2), 18–28.

McWilliam, R. A., & Bailey, D. B. (1992). Promoting engagement and mastery. In D. B. Bailey & M. Wolery (Eds.), *Teaching infants and preschoolers with disabilities* (2nd ed.). Englewood Cliffs, NJ: Merrill/Prentice Hall.

McWilliam, R. A., Trivette, C. M., & Dunst, C. J. (1985). Behavior engagement as a measure of efficacy of early intervention. *Analysis and Intervention in Developmental Disabilities, 5,* 59–71.

Miles, M. S., Funk, S. G., & Carlson, J. (1993). Parental Stressor Scale: Neonatal Intensive Care Unit. *Nursing Research, 42*(3), 148–152.

Mitchell, S. K., & Gray, C. A. (1981). Developmental generalizability of the HOME inventory. *Educational and Psychological Measurement, 41,* 1001–1010.

Moore, G. T. (1982). *Early childhood physical environment scales.* Center for Architecture and Urban Planning Research, P.O. Box 413, Milwaukee, Wisconsin 53201.

Moore, G. T. (1986). Effects of the spatial definition of behavior settings on children's behavior: A quasi-experimental field study. *Journal of Environmental Psychology, 6,* 205–231.

Moore, G. T. (1987). The physical environment and cognitive development in child-care centers. In C. S. Weinstein & T. G. David (Eds.), *Spaces for children: The built environment and child development* (pp. 41–72). New York: Plenum.

Mulligan, S., Miller-Green, K., Morris, S. L., Maloney, T. J., McMurray, D., & Kittelson-Aldred, T. (1992). *Integrated child care.* Tucson, AZ: Communication/Therapy Skill Builders.

Murdoch, D. R., & Darlow, B. A. (1984). Handling during neonatal intensive care. *Archives of Disease in Childhood, 59,* 957–961.

Murphy, M., & Vincent, L. J. (1989). Identification of critical skills for success in day care. *Journal of Early Intervention, 13*(3), 221–229.

National Academy of Early Childhood Programs. (1991). *Accreditation criteria and procedures.* Washington, DC: National Association for the Education of Young Children.

Nordquist, V. M., Twardosz, S., & McEvoy, M. (1991). Effects of environmental reorganization in classrooms for children with autism. *Journal of Early Intervention, 15,* 135–152.

O'Brien, M. O., Porterfield, J., Herbert-Jackson, E., & Risley, T. R. (1979). *The toddler center.* Baltimore, MD: University Park Press.

Odom, S. L., & McEvoy, M. A. (1988). Integration of young children with handicaps and normally developing children. In S. L. Odom & M. B. Karnes (Eds.), *Early intervention for infants and children with handicaps* (pp. 241–267). Baltimore, MD: Paul H. Brookes.

Olds, A. R. (1979). Designing developmentally optimal classrooms for children with special needs. In S. J. Meisels (Ed.), *Special education and development: Perspectives on young children with special needs* (pp. 91–138). Baltimore, MD: University Park Press.

Olds, A. R. (1987). Designing settings for infants and toddlers. In C. S. Weinstein and T. G. David (Eds.), *Spaces for children: The built environment and child development* (pp. 117–138). New York: Plenum.

Ostrosky, M. M., Skellenger, A. C., Odom, S. L., McConnell, S. R., & Peterson, C. (1994). Teachers' schedules and actual time spent in activities in preschool special education classes. *Journal of Early Intervention, 18,* 25–33.

Pearson, M. E., Pearson, A., Fenrick, N., & Greene, D. (1988). The implementation of sample, mand, and delay techniques to enhance the language of delayed children in group settings. *Journal of the Division for Early Childhood, 12,* 342–348.

Phillips, D. A. (Ed.). (1987). *Quality in child care: What does research tell us?* Washington, DC: National Association for the Education of Young Children.

Phillips, D. A., & Howes, C. (1987). Indicators of quality in child care: Review of research. In D. A. Phillips (Ed.), *Quality in child care: What does research tell us?* (pp. 1–20). Washington, DC: National Association for the Education of Young Children.

Phillips, D., McCartney, K., & Scarr, S. (1987). Child care quality and children's social development. *Developmental Psychology, 23,* 537–543.

Phyfe-Perkins, E. (1980). Children's behavior in preschool settings: A review of research concerning the influence of the physical environment. In L. G. Katz (Ed.), *Current topics in early childhood education* (Vol. III) (pp. 91–125). Norwood, NJ: Ablex.

Piper, M. C., & Ramsay, M. K. (1980). Effects of early home environment on the mental development of Down syndrome infants. *American Journal of Mental Deficiency, 85,* 39–44.

Polloway, E. A. (1987). Transition services for early age individuals with mild mental retardation. In R. N. Ianacone & R. A. Stodden (Eds.), *Transition issues and directions* (pp. 11–24). Reston, VA: Council for Exceptional Children.

Powell, M. L. (1981). *Assessment and management of developmental changes and problems in children.* St. Louis, MO: Mosby.

Quiltich, H. R., & Risley, T. R. (1973). The effects of play materials on social play. *Journal of Applied Behavior Analysis, 6,* 573-578.

Raab, M. M., Dunst, C. J., & Whaley, K. T. (1994). *Ecological characteristics of preschool settings.* Unpublished manuscript. Allegheny-Singer Research Institute, Pittsburgh, PA.

Raab, M. M., Dunst, C. J., Whaley, K. T., LeGrand, C. D., & Taylor, M. (1994). *Preschool Assessment of the Classroom Environment Scale–Revised.* Unpublished scale. Allegheny-Singer Research Institute, Pittsburgh, PA.

Ramey, C. T., Bryant, D. M., Wasik, B. H., Sparling, J. J., Fendt, K. H., & LaVange, L. M. (1992). Infant health and development program for low birth weight, premature infants: Program elements, family participation, and child intelligence. *Pediatrics, 89*(3), 454–465.

Ramey, C. T., Bryant, D. M., Sparling, J. J., & Wasik, B. H. (1985). Educational interventions to enhance intellectual development: Comprehensive day care versus family education. In S. Harel & N. J. Anastasiow (Eds.), *The at-risk infant: Psycho/socio/medical aspects* (pp. 75–86). Baltimore, MD: Paul H. Brookes.

Rogers-Warren, A. K. (1982). Behavioral ecology in classrooms for young, handicapped children. *Topics in Early Childhood Special Education, 2*(1), 21–32.

Rosenkoetter, S. E., Hains, A. H., & Fowler, S. A. (1994). *Bridging early services for children with special needs and their families: A practical guide for transition planning.* Baltimore, MD: Paul H. Brookes.

Rule, S., Innocenti, M. S., Coor, K. J., Bonem, M. K., & Stowitschek, J. J. (1989). Kindergartners' preacademic skills and mainstreamed teachers' knowledge: Implications for special educators. *Journal of Early Intervention, 13*(3), 212–220.

Sainato, D. M. (1990). Classroom transitions: Organizing environments to promote independent performance in preschool children with disabilities. *Education and Treatment of Children, 13*(4), 288–297.

Sainato, D. M., & Carta, J. J. (1992). Classroom influences on the development of social competence in young children with disabilities. In S. L. Odom, S. R. McConnell, & M. A. McEvoy (Eds.), *Social competence of young children with disabilities: Issues and strategies for intervention* (pp. 93–109). Baltimore, MD: Paul H. Brookes.

Sainato, D. M., Strain, P. S., Lefebvre, D., & Rapp, N. (1987). Facilitating transition times with handicapped preschool children: A comparison between peer-mediated and antecedent prompt procedures. *Journal of Applied Behavior Analysis, 20,* 285–292.

Sander, L. W. (1964). Adaptive relationships in early mother-child interaction. *American Academy of Child Psychiatry, 3,* 231–263.

Schumm, J. S., Vaughn, S., Haager, D., McDowell, J., Rothlein, L., & Saumell, L. (1995). General education teacher planning: What can students with learning disabilities expect? *Exceptional Children, 61*(4), 335–352.

Seideman, R. Y., Haase, J., Primeaux, M., & Burns, P. (1992). Using NCAST instruments with urban American Indians. *Western Journal of Nursing Research, 14*(3), 308–321.

Shiroiwa, Y., Kamiya, Y., Uchibori, S., Inukai, K., Kito, H., Shibata, T., & Ogawa, J. (1986). Activity, cardiac and respiratory responses of blindfolded preterm infants in neonatal intensive care units. *Early Human Development, 14,* 259–265.

Simeonsson, R. J. (1988). Assessing family environments. In D. B. Bailey & R. J. Simeonsson (Eds.), *Family assessment in early intervention* (pp. 167–183). Englewood Cliffs, NJ: Merrill/Prentice Hall.

Smith, P., & Connolly, K. (1976). Social and aggressive behavior as a function of crowding. *Social Science Information, 16,* 601–620.

Smith, P., & Connolly, K. (1981). *The behavioral ecology of the preschool.* Cambridge, England: Cambridge University Press.

Smith, B. J., & Rose, D. F. (1993). *Administrator's policy handbook for preschool mainstreaming.* Cambridge, MA: Brookline Books.

Snart, F., & Hillyard, A. (1985). Staff ratios and allocated instructional time for multi-handicapped students. *Exceptional Children, 51,* 289–296.

Spiker, D., Ferguson, J., & Brooks-Gunn, J. (1993). Enhancing maternal interactive behavior and child social competence in low-birth weight, premature infants. *Child Development, 64,* 754–768.

Stith, S. M., & Davis, A. J. (1984). Employed mothers and family day care: A comparative analysis of infant care. *Child Development, 55,* 1340–1348.

Strain, P. (1990). LRE for preschool children with handicaps: What we know, what we should be doing. *Journal of Early Intervention, 14,* 291–296.

Strauch, C., Brandt, S., & Edwards-Beckett, J. (1993). Implementation of a quiet hour: Effect on noise levels and infant sleep states. *Neonatal Network, 12,* 31–35.

Thoman, E. B. (1975, May). *Mother-infant adaptation: The first five weeks.* Paper presented at Perinatal Nursing Conference, Battelle Seattle Research Center, Seattle.

VandenBerg, K. A. (1982). Humanizing the intensive care nursery. In A. Waldstein, D. Gilderman, D. Taylor-Hersel, S. Prestridge, & J. Anderson (Eds.), *Issues in neonatal care* (pp. 83–105). Chapel Hill, NC: TADS, University of North Carolina.

Vincent, L. J., Salisbury, C. L., Strain, P., McCormick, C., & Tessier, A. (1990). A behavioral-ecological approach to early intervention: Focus on cultural diversity. In S. J. Meisels & J. P. Shonkoff (Eds.), *Handbook of early childhood intervention* (pp. 173–195). Cambridge: Cambridge University Press.

Vincent, L. J., Salisbury, C. L., Walter, G., Brown, P., Gruenewald, L. C., & Powers, M. (1980). Program evaluation and curriculum development in early childhood/special education. In W. Sailor, B. Wilcox, & L. Brown (Eds.), *Methods of instruction for severely handicapped students* (pp. 303–328). Baltimore, MD: Paul H. Brookes.

Wachs, T. D. (1979). Proximal experience and early cognitive-intellectual development: The physical environment. *Merrill-Palmer Quarterly, 25,* 3–41.

Weinstein, C. S., & David, T. G. (1987). *Spaces for children: The built environment and child development.* New York: Plenum.

Winton, P. J., Turnbull, A. P., & Blacher, J. (1984). *Selecting a preschool: A guide for parents of handicapped children.* Baltimore, MD: University Park Press.

Wolke, D. (1987a). Environmental and developmental neonatology. *Journal of Reproductive and Infant Psychology, 5*(1), 17–42.

Wolke, D. (1987b). Environmental neonatology. *Archives of Diseases in Childhood, 62,* 987–988.

CHAPTER

10

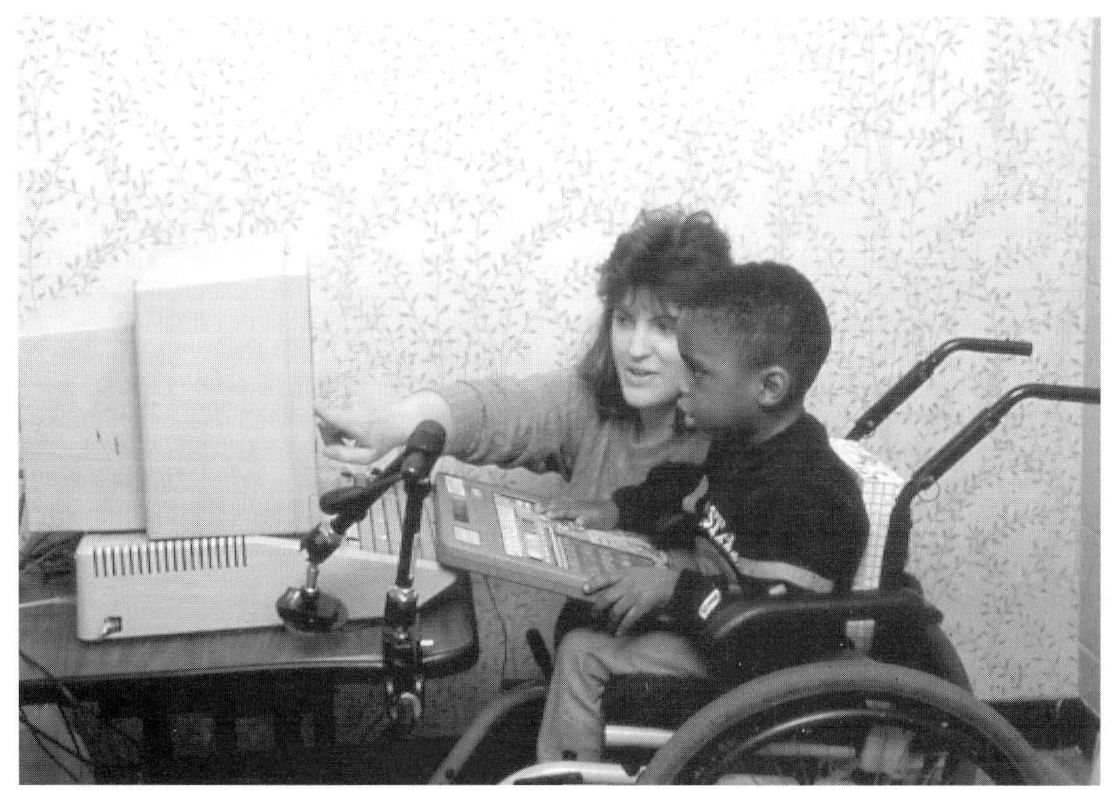

Assessing Cognitive Development

Katherine McCormick
Columbus College

RATIONALE

The assessment of cognition or intelligence has a long history in the fields of psychology, psychometrics, and education. As early as 1869, Sir Francis Galton began work in measuring and quantifying mental characteristics. In the 1990s many researchers and practitioners are still occupied with this task. Yet many of the questions asked by Galton and his contemporaries remain unanswered, and new areas of research and investigation are constantly being identified and explored. Why has so much thought and energy been expended toward the understanding and measurement of cognition? Three explanations are plausible. First, intelligence is valued as a human characteristic or capability. Second, cognition or intelligence is a multifaceted phenomenon confounded with many other domains of human behavior, thereby complicating its own identification. Finally, in order to arrive at an accurate measure of intelligence, the scientific community—educators, psychologists, developmental specialists—must agree on a common definition.

Defining intelligence is not an easy task. During a famous symposium in 1921, 13 eminent psychologists were asked to share their definitions of intelligence, which resulted in 13 different definitions. Science, however, has since made some progress toward consensus. In 1990, when asked to rate what they believed to be important elements of intelligence, 1,020 experts in psychology, sociology, education, and genetics rated three behavioral descriptions with greater than 96% agreement—abstract thinking or reasoning, the capacity to acquire knowledge, and problem-solving ability (Sattler, 1990). This chapter provides a brief historical perspective regarding the development of the concept of intelligence and cognition and the accompanying efforts to measure and validate this phenomenon.

Perspectives on the Assessment of Cognition

Traditional psychometric The psychometric assessment of young children began with Binet and Simon in 1905 (Kelly & Surbeck, 1991). Under contract from the educational system in Paris, Binet and Simon developed a 30-item instrument to discriminate between children who would benefit from instruction and those who would not. In 1908 these two pioneer psychometricians developed a second test, using the new concept of mental age. In the following years, researchers such as Lucy Sprague Mitchell, John B. Watson, Robert Yerkes, and J. C. Foster were active in the study of intelligence, concentrating on the early years of children's development (Kelly & Surbeck, 1991). Instruments such as the Merrill-Palmer Scale of Mental Tests (Stutsman, 1931), the Minnesota Preschool Scale (Goodenough, 1926), the Cattell Infant Intelligence Scale (Cattell, 1940), the Leiter International Performance Scale (Leiter, 1948), and the California First Year Mental Scales (Bayley, 1933) were the precursors of many of the psychometric assessments used with young children today. Later, psychologists, statisticians, and test publishers sought to make these instruments more methodologically sound and to make measurement more precise. These efforts were prompted by the need for effective evaluation of early intervention projects receiving significant federal, state, and local funds, such as Project Head Start. Through legislative efforts, programs receiving federal monies were mandated to include an evaluation component with appropriate instrumentation. Institutes such as the Battelle Institute and other private and public corporations responded to the growing need for measures to evaluate infants, toddlers, and preschoolers.

Developers of instruments to assess cognitive development have generally followed two theoretical models. The *global theory model* suggests that intelligence is best defined as the ability to think abstractly and to solve problems. Test authors include items that correlate with a large factor (typically referred to as "g"). This global factor is omnibus and encompasses many behaviors that are reflective of general intelligence. The earlier editions of the Stanford Binet incorporated this model. However, the second model, *the factor analytic model*, currently has a greater number of proponents. Researchers postulate a general factor with specific factors related to specific tasks. The number of these specific factors ranges from 2 (Horn, 1968; Wechsler, 1974) to 120 (Guilford, 1967). Factor analytic models with multiple factors, however, appear to have limited value for preschoolers. Multiple factors are not evidenced beyond two general ones (mental and motor) for many infants and toddlers (Snyder, Lawson, Thompson, Stricklin, & Sexton, 1993; Sheehan & Snyder, 1989–1990). The psychometric approach emphasizes standardized procedures with item selection based on statistical criteria. Norm-referenced assessments are the best examples of assessments with a psychometric foundation.

Cognitive stage/Piagetian In 1952 Jean Piaget wrote, "it is indisputable that (traditional) tests of mental age have, on the whole, lived up to what was expected of them: a rapid and convenient estimate of an individual's general level. But it is no less obvious that they simply measure a 'yield' without reaching constructive operation themselves" (Hoy & Gregg, 1994, p. 230). Piaget was interested in two types of problem solving: logico-mathematical and physical knowledge. He hypothesized that reasoning and problem solving developed through sequential stages. Organization and adaptation, two basic processes that were important to Piaget, result from the use and practice of *schemas* and through the processes of *assimilation* and *accommodation*. An infant possesses very immature sensorimotor organizational systems, or schemas; as he or she interacts with objects, people, and environments, these schemas change and mature. The acquisition of new information is termed *assimilation;* the use of information to modify existing organizational structures is called *accommodation. Adaptation* is the process of assimilating new information and accommodating old information to make sense of both the new and the old.

Piaget hypothesized that the presentation of new information that did not fit with the old would cause the individual some mental discomfort, or what Piaget termed "disequilibration." He proposed that disequilibration is a motivating process that drives an individual to make things fit or establish equilibrium. Therefore, a need to understand the world and fit the new with the old is seen as cognitive maturity and development.

Piaget classified cognitive behaviors into four stages of development: sensorimotor, preoperational, concrete operational, and formal operational. The first stage, *sensorimotor,* encompasses approximately the first 2 years and consists of six substages. The second stage, *preoperational,* is usually observed in typically developing children between the ages of 2 and 7. The hallmark of this stage is symbolic representation—the understanding that a symbol represents an object. The child is also able to think and talk about objects and people not physically present.

Piagetian approaches to cognitive development attempt to measure qualitative differences in a child's reasoning rather than quantitative differences. Tests are constructed according to age levels, with item clusters that attempt to measure multiple aspects of cognition such as seriation, conservation, number and spatial concepts, object permanence, deductive and inductive logic, classification, and decentration. The use of these assessments requires a broad understanding of Piagetian theory for accurate interpretation and administration; however, the richness of the information obtained is worth the effort. This approach holds particular utility for the assessment of children with disabilities, especially those with severe impairments. The most commonly used Piagetian assessment tool for the sensorimotor period (birth to 24 months) was developed by Uzgiris and Hunt (1975) and expanded on by Dunst (1980).

Information processing Information-processing models of intelligence have been greatly influenced by Soviet psychologists such as Vygotsky and Luria (Hoy & Gregg, 1994). Vygotsky suggests that memory, attention, and conceptualizations are the products of the child's organization of object and social interactions. Soviet psychologists believe strongly in the concept of mediated learning, especially when used by parents in early concept acquisition. Parents guide and mark or signal certain activities and objects for their child's attention. Therefore, intelligence is seen as the result of social learning experiences. Cognition develops through the child's internalization of social interactions and experiences (Hoy & Gregg, 1994). A second example of an information-processing model is provided by the work of Campione and Brown (1978), who developed their theory of intelligence using two basic components: an architectural system (the structural component) and an executive system (the control component). The architectural system acts as a scaffold comprised of capacity, durability (retention), and efficiency (speed of information encoded); the executive operates as the learned components, including knowledge, schemes, control processes, and metacognition (Sattler, 1990). The use of schemes appears again in this theory and is used to describe the active construction of the rules of thinking. The architectural system may be considered as the biologically/genetically based component of intelligence; the executive system refers to environmentally based components.

Social learning Soviet psychologists have also conceptualized cognitive development in a social context. The concept of a "proximal zone of development" suggests that there is a zone that reflects the distance between the actual developmental level (determined by independent problem solving) and the level of potential development (determined through problem solving under adult guidance or in collaboration with more capable peers). In other words, development occurs when a problem is presented that is just beyond the child's ability and an adult or peer is able to mediate the experience to move the child to a new level of understanding (Anastasiow, 1986). Bandura (1978) also describes development through a social learning model termed *reciprocal determinism,* in which learning develops through the interaction of socialization, developmental status, environmental factors, and the child's motivation. In other words, the characteristics and properties of the environment in interaction with one another and with the child's thinking and judgment about his behavior account for the learning of new behavior and understanding of past and present behavior (Gage & Berliner, 1991).

Maturational/developmental A major effort to establish developmental markers during the preschool years was undertaken in 1925 at the Yale Clinic for Child Development under the leadership of Arnold Gesell. Gesell and his fellow researchers postulated that development and growth were biologically predetermined. This maturational perspective hypothesized a time-bound developmental model in which qualitative change occurred in the young child at the "appropriate time"—that as children age and mature, their capabilities, behaviors, and cognitive development change. To document this maturational model,

Gesell and his colleagues identified 150 items in four areas—motor, language, adaptive, and personal-social—and presented them as developmental schedules for 10 age levels (birth and 4, 6, 9, 12, 18, 24, 36, 48, and 60 months) (Kelly & Surbeck, 1991).

Functional The functional model of development owes its origin to operant learning theory from the field of psychology, typically referred to as behaviorism. In this model, all behavior is considered as learned behavior. All living organisms repeat behavior that is satisfying and avoid behavior that is not. Learning occurs as children practice a new behavior, find it functional, and experience reinforcing consequences (Peterson, 1987). The functional model is derived from the notion that the most critical and functional behaviors for the developing child are those that produce pleasing and positive interactions with people, objects, and environments. This model has as its major assumption that behavior is determined by the interaction of people and their environment. The most important principle associated with this approach is reinforcement—an event that follows a response and that changes the probability of a response occurring again. For example, Skinner's explanation of learning is based on the premise that the consequences of behavior determine the probability that the behavior will occur again (Lefrancois, 1995).

Conclusions Witt, Elliott, Kramer, and Gresham (1994) suggest that in a general sense, cognition includes a broad spectrum of mental abilities that are often referred to as intelligence. In practice, however, it is the subsets of cognition, such as attention, memory, comprehension, and reasoning, that are of concern to educators and psychologists. Regardless of one's theoretical foundation, the assessment of cognition in young children is important for intervention planning and for describing children's current developmental repertoire. Assessments may be used to determine program eligibility, to plan interventions, to identify environments and techniques by which development is facilitated, and to evaluate progress. By determining the abilities and information children possess and in what environments they are most likely to demonstrate these abilities, the most effective interventions can be designed, using the most efficient methods in the most natural environments. To attempt to provide intervention without an understanding of a child's present level of functioning would waste both resources and time. Because the cognitive development of young children is closely enmeshed with motor and communication behavior, the reader is directed to Chapters 11 and 12 to more fully understand this important area of development.

DIMENSIONS OF ASSESSMENT

Behaviors Typically Sampled by Cognitive Assessments

Discrimination, generalization, motor behavior, general information, vocabulary, comprehension, sequencing, analogies, abstract reasoning, and paired-associate learning are some of the behaviors typically sampled by cognitive assessments. Test developers must meet a level of adequacy in behaviors sampled while dealing with the attentional constraints of young children and examiners. As children age, the number of items must increase to measure more stable traits. Behavior sampling for infants and toddlers may include behaviors that require motor and sensory awareness and integration. During the early months, these motor and sensory behaviors are indicative of cognitive development. As children age and their behavioral repertoire expands, cognitive skills may be measured by a broader spectrum of behaviors, such as language, problem-solving tasks, vocabulary usage, and memory items.

Measurement Scales

There are four scales of measurements typically used in assessment: nominal, ordinal, ratio, and equal interval. *Nominal scales* use names or numbers to represent the variables; they use numbers without an inherent relationship to one another to name people or objects (Salvia & Ysseldyke, 1995). *Ordinal scales* order or rank objects, persons, or events. Numbers that are adjacent indicate higher or lower value; however, the value is not always equivalent. For example, children can be ranked from first to last based on their ability to name the days of the week, but the difference in the rank between the first child and the second child may not be equal to the difference between the second and third children. The first child may have named all seven days, the second child only six, and the third child only two.

The magnitude of the difference between two adjacent values on *ratio scales* is equivalent. Weight is measured on a ratio scale; the difference between 15 and 16 pounds is the same as the difference between 150 and 151 pounds. Ratio scales have a second important attribute; they have an absolute zero (Salvia & Ysseldyke, 1995). A ratio scale without the absolute zero is an *equal-interval scale.* The important characteristic of this scale is that ratios cannot be derived from an equal-interval scale. Since intelligence is typically measured with an equal-interval scale, and there is no absolute zero, we cannot make comparisons using a ratio system. Therefore, an IQ of 100 is not twice as large as an IQ of 50. Many of the assessments described in this chapter are equal-interval scales; however, assessments that use an ordinal scale of measurement are becoming more widely used, especially for infants and young children with severe disabilities.

Quantification of Performance and Accompanying Cautions

It is difficult to accurately reflect the behavioral and developmental status of infants and young children. Several assumptions must be recognized: (a) young children are bound more closely to biological development than are their older peers; (b) the limited communication abilities of young children may interfere with their ability to respond to or to understand verbal instruction; (c) distractibility and short attention span may compromise assessment outcomes; (d) separation issues occur throughout the preschool years; and (e) a lack of compliance or understanding of social relationships may also be evidenced (Lidz, 1991). When these problems are compounded by the presence of a disability, the examiner faces an especially challenging task in assessing a young child's cognitive ability.

Professionals must also be cautious in interpreting and ascribing an unwarranted level of confidence and meaning to the outcomes generated by evaluation or assessment tools. A test score tells only a small part of the story. For example, children can achieve the same score for entirely different reasons. Bobby might get all the items correct until a certain point and then miss them all; Joey, on the other hand, misses items throughout the test. Thus equivalent scores could result from very different responses. Closer examination may show that Joey missed only those items that required physical manipulation of objects or visual acuity. These tasks require a different and more difficult response if Joey has cerebral palsy or low vision. A discussion of various types of scores and accompanying information on validity and reliability is included in Chapter 2.

Stability of IQ

Discontinuity, which is important to the issue of stability of cognitive development, characterizes the wide variety of behaviors in individual children and among children considered to be typically developing or "normal" (Neisworth & Bagnato, 1992). Young children display great variability in day-to-day performance; furthermore, their development is seldom parallel across developmental domains. Observations of young children and discussions with their parents suggest that development is often delayed in one area while the child uses his or her energies to master a behavior in another. Parents frequently describe a lapse in language development during the period when their children begin to walk and, similarly, a slower rate of motor development is reported when language development is expanding. This uneven pattern of development, which is normal for young children, cannot be accurately reflected in a single number.

The stability of cognitive development is even more important when considered in the context of transition periods—when a behavior is emerging but is not fully integrated in the child's repertoire. If assessment takes places during a developmental transition, the assessment may capture a less advanced version of the skill undergoing rapid change and progress. The more advanced skill may be displayed and preferred by the child within the next week (Neisworth & Bagnato, in press). As children age, developmental rates decrease and the range of behaviors considered normal narrows (Bracken, 1991a).

PROCEDURAL CONSIDERATIONS

Assumptions Underlying Assessment

In 1988 Salvia and Ysseldyke identified five assumptions that must be met for assessment information to be valid and reliable: The administrator is skilled; error will be present; acculturation is comparable; behavior sampling is adequate; and present behavior is observed, future behavior is inferred.

Administrator is skilled When children are tested, at least three assumptions concerning the skills of the person administering the test are made: The person is (a) adequately trained, (b) proficient in establishing rapport, and (c) knowledgeable to administer the test, score the responses, and interpret the outcomes (Salvia & Ysseldyke, 1988). These characteristics are critical in the assessment of infants and young children. Adequate training of personnel is a critical issue for many states that have not had a long history of providing services to infants, toddlers, and preschoolers with special needs. States must develop strategies that ensure appropriate licensure and certification for individuals administering cognitive or intelligence tests. Decisions that affect the provision of services for children and their families must be made by individuals with adequate training. The establishment of rapport is equally important in the assessment of young children. Best practice requires the ability to observe children's behavior, respond, expand on their behavior, and elicit other behaviors in their repertoires. Rapport building and maintenance is a dynamic balance of interactions among the examiner, the child, and the family. As children age, this balance moves from observations of sensory, motor, and prelinguistic behaviors to those of concept development, language, and interaction with objects and social environments. The examiner must be able to adjust the rate of stimulus presentation, verbal input, and other variables that may affect the quality of the interaction between examiner and child and, therefore, the outcome of the assessment. The examiner must also be patient to increase the opportunities for observation and be skilled in eliciting information from caregivers and family members.

Administering, scoring, and interpreting standardized assessments are also skills the examiner must demonstrate. Proper administration and scoring ensure that the outcomes are an accurate measure of the child's performance against a norm group or criterion measure and provide useful information for programming. Assessments are continually being developed, revised, and restandardized. Individuals responsible for the administration of these assessments must maintain knowledge of current and available assessments and choose those most appropriate to the purpose of the assessment as well as to each child's characteristics. The interpretation of behaviors demonstrated by young children in a standardized assessment requires knowledge of both typical and atypical developmental patterns. The examiner must possess skill in evaluating a response within these parameters. Cohen and Gross (1979a, 1979b) provide a useful guide for the identification of typical developmental sequences; useful information regarding developmental sequences for children with disabilities can be found in Wachs and Sheehan (1988).

Error will be present Few psychological phenomena or constructs can be measured without error, either examiner error or instrument error. No matter how skilled and well trained they may be, examiners will make some errors—in the administration of an item, the tabulation of the responses, or the scoring of the test. The amount of this deviance is reported as an error term. The size of this term is dependent on several factors, one of which is the age of the child being tested. For example, the error term for a 5-year-old on the Kaufman Intelligence Test for Children (Kaufman & Kaufman, 1983) is 8 points, while the error term for an 8-year-old is 5. The reported scores then might be 69 ± 8 and 69 ± 5. We can assume that the scores generated for 5-year-olds were less stable and therefore needed a wider band of error than those for 8-year-olds. Also important is the degree of certainty with which we want to treat the assigned score. For example, if we want to be right 99 times out of 100, the error term will be larger than if we widen our level of tolerance to 95 out of 100. Error can be systematic or random. The degree of systematic error indicates a bias that can be predicted; the degree of random error is less predictable and indicates the extent of the reliability of the outcome. Assessments demonstrate varying degrees of reliability. Reliability may also be dependent on the age and characteristics of the child being assessed.

Acculturation is comparable The issue of comparable acculturation or experiences is possibly the most problematic assumption in the administration of norm-referenced tests of cognition or intelligence for young children with special needs. Simply stated, this assumption requires that the children being tested have participated in experiences similar to those of the group of children on which the assessment was normed; this is questionable in a country with vast regional, cultural, linguistic, and social diversity. When children who learn in different ways and possess alternative strategies to process sensory, motor, or social information are included, the assumption may be stretched further than is reasonable. To assume comparable acculturation is even more tenuous when preschoolers are involved. Schooling provides somewhat common experiences in the 6-hour school day. As children proceed through these standard experiences, the appropriateness of comparisons increases, but for preschoolers this common experience is absent. The presence of the disability and the probable differences in acculturation pose real problems in the assessment of children with disabilities. Therefore, many examiners and test developers are turning to assessments that allow for administration within the child's natural environment. Use of familiar toys, typical communication partners, and everyday environments may decrease this discrepancy. Professionals involved in the use of norm-referenced instruments must be cognizant of the issue of acculturation and explain possible problems when discussing assessment results with other professionals and parents.

Cultural uniqueness further complicates this assumption of comparable acculturation. In her classic work, Mercer (1979) suggests that intelligence tests used with children from culturally diverse backgrounds measure the level of acculturation rather than cognitive ability. The longer a family or a child has had to acquire behaviors valued by the dominant culture, the more valid the assessment will be. Limited experience in the dominant culture calls for considerable caution in the generation of indices of cognitive development.

Behavior sampling is adequate Assessment must provide adequate opportunities for young children to demonstrate their unique abilities across multiple behaviors and response sets. For example, good cognitive assessments are neither completely verbal nor completely nonverbal in their makeup, but strive for adequate sampling of multiple behaviors indicative of cognitive development. Adequate behavioral sampling must, however, be balanced with efficiency. If five items provide equivalent information, test publishers will delete four, using only one, since the four are redundant. On the other hand, if each provides a unique opportunity for the child to demonstrate a particular skill, the inclusion of all five may be warranted. This balance is not an easy one and often is cause for caution when using assessments that attempt to measure abilities across a broad age range with few items.

The types of behavior that are sampled are important; the level of specificity of items is equally important. The sensitivity of an instrument to small differences in ability is indicated by the amount of change in a standard score when an additional item is passed or failed. Bracken (1987) uses the term *item-gradient* to describe this phenomenon. This difficulty is experienced frequently when norm-referenced instruments are used with young children. Examiners, early interventionists, teachers, and parents complain that a child "falls through the cracks" to describe a lack of item specificity or gradient. In other words, there are insufficient items to accurately reflect a child's ability. This problem is particularly evident with assessments such as the Battelle Developmental Inventory (Newborg, Stock, Wnek, Guidubaldi, & Svinicki, 1984) that force scales downward with limited items to allow accurate discriminations between children at the younger ages.

Bracken also describes another important criterion related to behavioral sampling for preschool instruments. The term *floor* describes the degree to which a test discriminates among children at the lower range of ability (Bracken, 1987, p. 320). A test with a limited floor does not accurately sort children of differing ability levels who are functioning significantly below the mean (typically at least two standard deviations) or who are at the lowest age level. A parallel term, *ceiling,* applies to this problem at the upper end of ability or age levels. An inadequate floor is particularly troublesome in the assessment of preschoolers with disabilities, many of whom are performing significantly below the mean. The Battelle Developmental Inventory again provides an excellent example of this problem. The lowest deviation quotient provided by the Battelle is 65; therefore, many examiners assign this score to children who in fact demonstrate abilities far below this cutoff. Although this strategy is not inappropriate, it may be very misleading to parents and other team members. To remedy this difficulty, many examiners extrapolate raw scores below this cutoff for a more accurate reflection of the performance of the children tested (McLean, McCormick, Bruder, & Burdg, 1987). Extrapolation, however, does not produce normalized scores with equivalent psychometric characteristics. For assessments such as the Battelle, which can be used with children from birth to 8 years of age, we may assume that children in the middle of the age range (3 to 5 years) may experience the least difficulty with a floor or ceiling effect, while those at the extremes would be most affected.

Present behavior is observed; future behavior is inferred It is this issue that appears to be the most difficult to address in the assessment of the cognitive development of preschoolers. The years between 3 and 5 provide a transition between poor and relatively good predictions of later cognitive development (Clark, 1982; Lidz, 1991). Lidz (1991) states: "If preschool children were stable responders (which frequently they are not) and the assessment tools reliable and valid (which frequently they are not) diagnostic labels might at least be valid descriptors of the child's current levels of functioning, if not good predictors of future levels of functioning" (p. 20).

Factors Important in Assessment

Developmental history Preassessment strategies include good information gathering and discussion with parents, caregivers, daycare providers, and other team members. Parents and other caregivers can provide information concerning the acquisition of developmental milestones, medical history, names of family members, daily routines, occupations, and typical environments. This information is critical to the assessment process and provides the beginning building blocks for hypothesis generation and diagnostic planning. For children with motor or sensory disabilities, developmental histories can provide information regarding appropriate adaptations, aids, prosthetics, and test selection. Current medical and nutritional status as well as information regarding medications and daily schedules are also very important in guiding assessment planning.

Cultural uniqueness Early intervention in the United States must respond to the increasing diversity of infants, toddlers, and preschoolers with disabilities. By the year 2000, approximately one third of the U.S. population will be people who define themselves as African American, Native American, Asian Pacific, Hispanic, or as other people of color (Chang, 1990). Accurate and appropriate assessment of children from culturally diverse environments requires attention to the uniqueness of a child's culture and acknowledgment of the requirements of standardization. For example, attention to task or directions, solutions to social problems, and social interactions may be influenced by culture. Expressive skills and styles of interacting with adults are also influenced by cultural membership. Specific culturally dependent behaviors such as eye contact may carry distinctly different messages. These differences are closely associated with the issue of comparable acculturation mentioned previously. The reader is referred to Chapter 4 for more information on this topic.

Impact of disability The greatest concern for the examiner testing children with motor or sensory impairments is that the assessment reflect the child's cognitive ability rather than the degree of disability. Neisworth and Bagnato (1992) suggest that most cognitive assessments "measure the child's disability rather than his ability" (p. 8). Psychologists and other examiners have historically been challenged to establish techniques and instruments that effectively evaluate a child's cognitive status without violating the principles of standardization. The process of modifying materials and instruments for the purpose of gaining more information about the child's cognitive status without the impact of the disability is sometimes called "testing the limits." For example, for an infant who is slow to alert or attend, the examiner may first score the item under the standardized conditions and then attempt to gain the infant's attention through alternative alerting behaviors. At issue, especially for children with disabilities, is not whether the child can pass or fail the item attempted but whether the child truly has acquired the critical function of the item measured.

The question "What is this item really measuring?" will provide insight into the critical function of the item, although often multiple behaviors other than the critical function are also required to pass the item. For example, the task of picking up a cup to retrieve a hidden object involves multiple behaviors and abilities other than the critical function of object permanence. If the child has motor impairments, difficulties with grasp, reach, and upper body strength may prevent the demonstration of object permanence. The child with impaired vision may have the concept of object permanence but have difficulty locating the cup. Haring et al. (1981) described three techniques to modify test items in *The Uniform Performance Assessment System.* Support adaptations provide positional and physical support, prosthetic adaptations involve the use of equipment or aids, and general adaptations represent any change in the requirements of the task. Others, such as Thurlow, Ysseldyke, and Silverstein (1993), suggest modification of materials, modifications of the manner in which the items are administered, and modifications in the response required by the child. If modifications are used, the examiner must be extremely careful to document them and should not assume that they do not alter the standardization process. Some test publishers have attempted to provide a standardized format for modifications. Two such instruments are the Battelle Developmental Inventory and the Adaptative Performance Inventory, which include adaptations appropriate for children with hearing, vision, and motor impairments.

Examiners must also be cognizant of the unique influence that specific disability conditions may have on the young child's behavior. For example, fatigue may be exacerbated by the effort of the child to move, visually track, or auditorily localize. The effects of medication may further complicate readiness or desire to participate in social interaction or object play required during most assessments. In addition, disabilities may produce a differential developmental sequence for the acquisition of some cognitive skills. Robinson and Fieber (1988) suggest that limited motor behavior may constrain object exploration, which is typically believed to precede concept development, but that concept development may still be evidenced without the fine motor behavior necessary for object manipulation. In other words, some children may compensate through other developmental pathways for the missing information typically gained through motor behavior (McLean & McCormick, 1993). The limitations that a missing pathway of information place on a child's interpretation of his social and physical environment must be carefully considered when selecting assessment tools and interpreting their outcomes (Robinson & Fieber, 1988, p. 130).

In the evaluation of children with hearing impairments, examiners should present tasks in a consistent and organized manner in order to facilitate habituation and response expectations. It is also important to note that many children with hearing impairments have learned socially appropriate responses (such as nodding and smiling) to verbal directions that they do not hear or understand. Children with visual impairments often have developed abilities in using tactile cues in tandem with auditory cues. Older children with visual impairments often have visual aids or glasses that will facilitate the use of their vision during assessment. The skilled evaluator will question family members or caregivers concerning the use of these devices. Psychologists who are remiss in this area can be faced with "Oh, I forgot to tell you, his glasses are in my purse" following a lengthy (and invalid) assessment. Examiners should make the best use of residual vision, using strategies such as high-contrast visual stimuli, materials of increased size, and ample time to explore material (Fewell, 1983).

In evaluating children with physical impairments, the evaluator must first determine the extent to which the impairment interferes with the response demands of the evaluation. Issues of head control and postural stability are important in making children comfortable and enabling/preparing them to move. Alternative seating or support is encouraged, especially if the child has difficulty moving to midline or focusing his vision. Assessments with time limits are particularly problematic for children with motor difficulties. For children with physical impairments at least seven issues must be addressed: primary response mode, sensory input, degree of motor impairment, positioning, fatigue, medical problems, and signs of learning disabilities (Venn & Dykes, 1987).

Approaches to Assessment

In the early 1990s researchers began to identify emerging trends in the evaluation and assessment of young children with disabilities—play-based assessment, ecological assessment, arena assessment, judgment-based assessment, and adaptive (sometimes called adaptive-to-handicap) assessment (Fewell, 1991; Neisworth & Bagnato, 1992). Common among many of these trends was the use of naturalistic environments, community and home settings where children and their families could interact as active participants in familiar environments in preferred ways. Some of these trends are discussed in this section.

Free-play and elicited and structured play Linder (1993) provides an approach to using play as a medium for a more naturalistic and authentic evaluation of a child's developmental status. Linder's model (1992) includes an adjustable six-phase process. The first phase is *unstructured facilitation,* lasting about 25 minutes, when the child takes the lead. The facilitator for the assessment interacts with the child, attempting to move him or her to higher skill levels through modeling. In the second phase, *structured facilitation,* cognitive and language behaviors that were not observed are elicited. In this phase the facilitator takes a direct approach, with specific requests made to the child, while maintaining play as the vehicle for assessment. *Child-to-child interaction* in an unstructured situation describes the third phase; the fourth phase is *parent-child interaction,* with some opportunity provided to observe separation and greeting behaviors. The fifth phase consists of *motor play,* and the sixth is *snack*.

The advantages of naturalistic environments and behavioral response sets such as play in the assessment of cognition are obvious. Children are free to interact with objects and environments that are interesting and motivating to them. Examiners are free to observe, to model, and to expand infant and child behaviors to more accurately ascertain the child's level of engagement with and understanding of familiar and novel physical and social environments. However, examiners must be judicious in their choice of settings in which to conduct the evaluations and assessments. Paget (1991) suggests that the ideal setting for the assessment of young children is an area that is familiar to the child, where he or she is at ease, and where distractions are at a minimum. Natural environments meet the first two of these three requirements. Examiners must work with family members to meet the requirements of minimum distractions. As evaluations take place more and more frequently in the home and community, creative and family-centered decisions regarding the best environments for evaluation and assessment will be evidenced.

Traditional assessments remove children from the environments where they have learned and practiced behaviors. Naturalistic environments provide children with opportunities to display behaviors that have functional utility in their environments. Compensatory efforts and strategies can also be observed. The opportunity to observe behaviors that are transitional or emerging are also afforded the examiner in natural environments. Furthermore, the benefits of using family members and caregivers in providing assessment information and in active participation in the evaluation and assessment process cannot be overstated.

Test-teach-test models Curriculum assessments that use a test-teach-test model hold tremendous promise in allowing teachers and interventionists to measure more accurately the cognitive ability of young children. This model, which Feuerstein (1979) describes as a *dynamic assessment,* determines a child's level of functioning, provides training, and then re-evaluates the child in a structured situation. Proponents of this model believe that a more accurate measure of potential rather than performance can be obtained. An example of an instrument developed and now widely used by Feuerstein and his colleagues is the Learning Potential Assessment Device (LPAD) (Feuerstein, 1979). The LPAD is designed to estimate the child's cognitive deficits, preferred cognitive strategies and perceptual modalities, capacity for modifiability under optimal training conditions, and the generalizability of strategies to new tasks. Feuerstein's model is also referred to as an instrumental enrichment model.

Other researchers (Campione & Brown, 1987; Lidz, 1987) suggest that this second assessment in the test-teach-test paradigm provides a far more valid measure of children's cognitive abilities than the initial one, and they have attempted to quantify this change by identifying factors such as the level of prompts, the number of models needed to accomplish the task and meet criteria, and the child's ability to generalize this new information to similar tasks. Benner (1992) describes two assessments designed for preschoolers that use a test-teach-test model: The Children's Analogical Thinking Modifiability (CATM), which was developed by Tzuriel and Klein in 1987, and the Preschool Learning Assessment Device, developed in 1987 by Lidz and Thomas. Each uses a mediated learning experience task to evaluate the child's level of cognitive modifiability (the ability to improve performance). According to Benner (1992), kindergartners from low socioeconomic environments demonstrate high modifiability on the CATM using this model. Dynamic assessments often use a test-teach-test paradigm and emphasize the process a child uses to produce a response rather than the correctness of the product/response. These assessments also focus on the specification of conditions that produce effective performance and on obstacles to such performance.

Considerations in Test Selection and Administration

Response demands The response demands of an assessment instrument must be carefully analyzed prior to the evaluation and assessment of the cognitive abilities of children with disabilities. Some tests require verbal fluency and expressive communication; others place demands on the child's sensory and motor systems. Most will include items that require a broad range of behaviors across sensory, motor, and communication domains. Assessment instruments should be chosen that will best reveal the child's cognitive ability while minimizing the impact of one or multiple disabilities.

Representation of children with disabilities Norm-referenced testing assumes that development progresses in a predictable and orderly manner. For some children with disabilities, especially those with limited motor or sensory ability but adequate cognitive ability, this may be a faulty assumption. Norm-referenced assessments, according to their publishers, are not supposed to include a "clinical" population; the purpose of the test is to discriminate the "clinical" from the "norm."

Therefore, there are few children who "match" the children with whom these tests are used. For this reason some psychologists and special educators have suggested that norm-referenced tests may not be valid for children with disabilities.

Assessments for children with specific disabilities are few and the majority of them are dated. Many have items that are obsolete and would not be understood by children today (Hoy & Gregg, 1994). Some nonverbal measurements are also out of date because they include tasks and/or behaviors that are not typically in the experiences of children with disabilities. Furthermore, older assessments, such as the Columbia Mental Maturity Scale (Burgemeister, Blum, & Lorge, 1972), and French's Pictorial Test of Intelligence (French, 1964), use black-and-white photographs or line drawings and provide little that is stimulating or motivating for the young child. The newer Differential Abilities Scale (Elliott, 1990) is a noteworthy exception, however, and includes children with disabilities in the normative sample in sufficient numbers to represent special education categories present in the 1984 school population.

REPRESENTATIVE METHODS

As programs for infants, toddlers, and preschoolers with disabilities grow in number, test publishers and researchers will respond to the demands for assessment tools to determine eligibility, to plan interventions, and to document progress. It must be remembered that few tests currently available can meet all three of these requirements. Included in this section are instruments currently available to the field, and new instruments and revisions are constantly being marketed. Early intervention team members should be cautious in the selection and interpretation of tools to measure cognitive development. They must recognize the limitations of the instruments they use and share their cautions and concerns with all team members, especially family members, being ever-mindful of the power these assigned numbers take on. Children are not defined by the outcomes of assessments nor is their behavioral repertoire always accurately reflected. The use of a multimeasure, multisource, multisetting, and multisituation model alleviates some of the inherent difficulties in the assessment of young children. However, the dynamic nature of development during this period cannot be overstated. One should remember that children with disabilities are children first, and that their cognitive, language, or motor development is only a part of who they are within their families and culture.

Accurate evaluation and assessment of young children are critical to good interventions. While these terms are often used interchangeably, they connote two different processes. *Evaluation* may be defined as the procedures used to determine a child's initial and continued eligibility for services; *assessment* is the ongoing process used by qualified personnel throughout the period of a child's eligibility to identify the family's resources, priorities, and concerns as well as the child's unique needs (McLean & McCormick, 1993). The examiner must choose which instruments are appropriate to fulfill the requirements of each of these processes, which are thoroughly reviewed in Chapter 1 of this text.

Norm-Referenced Measures

Norm-referenced instruments have two attributes: They are developed based on the performance of a norming group, and they typically use a standardized score to report outcomes. They are most appropriately used as evaluation tools. The issues previously mentioned in the chapter are important in the selection of appropriate norm-referenced measures of cognitive development. Best practice would advocate instruments that provide the best match between the child and the requirements of the assessment or evaluation tool. Several measures are identified in this section. Examiners should choose the instrument that will yield the most reliable and valid information about the individual child, keeping in mind the assumptions underlying the test development, test characteristics (normative sample, adequate floor, predictive validity), and response requirements.

A note of caution is appropriate here in regard to the use of norm-referenced assessments for children with severe or profound disabilities. Berdine and Meyer (1987) suggest that the use of norm-referenced assessment to label and classify children with severe or profound disabilities is gratuitous at best and potentially damaging in the worst case. The use of a comparison group of individuals who function within a normal range of abilities may be irrelevant to the assessment of the abilities of children with severe or profound disabilities. The unexamined use of norm-referenced assessments with this population, which leads to statements such as "This child is untestable," is indefensible. Informed examiners and team members recognize the limits of such assessments and will develop alternative and appropriate assessment models that can reflect accurately the ability levels of children with severe or profound disabilities. A further caution relates to the use of items from norm-referenced instruments as instructional targets.

Battelle Developmental Inventory

The Battelle Developmental Inventory (Newborg et al., 1984) is a developmentally based norm-referenced assessment appropriate for the measuring of the development of children from birth to age 8. It consists of 341 items grouped within five domains and 22 subdomains, and provides a variety of standard scores (including developmental quotients), percentile ranks, and age equivalents. Scores can be obtained for the full scale as well as domains and subdomains (10 summary scores).

The normative sample consisted of 800 children selected by stratification variables based on 1980 census data. The Battelle has three distinct advantages: First, it is a multidomain assessment (cognitive, communication, motor, personal-social, and adaptive); second, a 3-point scoring system is used that allows for the crediting of emerging abilities; and third, three procedures for obtaining information (traditional administration, observation, and interview) provide a more ecologically appropriate assessment.

Test authors suggest that the subtests/domains can be administered independently to measure independent traits or abilities; however, a recent study suggests that for children with severe disabilities these domains are less independent and caution should be used, especially when interpreting domain scores in communication, cognition, and social-emotional development for this population (Snyder, Lawson, Thompson, Stricklin, & Sexton, 1993). Boyd (1989) has reported that age-related discontinuities could produce radically different scores on a child from one day to the next despite identical item performance. He hypothesizes that this problem may be the result of an insufficient number of infants included in the normative sample. For example, the 1984 Bayley Scales of Infant Development used 450 infants between the ages of birth and 6 months, while the Battelle Developmental Inventory (BDI) used only 50. "Depending upon whether the BDI is given prior to or after a particular cut-off point, BDI results can make the child appear relatively better or worse than a companion instrument" (Boyd, 1989, p. 118). Sheehan and Snyder (1989–1990) support Boyd's research and caution against the use of the assessment for all children below the age of 2 because of limited item sampling.

Bailey, Vandiviere, Dellinger, and Munn (1987) identify three problems with the Battelle inventories. First, for 247 protocols scored by 76 teachers, only 20.2% were scored without errors; second, of 247 children, 174 (75%) required extrapolated scoring; and third, 49 children (20%) received negative developmental quotients as a result of extrapolation. Extrapolated scores are sometimes necessary evils when evaluating children with disabilities. However, two cautions are appropriate. First, these scores do not have the psychometric integrity of scores generated within standardization and norming procedures; they are only estimates of scores that might have been obtained. Second, logic would dictate that a minimal range of raw scores must be earned (Bailey & Wolery, 1989). It would be unreasonable to extrapolate scores on the basis of multiple scores of zeros.

The Battelle is an example of a unique hybrid of norm-referenced and developmental/criterion-based assessment. The distinction between criterion-based and norm-referenced is easily seen in school-age assessments. For example, the Key Math (Connolly, 1988) is readily identified as a criterion measure of mathematical ability; the Wechsler Intelligence Scales for Children (Wechsler, 1991) measures cognitive abilities. This distinction is less obvious in assessments for preschoolers, and the use of the generic term *developmental assessment* for both kinds of measures makes the distinction even more difficult. Furthermore, many of the items included in norm-referenced developmental assessments may be seen as intervention targets. The key to understanding this distinction is the way in which the outcomes/scores are generated. Norm-referenced outcomes are comparisons with the performance of the norm group; developmental/age equivalents from a non-norm-referenced developmental assessment are generated based on what we assume to be ages when these skills typically develop. Again, these arbitrarily assigned expectations or assumptions are problematic for children with disabilities. Critical to the appropriate use of age equivalents based on developmental milestones or schedules is a sound knowledge of child development. The Battelle authors suggest that this assessment inventory can be used for the purposes of evaluation and assessment. In other words, it can be used for eligibility determination and for program planning. It is naive, however, to believe that one assessment can adequately fulfill both of these missions. Despite these difficulties, the Battelle continues to enjoy widespread usage and appears to meet psychometric standards for use with children age 2 and older with mild to moderate disabilities.

Bayley Scales of Infant Development

The Bayley Scales of Infant Development II, the 1993 revision of the original Bayley Scales of Infant Development (Bayley, 1969), provides a comprehensive assessment of the development of children ages 1 through 42 months. The second edition, similar to the first, contains three scales: (1) a mental scale includes the assessment of perceptual acuity, discrimination, object constancy and memory, learning and problem solving, verbal ability, generalization, and classification; (2) a motor scale assesses muscle control and coordination; and (3) a behavior rating scale contains four subscales: orientation/engagement, attention, motor quality, and emotional regulation.

The Bayley uses a two-tiered theoretical model and provides developmental age equivalents for motor, personal/social, language, and cognition. No studies have yet reported on the validity of this model, although reliability and validity studies reported by the publishers demonstrate adequacy. Scale scores are also provided for the mental and motor scales. The normative sample included 1,700 children stratified by race, gender, parental education level, and geographic region. A clinical sample was assessed to validate the normative sample. This sample included children with autism and developmental delay, as well as children who were premature, HIV positive, prenatally exposed to drugs, and asphyxiated at birth (Cohen & Spenciner, 1994).

Cattell Infant Intelligence Scale The Cattell Infant Intelligence Scale (Cattell, 1960, 1980) uses a single-factor model of intelligence and includes items from the Gesell schedules. The Cattell was initially designed as a downward extension of the Stanford-Binet and is very similar to the early Bayley Scales of Infant Development. Many of the items on the Cattell are almost identical to those on the Bayley; however, the number of items is less comprehensive. For many of the age levels, the Cattell contains two additional items to be used as substitutions if a previous item is spoiled during administration (Langley, 1989). Norms are provided for months 2 to 12, every 2 months to 24 months, and every 3 months to 30 months. Benner (1992) provides correlations with the Stanford-Binet (Form L-M), ranging from .10 at 3 months to .56 at 12 and .71 at 24 months.

Differential Ability Scales The Differential Ability Scales (Elliott, 1990) is a revision of the British Ability Scales (Elliott, Murray, & Pearson, 1979) for children ages 2 years 6 months through 17 years. The DAS contains two components: a cognitive battery with two levels, one for preschool and one for school-age children, and a set of academic achievement tests for school-age children. The cognitive battery provides a composite score (the General Conceptual Ability score), cluster ability scores, and individual subtest scores, similar to the three-tiered model used in the Stanford Binet, Fourth Edition. The cognitive battery is composed of two types (core and diagnostic) of subtests. Only the core subtests are used in calculating the GCA composite (mean of 100 and standard deviation of 15). The authors of the DAS suggest that it provides greater subtest specificity than other cognitive measures due to an increased effort to design subtests that were "relatively pure" (Elliott, Daniel, & Guiton, 1991, p. 134). However, poor subtest specificity is still an issue in the assessment of preschoolers. According to Elliot et al. (1991), as children age and ability increases, the general factor underlying core subtests becomes more differentiated. For example, at the early level (2 years, 6 months to 3 years, 5 months) the four core tests measure a single factor. For ages 3 years, 6 months to 5 years, 11 months, the six core tests measure two factors—verbal and nonverbal. By age 6, three factors emerge—verbal, nonverbal, and spatial.

Test administration is somewhat different for the DAS. Rather than a basal and ceiling approach, starting and stopping points termed *decision points* are used in estimating the child's ability from the test results using a procedure based on the Rasch model of item response theory (Elliott et al., 1991). The aim is to administer items of moderate difficulty rather than working downward toward items that are "too easy" or upward until items become "too hard." DAS authors contend that the preschool level of the test is tailored for preschoolers rather than being a mere extension of school-age items. Brightly colored manipulatives and pictures are used to elicit and maintain the attention of young children. The DAS also provides sample items and allows for teaching following failure on initial items. Furthermore, the DAS provides a brief battery that can be used to obtain a special nonverbal composite score in place of the General Conceptual Ability (GCA) score. Directions for these items can be delivered through gestural communication and require only gestural responses from the child (pointing, drawing, and manipulating objects). In addition, the DAS makes use of extended norms that allow the calculation of GCAs as low as 25 (Platt, Kamphaus, Keltgen, & Gilliland, 1991) and provides for "out-of-level" testing when evaluating children who are performing considerably lower (or higher) than others of the same chronological age (Elliott et al., 1991).

The normative sample for the DAS included children who exhibited learning disabilities, speech and language impairments, mild mental retardation, emotional disturbance, and/or mild visual, hearing, or motor impairments. This produced a sample that closely matched the 1984 percentage for special education categories in the population and a percentage of other children representative of the general population (Elliott et al., 1991). In all, 3,475 children, reflecting the population distribution of race, socioeconomic status, and region, as measured by 1988 U.S. census data, were included in the sample. Item bias ascribed to race or gender was analyzed, and items that were differentially difficult were excluded from the test.

Concurrent validity studies were conducted using other cognitive measures such as the Wechsler Preschool and Primary Scales of Intelligence, the Kaufman Assessment Battery for Children, the Stanford-Binet, Fourth Edition, and the McCarthy Scales of Children's Abilities as the criterion measures. Coefficients ranged from .68 to .89, indicating moderate to strong relationships (Elliott et al., 1991).

Griffiths Mental Development Scales The Griffiths Mental Development Scales (Griffiths, 1954, 1979), which includes five independent measures—locomotor, person-social, hearing and speech, eye-hand coordination, and performance—was developed in post–World War II England and has not been standardized on an American population. Concurrent validity efforts, however, suggest that the Griffiths scales are consistent with other multidomain measures typically used in the United States, such as the Bayley Scales of Infant Development and the Battelle Developmental Inventory. Some research has also suggested that scores obtained on the Griffiths are somewhat inflated (McLean, McCormick, & Baird, 1991). The scales include The Abilities of Babies (birth to 24 months) and The Abilities of Young Children, expanding the scale to 8 years. Each of the scales produces a developmental quotient and a general intelligence quotient.

Kaufman Assessment Battery for Children The Kaufman Assessment Battery for Children (K-ABC) (Kaufman & Kaufman, 1983) contains four scales: sequential processing, simultaneous processing, achievement, and nonverbal for children ages 2 years, 6 months to 12 years, 5 months. The authors used this four-factor model to minimize the effect of verbal processing, ethnic bias, and gender bias on the estimate of cognitive development. A mental processing composite of the sequential and simultaneous scales is produced with a mean of 100 and a standard deviation of 15. Subtest scaled scores have a mean of 10 and standard deviation of 3.

The normative sample consisted of 2,000 children chosen by a stratification procedure based on race and ethnicity, age, gender, geographic region, socioeconomic status as measured by parent education, and community size according to 1980 census data. However, African Americans from lower-socioeconomic environments and Hispanic Americans were underrepresented by 24% and 10% (Benner, 1992). Reliability and validity studies suggest moderate to strong correlations with other measures such as the WPPSI. However, there is some concern that the exclusion of verbal ability (to support a more culture-fair measure) severely limits the behavioral sampling of the mental processing composite. Furthermore, difficulties with an inadequate floor have also been cited when the test is used with preschoolers with below-average abilities (Bracken, 1987). As with other multiple-factor models, the factor structure for preschoolers is questionable. Gridley, Miller, Barke, Fischer, and Smith (1990) found no evidence of the two factors for a sample of preschoolers; Kamphaus and Kaufman (1991) report that the K-ABC produces two factors (sequential and simultaneous) for young children (ages 2 and 3) with a third (achievement) emerging at age 4.

The K-ABC was developed with great attention to the uniqueness of preschool assessment. Test materials are colorful and use colorful photographs rather than line drawings. The attentional demands of standardized assessments with young children are also accommodated by the use of only seven subtests for younger children. As children age and attention spans increase, the number of subtests increases. Instructions were simplified to remove any embedded concepts such as "middle" or "after." Sample and teaching items facilitate test administration and validity. Furthermore, the K-ABC Nonverbal Scale may provide examiners with supporting information about the cognitive abilities of children with limited English proficiency and children with language or hearing impairments. However, caution should be exercised when using the K-ABC with preschoolers with hearing impairments because of a limited number (three) of subtests (Telzrow, 1984). In summary, limitations for preschoolers include too few manipulative tasks; too few easy items (limited floor); a heavy emphasis on visual stimuli, making the test difficult for children with visual impairments; and too little opportunity to sample verbal reasoning and spontaneous expression (Kaufman, Kamphaus, & Kaufman, 1985).

The Learning Accomplishment Profile–Diagnostic Standardized Assessment (LAP–D) The LAP–D (Nehring, Nehring, Bruni, & Randolph, 1992), an instrument with characteristics similar to the BDI, was originally developed as a criterion-referenced measure of developmental status. The LAP–D Standardized Assessment, according to the authors, may be used for educational decisions concerning placement and developmental profile. The LAP–D includes four domains: fine motor (writing and manipulation), cognitive (matching and counting), language (naming and comprehension), and gross motor (body movement and object movement). Like the Battelle, each domain has its own manual with accompanying materials.

The LAP–D yields age equivalents, percentile ranks, and z and t scores. Normative data were generated for 792 children ages 30 to 72 months, stratified by gender and race. Stratification procedures did not include geographic region or the socioeconomic or educational status of parents. Subtest floors and total test floor appear to be adequate; however, item gradient problems were noted for the lowest age range (30 to 35 months). A concurrent validity study with 60 children ages 30 months to 72 months conducted by Mayfield, McCormick, and Cook (1993) suggests moderate to strong correlations between subtest age equivalents reported by the LAP–D and the Battelle Developmental Inventory. The Learning Accomplishment Profile (LAP) (Sanford & Zelman, 1981) and the Early Learning Accomplishment Profile (Glover, Preminger, & Sanford, 1978) have enjoyed a long history of use as assessments for program planning and measurement of child progress in many preschool programs, particularly in Head Start. Perhaps because of this previous familiarity with the instrument as a criterion-referenced assessment, its use as an evaluation for eligibility has not as yet become widespread.

McCarthy Scales of Children's Abilities The McCarthy Scales of Children's Abilities (McCarthy, 1972) contains five scales: verbal, perceptual-performance, quantitative, memory, and motor. Three of the five scales—verbal, perceptual-performance, and quantitative—are combined to form a composite score termed a general cognitive index (mean of 100 and standard deviation of 16). Profile subtest scaled scores (mean of 50 and standard deviations of 10) are also generated. Included in the normative sample were 1,032 children, selected on the stratification variables of race, geographic region, father's occupation, urban-rural residence, age, and gender, using the 1970 census data. Moderate reliability is reported; concurrent validity coefficients range from

.45 to .91 (Sattler, 1990). Bracken (1991b) points to the limited floor for young or developmentally delayed children for most of the subtests. However, the general cognitive index does provide an adequate floor and item gradation.

Stanford-Binet Intelligence Scale: Fourth Edition The fourth edition of the Stanford-Binet (Thorndike, Hagen, & Sattler, 1985) continues the work begun in 1905 by Binet and Simon. The new Stanford-Binet can be given to individuals ages 2 to 23. The test authors deviated from the original general-factor model by using a three-level hierarchical model, which consists of a general factor, followed by three factors—crystallized, fluid, and short-term memory—with specific factors identified at the third level. Fifteen subtests can be administered that assess abilities in verbal reasoning, quantitative reasoning, abstract visual reasoning, and short-term memory. Standard scores are provided for each of these levels; the composite and area scores have means of 100 with standard deviations of 16; the subtest means are 50 with a standard deviation of 8. Numerous studies support the validity and reliability of the outcomes generated by this assessment. However, the technical properties are less strong for preschool children; limited subtest floors fail to discriminate among children younger than 3 years, 6 months (McCallum, 1991). One other technical consideration, the lack of subtest specificity, is noteworthy. As indicated previously, the factor model used to generate subtest specificity may not be reflective of the development of young children.

Wechsler Preschool and Primary Scale of Intelligence–Revised The WPPSI–R (Wechsler, 1989) provides a full-scale intelligence quotient, with quotients also derived for the two supporting scales of performance and verbal and is useful for children ages 3 years to 7 years, 3 months. The normative sample was stratified based on the 1986 U.S. Census. Stratification factors included occupation and educational level of parents, region, and ethnicity. The publishers used an oversample of 400 children from minority populations to further investigate item bias. The full performance and verbal scales, which are standardized to yield a mean of 100 with a standard deviation of 15, contain six subscales generating standard scores with a mean of 10 and a standard deviation of 3. The performance scale is composed of the following: object assembly, geometric design, block design, mazes, picture completion, and animal pegs. The verbal scales include information, comprehension, arithmetic, vocabulary, similarities, and sentences.

For examiners familiar with the WPPSI, the WPPSI–R is a pleasant surprise. The revision focused on making the test more attractive and motivating for young children and still has all of the advantages of the WPPSI, such as strong reliability and validity, excellent normative sample, and strong psychometric properties consistent with the other Wechsler scales. Gyurke (1991) reports a weak floor for some of the subtests at age 3; however, by the 3.5-year level, almost all demonstrate an adequate floor. Concurrent validity studies using the WPPSI, WISC–R, Stanford-Binet (Fourth Edition), McCarthy Scales of Children's Abilities, and Kaufman Assessment Battery for Children produced moderate to strong correlations (.54 to .87) with the exception of the K-ABC (.31 to .49) (Gyurke, 1991).

Other norm-referenced cognitive assessments include the Detroit Tests of Learning Aptitude–P (Hammill & Bryant, 1991, 1986) and the Woodcock-Johnson Psychoeducational Battery–Revised (Woodcock & Johnson, 1989). The Woodcock-Johnson is a wide-range set of tests designed to measure cognitive abilities, scholastic aptitude, and achievement of children 2 years through adult. The cognitive assessment was based on the Horn-Cattell theory; however, there is not yet sufficient information regarding the use of this assessment with young children (Taylor, 1993).

Developmental Scales and Checklists

Brigance Diagnostic Inventory of Early Development–Revised The Brigance Inventory of Early Development–Revised (Brigance, 1991) measures abilities in 11 areas and includes 84 skills sequences. Supplemental and comprehensive sequences are also available and are useful with children for whom more specific task analysis is needed. Developmental age equivalents can be obtained; however, these are not norm-based and can be considered only as estimates of developmental status.

The Carolina Curriculum for Handicapped Infants and Infants at Risk and The Carolina Curriculum for Preschoolers The Assessment Log and Developmental Progress Chart–Infants (Second Edition) (Johnson-Martin, Jens, Attermeier, & Hacker, 1991) is part of The Carolina Curriculum for Handicapped Infants and Infants at Risk. Items are included that are correlated with 24 curriculum sequences and are presented in a checklist format. Cognition (using a Piagetian model), language/communication, fine and gross motor, and self-help/social skills are included. The Assessment Log and Developmental Progress Chart–Preschoolers (Johnson-Martin, Attermeier, & Hacker, 1990) measures five domains with 25 skills sequences. These assessments may be completed using observation and direct testing with corresponding program areas for intervention.

Gesell Developmental Schedules The Gesell Developmental Schedules (revised by Knobloch & Pasamanick in 1974 and in 1980 by Knobloch, Stevens, & Malone) describe development across motor (gross and fine), communication, personal-social, and adaptive behavior for children between the ages of 4 weeks and 72 months. Gesell intended that the schedules be used as benchmarks, in the same manner as criterion-based instruments, to determine the current functioning of the child rather than to predict future status. A Developmental Quotient (DQ) can be derived from a ratio formula using the mental and chronological ages. A parent questionnaire can also be used to validate direct test administration (Gibbs, 1990).

Hawaii Early Learning Profile The Hawaii Early Learning Profile (HELP) (Furuno et al., 1988) provides an assessment of development in cognitive (which includes receptive language), expressive language, fine and gross motor, self-help, and social domains. In addition to assessment information, the HELP provides a helpful linkage to intervention planning through the inclusion of teaching activities for each of the test items. Furthermore, there appears to be an adequate number of items to assess the emergence of sensorimotor behavior in the young child. In addition to the HELP, there is HELP at HOME, which provides information for parents and professionals in facilitating development within specific skill areas. The Hawaii for Special Preschoolers Assessment Checklist (Santa Cruz County Office of Education, 1987) is a criterion-referenced assessment that focuses on five skill areas: learning/cognition, self-help, motor development, communication, and social skills, with accompanying developmental activities.

Vulpé Assessment Battery The Vulpé Assessment Battery (Vulpé, 1977), a developmental assessment of the behavior of children from birth to age 6, contains 1,230 items across eight domains: basic senses and functions; gross-motor behaviors, fine-motor behaviors; language behaviors; cognitive processes and specific concepts; organization of behavior; activities of daily living; and assessment of environment. The cognitive processes and specific concepts contain a number of Piagetian concepts as well as a number of items more typically found in assessments of information processing, such as concepts of object, body, color, shape, size, space, time, amount, and number, as well as visual memory, auditory discrimination, auditory attention, comprehension and memory, cause/effect or means/end behavior, and categorizing/combining schemes. The Vulpé uses a 7-point scoring system similar to a most-to-least prompt system. For example, the lowest score is a *no score* if a child doesn't attend to the task through *attention, physical, socio-emotional, and verbal assistance* to *independent* and *transfer* (generalization) scores. Age equivalents are assigned to the items.

Assessments that are primarily measures of concept development and readiness for school are also available for preschoolers. The Basic School Skills Inventory–Diagnostic (Hammill & Leigh, 1983) was designed to be used as both a norm-referenced and criterion-referenced assessment. The test includes 110 items in six areas: daily living skills, spoken language, reading, writing, and math readiness, and classroom behavior. The Boehm Test of Basic Concepts–Preschool Version (Boehm, 1986a, 1986b) and the Bracken Basic Concept Scale (Bracken, 1986) also measure basic concept attainment for preschoolers and early elementary-age children. The Boehm Test of Basic Concepts–Preschool Version is a downward extension of the Boehm–R, an instrument that provides information regarding a child's mastery of concepts important for successful performance early in school. This assessment surveys the child's understanding of 26 basic relational concepts that help children understand and describe the world around them. The results were intended by the author to be used by teachers to plan interventions and as indicators of school readiness (Boehm, 1991). The Bracken Basic Concept Scale assesses 258 concepts in 11 areas: color, letter identification, numbers/counting, comparison, shapes, direction/position, social emotional, size, textural/material, quantity, and time/sequence. The test is divided into two instruments—a diagnostic full-scale instrument and an alternate form screening test—and can be used with children 2 years, 6 months to 8 years.

Ordinal Scales

Assessment in Infancy: Ordinal Scales of Psychological Development (Uzgiris & Hunt, 1975) are comprised of six scales: visual pursuit and permanence of objects, means for obtaining desired environmental events, imitation (vocal and gestural), operational causality, construction of object relations in space, and relation to objects. These scales are further broken into steps or test items. Items include an activity, directions for eliciting the response, and suggested location and materials. The criterion behavior is also included.

These scales are individually administered and may be presented in a single session or in multiple ones. No norms are provided; however, in 1980 Dunst assigned for each of the scale steps estimated developmental age placements that provided a reasonable estimate of current functioning and have demonstrated moderate to high correlations with norm-referenced instruments such as the Bayley Scales of Infant Development and the Griffiths Mental Development Scales (Dunst, Rheingrover, & Kistler, 1986). These scales are based primarily on Piaget's theory of intelligence, which suggests that the acquisition of competencies is dependent on the mastery of prior competencies at a lower level of functioning. Learning is hierarchical with increasing sophistication and expansion of previous learning.

Dunst and Gallagher (1983) describe ordinal scales in this way: "The test items on ordinal assessment scales consist of eliciting situations designed to evoke a possible range of critical actions and behaviors from the infant" (p. 45). Developmental status is obtained by noting the highest item passed on each scale. Ordinal scales have a distinct advantage for testing children with disabilities. Test procedures are much more flexible and permit the examiner to vary materials and create situations that elicit the required response/behavior.

Although the Ordinal Scales were originally developed for use with infants functioning within the sensorimotor stage, they are also frequently used with older children, especially those with severe delays or disabilities. To provide greater specificity, Dunst (1980) developed a manual that offers additional items to make the scales more sensitive to the smaller changes in development often evidenced by children with severe or profound disabilities.

The Observation of Behavior in Socially and Ecologically Relevant and Valid Environments (OBSERVE) (Dunst & McWilliam, 1988) provides an observational method of evaluation based on Piagetian stage theory that is particularly useful for children with multiple disabilities (Benner, 1992). The OBSERVE assesses interactive competencies in social and nonsocial environments, using a hierarchical system comprised of five levels of behavioral capabilities: attentional interactions, contingency interactions, differentiated interactions, encoded interactions, and symbolic interactions. The assessment provides a mechanism for observing ongoing interactions of the child and the social and nonsocial environment, and a set of "eliciting" situations (Dunst, Holbert, & Wilson, 1990). Using five mutually exclusive levels of behavior capabilities (following Piaget's cognitive development sequence), the system provides a running record of behaviors demonstrated by the child in adapting to natural and elicited environmental demands in daily routines. These five levels and four transition levels/points provide a nine-level model to describe the capabilities of young children with or without disabilities. By closely matching learning conditions to the child's ability to interact with the environment and response capabilities, a more accurate measure of his ability to learn new behaviors may be obtained (McLean, Bruder, Baird, & Dunst, 1991). In other words, the response demands of the assessment are designed to match the response capabilities of the child, rather than the reverse.

Special Populations

Hearing impairments The Hiskey-Nebraska Tests of Learning Aptitude (Hiskey, 1966) provide assessment information for children ages 3 through 17. Deaf and hard-of-hearing norms are provided. The Hiskey-Nebraska can be administered by pantomime or verbal directions. Subtests include bead patterns, memory for color, picture identification, picture association, paper folding, visual attention span, block patterns, and completion of drawings. Derived scores (mean of 100 and standard deviation of 16) depend on the type of administration. When the test is administered in pantomime, a learning age and learning quotient are obtained; when it is administered verbally, a mental age and intelligence quotient are generated.

This test was originally developed in 1941 and was restandardized in 1966. The normative sample consisted of 1,079 children with hearing impairments and 1,074 hearing children between the ages of 2 years, 6 months and 17 years, 5 months from 10 states. Available data for the norming group are limited. The children with hearing impairments were primarily from state schools for the deaf, while the hearing children were selected based on the 1960 census data. No efforts were made to include representative numbers of children from minority populations. Sattler (1990) reports high reliability and validity coefficients for reported studies (.78 to .93), although information on reliability and validity of the scales is limited.

Other assessments for children with hearing impairments are the Nonverbal Performance Scale (Smith & Johnson, 1977) and the Adaptation of WPPSI for Deaf Children (Ray & Ulissi, 1982). The Nonverbal Performance Scale is appropriate for children ages 2 to 4 years and consists of 14 task categories. Norms for hearing children and children with hearing impairments are provided. The Adaptation of WPPSI for Deaf Children also provides performance IQ and subscale scores similar to those of the WPPSI for young children ages 4 years to 6 years, 6 months. Children with prelingual hearing impairments with loss greater than 70 dB made up the normative sample. Because of the high level of psychometric integrity of the Wechsler Scales, this may be the preferred measure of cognitive development of children with hearing impairments.

Visual impairments The Perkins-Binet Intelligence Scale (Davis, 1980) provides two forms. Form N, for ages 4 through 18, is used for children with nonusable vision; Form U, for ages 3 through 18, is appropriate for children with usable vision. Mental age and IQ scores are obtained, using a normative sample of blind and partially sighted children. The Reynell-Zinkin Developmental Scales for Young Visually Handicapped Children (Reynell, 1983) is appropriate for children from birth to 5 years and provides six age scales for cognitive and linguistic development. The norming group was composed of blind and partially sighted children.

Physical impairments and multiple disabilities The Callier-Azusa Scale (Stillman, 1978) was designed to assess the developmental status of children with dual sensory impairments and children with severe or profound disabilities, from birth through 9 years. Accurate assessment and evaluation of the behavioral repertoire of this population requires thorough familiarity with the child. Stillman states that the examiner should observe the child for at least two weeks before the evaluation. The Callier-Azusa Scale is composed of 18 subscales in five areas and contains sequential items to measure developmental milestones within each subscale. Subtest scores may be used to calculate age equivalents.

The Columbia Mental Maturity Scale (Burgemeister, Blum, & Lorge, 1972) and The Pictorial Test of Intelligence (French, 1964) are also available supporting tools for children with motor and language deficits. Both require only a pointing response and can be used with a yes/no question-and-answer format. The Columbia Mental Maturity Scale, Third Edition, requires children to make visual-perceptual discriminations. Ninety-two cards are arranged in eight levels for the assessment of children between the ages of 3 years, 6 months and 9 years, 11 months. The child is asked to select a drawing on each card that is different from the others. The opportunity to establish a reliable response set and communication between examiner and child is provided by using practice cards. A standard score and an age deviation score are obtained (mean of 100 and a standard deviation of 16), as well as a maturity index indicating age equivalents.

The Columbia scales were standardized on 2,600 children from 25 states with inclusion based on race, parental occupation, gender, age, and geographic region, to approximate the 1960 census data. Sattler (1990) reports moderate reliability coefficients and moderate-to-weak concurrent validity estimates (.30 to .74). The Columbia offers an alternative approach to assessing children with limited language, motor, or hearing abilities; however, as noted previously, the line drawings are not extremely motivating for many children and may include items or exemplars unfamiliar to children from diverse cultural environments. The Columbia has traditionally been used as an adjunct measure to estimate the intellectual abilities of children with communication difficulties. Advantages include easy administration and scoring and psychometric soundness. However, it is dated (standardized in 1972) and samples only a limited range of cognitive abilities, primarily discrimination and classification.

The Pictorial Test of Intelligence includes six subtests: picture vocabulary, form discrimination, information and comprehension, similarities, size and number, and immediate recall. The test provides deviation IQs (mean of 100 and standard deviation of 16), mental ages, and percentiles. The stratified normative sample consisted of 1,830 children, ages 3 to 8, representative of the U.S. population according to the 1960 census. Although the Pictorial Test is somewhat dated in norms and materials, it does provide an alternative for assessing children with motor and speech impairments.

The Arthur Adaptation (Arthur, 1949) of the Leiter International Performance Scale (Leiter, 1948, 1979) is an untimed, nonverbal age scale consisting of 60 items ranging from the 2-year to the 12-year level. The AALIPS provides two scores, a mental age and a ratio intelligence quotient. The normative sample consisted of 289 children from a middle-class, metropolitan background in a midwestern state. No reliability or validity data were published in the manual, but later research indicates coefficients ranging from .37 to .92 (Sattler, 1990). This nonverbal scale includes 54 items that require children to arrange blocks in a form-board. Early items require matching; later items test sequential and logical relations. Use of the Leiter presents a number of difficulties, including inadequate item gradation, inadequate validity and reliability data, poor standardization, reliance on a ratio IQ, and out-of-date norms and items. These difficulties make its use for evaluation purposes questionable; however, it may provide useful diagnostic information.

Perhaps one of the most useful of these assessments is the Uniform Performance Assessment System by Haring et al. (1981), which can be used with individuals who display behaviors similar to those of children below a developmental age of 6. The authors of this curriculum-referenced assessment system believe the test is most useful as a mechanism for parents and teachers to select skills and behaviors for instruction. Support adaptations provide positional and physical support, prosthetic adaptations involve the use of equipment or aids, and general adaptations represent any change in the requirements of the task. The Uniform Performance Assessment System contains 250 items in preacademic, communication, social/self-help, and gross motor domains and can be used with individuals who display behaviors similar to those of children below a developmental age of 6. The authors of this curriculum-referenced assessment system believe the test is most useful as a mechanism for parents and teachers to select skills and behaviors for instruction.

TRANSLATING ASSESSMENT INFORMATION INTO INSTRUCTIONAL GOALS

Linking Assessment to Intervention

The future of assessment instruments will depend on their usefulness in planning and evaluating programs for young children (Kelly & Surbeck, 1991). The use of norm-referenced assessments in isolation is becoming increasingly challenged (Neisworth & Bagnato, in press). School psychologists and educational diagnosticians are using alternative assessment instruments more frequently to determine a child's abilities and to plan intervention (Neisworth & Bagnato, 1992). Alternative methods of assessment may include authentic, dynamic, portfolio, curriculum-based, process, and performance assessments as well as task analysis (Cohen & Spenciner, 1994).

A systematic mechanism to use the information provided by norm-referenced instruments in conjunction with other assessments, such as interviews, observations, and criterion-referenced tests and other alternative procedures, to plan intervention services is contained in the System to Plan Early Childhood Services (SPECS) by Bagnato, Neisworth, and Gordon (1990). The convergent assessment model described by these authors provides a link to intervention through the establishment of a developmental content, behavioral strategies hypothesized to be effective for intervention, and appropriate data-keeping methods. There is strong support for the use of a more convergent model in linking assessment and evaluation to intervention. Best practice suggests the use of multiple measures: (a) *norm-referenced*; (b) *criterion-referenced*; (c) *judgment-based*; and (d) *ecological-based*. Multiple sources such as parents and other family members, caregivers, and early care and education providers must also be used to gather information concerning the abilities of the child in multiple settings—home, preschool, church, grandmother's house, and the grocery store. A convergent model of multiple measures for children ages 36 to 48 months is included in Figure 10.1.

Norm-based	Battelle Developmental Inventory (1984) or McCarthy Scales of Children's Abilities (1972)
Curriculum-based	Help for Special Preschoolers (1987) or Carolina Preschool Curriculum (1990)
Judgment-based	System to Plan Early Childhood Services (1990) and Child Behavior Checklist (1986) or Social Skills Rating System (1990)
Eco-based	Home Observation for Measurement of the Environment—Form II (1978) and Early Childhood Environment Rating Scale (1980)

FIGURE 10.1
Sample assessment battery for preschool (36–48 months)
Source: From *Assessment for Early Intervention: Best Practices for Professionals* by S. Bagnato and J. Neisworth, 1991, London: Guilford Press.

Convergent assessment refers to the synthesis of information gathered from several sources, instruments, settings, and occasions to produce the most valid appraisal of developmental status and to accomplish the related assessment purposes of identification, prescription, and progress evaluation (Bagnato & Neisworth, 1991). The convergent model establishes an organized context in which information from multiple sources may be used in a systematic way. The System to Plan Early Childhood Services is comprised of three main components: Developmental Specifications, Team Specification, and Program Specifications. Team members use one of three rating scales included in the SPECS system to rate the child on 19 functional dimensions. The individual professionals share their findings and information with the other members to form a collective pooling resulting in a team rating consensus. The program-specific component is then used to plan the child's program and to document child progress and program effectiveness. Figure 10.2 provides a graphic representation of each of these phases and illustrates this interdisciplinary model of convergent assessment.

Bricker and her colleagues have also developed a system for linking assessment to program planning and progress evaluation. The Assessment, Evaluation, and Programming System (AEPS) for Infants and Children is a comprehensive system that encompasses the assessment, intervention, and evaluation process and provides strong linkages between a curriculum-referenced instrument and intervention planning and implementation. The system, which is described in two volumes (Bricker, 1993; Cripe, Slentz, & Bricker, 1993), includes (a) the AEPS Test; (b) a set of IEP/IFSP goals and objectives; (c) data recording forms; (d) the AEPS Family Report—an assessment designed to be completed by families; (e) the AEPS Family Interest Survey; (f) the AEPS Child Progress Form; and (g) the AEPS Curriculum for Birth to Three Years.

The AEPS Test, which is designed to measure functional abilities, is comprehensive (1 month to 3 years), uses observation as the primary method of obtaining information, and allows the examiner to adapt or modify the presentation format. In addition, a parallel form of the assessment may be used by family members to assist them in the identification of IEP/IFSP goals and objectives. Accompanying materials also include assessment activity plans that provide suggestions for the acquisition of assessment information in natural environments and during typical routines such as group play.

The cognitive domain of the AEPS contains seven strands based largely on Piagetian theory—sensory stimuli, object permanence, causality, imitation, problem solving, preacademic skills, and interaction with objects. Each strand is comprised of goals and more specific objectives. Sample items contained in the cognitive domain of the AEPS Test are included in Figure 10.3.

The system allows for easy transition from the assessment sequences to identification of goals and objectives and finally to intervention strategies. For example, the first goal in the cognitive domain of the AEPS is "orients to auditory, visual, and tactile events." Accompanying objectives are "orients to auditory events, orients to visual events, orients to tactile events, and responds to auditory/visual/tactile events" (Cripe et al., 1993, p. 255). Figure 10.4 provides accompanying curriculum considerations for the objective "orients to auditory events."

The assessments and materials developed by Bricker and her colleagues provide a comprehensive and unified approach to assessment, intervention, and program evaluation. The AEPS Test provides an opportunity to assess young children comprehensively within naturally occurring routines and environments. As is evidenced in Figure 10.4, the AEPS Curriculum is a source of information for interventionists. It includes (a) a rationale for the inclusion of the behavior in the child's intervention program; (b) objectives in other domains that may be concurrently addressed; (c) teaching suggestions; (d) environmental arrangements; (e) instructional sequences; and (f) general teaching considerations. This is an exciting development in the assessment of infants and toddlers, and it is hoped that the authors will expand their work to include other populations.

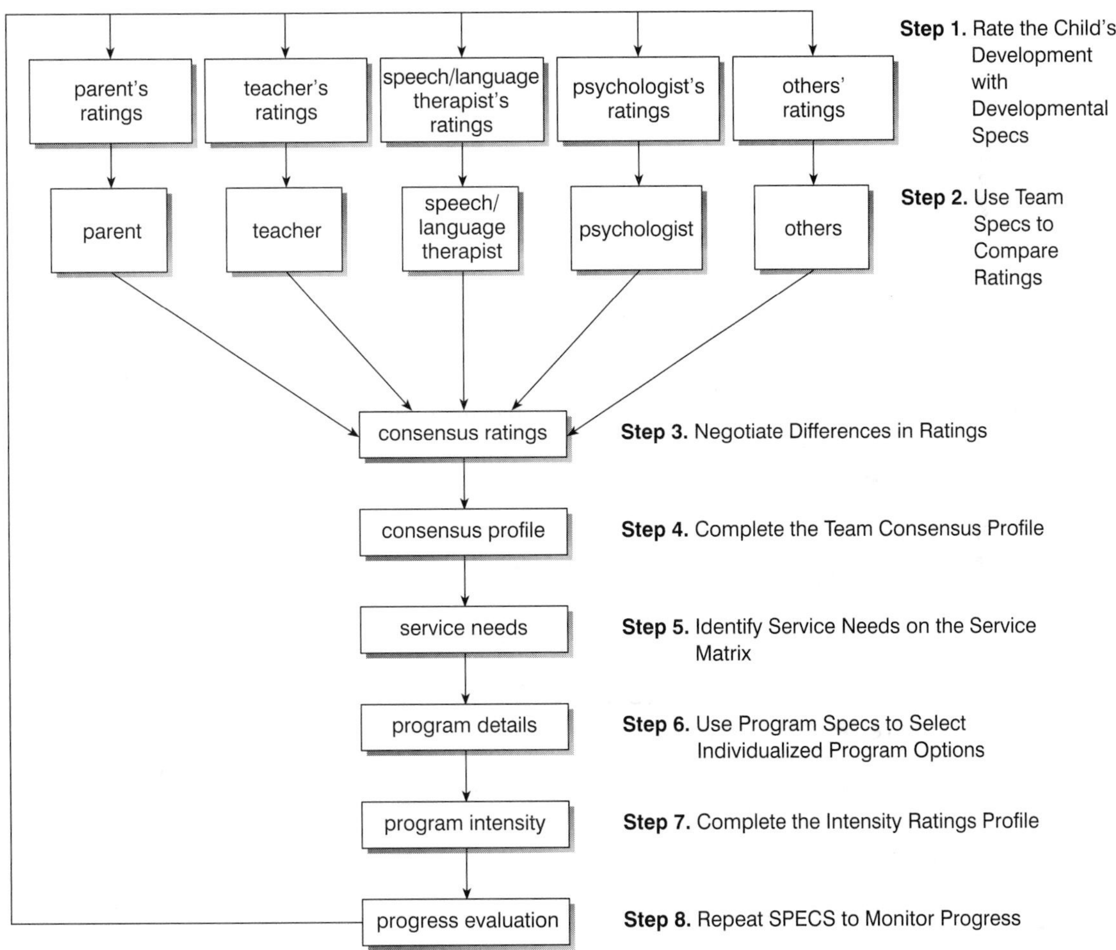

FIGURE 10.2
Steps to follow in using the SPECS system
Source: From *System to Plan Early Childhood Services (SPECS)* by S. J. Bagnato, J. T. Neisworth, and J. Gordon, 1990, Circle Pines, MN: American Guidance Service. Copyright 1990 by American Guidance Service. Reprinted by permission.

Cognitive Domain

S = Scoring Key	Q = Qualifying Notes
2 = Pass consistently 1 = Inconsistent performance 0 = Does not pass	A = Assistance provided B = Behavior interfered R = Reported assessment M = Modification/adaptation D = Direct test

Name: ______________ Test Period: / Test Date: / Examiner:

	IEP	S	Q	S	Q	S	Q	S	Q
Test Period:		____		____		____		____	
Test Date:		__/__		__/__		__/__		__/__	
Examiner:		____		____		____		____	
A. Sensory stimuli									
1. Orients to auditory/visual/tactile events									
1.1 Orients to auditory events									
1.2 Orients to visual events									
1.3 Orients to tactile events									
1.4 Responds to auditory/visual/ tactile events									
B. Object permanence									
1. Visually follows object or person to point of disappearance									
1.1 Visually follows object moving in horizontal/vertical/circular direction									
1.2 Focuses on object or person									
2. Locates object in latter of two successive hiding places									
2.1 Locates object or person who hides while child is watching									
2.2 Locates object or person who is partially hidden									
2.3 Reacts when object or person hides from view									
3. Maintains search for object that is not in usual place									
3.1 Looks for object in usual location									

FIGURE 10.3
AEPS Test protocol items within the cognitive domain
Source: From "AEPS Test" by D. Bricker (Ed.), in D. Bricker (Ed.) *Assessment, Evaluation, and Programming System (AEPS) for Infants and Children: Vol. 1. AEPS Measurement for Birth to Three Years,* 1992, Paul H. Brookes, P.O. Box 10624, Baltimore, MD 21285-0624. Used by permission.

Objective 1.1 Orients to auditory events

DEVELOPMENTAL PROGRAMMING STEPS

✓ The objective above is the most basic step for the skill to be taught. Most children will benefit from the activities outlined here that emphasize this skill. For children who need more instruction, consider designing programming steps from the *environmental arrangements* suggestions or from the *instructional sequence* outlined.

IMPORTANCE OF SKILL

Orientation to auditory stimuli is essential for the acquisition of practical communication skills. A child needs to be attentive to sounds in the environment to comprehend and develop verbal language. The child establishes a socially appropriate nonverbal interaction by focusing on the person speaking.

PRECEDING OBJECTIVE

Cog A:1.4	Responds to auditory, visual, and tactile events

CONCURRENT OBJECTIVES

FM A:1.2	Makes nondirected movements with each arm
GM A:1.1	Turns head past 45° to the right and left from midline position
Cog A:1.2	Orients to visual events
Cog A:1.3	Orients to tactile events
Cog B:1.2	Focuses on object and/or person
SC A:1.2	Turns and looks toward noise-producing object
Soc A:1.1	Responds appropriately to familiar adult's affective tone

TEACHING SUGGESTIONS

Activity-Based

- Play with noise-producing objects (e.g., bells, rattle, crinkly paper, music box, squeeze-toy).
- Encourage the child to orient to sounds that occur near him or her by turning, looking, reaching, or moving in the direction of the sound.
- Expose the child to noises in the daily environment, such as vacuum cleaners, doorbell, garbage disposal, mixer, train, and animals.
- Talk to the child frequently during daily caregiving routines (bathing, dressing, feeding, play) and vary pitch, intonation, and intensity.
- Use a variety of sounds by varying the pitch of your voice, sounding bells or maracas, playing soft and loud music, to determine the cues to which the child most readily responds. Begin with auditory cues to which the child most readily responds and gradually present other cues until the skill is generalized across a variety of auditory cues.
- Make funny sounds (tongue clicks, animal imitations) while interacting with the child.
- Call to the child from behind or the side; whisper in the child's ear.

FIGURE 10.4

AEPS curriculum for the objective: Orients to auditory events

Source: From "Cognitive Domain" by A. Notari, J. Cripe, K. Slentz, and B. Ryan-Seth, in J. Cripe, K. Slentz, and D. Bricker (Eds.) *Assessment, Evaluation, and Programming System (AEPS) for Infants and Children: Vol. 2. AEPS Curriculum for Birth to Three Years,* 1992, Paul H. Brookes, P.O. Box 10624, Baltimore, MD 21285-0624. Used by permission.

✓ If your data indicate the child is not making progress toward the objective, provide additional structure within the suggested activities by incorporating the following *environmental arrangements*:

Environmental Arrangements

- Help the child differentiate between sounds and silence. Speak and then pause, turn on the radio and then shut it off and wait for the child to respond.
- Cease activity and listen to dogs barking, children shouting, airplanes, appliances: take the child to locate the noises.
- Alternate low tones (use wooden objects) and high tones (use plastic objects), and loud sounds (sing) and soft sounds (whisper).
- Give the child a noise-producing object to manipulate (e.g., rattle, crinkly paper).
- Attach noise-producing objects to child's arms or legs (e.g., jingle-bells on socks or wrist).
- Hide yourself or a toy and continue to speak or make a noise with the toy.

✓ If this objective is particularly difficult for a child, it may be necessary, within activities, to use *an instructional sequence*.

Instructional Sequence

- Increase intensity of auditory cues by using louder, more distinct sounds (e.g., drum, shout, larger bells) in place of speech and music.
- Pair auditory events with visual or tactile cues. For example, talk to the child while moving your face within the child's visual field.
- Gently assist the child to move, turn, or reach toward noise-producing objects or to touch the mouth of a person speaking.

✓ Combining or pairing different levels of instructions may be helpful when begining to teach a new and difficult skill. Fade to less intrusive instructions as soon as possible to encourage more independent performance.

TEACHING CONSIDERATIONS

1. The child should be in a quiet and alert state.
2. The environment should be free of auditory, visual, or tactile events that compete with the auditory event presented.
3. When presenting paired cues to elicit a response to an auditory event, select those cues to which the child is most responsive (visual or tactile).
4. Be cautious about scaring the child or eliciting a startle with loud or sudden noises.
5. The child with a hearing impairment may require instructions that are more intense (louder) and are paired with tactile or visual cues.
6. Consult a qualified specialist for techniques for a child with a visual or motor impairment.
7. Consider safety with all objectives that the child handles. Never leave the child unattended with potentially hazardous objects.

FIGURE 10.4
Continued

SUMMARY OF KEY CONCEPTS

- New methods of assessing and evaluating infants and young children with disabilities are being developed and used to capture reliable and realistic child and family information.
- An awareness of the theoretical issues in the assessment of cognitive development allows early interventionists to examine their philosophy and to become more knowledgeable consumers of instruments and tools.
- The assessment of cognition can be viewed from a number of perspectives, including traditional psychometrics, cognitive stage or Piagetian, information processing, social learning, maturational/developmental, and functional.
- If assessment information is to be valid and reliable, five important assumptions must be met, and these are described.
- When assessing children, interventionists must attend to children's developmental histories, their cultural uniqueness, and the impact of their disabilities.
- Emerging trends in the evaluation and assessment of young children with disabilities include play-based assessment, ecological assessment, and judgment-based assessment. Common among these is the use of naturalistic environments—community and home settings where children can interact and participate in preferred ways in familiar surroundings.
- Early interventionists should be familiar with representative norm-referenced instruments, developmental scales and checklists, ordinal scales and instruments, and tools designed for specific populations.
- Alternative methods of assessment such as curriculum-based, process, and performance assessments are increasingly becoming a part of the assessment battery.
- The System to Plan Early Childhood Services and the Assessment, Evaluation, and Programming System are two methods for linking assessment information with intervention planning.

REFERENCES

Anastasiow, N. (1986). *Development and disability.* Baltimore, MD: Paul H. Brookes.

Arthur, G. (1949). The Arthur adaptation of the Leiter International Performance Scale. *Journal of Clinical Psychology, 5,* 345–349.

Bagnato, S. J., Neisworth, J. T., & Gordon, J. (1990). *System to Plan Early Childhood Services (SPECS).* Circle Pines, MN: American Guidance Service.

Bagnato, S., & Neisworth, J. T. (1991). *Assessment for early intervention: Best practices for professionals.* London: Guilford Press.

Bailey, D. B., Vandiviere, P., Dellinger, J., & Munn, D. (1987). The Battelle Developmental Inventory: Teacher perceptions and implementation data. *Journal of Psychoeducational Assessment, 3,* 217–226.

Bailey, D., & Wolery, M. (1989). *Assessing infants and preschoolers with handicaps.* Englewood Cliffs, NJ: Merrill/Prentice Hall.

Bandura, A. (1978). The self system in reciprocal determinism. *American Psychologist, 33,* 344–358.

Bayley, N. (1933). *The California first year mental scale.* Berkeley, CA: University of California Press.

Bayley, N. (1969). *Bayley Scales of Infant Development.* San Antonio, TX: The Psychological Corp.

Bayley, N. (1993). *Bayley Scales of Infant Development—II.* San Antonio, TX: The Psychological Corp.

Benner, S. (1992). *Assessing young children with special needs: An ecological perspective.* New York: Longman.

Berdine, W. H., & Meyer, S. A. (Eds.). (1987). *Assessment in special education.* Boston: Little, Brown.

Boehm, A. E. (1986a). *Boehm Test of Basic Concepts—Preschool Version.* San Antonio, TX: The Psychological Corp.

Boehm, A. E. (1986b). *Boehm Test of Basic Concepts—Revised.* San Antonio, TX: The Psychological Corp.

Boehm, A. E. (1991). Assessment of basic relational concepts. In B. Bracken (Ed.), *The psychoeducational assessment of preschool children* (2nd ed.) (pp. 241–258). Boston: Allyn and Bacon.

Boyd, R. D. (1989). What a difference a day makes: Age-related discontinuities and the Battelle Developmental Inventory. *Journal of Early Intervention, 13*(2), 114–119.

Bracken, B. A. (1986). *Bracken Basic Concept Scale.* San Antonio, TX: The Psychological Corp.

Bracken, B. A. (1987). Limitations of preschool instruments and standards for minimal levels of technical adequacy. *Journal of Psychoeducational Assessment, 5,* 313–326.

Bracken, B. (1991a). The clinical observation of preschool assessment behavior. In B. Bracken (Ed.), *The psychoeducational assessment of preschool children* (2nd ed.) (pp. 40–52). Boston: Allyn and Bacon.

Bracken, B. (1991b). The assessment of preschool children with the McCarthy Scales of Children's Abilities. In B. Bracken (Ed.), *The psychoeducational assessment of preschool children* (2nd ed.) (pp. 53–85). Boston: Allyn and Bacon.

Bricker, D. (Ed.) (1993). *Assessment, evaluation, and programming system (AEPS) for infants and children: Vol. I. AEPS measurement for birth to three years.* Baltimore, MD: Paul H. Brookes.

Brigance, A. H. (1991). *Brigance Diagnostic Inventory of Early Development—Revised.* North Billerica, MA: Curriculum Associates.

Burgemeister, B., Blum, L., & Lorge, I. (1972). *Columbia Mental Maturity Scale.* San Antonio, TX: The Psychological Corp.

Campione, J. C., & Brown, A. L. (1978). Toward a theory of intelligence: Contributions from research with retarded children. *Intelligence, 2,* 279–304.

Campione, J. C., & Brown, A. L. (1987). Linking dynamic assessment with school achievement. In C. S. Lidz (Ed.), *Dynamic assessment: An interactional approach to evaluating learning potential* (pp. 82–115). New York: Guilford Press.

Cattell, P. (1940). *The measurement of intelligence of infants and young children.* New York: The Psychological Corp.

Cattell, P. (1960). *Cattell Infant Intelligence Scale.* San Antonio, TX: The Psychological Corp.

Cattell, P. (1980). *The measurement of intelligence of infants and young children* (5th reprint). San Antonio, TX: The Psychological Corp.

Chang, P. (1990). Early intervention with culturally diverse families of infants and toddlers with disabilities. *Infants and Young Children, 3*(2), 78–87.

Clark, A. M. (1982). Developmental discontinuities: An approach to assessing their nature. In L. A. Bond and J. M. Joffe (Eds.), *Facilitating infant and early childhood development* (pp. 58–77). Hanover, NH: University Press of New England.

Cohen, M., & Gross, P. (1979a). *The developmental resource: Behavioral sequences for assessment and program planning (Vol. 1).* New York: Grune & Stratton.

Cohen, M., & Gross, P. (1979b). *The developmental resource: Behavioral sequences for assessment and program planning (Vol. 2).* New York: Grune & Stratton.

Cohen, L., & Spenciner, L. (1994). *Assessment of young children.* New York: Longman.

Connolly, A. J. (1988). *Key Math—Revised: A diagnostic inventory of essential mathematics.* Circle Pines, MN: American Guidance Service.

Cripe, J., Slentz, K., & Bricker, D. (Eds.). (1992). *Assessment, evaluation, and programming system (AEPS) for infants and children: Vol. 2. AEPS curriculum for birth to three years.* Baltimore, MD: Paul H. Brookes.

Davis, C. (1980). *Perkins-Binet Test of Intelligence for the Blind.* Watertown, MA: Perkins School for the Blind.

Dunst, C. J. (1980). *A clinical and educational manual for use with the Uzgiris and Hunt scales of infant psychological development.* Austin, TX: PRO-ED.

Dunst, C. J., & Gallagher, J. (1983). Piagetian approaches to infant assessment. *Topics in Early Childhood Special Education, 3*(1), 44–62.

Dunst, C. J., Holbert, K. A., & Wilson, L. L. (1990). Strategies for assessing infant sensorimotor interactive competencies. In E. D. Gibbs & D. M. Teti (Eds.), *Interdisciplinary assessment of infants: A guide for early intervention professionals.* Baltimore, MD: Paul H. Brookes.

Dunst, C. J., & McWilliam, R. A. (1988). Cognitive assessment and multiply handicapped young children. In T. D. Wachs & R. Sheehan (Eds.), *Assessment of developmentally disabled children* (pp. 213–238). New York: Plenum Press.

Dunst, C. J., Rheingrover, R. M., & Kistler, E. D. (1986). Concurrent validity of the Uzgiris-Hunt Scales: Relationship to Bayley Scales mental age. *Behavioral Science Documents, 16,* 65.

Elliott, C. D. (1990). *The Differential Ability Scales.* San Antonio, TX: The Psychological Corp.

Elliott, C. D., Daniel, M. H., & Guiton, G. W. (1991). Preschool cognitive assessment with the Differential Ability Scales. In B. Bracken (Ed.), *The psychoeducational assessment of preschool children* (2nd ed.) (pp. 133–153). Boston: Allyn and Bacon.

Elliott, C. D., Murray, D. J., & Pearson, L. S. (1979). *The British Ability Scales.* Windsor, England: National Foundation for Educational Research.

Feuerstein, R. (1979). *The dynamic assessment of retarded performers.* Baltimore: University Park Press.

Fewell, R. (1983). Assessing handicapped infants. In G. Garwood & R. Fewell (Eds.), *Educating handicapped infants* (pp. 257–297). Rockville, MD: Aspen Systems.

Fewell, R. R. (1991). Some new directions in the assessment and education of young handicapped children. In J. M. Berg (Ed.), *Science and service in mental retardation* (pp. 179–188). London: Methuen.

French, J. L. (1964). *Pictorial Test of Intelligence.* Boston: Houghton Mifflin.

Furuno, S., O'Reilly, K. A., Hosaka, C. M., Inatsuka, T. T., Zeisloft-Falbey, B., & Allman, T. (1988). *Hawaii Early Learning Profile (HELP).* Palo Alto, CA: VORT.

Gage, N. L., & Berliner, D. C. (1991). *Educational psychology.* Boston: Houghton Mifflin.

Gibbs, E. D. (1990). Cognitive language and developmental assessment. In E. D. Gibbs & D. M. Teti (Eds.), *Interdisciplinary assessment of infants: A guide for early intervention professionals* (pp. 77–91). Baltimore, MD: Paul H. Brookes.

Glover, M. E., Preminger, J. L., & Sanford, A. R. (1978). *Early Learning Accomplishment Profile for Young Children (Early LAP).* Lewisville, NC: Kaplan Press.

Goodenough, F. L. (1926). *Measurement of intelligence by drawings.* Chicago: World Book.

Gridley, B., Miller, G., Barke, C., Fischer, W., & Smith, D. (1990). Construct validity of the K-ABC with an at-risk preschool population. *Journal of School Psychology, 28,* 39–49.

Griffiths, R. (1954). *The abilities of babies.* High Wycombe, United Kingdom: The Test Agency.

Griffiths, R. (1979). *The abilities of young children.* London: Child Development Research Center.

Guilford, J. P. (1967). *The nature of human intelligence.* New York: McGraw-Hill.

Gyurke, J. (1991). The assessment of preschool children with the Wechsler Preschool and Primary Scale of Intelligence—Revised. In B. Bracken (Ed.), *The psychoeducational assessment of preschool children* (2nd ed.) (pp. 86–106). Boston: Allyn and Bacon.

Hammill, D. D., & Bryant, B. R. (1986). *Detroit Tests of Learning Aptitude—Primary.* Austin, TX: PRO-ED.

Hammill, D. D., & Bryant, B. R. (1991). *Detroit Tests of Learning Aptitude—Primary* (2nd ed.). Austin, TX: PRO-ED.

Hammill, D., & Leigh, J. (1983). *Basic School Skills Inventory—Diagnostic.* Austin, TX: PRO-ED.

Haring, N. G., White, O. R., Edgar, E. B., Affleck, J. Q., Hayden, A. H., Munson, R. G., & Bendersky, M. (Eds.). (1981). *Uniform Performance Assessment System.* Englewood Cliffs, NJ: Merrill/Prentice Hall.

Hiskey, M. S. (1966). *Hiskey-Nebraska Test of Learning Aptitude.* Lincoln, NE: Author.

Horn, J. L. (1968). Organization of abilities and the development of intelligence. *Psychological Review, 75,* 242–259.

Hoy, C., & Gregg, N. (1994). *Assessment: The special educator's role.* Pacific Grove, CA: Brooks-Cole.

Johnson-Martin, N. M., Attermeier, S. M., & Hacker, B. J. (1990). *The Carolina Curriculum for Preschoolers with Special Needs* (2nd ed.). Baltimore, MD: Paul H. Brookes.

Johnson-Martin, N. M., Jens, K. G., Attermeier, S. M., & Hacker, B. J. (1991). *The Carolina Curriculum for Infants and Toddlers with Special Needs* (2nd ed.). Baltimore, MD: Paul H. Brookes.

Kamphaus, R. W., & Kaufman, A. S. (1991). The assessment of preschool children with the Kaufman Assessment Battery for Children. In B. Bracken (Ed.), *The psychoeducational assessment of preschool children* (2nd ed.) (pp. 154–167). Boston: Allyn and Bacon.

Kaufman, A., Kamphaus, R., & Kaufman, N. (1985). The Kaufman assessment battery for children. In C. Newmark (Ed.), *Major psychological assessment instruments.* Boston: Allyn and Bacon.

Kaufman, A. S., & Kaufman, N. L. (1983). *Kaufman Assessment Battery for Children.* Circle Pines, MN: American Guidance Service.

Kelly, M. F., & Surbeck, E. (1991). History of preschool assessment. In B. Bracken (Ed.), *The psychoeducational assessment of preschool children* (2nd ed.) (pp. 1–17). Boston: Allyn and Bacon.

Knobloch, H., & Pasamanick, B. (1974). *Gesell and Amatruda's Developmental Diagnosis: The evaluation and management of normal and abnormal neuropsychological development in infancy and early childhood* (3rd ed.). New York: Harper & Row.

Knobloch, H., Stevens, F., & Malone, A. F. (1980). *Manual of developmental diagnosis.* New York: Harper & Row.

Langley, M. B. (1989). Assessing infant cognitive development. In D. Bailey & M. Wolery (Eds.), *Assessing infants and preschoolers with handicaps* (pp. 249–274). Englewood Cliffs, NJ: Merrill/Prentice hall.

Lefrancois, G. R. (1995). *Theories of human learning.* Pacific Grove, CA: Brookes/Cole.

Leiter, R. G. (1948). *International Performance Scale.* Chicago: Stoelting Co.

Leiter, R. G. (1979). *Leiter International Performance Scale* (rev. ed.). Wood Dale, IL: Stoelting Co.

Lidz, C. S. (Ed.). (1987). *Dynamic assessment: An interactional approach to evaluating learning potential.* New York: Guilford.

Lidz, C. S. (1991). Issues in the assessment of preschool children. In B. Bracken (Ed.), *The psychoeducational assessment of preschool children* (2nd ed.) (pp. 18–32). Boston: Allyn and Bacon.

Lidz, C. S., & Thomas, C. (1987). The Preschool Learning Assessment Device: Extension of a static approach. In C. S. Lidz (Ed.), *Dynamic assessment: An interactional approach to evaluating learning potential.* New York: Guilford.

Linder, T. (1993). *Transdisciplinary play-based assessment: A functional approach to working with young children* (2nd ed.). Baltimore, MD: Paul H. Brookes.

Mayfield, P., McCormick, K., & Cook,. M. (1993). *A comparison of the Battelle Developmental Inventory with the Learning Accomplishment Profile–Diagnostic Edition.* Unpublished manuscript. University of Alabama, Tuscaloosa, AL.

McCallum, R. S. (1991). The assessment of preschool children with the Stanford-Binet Intelligence Scale: Fourth Edition. In B. Bracken (Ed.), *The psychoeducational assessment of preschool children* (2nd ed.) (pp. 107–132). Boston: Allyn and Bacon.

McCarthy, D. (1972). *Manual for the McCarthy Scales of Children's Abilities.* San Antonio, TX: The Psychological Corp.

McLean, M., Bruder, M. B., Baird, S. M., & Dunst, C. J. (1991). Techniques for infants and toddlers with moderate or severe disabilities. In S. Raver (Ed.), *Strategies for teaching at-risk and handicapped infants and toddlers: A transdisciplinary approach* (pp. 234–259). Englewood Cliffs, NJ: Merrill/Prentice Hall.

McLean, M., & McCormick, K. (1993). Assessment and evaluation in early intervention. In W. Brown, S. K. Thurman, & L. F. Pearl (Eds.). *Family-centered early intervention with infants and toddlers: Innovative cross-disciplinary approaches* (pp. 43–81). Baltimore, MD: Paul H. Brookes.

McLean, M., McCormick, K., & Baird, S. (1991). Concurrent validity of the Griffith's Mental Development Scales with a population of children under 24 months. *Journal of Early Intervention, 15*(4), 338–344.

McLean, M., McCormick, K., Bruder, M. B., & Burdg, N. (1987). An investigation of the validity and reliability of the Battelle Developmental Inventory with a population of children younger than 30 months with identified handicapping conditions. *Journal of the Division for Early Childhood, 11*(3), 238–246.

Mercer, J. R. (1979). *System of multicultural pluralistic assessment technical manual*. New York: The Psychological Corp.

Nehring, A. D., Nehring, E. F., Bruni, J. R., & Randolph, P. L. (1992). *Learning Accomplishment Profile Diagnostic Standardized Assessment.* Lewisville, NC: Kaplan School Supply Corporation.

Neisworth, J., & Bagnato, S. (in press). Assessment for early intervention: Emerging themes and practices. In S. Odom & M. McLean (Eds.), *Recommended practices in early intervention*. Austin, TX: PRO-ED.

Neisworth, J. T., & Bagnato, S. J. (1992). The case against intelligence testing in early intervention. *Topics in Early Childhood Special Education, 12*(1), 1–20.

Newborg, J., Stock, J. R.. Wnek, L., Guidubaldi, J., & Svinicki, J. (1984). *Battelle Developmental Inventory.* Allen, TX: DLM.

Paget, K. (1991). The individual assessment situation: Basic considerations for preschool-age children. In B. Bracken (Ed.), *The psychoeducational assessment of preschool children* (2nd ed.) (pp. 32–39). Boston: Allyn and Bacon.

Peterson, N. (1987). *Early intervention for handicapped and at-risk children*. Denver: Love.

Platt, L., Kamphaus, R., Keltgen, J., & Gilliland, F. (1991). Overview of and review of the Differential Ability Scales: Initial and current research findings. *Journal of School Psychology, 29,* 271–278.

Ray, S., & Ulissi, S. M. (1982). *Adaptation of the Wechsler Preschool and Primary Scales of Intelligence for Deaf Children.* Natchitoches, LA: Steven Ray.

Reynell, J. (1983). *Manual for the Reynell-Zinkin Developmental Scales for Young Visually Handicapped Children*. Windsor, Berks, UK: NFER-NELSON Publishing Company.

Robinson, C., & Fieber, N. (1988). Cognitive assessment of motorically impaired infants and preschoolers. In T. Wachs & R. Sheehan (Eds.), *Assessment of young developmentally disabled children* (pp. 127–162). New York: Plenum.

Salvia, J., & Ysseldyke, J. (1988). *Assessment in special and remedial education.* Boston: Houghton Mifflin.

Salvia, J., & Ysseldyke, J. (1995). *Assessment* (2nd ed.). Boston: Houghton Mifflin.

Sanford, A. R., & Zelman, J. G. (1981). *The Learning Accomplishment Profile.* Winston-Salem, NC: Kaplan School Supply.

Sattler, J. (1990). *Assessment of children* (3rd ed.). San Diego, CA: Jerome M. Sattler.

Sheehan, R., & Snyder, S. (1989–1990). Battelle Developmental Inventory and the Battelle Developmental Inventory Screening Test. *Diagnostique, 15,* 16–30.

Smith, A. J., & Johnson, R. E. (1977). *Smith-Johnson Nonverbal Performance Scale.* Los Angeles: Western Psychological Services.

Snyder, P., Lawson, S., Thompson, B., Stricklin, S., & Sexton, D. (1993). Evaluating the psychometric integrity of instruments used in early intervention research: The Battelle Developmental Inventory. *Topics in Early Childhood Special Education, 13*(2), 216–232.

Stillman, R. (1978). *The Callier-Azusa Scale.* Dallas, TX: South Central Regional Center for Services to Deaf-Blind Children.

Stutsman, R. (1931). *Mental measurement of preschool children.* New York: World Book.

Taylor, R. L. (1993). *Assessment of exceptional students: Educational and psychological procedures* (3rd ed.). Boston: Allyn and Bacon.

Telzrow, C. F. (1984). Practical applications of the K-ABC in the identification of handicapped preschoolers. *The Journal of Special Education, 18,* 311–324.

Thorndike, R. L., Hagen, E. P., & Sattler, J. M. (1985). *Stanford-Binet Intelligence Scale: Fourth Edition*. Chicago: Riverside Publishing Company.

Thurlow, M. L, Ysseldyke, J. E., & Silverstein, B. (1993). *Testing accommodations for students with disabilities: A review of the literature (Synthesis Report 4).* Minneapolis: National Center on Educational Outcomes, University of Minnesota.

Tzuriel, D., & Klein, P. S. (1987). Assessing the young child: Children's analogical thinking modifiability. In C. S. Lidz (Ed.), *Dynamic assessment: An interactional approach to evaluating learning potential*. New York: Guilford.

Uzgiris, I., & Hunt, J. McV. (1975). *Assessment in infancy: Ordinal scales of psychological development*. Urbana: University of Illinois Press.

Venn, J., & Dykes, M. K. (1987). Assessment of the physically handicapped. In W. H. Berdine & S. A. Meyer (Eds.), *Assessment in special education* (pp. 278–308). Boston: Little, Brown.

Vulpé, S. G. (1977). *Vulpé Assessment Battery*. Toronto: National Institute of Mental Retardation.

Wachs, T., & Sheehan, R. (1988). *Assessment of young developmentally disabled children*. New York: Plenum Press.

Wechsler, D. (1974). *Manual for the Wechsler Intelligence Scales for Children–Revised*. San Antonio, TX: The Psychological Corp.

Wechsler, D. (1989). *Wechsler Preschool and Primary Scales of Intelligence–Revised*. San Antonio, TX: The Psychological Corp.

Wechsler, D. (1991). *Wechsler Intelligence Scale for Children–III.* San Antonio, TX: The Psychology Corp.

Witt, J. C., Elliott, S. N., Kramer, J. J., & Gresham, F. M. (1994). *Assessment of children: Fundamental methods and practices*. Dubuque, IA: Brown and Benchmark.

Woodcock, R. W., & Johnson, M. B. (1989). *Woodcock-Johnson Psychoeducational Battery–Revised*. Allen, TX: DLM.

CHAPTER

11

Assessing Motor Skills

Susan R. Harris
University of British Columbia
Irene R. McEwen
University of Oklahoma Health Sciences Center

Assessment of motor skills in young children who are at risk for motor disabilities or who demonstrate developmental motor delays is often conducted by pediatric physical or occupational therapists who have received specialized training in early identification or early intervention. Early childhood special education teachers should also be trained to administer standardized tools for screening or assessment of motor skills. The goal of this chapter is to provide an overview of current approaches to motor assessment that should be useful to a variety of early intervention professionals, including special education teachers, physical and occupational therapists, and paraprofessionals who work with young children with special needs.

In the initial portion of the chapter, the rationale for assessing motor skills will be discussed, including the interrelationships among motor, cognitive, and communication skills. Three different types of assessment indices will be presented, followed by a discussion of the various domains of motor assessment. The next section of the chapter will examine procedural considerations, including the purpose of the assessment, the test environment, the child's age, and the degree of family involvement in selecting the specific test or assessment strategy. As a framework for examining different purposes of motor assessment, the World Health Organization's International Classification for Impairment, Disability, and Handicap (1980) will be described in this section.

Representative methods of motor assessment will be presented next, including examples of tests that attempt to *predict* later motor performance, as well as standardized, norm-referenced tools that are designed to *discriminate* children with motor delay from those who are typically developing. Measurement strategies for evaluating change in motor performance are described, including several recently published tools that are designed to be *evaluative* in nature.

The final section of the chapter will illustrate how motor assessment information can be translated into functional motor goals for young children with special needs. Both the team process in determining functional goals and family participation in selecting intervention outcomes will be highlighted.

RATIONALE FOR ASSESSING MOTOR SKILLS

Developmental motor milestones provide a clinical correlate for the underlying maturation of the central nervous system (CNS). Because motor skills are easy to observe and often serve as important developmental landmarks during the first year of life, it is important to assess their acquisition. Most parents or caregivers can remember the ages of attainment of important motor milestones such as when their baby first rolled over, sat independently, or walked. Delays in acquisition of these milestones may serve as the first sign of more global developmental delays or of delays in different domains, such as later mental retardation (von Wendt, Makinen, & Rantakallio, 1984). Delayed motor milestones, therefore, may serve as an indicator of an existing developmental delay or as a predictor of later developmental differences in other domains.

It may be important to assess other motor behaviors, such as primitive reflexes, in evaluating the presence of CNS immaturity or damage. Primitive reflexes are coordinated patterns of movement that are demonstrated spontaneously or elicited by external stimuli (Crutchfield & Barnes, 1993) such as a loud noise or change of position of the head in space. They occur in typically developing infants but gradually disappear during the first year of life (see Table 11.1). Retention of primitive reflexes, such as the asymmetrical tonic neck reflex (ATNR), beyond the time when they should typically disappear may be important in the early diagnosis of some types of cerebral palsy (Harris, 1987b), as well as in disorders often associated with mental retardation, such as fetal alcohol syndrome (FAS) (Harris, Osborn, Weinberg, Loock, & Junaid, 1993).

Delays in attainment of motor skills occur in children who are typically served in early intervention settings, such as those with Down syndrome or cerebral palsy, as well as in those with less prevalent and often difficult-to-diagnose disabilities, such as Prader-Willi syndrome or Duchenne muscular dystrophy (Dubowitz, 1980). Thus, the assessment of motor skills may be important diagnostically because delays in the attainment of important motor milestones may be the first observable manifestation of a variety of developmental disabilities. Again—delayed attainment of motor milestones may serve as a discriminative index or as an initial screen to alert the parent or the examiner to the need for conducting a more comprehensive assessment of the child in a variety of different domains.

TABLE 11.1
Terms Sometimes Used in Motor Assessment of Infants and Preschoolers

Term	Definition
Automatic reactions or movements	Coordinated patterns of movement that occur in response to a stimulus, such as reactions that maintain balance (equilibrium reactions) or align the head and body (righting reactions). May include primitive reflexes, below (Palisano, 1993a).
Distal	Farthest away from the center of the body, such as the hand is distal to the elbow.
Force production	Muscle performance that produces movement or stability at a joint. Force is necessary for movement. Force = mass × acceleration (Campbell, 1991; Mayhew & Rothstein, 1985).
Muscle tone	Tension or stiffness of muscles at rest; resistance to quick passive movement. Stiffness may be abnormally high (hypertonia), low (hypotonia), or fluctuating. Muscle tone varies with position and activity. It is unclear how passive stiffness at rest relates to active movement (Palisano, 1993a).
Postural control	Regulation of the body's position in space for stability and orientation. *Stability* (or balance) maintains or regains the position of the body over the base of support. *Orientation* aligns the body parts in relation to one another, so they are appropriate for the movement or task being accomplished (Shumway-Cook & Woollacott, 1993).
Primary, early, or primitive reflexes	Coordinated patterns of movement demonstrated spontaneously by normally developing infants that may also be elicited by external stimuli. Examples include the rooting, Moro, and asymmetrical tonic neck reflexes (Crutchfield & Barnes, 1993).
Proximal	Nearest to the center of the body, such as the shoulder is proximal to the elbow.
Range of motion	Movement of a joint through its possible extent, such as from full flexion to full extension. Movement may be either active (by the child) or passive (by someone else).
Spasticity	Excessive muscle stiffness (hypertonus) resulting from a combination of central nervous system damage, and the passive viscoelastic properties of muscle and connective tissue (Campbell, 1991; Palisano, 1993a).

The interrelationship of motor skills to other areas of development, such as cognitive, communication, and social domains, is another reason that it is important to assess a child's motor abilities. The influence of movement on other aspects of development, particularly cognitive development, was emphasized by Piaget, who postulated that "all intelligence has as its source the infant's motor actions on the environment" (Ramey, Breitmayer, & Goldman, 1984, p. 243). The impact of movement (or the child's innate motor abilities) on other aspects of development is particularly important during the first 2 years of life, or what Piaget has termed the *sensorimotor phase* (Gallahue, 1989).

For children with motor impairments or delays, movement and environmental exploration may be compromised, suggesting that other aspects of development, such as communication and self-initiated interactions, may be hindered as well (Butler, 1986). Therefore it is important not only to assess motor milestones per se, but also to assess functional motor skills, such as patterns of locomotion or methods used to acquire mobility in the environment (Haley, Coster, Ludlow, Haltiwanger, & Andrellos, 1992). Motor assessments conducted in early childhood special education settings should not be limited to the use of norm-referenced tools designed to examine the attainment of motor milestones, but should be broadened to include assessment of the children's abilities to move in their environment, to act on their environment, and to make meaningful use of information from their environmental interactions. With these different goals in mind, three different types of motor assessment indices will be discussed in further detail in the next section.

TYPES OF ASSESSMENT INDICES

In their methodological framework for assessing health indices, Kirshner and Guyatt (1985) described three different types of measures or indices: discriminative, predictive, and evaluative. This same framework can be applied to the assessment of motor skills in infants at risk for motor impairments as well as the assessment of young children with identified motor disabilities or delays.

A *discriminative index* can be used to distinguish between children with or without a particular characteristic (Rosenbaum, 1992). Scores on norm-referenced tests of motor milestones, such as the Motor Scale of the Bayley Scales of Infant Development–II (Bayley, 1993) or the Peabody Developmental Motor Scales (Folio & Fewell, 1983), enable the assessor to distinguish whether or not a child has a motor delay based on his or her chronological age.

A *predictive index* allows for classification of individuals, either concurrently or prospectively, by comparison with established criteria for the purpose of determining the correctness of the original classification (Law, 1987). For example, Bleck developed a scale for preschool children with cerebral palsy that could be used to predict their ambulation status at age 7 years (Bleck, 1975). The ability of the Movement Assessment of Infants (Chandler, Andrews, & Swanson, 1980) (a neuromotor instrument that has been used extensively in the assessment of premature infants) to predict later cerebral palsy has been examined retrospectively (Harris, 1987a; Harris, 1989).

An *evaluative measure* is used to assess change over time or change as the result of intervention (Kirshner & Guyatt, 1985). One exciting new tool that has been developed to detect small changes in gross motor function over time in children with cerebral palsy is the Gross Motor Function Measure (GMFM) (Russell et al., 1990).

All three types of indices are important in assessing motor skills in different types of early intervention settings. Although predictive measures may be used more commonly in clinical studies involving longitudinal follow-up of infants at high risk for neuromotor disabilities, such as cerebral palsy, both discriminative and evaluative measures of motor skills are important in assessing children with special needs in typical early intervention settings, such as integrated preschools.

DOMAINS OF MOTOR ASSESSMENT

The three areas that typically comprise the assessment of motor skills are gross motor, fine motor, and oral-motor domains. Traditionally, these terms have been used to describe or differentiate components or subscales within tests of motor milestones, such as the Gross Motor and Fine Motor Scales of the Peabody Developmental Motor Scales (Folio & Fewell, 1983). More recently, however, the terms have been used to describe criterion-referenced tests that examine more detailed aspects of gross motor performance, such as the Gross Motor Function Measure (Russell et al., 1990).

Gross motor skills typically refer to activities that involve the large muscles of the body, including the neck and trunk muscles and proximal muscles of the limbs. Gross motor developmental milestones include rolling, creeping, walking, and running. Functional gross motor activities might include transferring (e.g., from wheelchair to toilet) and various methods of locomotion. Fine motor skills involve the use of the smaller and more distal muscles, particularly the muscles of the arms and hands. Fine motor developmental milestones include reaching, grasping, and releasing. Functional fine motor activities include eating, drinking, and writing. Oral-motor skills involve the use of the lips, mouth, tongue, teeth, and facial and jaw muscles. Oral-motor developmental milestones include sucking, swallowing, biting, and chewing. Functional oral-motor skills include eating and talking.

In determining the appropriate tool or method for assessing motor skills, a number of procedural considerations, such as the level of the disability, the purpose of the assessment, the test location and environment, the child's age, and the degree of family involvement, must be addressed. These procedural considerations will be discussed in the next section of the chapter.

PROCEDURAL CONSIDERATIONS

Level of Disability

An important consideration in the selection of the appropriate assessment tool or instrument is the level of disability at which the assessment is aimed. A common and universal method of classifying disabling conditions into different levels (disease, impairment, disability, handicap) is the World Health Organization's International Classification of Impairments, Disabilities, and Handicaps (ICIDH), which was published in 1980.

According to the ICIDH system, disease is represented as "any pathologic process associated with a characteristic and identifiable set of symptoms and signs" (Jette, 1989, p. 968). In describing a 4-year-old girl with spinal muscular atrophy (SMA) of intermediate severity (Dubowitz, 1980), for example, the diagnosis of SMA would constitute the disease. The second level or category in the ICIDH classification system is impairment, defined by Jette (1989) as "any loss or abnormality of psychologic, physiologic, or anatomic structure within a specific organ or system of the body" (p. 968). The weakness, hypotonia, and muscle wasting that accompany SMA would be considered impairments. The third level in the classification system is disability, defined as the loss of or restriction in ability to accomplish daily activities in the normal or typical manner. The inability to walk, a characteristic that typifies a child with intermediate-level SMA, would be considered a disability.

The final element of the ICIDH is handicap, "a disadvantage that limits or prevents an individual's fulfillment of a role that is normal"

(Jette, 1989, p. 968). Because the normal role for a preschool-age child is to play with other children, the inability of this child to run and play tag at the community playground, for example, might be considered a handicap for her. However, if modifications in the game of tag were made so that this little girl could use her powered wheelchair to compete, the disability (inability to walk) would no longer result in a handicap.

The ICIDH system has been modified slightly and expanded by the National Center for Medical Rehabilitation Research (NCMRR) of the National Institutes of Health (Research Plan for the National Center for Medical Rehabilitation Research, 1993). The NCMRR classification system contains five domains: pathophysiology, impairment, functional limitations, disability, and societal limitations. The first four correspond to the four levels of the ICIDH system. Societal limitations, the fifth domain, have been defined as "restrictions attributable to social policy or barriers (structural or attitudinal) which limit fulfillment of roles or deny access to services and opportunities associated with full participation in society" (Research Plan for the NCMRR, 1993, p. 38). These five domains are displayed in Figure 11.1.

To continue the example of the 4-year-old girl with SMA—if the community playground surface was rough or uneven and it was impossible for her to maneuver her powered wheelchair on it so that she could play with other children, it would be considered a societal limitation. Use of a disability classification scheme, as in either the ICIDH or NCMRR model, is an important dimension to consider in deciding what type of motor assessment to use.

With reference to these models, a compelling reason for having a thorough knowledge of a disorder is to understand its expected effect on impairment, disability, and handicap. In the case of the little girl with SMA, for example, the proximal muscles of the neck, trunk, shoulders, and hips are more impaired by weakness and wasting than the distal muscles are. This impairment results in relatively greater gross motor disability (with relatively intact fine motor abilities). If one were to use a norm-referenced test of gross motor milestones to assess this child's ability to walk, it could be assumed that her inability to walk might be considered a handicap that would limit the exploration of her environment. However, if one assessed her fine motor abilities to maneuver a switch and could generalize those presumed skills into the use of a joystick to control a powered wheelchair, she would no longer be seen as having a handicap.

To use another example that would affect the type of motor assessment to be used, consider a young child with quadriplegia (paralysis of upper and lower extremities and trunk) secondary to spinal cord injury or spinal cord tumor at the level of C-5 or C-6 (fifth or sixth cervical level lesion). A child with this condition would have no use of the lower extremities and virtually no functional use of the upper extremities or, essentially, no gross motor or fine motor skills. The one domain that would be relatively spared would be the oral-motor domain. In this case, assessment could be aimed at analyzing the oral-motor abilities of the child to use a

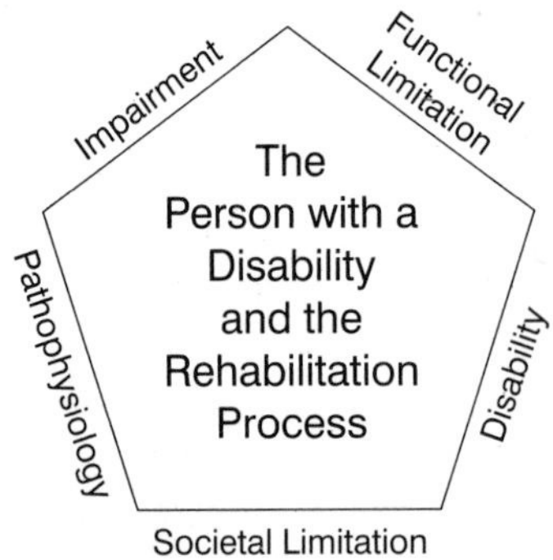

FIGURE 11.1
The domains of science relevant to medical rehabilitation.
Source: From *Research Plan for the National Center for Medical Rehabilitation Research* (p. 34), 1993, Bethesda, MD: National Institutes of Health. Copyright 1993 by the National Institutes of Health. Reprinted by permission.

mouth-stick to control a powered wheelchair for independent mobility. The use of a test of gross motor or fine motor developmental milestones would obviously be inappropriate for a child with such a variety of profound physical impairments; however, a functional assessment of oral-motor skills (as they pertained to the use of a mouth-stick) could be extremely relevant.

Purpose of the Assessment

Before beginning to assess a child's motor skills, the purpose of the assessment must be established. In early identification of developmental disabilities, such as in a follow-up clinic for infants at risk for neuromotor disabilities, the purposes of motor assessment will most likely be discriminative or predictive. A discriminative test, such as the Bayley Scales of Infant Development (Bayley, 1969; Bayley, 1993), is often used to identify infants with cognitive or motor delays (Harris et al., 1993), whereas a predictive test, such as the Movement Assessment of Infants (Chandler et al., 1980), may be more sensitive in predicting later cerebral palsy (Harris, 1987a).

In early intervention settings in which the child's motor delays or functional movement limitations have already been identified, the purpose of assessment is to monitor change over time. Therefore, an evaluative measure such as the Gross Motor Function Measure (Russell et al., 1990) or the Pediatric Evaluation of Disability Inventory (Haley et al., 1992) would be most appropriate. Other evaluative measures that have been used in motor outcomes research and that are very appropriate for use in early intervention settings include individualized therapy objectives (Harris, 1981) and goal-attainment scaling (Palisano, Haley, & Brown, 1992; Palisano, 1993b). Each of these evaluative measures is discussed in more detail in the following section on Representative Methods.

It is crucial that assessment instruments be used only for their intended purpose (Rosenbaum et al., 1990). The use of norm-referenced tests to evaluate change in an individual child as a result of motor intervention, such as physical or occupational therapy, does not make logical sense in that these measures are typically designed to be discriminative in nature. Similarly, an evaluative measure, such as the GMFM, cannot be used to predict later motor performance in a preschool child with cerebral palsy. In assessing motor skills, examiners should be familiar with the test's purpose and should use the test *only* for that purpose—in an effort to ensure that the test results are both meaningful and valid.

Age of the Child

One of the most important procedural considerations in selecting an appropriate motor skills assessment is the child's age. Each of the published motor assessment tools specifies the age range for which the test is appropriate. Although a specific chronological age range is provided, many test developers encourage the use of the test for children whose developmental motor skills fall within the age range even if the children are chronologically older than the test's upper limit. In the new Bayley–II, for example, it is explained that the test may be administered to children who are older than 42 months, providing that their developmental skills fall within the 1- to 42-month range. It will not be possible to determine a *developmental index* for a child who falls outside the age range of children on whom the test was normed, but it will be possible to determine a mental or motor *developmental age* for that child (Bayley, 1993). Similarly, Haley and colleagues (1992) suggest that the Pediatric Evaluation of Disability Inventory can be used for the functional evaluation of a child who is chronologically older than the 7.5-year upper limit, providing that the child's "functional abilities fall below that expected of 7.5-year-old children with no disabilities" (Haley et al., 1992, p. 3).

For children born at less than or equal to 37 weeks' gestation, it is important to "correct for prematurity" in determining the child's corrected or adjusted age; typical gestation is 38 to 42 weeks in length. Unfortunately, there are different methods for conducting this procedure, which can result in slightly different corrected ages. In the Movement Assessment of Infants manual, corrected age is calculated by subtracting the days of prematurity (number of weeks born prematurely × 7 days) from the child's current chronological age (Chandler et al., 1980). In the Bayley–II manual, the instructions are to subtract the number of months and days that the child was born early from the current chronological age (Bayley, 1993).

Regardless of the method used, it is extremely important to adjust for prematurity in all children who were born at less than or equal to 37 weeks' gestation. Correction for prematurity is particularly important during the early childhood years. The child's adjusted age may be several months younger than his or her chronological age, and this can make a dramatic difference when interpreting the norm-referenced developmental scores on different standardized tests. It is also important for parents of children born prematurely to learn to base their developmental expectations on the child's corrected age rather than on his or her chronological age.

Involvement of Family in Selecting Motor Assessments

As with all types of early childhood assessments, the child's family should be involved in the decision-making process of selecting appropriate tools or measures for assessing the child's motor skills (see Chapter 3). Once again, professionals are responsible for discussing with families the purposes of the assessment before proceeding with the selection of appropriate measures.

Because parents of children who are new to early identification or early intervention settings will most likely be unfamiliar with the variety of motor tests available, it is the responsibility of the physical or occupational therapist or teacher to explain the purposes and goals of the various assessment tools.

In addition to assisting in the selection of an appropriate norm-referenced or criterion-referenced motor assessment tool, a family-centered evaluation includes observation of the child's motor skills during play and activities of daily living, either in the home, in the classroom, or in some other natural environment (Chiarello, Effgen, & Levinson, 1992). Families themselves identify priorities and concerns regarding their child's functional motor capabilities in the areas of play, mobility, eating, toileting, dressing, and other areas of self-care (Chiarello et al., 1992).

Chiarello and colleagues (1992) have outlined the various steps that occur in providing parent-professional partnerships during the evaluation process with young children (see Table 11.2). This type of collaborative and family-centered approach is as important to the assessment of motor skills as it is to assessment in the other developmental domains.

Threats to Reliability and Validity

As with all types of assessments, there are a number of factors that may affect the reliability or consistency of the test results when assessing a child's motor skills. These generic threats to reliability include fatigue or illness of the child, unfamiliarity with the examiner or the test environment, and the length of the test. In addition, there are specific threats to a test's validity that must be considered when assessing a child with a neuromotor disability.

Children with neuromotor disabilities that are relatively common in early intervention settings, such as cerebral palsy or meningomyelocele, frequently have impairments that may

TABLE 11.2
Parent-Professional Partnership in the Evaluation Process

Initial Contact	Development of Evaluation Plan	Child and Family Evaluation	Development of IFSP
Exchange information Discuss concerns of parents Obtain written parental consent to conduct screening and evaluation Conduct screening of children/family Determine if child and family are eligible for evaluation	Establish service coordinator Determine areas to be evaluated Select evaluation instruments Determine which professionals will be involved Determine method of evaluation Select location, dates, and timeline	Perform: Interview Survey Observation Standardized evaluations Determine child's current level of functioning Identify family priorities, concerns, and resources Write up evaluation findings	Exchange information Prioritize child's needs in collaboration with family's priorities Translate needs and strengths into outcomes Determine intervention services including frequency, intensity, and method Develop intervention strategies Plan ongoing assessment and program evaluation Reestablish service coordinator Write IFSP Provide plans for smooth transition between early intervention and preschool services

Source: From "Parent-Professional Partnership in Evaluation and Development of Individualized Family Service Plans" by L. Chiarello, S. Effgen, and M. Levinson, 1992, *Pediatric Physical Therapy, 4,* 64–69. Reprinted by permission.

adversely affect their performance on standardized tests in other domains, such as the Mental Scale of the Bayley Scales of Infant Development. Tone differences, such as spasticity or fluctuating tone, and upper extremity coordination difficulties are extremely common. (See Table 11.1 for definitions of these and other terms sometimes used in motor assessment.) In tests of "mental" abilities that require both speed and accuracy for completion of some of the items (e.g., placing pegs in a pegboard in 22 seconds), the child with a neuromotor disability will be penalized because of the tone and coordination differences. In other words, the test score will not be a valid indicator of the child's true cognitive abilities.

Early childhood special educators must be cautious about the use and interpretation of tests of cognitive or communication abilities for children with neuromotor impairments. Involvement of a physical therapist or an occupational therapist in the assessment of skills in other domains (e.g., cognitive or speech/language) will assist in determining when the child's performance is compromised by a neuromotor impairment.

Test Environment

The choice of the test environment depends in part on the purpose of the test. In attempting to discriminate the presence or degree of motor delays, it is most logical to use a norm-referenced, standardized test, such as the Peabody Developmental Motor Scales (Folio & Fewell, 1983) or the Motor Scale of the Bayley Scales of Infant Development (Bayley, 1993). When administering a standardized test, one must use standardized test materials and conduct the assessment in a standardized fashion. For such purposes, a clinical setting may be more satisfactory than the child's natural environment. When evaluating the child's functional mobility skills, as with the Pediatric Evaluation of Disability Inventory, the child's natural environment is preferable.

Many motor assessments, particularly those that are administered for purposes of discrimination or prediction, take place in clinical settings such as university-affiliated child development centers or out-patient medical clinics. However, there is increased emphasis on conducting these assessments in more natural environments, such as the child's home, classroom, or community playground. As early as 1977, it was suggested that motor abilities of children with severe and profound handicaps were best assessed in natural environments (Sternat, Messina, Nietupski, Lyon, & Brown, 1977). Assumptions were that assessments in the child's natural environment provided "a more valid representation of general motoric functioning" and could then facilitate integration of therapy activities into the daily routine (Sternat et al., 1977, p. 265).

Once again, the purpose of the test will influence the choice of the assessment setting. Evaluative measures, in particular, are most appropriately administered in the natural setting. Norm-referenced, discriminative tests, however, must be administered in a standardized fashion, which often entails the use of standardized testing equipment that may only be available in a clinical setting (e.g., the Bayley stairs). In assessing children longitudinally for predictive purposes, such as in a high-risk infant follow-up clinic, the use of a standardized clinical setting will enhance the reliability or consistency of the measurement environment.

Regardless of the purpose of the assessment, the environment should be set up to facilitate the child's optimal performance. In a standardized clinical testing situation, environmental distractions such as nonstandardized toys, unexpected noises or visual stimuli, and the presence of siblings or other children should be minimized. In a natural environment, such as the home, classroom, or playground, these types of distractions are a normal part of the environment and should be included. The child's functional motor capabilities are better assessed in a natural, integrated setting, complete with real-world environmental stimuli, noises, and activities of daily living. A child who can ascend and descend the Bayley stairs independently but who is unable to climb the front-porch steps at home will succeed in the clinical setting but not in the real world. Assessment of motor skills in both types of environments is important for gaining an overall picture of the child's true abilities.

REPRESENTATIVE METHODS

Most tests of motor performance for infants and young children were designed to detect impairments or functional limitations (Campbell, 1993). These tools, whether norm- or criterion-referenced, sample motor behaviors that children of various ages are expected to be able to perform. A few tests examine aspects of motor impairment, such as postural control, force production, muscle tone, and primitive reflexes (see Table 11.1 for definitions of these terms), and there are a limited number of disability-level tools.

As discussed previously, the type of tool selected depends on the reason for the evaluation or assessment: (a) to predict future motor abilities, (b) to discriminate among children with and without motor problems, and (c) to evaluate change in motor performance (S. K. Campbell, 1991; Kirshner & Guyatt, 1985). As noted in Chapter 1, assessment is another type of appraisal that, as defined by Part H of the Individuals with Disabilities Education Act, is used to gain information for program planning purposes. Evaluation information may or may not be helpful for planning intervention for children with motor problems.

Tests That Attempt to Predict Future Motor Performance

Tests designed to predict future performance are most often used to evaluate young infants who are at risk for neuromotor dysfunction, but whose motor problems are not yet apparent. For the most part, these tests attempt to detect early signs of motor impairments that could later result in functional limitations and disability. A major problem, however, is that research has largely failed to support the capacity of any currently available evaluation tools to predict motor skills or problems of an individual infant (Campbell, 1993).

The Movement Assessment of Infants (MAI) (Chandler et al., 1980), which is one of the most widely used tools designed to identify children who will later be diagnosed as having cerebral palsy, is a 65-item test that evaluates four aspects of motor development during the first year of life. Examination of muscle tone, primitive reflexes, and automatic reactions addresses impairment level functions, while the volitional movement section looks at functional limitations in gross and fine motor behaviors. The MAI is usually administered by an occupational or physical therapist who has good knowledge of typical and atypical infant development and experience assessing infants' motor behaviors.

The MAI provides a total risk score and a risk score in each of the four sections, which for 4- and 8-month-old infants can be compared with risk profiles of infants who were later diagnosed to have motor dysfunction. In a retrospective study of 153 low-birthweight infants, Harris compared the ability of the 4-month MAI total risk scores and the Bayley Motor Scale (Bayley, 1969) to identify infants who were eventually found to have cerebral palsy (Harris, 1987a). The MAI identified 73.5% of children with cerebral palsy, compared with 35.3% for the Bayley. The ability of a test to correctly identify children who will have the disability is called *sensitivity* (Stangler, Huber, & Routh, 1980); therefore, the MAI was more than twice as sensitive as the Bayley Motor Scale in detecting early signs of cerebral palsy. The Bayley Motor Scale, however, was better at identifying infants who would have normal motor outcomes (the specificity of a test); the specificity of the Bayley Motor Scale was 94.9% as compared with 62.7% for the MAI.

New evaluation tools are currently being developed to examine aspects of motor performance; preliminary data indicate that the new tests are better able to predict motor outcomes for an individual infant than tests that are presently available. One of these new tools, the Test of Infant Motor Performance (TIMP), examines postural control and alignment needed for functional movement of infants between 32 weeks gestational age and 3.5 months (Campbell, 1993).

Tests Used to Identify Children with Motor Delays

Most of the norm-referenced tests that can identify children who have motor delays are used to provide test scores necessary to document children's eligibility for early intervention or special education services. Such instruments rarely provide information useful for planning or evaluating intervention programs, especially for children with moderate or severe delays. They are also poor predictors of the future motor development of young infants (Bayley, 1969; Campbell, 1993).

Any team member can learn to administer most developmental tests and determine whether or not a child's motor performance is delayed. Physical or occupational therapists, however, can often determine not only *if* the child has delays, but by observing *how* the child performs test items, can determine *what* is contributing to the delays. Motor delays might be caused by such motor-related factors as inadequate strength, coordination, balance, flexibility, or motor planning abilities, but cognition, emotions, and other related developmental domains can also have an important impact on motor performance. Knowing simply that a child's motor performance is delayed compared with that of other children of the same age is usually not helpful for planning intervention programs; understanding what is preventing the child from performing age-level skills is much more important.

There are many tests whose reliability and validity have been determined to be adequate for evaluating the developmental performance of infants and preschoolers. Only a few will be described briefly in this chapter. Readers interested in additional details or information about other tests are referred to Chandler (1990), Stengel (1992), and Wilhelm (1993).

The Bayley Scales of Infant Development (Bayley, 1969) is one of the most widely used norm-referenced tests for evaluating both the mental and motor development of infants. Both the original test and the new Bayley–II (1993) have separate Mental and Motor Scales. The Bayley also includes an Infant Behavior Record, which was revised substantially and renamed the Behavior Rating Scale for the Bayley–II. The Bayley–II has updated normative data on 1,700 children and a number of new items. The age range has been expanded to cover infants and children from 1 to 42 months. The test manual indicates that professionals who administer the test should have training and experience in the administration and interpretation of comprehensive developmental tests, as well as experience in testing children whose ages and clinical or cultural backgrounds are similar to those they will be testing.

The Revised Gesell and Amatruda Developmental and Neurological Examination (Knobloch, Stevens, & Malone, 1987), another test that is widely used to evaluate the development of infants and toddlers, is descended from the pioneering observations of Arnold Gesell in the 1920s, whose work also provided the basis for many other developmental tests that are in use today. The revised Gesell has norms for children aged 4 weeks to 36 months in five domains of development: adaptive, gross motor, fine motor, language, and personal-social. The gross motor items assess postural reactions and developmental skills such as sitting and locomotion. The fine motor items assess reach, grasp, and manipulation. The Gesell takes approximately 30 minutes to administer and can be given by teachers, occupational and physical therapists, physicians, psychologists, and other members of early intervention or early childhood teams.

The Alberta Infant Motor Scale (AIMS) (Piper & Darrah, 1993) is a new tool that was designed to identify motor delay in infants, determine the severity of the delay, and monitor change in motor development. The AIMS provides a structure for observation of infants in various postural positions corresponding to the test's prone, supine, sit, and stand subscales. Normative data are provided for more than 2,000 infants, and percentile ranks can be determined. The AIMS was developed for administration by professionals with background in infant motor development and skill in observing components of movement.

The Peabody Developmental Motor Scales (PDMS) (Folio & Fewell, 1983) separately evaluate gross and fine motor performance and provide norms for children from birth to 83 months of age. The Gross Motor Scale is subdivided into five skill categories, including reflexes, balance, nonlocomotor, locomotor, and receipt and propulsion of objects. The Fine Motor Scale is subdivided into grasping, hand use, eye-hand coordination, and manual dexterity. In his review of several developmental tests, Palisano (1993a) concluded that the PDMS provides a more in-depth evaluation of motor performance than many other instruments.

Each PDMS scale takes approximately 20 to 30 minutes to administer and can be given on different days if a child is unable to complete 40 to 60 minutes of testing at one time. It can be administered by teachers, therapists, and other members of early intervention or preschool teams. In addition to being a norm-referenced evaluation tool, the PDMS can be a curriculum-referenced assessment when it is used in conjunction with a set of activity cards. Until recently, the activity cards were available only with the test kit, but they can now be purchased separately.

The Battelle Developmental Inventory (Newborg, Stock, Wnek, Guidubaldi, & Svinicki, 1984) is a comprehensive developmental evaluation that examines adaptive, cognitive, communication, motor, and personal-social skills. The BDI has norms for children aged 1 month to 9 years, an upper age limit that is above that of most other tools that can be used for infants. It takes about one hour to administer. Because of its limited number of motor items and small normative sample, Palisano (1993a) recommends that the BDI not be used for the purpose of diagnostic evaluation of infants. He suggests that it can be of value to determine eligibility for early intervention services, which is the primary value of all of the developmental tests designed to discriminate between children who do and who do not have delayed development. The BDI can be administered by a team of professionals or by an individual service provider.

The Transdisciplinary Play-Based Assessment (TPBA) (Linder, 1990) is a criterion-referenced tool that structures observations of the social-emotional, cognitive, language and communication, and sensorimotor domains of development. Observations are made by team members while the child plays with a facilitator, the parents, and a peer. The TPBA can be completed in 1 to 1½ hours.

The motor section of the TPBA focuses the observer's attention on the child's general appearance of movement; muscle tone, strength, and endurance; reactivity to sensory input; stationary play positions; mobility in play; other developmental achievements; prehension and manipulation; and motor planning. The author of the sensorimotor section (Hall, 1990) advises that an occupational or physical therapist assume responsibility for analyzing motor behaviors, but that another team member could gather motor information and refer the child to a therapist if necessary.

Linder (1990) suggests that the TBPA can be used to document eligibility for early intervention or special education services and may be of assistance in planning intervention programs and evaluating progress. The flexibility of the evaluation format, subjectivity of observations, and lack of reliability and validity data suggest caution, however, especially when using the TPBA to evaluate progress. The play-based format does appear to have unique potential for tapping a child's motor capabilities because behavior in a contextually and task-relevant play situation is more likely to represent typical or optimal levels of performance than testing under the artificial conditions required by most other evaluation instruments.

When using any of the widely available norm-referenced or criterion-referenced developmental tests designed to discriminate children with delayed motor development, it is important to remember that they were based primarily on the performance of children without disabilities. For this reason, although these tests can appropriately identify children whose development is delayed compared with that of most other children of the same age, they do not provide useful information about whether or not a child's development is typical of other children with the same disability. A noteworthy exception is the new Bayley–II (Bayley, 1993), which includes assessment data for samples of children with Down syndrome, children born prematurely, children with prenatal drug exposure, and children with autism. Other references have also provided ages at which certain motor skills can be accomplished for children with Down syndrome (Pueschel, 1990) and children with meningomyelocele (Sousa, Gordon, & Shurtleff, 1976).

Evaluation of Change in Motor Performance

Evaluation of change in a child's motor performance over time is another important purpose of motor evaluation. We expect a positive change in motor behaviors as a result of intervention, although maturation, the home environment, and a host of other factors may also influence a child's motor performance. If a child's motor deficits are mild and are relatively easily modified, it may be possible to detect improved performance by administering a developmental test used to discriminate children who have motor delays. Such tests, however, usually cannot detect change in children who have moderate or severe motor problems because there are relatively few items at each age level and developmental gaps between items are often large. Children with moderate and severe delays are usually unable to make progress to demonstrate change on developmental tests such as those described above.

An even greater problem with using developmental tests to determine whether or not intervention has been effective is that these tests do not examine a child's performance of functional activities in natural environments. Success of intervention must be evaluated by determining if a child's ability to perform meaningful skills in everyday environments improves (Fetters, 1991; Harris, 1991; McEwen, 1994). Contemporary theories of motor development and motor control maintain that motor behaviors are task- and context-dependent (Heriza, 1991). A child's improved performance on a developmental test does not necessarily mean that the improvement is meaningful to the child or that it will serve as a foundation for future motor skill development.

There are several methods by which infants' and children's acquisition of meaningful motor skills in natural environments can be evaluated. Methods that will be covered in this section include (a) tests designed specifically for children with disabilities that can be used both to aid in identifying skill deficits and to evaluate change; (b) use of behavioral objectives; (c) goal attainment scaling, a variation of a behavioral objective, which can detect even smaller gains; and (d) single-subject research methodologies that can easily be used in early intervention and early childhood settings to evaluate outcomes of intervention for individual children or small groups of children.

Tests for children with disabilities

The Gross Motor Function Measure (GMFM) (Russell et al., 1990) was designed for use by experienced pediatric therapists to evaluate change in the gross motor function of children with cerebral palsy. The criterion-referenced test contains items in five dimensions of motor performance that children without motor problems accomplish by the time they are 5 years old. These dimensions include lying and rolling; sitting, crawling, and kneeling; standing and walking; running; and jumping. The test can be administered in 45 to 60 minutes.

Because the GMFM is relatively new, it has been subjected to few reliability and validity studies. Palisano (1993a) suggests that it is best suited to children over the age of 2 years who can follow directions and have moderate to severe motor problems. The test is intended to detect slight change in gross motor skills, which may or may not relate to meaningful functional change for an individual child. A child may show improvement, for example, in kneeling or in sitting on a mat feet-first, neither of which is necessarily related to improvement in functional activities.

The Pediatric Evaluation of Disability Inventory (PEDI) (Haley et al., 1992), which was also developed specifically for children with disabilities, is a judgment-based evaluation of children's mobility, self-care, and social function. Haley, Baryza, and Blanchard (1993) distinguish judgment-based evaluations from criterion evaluations in that judgment-based evaluations do not require the evaluator to directly observe the child's behavior; rather, information about the child's abilities can be obtained from a parent, a teacher, a therapist, or another informant who knows the child well.

In addition to evaluating a child's performance of functional skills, the PEDI permits appraisal of the amount of caregiver assistance and environmental modification (such as use of walkers, bathtub rails, or other assistive equipment) that a child requires to perform functional tasks. Improvement may be demonstrated either by skill acquisition or by reduction in the amount of modification or assistance needed. The PEDI was designed for children between 6 months and 7.5 years. It can be administered by professionals with training in child development and experience with young children with disabilities. The PEDI manual recommends training in administration of the test, followed by practice with an experienced examiner.

Behavioral objectives A common method of evaluating whether a child's motor skills are improving is by monitoring accomplishment of behavioral objectives that lead to motor-related goals. If, for example, a child's goal is to go from the living room to her bedroom and get a toy out of her toy box, the task can be broken down into a series of activities that make up the goal. To develop behavioral objectives, five components of each activity are specified: *Who* will do *what,* under what *conditions, how well,* and by *when* (O'Neill & Harris, 1982).

In this example, one of the series of behavioral objectives might be "Tina will stand up from sitting on the floor without assistance five of five trials on five consecutive days by February 28, 199_." By comparing the child's performance with the objectives, it is relatively easy to determine if the child is progressing toward the goals in the projected time frame. Figure 11.2 illustrates a series of objectives that could have been developed for Tina to accomplish this motor-related goal. A method to determine meaningful functional goals is described later in this chapter in the section "Translating Assessment Information into Functional Goals."

If objectives are not being accomplished, they need to be examined, and the intervention, the objectives, and/or the time frame need to be modified. If it seems that the child should be able to accomplish the objectives but is not making the expected progress, the intervention may need to be modified. If the child is making steady progress but has not yet accomplished the objective, the time frame might need to be modified. If it seems that, given the most effective intervention, the child will be unable to accomplish an objective in a reasonable amount of time, more attainable objectives need to be identified. In some cases, it might not be necessary to change the goal. Tina, for example, might not be able to learn to walk from the living room to her bedroom to get

Outcome statement:	Tina will learn to play more independently.
Goal:	Tina will go from sitting on the living room floor to her bedroom and get a toy out of her toy box in 4 minutes or less on 5 consecutive days by May 17, 199_.
Objectives:	1. Tina will get a toy of her choice, after being assisted to stand beside her toy box, on 5 of 5 trials for 5 consecutive days by November 23, 199_.
	2. Tina will push open the door to her bedroom, while being assisted to walk from the hall to her toy box, on 5 of 5 trials for 5 consecutive days by December 15, 199_.
	3. Tina will stand up from sitting on the floor, 5 of 5 trials on 5 consecutive days by February 28, 199_.
	4. Tina will walk from the living room to her toy box 5 of 5 trials on 5 consecutive days by May 1, 199_.

FIGURE 11.2
Outcome statement, goal, and objectives for Tina, a 3-year-old with developmental delay

toys from her toy box. She might, however, be able to move around her home by learning to use a battery-powered car. Other goals and objectives related to standing and walking could be added at the present or a later time.

Goal-attainment scaling Goal-attainment scaling is a measure that is similar to a behavioral objective, but it permits more finely tuned assessment of motor outcomes (Palisano, 1993b). Goals are first identified that have all of the components of behavioral objectives, as described above. Then four additional outcomes for each objective are determined, two that exceed the goal and two that fall below it. By specifying goals both above and below a child's expected achievement, it is possible to assess a range of outcomes related to the same general goal (Palisano et al., 1992).

In the previous example, the behavioral objective was "Tina will stand up from sitting on the floor five of five trials on five consecutive days by February 28, 199_." This objective could be scaled and evaluated by goal-attainment scaling by adding four related objectives, as illustrated in Figure 11.3. When evaluating outcomes by use of goal-attainment scaling, a score of 0 is given if the child accomplishes the expected goal, +1 and +2 represent accomplishment of goals that exceed expectation, and -1 and -2 represent accomplishment of goals below expected levels (Palisano, 1993b). A change score can be calculated and expressed as a standard T-score, which is useful for examining the effectiveness of intervention across children or for assessing change across all goals of one child (Palisano et al., 1992).

Single-subject research methodologies Single-subject research methods can be as useful to service providers as they are to researchers to evaluate individually meaningful changes in children's motor skills. The advantage of single-subject research methods over simply retesting a child to evaluate change or observing whether or not a behavioral objective has been met is that single-subject research designs can help to determine if the intervention caused the change, rather than maturation or some other influence on motor skills. Single-subject designs can also help to identify which of two or more interventions is more effective in

Behavioral objective:	Tina will stand up from sitting on the floor, 5 of 5 trials on 5 consecutive days by February 28, 199_.
Goal attainment scaling:	Tina will crawl to the couch or other furniture and
	−2 put one hand on it (initial level of goal attainment)
	−1 pull to a kneeling position
	0 pull to a standing position
	+1 pull to a standing position and let go of the support
	Tina will
	+2 rise from the floor to a standing position without other support

FIGURE 11.3
Example of scaled objectives when using goal-attainment scaling to evaluate outcomes of intervention

improving a child's motor skills. Other characteristics of single-subject designs that make them useful in early intervention and early childhood programs are (a) they are easily used in natural settings, such as homes or classrooms; (b) they do not require control or comparison groups; (c) the data are graphed, so change or lack of change is often easy for parents and service providers to recognize; and (d) statistical analysis of data is usually not necessary (Barlow & Hersen, 1984).

Three basic single-subject research designs are the most common: A-B and withdrawal designs, multiple baseline designs, and alternating treatment designs. Each of these designs has many more variations and methods of interpretation than can be described in this chapter. An interested reader can find more information in Barlow and Hersen (1984), Ottenbacher (1986), and Wolery and Harris (1982).

A-B designs begin with a baseline phase, during which either there is no intervention or intervention is being provided that will be modified after baseline measures are complete. By convention, the *A* indicates a baseline phase of any single-subject design. During the baseline phase, data are collected and plotted on a graph until a line connecting the data points indicates that the data are stable.

Once the baseline is stable, the *B*, or intervention, phase begins. Intervention is initiated or modified and the behavior is again measured and data are plotted on a graph. If the plotted data show that the behavior changes after the intervention phase is begun (either a desirable behavior increases or an undesirable behavior decreases), it is possible that the intervention caused the change. With only one baseline and one intervention phase, however, the internal validity of the design is weak and various other factors, besides the intervention, could have caused the behavior change. To strengthen the internal validity, another baseline phase is added. This A-B-A design is also called a withdrawal design because the intervention is withdrawn to see if the behavior returns to baseline levels. If it does, there is reasonable assurance that the intervention caused the behavior change. A final intervention phase can be added, making it an A-B-A-B design, so that the successful intervention is again provided.

Horn, Warren, and Reith (1992) used an A-B-A-B design to examine motor skills of children with multiple disabilities. The motor skill measured was the children's use of a microswitch to activate a battery-powered toy under Condition A (behavioral teaching procedures) and Condition B (behavioral teaching procedures plus computer-mediated instruction and response-contingent toys). The graph in Figure 11.4 shows the averaged data across three children in each of two schools (Site 1 and Site 2). The data points indicate the percentage of 5-second intervals in which the children exhibited the motor behavior that activated the microswitch (such as sitting up straight) during each training session. The data graphs that under Condition A, the children exhibited the target motor behaviors during fewer of the 5-second intervals than they did when computer-mediated instruction and response-contingent toys were added to the instructional package.

The primary problem with A-B-A-B designs is that if the intervention results in permanent changes in motor behavior, which is what we usually intend, the behavior will not return to baseline levels once the intervention is withdrawn. If behavior is not expected to change when intervention is withdrawn, a multiple baseline design is another single-subject design that could be used. A multiple baseline design has A and B phases, but data are collected across two or more subjects, behaviors, or settings (Barlow & Hersen, 1984). By continuing to collect baseline data on the second and third behaviors while intervening on the first behavior, threats to internal

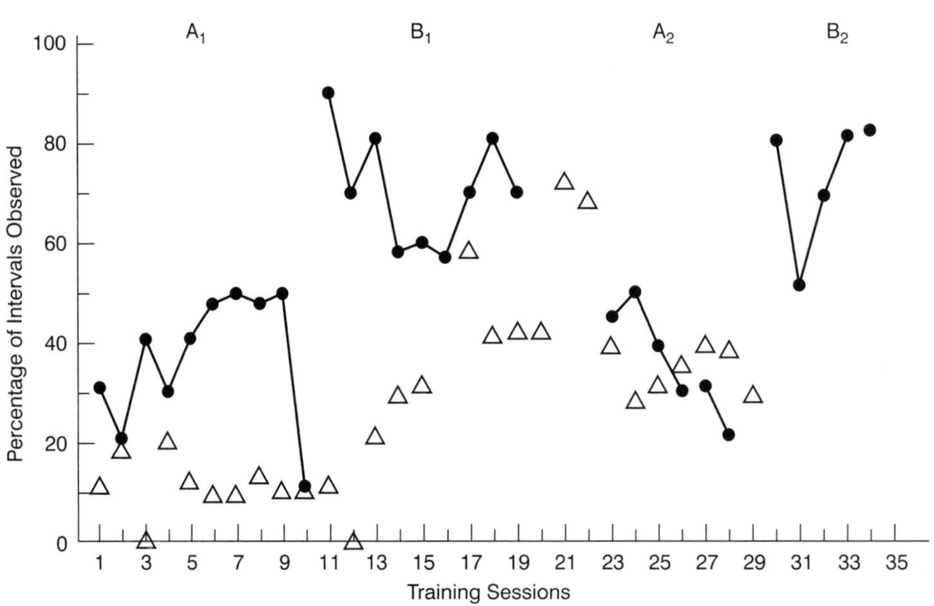

FIGURE 11.4
A single-subject A-B-A-B design showing the percentage of 5-second intervals in which children were performing their target motor behavior
Source: From "Effects of a Small Group Microcomputer-Mediated Motor Skills Instructional Package" by E. M. Horn, S. F. Warren, and H. J. Reith, 1992, *The Journal of The Association for Persons with Severe Handicaps, 17,* p. 139. Copyright 1992 by the Association for Persons with Severe Handicaps. Reprinted by permission.

validity are controlled and a cause-and-effect relationship can be established if baseline measures do not change until intervention is directly applied.

The third type of single-subject design is an alternating treatment design, in which two or more interventions are applied systematically, and effects are measured. Because effects must be reasonably immediate and strong, this type of design is not useful for assessing effects of interventions that take time to achieve measurable results. An alternating treatment design has been useful for assessing effects of assistive devices, as demonstrated by Harris and Riffle (1986), who compared standing balance of a child with cerebral palsy when he was wearing and was not wearing orthoses. Figure 11.5 shows first a baseline phase during which the child's standing balance when he was not wearing orthoses was measured in seconds, then an intervention phase during which the duration of his standing balance was measured with and without orthoses. As the graph indicates, the child was able to stand much longer when he was wearing the orthoses than when he was not.

McEwen and Karlan (1989) also used an alternating treatment design to evaluate the effect of assistive devices on motor behavior

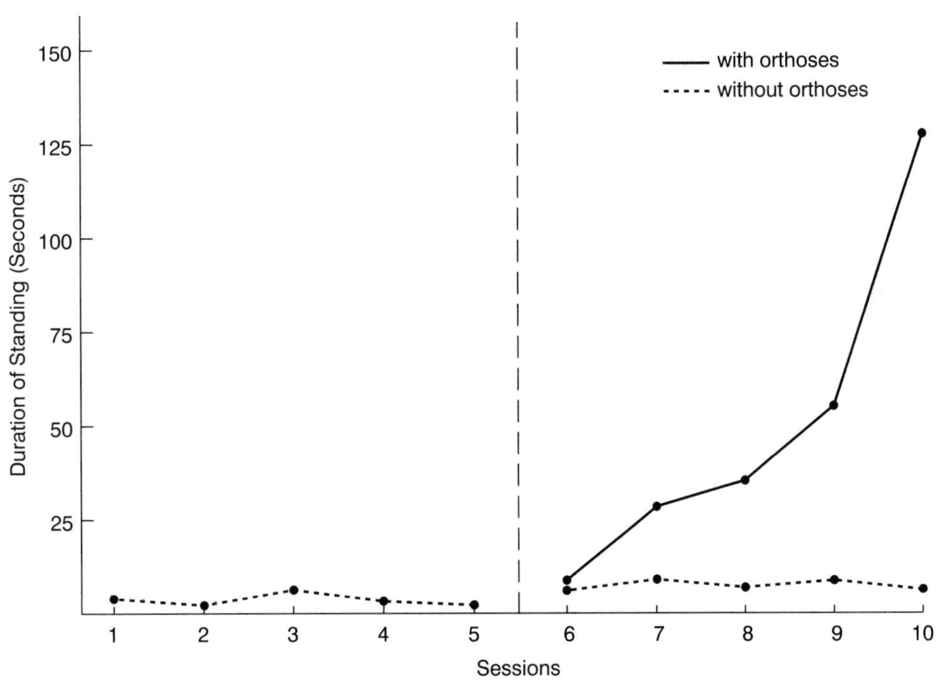

FIGURE 11.5
A single-subject alternating treatment design assessing standing balance of a child with cerebral palsy when wearing and when not wearing ankle-foot orthoses
Source: From "Effects of Inhibitive Ankle-Foot Orthoses on Standing Balance of a Child with Cerebral Palsy: A Single-Subject Design" by S. R. Harris and K. Riffle, 1986, *Physical Therapy, 66,* p. 665. Copyright 1986 by the American Physical Therapy Association. Reprinted with the permission of the American Physical Therapy Association.

of children with cerebral palsy. They compared the length of time it took two children to activate switches when they were positioned in a sidelyer, a chair, a stander, and a prone wedge. As Figure 11.6 shows, it took both children longer to activate the switches when they were positioned in the sidelyer than when they were in the other positions.

TRANSLATING ASSESSMENT INFORMATION INTO FUNCTIONAL GOALS

Goals of intervention for children with motor impairments have changed over the past decade from an emphasis on isolated components of movement and developmental milestones to a focus on achievement of functional activities that are meaningful to the child and the family (Harris, 1991). Therapists, teachers, parents, and other caregivers may need to help a child improve movement components to achieve functional skills (Fetters, 1991), but the functional activity needs to be the target of intervention and its accomplishment the means by which the success of intervention is measured.

Some examples may help to clarify distinctions between components of movement, developmental milestones, and functional activities. *Components of movement* include such aspects of neuromotor performance as force production (strength), muscle tone, reflexes, and balance reactions. Intervention goals that focus on these and similar aspects of movement have been common for children with cerebral palsy and other neuromotor problems, especially when neurodevelopmental treatment techniques are emphasized. Examples of goals that express a components-of-movement approach are for a child to lift his head when in a prone position, or for a child to right herself while sitting supported on a therapy ball. For

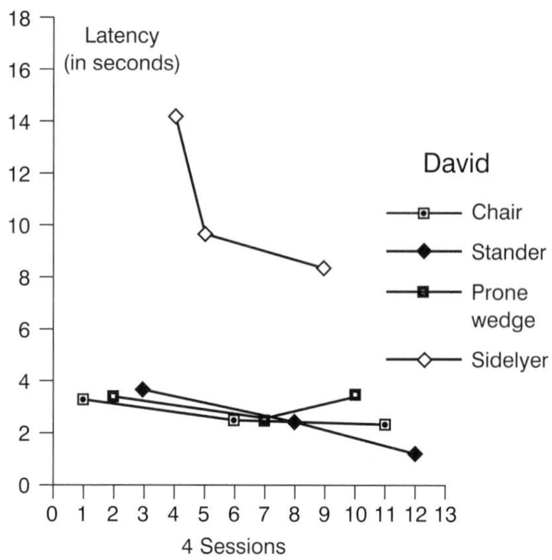

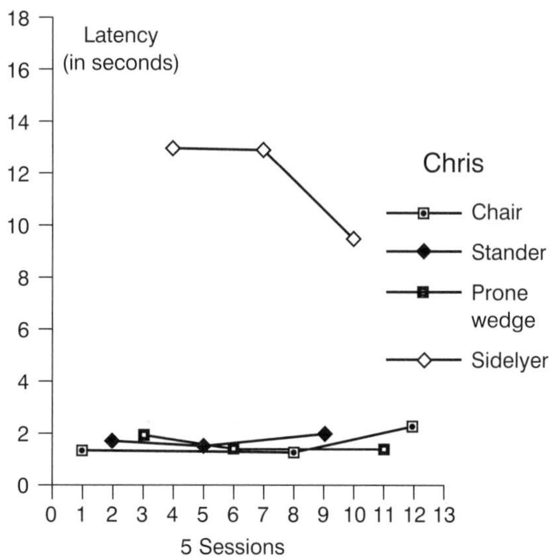

FIGURE 11.6
A single-subject alternating treatment design assessing means of switch activation latency when two children with cerebral palsy were positioned in a chair, a stander, a prone wedge, and a sidelyer.
Source: From "Assessment of Effects of Position on Communication Board Access by Individuals with Cerebral Palsy" by I. R. McEwen and G. R. Karlan, *Augmentative and Alternative Communication, 5,* pp. 238, 239. Copyright 1989 by the International Society for Augmentative and Alternative Communication. Reprinted by permission.

children with meningomyelocele, arthrogryposis, muscular dystrophy, and other conditions in which such components of movement as force production and range of motion are primary problems, the components-of-movement approach often led to such goals as maintaining range of motion or doing wheelchair push-ups.

These goals to improve components of movement were presumed to contribute eventually to a functional outcome, such as walking or transferring from a wheelchair to the toilet, but the functional outcomes were often only presumed to be accomplished some time in the future. They were not measured directly and may never have been achieved.

Another common method for determining goals related to motor performance has been the *developmental sequence* approach. With this approach, goals were selected from items that a child failed on a norm-referenced or criterion-referenced developmental test or checklist. If the child, for example, passed all items up to Item 42 on the Gross Motor Scale of the Peabody Developmental Motor Scales (Folio & Fewell, 1983), then Item 42, involving pivoting to get a toy while sitting, would be a goal of intervention.

The components of movement and developmental sequence approaches are based on several assumptions about motor development and motor control that have failed to be supported by recent research. The beliefs that motor development proceeds in cephalocaudal (head to toe) and proximal to distal (center of body outward) directions, and from gross motor to fine motor skills, for example, have been shown to be incorrect (Case-Smith, Fisher, & Bauer, 1989; Horowitz & Sharby, 1988). Rather, motor control develops relatively simultaneously and independently throughout the body. Development may appear to be directional, such as an infant gaining head control before being able to sit up, but factors other than cephalocaudal development have been shown to account for the timing of skill acquisition. Thelen (1979) demonstrated, for example, that infants' kicking is actually more skilled than their arm movements, but they are able to use their arm movements earlier, such as for reach and grasp, because the balance, strength, and other components necessary to use legs for standing and walking develop at a later time (Kamm, Thelen, & Jensen, 1990).

The components-of-movement and developmental approaches to identifying goals also assumed that functional goals would eventually be achieved once the building blocks of the movement were acquired. If a child could learn to balance while sitting on a large ball, for example, it was assumed that his or her overall balance would improve when sitting on a chair or when standing. Similarly, it was believed that moving through a developmental sequence of skills would eventually lead to movement required for self-care, mobility, communication, and other life activities. Contemporary theories of development suggest, however, that movement is organized to accomplish specific tasks within certain contexts (Haley et al., 1993; Heriza, 1991). There is no reason to believe that the movement required to maintain balance while sitting on a ball will carry over to other activities requiring balance, or that the specific movement necessary to sit on a ball will be helpful in maintaining balance while sitting on a chair or standing. Sitting on a ball, sitting on a chair, and standing are different tasks, and movement is uniquely organized to accomplish each of them.

The *functional approach* to determining intervention goals identifies skills that are immediately meaningful to children and their families. Wolery (1989) defined functional skills for children as behaviors that (a) are immediately useful, (b) enable a child to be more independent, (c) allow a child to learn other more complex skills, (d) allow a child to function in a less restrictive environment, and (e) enable a child to be cared for more easily by the family and others. He further specified that goals must also be meaningful to the child and the family, realistic, and achievable.

Functional outcomes have been emphasized in special education since at least the 1970s (Brown et al., 1979), but many occupational therapists and physical therapists, who frequently have a major influence on selection of motor-related goals, have focused on functional goals only recently (Haley et al., 1993; Harris, 1991). This is especially the case when children have cerebral palsy or some other neuromotor impairment. Contemporary theories of motor development, motor control, and motor learning largely support the importance of functional outcomes.

Team Process in Determining Functional Goals

The makeup of teams working with infants and young children varies with the service delivery setting. Physicians and other health-care professionals dominate hospital-based teams. Early childhood intervention programs often have a dozen or more professionals providing services directly or through consultation. Hospital-based teams are more likely to use multidisciplinary or interdisciplinary approaches, in which professionals evaluate and intervene directly, using discipline-specific approaches (as described in Chapter 3). Early intervention programs and school programs for children with severe disabilities often use a transdisciplinary approach, in which professionals and families cross disciplinary boundaries, and a primary service provider gains knowledge and implements strategies from various disciplines (Foley, 1990; Woodruff & McGonigel, 1988). Preschool teams are often interdisciplinary, with components of transdisciplinary collaboration among team members.

Regardless of the service setting and its model of team functioning, the child's family is always the most consistent team member and most critical to motor-related outcomes of intervention (Woodruff & McGonigel, 1988). The family's beliefs about their child and their hopes, dreams, and values must guide the intervention process, including the process to determine goals involving motor-related skills.

Family Participation in Determining Outcomes

When developing an individualized family service plan (IFSP) or individualized education program (IEP), it is helpful to identify the general outcomes of intervention before developing specific goals and objectives (P. H. Campbell, 1991). Depending on program requirements, long-term goals may need to be measurable, but objectives (or short-term goals) must always be measurable and conform to a format (O'Neill & Harris, 1982). These requirements can limit creative thinking about meaningful goals of intervention if they are determined too early in the process. Once general outcomes have been identified, goals and objectives can be written to accomplish them.

Outcomes are determined relatively independently of evaluation results, which P. H. Campbell (1991) describes as a top-down approach to intervention. This is in contrast to the bottom-up approach traditionally used by occupational therapists and physical therapists, in which sensorimotor components or milestones are identified through the evaluation process and then goals to remediate them are written. The problem with this approach, as discussed previously, is that such motor-related goals are unlikely to be meaningful to the child and the family, and often fail to lead to a child's accomplishment of functional skills, even after long periods of time.

If outcomes of intervention are to be meaningful to a child's family, the family must identify the outcomes. Because development of motor skills is one of the most prominent and celebrated accomplishments of infants and young children, families frequently identify motor activities as the outcomes they want young children to achieve. Parents of infants often identify developmental milestones, such as rolling, sitting, standing, and walking. For an infant, these can be functional outcomes because accomplishment of developmental milestones is the age-appropriate task of all babies.

Service providers are frequently concerned when they believe a family's expectations are too high or too remote, such as when the family of an 8-month-old with cerebral palsy says they want the child to walk. It is not the responsibility of the service provider to help families have "realistic" expectations, but it can be useful to help them focus on intermediate steps. One approach, *after* writing down walking as an outcome, is to ask the family what they think is preventing the child from walking. They will usually say something to the effect that "he can't even roll over yet" or "she probably needs to learn to sit up by herself first," which can be turned into a goal to be accomplished within the next few months.

Beyond the age of one year or so, accomplishment of early developmental milestones is no longer age-appropriate and may not be functional for a given child. This is especially true when children have moderate to severe motor impairments. If a 14-month-old has not learned to roll or sit without support, for example, the family probably has concerns other than accomplishment of developmental milestones. These concerns might be related to feeding, bathing, taking the child to the store, beginning self-care skills, playing with toys, and any of a number of functional tasks that the family and the child do together. This is not to say that intervention would not address sitting, only that sitting would not be the goal of intervention. We sit so that we are able to do something; the "something" needs to be the focus of intervention and its accomplishment the measure of success. In this case, the child might practice sitting on the floor while learning to use his hands to play with toys, which is an age-appropriate functional task for a 14-month-old. Even if the child never learns to sit, he will have learned to play with toys, which is an important skill for a child and one that he might have missed had intervention focused exclusively on sitting.

The biggest concern of a family of a 2-year-old who is unable to crawl or walk might be that they cannot leave the child alone without her crying. They would like the child to walk eventually, but in the meantime they think she needs some means of independent mobility so that she can go where she likes. Self-produced mobility is also related to cognitive, emotional, and social development (Bertenthal, Campos, & Barrett, 1984; Campos & Bertenthal, 1987), which could be affected by her inability to move about in her environment. In this case, mobility is the goal, which needs to be accomplished in the shortest time possible. A manual or power wheelchair or cart could provide this means of mobility until the child learns to walk, if she does. In the meantime, she will have the benefits of independent mobility. There is no evidence that use of a wheelchair will make children lazy or delay their walking. In fact, having early independent mobility may help children become more interested in their environments, have more interest in moving, and help prevent the passivity that is common among children who are immobile for long periods of time (Butler, 1991).

Developing Functional Motor Goals

Once the outcomes are identified, assessment specific to the outcomes may be necessary to identify goals and objectives and determine methods to accomplish them. Information from developmental evaluations is usually not very helpful in this process because test items rarely address the outcomes that families identify, and evaluation results generally reveal only that a child can perform certain skills and not others. Analysis of why the child cannot perform skills, judgment of whether or not the child is likely to be able to learn the skills, and the means to help the child accomplish the skills are the responsibility of the intervention team.

An ecological assessment is one of the most helpful methods of gathering the information necessary to determine goals and objectives that will lead to the desired outcome. To conduct an ecological assessment, one or more team members observe the child and family participating in the outcome activity. If, for example, the family identified self-feeding as one of the desired outcomes, the child and a parent would be observed during mealtime in the home. Interventionists could observe informally to determine an intervention approach, but various ecological assessment formats have been developed that formalize and facilitate the decision-making process (Baumgart et al., 1982; Dunn, Campbell, Berger, Hall, & Otter, 1989; Orelove & Sobsey, 1991).

Table 11.3 illustrates an ecological assessment for Kevin, who is a 4-year-old with meningomyelocele. His family identified increased independence as a high-priority outcome, and they, with the rest of the team, decided that one goal would be for Kevin to walk with his walker from the bus to his preschool classroom every morning. The ecological assessment was conducted to assist the team to determine objectives and intervention that would help Kevin accomplish this goal. The assessment is based on a format described by Baumgart et al. (1982), which begins with an analysis of the tasks required to accomplish the goal. This is followed by analysis of the steps that Kevin currently can and cannot accomplish and the steps that he may or may not be able to accomplish with intervention. Possible means to bypass or compensate for steps he may not be able to accomplish are then identified and, finally, the observer notes whether or not intervention is needed to accomplish each step. Goals and/or objectives are written for skills that the assessment indicates Kevin is likely to be able to accomplish with intervention, and team members arrange for compensatory strategies.

After the goals and objectives have been determined, the team will decide which team members are needed to help the child accomplish the goals. If goals and objectives relate to motor tasks, an occupational therapist and/or a physical therapist is likely to be involved. Depending on the needs of the child and the capabilities of the family and other team members, that involvement may be direct intervention with the child and consultation with the family and other team members, or may be consultation only. Kevin, for example, may require a physical therapist to work with him initially to determine how best to teach him the motor skills he needs to walk from the bus to his classroom. After he begins to learn the necessary skills, the teacher, a teaching assistant, and the family may be able to help him practice and gain proficiency, with consultation by the physical therapist. Because the family, the teacher, and an assistant are with Kevin for several hours each day, they will be able to provide him with many more opportunities to practice walking, which should help him learn the skills more quickly and learn to walk in more environments than if he only walked with the physical therapist. The therapist is responsible for ensuring that those helping Kevin have learned the skills that they need and for monitoring Kevin's progress.

TABLE 11.3

Ecological Assessment of Kevin Walking from the Bus to the Classroom

Name: Kevin **Environment: School, home, community**
Activity: Walking **Subenvironment: From bus to classroom**

Tasks Required	Kevin	Steps Can Acquire	Steps May Not Acquire	Compensatory Strategies	Objectives for Intervention
1. Walk down bus steps	Can bear weight as he is lifted down each step; cannot go down steps independently.	Go down steps independently	Going down steps reciprocally	None	Yes—going down bus steps
2. Walk from bottom of bus steps to the two steps of the school entrance	Can grasp walker and walk to steps.	Walk faster and without falling	Walking without walker	Will use a walker, which the bus driver will put at the bottom of the bus steps; evaluate whether or not another type of walker would be more helpful	Yes—walking faster and without falling
3. Walk up the two steps	Steps are wide and deep enough for the walker; he can put walker up on the first step, but cannot step up.	Walk up steps with a walker	Walk up without walker	No change	Yes—walk up steps with walker
4. Walk from the top of the steps to the door	Can do this, but loses balance occasionally and is slow.	Walk faster and without falling	Walk without walker	No change	Yes—see 2, above
5. Open the door of the school and go in	Cannot open door, or hold door to go through if it is opened for him; lacks needed strength, coordination, and balance.	May be able to learn to open the door and walk through		Team may need to request installation of automatic door	Yes—opening door and walking through
6. Walk from inside the door to the classroom (50 feet)	Can only walk about 15 feet before tiring and losing balance. With assistance can walk about 25 feet.	Walk faster and walk without falling from the door to the classroom	Walk without walker	No change	Yes—see 2, above

SUMMARY OF KEY CONCEPTS

- Assessment of motor skills in infants and young children has changed dramatically in the past few years.
- There is far less emphasis on attainment of motor milestones or measurement of muscle tone, strength, or balance reactions.
- Current assessments include a strong emphasis on functional motor skills that are important to the child and his or her caregivers.
- New assessment tools that are designed to assess functional activities, and family-centered therapy objectives are becoming the norm in North America.
- Physical and occupational therapists as well as early childhood special educators play important roles in assessment of motor skills for early identification of developmental disabilities and for program planning in early intervention.
- Motor assessment and intervention should occur more frequently in the child's natural environment with movement and therapeutic play activities integrated into daily life both at home and in the classroom.
- A shift is taking place from the traditional medical model that has been the cornerstone for training rehabilitation professionals toward more family-centered and ecologically relevant models of preparing entry-level occupational and physical therapists.
- Early childhood special educators need to become cognizant of and trained in the administration of the new evaluative tests that are being developed and used by primary health-care professionals.

REFERENCES

Barlow, D. H., & Hersen, M. (1984). *Single-case experimental designs* (2nd ed.). New York: Pergamon Press.

Baumgart, D., Brown, L., Pumpian, I., Nisbet, J., Ford, A., Sweet, M., Messina, R., & Schroeder, J. (1982). Principles of partial participation and individualized adaptations in educational programs for severely handicapped students. *The Journal of the Association for the Severely Handicapped, 7(2),* 17–27.

Bayley, N. (1969). *Bayley Scales of Infant Development.* New York: The Psychological Corp.

Bayley, N. (1993). *Bayley Scales of Infant Development* (2nd ed.). San Antonio, TX: The Psychological Corp.

Bertenthal, B. I., Campos, J. J., & Barrett, K. C. (1984). Self-produced locomotion: An organizer of emotional, cognitive, and social development in infancy. In R. N. Emde & R. J. Harmon (Eds.), *Continuities and discontinuities in development* (pp. 175–209). New York: Plenum.

Bleck, E. E. (1975). Locomotor prognosis in cerebral palsy. *Developmental Medicine and Child Neurology, 17,* 18–25.

Brown, L., Branston, M. B., Hamre-Nietupski, S., Pumpian, I., Certo, N., & Gruenewald, L. (1979). A strategy for developing chronological age appropriate and functional curricular content for severely handicapped adolescents and young adults. *Journal of Special Education, 12,* 81–90.

Butler, C. (1991). Augmentative mobility: Why do it? *Physical Medicine and Rehabilitation Clinics of North America, 2,* 801–815.

Butler, C. (1986). Effects of powered mobility on self-initiated behaviors of very young children with locomotor disability. *Developmental Medicine and Child Neurology, 28,* 325–332.

Campbell, P. H. (1991). Evaluation and assessment in early intervention for infants and toddlers. *Journal of Early Intervention, 15,* 36–45.

Campbell, S. K. (1991). Framework for the measurement of neurologic impairment and disability. In

M. Lister (Ed.), *Contemporary management of motor control problems: Proceedings of the II-STEP Conference* (pp. 143–153). Alexandria, VA: Foundation for Physical Therapy.

Campbell, S. K. (1993). Future directions for physical therapy assessment in infancy. In I. J. Wilhelm (Ed.), *Physical therapy assessment in infancy* (pp. 293–308). New York: Churchill Livingstone.

Campos, J. J., & Bertenthal, B. I. (1987). Locomotion and psychological development in infancy. In K. M. Jaffe (Ed.), *Childhood powered mobility: Developmental, technical and clinical perspectives: Proceedings of the RESNA First Northwest Regional Conference* (pp. 11–42). Washington, DC: RESNA.

Case-Smith, J., Fisher, A. G., & Bauer, D. (1989). An analysis of the relationship between proximal and distal motor control. *American Journal of Occupational Therapy, 43,* 657–662.

Chandler, L. S. (1990). Neuromotor assessment. In E. D. Gibbs & D. M. Teti (Eds.), *Interdisciplinary assessment of infants: A guide for early intervention professionals* (pp. 45–61). Baltimore, MD: Paul H. Brookes.

Chandler, L. S., Andrews, M. S., & Swanson, M. W. (1980). *Movement Assessment of Infants: A Manual.* Rolling Bay, WA: Infant Movement Research.

Chiarello, L., Effgen, S., & Levinson, M. (1992). Parent-professional partnership in evaluation and development of Individualized Family Service Plans. *Pediatric Physical Therapy, 4,* 64–69.

Crutchfield, C. A., & Barnes, M. R. (1993). *Motor control and motor learning in rehabilitation.* Atlanta, GA: Stokesville.

Dubowitz, V. (1980). *The floppy infant* (2nd ed.). Philadelphia, PA: J. B. Lippincott.

Dunn, W., Campbell, P. H., Berger, E., Hall, S., & Otter, P. (1989). *Guidelines for the practice of occupational therapy in early intervention.* Rockville, MD: American Occupational Therapy Association.

Fetters, L. (1991). Foundations for therapeutic intervention. In S. K. Campbell (Ed.), *Pediatric neurologic physical therapy* (2nd ed.) (pp. 19–32). New York: Churchill Livingstone.

Foley, G. M. (1990). Portrait of the arena evaluation: Assessment in the transdisciplinary approach. In E. D. Gibbs & D. M. Teti (Eds.), *Interdisciplinary assessment of infants: A guide for early intervention professionals* (pp. 271–286). Baltimore, MD: Paul H. Brookes.

Folio, R. M., & Fewell, R. (1983). *Peabody Developmental Motor Scales.* Allen, TX: DLM Teaching Resources.

Gallahue, D. L. (1989). *Understanding motor development: Infants, children, and adolescents* (2nd ed.). Carmel, IN: Benchmark Press.

Haley, S. M., Baryza, M. J., & Blanchard, Y. (1993). Functional and naturalistic frameworks in assessing physical and motor disablement. In I. J. Wilhelm (Ed.), *Physical therapy assessment in early infancy* (pp. 225–256). New York: Churchill Livingstone.

Haley, S. M., Coster, W. J., Ludlow, L. H., Haltiwanger, J. T., & Andrellos, P. J. (1992). *Pediatric Evaluation of Disability Inventory (PEDI): Development, standardization, and administration manual.* Boston, MA: New England Medical Center Hospitals, Inc.

Hall, S. (1990). Observation of sensorimotor development. In T. Linder (Ed.), *Transdisciplinary Play-Based Assessment: A functional approach to working with young children* (pp. 201–246). Baltimore, MD: Paul H. Brookes.

Harris, S. R. (1981). Effects of neurodevelopmental therapy on motor performance of infants with Down's syndrome. *Developmental Medicine and Child Neurology, 23,* 477–483.

Harris, S. R. (1987a). Early detection of cerebral palsy: Sensitivity and specificity of two motor assessment tools. *Journal of Perinatology, 7,* 11–15.

Harris, S. R. (1987b). Early neuromotor predictors of cerebral palsy in low-birthweight infants. *Developmental Medicine and Child Neurology, 29,* 508–519.

Harris, S. R. (1989). Early diagnosis of spastic diplegia, spastic hemiplegia, and quadriplegia. *American Journal of Diseases of Children, 143,* 1356–1360.

Harris, S. R. (1991). Functional abilities in context. In M. J. Lister (Ed.), *Contemporary management of motor control problems: Proceedings of the II-STEP conference* (pp. 253–259). Alexandria, VA: Foundation for Physical Therapy, Inc.

Harris, S. R., Osborn, J. A., Weinberg, J., Loock, C., & Junaid, K. (1993). Effects of prenatal alcohol exposure on neuromotor and cognitive development during early childhood: A series of case reports. *Physical Therapy, 73,* 608–617.

Harris, S. R., & Riffle, K. (1986). Effects of inhibitive ankle-foot orthoses on standing balance of a child with cerebral palsy. A single-subject design. *Physical Therapy, 66,* 663–667.

Heriza, C. (1991). Motor development: Traditional and contemporary theories. In M. J. Lister (Ed.), *Contemporary management of motor control problems: Proceedings of the II STEP conference* (pp. 99–126). Alexandria, VA: Foundation for Physical Therapy, Inc.

Horn, E. M., Warren, S. F., & Reith, H. J. (1992). Effects of small group microcomputer-mediated motor skills instructional package. *The Journal of the Association for Persons with Severe Handicaps, 17,* 133–144.

Horowitz, L., & Sharby, N. (1988). Development of prone extension postures in healthy infants. *Physical Therapy, 68,* 32–39.

Jette, A. (1989). Diagnosis and classification by physical therapists: A special communication. *Physical Therapy, 69,* 967–969.

Kamm, J., Thelen, E., & Jensen, J. I. (1990). A dynamical systems approach to motor development. *Physical Therapy, 70,* 763–775.

Kirshner, B., & Guyatt, G. H. (1985). A methodologic framework for assessing health indices. *Journal of Chronic Diseases, 38,* 27–36.

Knobloch, H., Stevens, F., & Malone, A. F. (1987). *Manual of developmental diagnosis: The administration and interpretation of the revised Gesell and Amatruda developmental and neurologic examination.* Houston, TX: Gesell Developmental Materials.

Law, M. (1987). Measurement in occupational therapy: Scientific criteria for evaluation. *Canadian Journal of Occupational Therapy, 54,* 133–138.

Linder, T. (1990). *Transdisciplinary Play-Based Assessment: A functional approach to working with young children*. Baltimore, MD: Paul H. Brookes.

Mayhew, T. P., & Rothstein, J. M. (1985). Measurement of muscle performance with instruments. In J. M. Rothstein (Ed.), *Measurement in physical therapy* (pp. 57–102). New York: Churchill Livingstone.

McEwen, I. R. (1994). Mental retardation. In S. K. Campbell (Ed.), *Physical therapy for children* (pp. 457–488). Philadelphia: W. B. Saunders.

McEwen, I. R., & Karlan, G. R. (1989). Assessment of effects of position on communication board access by individuals with cerebral palsy. *Augmentative and Alternative Communication, 5,* 235–242.

Newborg, J., Stock, J. R., Wnek, L., Guidubaldi, J., & Svinicki, J. (1984). *Battelle Developmental Inventory.* Chicago, IL: Riverside Publishing.

O'Neill, D. L., & Harris, S. R. (1982). Developing goals and objectives for handicapped children. *Physical Therapy, 62,* 295–298.

Orelove, F. P., & Sobsey, D. (1991). Curriculum and instruction. In F. P. Orelove & D. Sobsey (Eds.), *Educating children with multiple disabilities: A transdisciplinary approach* (2nd ed.) (pp. 231–258). Baltimore, MD: Paul H. Brookes.

Ottenbacher, K. J. (1986). *Evaluating clinical change: Strategies for occupational and physical therapists.* Baltimore, MD: Williams & Wilkins.

Palisano, R. J. (1993a). Neuromotor and developmental assessment. In I. J. Wilhelm (Ed.), *Physical therapy assessment in early infancy* (pp. 173–224). New York: Churchill Livingstone.

Palisano, R. J. (1993b). Validity of goal attainment scaling in infants with motor delays. *Physical Therapy, 73,* 651–660.

Palisano, R. J., Haley, S. M., & Brown, D. A. (1992). Goal attainment scaling as a measure of change in infants with motor delays. *Physical Therapy, 72,* 432–437.

Piper, M. C., & Darrah, J. (1993). *Motor assessment of the developing infant.* Philadelphia: W. B. Saunders.

Pueschel, S. M. (1990). *A parent's guide to Down syndrome.* Baltimore, MD: Paul H. Brookes.

Ramey, C. T., Breitmayer, B. J., & Goldman, B. D. (1984). Learning and cognition during infancy. In M. J. Hanson (Ed.), *Atypical infant development* (pp. 237–279). Baltimore, MD: University Park Press.

Research Plan for the National Center for Medical Rehabilitation Research. (1993). NIH Publication No. 93-3509. Bethesda, MD: National Institutes of Health.

Rosenbaum, P. L. (1992). Clinically based outcomes for children with cerebral palsy: Issues in the measurement of function. In M. Sussmann (Ed.), *The diplegic child* (pp. 125–132). Park Ridge, IL: American Academy of Orthopaedic Surgeons.

Rosenbaum, P. L., Russell, D. J., Cadman, D. T., Gowland, C., Jarvis, S., & Hardy, S. (1990). Issues in measuring change in children with cerebral palsy: A special communication. *Physical Therapy, 70,* 125–131.

Russell, D., Rosenbaum, P., Gowland, C., Hardy, S., Lane, M., Plews, N., McGavin, H., Cadman, D., & Jarvis, S. (1990). *Gross Motor Function Measure Manual.* Hamilton, Ontario: McMaster University.

Shumway-Cook, A., & Woollacott, M. (1993). Theoretical issues in assessing postural control. In I. J. Wilhelm (Ed.), *Physical therapy assessment in early infancy* (pp. 161–171). New York: Churchill Livingstone.

Sousa, J. C., Gordon, L. H., & Shurtleff, D. B. (1976). Assessing the development of daily living skills in patients with spina bifida. *Developmental Medicine and Child Neurology, suppl. 18, 37,* 134–142.

Stangler, S. R., Huber, C. J., & Routh, D. K. (1980). *Screening growth and development of preschool children: A guide for test selection* (pp. 34–60). New York: McGraw-Hill.

Stengel, T. J. (1992). Assessing motor development in children. In S. K. Campbell (Ed.), *Pediatric neurologic physical therapy* (pp. 33–65). New York: Churchill Livingstone.

Sternat, J., Messina, R., Nietupski, J., Lyon, S., & Brown, L. (1977). Occupational and physical therapy services for severely handicapped students: Toward a naturalized public school service delivery model. In E. Sontag, J. Smith, & N. Certo (Eds.), *Educational programming for the severely and profoundly handicapped* (pp. 263–287). Reston, VA: Council for Exceptional Children.

Thelen, E. (1979). Rhythmical stereotypes in normal human infants. *Animal Behavior, 27,* 699–715.

von Wendt, L., Makinen, H., & Rantakallio, P. (1984). Psychomotor development in the first year and mental retardation. *Journal of Mental Deficiency Research, 28,* 219–225.

Wilhelm, I. J. (Ed.) (1993). *Physical therapy assessment in early infancy.* New York: Churchill Livingstone.

Wolery, M. (1989). Using assessment information to plan instructional programs. In D. B. Bailey & M. Wolery (Eds.), *Assessing infants and preschoolers with handicaps* (pp. 478–495). Englewood Cliffs, NJ: Merrill/Prentice Hall.

Wolery, M., & Harris, S. R. (1982). Interpreting results of single-subject research designs. *Physical Therapy, 62,* 445–452.

Woodruff, G., & McGonigel, M. J. (1988). Early intervention team processes: The transdisciplinary model. In J. B. Jordan, J. J. Gallagher, P. L. Huntinger, & M. B. Karnes (Eds)., *Early childhood special education: Birth to three* (pp. 163–181). Reston, VA: The Council for Exceptional Children.

World Health Organization. (1980). *International Classification of Impairments, Disabilities, and Handicaps.* Geneva, Switzerland: Author.

CHAPTER

12

Assessing Communication Skills

Elizabeth R. Crais
Joanne Erwick Roberts
The University of North Carolina at Chapel Hill

Communication is integral to everyday functioning; through it we exchange ideas, information, and feelings, achieve goals, share past events, and make plans for the future. Basic communication skills are critical for accessing and enjoying others and for managing everyday activities. For many young children with special needs, learning to communicate is not easy or natural; therefore, focusing on communication skills in assessment and intervention becomes an important component of the overall early intervention process.

The focus of this chapter is on the assessment of communication skills for the purpose of determining appropriate instructional goals for infants and preschool children with special needs. First, a rationale is provided for involvement across professionals in assessing and facilitating communication skills. Next, the dimensions and nature of communication development are presented. Finally, procedural considerations and representative methods of assessing communication are highlighted, along with suggestions for translating assessment information into instructional goals.

RATIONALE FOR ASSESSING COMMUNICATION

The recent shift toward transdisciplinary or multidisciplinary service delivery models has challenged many professionals to gain new knowledge and skills for working with young children with special needs and their families (Fenichel & Eggbeer, 1991; McCollum & Thorp, 1988). A critical component of all interactions with children and their families is communication, including the ways the child communicates with others and the ways others communicate with the child. Of particular importance is the enhancement of communicative and social interactions that are necessary for development across a variety of related areas (e.g., cognitive, affective, academic). By attending to the child's and their own communication skills, professionals can influence development directly by working with the child and indirectly by working with the child's caregivers.

To enhance the child's overall development, professionals should be familiar with communication concepts and assessment for a variety of reasons. First, because communication develops in accordance with a child's social, cognitive, and motor skills (McLean & Snyder-McLean, l978), professionals must look at communication in relation to the child's overall development and needs, as well as the intervention plans made for the child. For example, in the case of a young child with cerebral palsy who has difficulty pointing and communicating, professionals can work with the family to facilitate the child's overall development. As the occupational therapist coaches the parents and others in developing the child's pointing response, the physical therapist can help with trunk stability to enable pointing. The speech-language pathologist can then help combine pointing and vocalizing to request a desired object, and the special educator can focus on helping the child point to the object to indicate recognition of its name. As these facilitators work together, goals and activities can be coordinated to meet the child's overall needs.

A second reason for understanding communication development and assessment is that all professionals and family members interact and intervene with the child through communication. Professionals should, therefore, be able to recognize the child's overall level of communication (e.g., how the child communicates with and understands others) and modify their own communication and task demands accordingly. The closer the adult is to the child's level(s) of communicating, the more likely it is that the child will take part in and gain from the interaction.

Third, a large number of preschool children have communication needs. Before 1987, when noncategorical reporting was initiated, 70% of the children aged 3 to 5 who were served under the Individuals with Disabilities Education

Act (IDEA) were classified as having a speech or language impairment as their primary disability (U.S. Department of Education, l987). Based on the prevalence of communication disorders among disabling conditions, one can assume that a large number of the children with other disabilities also have communication problems.

Fourth, children with language disorders in the preschool years often have later academic, emotional, and behavioral difficulties (Aram & Hall, 1989). Indeed, Aram and Hall reported that 60% of the children who exhibited language disorders in preschool received special education services during the school years. Recent work has indicated that intervention to facilitate communication skills in the early years may prevent or mitigate later learning, emotional, and behavioral difficulties (Baker & Cantwell, 1987; Guralnick & Bennett, 1987; Prizant & Wetherby, 1993).

Finally, interventionists should be familiar with communication development and assessment because of the current focus on facilitating communication in natural settings such as the classroom and the home. It is commonly accepted that communication difficulties cannot typically be remediated with a few hours a week of speech-language therapy. Moreover, unless the environment where communication skills are taught is similar to the environment where they are used, most children with special needs will not generalize the newly acquired skills (Fey, 1986; Leonard, l981; Stokes & Baer, l977; Rogers-Warren & Warren, l984). Recent research (Warren & Kaiser, l986; Rogers-Warren & Warren, l984; Halle, Alpert, & Anderson, l984), therefore, has indicated that most communication assessment and teaching be taken out of highly structured and isolated settings and moved to more natural communication environments where a child actually uses communication. In the classroom, children have many opportunities to interact with their teachers and peers, as do children at home with their families. In addition, with the use of noncategorical labeling, fewer children may be specifically identified as speech delayed or communication impaired and therefore may not directly receive the services of a speech-language pathologist. Thus, all professionals need to be familiar with communication development and assessment because they will be responsible for facilitating communication skills in children, helping caregivers recognize and use appropriate techniques, and knowing when to make referrals to and seek assistance from speech-language pathologists.

DIMENSIONS OF COMMUNICATION ASSESSMENT

Definitions of Communication, Language, and Speech

Communication is a social act, the primary function of which is interaction with another living being. It is an active process with a sender who encodes or formulates a message and a receiver who decodes or comprehends the message. Communication can also occur, however, without the intent or the knowledge of the sender (e.g., a sender who inadvertently frowns may communicate displeasure). Communication can occur between and among many species (e.g., dogs, bees, humans); however, for it to be considered language, a mutually understood symbol system is necessary. Thus, language is a code of symbols and rules for combining those symbols. For example, English and Japanese are both languages with their own symbol and rule systems.

Communication and language also require a means for expression. Speech, the production of vocal sound patterns, is the most common means of human communication, although many other types exist, including gestures (e.g., pointing), facial expression (e.g., smiling), vocalizations (e.g., "baba"), nonspeech sounds (e.g., laughter), writing (e.g., "Dear Matthew"), signing (e.g., American Sign Language), and singing (e.g., "Rock-a-bye baby").

Components of Language

When acquiring any language, children must learn rules about its sounds, grammar, meanings, and uses. These rules are reflected in four components of language: phonology, syntax, semantics, and pragmatics. Phonology and syntax relate to the form of language, semantics to the meaning of language, and pragmatics to the use of language. *Phonology* refers to the rules for the formation of speech sounds, or phonemes, and how phonemes are joined together into words. Phonological rules govern what sounds can appear in various positions within a word (e.g., in English, *ft* can occur in the medial and final positions of words, but never in the initial position) and also in what sequences they can occur (e.g., *sl* is a permissible sequence, but *sd* is not). *Syntax* is the rule system for combining words into phrases and sentences. These rules specify parts of speech (e.g., noun, adjective, verb), word order, and sentence constituents (e.g., noun phrase, verb phrase). Someone who knows the syntax of a language can generate any number of sentences and identify those that are grammatically incorrect (e.g., The boy ball the threw). *Semantics* refers to the rules for meanings of words and their joint relationship to one another. A particular word has many characteristics that establish its meaning, and a child's task is to learn which factors are critical in acquiring the use of a word. Some words (e.g., *glasses)* take on very different meanings depending on the context in which they are uttered (eye glasses, drinking glasses). Further, just as the words in the utterance "Johnny jumps" can be described as a noun and a verb in a syntactic approach, they can also be described as agent (Johnny) and action (jumps) in a semantic approach. See Table 12.1 for a list of common semantic relations.

Pragmatics refers to the rules that govern the use of language in social contexts and for the purpose of communication. Two different levels of pragmatics are commonly assessed: intentions and discourse. Communicative intentions are the reasons that someone talks (e.g., to request an object, to protest something, or to share information). Because intentions are expressed through a variety of means (e.g., vocal, gestural, verbal), even children who are not yet using words may be intentionally communicating. For example, when a child points to a truck on the floor, he could either be requesting the truck or commenting about it. When a child shakes her head and screams as a peer takes away a toy, she is clearly using the intention of protesting. A second area of pragmatics is discourse, specifically, how to participate in interaction by taking turns. A conversation or interaction between two or more individuals is made up of turns, with each person taking the floor to communicate. To eventually become an effective conversationalist, a child must first learn how and when to begin, maintain, and end an interaction. The length of the turn, how to take a turn, when it is acceptable to take a turn, and when it is not acceptable for turn-taking are all examples of the rules for conversation (Keenan & Schieffelin, 1976).

Development of Communication and Language

The following section briefly describes the development of the four language components. The area of pragmatics receives the most detail, because many have argued that it has the greatest implications for young children (Miller, l981; McLean & Snyder-McLean, l978).

Pragmatics Although infants do not typically produce meaningful words until the end of their first year, they become actively involved in interactions with people in their environment early in life. During the first few months, caregivers respond to infants' unintentional signals (e.g., eye gaze, facial expressions) as if they were purposeful. For example, infant crying or repetitive sucking appear to be reflexive reactions rather than intentional communication,

TABLE 12.1
Semantic Relations Expressed in Prelinguistic, One-Word, and Multiword Utterances

General Relationship	Function/Meaning	Child Behavior: Prelinguistic	Child Behavior: One-Word	Child Behavior: Multiword
Agent	The individual performing the action	Throws ball to teacher and smiles proudly	Throws ball and says "Me"	"Me throw."
Action	Requests action	Holds hands up to be picked up	"Up," to indicate "pick me up"	"Up Mommy."
Object	Comments on the object of action	Points to ball being pushed	"Ball," as ball is pushed	"Ball go."
Recurrence	Requests/comments on repetition of activity/object	Drinks milk and holds up empty bottle	"More," to indicate "more milk"	"Me more milk."
Nonexistence	Comments on nonexistence/disappearance of object or person	Points to missing wheel on car	"Wheel," while pointing to car	"No wheel."
Cessation	Comments on cessation of activity	Points to top that stopped spinning	"Stop," to indicate top is no longer spinning	"Top stop."
Rejection	Protests/comments on undesired action or something forbidden	Turns head away from food	"No," in response to peas	"No peas."
Location	Comments on spatial location	Holds truck and points to box	"Box," while pointing to toy box	"Put box."
Possession	Comments on possession of object	Reaches for own shoes among others' shoes and points	"Mine," while getting own shoes	"My shoes."
Agent action*	Comments on agent and action			"Boy hit."
Action object*	Comments on action and object			"Kick ball."
Agent action object*	Comments on agent, action, and object			"Mommy throw ball."
Action object location*	Comments on agent, action, and location			"Put ball chair."

* These are more commonly used examples of relational combinations; many possibilities exist.

but caregivers typically interpret these behaviors as purposeful expressions of hunger or of a desire to be picked up. As noted by Goldberg (1977), readability, or the ability of caregivers to recognize and respond to the infant's behaviors, is an important factor in the infant's ability to learn the effects these behaviors can have on others. These early nonverbal exchanges between child and caregiver form the basis for later conversational turn-taking (Bruner, 1978). From 3 to 8 months, there are dramatic increases in the child's interactions with caregivers, clarity of signals, and ability to participate in turn-taking sequences.

Between 9 and 12 months, children's gestures and sound vocalizations (e.g., extending arms to be picked up, saying "ah" while pointing to a desired object) begin to be used consistently and others begin to understand what the infant is intentionally communicating. Thus, the infant's communicative attempts begin to serve particular communicative functions. Wetherby and Prizant (1993), based on Bruner's (1981) work, describe three types of functions children use by the end of their first year: (a) behavior regulation serves to regulate the behavior of another individual to do something (e.g., requests a ball on a shelf) or to stop doing something (e.g., while eating, the child pushes away offered food); (b) social interaction attracts and maintains attention to the child so an individual will look at or notice the child (e.g., waving bye-bye as father leaves); and (c) joint attention attracts and maintains attention of an individual to an object or event (e.g., the child points to a picture in a book). See Chapman (1981), McLean and Snyder-McLean (1978), and Roth and Spekman (1984) for a review of other taxonomies of communicative intentions.

Because it may be difficult at times to determine whether a young child is intentionally communicating, Wetherby and Prizant (1989) suggest the following criteria: the child (a) alternates eye gaze between the listener and the goal, (b) persists in signaling or changes the signal until a goal is accomplished, (c) uses a conventional (e.g., waving bye) or ritualized (e.g., "ba" for dog) form of signal, (d) pauses for a response from a listener, (e) terminates a signal and/or displays satisfaction when a goal is met, and (f) displays dissatisfaction when a goal is not met. Examples of communicative intentions expressed at the prelinguistic stage appear in Table 12.2.

At approximately 12 to 15 months, children begin to use words (e.g., *up, mama)* and word approximations (e.g., "ba" for *ball)* to indicate the same intentions expressed in the prelinguistic stage. Thus, when a child wants a cookie, instead of putting the adult's hand on the jar to get it open, the child says "open" or "oh." The infant's signals are now easier to interpret, and if a signal is not understood, the infant can repeat and vary the communication.

At about 18 months, children begin to combine words and to indicate their communicative intentions with word combinations. Children also learn to use words to express intentions in relation to preceding utterances in conversation. As shown in Table 12.2, these discourse functions include requesting information (e.g., "What's that?"), answering (e.g., child says "juice" in response to "What do you want?"), and acknowledging (e.g., child says "okay" to a request to sit down). Although the ability to maintain a conversation is not typically established until the third year of life, children now show increasing ability to maintain a topic for a greater number of turns. Bloom, Rocissano, and Hood (1976) found that at 21 months, children maintained the topic approximately 50% of the time.

The 3- to 3½-year-old shows increasing sophistication in discourse skills. Children can at this point maintain the topic of a conversation 75% of the time (Bloom et al., 1976) and can provide new information on the topic. Their language use shifts from a focus on things in their environment to events and people more distant in time. They use language to report on present and past events, describe imaginative situations, identify their own and others' feelings, plan

TABLE 12.2
Communicative Intentions Expressed in Prelinguistic, One-Word, and Multiword Utterances

Intention	Definition	Prelinguistic	One-Word	Multiword
Attention seeking	Solicits attention to self or aspects of the environment; has no other intent	Child tugs on her mother's skirt	"Mommy," as she tugs on skirt	"You know what?"
Request object	Demands desired tangible object; includes requesting consumable and nonconsumable objects	Child points to a dog he wants	"Dog"	"Give me dog."
Request action	Commands another to carry out an action; includes requesting assistance and other actions involving another person or between another person and an object	Child puts adult's hand on lid of jar while looking at the adult	"Open," while giving jar to adult	"Mama, open bottle."
Request information	Finds out something about an object or event; includes *wh-* questions and other utterances having the intonation contour of an interrogative		"Shoe?" as he points to shoe box	"Where shoe?"
Protest	Commands another to cease an undesired action; includes resisting another's action and rejection of object that is offered	Child pushes the adult's hand away when an undesired food item is offered	"No," in response to undesired food	"No peas, Mama."
Comment on object	Directs another's attention to an object; includes pointing, showing, describing, informing, and interactive labeling	Child holds up toy car toward the adult and smiles while looking at the adult	Child points to the car in his hand and says "Car"	"My car."
Comment on action	Calls listener's attention to the movement of some object or action of others or self	Laughs and looks at adult while adult falls down	"Down," as adult falls	"Bobbie fall down."
Greeting	Communicates salutation and offers conversational rituals "hi," "bye," "please," and "thank you"	Child waves as mother leaves	"Bye"	"Bye, mom."
Answering	Responds to request for information		Child says "nose" in response to "Where's your nose?"	"Here my nose."
Acknowledgement of other's speech	Acts or utterances used to indicate that the other's utterance was received, not in response to a question; includes repetition of an utterance		Child says "yea" when favorite song is mentioned	"My song."
Other	Tease, warn, alarm, exclaim, or convey humor	Child giggles as she takes a turn in a tickle routine	Child says "no" as she sticks her tummy out to be tickled	"No tickle me."

Source: Adapted from "The Communication Intention Inventory: A System for Coding Children's Early Intentional Communication" by T. Coggins and R. Carpenter, 1981, *Applied Psycholinguistics, 2;* "A Pragmatic Description of Early Language Development" by J. Dore, 1974, *Journal of Psycholinguistic Research, 4;* and "Assessing the Pragmatic Abilities of Children: Part I. Organizational Framework and Assessment Parameters" by F. Roth and N. Spekman, 1984, *Journal of Speech and Hearing Disorders, 49.*

events, and anticipate what will happen in the future. They can also recognize and respond appropriately to a listener's request for clarification in conversations. Thus the 4-year-old has some awareness of the linguistic and cognitive abilities of the listener and can modify speech and language accordingly. The child can now tell jokes, tease, and provide warnings, and shows increasing ability to use language for abstract purposes not tied to the present context.

Phonology During the first few months of life children coo and gurgle and produce some single syllables such as "na" and "ya." Infants typically begin to babble, using consonant-vowel combinations such as "mama" or "bababa" at around 6 to 8 months and produce different vocalizations that include both nonspeech (e.g., raspberries and squeals) and speech sounds. At 9 to 12 months, they begin to use wordlike sounds consistently (e.g., "ah" to indicate a desired object or "da" for *dog).* As children begin to use words, speech sounds generally develop in a predictable sequence at certain ages. For example, most children by 3 years of age produce many sounds, although the "r" sound is not produced correctly until at least 4 years. By age 4, children can produce most sounds accurately, although continued refinements of words with multisyllables take place over the next few years. As children acquire adult speech, they often fail to produce sounds or sound sequences in accordance with the adult form. For example, a child may consistently say "wabbit" for *rabbit* or "pusketti" for *spaghetti.* These errors have been described as resulting from phonological processes, which are patterns of simplifications that children use when learning words. For example, omitting the final "g" in *dog* and the "s" in *house* are instances of the phonological process of deletion of final consonants. Bernthal and Bankson (1988), Shriberg and Kwiatkowski (1980), and Stoel-Gammon and Dunn (1985) provide further descriptions of sound development and phonological processes.

Syntax The rules of syntax are acquired gradually as children learn to put words together. One-word utterances are typically produced at about 12 months, two-word utterances at about 18 months, and three-word utterances at about 2 years. The 2- to 2½-year-old may produce many two- and three-word utterances, but is also still producing one-word utterances and may occasionally use a six-word utterance. At this point, the child begins to use different types of sentences such as questions, negatives, and imperatives. At first, early forms are not grammatically correct. For example, negatives are formed by using *no* or *not* in utterances such as "No go eat" or "He not big." Early yes-no questions are signaled by a rising intonation (e.g., "Mommy going?" for "Is mommy going?"); *wh-* questions lack a copula or auxiliary verb (e.g., "Where my hat?" for "Where is my hat?"). At about age 3, children begin to learn complex sentence structures so that clauses can be joined and embedded in one another. Now sentences sound like "My mommy says that the baby's crying" and "Why don't you like chocolate on it?" By the time children are 5, basic and complex syntactic structures are established, yet the refinement of complex sentence usage continues into the early elementary school years.

A good estimate of young children's syntactical complexity is mean length of utterance (MLU) in words. MLU is computed by dividing the number of words in a sample of the child's language by the number of utterances in the sample (150 words/50 utterances = 3.0 MLU). MLU in words is a valid index of language development when the MLU is between 1.0 and 4.5 words (Miller, 1981). However, as children get beyond this upper MLU level, complex sentence structure is a more appropriate index of language development. See Miller (1981) for further discussion of the development of sentence structure.

Semantics Children's early words relate to the things that are most meaningful to them, such as the names of people and objects in their environment. For example, early words such as *mommy, daddy, doggie,* and *milk* are common and may be present for a time and then drop out of use. Around 18 months, children may use about 50 words although they may comprehend as many as 300. At this time, children talk about things that exist (e.g., wheel), no longer exist (e.g., pointing to missing wheel on car), recur (e.g., "more juice") and are rejected ("no" in response to bedtime). Around 18 months, children are also beginning to combine words into multiword utterances that consist of combinations of semantic categories such as agent-action ("Doggie bark"), and agent-action-object ("Mommy eat cookie"). Some of the common semantic categories children use in their prelinguistic communication and their one-word and multiword utterances are summarized in Table 12.1.

After 2 years of age, word knowledge increases dramatically. For example, a child can have a production vocabulary of 500 words at 2½ to 3 years and can comprehend as many as 1,000. Children now learn about complex concepts such as color, quantity, and spatial and temporal relations; they also begin to talk about causality. At around 4 years, they begin to develop metalinguistic knowledge—how to use language as a tool to focus on language form and content. This includes the ability to identify grammatical versus ungrammatical utterances, segment words into phonemes and sentences into words, and to rhyme words.

Language Comprehension

The description above focuses primarily on the development of language production in young children. It is also important to identify the child's development of comprehension in these early stages, from both linguistic and nonlinguistic standpoints. Chapman (1978) provides an excellent overview of young children's response strategies utilized in comprehending the world around them. Early nonlinguistic strategies used between 8 and 12 months include looking at objects looked at by another, acting on objects that are noticed, and imitating ongoing action. Strategies used in the 12- to 18-month period are typically based on some linguistic element and include attending to an object mentioned, giving evidence of notice to objects or actions, and doing what is usually done in a situation (e.g., child puts on coat when others do). In addition to these strategies, those used from 18 to 24 months include acting on objects as the agent (e.g., child lies down when asked to "Put the baby to sleep") and using conventional behaviors (e.g., combing hair with a brush). Strategies used during the 2- to 4-year period include using probable location (e.g., child puts things where they usually go) and probable event strategies (e.g., when asked to point to "boy bites dog," child selects picture of "dog bites boy"). At this stage, children can also give information in response to a question, although not always correctly. For example, to the question "How do you eat?" a child may respond "cereal." Between 3½ and 5, children begin to use word order ("boy bites dog") as a cue to sentences heard. For a more complete description of the development of comprehension skills, see Chapman (l978) and Paul (l987).

Communication-Related Domains

Hearing Due to the impact that a hearing loss can have on speech and language development, it is important that all children suspected of developmental delays have their hearing checked periodically (American Speech-Language-Hearing Association, 1991a). Hearing loss may be identified when an infant is in the newborn nursery, but only if the hospital employs screening procedures for neonates, and, in some instances, only if the neonate is at risk for a hearing loss. The hearing status of neonates can be screened by measuring the auditory brain stem response (ABR) evoked by electrodes placed on the child's scalp. By 6 months, infants can be tested with visual reinforcement audiometry (VRA), which involves sounds emitted from a loudspeaker and an animated, lighted toy that is turned on when the child looks in the direction of the sound signal. Children 2 years and older can be assessed using pure tone audiometry; the child wears earphones and is taught to drop a block or perform a similar task when a sound is heard. Although the hearing of older children can be screened by a health-care professional, screening of children under the age of 3 should be performed by an audiologist. For more information about hearing testing, see American Speech-Language-Hearing Association (1990, 1991a), Northern and Downs (1991), and Roush (1990). Chapter 6 includes more information on hearing screening and assessment.

Otitis media with effusion, which is one of the most common illnesses of early childhood (Bluestone & Klein, 1990), is of concern for children's language development because it is often accompanied by fluid in the middle ear, which can cause a mild to moderate fluctuating hearing loss (Roberts, Burchinal, Davis, Collier, & Henderson, 1991; Roberts, Wallace, & Zeisel, 1993). Children who have or are suspected of having recurrent middle ear problems should be monitored by a physician to minimize the risk of hearing loss.

Symbolic play Increasingly, there is evidence that language and play skills are highly correlated and that during some stages of development, they reflect common underlying cognitive processes (Kennedy, Sheridan, Radlinski, & Beeghly, 1991; Westby, 1988). For example, as first words are appearing along with more consistent communicative gestures (13 to 20 months), single pretend schemes (e.g., child feeds self with spoon) are emerging during play (Kennedy et al., 1991). As children begin to use language for interactional purposes, they also develop the ability to represent objects, actions, and feelings in symbolic play, using one object to stand for or represent an absent object during dramatic or make-believe play. As children begin to combine words (20 to 24 months), they also combine single pretend schemes (e.g., child feeds self with spoon, then drinks from cup). By 28 months, children are learning the rules for syntax, producing ordered play sequences, and showing an increase in productivity in language and other symbolic domains (Kennedy et al., 1991; McCune-Nicholich & Bruskin, 1982). In addition, for typically developing children (Bates, Bretherton, & Snyder, 1988) and children with developmental delays (Kennedy et al., 1991), higher levels of comprehension have been associated with higher levels of gestural production and play maturity. Westby (1988) has described seven stages of symbolic play that correspond to stages in children's language development. See Chapter 14 for a description of the assessment of play skills.

Social, motor, and cognitive skills
When planning assessment and intervention for infants and young children, the interventionist should consider the mutual influences of social, motor, and cognitive development on the child's efforts to communicate and learn language. The infant's interactions with people and objects in the environment set the stage for the development of many nonverbal behaviors considered to be the antecedents of "language" (Carlson & Bricker, 1982; Seibert & Hogan, 1982). For example, eye gaze, touch, and attention getting are important antecedents of social and communicative development in the first 2 years of life. The development of communicative competence in the infant depends on the caregiver's social responsiveness, which in turn is influenced by the child's behaviors (Dunst, Lowe, & Bartholomew, 1990). As suggested by Siegel-Causey, Ernst, and Guess (1987), contingency relationships between infants with special needs and their caregivers may be compromised by (a) the infant's medical involvement, which decreases the opportunity for social interaction; (b) parental attitudes and feelings that limit the parents' provision of

associated events; (c) the limited response repertoire of the infant, which makes both social and object co-occurrences less likely; (d) the limited ability of some children to detect and remember co-occurrences; and (e) the complex interactions of the infant and the environment, which may reduce the frequency of social co-occurrences. Thus, infants with special needs may have difficulty integrating the social, cognitive, and motor components necessary to gain communicative competence. For more information on the development of social skills and their effect on development, see Chapter 13, Dunst et al. (1990), Tronick (1989), and Wetherby and Prizant (1992).

Impairments in motor skills further compromise integration of cognitive, social, and communicative skills. In children with multiple special needs, it is difficult to differentiate the influence of the motor impairment from other factors (Nelson, 1993). For some children with severe physical impairment, such as cerebral palsy, their ability to speak may be impaired although their underlying cognitive and linguistic abilities are intact. For children with motor impairments, it is important to consider the effect of the motor impairment on both the conceptual development underlying their language and their speech production abilities. For more information on the effects of motor difficulties on communication, see the augmentative communication section in this chapter, Chapter 11, Blackstone (1986), and Light, Collier, and Parnes (1985).

A recent trend in assessment is to incorporate nonstandard measures of nonverbal cognitive skills such as those described by Piaget, as well as the scores of nonverbal (performance) mental ages on standardized intelligence tests (see Chapter 10). This practice typically allows for comparison between verbal and nonverbal skills and between cognitive and other developing skill areas. Although there is disagreement as to the exact relationship between language and cognitive development, the correlation between measures of cognition and language takes on particular importance when assessing children whose development appears to be delayed (Miller, Chapman, Branston, & Reichle, 1980). Gill and Dihoff (1982) suggest that when a child's language level is significantly below that of his or her cognitive level, the professional should suspect the presence of a disorder such as a hearing impairment, an auditory processing problem, or a potential learning disability. For practical guides to cognitive development and assessment within the framework of an overall communication assessment, see Miller et al. (1980) and Gill and Dihoff (1982); for general cognitive assessment, see Chapter 10.

PROCEDURAL CONSIDERATIONS IN ASSESSING COMMUNICATION

During the past several years, assessment of infants and preschoolers with special needs has undergone substantial changes in the ways information is gathered and shared by family members and professionals. Several characteristics of assessing communication skills in young children reflect these trends, such as the current emphasis on ecological validity of assessment tools and practices, the ongoing nature of assessment, the increased emphasis on active participation of family members and other caregivers, and the collaborative nature of the assessment and intervention planning process. In addition, changes in assessment practices in the area of communication reflect the broadening view of what constitutes communication in young children. Moreover, the terms *evaluation* and *assessment* have come to have differing definitions according to recent legislation. Evaluation activities, which are defined as the procedures to determine a child's initial and continuing eligibility, include determining the child's status in each developmental area (McLean & McCormick, 1993). Assessment is defined as the ongoing procedures used to identify a child's strengths and needs; the family's resources, priorities, and concerns; and the intervention services necessary to the child and the family. In this chapter, the term *assessment* is defined broadly to include *all* types of activities used to gather information about the child and the family, whereas *evaluation* is used only to indicate the process of determining eligibility. The following sections highlight these trends in assessment practices.

Concerns Related to Traditional Assessment Approaches

Traditionally, the assessment of communication skills in young children included the primary use of standardized instruments with some observational information gathered. Bricker (1992) suggests that standardized measures can be useful when establishing eligibility, in comparing children with a normative group, and for providing a general index of change over time. Standardized measures, however, were not generally designed to provide information for intervention planning. Indeed, these measures were developed to provide information under a "standard" set of conditions; therefore, an examination of a child's skills in contexts that represent his or her daily interactions is not fostered. Regarding communication assessment, standardized testing typically does not describe how the child actually uses language to communicate (verbally or nonverbally), nor are there any standardized tests available for examining all aspects of language.

An additional area of concern with traditional assessment measures is their poor predictive validity (Neisworth & Bagnato, 1992; Widerstrom, Mowder, & Sandall, 1991), especially for infants and young children with delays and disabilities (Maistro & German, 1986). Moreover, few standardized measures have included children with disabilities in the norming population (Fuchs, Fuchs, Benowitz, & Barringer, 1987; Neisworth & Bagnato, 1992); thus, the question of whether they are appropriate for *assessing* children with disabilities has not been adequately addressed.

A further problem arises for children with communication difficulties. As indicated by the work of Fuchs, Fuchs, Power, and Dailey (1985), although preschool children without disabilities performed equally well with familiar and unfamiliar examiners, children with communication difficulties performed more poorly with unfamiliar examiners. Moreover, for children with communication difficulties, the professional needs to consider the child's level of comfort with the examiner and the assessment context, the response type expected from the child (pointing, answering), and the type of stimulus materials (pictures, objects) used for the assessment activities. Children, unlike most adults, may not be willing or capable of talking freely to an unfamiliar adult, and helping them feel comfortable in a new and possibly threatening setting is not always easy. Figure 12.1 provides a list of suggestions for engaging children in interaction. Some children may be more comfortable communicating nonverbally, although they are capable of speaking. In this case, the administration of nonverbal tasks first in the assessment process may be useful. Children's responses also may vary according to the type of stimuli used. For young children, objects may be more interesting and may elicit better responses than pictures. For all assessments, the type of stimuli used, the nature of the accompanying instructions, and the mode of communication should be noted in the protocol and report.

The final issue of concern with most traditional communication assessment measures is their limited profiling of the child's strengths and needs across and within domains related to communication (Wetherby & Prizant, 1992). Where once syntax and semantics were the primary areas of assessment, additional areas such as social-affect, communicative intent, symbolic skills, turn-taking, eye contact, number and types of initiations, and level of overall communication skills have become increasingly important. As indicated by Wetherby and Prizant

1. Choose developmentally appropriate toys and materials. Use play and motor scales to help in the selection.
2. Limit your own talking, especially questions. Pause often to encourage the child to initiate communication and take a turn.
3. Watch for and encourage any means of communication demonstrated by the child (eye gaze, point, shrug, word, etc.).
4. Parallel play with the child, mimicking his/her actions. Play animatedly with object or toy and occasionally comment on an object or action.
5. Place a few items within eye gaze but out of reach, as well as partially hide a few objects. If necessary, point to or comment on objects to encourage a comment or request by the child.
6. Let child choose objects and/or activities, particularly in the beginning (and throughout the interaction if possible). Be prepared to watch and interact/comment when the child shows interest.
7. Include parent or another child to help "break the ice." Stay in the background and slowly get into the interaction.
8. Begin interaction with activities that require little or no talking and gradually move to more vocal or verbal tasks.
9. Be genuine in your questions and stay away from asking what is obvious to both you and the child.
10. Follow the child's lead in the interaction by maintaining the child's focus on particular topics and meanings.
11. Show warmth and positive regard for the child and value his/her comments.

FIGURE 12.1
Guidelines for interactions with children

(1992), most of the traditional instruments used to assess the communication skills of newborns to 3-year-olds fail to provide a profile of the child's strengths and needs across these critical areas.

Ecological Approach to Assessment

As noted in previous chapters, when professionals talk about the ecology of the child, they often refer to Bronfenbrenner's (1977) concept of the child nested within the family, which is itself embedded in a larger community system. Taking an ecological perspective, Bronfenbrenner suggested that to understand human development, one must go beyond observation of one or two people in the same location. In considering the ecologies that surround the child (e.g., home, daycare, preschool), professionals are urged to take into account the child's interactions across multiple settings and the facilitators and constraints inherent in those settings.

In recent years a number of professionals have recognized the need to view assessment as ongoing rather than as a one-time set of activities. Due to the high variability shown by young children, the need to be representative in assessment, and the difficulty of seeing a child's best or even typical performance under testing conditions, assessment strategies need to be viewed as serial. In addition, a child's communication skills need to be examined across a variety of contexts and with multiple sources contributing to the information gained. The use of multiple methods of assessment (e.g., observation, naturalistic interaction, direct assessment by professionals and family members, communication sampling, discussions with caregivers) can both add to the information available and contribute to the overall reliability and validity of the process. Indeed, the move toward more naturalistic activities and settings can increase the ecological validity of assessment and intervention planning. The opportunity to view a child over time and to gather information under different conditions allows the team the chance to develop a more accurate picture of the child.

Sociocultural Awareness

Professionals should be sensitive to the social, cultural, linguistic, and ethnic characteristics of the children and families they serve. Increasingly, professionals are interacting with families of diverse backgrounds that often differ from their own. One of the challenges in considering a child's communication skills is the need to understand the effects of culture on communication (Harris, 1985). Sociocultural background influences many aspects of communication, including when and how a child interacts with adults or strangers, the dialect used, and the ways the child views the communication process. For example, Cheng (1987) noted that for children from Asian-American families, communication is to be carried out with the fewest words possible and nonverbal cues are critical to the accuracy of the message. A child's background also influences the types of materials and toys available and thus can influence early cognitive and literacy experiences (Wells, 1986).

For children with special needs who are non-English speaking or who have limited English proficiency, it is critical to determine whether communication difficulties occur in the primary language and specifically whether the child's own communicative behaviors differ substantially from the norms and expectations of the child's own language community (Nelson, 1993; Taylor, 1985). In addition, there are many dialects in use in the United States (e.g., African-American Vernacular English, Hispanic English), and each represents a rule-based variant of Standard American English (SAE). Clearly, the results of tests based on standard English would provide an invalid picture of the communication skills of children who are used to speaking and hearing a dialect (Nelson, 1993).

In spite of the mandate that test materials and procedures be nondiscriminatory, few standardized communication assessment instruments are available that are dialectally or culturally sensitive (Vaughn-Cooke, 1983; Taylor, 1985; Terrell & Terrell, 1983). Some tests have alternative scoring protocols for syntax and phonology (for examples, see Table 12.3). Yet, as indicated in Chapter 4, test results must be interpreted carefully, because children may not have the same perspective or familiarity with taking tests. For these and other reasons, it is important to be familiar with the dialect and cultural expectations and behaviors of the child's community and family in order to determine if a child is having communication difficulties. Although it is possible to consult reference texts (e.g., Owens, 1992) to determine if a feature (e.g., omission of plural *s)* is characteristic of the child's community, the specific rules may not represent all individuals in the community or region. Determining the family's perspective of the child's communication skills is also essential if the child has language that is different from his or her own language community. Immersing oneself in the child's culture by observing other members of the cultural group, asking adults who use (or are familiar with) the dialect, using ethnographic observation, showing sensitivity to the family's style of communication, and using toys and other materials that are familiar and culturally appropriate should help to provide a nonbiased assessment (Nelson, 1993; Westby, 1990). In addition, Westby (1990) provides guidelines for using ethnographic interviewing to gather information from families about their concerns and priorities. For more information about culturally appropriate assessment, see Chapter 4, Battle (1993), Taylor (1985), and Vaughn-Cooke (1983).

Family Priorities

As suggested in Chapters 3 and 8, it is critical that assessment activities be based on what the family wants and needs and would find useful. In this sense, the contexts of the family's concerns become the context for assessment. There are many reasons for assessment; for example, some families may want to know whether their child's language is delayed relative to other children. Others may want to know why their child's communication skills are not developing typically and/or what they can do to help the child achieve. And still others may recognize their child's difficulties and simply want help in determining which preschool program is best for him or her. Professionals perform assessment to meet the family's goals, ensure a child's eligibility, document progress in therapy, or seek information to facilitate intervention planning. Although some professionals may be constrained by meeting certain eligibility requirements (e.g., use of two standardized tests), careful selection and use of assessment measures and techniques can provide some flexibility.

Active Participation of Caregivers

A recent trend in assessment practices is the move toward greater reliance on and participation of caregivers. Within the area of communication skills, caregivers and others familiar with the child often have unique insights into the ways and reasons the child communicates and the best strategies to engage the child in interaction. In contrast, professionals are at a disadvantage in the assessment process because they typically have limited opportunities to see the child, may be strangers to him or her, and may be unfamiliar with his or her behaviors. Increasingly, professionals across many disciplines are relying on caregivers to provide information that may not be easily observed or obtained in a brief assessment session. In addition, recent research has indicated that parents can be reliable when asked to indicate whether their child currently performs specific behaviors or has acquired language patterns such as specific vocabulary (Bricker & Squires, 1989; Dale, 1991; Dale, Bates, Reznick, & Morisset, 1989). Caregivers are often indispensable in assessing a child's communication behaviors, which can be quite variable and/or limited in the presence of strangers.

In addition, it is helpful for the caregivers of young children to be physically present and to assist with the assessment itself. Caregivers are critical when the interventionist needs information on a child's level of mastery of communication skills as well as his or her likes, dislikes, and typical behaviors. Caregivers and others can be asked to play and interact with the child to allow the professional to view interactions with a familiar person. Parents and teachers can be asked to encourage the child's performance during a direct testing phase and to provide direct feedback on the representativeness of the child's performance. In later sections, tools and techniques that utilize parent report or evaluation of a child's behaviors (including communication skills) are highlighted (see Chapter 3 for a discussion of caregiver participation).

Collaborative Assessment and Intervention Planning

A further trend in assessment and intervention planning is the shift toward collaborative efforts among professionals and family members. Recent theoretical trends and legislative mandates have indicated the need for assessment and intervention planning to be a shared process that derives from the concerns and priorities of the family. In regard to communication skills, all caregivers and service providers who interact with the child should be encouraged to participate in the assessment and intervention process because of the overriding importance of communication to the child's overall development. Assessment instruments and techniques that encourage evaluation and discussion by professionals *and* caregivers may enhance both the assessment and intervention planning components of the process. Although some caregivers may be quite willing to participate actively in assessment, others may be less comfortable in taking an active role. As suggested in Chapter 3, professionals can describe various options for caregiver participation, but should always be respectful of caregivers' preferences.

Use of Augmentative/Alternative Communication

Children with severe cognitive, neurological, structural, emotional, or sensory impairments may have difficulties using spoken and, later, written modes of communication (Consensus Statement, 1992). In assessing these children, alternate or augmentative means of communication (AAC) such as gestures, signing, or communication systems may be necessary. The term *augmentative communication* refers to a general classification of procedures that are designed and utilized to supplement whatever vocal skills an individual possesses (American-Speech-Language-Hearing Association, 1991b). For children with severe disabilities, the use of AAC may be critical to development; AAC methods have been implemented with infants as young as 4 to 6 months (Hanrahan, Ferrier, & Jolie, 1987). Typical variables for consideration in determining candidacy for augmentative use are cognitive and sensory functioning, motor ability, oral motor skills (e.g., chewing, swallowing, sound production), imitation skills, social/emotional development, interactive and communication ages, chronological age, motivation to communicate, and caregivers' attitudes about an augmentative communication system. Because of the complex nature of the factors influencing the decision of whether and what type of system to use, an interdisciplinary team is necessary (American Speech-Language-Hearing Association, 1991b). See Blackstone (1986), Consensus Statement (1992), and Nelson (1993) for criteria and guidelines for use of AAC.

REPRESENTATIVE METHODS OF ASSESSMENT

A variety of methods are currently available for the assessment of communication skills, and professionals are encouraged to use multiple sources of information and multiple means to gather that information. This section begins with an overview of the broad areas to be assessed, followed by a brief discussion of traditional assessment tools and their limitations regarding the preferred areas of assessment. A series of alternative tools and techniques are then presented in an effort to broaden the scope of available methods of assessment. Finally, communication sampling and decision trees are described, and examples of how these two techniques might be used by professionals are provided.

Overview of Areas to Assess

Preverbal child To gain information on a child's communication skills, the child's primary means (ways to communicate) and functions (reasons for communicating) need to be identified. Does the child primarily use nonverbal behaviors (e.g., body movements, grimaces) and vocalizations that do not make clear to caregivers what he or she is signaling? In such a case, the child may be preintentional; therefore, the assessment may focus on identifying consistent communicative behaviors or those that could be used to develop a means of communication (Wilcox, 1992). As suggested by Wilcox, caregivers and professionals can work together to identify a single behavior to interpret as meaningful (e.g., using a particular vocalization), then systematically reinforce the behavior in a particular context (e.g., during mealtime) to help the child develop intentional behavior (e.g., requesting food). See Wilcox (1992) for an overview of strategies for establishing and/or increasing productive use of intentional communication in young children with special needs.

For children in the early stages of intentionality, it is important for the assessor to identify the range of communicative functions and means used. For those who are prelinguistic and using gestures and vocalizations meaningfully (e.g., pointing or vocalizing for something), expanding the child's means and functions of communication can increase overall communicative efficiency. For this to happen most effectively, however, caregivers and professionals must recognize the child's *existing* means and functions and expand them. For example, for a child who vocalizes "uh" to request objects, the caregiver may model "uh-uh" when the child shakes her head to protest undesired foods or actions and may thereby prompt her to use "uh-uh" for protesting. A child who either points *or* vocalizes "da" to request an object may begin to use both *together* after caregivers model the vocalization "da" while pointing. For children in the early intentional stage who are also using word approximations (e.g., "ba" for *ball),* the professionals and caregivers can identify the sounds, sound combinations, and word approximations attempted by the child. In recognizing that new skills are built from existing ones, professionals can help caregivers extend the child's existing repertoire by encouraging the sounds and word approximations that are already used and attempting to shape or add to them in a systematic way. In working with young children whose parents report that they do not use "words," it is critical to help the caregivers recognize and reinforce the many ways the child already communicates (e.g., pointing, shaking or turning his or her head).

Verbal child For children in later stages of development who use primarily words and word combinations, it continues to be important to identify the *reasons* that they communicate as well as the words they use. The examiner should look for requests for objects and actions, but also for more sophisticated communicative functions such as requests for information. The child's words can also be classified into semantic categories, such as animals, people, actions, and animal sounds to get an idea of the variety of categories used. Identifying the semantic relations expressed by a child in prelinguistic, one-word, and multiword utterances can also be beneficial (see Table 12.1). For the interventionist to be able to build from a child's existing verbal skills, it is important to recognize and use what the child is currently doing. For example, if the child currently uses single words to express the semantic relations of agency *(baby),* action *(eat),* and object *(cup),* it is natural that caregivers could model word combinations using two of these relational words together ("baby eat," "baby cup," "eat cup"). To further expand the child's use of semantic relations, possession may be introduced ("baby's cup," "mommy's cup").

As the child develops, it will be necessary to look at syntactic skills including morphological markers (e.g., *-ed,* plural *s, -ing*) and the complexity of sentences (e.g., simple versus complex) as well as phonological skills. At all levels, the child's comprehension abilities also need to be documented either through informal activities (e.g., "Which one is the cow?," "Show me the baby is drinking") or formal measures. In addition, skill areas related to communication, such as motor, play, social, and cognitive skills, should be examined. See individual chapters in this text for extensive assessment information related to these areas.

Communication partners A necessary part of all assessment will include observation of children with their interactional partners in their daily environments. As suggested by McLean (1990), the nature of communication and communication development is transactional, and both partners influence the amount and type of interaction. The literature in adult/child interaction has indicated that behaviors that facilitate communication include contingent responses, provision of positive models, imitation or expansion of the child's actions or words, acceptance of the child's attempts, and adequate time provided for the child to initiate and respond (Duchan, 1989; Dunst et al., 1990; Peck, 1989). This is not to say, however, that there is one best way to interact with a child or to encourage practitioners to judge caregivers by how they interact with the child. Rather, the focus in observing caregiver/child or teacher/child interactions is to identify the behaviors that may be facilitating interaction and communication and to encourage and perhaps refine such behaviors.

With the recent attention to the interplay of child and caregiver characteristics and the individual nature of caregiver/child interactions, practitioners should be careful in drawing conclusions and suggesting interventions. For example, parents may be controlling or directive in their interactions with their child because this style seems more effective in getting and keeping the child's attention and participation. In addition, Plapinger and Kretschmer (1991) have reported that some caregiver behaviors differ across contexts and are more a factor of the parents' expectations of their role in an activity (e.g., teacher or therapist) than of caregiver interactional style. Indeed, Sorsby and Martlew (1991) reported a low incidence of directive comments produced during bookreading versus play with toys. In addition, the fact that some children produce very few vocalizations may serve to limit the responsivity of their caregivers (Konstantareas, Zajdeman, Homatidis, & McCabe, 1988; Zirpoli & Bell, 1987). Speech intelligibility has also been shown to be a factor in responsivity as indicated by Conti-Ramsden (1990), who examined the contingency of responses of mothers of children with and without language impairments and revealed that the greater the child's intelligibility, the greater the likelihood that the mother used semantically contingent utterances. As suggested by Conti-Ramsden (1993), attempts to assess and modify parental conversational behaviors may carry the implication that the parents have somehow failed to provide what their child needed, or worse, that they may have somehow contributed to the "problem." Thus, as she suggests, it is necessary to share with families that their interactional behaviors are not wrong and to remind them that "special children have special needs and that changes are needed in order to help their child to better learn language" (p. 292). Positive ideas for examining and influencing caregiver/child interactions can also be found in Calhoun, Rose, and Prendergast (1991), Duchan (1989), MacDonald (1989), Peck (1989), and Wilcox (1992).

Traditional Standardized Tests of Language

As noted previously, standardized testing is particularly useful for evaluation (e.g., identifying developmental levels and determining eligibility), but less useful for identifying instructional targets. Standardized tests, however, can be used to supplement the information gained from other measures and activities. Table 12.3 contains a list of representative standardized speech and language diagnostic and screening tests that can be used to assess the communication of infants and preschoolers. Indicated for each test are the areas assessed, age range, format of the test, type of score obtained, and unique aspects.

TABLE 12.3
Summary of Speech and Language Instruments

Test Name	Areas Assessed	Age Range	Format	Scores Obtained	Unique Aspects
A. *Standardized Language Diagnostic Instruments*					
Battelle Developmental Inventory (BDI) (Newborg, Stock, Wnek, Guidubaldi, & Svinicki, 1984)	personal-social, adaptive, motor, communication and cognitive	0–8:0	observation, structured interaction, and caregiver/teacher interview	percentile, standard score, age equivalent	includes screening test
Carrow Elicited Language Inventory (Carrow, 1974)	grammatical form and structure	3:0–7:11	elicited imitation	percentile, stanine, age equivalent	
Clinical Evaluation of Language Fundamentals–Preschool (Wiig, Secord, & Semel, 1992)	expressive and receptive language skills	3:0–6:0	picture identification, sentence comprehension, grammatical completion, question answering, recalling sentences in context, comprehension of linguistic concepts	standard score, percentile, age equivalent; receptive, expressive, and total score	
Communication and Symbolic Behavior Scales (Wetherby & Prizant, 1993)	communication functions and means, comprehension, symbolic and constructive play, social-affective signaling, reciprocity	8 mos–2:0	observation and elicited interaction	standard score, percentile, age equivalent	caregiver perception rating scale
Detroit Tests of Learning Aptitude–Primary: 2 (Hammill & Bryant, 1991)	cognitive, attention, linguistic, and motor	3:0–9:0	picture identification, object identification, object manipulation, observation, drawing	percentile and standard score for general intelligence and specific skills, age equivalent	
Developmental Observation Checklist System (Hresko, Miguel, Sharbenou, & Burton, 1994)	motor, social, language, and cognition	0–6:11	parent/caregiver completed checklist	standard score, percentile rank	computer scoring available (IBM, Macintosh); linked with adjustment behavior checklist, and parental stress and support checklist

Expressive One-Word Picture Vocabulary Test–Revised (Gardner, 1990)	expressive vocabulary	2:0–11:11	picture naming	mental age, percentile, stanine, IQ, age equivalent, standard score, scaled score	
Infant Mullen Scales of Early Learning (Mullen, 1989)	fine and gross motor; speech and communication; visual and auditory reception, organization and memory	0–3:0	picture identification, observation, labeling pictures, following directions, manipulation of objects, responses to questions	age score, T-score	
Kaufman Survey of Early Academic and Language Skills (Kaufman & Kaufman, 1993)	receptive and expressive vocabulary, some concepts (numbers, letters, words, counting), articulation survey	3:0–6:0	picture identification, labeling, pictures	standard score, percentile	
MacArthur Communicative Development Inventories, Infant & Toddler Versions (Fenson, Dale, Reznick, Bates, Thal, Hartung, & Reilly, 1991)	vocabulary comprehension and production, word endings and forms, syntactic development	10 mos–3:0	parent-completed checklist	percentile, mean	evaluation by parent
Miller-Yoder Language Comprehension Test (Miller & Yoder, 1984)	comprehension of grammatical form and structure	4:0–8:0	picture identification	receptive developmental age and error analysis by grammatical form	
Peabody Picture Vocabulary Test–Revised (Dunn & Dunn, 1981)	receptive vocabulary	2:5–adult	picture identification	receptive vocabulary age, standard score, percentile, stanine	adaptable for children with motor impairment, Spanish translation
Preschool Language Scale–3 (Zimmerman, Steiner & Pond, 1992)	developmental aspects of auditory comprehension, articulation, grammatical form and structure, basic concepts	0:1–3:0	responses to pictures, object manipulation, picture identification, following directions	total language, auditory comprehension expression scores, standard score, percentile, rank by age, language age equivalent	Spanish translation

TABLE 12.3
Continued

Test Name	Areas Assessed	Age Range	Format	Scores Obtained	Unique Aspects
Reynell Developmental Language Scales (Reynell & Gruber, 1969)	general expressive and receptive language skills	1:0–6:0	observation, picture identification, object identification, object manipulation	communication age equivalent, standard score, percentile, developmental age score	normed verbal comprehension version for children responding only by pointing
Sequenced Inventory of Communicative Development–Revised (Hedrick, Prather, & Tobin, 1984)	sound awareness and discrimination, comprehension, motor, vocal, and verbal expressions (i.e., responses, initiations, imitations)	0:4–4:0	parent report, object manipulation, picture identification, following directions	receptive communication age, expressive communication age	assesses some prelinguistic skills, uses elicited and parent report information
Test for Auditory Comprehension of Language–Revised (Carrow-Woolfolk, 1985)	comprehension of grammatical form and structure, content, and vocabulary	3:0–adult	picture identification, object manipulation, best choice	percentile rank, comprehension age equivalent, percentile ranks for grade equivalents	computer scoring available (Apple and IBM)
Test of Early Language Development–2 (Hresko, Reid, & Hammill, 1991)	receptive and expressive grammatical forms, content of language, and word knowledge	2:0–7:11	picture identification, answering questions, object manipulation, imitation, picture description, best choice, sentence completion, synonyms, sentence formulation, defining words	percentile, language age, language quotient, standard score, age equivalent	
Test of Language Development–Primary–2 (Newcomer & Hammill, 1988)	grammatical understanding, receptive and expressive vocabulary, expressive grammatical structure	3:0–8:11	picture identification, imitation, grammatical completion, defining words, word discrimination, word articulation	language ages for each subtest, standardized global index of language ability	computer scoring available (Apple and IBM)
Test of Pragmatic Skills–Revised (Shulman, 1986)	how children verbally adapt to various communicative contexts	3:0–8:11	four guided play interactions	means, percentile	computer scoring available (Apple)

B. *Standardized Language Screening Instruments*					
Ages and Stages Questionnaires (ASQ): A Parent-Completed Monitoring System (Bricker, Squires, & Mounts, 1995)	fine and gross motor, communication, problem solving, personal-social, and overall	4 mos–4:0	parent-completed checklist	pass/fail	evaluation by parent Spanish version
Bankson Language Screening Test–2 (Bankson, 1990)	vocabulary, grammatical form, content, and visual and auditory perception, semantic knowledge, morphological and syntactic rules, pragmatic knowledge	3:0–8:0	picture identification, object identification, best choice, imitation, sequencing, matching	standard deviation scores, percentiles	
Birth to Three Assessment & Intervention System (Bangs, 1986)	problem solving, personal-social skills, motor skills, general receptive and expressive language	0:0–3:0	observation, following directions, motor and verbal imitation, picture identification, naming body parts, object identification, parental report	standard score, percentile rank, stanine	norm-referenced screening test, criterion-referenced checklist
Compton Speech and Language Evaluation (Compton, 1978)	articulation, vocabulary, colors, shapes, fluency, voice, oral mechanism, auditory-visual memory, expressive grammatical structure, and grammatical understanding	3:0–6:0	object identification, object labeling, oral mechanism exam	pass/fail	Spanish version
Fluharty Preschool Speech and Language Screening Test (Fluharty, 1968)	articulation, vocabulary, receptive and expressive language ability	2:0–6:0	object identification, picture identification, sentence repetition	cut-off scores for each age group	
Northwestern Syntax Screening Test (Lee, 1971)	receptive and expressive grammatical form and structure	3:0–7:11		age equivalent	

TABLE 12.3
Continued

Test Name	Areas Assessed	Age Range	Format	Scores Obtained	Unique Aspects
Pragmatics Screening Test (Prinz & Weiner, 1987)	maintaining topic, formulating speech acts, politeness, establishing a referent for listener, narration, revising a directive when listener does not understand	3:5–8:5	gamelike tasks (ghost trick, absurd requests, referential communication)		
Receptive-Expressive Emergent Language Test–2 (Bzoch & League, 1991)	prelinguistic skills	0:1–3:0	parent report	receptive and expressive communication age, quotients, combined language age	
C. *Criterion-Referenced Instruments*					
Assessment, Evaluation, and Programming System: AEPS Measurement for Birth to Three Years (Bricker, 1993)	fine and gross motor, adaptive, cognitive, social-communication, and social	0–3:0	observation and elicited interaction, parent evaluation	criterion-referenced age equivalents	parent and professional evaluation, Family Interest Survey included
Carolina Curriculum for Infants and Toddlers with Special Needs (Johnson-Martin, Jens, Attermeier, & Hacker, 1991)	cognition, fine and gross motor, communication, social adaptation	0–2:0	observation and elicited interactions	criterion-referenced age equivalents	assessment log and curriculum guide for intervention
Carolina Curriculum for Preschoolers with Special Needs (Johnson-Martin, Attermeier, & Hacker, 1990)	cognition, communication, social adaptation, fine and gross motor	2:0–5:0	observation, elicited interactions	criterion-referenced age equivalents	assessment log and curriculum guide for intervention
Hawaii Early Learning Profile (Furuno, O'Reilly, Inatsuka, Hosaka, Allman, & Zeisloft-Falbey, 1987)	cognition, receptive and expressive language, fine and gross motor, social, and self-help	0–3:0	checklist	criterion-referenced age equivalents	

HELP for Special Preschoolers (1987)	self-help, motor, communication, social, and learning/cognitive	3.0–6.0	checklist	criterion-referenced age equivalents	
Parent/Professional Preschool Performance Profile (Bloch, 1987)	social, motor, cognitive, self-help, language, and classroom adjustment	6 mos–6 yrs	parent and professional checklist	criterion-referenced age equivalents	parent and professional evaluation
D. *Nonstandardized Assessment Instruments*					
Assessing Prelinguistic and Linguistic Behaviors (Olswang, Stoel-Gammon, Coggins, & Carpenter, 1987)	cognitive antecedents, play, communicative intention, language production and comprehension	0–2:0	observation, elicited interactions	criterion-referenced age equivalents	video training tapes available
Infant-Toddler Language Scale (Rossetti, 1990)	play, gesture, interaction-attachment, pragmatics, language comprehension and expression	0–3:0	observation, elicited interaction, and parent report	age equivalents	includes parent questionnaire
Preschool Language Assessment Instrument (Blank, Rose, & Berlin, 1978)	discourse, general language ability, language skills needed in teaching environment	3:0–5:11	responses to pictures, questions	profile of discourse skills, qualitative rating of language adequacy	can be used with children who have poor school performance and whose language skills are questionable (up to 10 years old), Spanish version
Pre-Speech Assessment Scale (Morris, 1982)	feeding, sucking, swallowing, biting and chewing, respiration-phonation, sound play		rating scale	levels of development	
Transdisciplinary Play-Based Assessment (Revised Edition) (Linder, 1993)	cognitive, communication and language, sensory-motor, and social-emotional	6 mos–6:0	play-based arena assessment	age equivalencies available from developmental charts	

TABLE 12.3
Continued

Test Name	Areas Assessed	Age Range	Format	Scores Obtained	Unique Aspects
E. *Standardized Speech Diagnostic Instruments*					
Arizona Articulation Proficiency Scale–Revised (Fudala & Reynolds, 1986)	determining misarticulations and total articulation proficiency	any age, norms for 1:5–13 years	picture identification	total score, weighted for percent each error sound is used in English; intelligibility descriptions, severity designations, developmental age equivalents, percentile, standard scores	
Assessment of Phonological Processes–Revised (Hodson, 1986)	phonological processes	2–9 yrs	labeling objects	percentage of occurrence, phonological deviancy score, phonological process average	computer analysis available (Apple)
Bankson-Bernthal Test of Phonology (BBTOP) (Bankson & Bernthal, 1990)	articulation and phonological processes	3:00–9:0	labeling pictures	standard scores, percentile ranks	
Compton-Hutton Phonological Assessment (Compton & Hutton, 1978)	broad patterns of articulation errors and linguistic analyses of misarticulation	any age	picture identification	summary of phonological pattern analysis, phonological rule analysis	
Goldman-Fristoe Test of Articulation (Goldman & Fristoe, 1986)	articulation errors and stimulability for correct production of error sounds	2:0–16:0+	picture identification, story retell, imitation	percent of speech in error	
Khan-Lewis Phonological Analysis (Khan & Lewis, 1986)	diagnosis and description of phonological processes	any age, norms for 2:0–5:11	uses stimulus material from *Goldman-Fristoe Test of Articulation*, test yields error scores, percentage ranks	developmental phonological process rating	

Most Frequently Used Assessment Tools

In an attempt to identify the instruments used routinely to assess the communication skills of infants and toddlers, Crais and Leonard (1990) asked respondents to a survey of speech-language pathology graduate programs which tools they used most frequently. The 10 most frequently used tools (which appear in Table 12.4) were then rated by Wetherby and Prizant (1992) according to seven characteristics of assessment content and strategies (Table 12.4).

As can be seen in Table 12.4, a number of the characteristics that may be viewed as representing best practice in assessing young

TABLE 12.4
Rating of Traditional Instruments for Assessing Infants and Toddlers

	Assessment Instrument									
Feature	**SICD**	**PLS**	**REEL**	**Denver**	**Birth to Three**	**Bayley Scales**	**ACLC**	**Ordinal Scales**	**Vineland**	**ELI**
Assesses functions of communication	L	—	L	L	L	L	—	L	L	—
Analyzes preverbal communication	L	—	L	L	+	L	—	—	L	—
Assesses social-affective signaling	—	—	—	L	L	L	—	—	L	—
Profiles social, communicative, and symbolic abilities	—	—	—	L	+	—	—	—	L	—
Uses caregivers as informants and assesses child directly	+	—	+	+	L	—	—	—	L	—
Uses spontaneous child-initiated communicative interactions	L	—	—	—	—	—	—	—	—	+
Uses caregivers as active participants	—	—	—	L	—	—	—	—	—	L

Ten routinely used assessment instruments for developmentally young children, rated for characteristics of assessment content and strategies. The assessment instruments are listed from left to right in descending order by number of university programs in speech-language pathology that use each instrument routinely (Crais & Leonard, 1990). (SICD = Sequenced Inventory of Communication Development; PLS = Preschool Language Scale; REEL = Receptive-Expressive Language Scale; Denver = Denver Developmental Screening Test; Birth to Three = Birth to Three Checklist of Learning and Language Behavior; Bayley Scales = Bayley Scales of Infant Development; ACLC = Assessment of Children's Language Comprehension; Ordinal Scales = Ordinal Scales of Psychological Development; Vineland = Vineland Adaptive Behavior Scales; ELI = Environmental Language Inventory; + = characteristic addressed in depth; L = characteristic addressed to a limited extent; — = characteristic not addressed.)

Source: From "Profiling Young Children's Communicative Competence" by A. Wetherby and B. Prizant, in S. Warren and J. Reichle (Eds.) *Causes and Effects in Communication and Language Intervention,* 1992, Baltimore, MD: Paul H. Brookes Publishing Company, P.O. Box 10624, Baltimore, MD 21285-0624.

children are either not addressed or are addressed only to a limited degree by many of the instruments. In recent efforts to update the list of currently used instruments, Crais (1994a, 1994b) asked over 100 speech-language pathologists working with infants and toddlers to identify from a list provided which instruments they used "routinely" to assess children in the birth-to-3-year range. The top 10 instruments selected appear in Figure 12.2. Although two of the tools listed, the Infant-Toddler Language Scale (Rossetti, 1990) and the Transdisciplinary Play-Based Assessment (Linder, 1993), do represent a number of the best practice characteristics identified by Wetherby and Prizant (1992), most of the remaining tools reflect a continued focus on standardized techniques with limited attention to recent trends in assessment. Thus, a number of professionals (Crais, 1995; Crais & Roberts, 1991; Norris, 1992; Prizant & Wetherby, 1993) have argued against the sole use of standardized testing and suggest adding observational and informal assessment measures. In particular, they suggest a blend of standardized testing and nonstandardized assessment, including direct observation, interaction with the child, and caregiver interviews. For professionals who have naturalistic contexts in which to observe and informally assess children, nonstandardized measures are particularly appropriate for analyzing a child's communication skills.

Criterion-Referenced and Nonstandardized Instruments

Criterion-referenced instruments and developmental scales are typically not standardized and are often developed by compiling information taken from standardized tests, other developmental charts and scales, and clinical experiences. This type of information can be particularly useful in assessment and later intervention planning, although care should be

Preschool Language Scale–3 (Zimmerman, Steiner, & Pond, 1992)

Receptive-Expressive-Emergent Language–2 (Bzoch & League, 1991)

Sequenced Inventory of Communication Development–Revised (Hedrick, Prather, & Tobin, 1984)

Infant-Toddler Language Scale (Rossetti, 1990)

Expressive One-Word Picture Vocabulary Test–Revised (Gardner, 1990)

Clinical Evaluation of Language Fundamentals–Preschool (Wiig, Secord, & Semel, 1992)

Peabody Picture Vocabulary Test–Revised (Dunn & Dunn, 1981)

Transdisciplinary Play-Based Assessment (Linder, 1993)

Receptive One-Word Picture Vocabulary Test (Gardner, 1985)

Birth to Three Assessment and Intervention System (Bangs, 1986)

(See Table 12.3 for further information.)

FIGURE 12.2

Top 10 instruments used to assess communication skills in infants and toddlers

Source: From *Birth to Three: Assessment Tools and Techniques* by E. Crais, 1994a, presentation to Charlotte Area Health Education Center, Charlotte, NC; *Birth to Three: Current Assessment Tools and Techniques* by E. Crais, 1994b, presentation to the Tennessee Association of Audiologists and Speech-Language Pathologists, Gatlinburg, TN.

taken when using developmental scales as anything more than rough guidelines to development. Table 12.3 provides a list of commercially available criterion-referenced and nonstandardized speech and language instruments. In addition to assessing communication skills, many of these instruments also examine social, cognitive, and motor skills. Examples are the Assessment, Evaluation, and Programming System (Bricker, 1993), the Hawaii Early Learning Profile (Furuno, O'Reilly, Inatsuka, Hosaka, Allman, & Zeisloft-Falbey, 1987), and the Parent/Professional Preschool Performance Profile (Bloch, 1987). Some instruments, such as the Battelle Developmental Inventory (Newborg, Stock, Wnek, Guidubaldi, & Svinicki, 1984), are both standardized and criterion-referenced.

Alternative Assessment Tools and Techniques

With the recent focus on more informal and observational approaches, a number of alternative assessment tools and techniques have been developed. This section highlights a representative sample of these instruments in an attempt to encourage professionals to broaden their use of available assessment measures. Whereas Table 12.3 provides a brief description of most of these tools, Table 12.5 displays these alternative tools and techniques rated according to the seven best-practice characteristics identified by Wetherby and Prizant (1992) in addition to six characteristics identified by Crais (1995). As can be seen, many of the alternative tools do address a number of the best-practice characteristics, particularly emphasizing naturalistic assessment contexts and more active roles played by family members.

Finally, the reader will note that two assessment techniques listed in Table 12.5 are not described in Table 12.3 because they were not originally designed for assessing children with special needs. Both the Family Administered Neonatal Activities (Cardone & Gilkerson, 1989) and the Social Action Games (Platt & Coggins, 1990), described in Chapter 3, also provide alternatives to traditional assessment approaches. The following section highlights an additional alternative strategy that has been available for years and has received renewed attention with the current emphasis on observational and informal measures.

Communication Sampling

Collecting a communication sample is a frequently used method for obtaining information about a child's communication. These samples provide a running record of communication efforts during a set period of time and can be collected in such natural settings as the child's home with the family or the child's classroom with peers. Communication samples are particularly useful for assessing the frequency and manner in which children communicate in their daily environments. The ultimate goal is to collect information that is representative of a child's communicative performance.

Several issues should be considered before collecting a communication sample. First, what is the purpose of the sample? Is it to identify the child's overall level of communication or primarily to pinpoint the use of specific communication behaviors? Second, how will the behaviors of interest be measured? That is, will all the occurrences of a behavior be counted or only those occurring during specific points in time? Third, how will the sample be collected? The context, participants, and nature of the interaction can all influence a child's communication. Fourth, how will the sample be recorded? Will on-line notes or transcription be performed or will video or audio recording be done? Finally, how will the information be analyzed? Will the target behaviors be totaled or will further analysis be necessary in the areas of communication or play, such as coding the type of communication attempts or play behaviors exhibited during play?

TABLE 12.5
Alternative Infant/Toddler Assessment Tools and Techniques Rated Against Thirteen Best-Practice Characteristics

	AEPS	APLB	CCIT	CSBS	FANA	IMQ	ITLS	LDS	MCDI	5PS	SAG
Opportunities for child initiations	+	+	+	+	+	+	+	+	+	+	+
Focuses on preverbal communication	+	+	+	+	+	+	+	–	+	+	+
Focuses on communicative function	+	+	–	+	–	–	+	–	+/–	+/–	–
Focuses on social-affective behaviors	+/–	–	+	+	+	+	+	–	–	+	+/–
Profiles strengths and needs within communication	+	+	+	+	–	–	+	–	+	+	+
Documents emerging skills	+	+	+	+	+	+	+	–	+/–	+/–	+
Corresponds to day-to-day activities	+	+	+	+	+	+	+	+	+	+	+
Active role for caregiver	+	+	+	+	+	+	+	+	+	+	+
Includes caregiver assessment	+	+/–	+/–	+/–	+	+	+	+	+	+	+/–
Dynamic assessment process	+	+/–	+/–	+	+	–	+/–	–	–	+/–	+
Caregiver validates findings	+	+/–	+	+	+	+	+/–	+	+	+	+/–
Allows individual variation	+	+	+	+	+	+	+	+	+	+	+
Predictable of later communication	NA	NA	NA	NA	NA	NA	NA	NA	+	NA	NA

AEPS = Assessment, Evaluation, and Programming System (Bricker, 1993)
APLB = Assessing Prelinguistic and Linguistic Behavior (Olswang, Stoel-Gammon, Coggins, & Carpenter, 1987)
CCIT = Carolina Curriculum for Infants and Toddlers with Special Needs (Johnson-Martin, Jens, Attermeier, & Hacker, 1991)
CSBS = Communication and Symbolic Behavior Scales (Wetherby & Prizant, 1993)
FANA = Family Administered Neonatal Activities (Cardone & Gilkerson, 1989)
IMQ = Infant Monitoring Questionnaire (Bricker, 1989)
ITLS = Infant-Toddler Language Scale (Rossetti, 1990)
LDS = Language Development Survey (Rescorla, 1989)
MCDI = MacArthur Communicative Development Inventories (Fenson, Dale, Reznick, Thal, Bates, Hartung, Pethick, & Reilly, 1991)
5PS = Parent/Professional Preschool Performance Profile (Bloch, 1987)
SAG = Social Action Games (Platt & Coggins, 1990)

\+ = characteristic is addressed
+/– = characteristic can be addressed by adaptation of tool
– = characteristic is not addressed
NA = information not yet available

Identifying the purpose of the sample The sample can examine any area of communication that is of interest to the early interventionist and other team members. Sampling, for example, could determine how a child intentionally communicates (e.g., requests, protests), a child's typical form of communication (e.g., gesture, vocalization, or speech) or the diversity of communicative functions used. The sample can also address specific communication areas such as how the child responds to teacher requests or how he or she protests when a peer grabs a toy during playtime. Once the purpose of the sample is determined, the behaviors of interest should be behaviorally defined. For example, if the child's requesting behavior in the classroom is of interest, should the number of times he or she makes a request, the types of requests used (e.g., gestures vs. speech), or the proportion of communication attempts that are requests be studied?

Collecting the sample Variables associated with the collection of the sample are critical because the context of the interaction can influence the child's communication and thus the representativeness of the sample. The sample can be collected almost anywhere (e.g., classroom, home, playground), during any activity (free-play, block building, book-reading, diapering), and with any partners (peers, siblings, teachers, parents, other caregivers). Familiar contexts and activities that are both age-appropriate and interesting can increase the child's level and type of communication. Children tend to talk more with conversational partners who follow their topic, respond to their communicative attempts, pause for the child to take a turn, and use open-ended rather than closed-ended questions (Coggins, Olswang, & Guthrie, 1987). The suggestions in Figure 12.1, Miller (l981), and Lund and Duchan (1988) can be useful for engaging a child in interaction. Because context, activities, and partners influence a child's communication, it is advantageous, although not necessary, to sample more than one context in a setting, for example, by varying the setting as well as changing the communicative partner or activity. A further variable is how long the sample should last. The time can be as short as 5 minutes or as long as needed, depending on the sample's purpose. For a representative sample, Miller (1981) suggests at least two 15-minute sampling sessions with a minimum of 50 to 100 utterances recorded.

Once the context is selected, the technique for eliciting the sample should be identified. One technique available is naturalistic observation, in which the interventionist observes the child in a natural environment and does not actively engage the child. For example, the child may be observed during free-play in the classroom, during games such as peek-a-boo with a parent, or playtime with a sibling. The professional can provide a set of toys or the child can play with familiar toys available in the sampling context. With naturalistic observation, however, certain types of communicative behaviors (e.g., question asking) may occur infrequently or not at all (Coggins et al., 1987). In such cases, the professional might use a second technique, structured interaction, in which the situation is structured to increase the likelihood that particular types of behaviors will occur. This technique can be used to elicit behaviors such as the communication functions of requests or protests or specific language structures such as use of negatives. For example, if the professional desires information about requesting behavior, the child can be given a tightly closed plastic jar with Cheerios inside to see if and how he or she requests assistance. Creaghead (l984), Fey (l986), Miller (1981), and Prizant and Wetherby (1993) describe other procedures for eliciting communication in structured interactions.

Recording the sample Communication samples can be recorded on-line, with the observer writing down the information from the session or using video or audio recorders. For on-line transcription, the professional can either note what the child says or does that relates to the target behaviors or code the target behaviors, using predetermined categories. If continuous sampling is used, the coder writes down everything that happens or codes every target event; if interval sampling is used, the examiner records whether a behavior occurred within a set interval of time (e.g., during a 10-second time block). Audio or video recording can be used to supplement on-line transcription or for later analysis. Clearly, audio or video recording provides more accurate retrieval of the child's communicative interactions; however, it may not be necessary for the sample's purpose. Further, the difficulty of using recorders in natural settings and the time needed for transcription and/or coding may make their use impractical. A form for collecting a communication sample is shown in Figure 12.3 (pp. 366–367). The form can help the observer identify the speaker, the communication itself, the type of turn, the communication function, and the means used to communicate. Nonverbal behaviors and other contextual information can be noted in parentheses; this is often necessary, because the meaning of an utterance may differ depending on the context.

Analyzing the sample For the professional who is primarily interested in an overview of a child's communicative behavior (e.g., whether a child communicates by vocalizing or gesturing), the collected sample itself may provide adequate and interpretable information. For some children, however, more detailed analyses are necessary in the areas of pragmatics, semantics, syntax, phonology, or play. Below are examples of the kinds of information that can be derived from a sample in each of these domains.

In analyzing pragmatic behavior, for example, children's communicative functions can be coded into specific categories, using Wetherby and Prizant's (1993) taxonomy outlined previously. The communication sample can then be examined for three indices: the frequency of communication (e.g., 5 times in 10 minutes), the diversity of communication functions expressed (e.g., 2 requests, 1 protest, 1 comment, 1 answer), and the diversity of means used to express the communicative functions (e.g., 2 vocalizations, 3 gestures). The sample can also be analyzed for discourse skills; for example, determining the percentage of the times a child responds or initiates and with whom the child communicates (e.g., adults only, never with peers). The average number of turns that a child takes in routines such as patty-cake, in vocal play, or in conversational exchanges can also be useful. Table 12.6 shows how communicative functions and turn-taking can be coded in a communication sample. For additional information on coding pragmatic behaviors, see Roth and Spekman (1984) and Paul (1987).

For semantic abilities, the analysis can include the total number of words used in the sample, the number of different words, and the number and type of semantic relations. Using Table 12.1, each utterance can be examined to determine the semantic categories used in prelinguistic, one-word, and multiword utterances, as well as whether a variety of semantic roles are used. If, for intervention purposes, the professional is interested in a specific category of words such as common foods or action words, these categories can also be included in the analysis. An index of vocabulary diversity often computed is the Type Token Ratio (TTR), which is the number of different words used in a sample divided by the total number of words. A TTR of .45 to .50 is common for children 3 to 8 years of age and shows a typical amount of vocabulary diversity in a sample (Templin, 1957). A low ratio of .20, on the other hand, indicates that in this sample the child used only a few words, although repeatedly, and thus may be limited in vocabulary diversity.

When analyzing the sample for syntax, the professional can look at both the child's overall utterance length or mean length of utterance (as described earlier) and the basic sentence structures used. For a child using only one- or two-word utterances, syntactic analysis is not necessary. For a child using three-word or multiword constructions, the analysis could include the use of grammatical morphemes (e.g., *ing, ed),* negatives, questions, and simple versus complex sentence structures, as described in Miller (1981).

In analyzing the sample for phonological skills, the professional can note both the sounds the child does and does not produce and the number of syllables generally used (e.g., two in *uh-oh,* one in *up).* An increase in the number of syllables used is an indication of advancing phonological skills. It is also helpful to note how often the child's speech is intelligible, that is, understandable (e.g., all, most, some, or none of the time) and whether it varies depending on the context (e.g., home versus school), conversational partner (e.g., parent versus peer), or utterance length (e.g., one-word versus multiword utterances). Although a communication sample can be analyzed for specific sounds and error patterns, a detailed analysis is generally performed by a speech-language pathologist. Developmental information on phonology can be found in Bernthal and Bankson (1988), Creaghead, Newman, and Secord (1989), and Stoel-Gammon and Dunn (1985).

Analyses illustrated An example of how information from a communication sample can be analyzed is illustrated for a 4-year-old child, Bob, who has cerebral palsy. The communication sample was collected during two 10-minute classroom activities (e.g., snack time and free-play). A portion of the snack-time sample is shown in Table 12.6 (p. 368). Bob communicated 20 times during the two observations, using speech most frequently and gestures on occasion. His speech consisted primarily of one- and two-word utterances and an occasional three-word utterance. Except for very structured interactions, Bob infrequently initiated communication to his teacher and less frequently to peers. If an adult started and controlled the interaction, however, Bob responded by taking as many as five turns using speech. He often used repetition of the adult's utterance as a means for continuing the interaction. He responded appropriately to many adult requests by answering questions with words and gestures; however, he typically responded to peers nonverbally through smiling or gestures (especially grabbing), and when frustrated, cried rather than verbalized his desires.

The semantic analysis indicated that Bob used a total of 30 words and that there were 15 different words, for a type token ratio (TTR) of .50. Bob expressed a range of semantic relations at the two-word level, such as agent + object, action + object, recurrence + object, and one at the three-word level (agent + action + object). His words included the names of people and common objects, actions, social words, and modifiers. The syntactic analysis of the 15 utterances indicated that during the sample Bob's mean length of utterance (MLU) in words was 1.75, although this figure should be interpreted cautiously. As recommended by Miller (1981), MLU should be based on at least 50 utterances. The phonological analysis indicated that Bob used age-appropriate initial and medial consonants but omitted most final consonants.

In summary, the information derived from a communication sample can provide important information about how a child communicates in everyday situations and can be a working basis for later intervention decisions. The following section provides an additional means for practitioners to gain information about a child's communication skills.

FIGURE 12.3
Communication report form

Instructions: Please check under level of use each communicative function and write in the communication mode.

	Level of Use			Communication Mode Used*		Situations	
Functions	Yes does this	Is learning this	Does not do this	Most often	Least often	In what situations?	Give example
1. *Requests objects*—Does your child communicate that he wants an object that is out of reach? (e.g., pushes adult's hands toward a cookie or says "cookie")							
2. *Requests action*—Does your child communicate that she wants help doing something? (e.g., hands adult a jar to open or says "open")							
3. *Attention seeking*—Does your child communicate that he wants you to attend to him or to something in the environment? (e.g., tugs on mother's pants or says "mama")							
4. *Comment on object*—Does your child communicate that she wants you to notice or comment on an object? (e.g., points to "dog" and smiles or says "dog")							
5. *Comment on action*—Does your child communicate that he is interested in something another person or object has done or does he try to get you to notice? (e.g., flies plane in air and claps or says "up")							

Instructions: Please check under level of use each communicative function and write in the communication mode.

	Level of Use			Communication Mode Used*		Situations	
Functions	Yes does this	Is learning this	Does not do this	Most often	Least often	In what situations?	Give example
6. *Protests*—Does your child communicate that she does not like or does not want something? (e.g., pushes your hand away or says "no")							
7. *Requests information*—Does your child ask for names and locations of things, animals, or people? (e.g., points to picture in book and looks at adult or asks "what that?")							
8. *Answers*—Does your child respond to your questions about name and locations of things, animals, or people? (e.g., when asked, "What do you want?" points to chocolate cookie or says "cookie")							
9. *Acknowledges*—Does your child do something to indicate that he has heard you speaking to him? (e.g., nods his head or says "yes")							
10. *Social Routines*—Does your child communicate routines such as "please," "thank you," "hi," and "bye"? (e.g., to indicate "bye-bye" waves or says "bye")							

* GE = gesture, SP = speech, SO = sounds, SI = signing

TABLE 12.6
Communication Sample Analysis

Child: Bob (B) Other participant: Teacher (T) Setting: Classroom Date: 7/7/94
Activity: Snack Length of observation: 10 minutes Observer: JR
Notes: Bob has a cold and an ear infection.

Speaker	Communication Behavior	Turn*	Function†	Mode‡
T	"It's snack time. Look." (teacher puts cookies on table out of reach of children)			
B	Reaches for cookie as looks at teacher.	I	RO	GE
T	"What do you want?"			
B	(points to package as looks at teacher)	R	RO	GE
T	"Cookie?"			
B	"Yeah, cookie."	R	AN	SP
T	"Do you want chocolate chip or sugar?"			
B	"Chocolate."	R	AN	SP
T	Gives Bob cookie.			
B	"Cookie good."	I	CO	SP
T	"Yes. The cookie is good!"			
B	"More cookie." (pointing toward others on plate)	I	RO	SP

* Turn–I = Initiation, R = Response
† Function–RO = Request for object, AN = answer, CO = comment on object
‡ Mode–GE = gesture, SP = speech

Decision Trees

Three decision trees developed by Crais and Roberts (1991) for children functioning at the prelinguistic, one-word, and multiword levels appear in Figures 12.4, 12.5, and 12.6. They incorporate questions to help identify a child's level of communication functioning, for the purpose of guiding intervention planning. The key points in assessing young children are *whether* a child communicates and *when, what,* and *how* information is transmitted. As noted for prelinguistic children, the focus is on early-developing social and interactive aspects of communication. For example, if a child uses only gestures and vocalizations, the focus in assessment would be primarily on determining whether those behaviors represent functional communication. For verbal children, although words are important, the focus still remains on functional and interactive aspects; therefore, assessments of semantics and pragmatics rather than phonology or syntax are highlighted. Furthermore, the decision trees were designed for use with children functioning *developmentally* between 6 months and 3 years of age. For children functioning at a higher level, the assessment tools in Table 12.3 can be utilized.

Each decision tree includes three major skill areas: social interaction, comprehension, and production. For practical purposes, production has been divided into two areas, spontaneous and imitation, although imitation crosses each of the other areas. Within each skill area is a list of behaviors that can be observed or elicited. The individual behaviors are generally listed in a developmental sequence from early- to later-developing; however, since some behaviors develop simultaneously, the sequence may vary. Although each skill area is presented as discrete, any one behavior *within* a skill area may incorporate aspects of the other skill areas.

The professional should generally move vertically through each list of behaviors, stopping where the child either does not exhibit a few consecutive behaviors, or does so in a limited or inconsistent manner. Once this point, which is the child's current level of functioning, is established, the interventionist can then move through the other two areas of the decision tree. At any point in the process, further analysis in any of the areas can be initiated. Developmental charts and scales and interactive assessment techniques (described in the previous sections) can be used to identify additional behaviors between achieved and unachieved behaviors. Most of the behaviors can be elicited through interaction with the child or gained from discussion with parents and other caregivers.

When moving through the decision trees, the interventionist should remember that each child is unique and will therefore display some degree of individual variability. Thus the decision questions are basic guidelines and are not presented as hard-and-fast rules for each child's absolute progression of skills. Although the three decision trees are presented separately, interventionists may need to move back and forth between them to explore a child's full range of communication skills. It is also important to remember that opportunity plays a part in *which* skills will be exhibited by an individual child. The type and number of interactions that are initiated by, responded to, and encouraged by a child's caregivers or teachers can shape the kinds of behaviors displayed. It is often helpful to observe the caregiver(s) or teacher(s) interacting with the child to get an idea of the typical opportunities the child may have available.

An example of how one might use the decision trees to assess communicative behavior in a child at a prelinguistic level is demonstrated for the Social Interaction area. The interventionist could set up situations to elicit specific communicative means and functions, observe the means and functions that are readily used by the child, and look for evidence of those not yet developed. The interventionist could also rely on caregiver or teacher report through the use of a form like that shown in Figure 12.3. The interventionist can ask the caregiver or teacher to describe (a) *what functions* the child does or does not use, or is learning to express (e.g., requests for objects or actions, protests); (b) *what means* are used to express those functions: nonverbal (gesture, body movement, facial expression), verbal (speech, signing), or vocal (speech sounds, nonspeech sounds); and (c) in *what situations* the child expresses these functions.

Using the Decision Trees

To illustrate the use of the decision trees in identifying a child's current communicative means and functions, the process of observing and interacting with a 20-month-old child named Susan will be described. Because Susan's parents (Ella and Matt) reported that what they primarily wanted from the assessment was ideas for how they and their child-care provider (Terry) could work to improve Susan's communication skills at home, it was suggested that Susan should be observed interacting with her parents, her 4-year-old sister, the child-care provider, and the examiners in free-play, and with her parents during mealtime and dressing. In discussing options for assessment tools and techniques, Ella and Matt liked the idea of using informal observations and the

FIGURE 12.4
Decision tree for a child at the prelinguistic stage

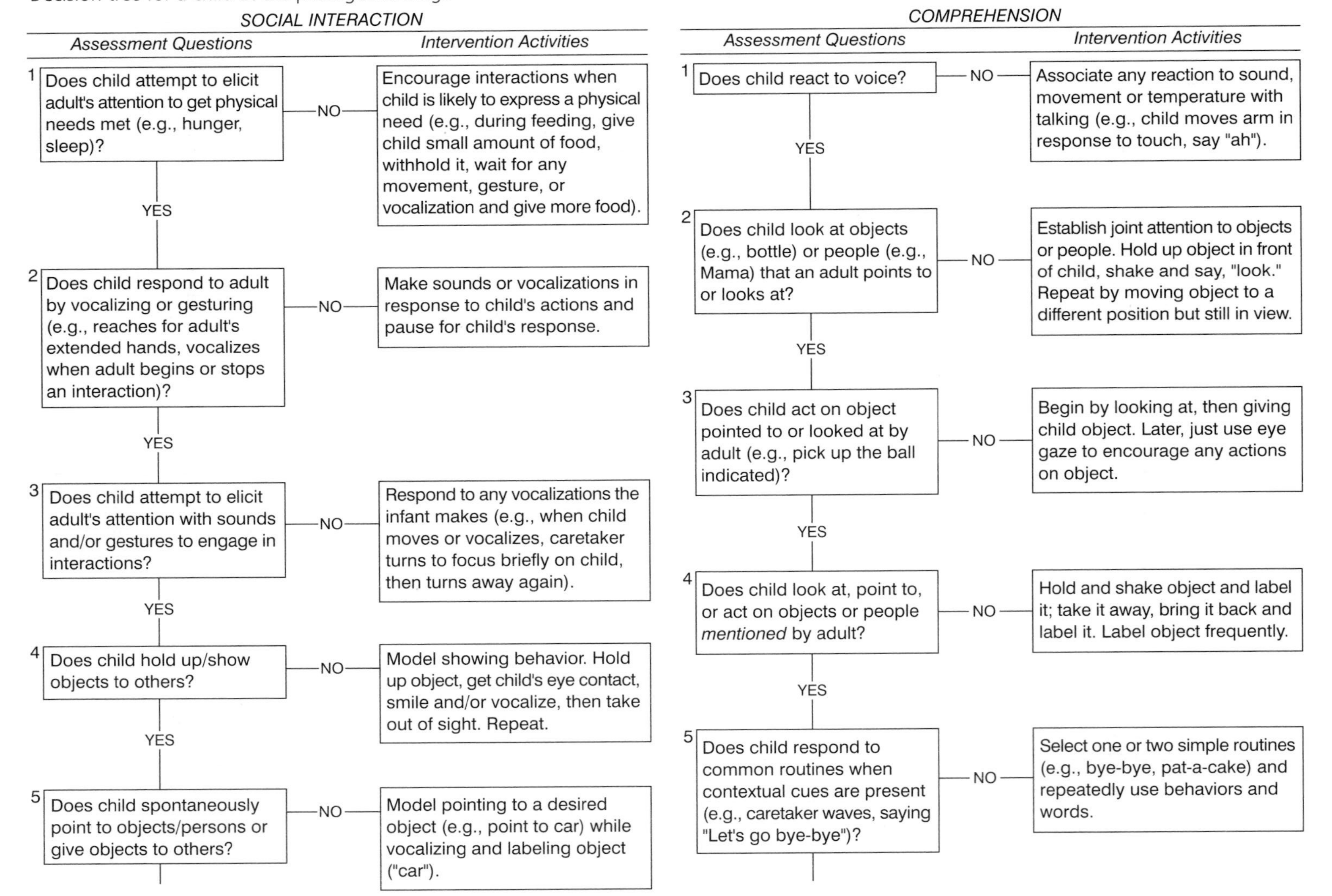

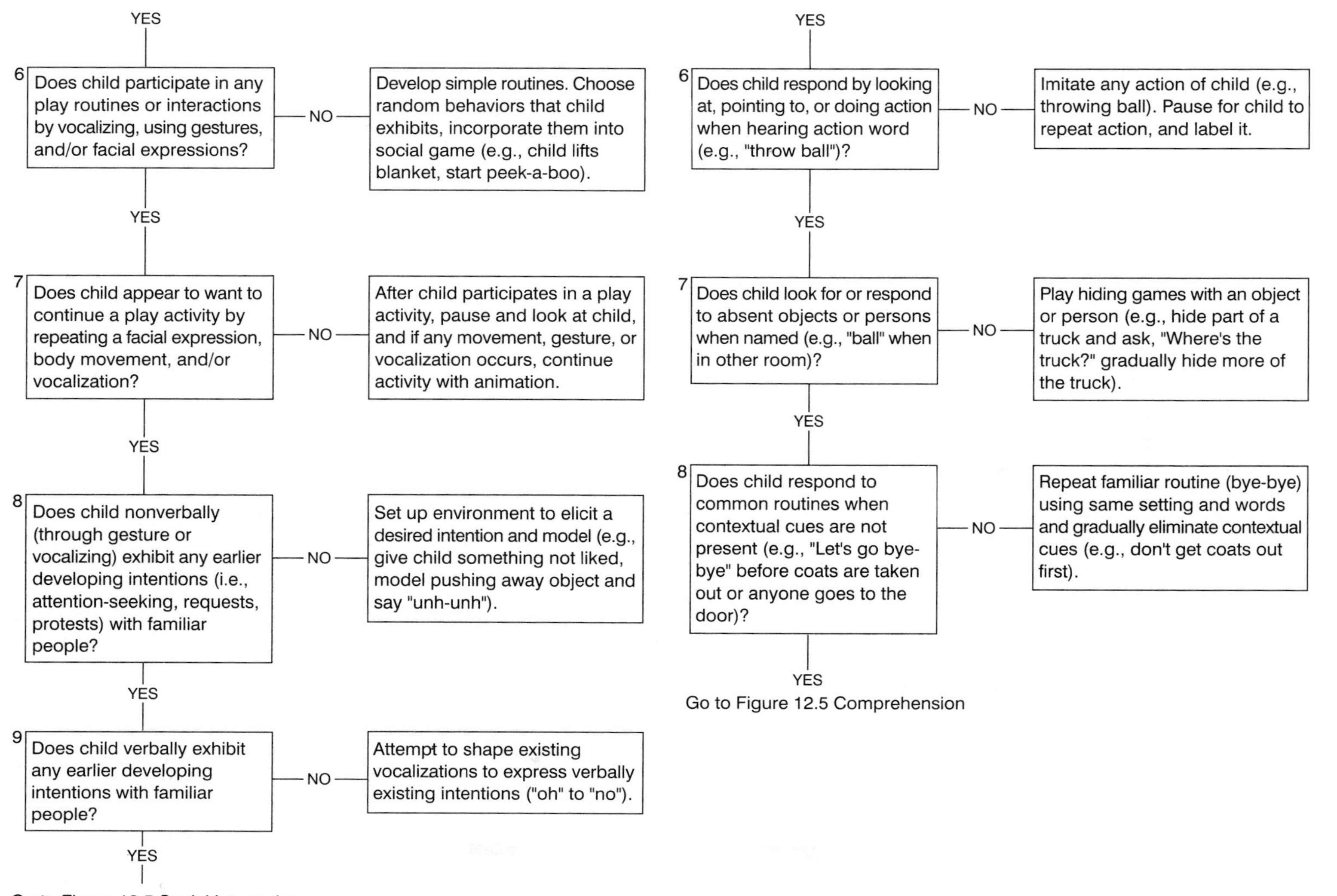
YES
6 Does child participate in any play routines or interactions by vocalizing, using gestures, and/or facial expressions?
NO
Develop simple routines. Choose random behaviors that child exhibits, incorporate them into social game (e.g., child lifts blanket, start peek-a-boo).
YES
7 Does child appear to want to continue a play activity by repeating a facial expression, body movement, and/or vocalization?
NO
After child participates in a play activity, pause and look at child, and if any movement, gesture, or vocalization occurs, continue activity with animation.
YES
8 Does child nonverbally (through gesture or vocalizing) exhibit any earlier developing intentions (i.e., attention-seeking, requests, protests) with familiar people?
NO
Set up environment to elicit a desired intention and model (e.g., give child something not liked, model pushing away object and say "unh-unh").
YES
9 Does child verbally exhibit any earlier developing intentions with familiar people?
NO
Attempt to shape existing vocalizations to express verbally existing intentions ("oh" to "no").
YES
Go to Figure 12.5 Social Interaction
YES
6 Does child respond by looking at, pointing to, or doing action when hearing action word (e.g., "throw ball")?
NO
Imitate any action of child (e.g., throwing ball). Pause for child to repeat action, and label it.
YES
7 Does child look for or respond to absent objects or persons when named (e.g., "ball" when in other room)?
NO
Play hiding games with an object or person (e.g., hide part of a truck and ask, "Where's the truck?" gradually hide more of the truck).
YES
8 Does child respond to common routines when contextual cues are not present (e.g., "Let's go bye-bye" before coats are taken out or anyone goes to the door)?
NO
Repeat familiar routine (bye-bye) using same setting and words and gradually eliminate contextual cues (e.g., don't get coats out first).
YES
Go to Figure 12.5 Comprehension

FIGURE 12.4
Continued

*PRODUCTION**

SPONTANEOUS

	Assessment Questions	If NO	*Intervention Activities*
1	Does child produce any vocalizations (e.g., "ah", "eh")?	NO	Attend to any sounds made by the child and reinforce with smiles, touches, and vocalizations.
	YES		
2	Does child produce any consonant sounds (e.g., "da", "ga")?	NO	Listen for and reinforce any sounds which are consonant-like (e.g., gurgles, lip smacking).
	YES		
3	Does child use the same sounds/syllables in sound strings (e.g., "a-a-a" or "bababa")?	NO	Listen for any sound or syllable used frequently and model repetition of sound/syllable.
	YES		
4	Does child use alternating vowels or consonants in strings (e.g., "ba-da-ba" or "be-ba-be")?	NO	Listen for sounds or syllables used frequently and model alternating repetitions.
	YES		
5	Does child vocalize when refusing or commenting on an object/person/food?	NO	Model refusal behavior, using both gesture and vocalization during play activity or interaction (e.g., give food child doesn't desire, model "unh-unh" and shake head).

IMITATION

	Assessment Questions	If NO	*Intervention Activities*
1	Does child imitate motor actions (e.g., reaching, clapping)?	NO	Imitate natural actions in child's repertoire (e.g., reaching for toy) and build sequence of turns imitating child.
	YES		
2	Does child imitate oral motor actions (e.g., lip smack, raspberry)?	NO	Imitate playfully any oral motor action that child performs (e.g., smacks lips after drinking). Wait for child to do again and imitate again.
	YES		
3	Does child imitate any nonspeech sounds (e.g., cough, squeal?)	NO	Imitate playfully any nonspeech sounds in child's repertoire. Wait for child to do again and imitate.
	YES		
4	Does child imitate speech sounds or syllables [e.g., vowel ("a"), consonant ("b") or consonant + vowel combinations ("ba")]?	NO	Imitate nonspeech sounds first and encourage child to make sound again. Add speech sounds to sequences (e.g., child squeals, caretaker squeals and adds "ee").
	YES		
5	Does child imitate approximations of sound combined with motor acts (e.g., "m-m" for motor sound while pushing car)?	NO	Use sounds in child's repertoire and try to combine with motor actions within child's repertoire (e.g., say "no" or "oh" as shakes head when cookie is taken away).

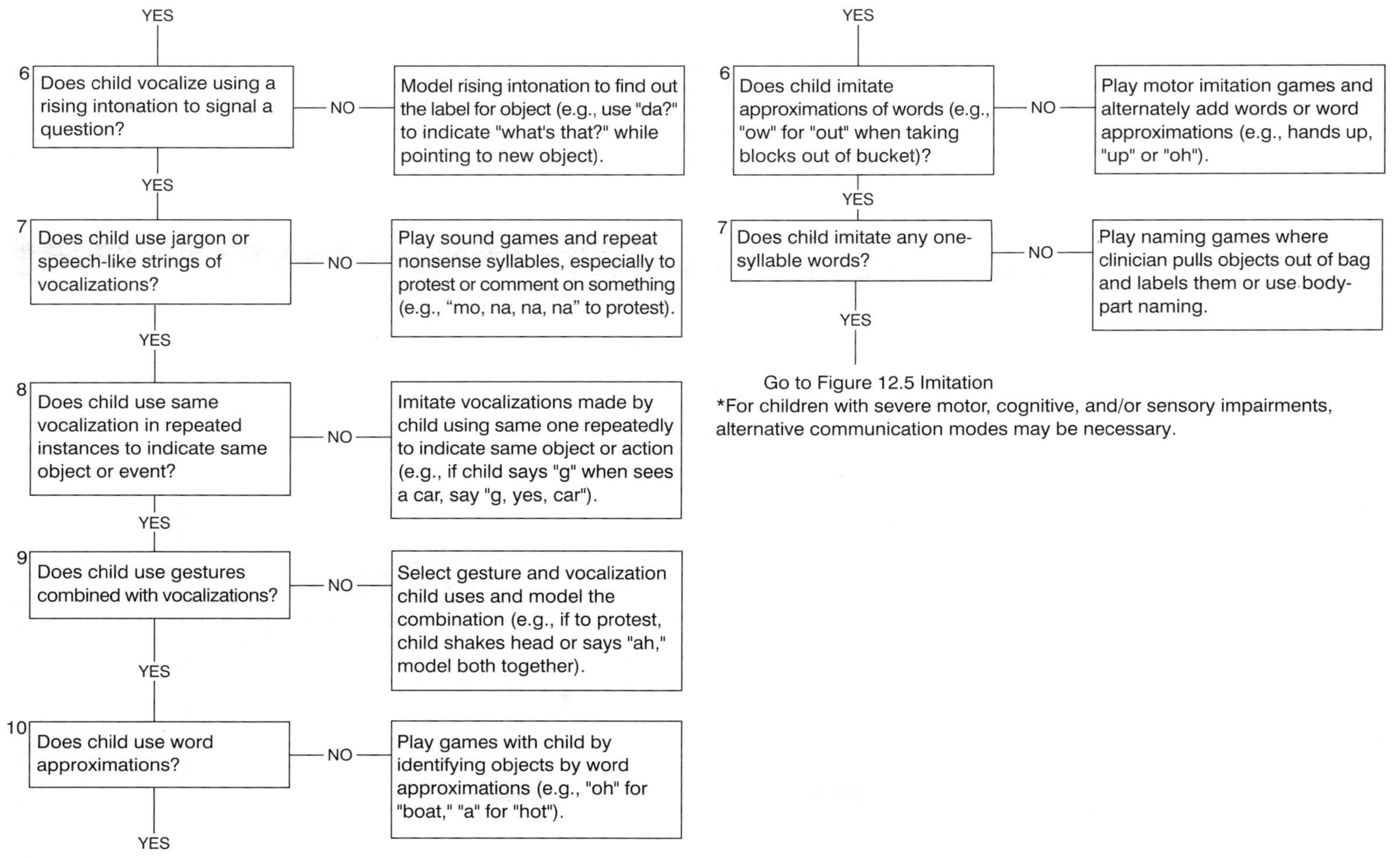

Source: From "Decision Making in Assessment and Early Intervention" by E. Crais and J. Roberts, 1991, *Language, Speech, Hearing Services in Schools, 22,* pp. 25–30. Copyright 1991 by ASHA. Reprinted by permission.

FIGURE 12.5
Decision tree for a child at the one-word utterance stage

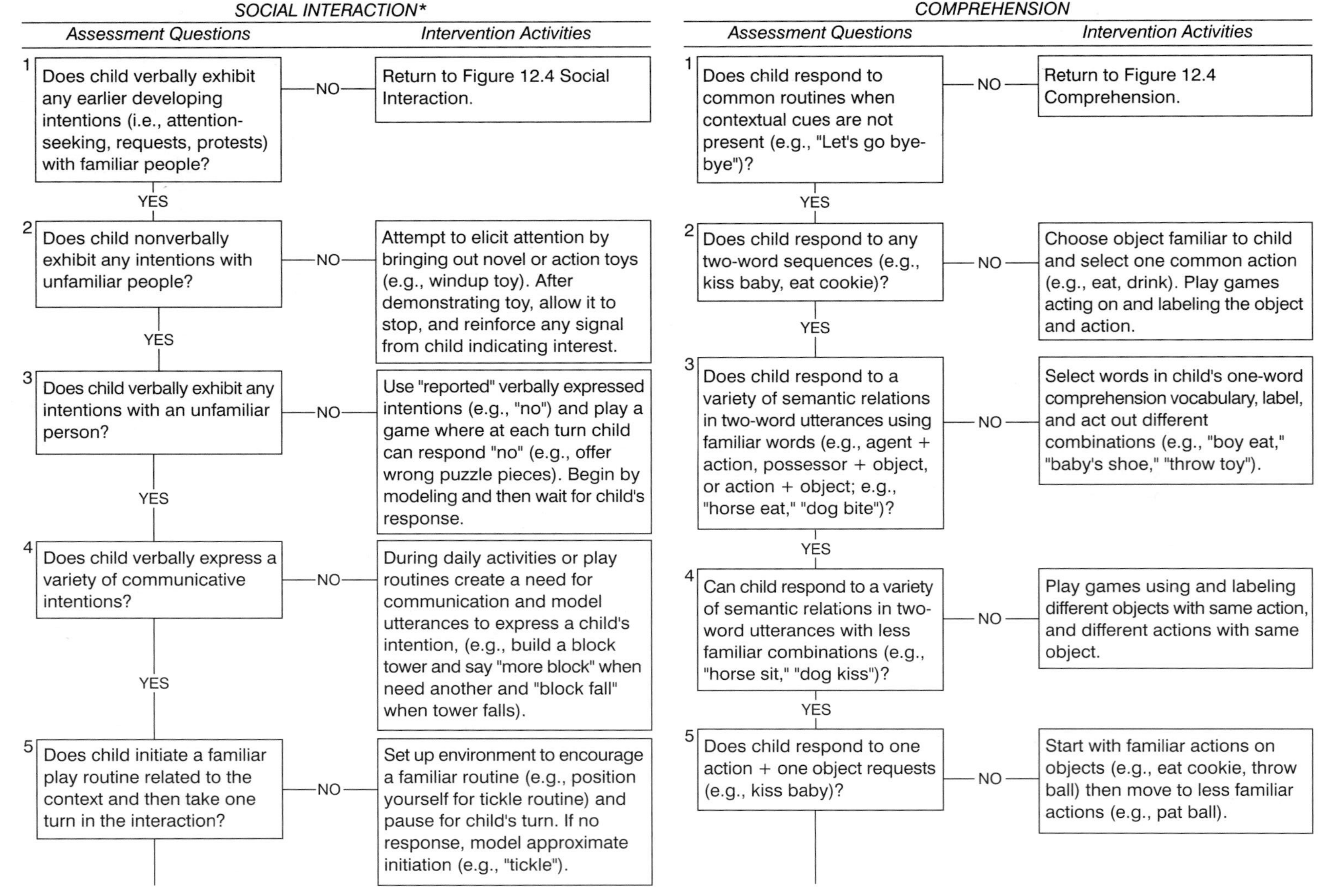

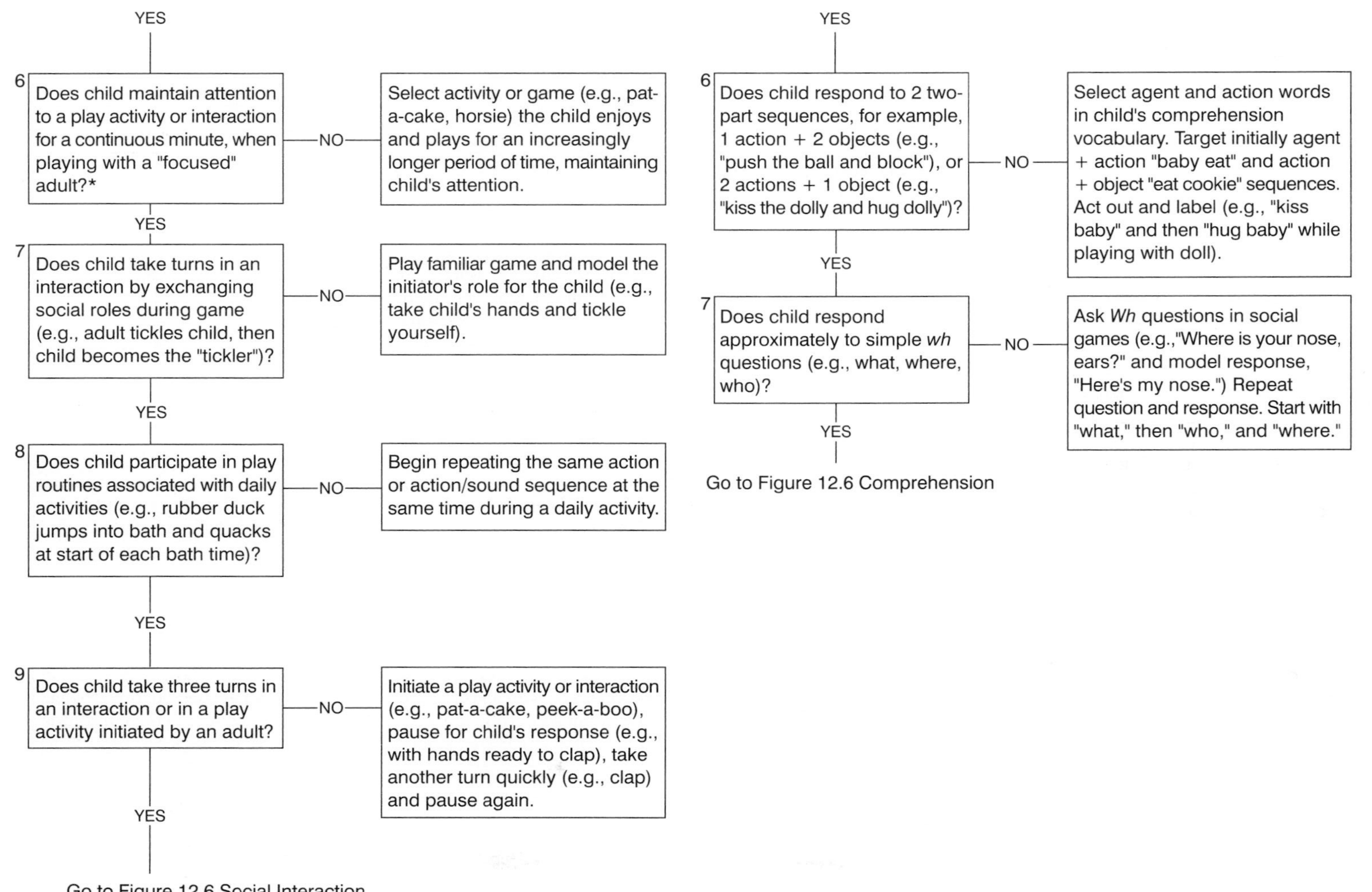
YES
6 Does child maintain attention to a play activity or interaction for a continuous minute, when playing with a "focused" adult?*
NO
Select activity or game (e.g., pat-a-cake, horsie) the child enjoys and plays for an increasingly longer period of time, maintaining child's attention.
YES
7 Does child take turns in an interaction by exchanging social roles during game (e.g., adult tickles child, then child becomes the "tickler")?
NO
Play familiar game and model the initiator's role for the child (e.g., take child's hands and tickle yourself).
YES
8 Does child participate in play routines associated with daily activities (e.g., rubber duck jumps into bath and quacks at start of each bath time)?
NO
Begin repeating the same action or action/sound sequence at the same time during a daily activity.
YES
9 Does child take three turns in an interaction or in a play activity initiated by an adult?
NO
Initiate a play activity or interaction (e.g., pat-a-cake, peek-a-boo), pause for child's response (e.g., with hands ready to clap), take another turn quickly (e.g., clap) and pause again.
YES
Go to Figure 12.6 Social Interaction
*As the child's communicative skills improve, these turn-taking behaviors should first be seen vocally and later verbally.
YES
6 Does child respond to 2 two-part sequences, for example, 1 action + 2 objects (e.g., "push the ball and block"), or 2 actions + 1 object (e.g., "kiss the dolly and hug dolly")?
NO
Select agent and action words in child's comprehension vocabulary. Target initially agent + action "baby eat" and action + object "eat cookie" sequences. Act out and label (e.g., "kiss baby" and then "hug baby" while playing with doll).
YES
7 Does child respond approximately to simple *wh* questions (e.g., what, where, who)?
NO
Ask *Wh* questions in social games (e.g.,"Where is your nose, ears?" and model response, "Here's my nose.") Repeat question and response. Start with "what," then "who," and "where."
YES
Go to Figure 12.6 Comprehension

FIGURE 12.5
Continued

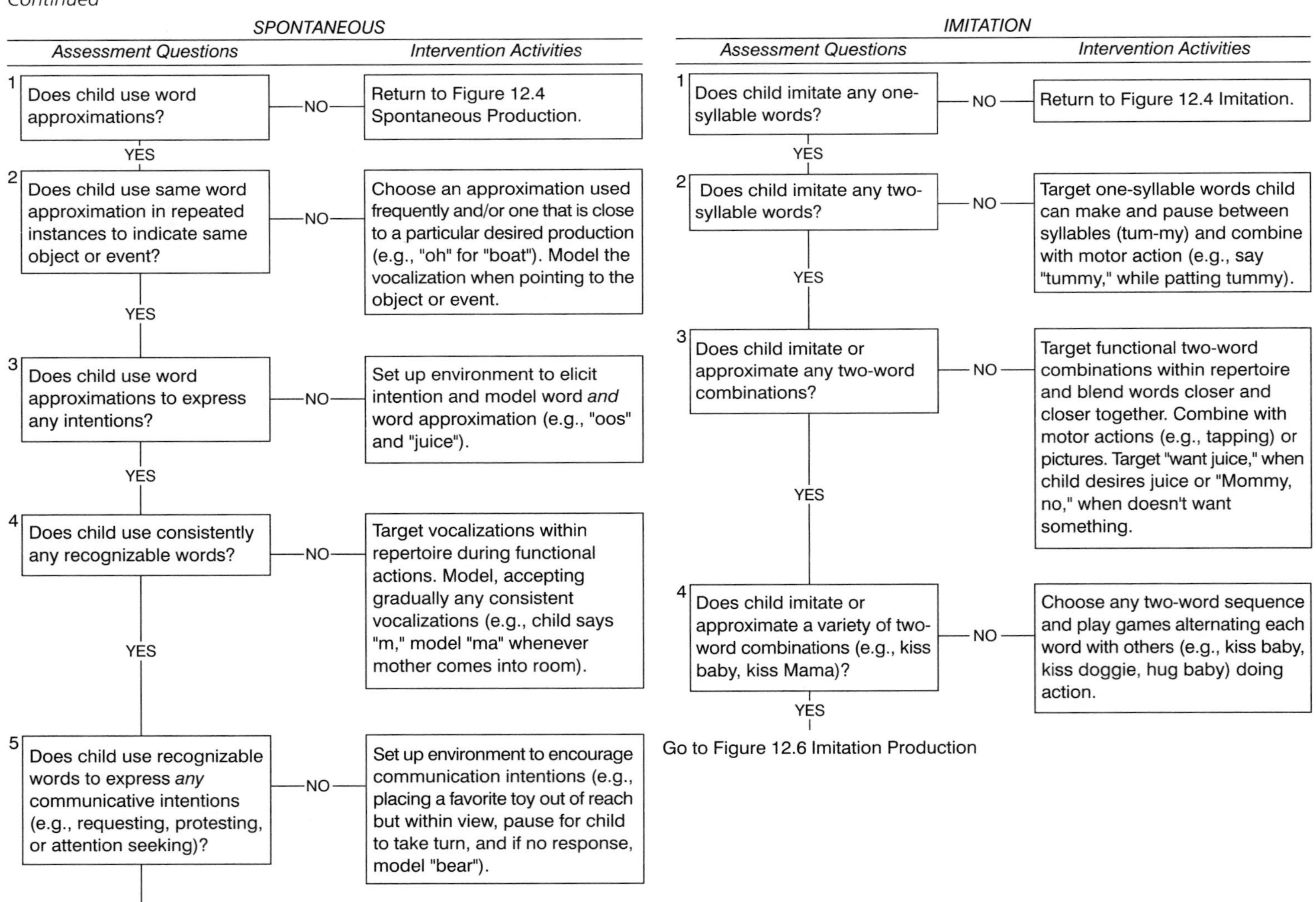

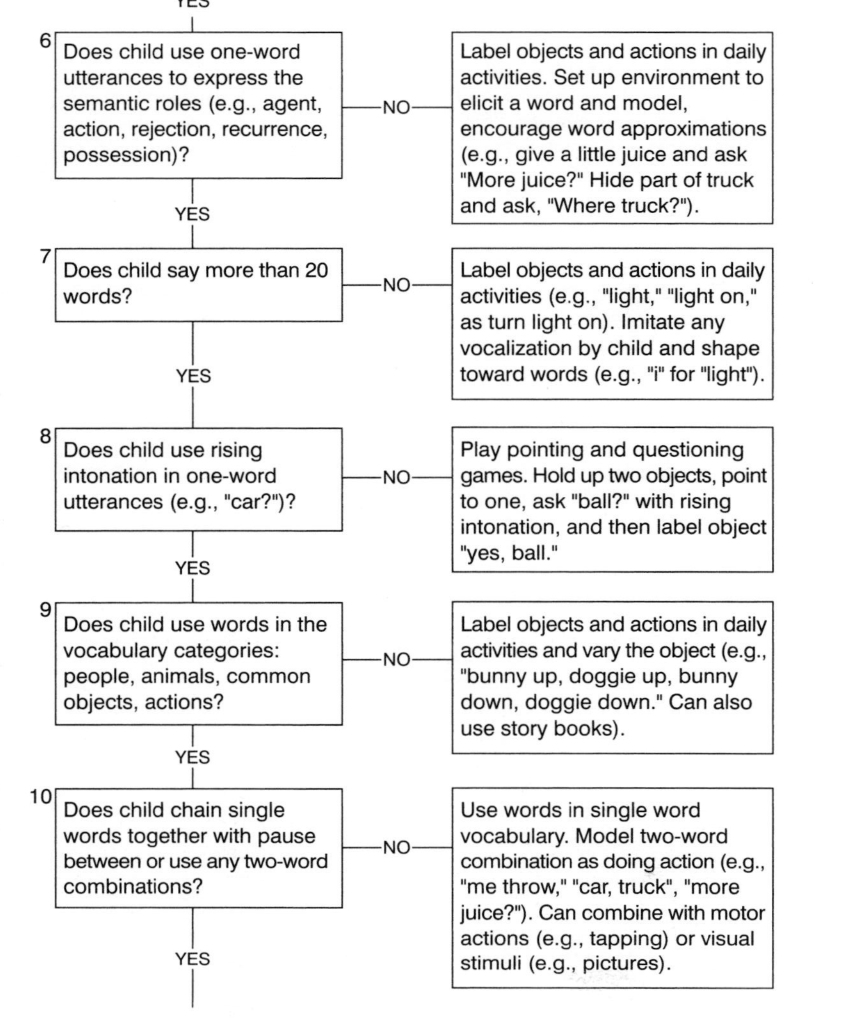

Go to Figure 12.6 Spontaneous Production

Source: From "Decision Making in Assessment and Early Intervention" by E. Crais and J. Roberts, 1991, *Language, Speech, Hearing Services in Schools, 22,* pp. 25–30. Copyright 1991 by ASHA. Reprinted by permission.

FIGURE 12.6
Decision tree for a child at the two-word utterance stage and above

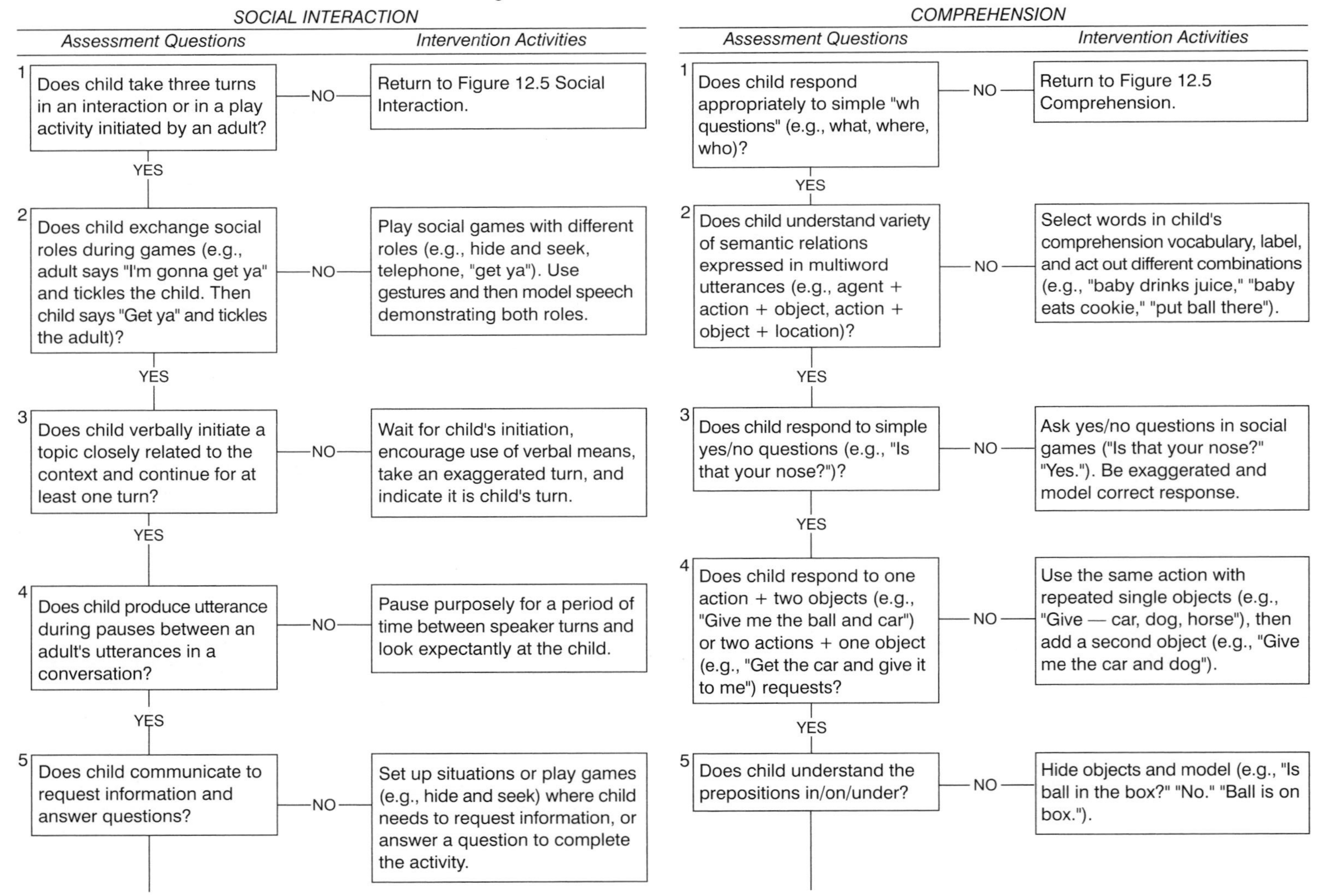

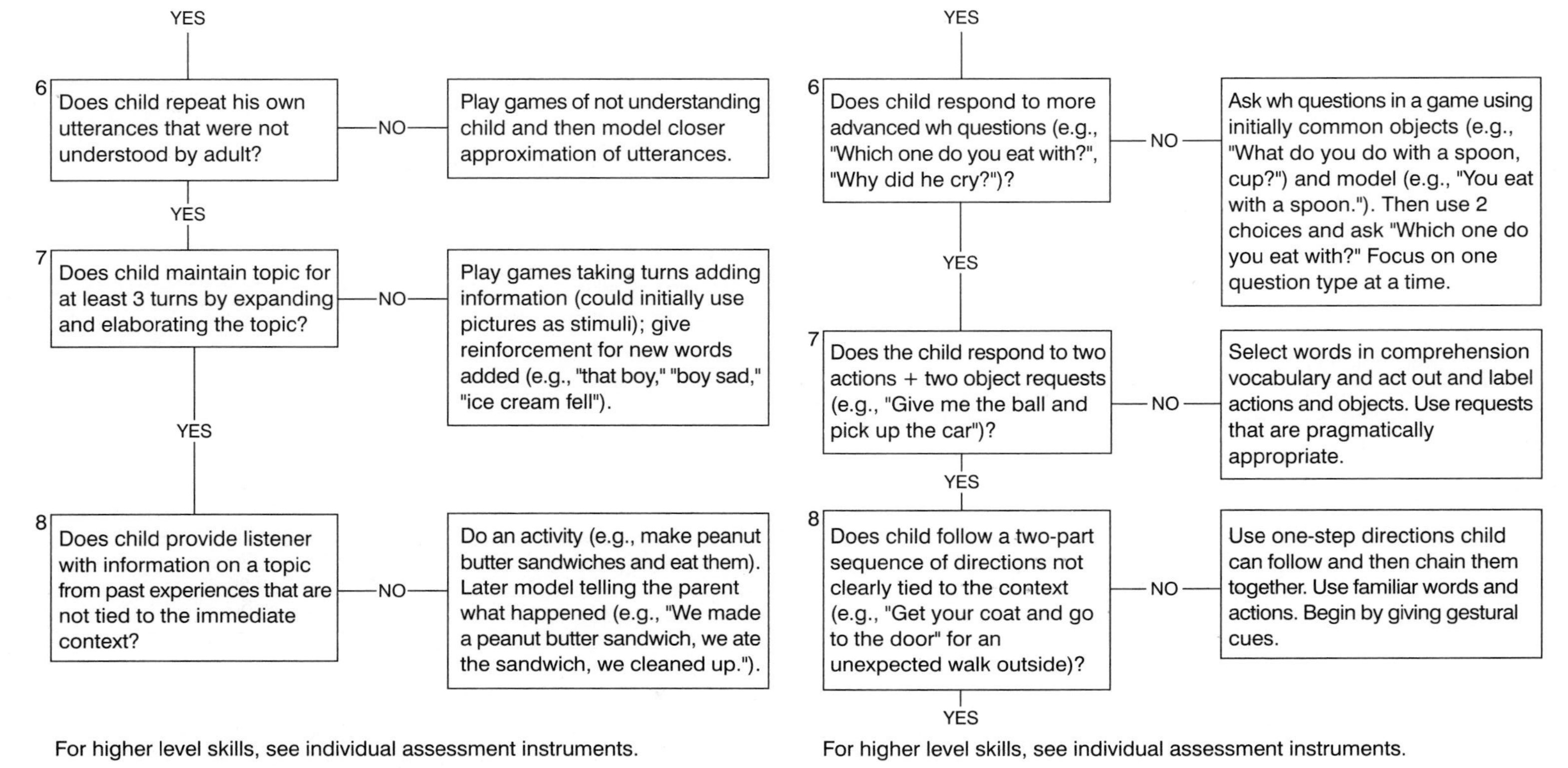
YES
6
Does child repeat his own utterances that were not understood by adult?
NO
Play games of not understanding child and then model closer approximation of utterances.
YES
7
Does child maintain topic for at least 3 turns by expanding and elaborating the topic?
NO
Play games taking turns adding information (could initially use pictures as stimuli); give reinforcement for new words added (e.g., "that boy," "boy sad," "ice cream fell").
YES
8
Does child provide listener with information on a topic from past experiences that are not tied to the immediate context?
NO
Do an activity (e.g., make peanut butter sandwiches and eat them). Later model telling the parent what happened (e.g., "We made a peanut butter sandwich, we ate the sandwich, we cleaned up.").
For higher level skills, see individual assessment instruments.
YES
6
Does child respond to more advanced wh questions (e.g., "Which one do you eat with?", "Why did he cry?")?
NO
Ask wh questions in a game using initially common objects (e.g., "What do you do with a spoon, cup?") and model (e.g., "You eat with a spoon."). Then use 2 choices and ask "Which one do you eat with?" Focus on one question type at a time.
YES
7
Does the child respond to two actions + two object requests (e.g., "Give me the ball and pick up the car")?
NO
Select words in comprehension vocabulary and act out and label actions and objects. Use requests that are pragmatically appropriate.
YES
8
Does child follow a two-part sequence of directions not clearly tied to the context (e.g., "Get your coat and go to the door" for an unexpected walk outside)?
NO
Use one-step directions child can follow and then chain them together. Use familiar words and actions. Begin by giving gestural cues.
YES
For higher level skills, see individual assessment instruments.

FIGURE 12.6
Continued

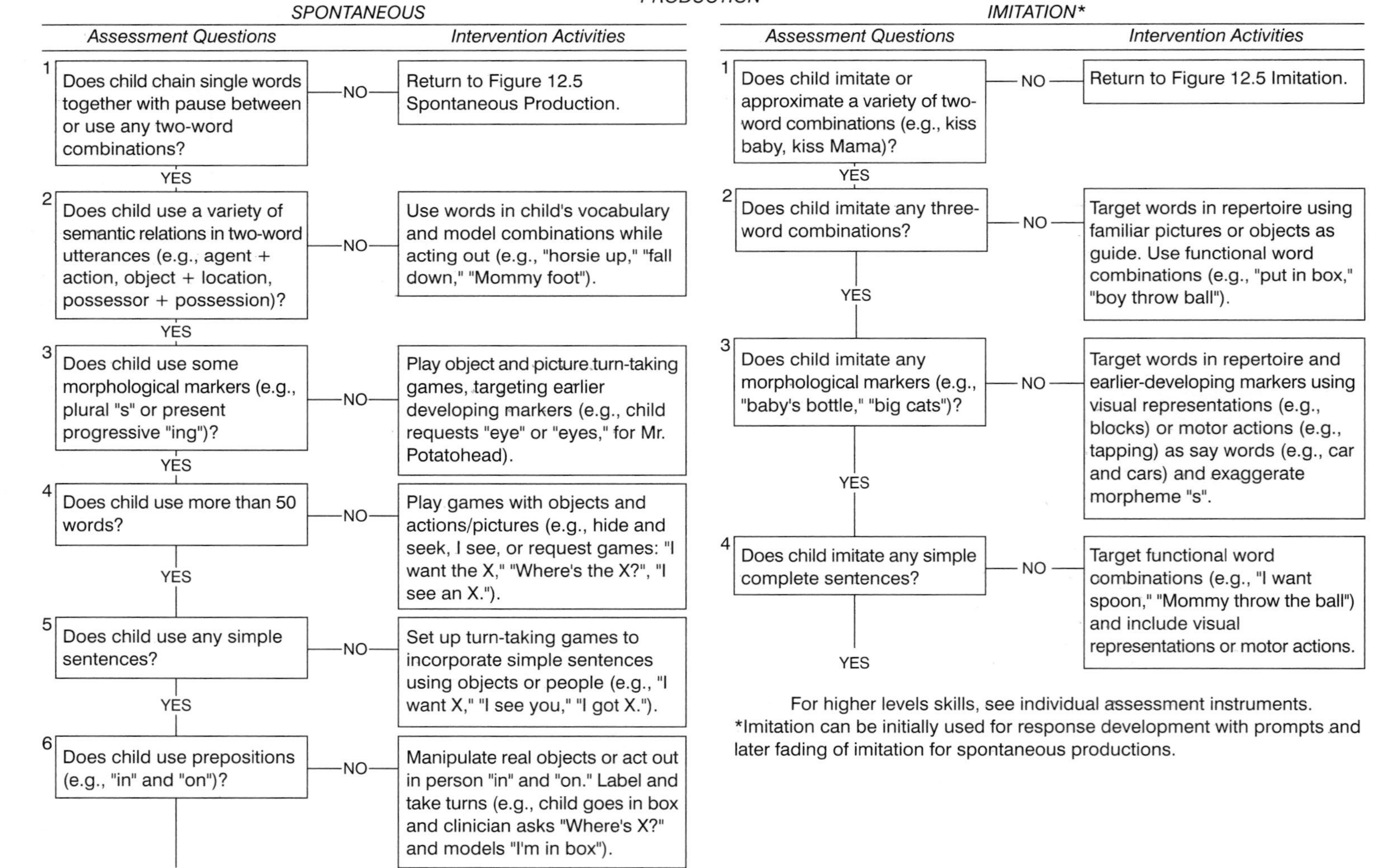

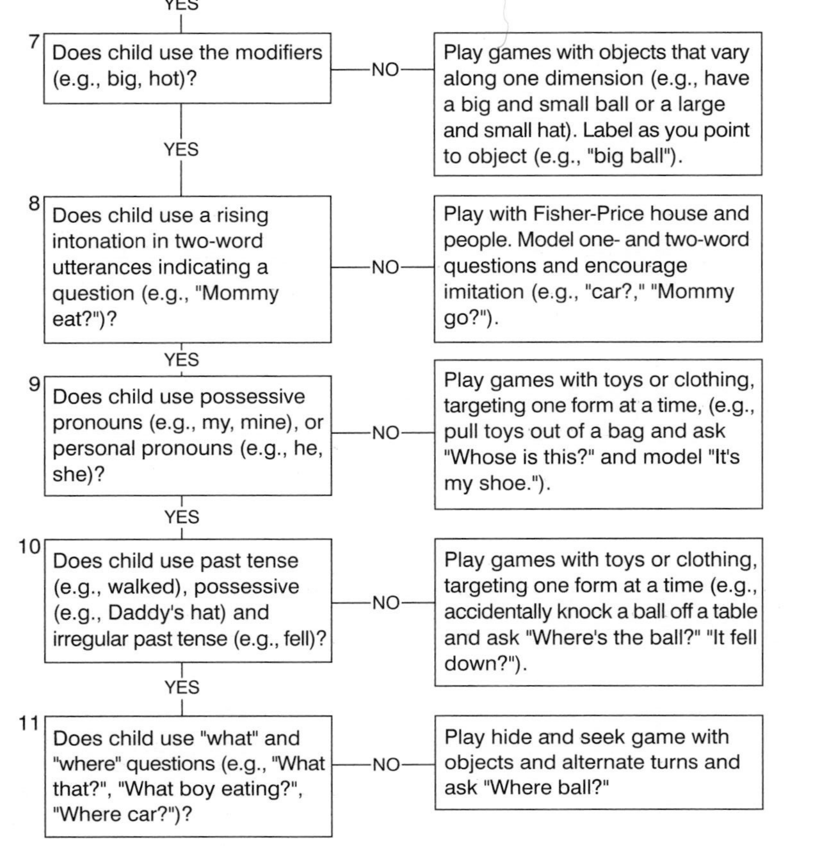

Source: From "Decision Making in Assessment and Early Intervention" by E. Crais and J. Roberts, 1991, *Language, Speech, Hearing Services in Schools, 22,* pp. 25–30. Copyright 1991 by ASHA. Reprinted by permission.

decision trees. Because they related that Susan does not use any "words" and that she primarily gets her needs met by gesturing and vocalizing, the decision tree for a child at the prelinguistic stage (Figure 12.4) was selected. The professionals and caregivers briefly reviewed the decision tree and agreed that they would each contribute to identifying the items Susan was able to do. The parents and the child-care provider were given a copy of the decision tree so they could begin to identify the items that Susan readily performed and could watch for those behaviors during the upcoming observations. Three observation and interaction sessions were performed over a 2-week period. Following the observations, Ella, Matt, Terry, and the professionals met to discuss their observations. For each skill area and the items in each area, Susan's typical and observed behaviors were pinpointed and written directly on a copy of the decision tree.

In the Social Interaction skill area, the parents and the professionals were specifically looking for the means and functions Susan uses to communicate and the type of social games in which she participates. By caregiver report and observation, Susan elicited adult attention by vocalizing "ah," showed and gave objects to others, played two social interaction games (e.g., tickle and peek-a-boo), and used a vocalization ("ba") to protest when a favorite food was taken away and a pushing-away gesture when she did not want a cracker. She requested an object by vocalizing or gesturing, and once by vocalizing *and* gesturing. When Susan wanted an activity to continue (peek-a-boo) she held up the blanket to her mother. All observers agreed that she did not yet use any verbal means to get her needs met.

In the Comprehension area, Susan looked at objects mentioned, reacted to "bye-bye" when context cues were present (e.g., the examiner put on her coat and moved toward the door), and when her sister was not in the room, looked for her after hearing her name. All observers agreed that Susan did not respond to any action words or indicate a recognition of routines without the presence of contextual cues. In the Spontaneous Production area, Susan vocalized when refusing a cracker and when pointing to a new object held by the examiner, used a rising intonation when vocalizing to put a block in a box as if to ask "in here?", used speech-like strings of vowels and consonants, and on one occasion used a vocalization with a gesture (drinking gesture and "da" when requesting juice). She did not use consistent vocalizations or word approximations. In the Imitation area, Susan imitated motor and oral motor actions, some nonspeech sounds ("grr" for a tiger, buzzing sound for a bee) and a few speech sounds ("bu," "mu," "da") during a game with the examiner. She imitated two sounds combined with a motor act (buzzing "zz" while holding fingers together like a bee and "grr" while scratching like a tiger), but did not imitate any word approximations or words. Figure 12.7 (pp. 384–385) provides a summary of Susan's observed and reported communicative behaviors.

After confirming and reviewing the behaviors Susan did and did not exhibit on the prelinguistic decision tree, the professionals and caregivers then began to evolve an intervention plan for Susan. They also discussed how Susan and her caregivers interacted (e.g., how she gained their attention, how they gained hers, how she responded to their initiations and they to hers, and the kinds of sounds and words they modeled for her). An example of goal planning with the information gained from using the prelinguistic decision tree with Susan is provided in the final section of the chapter. In regard to utilizing the decision trees, one additional comment should be made. As with most assessment tools and techniques, use of the decision trees typically involves only brief interactions between a child and other individuals, and so the examiner and caregivers may need to gather further information. If developmental levels are desired by the family or needed by the professionals in terms of determining eligibility, standardized tests, developmental charts, and/or some of the alternative techniques suggested can be used in conjunction with the decision trees.

TRANSLATING ASSESSMENT INFORMATION INTO INSTRUCTIONAL GOALS

As with assessment planning, intervention planning must begin with the family's concerns and priorities. Once the assessment has been completed, Kjerland and Kovach (1990) suggest that the postassessment discussion include critiquing the assessment, describing the child (strengths and needs), drawing conclusions, and setting priorities. To help set priorities, the family may be asked questions such as "What seems most important to you at this point?" or "What would you like your child to learn or to change within the next few months?" The family and the professionals can then begin identifying the specific goals and strategies used to reach the broad goals. For each goal, the team first discusses the child's current behaviors and ideas for how change can be made and who will help facilitate that change (Kjerland & Kovach, 1990).

In the area of communication, as with many other areas, families typically have broad skills or achievements that they would like their child to attain. For example, they may say that they want their child to be able to "use words instead of all these sounds," "let us know what he wants," or "talk in a way that other people can understand her." They may not, however, know the discrete skills or the individual activities that could help their child achieve these broader outcomes. With the recent focus on providing family-centered services, professionals are often challenged to provide information and ideas and yet to do so in a way that is responsive to the concerns and priorities of the family. When considering the broad outcomes identified by the family, the following questions may help professionals think about what subgoals might be identified to help the child attain the larger outcomes.

1. What outcomes are most important to the caregiver(s)?
2. What modifications would have the most effect on communication?
3. What modification in behavior will have the greatest effect on other skill areas?
4. What skill areas or behaviors are being worked on by other professionals?
5. What behaviors have the best possibility of generalization to other contexts?
6. Which behavior is the most easily modified?
7. On which outcome could the child and/or the family be most successful?
8. What goal would be the most motivating for the child and/or the family?

In working closely together, the family and the professionals can identify the types of subgoals that will help the child achieve the broader outcomes and can bring together the expertise of both the family and the professionals.

Illustration of Goal Planning

When professionals and families are planning intervention, there are two alternative approaches. The first is to focus on the child's *needs* compared with children of the same chronological age level. In this method, the interventionist and family primarily examine standardized measures, developmental charts, or the decision trees to identify the skills and behaviors that the child does not exhibit. Intervention planning then consists of working on teaching those deficient skills in order to get the child closer to age level.

I. *SOCIAL INTERACTIONS*

Behavioral Regulation

Requests = vocalization "uh uh," gestures (e.g., pointing to objects and people)
vocalization + gesture (e.g., "da" + reach for cookie, "da" + "drinking" motion for juice)

Protests = vocalization (e.g., "uh" when food taken away, "ah" when refusing cracker), gestures (e.g., pushing away unwanted cracker)

Social Interaction

Calling attention = vocalization (squeals)

Social/Play Routines: peek-a-boo, tickle

Joint Attention

Comments = gesture (showing and giving an object)
vocalization + gesture (e.g., "ah" when pointing to new object)

Request Info = vocalization ("di?" rising intonation when putting block in box)

II. *COMPREHENSION*

Looked at objects mentioned (ball, juice)
Waved "bye-bye" with context cues
Looked for absent sister
Semantic relations observed:

4 agents = Mama, Daddy, doggie, baby
6 objects = ball, juice, cookie, car, cup, boat

III. *PRODUCTION*

Spontaneous

Vocalizations = when refusing cracker
when pointing at object
when putting block in box
to get attention
speech-like string of vowels and consonants
vocalization + gesture (see above)

Observed sound inventory = /m/, /b/, /g/, /d/ with some vowels
Babbling of consonant-vowel combinations
Nonspeech sounds = raspberries, play cough, tongue clicks, laugh

Imitation

Vocalizations = motor acts (clapping, swaying body)
oral motor acts (stick out tongue, open mouth)
nonspeech sounds ("grr" for tiger, "zz" for bee)
speech sounds (bu, mu, da)
sounds and motor acts ("zz" with fingers like bee, "grr" while scratching like tiger)

FIGURE 12.7
Analysis of communication behaviors for Susan based on the decision tree

Outcome 1. Susan will use sounds and gestures more often and more consistently so that Matt, Ella, and Terry will be able to understand her needs throughout the day.

Strategies/Activities

a. Matt, Ella, and Terry will respond immediately and very positively to Susan whenever she uses any gesture or sound to communicate her needs.
b. Ella, Matt, and Terry will respond immediately and very positively to Susan whenever she uses a gesture and a sound together.
c. Ella, Matt, and Terry will model some of Susan's familiar gestures and sounds combined together (e.g., "uh uh" while reaching for toy).
d. Matt, Ella, and Terry will model simple gestures for Susan (e.g., shaking head to mean "no").

Outcome 2. Susan will imitate sounds, actions, and words used by Ella, Matt, and Terry during play and social games.

Strategies/Activities

a. Matt, Ella, and Terry will imitate Susan's sounds and actions during play activities.
b. Ella, Matt, and Terry will play "sound games" with Susan to encourage her imitation of them making sounds that she can already produce (e.g., "uh," "da," "di").
c. Matt, Ella, and Terry will use word approximations along with the names of people and things in the home (e.g., "bo" for bottle, "di" for diaper).
d. Ella, Matt, and Terry will continue to expand Susan's social routines (e.g., this little piggie, "gotcha," bounce on knee for "horsie") and will use sounds and word approximations (e.g., "pee" and "boo" for peek-a-boo).

Outcome 3. Terry, Matt, and Ella want ideas for toys, books, activities to keep Susan's interest during play and social games.

Strategies/Activities

a. Matt and Ella will bring some of Susan's toys and books to Terry's house for Susan.
b. Terry, Matt, and Ella will access the materials in the Center's resource library.
c. Matt, Ella, and Terry will use simple words and phrases with Susan to encourage her participation in play activities and social games.
d. Ella, Matt, and Terry will use gestures when possible to help Susan understand the ongoing activity.
e. Ella, Matt, and Terry will repeat words and phrases for Susan during play activities.

Outcome 4. Matt and Ella want Barbara to help them monitor Susan's progress over time and to help them find new ideas to help Susan develop.

Strategies/Activities

a. Barbara will go to observe Susan once a month, alternating months in Ella and Matt's home, and Terry's home.
b. In the months that Barbara does not go to Matt and Ella's home, she will contact them regarding the ideas developed by Terry and herself (and the same will go for visiting Terry's house and calling Ella and Matt).

FIGURE 12.7
Continued

The other, and preferable, approach to planning is to focus on what the child *can* do and then begin expanding the already available skills. In this way the family and the interventionist start at the child's level and build in a vertical and horizontal fashion from where the child is currently functioning. The latter method of planning instructional goals will be illustrated for the 20-month-old child, Susan, previously discussed (see "Using the Decision Trees").

To help begin the intervention planning process, the parents, the child-care provider, and the professionals discussed Susan's overall strengths, which included her ability to get some of her needs met by gesturing and vocalizing, her frequent and varied vocalizations, her positive social affect in interactions with adults, her interest in interacting with people (even strangers), her willingness to attempt to imitate sounds and motor acts, and her recognition of the names of people and objects around her. The professionals also pointed out her persistence in trying to gain others' attention and her ability to use different means (e.g., gesture, vocalization) to get something she wanted. The group then discussed their perspectives on Susan's needs. Her parents noted that sometimes she has difficulty letting them know what she wants and they would like to be able to understand her better. They also reported that she is not able to imitate words they say and they felt that this was important to her development. The child-care provider suggested that she would like some ideas for toys and books that might hold Susan's interest during play activities. The broad outcomes identified by the group are listed in Figure 12.8.

For each outcome they identified, the caregivers and the professionals talked about strategies and activities that could help Susan or them attain the outcome. Concerning Ella and Matt's desire to be able to better understand Susan, several ideas were generated by the group. First, everyone agreed that one way to understand Susan better was to get her to use the sounds and gestures she can already produce more frequently and consistently. Through discussion, the group agreed that everyone would try to respond positively and at times imitate Susan's sounds and gestures. When asked how Susan was progressing in her communication skills, Matt and Ella noted that she was just beginning to use sounds and gestures combined together (an item from the decision tree), and they felt that this improved their ability to understand her. They suggested that everyone also reinforce Susan's use of gestures and sounds together. When asked for ways that have helped Susan learn new things, both parents said she usually tries to imitate their actions. Thus they were encouraged to model the gestures Susan currently uses combined with some of her sounds and to model some new simple gestures that may help her communicate (e.g., shaking her head for "no," taking an adult's hand to indicate a need for help).

In talking about why they think Susan does not imitate words, Matt and Ella suggested that maybe she did not want to or could not imitate words when asked. Given that she imitates some things, it was suggested that perhaps words were too hard for her at this time and that encouraging the imitation of any actions or sounds might be useful. All three caregivers were encouraged to use play activities with familiar actions and sounds to encourage her to imitate them. For example, the caregivers can watch for naturally occurring motor acts such as patting, tapping, or nonspeech sounds (e.g., squeals, snorts), playfully and explicitly imitate the action or sound (e.g., tapping, giggling), and encourage the child to repeat the behavior. Social routines are perfect for motor and sound imitation (see Calhoun et al., 1991; Fey, 1986; and Platt & Coggins, 1990,

I. *SOCIAL INTERACTION*
   1. Increase number, length, and diversity of social interactions
      a. Increase number of interactive games (e.g., "this little piggie," bounce on knee for "horsie")
      b. Increase number of games incorporating recurrence (e.g., child bounces for "more," holds up blanket for more actions)
      c. Increase use of vocalizations in games; adult will model consistent word or syllable to express the game (e.g., pee = peek-a-boo, ti = tickle)
      d. Expand imitation of motor acts (e.g., begin with imitation of acts already in child's repertoire) try to incorporate into social games (e.g., wave "bye-bye" as part of peek-a-boo)
      e. Increase number of nonverbal acts (e.g., commenting = pointing to unusual happening, requesting = reaching for new objects and agents)

II. *COMPREHENSION*
   1. Expand comprehension vocabulary and increase recognition of a variety of semantic relations
      a. Increase identification of objects, actions, agents: play games of hiding, finding different items and labeling
      b. Increase comprehension of different actions on the objects already in comprehension vocabulary (e.g., kiss baby, hug baby)
      c. Increase recognition of different agent + action combinations (e.g., Susan eat, Mommy eat)
      d. Introduce locations, attributes (e.g., hot, big) into games

III. *PRODUCTION*
   1. Increase frequency, consistency, and diversity of vocalizations and word approximations
      a. Expand use of existing vocalizations to express similar communicative acts (e.g., protests = "uh" used when toy taken away, when drink taken away; "ah" used when refusing other food or actions)
      b. Increase consistent use of existing vocalizations + gestures through imitation and modeling
      c. Expand protests to combine vocalization + gesture (e.g., model "ah" and pushing away cracker)
      d. Introduce "no" or "oh" with nonverbal gesture of pushing away
      e. Increase use of word approximations for common objects and agents (e.g., "bo" = "boat," "Ma" for Mama)
   2. Increase imitation of sounds in play activities
      a. Increase imitation of nonspeech sounds
      b. Increase imitation of sounds within speech repertoire
      c. Increase imitation of new sounds and sound combinations

FIGURE 12.8
Possible goals and objectives for intervention with Susan

for ideas for developing infants' and young children's early social routines). The caregivers can also play sound games by performing an action (e.g., patting the floor, putting a ring on a ring stack, throwing blocks into a bucket) while vocalizing a sound from the child's repertoire. As the child does the motor action combined with vocalizations, the vocalizations can gradually be shaped to new sounds. In addition, the caregivers were encouraged to use both the name and a word approximation for simple objects and people in Susan's environment ("You want the milk," "Here's the mi") and then to encourage her for any attempt she makes to vocalize.

As for additional ideas for toys and books, Ella and Matt noted that they would lend some of Susan's favorite books and toys to Terry and the professionals suggested that she could borrow from their program's resource library. The group also discussed ways to encourage Susan's participation by making activities simpler for her. Examples included simplifying what was said to her to include single words or short phrases (e.g., "boat," "look at the boat"), using gestures and eye gaze to help her understand what was said (Patting chair while saying, "Come here"), and using frequent repetition. Finally, Ella and Matt indicated an interest in having the speech-language pathologist, Barbara, help them monitor Susan's progress over time and continue to provide them with suggestions for ways to help her.

To further the application of assessment information to intervention planning, the following section highlights several guidelines for use by professionals and families when developing communication goals and activities for intervention. Although many of the guidelines can be applied to any type of intervention, some are specific to communication abilities. It may be useful for both professionals and family members to read over the guidelines when developing intervention plans.

Intervention Guidelines

Start at the child's level Children cannot be expected to achieve skills beyond their cognitive, motor, social, or communicative levels, and sometimes it is hard for both professionals and caregivers to recognize the child's current levels, particularly if they are below the child's chronological age. A concrete example of starting at a level that is too high is when the parent, teacher, or professional prompts a child who typically only produces vocalizations to use entire words. Although prompting words or structures that are slightly beyond the child's current capabilities can be facilitatory, it is also important to meet the child at his or her level of functioning and to provide a bridge to the next higher skill level. An example of bridging for this child would be to (a) model an entire word ("boat"), (b) reduce the whole word to a shortened form ("bo" or "ot"), (c) encourage and reinforce the child for *any* communication attempts, and (d) guide the child to make closer and closer approximations of the word. In essence, it is important to be aware of the child's overall developmental and communicative skills and balance instructional goals to encompass both the current level of functioning and behaviors at a slightly higher or more complex level.

Move vertically and horizontally When planning intervention, consider both vertical and horizontal movement in various skill areas. As the previous example illustrates, if the child is not ready or able to move vertically to the next level (from vocalization to verbalization), the adult can encourage either smaller vertical behaviors (e.g., word approximations, any consistent vocalization, pairing vocalization with gesture) or other horizontal skills (e.g., if the child requests objects or actions, caregivers can model protesting and can encourage the use of vocalizing to meet other needs). For practical guides to communication development, the interventionist can turn to the developmental scales listed in Table 12.3, the decision trees (Figures 12.4 through 12.6), Nelson (1993), and Wetherby (1992).

Watch the child for cues Readability, the ability of the professional to recognize and respond to the child's behaviors, is an important part of the intervention process (Goldberg, 1977). The better the adult is at "reading" the infant, the more likely the adult's response is to get or keep an interaction going. In addition, reading cues more accurately can help the interventionist establish the child's level of communication functioning. Parents are often good at reading their child's cues, but with some infants (or for some parents) this may not be an easy task. Clearly, interventionists need to orient their own skills to reading infants and also, at times, to helping caregivers develop or expand their abilities. It is also important for all caregivers and interventionists to look for *all* means (nonverbal and vocalizations) used by the child to communicate and to take the focus off words as the *only* means. Refer to Goldberg (1977), Dunst and Wortman-Lowe (1986), Wetherby and Prizant (1992), and Wilcox (1992) for ideas for recognizing communicative efforts in young children.

Be functional Use naturalistic settings, materials, and procedures as often as possible. As described in earlier chapters, the acquisition and generalization of newly acquired skills are facilitated when the context for training is closest to the setting in which the behavior actually occurs. With communication skills, for example, the context for teaching a child to request an action should occur at the time when and in the place where the child actually needs someone to perform that action. Language is typically acquired in a context in which the child is motivated to communicate to achieve a desired response from others; therefore, always provide the child with a reason to communicate. In this way, the achievement of the desired response often becomes its own reinforcement. Fey (1986), McWilliam (1992), and Nelson (1993) provide excellent guides to the use of naturalistic contexts for intervention.

Follow the interests of the child Use developmental and play scales as a guide to toys, materials, and activities that are of interest to children at different developmental levels. As noted previously, the closer the match between a child's cognitive and developmental level and the tasks and materials, the more likely it is that the child will succeed and enjoy the activity. A major tenet of incidental teaching—one that has considerable empirical support in facilitating children's communication (Warren & Kaiser, 1986; Hart & Risley, 1978)—is following a child's interests when selecting communication targets. Sources such as Cripe, Slentz, and Bricker (1993); Johnson-Martin, Jens, Attermeier, and Hacker (1991); and Patrick (1993) are useful for guiding decisions about children's interests and developmental skills.

Target behaviors for success Target either frequently occurring behaviors that need modification or desired but nonexisting behaviors that have many opportunities for practice and reinforcement. Clearly, new behaviors that can be used frequently and those that build from the child's existing repertoire are more likely to be acquired. For example, modeling vocalizations to request objects that the child likes and is exposed to frequently is an appropriate target for a child who uses vocalizations to protest but not to make requests. To facilitate success, the modeled vocalizations should at first be ones already used by the child for other purposes and can later be new ones created from the sounds the child produces.

Consider the content of the activities Keep in mind the developmental level and functionality of the topics chosen for intervention. Some preschool programs for children with special needs continue to focus on colors or shapes or the days of the week, when more functional skills such as requests for information or how to ask a peer for a toy could be more useful targets. In other words, when planning content for intervention, consider how and when that content could be used by the child. Choose topics that he or she can benefit from frequently in everyday life.

Be efficient Plan goals that focus on more than one skill area or aspect of an area. For example, plan goals that focus on communication as well as cognitive skills and embed them both in a play activity, or, while focusing on word approximations and requests for objects, use words with sounds the child has already acquired to increase the likelihood that he or she will be able to produce the approximation.

Use direct training at times Remember that many children with special needs have had difficulty learning some skills in an incidental manner, that is, through naturalistic interactions with people and objects in their environment. Therefore, it may be appropriate to teach some skills more directly. This may be true, for example, of articulation skills (correct production of *s*) or syntactic structures (use of *ed*) for some children. In addition, the use of imitation, particularly for sound, word, word approximation, phrase, or grammatical learning can be extremely productive. As noted previously, imitation is often used for items that the child is in the process of learning (Owens, 1992). Thus, the use of imitation training and later generalization to more natural and spontaneous contexts has empirical support from the language acquisition literature.

Be facilitative To facilitate interaction, use techniques such as modeling desired verbal and nonverbal behaviors, describing your own or a child's actions, expanding communications used by the child, allowing the child time to take a turn, and revising a child's communication attempt in your next utterance. Nonverbal behaviors and vocalizations can be modeled as easily as verbalizations. For example, hold a toy to trade while vocalizing "uh?" and pointing to the desired toy, or model only what you want the child to *say,* such as "That's mine," while demonstrating a pulling-away gesture with the toy, rather than using, "Say, 'that's mine'." You are a model of communication for the child; remember to consider carefully *what* and *how* you communicate. As often as possible, use vocalizations, words, phrases, and sentences that children would be likely to use in their own interactions. Fey (1986) is an excellent source for a variety of facilitation techniques. For further information on intervention planning, see Crais (1993), Kjerland and Kovach (1990), McWilliam (1992), and Norris (1992).

CONCLUSION

In this chapter, standard and "nonstandard" ways of looking at communication assessment and intervention planning have been presented with a few suggestions for going about these activities. In closing, there are a few final suggestions for the interventionist. First, use continuous reality checking to remember the real world. Keep asking (a) Is this outcome important to the child's development? (b) Will it improve communication in a substantial manner? and, finally (c) Why should this outcome be selected for intervention above all others possible? If the answers are "yes," "yes," and a worthwhile "because . . . ," follow through with the outcome. If the answers are "no," "no," and "I'm not sure," rethink the implementation of this outcome.

Second, children will usually try to communicate the best way they know how. Interventionists, families, and other professionals need to be aware of the many and varied means through which children communicate. For children with communication difficulties, the interventionist must discover what the best means of communication are and then help the child and the caregivers expand and develop those communication means. Third, remember that you serve as a model for the child in an interaction, so think carefully about what you want to model and how you will do it. Finally, remember that you are an experienced communicator and therefore you can use your own knowledge of what promotes or hinders communication to guide the assessment and goal planning process.

SUMMARY OF KEY CONCEPTS

- Communication is a social act, the primary function of which is interaction; language is the symbol system used in communication; and means of communication can include verbal, vocal, and nonverbal ways to communicate.
- Interventionists should be familiar with communication concepts and assessment because communication occurs within the context of other developmental domains; all professionals and families interact and intervene with the child through communication; a large number of preschool children have communication needs; children with language disorders often have later academic, emotional, and behavioral difficulties; and the current focus in intervention is on facilitating communication in natural settings (e.g., classroom and home).
- Components of language include pragmatics, phonology, semantics, and syntax; pragmatics and semantics should receive the most attention in assessment and the greatest emphasis in intervention for many preschool children.
- With the current emphasis on ecologically valid assessment, issues related to sociocultural awareness, family priorities, active participation of caregivers, and collaborative assessment and intervention planning play greater roles than in more traditional assessment approaches.
- Professionals are encouraged to use multiple sources and multiple means for gathering assessment information, including standardized and nonstandardized activities. Recognizing the limitations to many standardized instruments, professionals are encouraged to seek alternative assessment strategies.
- Different areas of assessment are highlighted for children, depending on their existing level of communication (preverbal and verbal); a necessary part of assessment for all children is the observation of the child with his or her communication partners.
- Collection and analysis of communication samples is one of the more in-depth methods of assessing children's communication skills.
- Three separate decision trees were described for guiding assessment efforts and one was illustrated through a case example.
- Information gathered during the assessment of communication skills should be used for planning intervention. Guidelines for intervention are (a) start intervention at the child's level, (b) move vertically and horizontally in planning intervention targets, (c) watch the child for cues, (d) use functional goals and activities, (e) follow the child's interest, (f) target behaviors that will result in success, (g) consider the content of the activities, (h) use efficient strategies, (i) use direct teaching at times, and (j) use techniques that facilitate interaction and communication.

REFERENCES

American Speech-Language-Hearing Association. (1990). Guidelines for screening for hearing impairments and middle ear disorders. *ASHA, 32* (Suppl. 2), 17–24.

American Speech-Language-Hearing Association. (1991a). Joint committee on infant hearing 1990 position statement. *ASHA 33*(5), 3–6.

American Speech-Language-Hearing Association. (1991b). Report: Augmentative and alternative communication. *ASHA, 33* (Suppl. 5), 9–12.

Aram, D., & Hall, N. (1989). Longitudinal follow-up of preschool communication disorders: Treatment implications. *School Psychology Review, 18,* 487–501.

Baker, L., & Cantwell, D. (1987). A prospective psychiatric follow-up of children with speech/language disorders. *Journal of the American Academy of Child and Adolescent Psychiatry, 26,* 546–553.

Bangs, T. (1986). *Birth to Three Assessment and Intervention System.* Chicago, IL: Riverside Publishing Co.

Bankson, N. (1990). *Bankson Language Screening Test—2.* Los Angeles, CA: Western Psychological Services.

Bankson, N., & Bernthal, J. (1990). *Bankson-Bernthal Test of Phonology (BBTOP).* Chicago, IL: Riverside Publishing Co.

Bates, E., Bretherton, I., & Snyder, L. (1988). *From first words to grammar: Individual differences and dissociable mechanisms.* New York: Cambridge University Press.

Battle, D. E. (1993). *Communication disorders in multicultural populations.* Stoneham, MA: Andover Medical Publishers.

Bernthal, J. E., & Bankson, N. W. (1988). *Articulation and phonological disorders.* Englewood Cliffs: Prentice Hall.

Blackstone, S. (Ed.). (1986). *Augmentative communication: An introduction.* Rockville, MD: American Speech, Language and Hearing Association.

Blank, M., Rose, S., & Berlin, L. (1978). *Preschool Language Assessment Instrument.* San Antonio, TX: The Psychological Corp.

Bloch, J. (1987). *Parent/Professional Preschool Performance Profile (5ps).* Syosset, NY: Variety Pre-Schooler's Workshop.

Bloom, L., Rocissano, L., & Hood, L. (1976). Adult-child discourse: Developmental interaction between information processing and linguistic knowledge. *Cognitive Psychology, 8,* 521–552.

Bluestone, C., & Klein, J. (1990). Otitis media, atelectasis and eustachian tube dysfunction. In C. Bluestone, S. Stool, & M. Scheetz (Eds)., *Pediatric otolaryngology* (pp. 320–400). Philadelphia: W. B. Saunders.

Bricker, D. (1992). The changing nature of communication and language intervention. In S. Warren & J. Reichle (Eds.), *Causes and effects in communication and language intervention* (pp. 361–375). Baltimore, MD: Paul H. Brookes.

Bricker, D. (1993). *AEPS Measurement for Birth to Three Years* (Vol. 1). Baltimore, MD: Paul H. Brookes.

Bricker, D., & Squires, J. (1989). The effectiveness of parental screening of at-risk infants: The infant monitoring questionnaires. *Topics in Early Childhood Special Education, 9,* 67–85.

Bricker, D., Squires, J., & Mounts, L. (1995). *Ages and Stages Questionnaires (ASQ): A Parent-Completed Monitoring System.* Baltimore: MD: Paul H. Brookes.

Bronfenbrenner, U. (1977). Toward an experimental ecology of human development. *American Psychologist, 32,* 513–531.

Bruner, J. (1978). The role of dialogue in language acquisition. In A. Sinclair, R. J. Jarvella, & W. J. M. Leveit (Eds.), *The child's conception of language* (pp. 241–256). Berlin: Springer-Verlag.

Bruner, J. (1981). The social context of language acquisition. *Language Communication, 1,* 155–178.

Bzoch, K., & League, R. (1991). *Receptive-Expressive-Emergent Language Test–2.* Los Angeles, CA: Western Psychological Services.

Calhoun, M., Rose, T., & Prendergast, D. (1991). *Charlotte circle intervention guide for parent-child interactions.* Tucson, AZ: Communication Skill Builders.

Cardone, I., & Gilkerson, L. (1989). Family Administered Neonatal Activities. *Zero to Three, 10*(1), 23–28.

Carlson, L., & Bricker, D. (1982). Dyadic and contingent aspects of early communicative intervention.

In D. Bricker (Ed.), *Intervention with at-risk and handicapped infants: From research to application* (pp. 291–309). Austin, TX: PRO-ED.

Carrow, E. (1974). *Carrow Elicited Language Inventory.* Chicago, IL: Riverside Publishing Co.

Carrow-Woolfolk, E. (1985). *Test for Auditory Comprehension of Language–Revised.* Chicago, IL: Riverside Publishing Co.

Chapman, R. (1978). Comprehension strategies in children. In J. Kavanagh & P. Strange (Eds.), *Language and speech in the laboratory, school, and clinic* (pp. 308–327). Cambridge, MA: MIT Press.

Chapman, R. (1981). Exploring children's communicative intents. In J. F. Miller (Ed.), *Assessing language production in children* (pp. 111–136). Baltimore: University Park Press.

Cheng, L. (1987). *Assessing Asian language performance: Guidelines for evaluating limited-English-proficient students.* Gaithersburg, MD: Aspen Publishers.

Coggins, T., & Carpenter, R. (1981). The communication intention inventory: A system for coding children's early intentional communication. *Applied Psycholinguistics, 2,* 235–252.

Coggins, T. E., Olswang, L. B., & Guthrie, J. (1987). Assessing communicative intents in young children: Low structured or observation tasks? *Journal of Speech and Hearing Disorders, 52,* 44–49.

Compton, A. (1978). *Compton Speech and Language Evaluation.* San Francisco, CA: Carousel House.

Compton, A., & Hutton, S. (1978). *Compton-Hutton Phonological Assessment.* San Francisco, CA: Carousel House.

Consensus Statement on Augmentative and Alternative Communication Intervention. (1992). Washington, DC: National Institute on Disability and Rehabilitation Research.

Conti-Ramsden, G. (1990). Maternal recasts and other contingent replies to language-impaired children. *Journal of Speech and Hearing Disorders, 55,* 262–274.

Conti-Ramsden, G. (1993). Using parents to foster communicatively impaired children's language development. *Seminars in Speech and Language, 14,* 289–295.

Crais, E. (1993). Families and professionals as collaborators in assessment. *Topics in Language Disorders, 14*(1), 29–40.

Crais, E. (1994a, February). *Birth to three: Assessment tools and techniques.* Presentation to Charlotte Area Health Education Center, Charlotte, NC.

Crais, E. (1994b, April). *Birth to three: Current assessment tools and techniques.* Presentation to the Tennessee Association of Audiologists and Speech-Language Pathologists, Gatlinburg, TN.

Crais, E. (1995). Expanding the repertoire of tools and techniques for assessing the communication skills of infants and toddlers. *American Journal of Speech-Language Pathology, 4*(3), 47–59.

Crais, E., & Leonard, R. (1990). P.L. 99-457: Are speech-language pathologists prepared for the challenge? *ASHA, 32*(4), 57–61.

Crais, E., & Roberts, J. (1991). Decision making in assessment and early intervention. *Language, Speech, Hearing Services in Schools, 22*(2), 19–30.

Creaghead, N. (1984). Strategies for evaluating and targeting pragmatic behaviors in young children. *Seminars in Speech and Language, 5*(3), 241–252.

Creaghead, N., Newman, P., & Secord, W. (1989). *Assessment and remediation of articulatory and phonological disorders* (2nd ed.). Englewood Cliffs, NJ: Merrill/Prentice Hall.

Cripe, J., Slentz, K., & Bricker, D. (1993). *AEPS curriculum for birth to three years* (Vol. 2). Baltimore, MD: Paul H. Brookes.

Dale, P. (1991). The validity of a parent report measure of vocabulary and syntax at 24 months. *Journal of Speech and Hearing Research, 34,* 565–571.

Dale, P., Bates, E., Reznick, S., & Morisset, C. (1989). The validity of a parent report instrument on child language at twenty months. *Journal of Child Language, 16,* 239–249.

Dore, J. (1974). A pragmatic description of early language development. *Journal of Psycholinguistic Research, 4,* 343–350.

Duchan, J. (1989). Evaluating adults' talk to children: Assessing adult attunement. *Seminars in Speech and Language, 10,* 17–27.

Dunn, L., & Dunn, L. (1981). *Peabody Picture Vocabulary Test–Revised.* Circle Pines, MN: American Guidance Service.

Dunst, C., Lowe, L., & Bartholomew, P. (1990). Contingent social responsiveness, family ecology, and infant communicative competence. *National Student Speech, Language, and Hearing Association Journal, 17,* 39–49.

Dunst, C., & Wortman-Lowe, L. (1986). From reflex to symbol: Describing, explaining, and fostering communicative competence. *Augmentative and Alternative Communication, 2,* 11–16.

Fenichel, E., & Eggbeer, L. (1991). Preparing practitioners to work with infants, toddlers, and their families: Four essential elements of training. *Infants and Young Children, 4*(2), 56–62.

Fenson, L., Dale, P., Reznick, S., Thal, D., Bates, E., Hartung, J., Pethick, S., & Reilly, J. (1993). *MacArthur Communication Development Inventories.* San Diego, CA: Singular Publishing Group, Inc.

Fey, M. (1986). *Language intervention with young children.* San Diego, CA: College-Hill Press.

Fluharty, N. (1968). *Fluharty Preschool Speech and Language Screening Test.* Chicago, IL: Riverside Publishing Co.

Fuchs, D., Fuchs, L., Benowitz, S., & Barringer, K. (1987). Norm-referenced tests: Are they valid for use with handicapped students? *Exceptional Children, 54,* 263–271.

Fuchs, D., Fuchs, L., Power, M., & Dailey, A. (1985). Bias in the assessment of handicapped children. *American Educational Research Journal, 22,* 185–197.

Fudala, J., & Reynolds, W. (1986). *Arizona Articulation Proficiency Scale–Revised.* Los Angeles, CA: Western Psychological Services.

Furuno, S., O'Reilly, K., Inatsuka, T., Hosaka, C., Allman, T., & Zeisloft-Falbey, B. (l987). *Hawaii Early Learning Profile.* Palo Alto, CA: VORT Corporation.

Gardner, M. (1990). *Expressive One-Word Picture Vocabulary Test–Revised.* Los Angeles CA: Western Psychological Services.

Gill, G., & Dihoff, R. (1982). Nonverbal assessment of cognitive behavior. In B. Campbell & V. Baldwin (Eds.), *Severely handicapped/hearing impaired students: Strengthening service delivery* (pp. 77–ll3). Baltimore: Paul H. Brookes.

Goldberg, S. (1977). Social competence in infancy: A model of parent-infant interaction. *Merrill-Palmer Quarterly, 23,* 163–177.

Goldman, R., & Fristoe, M. (1986). *Goldman-Fristoe Test of Articulation.* Circle Pines, MN: American Guidance Service.

Guralnick, M., & Bennett, F. (1987). *The effectiveness of early intervention for at-risk and handicapped children.* New York: Academic Press.

Halle, J., Alpert, C., & Anderson, S. (1984). Natural environment language assessment and intervention with severely impaired preschoolers. *Topics in Early Childhood Special Education, 4*(2), 36–56.

Hammill, D., & Bryant, B. (1991). *Detroit Tests of Learning Aptitude–Primary: 2.* Austin, TX: PRO-ED.

Hanrahan, L., Ferrier, L., & Jolie, K. (1987, November). *Infants, caregivers and augmentative communication: We must intervene earlier.* Paper presented at the American Speech-Language Hearing Association Annual Convention, New Orleans.

Harris, G. (1985). Considerations in assessing English language performance of Native American children. *Topics in Language Disorders, 5*(4), 42–52.

Hart, B., & Risley, T. (1978). Promoting productive language through incidental teaching. *Educational Urban Society, l0,* 407–432.

Hedrick, D., Prather, E., & Tobin, A. (1984). *Sequenced Inventory of Communicative Development–Revised.* Los Angeles, CA: Western Psychological Services.

HELP for Special Preschoolers. Santa Cruz County Office of Education. (1987). Palo Alto, CA: VORT Corporation.

Hodson, B. (1986). *Assessment of Phonological Processes–Revised.* Danville, IL: Interstate Printers & Publishers, Inc.

Hresko, W., Miguel, S., Sharbenou, R., & Burton, S. (1994). *Developmental Observation Checklist System.* Austin, TX: PRO-ED.

Hresko, W., Reid, D., & Hammill, D. (1991). *Test of Early Language Development–2.* Austin, TX: PRO-ED.

Johnson-Martin, N., Attermeier, S., & Hacker, B. (1990). *Carolina Curriculum for Preschoolers with Special Needs.* Baltimore, MD: Paul H. Brookes.

Johnson-Martin, N., Jens, K., Attermeier, S., & Hacker, B. (1991). *The Carolina Curriculum for Infants and Toddlers with Special Needs* (2nd ed.). Baltimore, MD: Paul H. Brookes.

Kaufman, A., & Kaufman, P. (1993). *Kaufman Survey of Early Academic and Language Skills.* Circle Pines, MN: American Guidance Service.

Keenan, E., & Schieffelin, B. (1976). Topic as a discourse notion: A study of topic in the conversations of children and adults. In C. Li (Ed.), *Subject and topic* (pp. 337–384). New York: Academic Press.

Kennedy, M., Sheridan, M., Radlinski, S., & Beeghly, M. (1991). Play-language relationships in young children with developmental delays: Implications for assessment. *Journal of Speech and Hearing Research, 34,* 112–122.

Khan, L., & Lewis, N. (1986). *Khan-Lewis Phonological Analysis.* Circle Pines, MN: American Guidance Service.

Kjerland, L., & Kovach, J. (1990). Family-staff collaboration for tailored infant assessment. In E. Gibbs & D. Teti (Eds.), *Interdisciplinary assessment of infants: A guide for early intervention professionals.* Baltimore, MD: Paul H. Brookes.

Konstantareas, M., Zajdeman, H., Homatidis, S., & McCabe, A. (1988). Maternal speech to verbal and high functioning versus nonverbal and lower functioning autistic children. *Journal of Autism and Developmental Disorders, 18,* 647–657.

Lee, L. (1971). *Northwestern Syntax Screening Test.* Evanston, IL: Northwestern University Press.

Leonard, L. (1981). Facilitating linguistic skills in children with specific language impairment. *Applied Psycholinguistics, 2*(2), 89–118.

Light, J., Collier, B., & Parnes, P. (1985). Communicative interaction between young nonspeaking physically disabled children and their primary caregivers: Parts I–III. *Augmentative Communication, 1,* 74–133.

Linder, T. (1993). *Transdisciplinary Play-Based Assessment* (rev. ed.). Baltimore, MD: Paul H. Brookes.

Lund, N., & Duchan, J. (1988). *Assessing children's language in naturalistic contexts.* Englewood Cliffs, NJ: Prentice Hall.

MacDonald, J. (1989). *Becoming partners with children.* San Antonio, TX: Special Press.

Maistro, A., & German, M. (1986). Reliability, predictive validity, and interrelationships of early assessment indices used with developmentally delayed infants and children. *Journal of Clinical Child Psychology, 15,* 327–332.

McCollum, J., & Thorp, E. (1988). Training of infant specialists: A look to the future. *Infants and Young Children, 1*(2), 55–65.

McCune-Nicholich, L., & Bruskin, C. (1982). Combinatorial competency in symbolic play and language. In D. Pepler & K. Rubin (Eds.), *The play of children: Current theory and research* (pp. 30-45). Basel, Switzerland: S. Karger.

McLean, L. (1990). Communication development in the first two years of life: A transactional process. *Zero to Three, 11,* 13–19.

McLean, J., & Snyder-McLean, L. (1978). *A transactional approach to early language training.* Englewood Cliffs, NJ: Merrill/Prentice Hall.

McLean, M., & McCormick, K. (1993). Assessment and evaluation in early intervention. In W. Brown, S. Thurman, & L. Pearl (Eds.), *Family-centered early intervention with infants and toddlers* (pp. 43–79). Baltimore, MD: Paul H. Brookes.

McWilliam, R. (1992). *Family-centered intervention planning.* Tucson, AZ: Communication Skill Builders.

Miller, J. (1981). *Assessing language production in children: Experimental procedures.* Baltimore, MD: University Park Press.

Miller, J., Chapman, R., Branston, M., & Reichle, J. (1980). Language comprehension in sensorimotor stages V and VI. *Journal of Speech and Hearing Research, 23,* 284–311.

Miller, J., & Yoder, D. (1984). *Miller-Yoder Language Comprehension Test.* Austin, TX: PRO-ED.

Morris, S. (1982). *Pre-Speech Assessment Scale.* Clifton, NJ: Preston.

Mullen, E. (1989). *Infant Mullen Scales of Early Learning.* Cranston, RI: T.O.T.A.L. Child, Inc.

Neisworth, J., & Bagnato, S. (1992). The case against intelligence testing in early intervention. *Topics in Early Childhood Special Education, 12*(1), 1–20.

Nelson, N. (1993). *Childhood language disorders in context.* Englewood Cliffs, NJ: Merrill/Prentice Hall.

Newborg, J., Stock, J. R., Wnek, L., Guidubaldi, J., & Svinicki, J. (1984). *The Battelle Developmental Inventory.* Allen, TX: DLM/Teaching Resources.

Newcommer, P., & Hammill, D. (1988). *Test of Language Development–Primary–2.* Austin, TX: PRO-ED.

Norris, J. (1992). Assessment of infants and toddlers in naturalistic contexts. *Best Practices in School Speech-Language Pathology, 2,* 21–31.

Northern, J., & Downs, M. (1991). *Hearing in children.* Baltimore, MD: Williams & Wilkins Co.

Olswang, L., Stoel-Gammon, C., Coggins, T., & Carpenter, R. (1987). *Assessing Prelinguistic and Linguistic Behaviors.* Seattle, WA: University of Washington Press.

Owens, R. (1992). *Language development: An introduction.* Englewood Cliffs, NJ: Merrill/Prentice Hall.

Patrick, S. (1993). Facilitating communication and language development. In T. Linder, *Trandiscipli-*

nary play-based intervention (pp. 287–396). Baltimore, MD: Paul H. Brookes.

Paul, R. (1987). A model for the assessment of disorders in infants and toddlers. *National Student Speech Language Hearing Association Journal, l5,* 88–105.

Peck, C. (1989). Assessment of social communicative competence: Evaluating environments. *Seminars in Speech and Language, 10,* 1–15.

Plapinger, D., & Kretschmer, R. (1991). The effect of context on the interactions between a normally-hearing mother and her hearing-impaired child. *Volta Review,* February/March, 75–87.

Platt, J., & Coggins, T. (1990). Comprehension of social-action games in prelinguistic children: Levels of participation and effect of adult structure. *Journal of Speech and Hearing Disorders, 55,* 315–326.

Prinz, P., & Weiner, F. (1987). *Pragmatics Screening Test.* Englewood Cliffs, NJ: Merrill/Prentice Hall.

Prizant, B., & Wetherby, A. (1993). Communication and language assessment for young children. *Infants and Young Children, 5*(4), 20–34.

Rescorla, L. (1989). The language development survey: A screening tool for delayed language in toddlers. *Journal of Speech and Hearing Disorders, 54,* 587–599.

Reynell, J., & Gruber, C. (1969). *Reynell Developmental Language Scales.* Los Angeles, CA: Western Psychological Services.

Roberts, J., Burchinal, M., Davis, B., Collier, A., & Henderson, F. (1991). Otitis media in early childhood and later language. *Journal of Speech and Hearing Research, 34,* 1158–1168.

Roberts, J., Wallace, I., & Zeisel, S. (1993). Otitis media: Implications for early language. *Zero to Three, 13*(4), 24–28.

Rogers-Warren, A., & Warren, S. (1984). The social basis of language and communication in severely handicapped preschoolers. *Topics in Early Childhood Special Education, 4*(2), 57–72.

Rossetti, L. (1990). *Infant-Toddler Language Scale.* East Moline, IL: LinguiSystems.

Roth, F., & Spekman, N. (1984). Assessing the pragmatic abilities of children: Part I. Organizational framework and assessment parameters. *Journal of Speech and Hearing Disorders, 49,* 2–11.

Roush, J. (1990). Acoustic amplification for hearing-impaired infants and young children. *Infants and Young Children, 2*(4), 59–71.

Seibert, J., & Hogan, A. (1982). A model for assessing social and object skills and planning intervention. In D. McClowry, A. Guilford, & S. Richardson (Eds.), *Infant communication, development, assessment, and intervention* (pp. 21–53). New York: Grune & Stratton.

Shriberg, L., & Kwiatkowski, J. (1980). *Natural process analysis: A procedure for phonological analysis of continuous speech samples.* New York: John Wiley & Sons.

Shulman, B. (1986). *Test of Pragmatic Skills–Revised.* Tucson, AZ: Communication Skill Builders.

Siegel-Causey, E., Ernst, B., & Guess, D. (1987). Elements of nonsymbolic communication and early interactional processes. In M. Bollis (Ed.), *Communication development in young children with deafness/blindness: Literature review III* (pp. 57–102). Monmouth, OR: Oregon State System of Higher Education.

Sorsby, A., & Martlew, M. (1991). Representational demands in mothers' talk to preschool children in two contexts: Picture book reading and a modeling task. *Journal of Child Language, 18,* 373–396.

Stoel-Gammon, C., & Dunn, C. (1985). *Normal and disordered phonology in children.* Baltimore, MD: University Park Press.

Stokes, T., & Baer, D. (1977). An implicit technology of generalization. *Journal of Applied Behavior Analysis, 10,* 349–367.

Taylor, O. L. (1985). *Nature of communication disorders in culturally and linguistically diverse populations.* San Diego, CA: College Hill Press.

Templin, M. (1957). *Certain language skills in children.* Minneapolis, MN: University of Minnesota Press.

Terrell, S., & Terrell, F. (1983). Distinguishing linguistic differences from disorders: The past, present, and future of nonbiased assessment. *Topics in Language Disorders, 3*(3), 1–7.

Tronick, E. (1989). Emotions and emotional communication in infants. *American Psychologist, 44,* 112–119.

U.S. Department of Education. (1987). *Ninth Annual Report to Congress on the Implementation of the Education of the Handicapped Act.* Washington, DC: Office of Special Education Programs.

Vaughn-Cooke, F. B. (1983). Improving language assessment in minority children. *ASHA, 25,* 29–34.

Warren, S., & Kaiser, A. (1986). Incidental language teaching: A critical review. *Journal of Speech and Hearing Disorders, 51*(4), 291–299.

Wells, G. (1986). *The meaning makers: Children learning language and using language to learn.* Portsmouth, NH: Heinemann.

Westby, C. (1988). Children's play: Reflections of social competence. *Seminars in Speech and Language, 9,* 1–14.

Westby, C. (1990). Ethnographic interviewing: Asking the right questions to the right people in the right ways. *Journal of Childhood Communication Disorders, 13*(1), 101–111.

Wetherby, A. (1992). *Communication and language intervention for preschool children.* Manual for inservice workshop. Buffalo, NY: Educom Associates.

Wetherby A., & Prizant B. (1989). The expression of communication intent: Assessment guidelines. *Seminar in Speech and Language, 10,* 77–91.

Wetherby, A., & Prizant, B. (1992). Profiling young children's communicative competence. In S. Warren & J. Reichle (Eds.), *Causes and effects in communication and language intervention* (pp. 217–253). Baltimore, MD: Paul H. Brookes.

Wetherby A., & Prizant B. (1993). *Communication and Symbolic Behavior Scales.* Chicago, IL: The Riverside Publishing Co.

Widerstrom, A., Mowder, B., & Sandall, S. (1991). *At-risk handicapped newborns and infants.* Englewood Cliffs, NJ: Prentice Hall.

Wiig, E., Secord, W., & Semel, E. (1992). *Clinical Evaluation of Language Fundamentals–Preschool.* San Antonio, TX: The Psychological Corp.

Wilcox, M. J. (1992). Enhancing initial communication skills in young children with developmental disabilities through partner programming. *Seminars in Speech and Language, 13,* 194–212.

Zimmerman, I., Steiner, V., & Pond, R. (1992). *Preschool Language Scale–3.* San Antonio, TX: The Psychological Corp.

Zirpoli, T., & Bell, R. (1987). Unresponsiveness in children with severe disabilities: Potential effects on parent-child interactions. *The Exceptional Child, 34,* 31–40.

CHAPTER

13

Assessing Social Performance

Samuel L. Odom
Leslie J. Munson
Vanderbilt University

. . . .

SCENE 1: Anna was so pleased to bring her baby home. Nicole was born 12 weeks early and had had a difficult hospital course. During the hospitalization, Nicole's fragile medical condition and Anna's own illness had prevented her from providing very much care. When Nicole first came home, she slept most of the time. Now she is 6 months old, and both she and Anna are having much difficulty. When Nicole cries, Anna attempts to soothe her by holding her, singing to her, and rocking her, but nothing seems to work. Medical routines and feeding take so much time that Anna has little time to play with the baby. When they do play, Nicole is sometimes unresponsive and often turns her gaze away. Even attempts to play peek-a-boo often end in tears for both of them.

. . . .

SCENE 2: Leon and Jared, who are both nearly 4 years old, began attending the Children's World Child Care Center in the fall. Leon, a child with autism, also receives weekly visits from a special education consulting teacher. During centers and playtime, Jared talks with his classmates, shares the toy he brought from home with the specific friend with whom he spends a lot of time, engages in activities planned by the teacher in which the other children participate, playfully chases his friend on the playground, and has to go to timeout with two other boys because they were "cutting up" in the bathroom. In contrast, during the same activities, Leon walks around the classroom, rarely picks up or looks at a toy or activity material, never talks with classmates (or adults), occasionally flicks his hands before his eyes, climbs on the outside play equipment, but never talks to another child. Classmates generally ignore Leon, but they take his hand and bring him back to the group when he leaves the class line during transitions, and they will help him when he appears to need help. In addition, they are persistent when he rejects their help.

. . . .

For infants and children with disabilities, becoming an active member of their social world is a major developmental achievement. Participation in social interaction with caregivers and peers provides the foundation for skills related to social competence in later years. However, for some infants and young children with disabilities, roadblocks exist that prevent the development of those skills. For Nicole, in the scenario above, the predictable behaviors that signal when she is ready for playful social experiences are not clear, which leads to frustration for her and her mother. For Leon, some of the necessary prerequisites for engaging in social interaction with peers may be missing; his social experience in the peer group differs substantially from Jared's. For both of the children with disabilities in these scenarios, a breakdown in the social development process exists.

Difficulties in developing social skills occur often for children with disabilities. Preschool teachers report that as many as 75% of their children with disabilities need to learn age-appropriate skills (Odom, McConnell, & Chandler, 1994). Guralnick (1990) and others (Odom, McConnell, & McEvoy, 1992) have recommended that promoting social competence of young children with disabilities should be a primary goal for early intervention programs. The first step in creating individualized programs that support social competence is to collect assessment information that may

This chapter was supported by Grant No. H024K40004 (the Early Childhood Research Institute on Inclusion) and Grant No. H024B10108 (Project BLEND) from the U.S. Department of Education. The authors wish to thank Scott McConnell for his contributions to an earlier edition version of this chapter.

determine the nature of the child's social participation (i.e., their performance) in interactions with caregivers or peers.

The purpose of this chapter is to describe assessment strategies and instruments that yield useful information about the social performance of infants and young children with disabilities. We will begin by describing the characteristics of social interaction and how it evolves over the infant and preschool years. Information that assessments provide about the different dimensions of social performance as well as procedural considerations in conducting social assessments will be examined. A review of methods for assessing social performance appears as the central part of this chapter. We will conclude with a discussion of ways in which assessment information may be used in early intervention and early childhood special education programs.

A SKETCH OF EARLY SOCIAL DEVELOPMENT

During the early childhood years, the two major influences on infants' and children's social development are their interactions with caregivers and their interactions with peers. These influences contribute to the acquisition of social skills and the development of social relationships. A brief description of the progress in social development appears in Table 13.1.

Parent-Infant Relationships

A primary task in social development is establishing positive styles of interaction with caregivers. Infants are influenced by the behavior of their caregivers, and their behavior influences their caregivers in a reciprocal and dynamic manner (Bell, 1968; Lewis & Lee-Painter, 1974). Through early positive interactions, infants develop an attachment relationship with a primary caregiver that assures survival, allows exploration, and provides stimulation (Ainsworth, Blehar, Waters, & Walls, 1978). Characteristics of successful parent-infant interactions include positive affect, active participation, facilitative positioning (Clarke-Stewart, 1973; O'Connor, Sigman, & Kasari, 1992), verbal exchanges (Olson, Bates, & Bayles, 1984), responsivity (Bakeman & Brown, 1980), sensitivity (Barrera, Rosenbaum, & Cunningham, 1986), turn-taking (Rutter & Durkin, 1987), and predictability (Goldberg, 1977). Failure of either partner to exhibit positive behaviors may result in less social behavior by the other member of the dyad. For example, when infants with a physical disability engage in less eye contact with their mothers, the mothers speak less to them during interaction (Barrera & Vella, 1987).

Peer Relationships

A major developmental task of the preschool years is to become a viable member of a peer group. Although there is evidence of peer social interaction (Mueller & Vandell, 1979) and peer preferences (Howes, 1983) in the infant and toddler years, peer interactions do not increase substantially in frequency or cohesion until the preschool years (Hartup, 1983). By 3 years of age, children will begin to show a preference for playing with peers in a coordinated and cooperative way (Howes, 1992). By 5 years of age, most typically developing children who have had peer group experiences have become relatively sophisticated social interactors. They know many social rules for interacting with a partner, although they may not be able to articulate them, and they can carry on sustained and reciprocal social interactions with their peers. The hallmark of this developmental period is social acceptance by peer groups and at least a small number of identified reciprocal friendships (Park, Lay, & Ramsay, 1993).

TABLE 13.1
Development of Social Interaction in Infants and Young Children

Age	Social Development
Birth–3 months	Infant born with predispositions toward social behavior (attends selectively to faces, some imitation abilities, crying as a natural elicitor of adult behavior, endogenous smiles).
3–6 months	Infant develops social smile.
6–9 months	Infant participates in adult/infant social games with adult as elicitor.
9–15 months	Infant/toddler increasingly becomes the imitator in parent/infant games. Developing motor skill allows infant/toddler to maintain physical proximity to mother or other attachment figure. Begins to discriminate unfamiliar adults (stranger anxiety). Some low rates of peer interaction begin to occur.
15–24 months	Increasing language skills allow parent/infant interactions to become increasingly verbal and more sophisticated. Increasing cognitive skills allow child to represent attachment figures in their absence.
24–36 months	Interest in peers increases. Sociodramatic play skills become more refined, allowing inclusion of peers in symbolic play. Parent/child interactions maintain.
36–48 months	Children become frequent social interactors with peer group. Elaboration of sociodramatic play skills continues. Child moves to attachment relationship involving mutual understanding between child and attachment figure about their absence.
48–60 months	Children typically are competent social interactors with peers. They are learning to play positively with peers and negotiate conflicts and are beginning to learn responses to aggression.

Social Development of Infants and Young Children with Disabilities

Infants who have a disability or who are at risk for a disability may have difficulty engaging in social interactions with their caregivers. Preschoolers with a disability may display delayed peer social interaction skills and achieve less social acceptance by peers than normally developing children in their peer group.

Parent-infant relationship Several factors may contribute to unsuccessful infant-caregiver interactions. When infants are developing in a typical pattern, their behavior (e.g., gazing, smiling, reaching) signals to the caregiver a readiness to interact. For infants with a disability or at risk for a disability, the signals may be diminished, different, or delayed. For example, infants who are deaf may be less active in their interactions with their caregiver (Wedell-Monig & Lumley, 1980). An infant who has a motor delay may provide signals that are unclear (Yoder, 1987).

In addition, caregivers may differ in their interactions with infants with disabilities relative to caregivers of typically developing infants. For example, mothers of premature infants gaze at their babies for longer periods than do mothers of full-term infants (Field, 1983). Mothers of infants who have Down syndrome are often more directive in their interactions than mothers of typical infants (Maurer & Sherrod, 1987). Similarly, the muted smiles that infants who are blind develop and the absence of eye contact early in life often prove distressful for parents (Fraiberg, 1975).

The development of the attachment relationship (i.e., identification of one or two adults as significant security figures) may be affected by a child's disability. Some children with disabilities appear to develop attachment, although it may be delayed or expressed in a manner different from that of typically developing children (Berry, Gunn, & Andrews, 1980; Sigman & Ungerer, 1984). For other children with disabilities, insecure and ambivalent attachment relationships develop (Spieker, 1986).

It should be noted that interactions occur during families' routine daily activities such as feeding, dressing, and playing. Factors related to daily activities and other variables within the family system influence the interactive behaviors and the subsequent relationships that develop. Among the factors that affect infant-caregiver interaction are setting (Seifer, Sameroff, Anagnostopolou, & Elias, 1992), support systems (Zarling, Hirsch, & Landry, 1988), cultural context (Fernald & Morikawa, 1993), and socioeconomic status (Parks & Bradley, 1991).

Peer relationships The social interactions of preschool-age children with disabilities differ in both quantity and quality from those of typical children of the same age. Research has repeatedly documented that preschoolers with disabilities interact less often than their nondisabled peers (Guralnick, 1980; Guralnick & Groom, 1987; Kopp, Baker, & Brown, 1992). In their study of integrated play groups, Guralnick and Groom (1988) found that the success in social interaction experienced by children with mild disabilities *decreased* across the time that the children participated in the play group. This decrease suggests that as the group became more familiar with its members, deficits in social skills led to impaired interaction patterns for the children with disabilities. To examine the social competence of preschool children with and without disabilities, Odom and McConnell (in press) used a multimethod approach to assess peer-related social competence. They found that the social performance of preschool children with disabilities was significantly lower on a central social competence factor than that of typically developing preschoolers. Researchers have noted both the unique competence (Salisbury, Britzman, & Kang, 1989) and concerns related to social interaction for preschool children with a range of disabilities (Antia & Kreimeyer, 1992; Goldstein & Gallagher, 1992; Skellenger, Hill, & Hill, 1992).

The development of peer relationships is undoubtedly based on participation in social interaction, as well as on other factors (e.g., appearance or attractiveness, reputation). In a study of friendships by Buysee (1993), teachers and parents reported that children with disabilities often have mutual friendships (each partner selects and is selected by another partner) as well as unilateral friendships (only one partner selects a child as a special friend). However, children with more severe developmental delays appeared to engage in fewer mutual friendships. The difference in formation of friendships may be related to these children's participation in social interaction. In a study of peer social interactions in mainstreamed settings, Strain (1983) found that children with disabilities who were chosen as "friends" on a sociometric measure exhibited a number of positive social behaviors that less preferred children with disabilities did not display. Similarly, in the study by Guralnick and Groom (1988) noted previously, the interaction patterns of children with mild disabilities were associated with preference scores that they received on peer rating assessments. Together, this research suggests that most preschool-age children with disabilities have social interaction delays that may exceed their other developmental delays. In addition, when placed in peer groups with normally developing children, children with disabilities may not automatically establish positive peer relationships.

DIMENSIONS OF SOCIAL INTERACTION ASSESSMENT

Assessments of children's social interaction skills reflect different levels of analysis. Like viewing a mountainside through a telescope and adjusting the focus to get a clear picture of the landscape's details, one can adjust the focus of an assessment to provide different views of a child's social development. Assessments can provide information at the most detailed, microscopic level (i.e., individual social behavior), at a microscopic but dynamic level (i.e., social interactions), or at a more macroscopic level (i.e., relationship/social status) (Suen & Ary, 1989). The assessor's choice of assessment will be determined by the purposes for which the information will be used. For example, a microscopic assessment approach might be used for planning or monitoring the immediate effects of intervention programs. More macroscopic approaches might be used for diagnostic or program evaluation purposes.

Individual Social Behaviors

When professionals assess the single social behaviors of infants and children, they focus on several aspects of social behavior. Most often, they count the *frequency* at which a social behavior occurs within a given time frame. Usually some judgment of a social behavior's *affective quality* (e.g., positive or negative) is made. Many assessments also indicate whether the child initiated an interaction or responded to the social behavior of another (Strain & Timm, 1974). Global (e.g., socially directed behavior) or specific (e.g., share/trade, leads peer) categories may be used. In their review of research from the 1980s, Odom and Ogawa (1992) found that over 240 behavioral categories of social behavior had been used by different researchers.

Interactional Level

The word *interactions* refers to the dynamic interchanges of behaviors among partners in a social interaction. At the interactional level, the concept of *social reciprocity* becomes significant. Social reciprocity has been defined in two ways. First, Strain and Shores (1977) referred to reciprocity as the immediate response of one child to the social behavior of another child. In analyzing social behavior at this level, the *sequence* or *order* of behaviors in an interaction is most important. Social interaction may be viewed as a chain of social behavior directed back and forth between social partners. Social behaviors that produce a response from a peer (or adult) are reciprocal; those that do not produce a response are not reciprocal. In their investigation of peer-related social behaviors, Tremblay, Strain, Hendrickson, and Shores (1981) identified the social behaviors that were most likely to result in a positive response from a peer. Similarly, Bakeman and Brown (1977) examined the conditional probabilities of mothers and infants responding to each other given a certain set of conditions.

A second type of reciprocity is assessed at a less microscopic level. Reciprocity defined at this level refers to the direction and frequency of social interactions with potentially available partners. Preschool-age children who direct positive social behaviors to peers receive positive social behavior from peers (Hartup, Glazer, & Charlesworth, 1967; Kohler & Fowler, 1985). In this sense, reciprocity means that the net effect of being positively social with a partner is that the partner will probably be positively social in return. To assess this type of reciprocity at the preschool level, the assessor looks at the number of social behaviors that a child directs to his peers and the number directed to him from his peers. At the parent-infant level, particularly after the child is about 9 months old, one might observe the amount of positive social exchanges that the infant initiates to the parent and the number that the parent initiates.

The last dimension of the assessment of social behavior at the interaction level is the concept of *duration of interactions.* Like reciprocity, duration has also been interpreted in two slightly different ways. First, it may refer to the length of time an interaction continues. To measure duration in this way, a teacher might start a stopwatch when an interaction begins and stop it when the interaction ends. For example, Brown, Ragland, and Fox (1988) measured the number of seconds that children were engaged in interactions. Second, duration may also refer to the number of behaviors in a social interaction chain. For example, if a mother begins a social game with her infant, the infant responds, the mother makes another verbalization to the infant, and the infant responds again, a four-unit chain of interaction has occurred. To measure duration in this way, an assessor would record and then count the number of behaviors in each interaction. In their studies of peer interaction, Odom and Strain (1986) and Rubenstein and Howes (1979) assessed the duration of the interactions by using this method.

At the interactional level, the peer preferences or relationships of toddlers and preschoolers can also be examined. Typically when a child interacts frequently with a peer, and the peer in turn directs a large percentage of his interactions to the original child, it reflects the development of a friendship. Friendships identified by observing social interaction have been shown to correlate with teacher ratings of peer preferences (Howes, 1983; Roopnarine & Field, 1984) and mothers' identifications of their children's preferred play partners (Hinde, Titmus, Easton, & Tamplin, 1985).

Social Relationships

Assessment of the social relationships of infants and young children with disabilities occurs at a macroscopic level and may measure the success with which children achieve the benchmark social developmental tasks of attachment and social acceptance within a peer group. As noted earlier, *attachment* refers to the relationship that develops between infants and their caregivers. The purpose of behaviors related to attachment (e.g., smiling, crying, locomotion to mother, talking to mother) is to ensure that the child stays in close proximity to the attachment figure, especially at times when the child feels insecure (Bowlby, 1969; Ainsworth et al., 1978). Assessment of attachment usually occurs through a laboratory procedure called the *strange situation.* In this assessment, the infant is exposed to various conditions in which the mother leaves him or her alone in a room and then returns to the room (Ainsworth & Bell, 1970). The critical indicator of the attachment relationship is the infant's behavior when mother and child are reunited. Research using the strange situation has revealed that different types of attachment relationships exist (i.e., secure, insecure, ambivalent) and are reflected in interactions that occur between infants and mothers in naturalistic settings (Isabella & Belsky, 1991).

At the preschool level, social relationships with peers are most often measured by the use of a sociometric assessment. These assessments may reveal the popularity of the child as well as the level of acceptance that the child has achieved in the peer group. Moreover, peer acceptance as measured by sociometrics has fairly substantial predictive validity (McConnell & Odom, 1986). A range of sociometric assessments, which are described in a later section, have been used with preschool-age children, and some evidence of reliability exists.

Social Competence versus Social Skill

Professionals have used the term *social competence* in many ways. It has been described as a myriad of skills that can be grouped under general competence (Anderson & Messick, 1974; Zigler & Trickett, 1978), as successful social behavior (Bailey & Simeonsson, 1985; Foster & Ritchey, 1979), and as interpersonal social problem solving (Shure, 1993). In their conceptualization of a performance-based assessment of social competence, Odom and McConnell (in press) have followed the lead of Hops (1983) in identifying social competence as a behavior that is effective and appropriate within a given social context, and they have incorporated McFall's (1982) concept of "performance" as the ultimate measure of competence. Performance implies that social behaviors are judged appropriate by significant social agents (e.g., teachers, parents) in the social environment (Odom & McConnell, 1985). Social competence is a summary dimension of social interaction skills, in that it incorporates information provided by multiple informants and collected through multiple methods.

PROCEDURAL CONSIDERATIONS IN ASSESSING SOCIAL INTERACTION

Assessment of children's social performance differs from assessment in most other developmental areas. The type of standardized assessment useful for measurement of cognitive or language development (e.g., individual administration of assessment, standard presentation of items) is neither available nor appropriate for assessing social interaction skills. Rather, these skills are usually observed in natural contexts and recorded by an observer or reported by the parent. The characteristics of the natural setting in which assessors observe infants and young children may affect the information obtained by the assessment. Similarly, the manner in which assessments are chosen or employed will affect the ultimate usefulness of the information obtained.

Setting of the Social Interaction

Since the setting of the interaction will affect the behaviors that are observed during the interaction, it is important to assess children's social behavior in the most natural setting. For infants, the most natural setting may be the home (Beal, 1991; Stern, 1974) or other location where mother and child feel most comfortable (Comfort, 1988). Since many infants are in child care, observations in that setting and with child-care staff may provide additional important information.

Because the presence of an observer may affect the interactions between infants and caregivers, observers should not begin collecting data until they have established positive rapport with the caregiver and the child. Otherwise, the partners in the dyad (particularly the adult) may interact in ways they perceive as socially appropriate or aligned with the observer's expectations. Some observations may involve videotaping the interaction. The additional presence of a video camera may further alter the interaction. Conducting several sessions with the video camera prior to actual recording may allow the dyad to become more comfortable.

Frequently, observations may occur during feeding and structured or unstructured play activities. For example, Farran, Kasari, Comfort, and Jay (1986) observed parent-infant interactions during free-play in order to complete their rating scale, the Parent/Caregiver Involvement Scale (P/CIS). Other activities observed include teaching a specific task, separation and reunion, and routine caregiving. Additional dimensions of the setting that are planned for some observations are the use of a standard set of toys and placement of mother and infant (e.g., face-to-face paradigm). As part of their assessment, observers should always document the setting and the activity in which the data are collected.

When observing preschoolers' interactions with peers, similar issues exist. The most typical setting in which preschool social interaction is observed is during free-play conditions (Odom & Ogawa, 1992). The types of toys and activities available in the setting may well affect the nature and frequency of interaction seen. For example, children will be more likely to play with peers when "high social" versus "low social" toys or activities are available. Odom, Peterson, McConnell, and Ostrosky (1990) found that children were significantly more interactive during play activities in which pretend play was occurring than during other activities during the day. In addition to the content of the activity, the structure of the activity (e.g., number in the group, definition of roles) will affect the level of interaction, with children being more interactive in high- versus low-structure activities. If observers are not part of the classroom staff (i.e., if the teacher is not collecting the information), their presence may have immediate but transitory affects on peer social interaction. Again, this is particularly true if videotaped data are being collected. Allowing time for children to get used to the observer in the classroom may well reduce the effect that the observer has on peer interactions.

Participants in the Social Interaction

Because social interaction is a reciprocal process, children's behavior will be affected by the partners with whom they may interact as well as by the history of interaction between the partners. For infants, both caregivers and infants contribute to the type of interactions occurring, and an assessment must capture the behavior of each participant. In addition, an infant may display very different behaviors with the mother, the father, and other caregivers (Belsky, Gilstrap, & Rovine, 1984; Field, 1978; Power & Parke, 1986). For preschool children, the skills of the peer group may affect the degree and nature of interaction. For example, if the peer group consists only of children with disabilities, the child being assessed may not have the opportunity to engage in positive, reciprocal interactions because the peer group may be less responsive than a typically developing peer group. In their study of children enrolled in early childhood education and special education classes, Odom et al. (1990) found that the proportion of time spent in interaction was nearly twice as great in the early childhood education classes, suggesting that more interaction opportunities might occur when a nondisabled peer group is available. At a minimum, assessors must report the participants in social interactions and, if possible, measure the relative contribution of each to the interactions recorded.

Use of Multiple Measures

As noted previously, Odom and McConnell (in press) and others (Gresham, 1986) have proposed that multiple sources of information be collected on children's social performance and that different informants (e.g., teachers, peers, caregivers) provide this information. The advantage of this approach is that it provides evidence of agreement or disagreement on socially competent behaviors from different perspectives and from different instruments (e.g., direct observation, teacher ratings, peer ratings, parent ratings, etc.). If agreement exists across assessments, more confidence can be placed in the information obtained. For example, direct observation and teacher ratings of the child's social interactions might indicate the same performance level. However, it is possible that assessment information will not agree. For example, the teacher's ratings and the parents' ratings might differ substantially, due to the difference in behaviors exhibited by the child in the home and in the school setting or to different standards imposed by the raters. In either case, differences provide unique information about the child's social skills across settings, and a comprehensive evaluation should capture such information.

METHODS FOR ASSESSING SOCIAL PERFORMANCE

A variety of techniques exist for assessing the social performance of infants and young children with disabilities. Each provides slightly different information but all depend on some level of observation of children or parents and infants. These observations may occur in single settings where the teacher or assessor steps away from the activity in which interaction may occur, watches the child, and records the information observed. Assessment information may be collected through (a) anecdotal notes, (b) questionnaires, (c) direct observation systems, (d) rating scales, (e) sociometric measures, (f) curriculum-based measures, or (g) norm-referenced assessments. Examples of each of these are provided in Table 13.2.

Anecdotal Data Collection

When observing infants and young children, teachers sometimes keep notes on the infants' or children's social behavior. These anecdotal notes should describe the setting, activity, participants, and behaviors observed during the interaction. If possible, the teacher should write the notes while observing the interaction or immediately after the observation period. Parents can also use anecdotal reporting to describe interactive behaviors observed in the home. For some early childhood education curricula, anecdotal records serve as the primary assessment information collected (Bredekamp, 1987; Schweinhart, 1993).

Questionnaires

Assessors sometimes use questionnaires to gather information from individuals who are knowledgeable about a child's behavior. These questionnaires differ from the rating scales discussed later in that they (a) do not require rating on a numeric scale, (b) usually do not have information related to reliability and validity, and (c) are sometimes used as clinical instruments for designing interventions. For example, to assess the friendships of young children with disabilities, Buysee (1991) developed the Early Childhood Friendship Survey, which provides information about the mutual and unilateral friendships of young children as well as factors related to making friends. Different forms are provided for parents and teachers. Buysee (1993) has used this survey to collect information about friendships of preschoolers with a range of disabilities.

A second example of an instrument that uses informal questionnaires is the Assessment of Peer Relations (APR) by Guralnick (1992a). Based on a hierarchical model of social competence (Guralnick, 1992b, 1993), this assessment gathers information about children's involvement and purposes of interaction, emotional regulation, shared understanding, peer group entry behavior, conflict resolution, and maintenance of play. Although a rating format is provided for some items, the rating anchors are not associated with numeric scores. The author stated that the APR is designed as a clinical tool for creating and monitoring intervention.

Direct Observation of Social Interaction

Observational systems that require the assessor to directly observe and immediately record infants' or children's social interaction provide detailed assessment information. Direct observational systems are similar to anecdotal systems in that they depend on observation of the child in a social context, but are different in that the categories for observation are predetermined and the observations are made within a temporal frame (i.e., a specific point in time or within a time interval). In addition, ongoing entries are recorded as the assessor observes the social interaction; in rating scales only a summary score is provided.

Three types of direct observation systems exist for assessing children's social interactions.

TABLE 13.2
Assessment of Social Behavior and Interactions of Infants and Young Children with Disabilities

Assessment Type	Title	Age Range	Information Generated	Description
Anecdotal	*Field Notes or Anecdotal Records*	Open	Behaviors determined by the teacher	Narrative recording or report of infants'/children's participation in social interaction with peers or caregivers
Questionnaires	*Early Childhood Friendship Survey* (Buysee, 1991)	Preschool	Mutual friendships Unilateral friendships Information about factors related to friendships	A questionnaire to be completed by caregivers (separate forms for parents and teachers)
	Assessment of Peer Relations (Guralnick, 1992)	Preschool	Range of information related to general overview of social behavior, emotional regulation, shared understanding, social strategies, tasks, and processes	A set of questionnaires to be completed by teacher or other individual knowledgeable about child's behavior. Both open-ended questions and rating forms included.
Direct Observation	*Social Interaction Assessment and Intervention* (McCollum & Stayton, 1985)	Infancy	Target behavior selected by assessor	Frequency count and overall rating
	Infant-Parent Social Interaction Code (Baird, Haas, McCormick, Carruth, & Turner, 1992)	Infancy	Parent (contingent responsivity, directiveness, intrusiveness, facilitation) Infant (initiation, participation, communication acts) Dyad (theme continuity)	Modified time sampling
	Parten/Smilansky Combined Scale (Rubin et al., 1976)	Preschool	See Table 13.3	An interval-sampling system designed to measure cognitive play within a social context
	Social Interaction Scan (Odom et al., 1988)	Preschool	Isolate/unoccupied Proximity Interactive Negative Teacher interaction	A system for scanning classrooms of children. Designed to measure both interaction play and social integration.

	Guralnick & Groom (1988)	Preschool	Gains attention Uses peers as resource Leads peers Imitates Expresses hostility Competes for attention Shows pride Follows peers' activities	Event recording system for measuring peers' interactions
	Bronson Social and Task Profile (Bronson, 1994)	Preschool	Helps Shares Trades Takes turns Joint effort Suggests activity Assigns roles States rules	Event recording system
Rating Scales	*Parent-Child Observation Guide* (Bernstein, Hans, & Percanksy, 1992)	Infancy	Parent (responsiveness to child's need and child's activity, positive feelings, helping child) Infant (expression, using parent, involvement, positive feelings, language)	Binary scoring Three age levels (birth to 3 months, 4 to 15 months, and 16 to 36 months) Developed in project for infants and mothers at environmental risk
	Infant-Caregiver Interaction Scale (ICIS) (Munson & Odom, 1994)	Infancy	Environment (positioning, distractions, planning) Parent (participation, predictability, sensitivity/ responsiveness/turn-taking, communicative intent, playful routines, imitation, affect) Infant (participation, predictability/ consistency, sensitivity/responsiveness/ turn-taking, communicative intent, playful routines, play behaviors, imitation, affect)	Five-point Likert scale Developed in a project for infants who were medically fragile
	Social Strategy Rating Scale (Beckman & Lieber, 1994)	Infancy and Preschool	21 social strategies, such as turn-taking, games, takes lead, invites, joins play	Rating scale completed after observing child in social interaction

TABLE 13.2
Continued

Assessment Type	Title	Age Range	Information Generated	Description
Rating Scales	*Teacher Impressions Scale* (Vanderbilt-Minnesota Social Interaction Project, 1993)	Preschool	16 social behaviors, such as converses appropriately, takes turns, plays cooperatively, smiles, shares materials	Rating scale completed after observing child in social interaction
	Social Skills Rating System (Gresham & Elliott, 1990)	Preschool	49-item scale that generates summary scores related to social skills and problem behavior	Alternate rating forms for teachers and parents
	Social Competence Scale (Kohn, 1988)	Preschool	Summary scores of cooperation vs. defiance and participation vs. disinterest	Scale completed by teacher or other individual familiar with the child
Sociometrics	McCandless & Marshall (1957)	Preschool	Summary score of peer nominations as friends	Peer nomination sociometric using photographs
	Asher, Singleton, Tinsley, & Hymel (1979)	Preschool	Summary score of peer rating by whole class	Peer rating scale using photographs
Curriculum-based Assessment	*The Carolina Curriculum for Infants and Toddlers with Special Needs,* Second Edition (Johnson-Martin et al., 1991)	Infancy	Five developmental domains including social Social adaptation (self-direction, social skills, self-help skills)	Teaching activities correspond to each item in the assessment
	The Carolina Curriculum for Preschoolers with Special Needs (Johnson-Martin et al., 1990)	Preschool	Five developmental domains including social Social adaptation (responsibility, self-concept, interpersonal skills)	Teaching activities correspond to each item in the assessment log

	Transdisciplinary Play-Based Assessment (rev. ed.) (Linder, 1993a)	Infancy and Preschool	Four developmental domains including social-emotional Social-emotional (temperament, mastery, motivation, social interaction with parents, social interactions with facilitator, characteristics of dramatic play in relation to emotional development, humor and social conventions, social interactions with peers)	Accompanying curriculum contains teaching activities (Linder, 1993b)
	AEPS (Bricker, 1993)	Infancy	Three subdomains related to interaction with adults, environment, and peers	Accompanying curriculum contains teaching activities (Cripe, Slentz, & Bricker, 1993)
Norm-referenced Assessment	*Battelle Developmental Inventory* (Newborg, Stock, Wnek, Guidubaldi, & Svinicki, 1988)	Infancy and Preschool	Personal-social domains contain subdomains related to adult-interaction, expression of feelings—affect, self-concept, peer interaction, coping, social role	Provides standard scores and age-equivalence on social domain
	Vineland Adaptive Behavior Scales (Sparrow, Balla, & Cicchetti, 1984)	Preschool	Age scores and percentile ranks for social age	General adaptive behavior scale with social competence subscale

Momentary time sampling systems require that the observer record at a specific point in time whether the infant, the child, or the parent is engaged in a specific social behavior or interaction (Sackett, 1978). Many data points are collected to gain a representative picture of the social interaction in which the infant or child engages.

In a momentary time sampling system called the Social Interaction Scan (SIS) (Odom et al., 1988), the teacher observes a child for 2 seconds and in the subsequent 4 seconds records the behavior in which the child was engaged. As can be seen from the coding sheet in Figure 13.1, the observer circles one of the letters that indicates a category of play behavior. These categories, based loosely on Parten's (1932) pioneering work, include isolate/unoccupied (I/U), proximity (P), interactive play (I), negative interaction (N), and teacher interaction (T). For the I and N categories, superscripts and subscripts indicate whether the child was playing with a child with disabilities (H) or a nondisabled child (N). For the teacher category, the observer indicates whether the child was talking to the teacher (C) or the teacher was talking to the child (T).

This system is called a *scan* because after the observer records the behavior for one child, he or she moves on to the next child, and when the behavior of the final child on the list is recorded, the observer begins again with the first child. This technique provides a more representative picture of the children's social behavior across a play session than does a single block of observations. An alternative way of using this system is to observe a single child for a certain number of observations (e.g., 10 observations) before moving on to the next child.

An advantage of time sampling is that it is usually less difficult to learn than either of the two other methods described below. Using the SIS, one can collect information on frequency of interactive play, the type of child involved in the interaction, and frequencies of other data (e.g., proximity, teacher interactions, etc.). In addition, information may be collected for the whole class in a short time. The SIS is a relatively simple scanning system, and more detailed and descriptive categories of social interaction could be developed.

Momentary time sampling systems do not allow the observer to collect information about the sequential nature of a child's social interaction (i.e., how many turns occurred in the interaction). Also, because the behavior is collected either instantaneously or within a very short interval, high-frequency behaviors tend to be overrepresented in the data and low-frequency behaviors tend to be underrepresented unless a substantial amount of data is collected for the assessment (Sackett, 1978). The authors of the SIS recommend that the teacher collect at least 100 to 150 data points per child in order to obtain a representative sample of children's behavior (Odom et al., 1988).

Interval sampling measures of social interaction require the observer to watch an infant or young child for a short period of time, usually between 6 and 15 seconds, and record whether the behavior occurred at all during the interval (i.e., partial interval sampling) or for the whole interval (i.e., whole interval sampling). In *discontinuous interval systems,* a short interval is provided after the observation interval to allow the observer to record the social behavior. In *continuous interval systems,* the observer records the behavior as it occurs and moves to the next observation interval without pausing. Usually an auditory tone (e.g., from an audiotape) cues the observer to change recording intervals.

An example of an interval sampling system for coding the social interactions of preschool children is provided in Figure 13.2 (McConnell, Sisson, & Sandler, 1984). This system is based on continuous 6-second intervals. When an interaction occurs in an interval, the observer records (1) whether the target child being observed (T) or a peer (P) initiated the interaction, (2) the type of initiation (starts, shares,

Classroom/Teacher: ______________________ Time Started: ______________________

Observer: ______________________ Activity: ______________________

Date: ______________________

Child's	T_t^c	T_t^c	T_t^c	T_t^c	T_t^c	T_t^c	T_t^c	Child's	T_t^c	T_t^c	T_t^c	T_t^c	T_t^c	T_t^c	T_t^c
Name	I_n^h	I_n^h	I_n^h	I_n^h	I_n^h	I_n^h	I_n^h	Name	I_n^h	I_n^h	I_n^h	I_n^h	I_n^h	I_n^h	I_n^h
	N_n^h	N_n^h	N_n^h	N_n^h	N_n^h	N_n^h	N_n^h		N_n^h	N_n^h	N_n^h	N_n^h	N_n^h	N_n^h	N_n^h
	P	P	P	P	P	P	P		P	P	P	P	P	P	P
	I/U	I/U	I/U	I/U	I/U	I/U	I/U		I/U	I/U	I/U	I/U	I/U	I/U	I/U

Child's	T_t^c	T_t^c	T_t^c	T_t^c	T_t^c	T_t^c	T_t^c	Child's	T_t^c	T_t^c	T_t^c	T_t^c	T_t^c	T_t^c	T_t^c
Name	I_n^h	I_n^h	I_n^h	I_n^h	I_n^h	I_n^h	I_n^h	Name	I_n^h	I_n^h	I_n^h	I_n^h	I_n^h	I_n^h	I_n^h
	N_n^h	N_n^h	N_n^h	N_n^h	N_n^h	N_n^h	N_n^h		N_n^h	N_n^h	N_n^h	N_n^h	N_n^h	N_n^h	N_n^h
	P	P	P	P	P	P	P		P	P	P	P	P	P	P
	I/U	I/U	I/U	I/U	I/U	I/U	I/U		I/U	I/U	I/U	I/U	I/U	I/U	I/U

Child's	T_t^c	T_t^c	T_t^c	T_t^c	T_t^c	T_t^c	T_t^c	Child's	T_t^c	T_t^c	T_t^c	T_t^c	T_t^c	T_t^c	T_t^c
Name	I_n^h	I_n^h	I_n^h	I_n^h	I_n^h	I_n^h	I_n^h	Name	I_n^h	I_n^h	I_n^h	I_n^h	I_n^h	I_n^h	I_n^h
	N_n^h	N_n^h	N_n^h	N_n^h	N_n^h	N_n^h	N_n^h		N_n^h	N_n^h	N_n^h	N_n^h	N_n^h	N_n^h	N_n^h
	P	P	P	P	P	P	P		P	P	P	P	P	P	P
	I/U	I/U	I/U	I/U	I/U	I/U	I/U		I/U	I/U	I/U	I/U	I/U	I/U	I/U

Child's	T_t^c	T_t^c	T_t^c	T_t^c	T_t^c	T_t^c	T_t^c	Child's	T_t^c	T_t^c	T_t^c	T_t^c	T_t^c	T_t^c	T_t^c
Name	I_n^h	I_n^h	I_n^h	I_n^h	I_n^h	I_n^h	I_n^h	Name	I_n^h	I_n^h	I_n^h	I_n^h	I_n^h	I_n^h	I_n^h
	N_n^h	N_n^h	N_n^h	N_n^h	N_n^h	N_n^h	N_n^h		N_n^h	N_n^h	N_n^h	N_n^h	N_n^h	N_n^h	N_n^h
	P	P	P	P	P	P	P		P	P	P	P	P	P	P
	I/U	I/U	I/U	I/U	I/U	I/U	I/U		I/U	I/U	I/U	I/U	I/U	I/U	I/U

Child's	T_t^c	T_t^c	T_t^c	T_t^c	T_t^c	T_t^c	T_t^c	Child's	T_t^c	T_t^c	T_t^c	T_t^c	T_t^c	T_t^c	T_t^c
Name	I_n^h	I_n^h	I_n^h	I_n^h	I_n^h	I_n^h	I_n^h	Name	I_n^h	I_n^h	I_n^h	I_n^h	I_n^h	I_n^h	I_n^h
	N_n^h	N_n^h	N_n^h	N_n^h	N_n^h	N_n^h	N_n^h		N_n^h	N_n^h	N_n^h	N_n^h	N_n^h	N_n^h	N_n^h
	P	P	P	P	P	P	P		P	P	P	P	P	P	P
	I/U	I/U	I/U	I/U	I/U	I/U	I/U		I/U	I/U	I/U	I/U	I/U	I/U	I/U

Child's	T_t^c	T_t^c	T_t^c	T_t^c	T_t^c	T_t^c	T_t^c	Child's	T_t^c	T_t^c	T_t^c	T_t^c	T_t^c	T_t^c	T_t^c
Name	I_n^h	I_n^h	I_n^h	I_n^h	I_n^h	I_n^h	I_n^h	Name	I_n^h	I_n^h	I_n^h	I_n^h	I_n^h	I_n^h	I_n^h
	N_n^h	N_n^h	N_n^h	N_n^h	N_n^h	N_n^h	N_n^h		N_n^h	N_n^h	N_n^h	N_n^h	N_n^h	N_n^h	N_n^h
	P	P	P	P	P	P	P		P	P	P	P	P	P	P
	I/U	I/U	I/U	I/U	I/U	I/U	I/U		I/U	I/U	I/U	I/U	I/U	I/U	I/U

FIGURE 13.1

Social Interaction Scan

Source: From *Integrated Preschool Curriculum* by S. L. Odom, M. Bender, M. Stein, L. Doran, P. Houden, M. McInnes, M. DeKlyen, M. Speltz, and J. Jenkins, 1988, Seattle, WA: University of Washington Press. Copyright 1988 by University of Washington Press. Reprinted by permission.

share request, play organizers, entries, negatives), (3) whether there was a response (yes, no, negative, ignores), (4) what general kind of social behavior occurred during the interval (parallel, social interaction, inappropriate social interaction, nonsocial), and (5) any teacher interaction (correction, prompt, praise). All of the data are collected on the same child, and samples of from 5 to 15 minutes are collected during a single session. For interval sampling systems such as this, Doll and Elliot (1994) recommend that at least four 10-minute sessions spread across 3 weeks be collected to provide a representative sample.

To assess parent interaction, Baird, Haas, McCormick, Carruth, and Turner (1992) developed an interval sampling observational system called the Infant-Parent Social Interaction Code (IPSIC), which measures four parent behaviors (contingent responsivity, directiveness, intrusiveness, and facilitation), four infant behaviors (initiation, participation, signal clarity, and intentional communicative acts), and one dyadic behavior (theme continuity). The selection of behaviors was based upon theoretical and empirical evidence of their importance for development.

The advantage of interval sampling systems is that they are less difficult to learn than the event recording systems noted below, but they are more difficult than time sampling systems. Interval sampling systems may provide more information about the reciprocal nature of social interactions than momentary time sampling systems, because the observer watches the interaction longer. However, interval sampling may be problematic when an interaction stretches across an interval, unless the code has a specific category for continuation.

The disadvantage for some interval sampling systems is that more than one behavior may occur in an interval. When this happens, the assessment data will actually underestimate the level of social interaction. Researchers sometimes make their intervals short (e.g., 6 seconds) so that the likelihood of more than one social interaction occurring per interval is reduced.

In *event recording systems* the observer records each instance of a social behavior or interaction. As in the other systems, these behaviors may be recorded within a specific time frame or interval, so that when interobserver agreement is collected, the teacher can determine the specific behaviors for which there is agreement or disagreement. However, within the time frame, the assessor records all the behaviors that occur rather then just the fact that the behavior occurred (i.e., as in interval sampling).

To collect information about preschool children's social interaction and independent goal-oriented task behavior, Bronson (1994) developed an event recording system entitled the Bronson Social and Task Skill Profile. Observers collect six 10-minute samples of a child's behavior over a 1- to 3-week period. For the social interaction portion of this system, the observer records behavior grouped within a *planning and organizing dimension* (suggests direction for activity, assigns roles or resources, states rules) and an *accommodating strategies dimension* (helps, shares, trades, trades off, takes turns, combines resources, joint effort).

The relative accuracy of the event recording systems, as compared with time and interval sampling systems, is a major advantage. By coding all behaviors (i.e., within the coding system) that occur, the teacher may gain clearer information about the child's social performance. Event recording systems are essential for coding the sequence of social behaviors that make up social interactions, because they allow the observer to record the behavior in real time.

The disadvantage of event recording systems is that they are more difficult than the other systems to learn and use. When collecting direct observation information, observers must

Target ______________________ Observer ______________________

Date ______________________ Tmt. Cond. ______________________

Setting ______________________ Session No. ______________________

			Initiations (Target & Peers)						Response (Target & Peers)					Summative (Target Only)		Teacher Atn to Target	
1	#	T	Aff	Sta	Sha-R	PlaO	Ent	Neg	T	Yes	No	Neg	Ign	Parallel	Inapp-SS	Corr/Prom	1
		P	Aff	Sta	Sha-R	PlaO	Ent	Neg	P	Yes	No	Neg	Ign	SocInter	NonSoc	Praise	
2	#	T	Aff	Sta	Sha-R	PlaO	Ent	Neg	T	Yes	No	Neg	Ign	Parallel	Inapp-SS	Corr/Prom	2
		P	Aff	Sta	Sha-R	PlaO	Ent	Neg	P	Yes	No	Neg	Ign	SocInter	NonSoc	Praise	
3	#	T	Aff	Sta	Sha-R	PlaO	Ent	Neg	T	Yes	No	Neg	Ign	Parallel	Inapp-SS	Corr/Prom	3
		P	Aff	Sta	Sha-R	PlaO	Ent	Neg	P	Yes	No	Neg	Ign	SocInter	NonSoc	Praise	
4	#	T	Aff	Sta	Sha-R	PlaO	Ent	Neg	T	Yes	No	Neg	Ign	Parallel	Inapp-SS	Corr/Prom	4
		P	Aff	Sta	Sha-R	PlaO	Ent	Neg	P	Yes	No	Neg	Ign	SocInter	NonSoc	Praise	
5	#	T	Aff	Sta	Sha-R	PlaO	Ent	Neg	T	Yes	No	Neg	Ign	Parallel	Inapp-SS	Corr/Prom	5
		P	Aff	Sta	Sha-R	PlaO	Ent	Neg	P	Yes	No	Neg	Ign	SocInter	NonSoc	Praise	
6	#	T	Aff	Sta	Sha-R	PlaO	Ent	Neg	T	Yes	No	Neg	Ign	Parallel	Inapp-SS	Corr/Prom	6
		P	Aff	Sta	Sha-R	PlaO	Ent	Neg	P	Yes	No	Neg	Ign	SocInter	NonSoc	Praise	
7	#	T	Aff	Sta	Sha-R	PlaO	Ent	Neg	T	Yes	No	Neg	Ign	Parallel	Inapp-SS	Corr/Prom	7
		P	Aff	Sta	Sha-R	PlaO	Ent	Neg	P	Yes	No	Neg	Ign	SocInter	NonSoc	Praise	
8	#	T	Aff	Sta	Sha-R	PlaO	Ent	Neg	T	Yes	No	Neg	Ign	Parallel	Inapp-SS	Corr/Prom	8
		P	Aff	Sta	Sha-R	PlaO	Ent	Neg	P	Yes	No	Neg	Ign	SocInter	NonSoc	Praise	
9	#	T	Aff	Sta	Sha-R	PlaO	Ent	Neg	T	Yes	No	Neg	Ign	Parallel	Inapp-SS	Corr/Prom	9
		P	Aff	Sta	Sha-R	PlaO	Ent	Neg	P	Yes	No	Neg	Ign	SocInter	NonSoc	Praise	

FIGURE 13.2
Observational Assessment of Reciprocal Social Interactions
Source: From *Category Definitions for Observational Assessment of Reciprocal Social Interactions* by S. R. McConnell, L. Sisson, and S. Sandler, 1984. Unpublished observer training manual, University of Pittsburgh. Reprinted by permission.

be trained to an acceptable level of agreement, and interobserver agreement must be collected on 20% to 30% of the sample. Hartman and Wood (1990) described well the issues related to measuring interobserver agreement and proposed a systematic plan for training observers.

It is probable that the level of detail generated by direct observation systems (especially event systems) may be more than is needed for designing and monitoring social interaction intervention programs for infants and young children with disabilities. More often, direct observation measures are used for research or very systematic program evaluations.

A note on a classic observational system Any discussion of assessing children's social interaction would be incomplete without an acknowledgement of Mildred Parten's work. The Parten Scale of Social Participation (Parten, 1932) was one of the earliest social interaction observational assessments

TABLE 13.3
Abbreviated Behavioral Categories of the Parten Scale of Social Participation and the Smilansky Scale, as Defined in Odom (1981)

Scale/Category	Definition
Parten Scale	
Unoccupied	Glancing around the room, but not focusing on an activity
Onlooker	Observing other children, but not interacting
Solitary	Playing alone with toys different from those being played with by children in the general proximity, not conversing
Parallel	Playing with toys similar to those used by children in the subject's vicinity
Associative	Playing with other children without role assignment, loosely organized
Cooperative	Playing with other children in an organized manner, roles assigned
Smilansky Scale	
Functional	Simple muscular activities, manipulating play objects
Constructive	Creative activities, appropriately manipulating academic materials
Dramatic	Manipulating objects in a symbolic manner
Games with rules	Playing games with prearranged rules

and has served as a basis for many other systems (e.g., the SIS scale described previously). The behavioral categories, presented in Table 13.3, denote the range of children's behavior from unoccupied to highly sophisticated cooperative play. In recent years, researchers have combined Parten's original social categories with Smilansky's measures of cognitive play to obtain an even more detailed description of the quality of children's social participation (Odom, 1981; Rubin, 1982; Rubin, Maioni, & Hornung, 1976; Guralnick, Connor, Hammond, Gottman, & Kinnish, in press).

Rating Scales

Rating scales assess behavior in a less microscopic manner than direct observation systems; they require observers to make a judgment about the quality or quantity of social behaviors or interactions that occur over a longer period of time rather than to record behaviors as they occur (Cairns & Green, 1979). With this methodology, developers initially define the construct assessed by the rating scale and the behaviors that compose those constructs. Although Guilford (1954) noted that five types of rating scales exist (i.e., graphic, standard, cumulated points, numerical, and forced-choice), numerical rating scales are used most frequently in rating social interactions. Raters make judgments about the quantity or quality of behaviors represented in specific items by using a numerical scale, such as a Likert scale (Likert, 1932). Finn (1972) suggested that 5 and 7 numerical points were optimal for Likert-type scales and reliability decreased beyond seven levels. However, some 3-point and binary scales have also yielded reliable results (Rasmussen, 1989).

Behavioral anchors provide the rater with a definition or description of what each number

Infant's Name ____________________

Infant's Age (AA) ____________________ (CA) ____________________

Date of Interaction ____________________

Activity ____________________

Observer ____________________

Score ____________________

Directions: Mark 1–5 as appropriate.

PARTICIPATION

1. Infant participates in social interaction

Infant never participates in social interaction.	1	2	3	4	5	Infant always participates in social interaction.

2. Infant initiates interaction with caregiver.

Infant never initiates.	1	2	3	4	5	Infant always initiates.

Note how the infant initiates the interaction.

PREDICTABILITY/CONSISTENCY

3. The infant's behaviors are consistent and identifiable.

Infant's behaviors are never consistent.	1	2	3	4	5	Infant's behaviors are consistent.

SENSITIVITY/RESPONSIVENESS/TURN-TAKING

4. Infant attends to caregiver's presence.

Infant never attends to caregiver.	1	2	3	4	5	Infant always attends to caregiver.

5. Infant responds to caregiver's social initiations.

Infant never responds to caregiver.	1	2	3	4	5	Infant always responds to caregiver.

FIGURE 13.3

Infant-Caregiver Interaction Scale

Source: From *Infant-Caregiver Interaction Scale* by L. Munson and S. Odom, 1994. Unpublished manuscript. Reproduced by permission.

represents. These behavioral anchors may be very general (e.g., 1 = rarely, 5 = frequently) or very specific (e.g., 1 = Parent shows pleasure in watching infant at least some of the time; 7 = Parent shows or reports pleasure in infant's enjoyment of his/her own activity). At a minimum, it is important that scale developers describe the behaviors especially at the low and high ends of the scale (Finn, 1972). Figure 13.3 provides an example of just such a rating scale of infant-caregiver interaction.

Raters may complete the scales immediately after observing the ratees for a specified period of time, or judgments may be based on accumulated observation occurring over a longer period of time and many opportunities to observe behaviors. For example, in a rating scale developed by Crawley and Spiker (1982), observers must watch 10-minute segments of mother-infant interaction during free-play before rating the quality of the infant's social initiative on a 5-point Likert scale. For the Social Skills Rating System (Gresham & Elliott, 1990), raters make judgments based on their multiple opportunities for observing the child.

Most rating scales include procedures for summarizing the ratings on individual items. This summary is done by adding the ratings and computing a total score, or, if the individual items are designed to measure different behaviors or attributes, by calculating specific subscale scores. For example, on the Parent-Infant Interaction Scale (PIIS) (Clark & Seifer, 1986), a rating scale that measures the quality of mother-infant interaction, the individual items are organized into three subsections: (1) interaction style, (2) social reference, and (3) assessment of context.

Ideally, a rating scale will provide information on the behaviors of both partners in a social interaction. The Parent-Child Observation Guide (PCOG) (Bernstein, Hans, & Percansky, 1992), Infant Caregiver Interaction Scale (ICIS) (Munson & Odom, 1994), and the PIIS (Clark & Seifer, 1986) offer such systems. Each scale varies on the number of infant behaviors that are measured. Other systems, such as the Maternal Behavior Rating Scale (MBRS) (Mahoney, 1992), measure behaviors of only one member of the dyad (e.g., the mother).

To provide information about the social strategies in which infants engage with caregivers and older children engage with peers, Beckman and Lieber (1994) developed the Social Strategy Rating Scale (SSRS), which has the advantage of assessing social interactions across the adult and peer social contexts. For assessing children's participation in a peer interaction context, McConnell and Odom developed the Teacher Impression Scales (TIS) (Vanderbilt/Minnesota Social Interaction Project, 1993) (see Figure 13.4). Both the SSRS and the TIS are designed to be completed immediately after observing a child in interaction. The Social Skills Rating System (Gresham & Elliott, 1990) and the Social Competence Scale (Kohn, 1988) are rating scales that rely on a more cumulative impression of preschool children's interaction with peers and adults. Both of these scales provide norms for interpreting the scores that are generated.

The advantages of using rating scales to measure social interaction is that they usually (a) are easier to use than observational measures, (b) are relatively quick to administer, (c) are easy to score, and (d) require less training for raters than observational measures. Some scales are designed specifically to be completed by teachers or parents. Rating scales may be useful for practitioners in ECSE programs where time is an important consideration (McCloskey, 1990). In addition, for some behaviors, rating scales may have higher predictive validity of later behavior than direct observation systems (Bakeman & Brown, 1980; Jay & Farran, 1981); some rating scales may have equal or higher stability over time (Schaefer, 1989; Clarke-Stewart & Hevey, 1981); and rating scales yield global information about social interaction development. As such, they may be useful for measuring general levels of social interaction, as the teacher might need to do when screening children for possible problems, identifying current functioning level, or measuring change in behavior across the year.

Rating scales also have some disadvantages. They are considered more subjective than direct observation systems (Cairns & Green, 1979), and they provide less detailed information about specific behaviors, which may make them less useful for designing or monitoring interventions on specific behavior. Another disadvantage of the rating scales that are presently available is the difficulty in finding complete validity and reliability data and training information.

A variation on the rating scale is a checklist that requires the observer to determine whether a behavior or set of behaviors occurred during an observation. Checklists typically

Child Name ______________________ Date ______________________

Teacher ______________________ Subject Number ______________________

Please read each item below and rate the degree to which it describes the child's behavior **in your classroom program**. *If you have not seen the child perform a particular skill or behavior, circle* **1**, *indicating* **Never**. If the child frequently performs the described skill or behavior, circle 5, indicating **Frequently**. If the child performs this behavior in between these two extremes, circle **2, 3,** or **4** indicating your best estimate of the rate of occurrence of the skill.

1 = Never Performs Skill 5 = Frequently Performs Skill

Circle only one number for each skill. Do not mark between numbers.

1 . . . 2 . . . 3 . . . 4 . . . 5	1. The child converses appropriately.
1 . . . 2 . . . 3 . . . 4 . . . 5	2. The child takes turns when playing.
1 . . . 2 . . . 3 . . . 4 . . . 5	3. The child plays cooperatively.
1 . . . 2 . . . 3 . . . 4 . . . 5	4. The child varies social behavior appropriately.
1 . . . 2 . . . 3 . . . 4 . . . 5	5. The child is persistent at social attempts.
1 . . . 2 . . . 3 . . . 4 . . . 5	6. The child spontaneously responds to peers.
1 . . . 2 . . . 3 . . . 4 . . . 5	7. The child appears to have fun.
1 . . . 2 . . . 3 . . . 4 . . . 5	8. Peers interacting with the child appear to have fun.
1 . . . 2 . . . 3 . . . 4 . . . 5	9. The child continues an interaction once it has begun.
1 . . . 2 . . . 3 . . . 4 . . . 5	10. Peers seek out the child for social play.
1 . . . 2 . . . 3 . . . 4 . . . 5	11. The child uses appropriate social behavior to begin an interaction.
1 . . . 2 . . . 3 . . . 4 . . . 5	12. The child enters play activities without disrupting the group.
1 . . . 2 . . . 3 . . . 4 . . . 5	13. The child suggests new play ideas for a play group.
1 . . . 2 . . . 3 . . . 4 . . . 5	14. The child smiles appropriately at peers during play.
1 . . . 2 . . . 3 . . . 4 . . . 5	15. The child shares play materials with peers.
1 . . . 2 . . . 3 . . . 4 . . . 5	16. The child engages in play activities where social interaction might occur.

FIGURE 13.4

Teacher Impression Scales

Source: From *Play Time/Social Time* by Vanderbilt/Minnesota Social Interaction Project. Copyright 1993 by Communication Skill Builders. Reproduced by permission of the authors.

require a yes/no response about a behavior's occurrence or nonoccurrence. They do not require finer judgments. The Nursing Child Assessment Teaching Scale (NCATS) (Barnard, 1978b) and Nursing Child Assessment Feeding Scale (NCAFS) (Barnard, 1978a) are examples of scales that have a binary or yes/no scoring system. Both were developed to measure parental behaviors during parent-infant interactions. In addition, both measure some infant behaviors.

Sociometric Assessments

In *sociometric assessment* procedures, children provide general evaluations of the social acceptance, social preference, or likability of other children. Typically, teachers gather sociometric information from intact groups of children, such as all the children enrolled in a particular class or all the children in a particular play group. As a result, sociometric measures cannot be used for children who are not enrolled in a preschool or child care.

There are four general types of sociometric assessment instruments: (a) peer nominations, (b) peer ratings, (c) peer assessments, and (d) paired comparisons (McConnell & Odom, 1986). Given the level of resources needed and the limited scope of their application, peer assessments and paired comparisons have little relevance to work in applied settings and will not be discussed further in this section.

Peer nominations Peer nominations are sociometric assessment procedures in which children are asked to identify a single classmate or several classmates who meet some general criterion. Children may be asked to identify classmates they consider their best friends, like to play or work with, or like the least. All the children in a class are asked to complete this nomination by selecting from a list of classmates' names or, for preschoolers, from a set of pictures of classmates (Marshall, 1957). Peer nomination scores are calculated as the proportion of nominations a child receives from all peers in his or her class or play group.

By using both positive (e.g., "Name your three best friends") and negative (e.g., "Name three children you don't like") nomination criteria, children can be classified into sociometric groups. These groups typically include (a) "popular" children, who receive many positive and few, if any, negative nominations, (b) "neglected" children, who receive few positive or few negative nominations, (c) "rejected" children, who receive few positive and many negative nominations, and (d) "controversial" children, who receive high numbers of both positive and negative nominations (Coie, Dodge, & Copotelli, 1982). It must be noted that the use of negative criteria in any sociometric assessment procedure, including nomination measures, is at times controversial (i.e., concerns may exist about the effect on children's behavior of making negative nominations). However, Hayvren and Hymel (1984) found no reactive effects on the interaction of peers after peer nomination assessment with elementary-age children. However, users of negative nomination sociometric procedures should be particularly attentive to concerns of parents and administrators and to the possible effects of these assessment procedures on the behavior of young children.

Peer ratings Unlike peer nominations, peer ratings require children to provide general qualitative ratings for each child in their classroom or play group. Like peer nominations, specific criteria vary as a function of the purpose of assessment; however, all ratings are completed to reflect general statements of preference (e.g., "How much do you like to play with _____?" or "How much do you like to talk with _____?"). These ratings, typically on a 3-point Likert-type scale (for preschool children), provide scores for each child in a particular group, with that score based on evaluations by all the other children in the group. A child's peer rating score is typically calculated as the sum or average rating received from all raters; however, other scoring procedures (e.g., sum of ratings by same-sex classmates, number of highest-preference ratings) are also used.

Peer ratings provide one way for avoiding the use of negative evaluations by children. All children in a group are rated on a common dimension; as a result, individual scores can be rank-ordered from most highly rated to least highly rated. However, as noted above, without negative nominations, specific sociometric subgroups cannot be formed.

Peer rating sociometrics also have been adapted for use with preschool children. Asher, Singleton, Tinsley, and Hymel (1979) developed and evaluated a picture rating procedure in which children sorted photographs of their individual classmates into marked boxes to indicate their relative ratings. This procedure proved to be quite useful and is now widely accepted as a standard procedure for collecting peer ratings among young children.

A note on reliability Preschool children are the informants for sociometric procedures and, given the complexity of the task, there may be some concern about the reliability or stability of these measures (McConnell & Odom, 1986). However, when suitable adaptations are made (e.g., training by rating pictures of foods and toys; the use of pictures of peers), it appears that these procedures do generate reliable information. When examining peer nomination, Denham and McKinley (1993) found positive evidence for the stability and convergent validity of the measures. In their original adaptation of the peer rating methodology, Asher et al. (1979) found acceptable test-retest reliability coefficients for two groups of children. These findings were replicated by Poteat, Ironsmith, and Bullock (1986). However, with young children the assessor should still attempt to determine if the child raters understand the task before completing the assessment, especially if the children are below 4 years of age.

Curriculum-Based Assessment

Curriculum-based assessment instruments provide a useful link among assessment, intervention, and evaluation (Neisworth & Bagnato, in press). These instruments usually take a criterion-referenced form and provide assessment of skills across developmental domains (with "social" as one domain). Assessment items are usually ordered according to when they typically appear in a child's development (or logically from simple to complex); this order may provide useful information for selecting skills for intervention (Bagnato & Murphy, 1989). Generally, curriculum-based assessments focus on functional skills (Bricker, 1989). In addition, some of these assessments include related curriculum activities that teachers can use to support the child's acquisition of identified skills.

Several curriculum-based assessment instruments and the related curricula are available. The Carolina Curriculum for Infants and Toddlers with Special Needs (CCITSN) (Johnson-Martin, Jens, Attermeier, & Hacker, 1991) and Carolina Curriculum for Preschoolers with Special Needs (CCPSN) (Johnson-Martin, Attermeier, & Hacker, 1990) are based on normal sequences of development. The Carolina, for infants from birth to 2 years, assesses social/adaptation skills. Subdomains are self-direction, social skills, and self-help skills. In the CCPSN, the interpersonal subdomain is most directly related to the assessment of children's social behavior. Both assessments have suggested modification of items to accommodate motoric or sensory impairments.

The HELP Strands (Parks, 1992) is a curriculum-based developmental assessment for children from birth to 36 months. The social-emotional domain of the HELP Strands includes the subdomains attachment/separation/autonomy, development of self, expression of emotions and feelings, learning rules and expectations, and social interactions and play. Additional materials that are available to be used with HELP Strands (Parks, 1992) include HELP at Home (Parks, 1988) and HELP Activity Guide (Furuno et al., 1985).

Additional curriculum-based assessments developed by Bricker (1993) and Linder (1993a) both include measures of the social domain. The Assessment, Evaluation, and Programming System for Infants and Children: AEPS Measurement for Birth to Three Years (AEPS) (Bricker, 1993) assesses children's social skills in the areas of interaction with adults, interaction with environment, and interaction with peers.

An accompanying volume, AEPS Curriculum for Birth to Three Years (Cripe, Slentz, & Bricker, 1993) provides a guide to developing intervention activities. Currently, an extension of the AEPS for preschool-age children is being developed. The Transdisciplinary Play-Based Assessment, Revised Edition (Linder, 1993a) assesses children's social skills in the subdomains of mastery motivation, attachment, separation and individuation, social relations with peers, and development of humor. The Transdisciplinary Play-Based Intervention (Linder, 1993b) provides curriculum guidelines.

Although curriculum-based assessment can provide some valuable information for identifying important goals for children's early intervention programs, McAllister (1991) has noted several inherent problems with this assessment approach. He proposes that the social skills domain is sometimes underrepresented in these assessments (i.e., merged with the adaptive behavior domain), may include too few items for a comprehensive assessment of social development, may not reflect the complexities inherent in social skills intervention (e.g., may not assess social performance across settings and partners), and may not reflect adequately the social development of children with certain specific disabilities (e.g., infants with visual impairments, young children with autism). Curriculum-based assessment may be a necessary and important first step in identifying the social skills of many young children with disabilities. Once those skills are identified, other assessment approaches described in this chapter might be more useful for monitoring children's actual performance in homes, classrooms, and communities.

Norm-Referenced Assessments

For certain purposes it is necessary to judge social behavior against established norms. In such situations the teacher is less concerned about specific interaction patterns or relationships than about the general performance of an infant or child as it relates to the performance of other children. Rather than describing specific skills that can be selected for intervention, norm-referenced measures tend to describe social functioning across a broad spectrum. These measures are used to compare the behavior, performance, or development of an individual child with the overall status of other children at similar ages, thus providing relative information regarding a child's current level of development. Typically, the norm-referenced assessment of social development and competence is seen as one part of a broader assessment of development of infants and preschool children with disabilities.

Norm-referenced measures of social development are included in several commonly used assessment instruments. For example, in the Battelle Developmental Inventory (BDI) (Newborg, Stock, Wnek, Guidubaldi, & Svinicki, 1988) social development is measured in the personal-social domain. The behaviors measured are adult interaction, expression of feelings/affect, self-concept, peer interaction, coping, and social role. Although these subdomains contain 85 items, with the exception of adult interaction, few items are included for developmental ages below 12 months. Administration of the BDI includes observation, parental and/or teacher interview, and structured tasks. In addition, specific adaptations are provided for children with sensory or motoric disabilities. Scores in each of the six subdomains are summed to obtain a total personal-social domain score. Scores can be expressed in percentile ranks, standard score, or age equivalents. The BDI is unique in that it has also been used as a criterion-referenced or curriculum-based assessment.

Norm-referenced assessments of adaptive behavior often include subsections related to social competence. The Vineland Adaptive Behavior Scale (Vineland) (Sparrow, Balla, & Cicchetti, 1984), one example of such a scale, is designed for use with individuals from birth to 18 years of age; it includes a survey form and an expanded edition that are completed during interviews with a parent or other informed adult. The socialization domain has three subdomains: (1) interpersonal relations, (2) play and leisure time, and (3) coping skills. Only interpersonal relations and play and leisure time include items beginning at birth. The Vineland offers age-level norms with raw scores being converted to standard scores (mean of 100 and standard deviation of 15), percentile ranks, stanines, and age equivalents.

In addition to the BDI and general scales of adaptive behavior, several of the rating scales mentioned previously also contain norms. The SSRS (Gresham & Elliott, 1990) yields standard scores and percentile ranks. The Social Competence Scale by Kohn (1988) also will generate percentile scores. Although the norms are fairly old, the California Preschool Social Competency Scale (Levine, Elzey, & Lewis, 1969) provides a general rating score and percentile ranking for preschool children.

USING SOCIAL INTERACTION ASSESSMENT INFORMATION

Information about children's social interaction is commonly used for screening, diagnosing social problems, designing instructional programs, monitoring instruction, program evaluation, and research. The assessment approaches discussed in this chapter are important for different purposes. Table 13.4 depicts the relationship between assessment approaches and purposes.

Screening

Professionals conduct screenings to identify infants and preschoolers who might be at risk for social interaction problems. When the teacher determines that a problem might exist, the infant or young child receives a more intensive assessment of social development. The information collected from a screening assessment is not sufficient for designing a social interaction intervention program; it should be used only for determining the need for further assessment.

Formal screening measures for infants and their caregivers are not available. Observations by teachers, anecdotal reports from parents and other caregivers, or interviews with parents and other caregivers may identify concerns about infant-caregiver interaction. For example, caregivers may report that the infant does not respond consistently to attempts to play, or the teacher may observe that the infant rarely smiles during interactions and turns away frequently. Such information indicates that the teacher needs to concentrate assessment activities on the social interactions occurring between the caregiver and the infant.

For preschool children, teachers may take a different approach to screening for social interaction problems. First, teachers, more than most other adults, are able to observe preschool children with their peer group, and they are very good at picking up problems through these observations. To confirm their concerns, teachers may use rating scales or direct observation to collect screening information on specific children. Second, teachers who work with a group of children for whom there is a risk of developmental or social problems (e.g., children who have been physically abused, children with prenatal exposure to cocaine or alcohol, etc.) might routinely collect screening information on all the children in the class. Third, from what we know about the development of children with disabilities (Guralnick & Groom, 1988), there is reason to suspect that these children will have delays in social development. Presence of a disability would be enough of a screening indicator for the teacher to plan for a more detailed assessment.

TABLE 13.4
Social Interaction, Assessment, Approaches, and Purposes

	Types of Assessment						
Purposes	Anecdotal	Direct Observation	Rating Scales	Sociometrics	Curriculum-based	Norm-referenced	Comments
Screening	X	X	X				
Diagnosis	X	X	X	X	X	X	Multimethod Assessment Important
Program Design	X	X	X		X		
Program Monitoring	X	X	X		X		
Program Evaluation		X	X	X		X	Multimethod Assessment Important
Research		X	X	X		X	Multimethod Assessment Important

Teacher rating scales seem to be the most efficient assessment approach for screening preschool-age children. The Social Interaction Rating Scale (Hops et al., 1979), the screening test of the BDI (Newborg et al., 1988), the "overview" section of the Assessment of Peer Relations (Guralnick, 1992b), and the Teacher Impressions Scale (Vanderbilt/Minnesota Social Interaction Project, 1993) are examples of teacher rating measures that can be completed quickly and can screen for potential social problems. Teacher rating scales routinely provide guidelines for interpreting scores and identifying children who should be considered for further assessment.

Diagnosing Social Interaction Difficulties

Social interaction assessment information may be used to document children's current skills and to diagnose a problem. To diagnose social interaction problems and to qualify children for special services, teachers often use norm-referenced assessments. For preschool-age children, assessments noted previously do include norms (Battelle Developmental Inventory, Social Skills Rating System, Vineland). This norm-referenced information should be supplemented by direct observation of the child in the classroom or naturalistic play setting.

Unfortunately, few norm-referenced assessments are available for identifying social interaction problems for infants and their caregivers. Formally identifying social interaction as a concern will require the teacher to become familiar with the infant and the caregiver and to develop a rapport prior to attempting any assessment. The teacher can interview the caregiver and observe the interactions, using instruments such as the rating scales or direct observation systems described previously. With this information, the teacher can attempt to document the discrepancy between normal and atypical development. Additional information may be gathered using a curriculum-based instrument. As with any assessment, infants should be alert and both caregiver and infant should be comfortable with their surroundings. As previously stated, the teacher should document the setting, the participants, and the activities of the interaction. In addition, he or she should observe interaction in more than one context and on more than one occasion.

Diagnostic assessment information on preschool children's social interactions with peers may be generated by rating scales, norm-referenced assessments, or direct observation. Most rating scales have specific instructions for collecting and interpreting the needed information. If the assessor collecting the assessment information is not the child's regular teacher and has not observed several free-play sessions, the regular teacher should complete the scale. Norm-referenced information, from adaptive behavior scales for example, may be collected by interviewing the child's regular teacher or parent. If direct observation information is used, it should be collected over multiple play sessions that are at least 15 minutes in length, although the specific amount of information needed will depend on the observational instrument used. Usually norms for observational data are not available and the teacher may have difficulty interpreting the assessment information collected. A solution is to establish local norms by collecting identical assessment information on one or two children in the class who are competent social interactors. The referred child's data may then be compared with the data from the socially competent peers.

Designing Intervention Programs

A teacher may use assessment information to develop goals and objectives for an intervention program. Although normative data could be important for identifying general areas of need, information from other assessment approaches may be more useful in planning intervention.

When working with infants and caregivers, assessors must remember that there is no best way for caregivers to interact with infants (Bromwich, 1981; McCollum & Stayton, 1985). When developing an intervention plan, the parent should participate in identifying the difficulties in interaction and developing possible solutions. Although intervention plans will probably require caregivers to change their behavior (since it is the adult members' behavior that is most amenable to initial change), the teacher must communicate to the caregivers that the plans do not represent a negative judgment of their interactive skills. Moreover, interventions should build on the positive behaviors already occurring in the interaction (Comfort, 1988). In addition, any intervention plan must respect cultural differences that influence the nature of infant-caregiver interactions.

Teachers working with preschool-age children should follow a similar process of basing their intervention on assessment information. Direct observation of children in play settings may reveal valuable information about the nature of social exchanges and potential intervention targets. Rating scales based on these observations, such as the Social Strategy Rating Scale (Beckman & Lieber, 1994) or the Teacher Impressions Scale (Vanderbilt/Minnesota Social Interaction Project, 1993), may assist teachers in identifying intervention objectives.

Monitoring the Intervention Program

Social interaction assessment information that is useful for screening, diagnosing, and selecting objectives may not be as useful for monitoring the intervention program once it has been implemented. Monitoring information must relate directly to goals and objectives of the IFSPs and IEPs, must be collected efficiently and frequently (e.g., daily, weekly), and must be sensitive to changes in the behavior of infants/children, caregivers, and peers. The information must be in a form that teachers can use to make decisions about the child's intervention programs (e.g., to continue the intervention, revise the program, determine that the child has met his or her objective). Chapter 17 provides more information on monitoring child programs.

For infants and their caregivers, monitoring information must reflect the nature and quality of the interactive episodes. Direct observation, parent report, and rating scales may assist the teacher in monitoring an intervention program. For example, the ICIS (Munson & Odom, 1994) can be completed periodically to provide consistent feedback on the progress of the intervention. In addition, following an intervention session, the teacher can record anecdotal information about the interactive behaviors that were observed.

Similarly, the teacher may observe preschool children with disabilities during play sessions with peers to note changes resulting (or not resulting) from the intervention sessions, then write anecdotal notes, record systematic direct observation data, or complete a rating scale (like the TIS [Vanderbilt/Minnesota Social Interaction Project, 1993], or SSRS [Beckman & Lieber, 1994]). Although collecting this information on a daily basis would be ideal, it may not be practical. Instead, the teacher might set aside one day a week to collect such information and use it to make decisions about the child's program.

Program Evaluation

Program evaluation may be either formative or summative. In formative evaluation, assessment information is used to reorganize the program. The assessment information described above for monitoring intervention programs would also be appropriate for use in formative evaluations.

Summative program evaluations of early intervention programs often require that assessment information of children's social behavior be collected at the beginning and at the end of the year. Evaluators may compute the differences between the pretest and posttest assessments and then compare this information either with the changes that occurred for similar children who were not in the program, or to the expected changes (i.e., based on preprogram rate of development) that would have occurred if the infants or young children had not been enrolled in the program (Odom, 1988). To conduct this type of evaluation, assessment information must be quantifiable. Direct observational data that can be summarized into one or a few scores, teacher rating scales that produce global scores, peer ratings scores, scores from norm-referenced assessments, and perhaps curriculum-based assessment information (i.e., number of criterion items passed) can be used to conduct summative evaluations for programs designed to teach social interaction skills. It should also be noted that naturalistic or ethnographic evaluation approaches may also be used in program evaluation (Guba & Lincoln, 1989). As we note in Table 13.4, and as a number of leaders in program evaluation have noted (Snyder & Sheehan, in press), collecting multiple sources of information is important.

Research

In conducting research on infants' social behavior, researchers have used rating scales (Lussier, Crimmins, & Alberti, 1994), direct observation (Garner & Landry, 1992), and a combination of methods (e.g., direct observation, rating scales, parent report) (Bakeman & Brown, 1980; O'Connor, Sigman, & Kasari, 1992). Many questions remain in the area of assessment of parent-infant interaction. To date, none of the available assessment methods is recognized as the standard method for research or for use in intervention programs. Rather, assessment methods are selected (or designed) to fit the research questions identified by the investigators. In recent years, a wider range of assessment instruments (particularly rating scales) have become available for use in research (Munson & Odom, 1995). Although these instruments are a valuable resource, they require that researchers continue to examine reliability and validity when the instruments are used in their studies.

For research with preschool-age children, assessment methods also continue to develop. Although the primary assessment methodology used in research with this group is direct observation of children's social behavior (Guralnick & Groom, 1988; Kopp et al., 1992), other methodologies are also being employed to examine the nature of children's social relationships (Buysee, 1993) and the nature of social competence (Guralnick, 1992a). In addition, multiple methodologies are employed to examine convergence of judgments of social competence across multiple perspectives (Odom & McConnell, in press) and to incorporate the qualitative technique of triangulation (Lincoln & Guba, 1985) across data sources when examining peer relationships.

CONCLUSION

A range of assessment methods exist for collecting information about the social interactions of infants and caregivers and preschool children and peers. The methods vary in the precision with which they generate information, labor intensiveness, and psychometric quality. Also, the information generated by these assessments may be relevant for different purposes, so assessors must match their choice of assessment instrument to the questions they are trying to address about the infants' or children's participation in social interaction with caregivers or peers.

SUMMARY OF KEY CONCEPTS

- A primary task in social development is establishing positive styles of interaction and secure attachment relationships with caregivers.
- Some infants and young children with disabilities may experience difficulties in establishing positive styles of interaction with caregivers and peers or forming secure attachment relationships with parents.
- During the preschool years, acquiring skills for engaging in positive interactions and positive social relationships with peers is also an important developmental task.
- Assessment of children's social development may occur at the levels of individual social behavior, social interactions, or social relationships.
- Social competence is the effective and appropriate use of social behaviors, as judged by appropriate members of an individual's social ecology.
- The nature of the social setting and participants in the interaction affect substantially the social performance of infants and young children.
- Assessment techniques often use observation of children in naturalistic settings to provide information about infants, children, and their social partners; these assessment techniques range from less formal anecdotal recordings to more formal structured direct observation measures.
- Sociometric assessments that employ photographs of classmates have often been used to assess social status of preschool-age children.
- Curriculum-based assessments may generate information about children's social performance that is useful for designing intervention programs.
- Norm-referenced instruments may provide information about children's social development that is useful for diagnosis, program evaluation, and research.
- Assessors must match their choice of assessment instruments to the questions they are trying to address about the infants' or children's participation in social interaction with caregivers or peers.
- Comprehensive assessments of children's social competence would include information provided by multiple sources and multiple informants.

REFERENCES

Ainsworth, M. D., & Bell, S. M. (1970). Attachment, exploration, and separation: Illustrated by behavior of one year olds in a strange situation. *Child Development, 41,* 49–67.

Ainsworth, M. D., Blehar, M. C., Waters, E., & Walls, S. (1978). *Patterns of attachment: A psychological study of the strange situation.* Hillsdale, NJ: Lawrence Erlbaum.

Anderson, S., & Messick, S. (1974). Social competency in young children. *Developmental Psychology, 15,* 443–444.

Antia, S. D., & Kreimeyer, K. H. (1992). Social competence intervention for young children with hearing impairments. In S. Odom, S. McConnell, & M. McEvoy (Eds.), *Social competence of young children with disabilities* (pp. 135–164). Baltimore, MD: Paul H. Brookes.

Asher, S. R., Singleton, L. C., Tinsley, B. R., & Hymel, S. (1979). A reliable sociometric measure for preschool children. *Developmental Psychology, 15,* 443–444.

Bagnato, S., & Murphy, J. (1989). Validity of curriculum-based scales with young neurodevelopmentally disabled children: Implications for team assessment. *Early Education and Development, 1,* 50–63.

Bailey, D. B., & Simeonsson, R. J. (1985). A functional model of social competence. *Topics in Early Childhood Special Education, 4*(4), 20–31.

Baird, S., Haas, L., McCormick, K., Carruth, C., & Turner, K. (1992). Approaching an objective system for observation and measurement: Infant-parent social interaction code. *Topics in Special Education, 12,* 544–571.

Bakeman, R., & Brown, J. (1980). Early interaction: Consequences for social and mental development at three years. *Child Development, 51,* 437–447.

Bakeman, R., & Brown, J. V. (1977). Behavioral dialogues: An approach to assessment of mother-infant interaction. *Child Development, 49,* 195–203.

Barnard, K. (1978a). *Nursing Child Assessment Feeding Scale.* Seattle, WA: University of Washington.

Barnard, K. (1978b). *Nursing Child Assessment Teaching Scale.* Seattle, WA: University of Washington.

Barrera, M., Rosenbaum, P., & Cunningham, C. (1986). Early home intervention with low-birth-weight infants and their parents. *Child Development, 57,* 20–33.

Barrera, M., & Vella, D. (1987). Disabled and nondisabled infants' interactions with their mothers. *American Journal of Occupational Therapy, 41,* 168–172.

Beal, J. (1991). Methodological issues in conducting research on parent-infant interaction. *Journal of Pediatric Nursing, 6,* 11–15.

Beckman, P. J., & Lieber, J. (1994). The Social Strategy Rating Scale: An approach to evaluating social competence. *Journal of Early Intervention, 18,* 1–11.

Bell, R. (1968). A reinterpretation of the direction of effects in studies of socialization. *Psychological Review, 75,* 81–95.

Belsky, J., Gilstrap, B., & Rovine, M. (1984). The Pennsylvania Infant and Family Development Project I: Stability and change in mother-infant and father-infant interaction in a family setting at one, three, and nine months. *Child Development, 55,* 692–705.

Bernstein, V., Hans, S., & Percansky, C. (1992). *Parent-Child Observation Guide.* (Available from Victor J. Bernstein, Department of Psychiatry, Box 411, The University of Chicago, Chicago, IL 60637.)

Berry, P., Gunn, P., & Andrews, R. (1980). Behavior of Down's syndrome infants in a strange situation. *American Journal of Mental Deficiency, 85,* 213–218.

Bowlby, J. (1969). *Attachment and loss: Attachment (Vol. 1).* New York: Basic Books.

Bredekamp, S. (1987). *Developmentally appropriate practice in early childhood programs serving children from birth through age 8.* Washington, DC: NAEYC.

Bricker, D. (1989). *Early intervention for at-risk and handicapped infants, toddlers, and preschool children* (2nd ed.). Palo Alto, CA: VORT.

Bricker, D. (1993). *AEPS measurement for birth to three years.* Baltimore, MD: Paul H. Brookes.

Bromwich, R. (1981). *Working with parents.* Austin, TX: PRO-ED.

Bronson, M. B. (1994). The usefulness of an observational measure of young children's social and mastery behaviors in early childhood classrooms. *Early Childhood Research Quarterly, 9,* 19–43.

Brown, W. H., Ragland, E. U., & Fox, J. J. (1988). Effects of group socialization procedures on the social interactions of preschool children. *Research in Developmental Disabilities, 9,* 359–376.

Buysee, V. (1991). *Early Childhood Friendship Survey.* Chapel Hill, NC: Frank Porter Graham Center, University of North Carolina.

Buysee, V. (1993). Friendship of preschoolers with disabilities in community-based child care settings. *Journal of Early Intervention, 17,* 380–395.

Cairns, R., & Green, J. (1979). How to assess personality and social patterns: Observations or ratings? In R. Cairns (Ed.), *The analysis of social interactions: Methods, issues, and illustrations* (pp. 209–226). Hillsdale, NJ: Lawrence Erlbaum.

Clark, G., & Seifer, R. (1986). *Parent-Infant Interaction Scale, a manual for analysis of videotapes of unstructured play.* (Available from Ronald Seifer, Institute for the Study of Developmental Disabilities, University of Illinois at Chicago, 1640 West Roosevelt Road, Chicago, IL 60680.)

Clarke-Stewart, K. (1973). *Interactions between mothers and their young children: Characteristics and consequences.* Monographs of the Society for Research in Child Development, 38(6-7, Serial No. 153).

Clarke-Stewart, K., & Hevey, C. (1981). Longitudinal relations in repeated observations of mother-child interactions from 1 to 2½ years. *Developmental Psychology, 17,* 127–145.

Coie, J. D., Dodge, K. A., & Copotelli, H. (1982). Dimensions and types of social status: A cross-age perspective. *Developmental Psychology, 18,* 557–570.

Comfort, M. (1988). Assessing parent-child interactions. In D. Bailey & R. Simeonsson (Eds.), *Family assessment in early intervention* (pp. 65–94). Englewood Cliffs, NJ: Merrill/Prentice Hall.

Crawley, S., & Spiker, D. (1982). *Mother-child rating scale.* Chicago, IL: University of Illinois. (ERIC Document Reproduction Service No. ED 221 978).

Cripe, J., Slentz, K., & Bricker, D. (Eds.). (1993). *AEPS curriculum for birth to three years.* Baltimore, MD: Paul H. Brookes.

Denham, S. A., & McKinley, M. (1993). Sociometric nominations for preschoolers: A psychometric analysis. *Early Education and Development, 4,* 109–122.

Doll, B., & Elliott, S. N. (1994). Representativeness of observed preschool social behaviors: How many data points are enough? *Journal of Early Intervention, 18,* 227–238.

Farran, D., Kasari, C., Comfort, M., & Jay, S. (1986). *Parent/Caregiver Involvement Scale.* (Available from Continuing Education, 209 Forney Building, University of North Carolina, Greensboro, NC 27412.)

Fernald, A., & Morikawa, H. (1993). Common themes and cultural variations in Japanese and American mothers' speech to infants. *Child Development, 64,* 637–656.

Field, T. (1978). Interaction behaviors of primary versus secondary caretaker fathers. *Developmental Psychology, 14,* 183–184.

Field, T. (1983). High-risk infants "have less fun" during early interactions. *Topics of Early Childhood Special Education, 3*(1), 77–87.

Finn, R. (1972). Effects of some characteristics in rating scale characteristics on the means and reliabilities of ratings. *Educational and Psychological Measurement, 32,* 255–265.

Foster, S. L., & Ritchey, W. L. (1979). Issues in the assessment of social competence in children. *Journal of Applied Behavior Analysis, 12,* 625–638.

Fraiberg, S. (1975). The development of human attachments in infants blind from birth. *Merrill-Palmer Quarterly, 21,* 315–324.

Furuno, S., O'Reilly, K., Hosaka, C., Inatsuka, T., Zeisloft-Falbey, B., & Allman, T. (1985). *Hawaii Early Learning Profile (HELP) activity guide.* Palo Alto, CA: VORT.

Garner, P., & Landry, S. (1992). Preterm infants' affective responses in independent versus toy-centered play with their mothers. *Infant Mental Health Journal, 13,* 219–230.

Goldberg, S. (1977). Social competence in infancy: A model of parent-infant interaction. *Merrill-Palmer Quarterly, 23,* 163–177.

Goldstein, H., & Gallagher, T. M. (1992). Strategies for promoting the social-communicative competence of young children with specific learning disabilities. In S. Odom, S. McConnell, & M. McEvoy (Eds.), *Social competence of young children with disabilities* (pp. 165–188). Baltimore, MD: Paul H. Brookes.

Gresham, F. M. (1986). Conceptual issues in the assessment of social competence in children. In P. S. Strain, M. J. Guralnick, & H. Walker (Eds.), *Children's social behavior: Development, assessment, and modification* (pp. 143–176). New York: Academic Press.

Gresham, F., & Elliott, S. (1990). *Social Skills Rating System.* Circle Pines, MN: American Guidance Service.

Guba, E. G., & Lincoln, Y. S. (1989). *Fourth generation evaluation.* Newbury Park, CA: SAGE Publications.

Guilford, J. (1954). *Psychometric methods.* New York: McGraw-Hill.

Guralnick, M. J. (1980). Social interaction among preschool handicapped children. *Exceptional Children, 46,* 248–253.

Guralnick, M. J. (1990). Social competence and early intervention. *Journal of Early Intervention, 14,* 3–14.

Guralnick, M. J. (1992a). A hierarchical model for understanding children's peer-related social competence. In S. Odom, S. McConnell, & M. McEvoy (Eds.), *Social competence of young children with disabilities* (pp. 37–64). Baltimore, MD: Paul H. Brookes.

Guralnick, M. J. (1992b). *Assessment of peer relations.* Seattle, WA: Child Development and Mental Retardation Center, University of Washington.

Guralnick, M. J. (1993). Developmentally appropriate practice in the assessment and intervention of children's peer relations. *Topics in Early Childhood Special Education, 13,* 344–371.

Guralnick, M. J., Connor, R., Hammond, M., Gottman, J. M., & Kinnish, K. (in press). Immediate effects of mainstreamed settings on the social interactions and social integration of preschool children. *American Journal on Mental Retardation.*

Guralnick, M. J., & Groom, J. M. (1987). The peer relations of mildly delayed and nonhandicapped preschool children in mainstreamed playgroups. *Child Development, 58,* 1556–1572.

Guralnick, M. J., & Groom, J. M. (1988). Friendships of preschool children in mainstream playgroups. *Developmental Psychology, 24,* 595–604.

Hartman, D. P., & Wood, D. D. (1990). Observational methods. In A. Bellack, M. Hersen, & A. Kazdin (Eds.), *International handbook of behavior modification and therapy* (pp. 107–138). New York: Plenum Press.

Hartup, W. W. (1983). Peer relations. In M. Heatherington (Ed.), *Handbook of Child Psychology, Vol. IV* (pp. 103–196). New York: John Wiley.

Hartup, W. W., Glazer, J., & Charlesworth, R. (1967). Peer reinforcement and sociometric status. *Child Development, 38,* 1017–1024.

Hayvren, M., & Hymel, S. (1984). Ethical issues in sociometric testing: Impact of sociometric measures on interaction behavior. *Developmental Psychology, 20,* 844–849.

Hinde, R. A., Titmus, G., Easton, D., & Tamplin, A. (1985). Incidence of friendship and behavior toward strong associates versus nonassociates in preschoolers. *Child Development, 56,* 234–245.

Hops, H. (1983). Children's social competence and skill: Current research practices and future directions. *Behavior Therapy, 14,* 3–18.

Hops, H., Guild, J., Fleishman, D. H., Paine, S., Street, A., Walker, H., & Greenwood, C. (1979). *Peers: Procedures for establishing effective relationship skills.* Eugene, OR: CORBEH.

Howes, C. (1983). Patterns of friendship. *Child Development, 54,* 1041–1053.

Howes, C. (1992). *Collaborative construction of pretend play.* Albany, NY: State University of New York Press.

Isabella, R. A. (1991). Interactional synchrony and the origins of infant-mother attachment: A replication study. *Child Development, 62,* 373–384.

Isabella, R. A., & Belsky, J. (1991). Interactional synchrony and the origins of infant-mother attachment: A replication study. *Child Development, 62,* 373–384.

Jay, S., & Farran, D. (1981). The relative efficacy of predicting IQ from mother-child interactions using ratings versus behavioral count measures. *Journal of Applied Developmental Psychology, 2,* 165–177.

Johnson-Martin, N., Attermeier, S., & Hacker, B. (1990). *Carolina Curriculum for Preschoolers with Special Needs.* Baltimore, MD: Paul H. Brookes.

Johnson-Martin, N., Jens, K., Attermeier, S., & Hacker, B., (1991). *The Carolina Curriculum for Infants and Toddlers with Special Needs* (2nd ed.). Baltimore, MD: Paul H. Brookes.

Kohler, F. W., & Fowler, S. A. (1985). Training prosocial behaviors to young children: An analysis of reciprocity with untrained peers. *Journal of Applied Behavior Analysis, 18,* 187–200.

Kohn, M. (1988). *Kohn problem checklist/Kohn Social Competence Scale.* San Antonio, TX: The Psychological Corp.

Kopp, C. B., Baker, B. L., & Brown, K. W. (1992). Social skills and their correlates: Preschoolers with developmental delays. *American Journal on Mental Retardation, 96,* 357–367.

Levine, S., Elzey, F. F., & Lewis, M. (1969). *California Preschool Social Competency Scale.* Palo Alto, CA: Consulting Psychologist Press.

Lewis, M., & Lee-Painter, S. (1974). An interactional approach to the mother-infant dyad. In M. Lewis & L. Rosenblum (Eds.), *The effect of the infant on its caregiver* (pp. 21–48). New York: John Wiley.

Likert, R. (1932). A technique for the measurement of attitudes. *Archives of Psychology, 22*(140), 1–52.

Lincoln, Y. S., & Guba, E. G. (1985). *Naturalistic inquiry.* Beverly Hills, CA: Sage Publications.

Linder, T. (1993a). *The Transdisciplinary Play-Based Assessment* (rev. ed.). Baltimore, MD: Paul H. Brookes.

Linder, T. (1993b). *The Transdisciplinary Play-Based Intervention.* Baltimore, MD: Paul H. Brookes.

Lussier, B., Crimmins, D., & Alberti, D. (1994). Effect of three adult interaction styles on infant engagement. *Journal of Early Intervention, 18,* 12–24.

Mahoney, G. (1992). *Maternal Behavior Rating Scale* (rev. ed.). (Available from Family Child Learning Center, 143 Northwest Avenue, Bldg. A, Tallmadge, OH 44278).

Marshall, H. R. (1957). An evaluation of sociometric-social behavior research with preschool children. *Child Development, 28,* 131–137.

Maurer, H., & Sherrod, K. (1987). Context of directives given to young children with Down syndrome and nonretarded children: Development over two years. *American Journal of Mental Deficiency, 91,* 579–590.

McAllister, J. R. (1991). Curriculum-based behavioral intervention for preschool children with handicaps. *Topics in Early Childhood Special Education, 11*(2), 48–58.

McCandless, B. R., & Marshall, H. R. (1957). A picture sociometric for preschool children and its relation to teacher judgments of friendship. *Child Development, 28,* 139–147.

McCloskey, G. (1990). Selecting and using early childhood rating scales. *Topics in Early Childhood Special Education, 10,* 39–64.

McCollum, J., & Stayton, V. (1985). Infant/parent interaction: Studies and intervention guidelines based on the SIAI model. *Journal of the Division for Early Childhood, 9,* 125–135.

McConnell, S. R., & Odom, S. L. (1986). Sociometrics: Peer-referenced measures and the assessment of social competence. In P. Strain, M. Guralnick, & H. Walker (Eds.), *Children's social behavior: Development, assessment, and modification* (pp. 215–286). New York: Academic Press.

McConnell, S. R., Sisson, L., & Sandler, S. (1984). *Category definitions for observational assessment of reciprocal social interactions.* Unpublished observer training manual. University of Pittsburgh.

McFall, R. M. (1982). A reformulation of the concept of social skill. *Behavioral Assessment, 4,* 1–33.

Mueller, E., & Vandell, D. (1979). Infant-infant interaction. In J. Osofsky (Ed.), *Handbook of infant development* (pp. 591–622). New York: John Wiley.

Munson, L., & Odom, S. (1994). *Infant-Caregiver Interaction Scale (ICIS) Manual.* Unpublished manuscript.

Munson, L. J., & Odom, S. L. (1995). *Evaluation of rating scales that measure parent-infant interaction.* Unpublished manuscript.

Neisworth, J. T., & Bagnato, S. J. (in press). Assessment for early intervention: Emerging themes and practices. In S. Odom & M. McLean (Eds.), *Early intervention for infants and young children with disabilities and their families: Recommended practices.* Austin, TX: PRO-ED.

Newborg, J., Stock, J. R., Wnek, L., Guidubaldi, J., & Svinicki, J. (1988). *Battelle Developmental Inventory with Recalibrated Technical Data and Norms.* Allen, TX: DLM.

O'Connor, M., Sigman, M., & Kasari, C. (1992). Attachment behavior of infants exposed prenatally to alcohol: Mediating effects of infant affect and mother-infant interaction. *Development and Psychopathology, 4,* 243–256.

Odom, S. L. (1981). The relationship of play to developmental level in mentally retarded children. *Education and Training of the Mentally Retarded, 16,* 136–142.

Odom, S. L. (1988). Research in early childhood special education: Methodologies and paradigms. In S. Odom & M. Karnes (Eds.), *Early intervention for infants and young children with handicaps: An empirical base* (pp. 1–21). Baltimore, MD: Paul H. Brookes.

Odom, S. L., Bender, M., Doran, L., Houden, P., McInnes, M., DeKlyen, M., Speltz, M., & Jenkins, J. (1988). *Integrated preschool curriculum.* Seattle, WA: University of Washington Press.

Odom, S. L., & McConnell, S. R. (1985). A performance-based conceptualization of social competence of handicapped preschool children: Implications for assessment. *Topics in Early Childhood Special Education, 4*(4), 1–19.

Odom, S. L., & McConnell, S. R. (in press). Promoting peer-related social competence of young children with disabilities. In M. Bambring, H. Rauh, & A. Beelman (Eds.), *Early childhood intervention: Theory, evaluation, and practice.* Berlin/New York: deGruyter.

Odom, S. L., McConnell, S. R., & Chandler, L. K. (1994). Acceptability and feasibility of classroom-based social interaction interventions for young children with disabilities. *Exceptional Children, 60,* 226–236.

Odom, S. L., McConnell, S. R., & McEvoy, M. A. (1992). Peer-related social competence and its implications for young children with disabilities. In S. Odom, S. McConnell, & M. McEvoy (Eds.), *Social competence of young children with disabilities* (pp. 3–36). Baltimore, MD: Paul H. Brookes.

Odom, S. L., & Ogawa, O. (1992). Direct observation of young children's social interaction with peers: A review of methodology. *Behavioral Assessment, 14,* 407–441.

Odom, S. L., Peterson, C., McConnell, S. R., & Ostrosky, M. M. (1990). Ecobehavioral analysis of early education/specialized classroom settings and peer social interaction. *Education and Training of Children, 13,* 316–330.

Odom, S. L., & Strain, P. S. (1986). Using teacher antecedents and peer initiations to increase reciprocal social interactions of autistic children: A comparative treatment study. *Journal of Applied Behavior Analysis, 19,* 59–71.

Olson, S., Bates, J., & Bayles, K. (1984). Mother-infant interaction and the development of individual differences in children's cognitive competence. *Developmental Psychology, 50,* 166–179.

Park, K., Lay, K. L., & Ramsay, L. (1993). Individual differences and developmental changes in preschoolers' friendships. *Developmental Psychology, 29,* 264–270.

Parks, P., & Bradley, R. (1991). The interaction of home environment features and their relation to infant competence. *Infant Mental Health Journal, 12,* 3–16.

Parks, S. (Ed.). (1988). *HELP at home.* Palo Alto, CA: VORT.

Parks, S. (1992). *Inside HELP: Administration and reference manual for the Hawaii Early Learning Profile (HELP).* Palo Alto, CA: VORT.

Parten, M. B. (1932). Social participation among preschool children. *Journal of Abnormal and Social Psychology, 27,* 243–269.

Poteat, G. M., Ironsmith, M., & Bullock, J. (1986). The classification of preschool children's social status. *Early Childhood Research Quarterly, 1,* 349–360.

Power, T. G., & Parke, R. D. (1986). Patterns of early socialization: Mother-infant and father-infant interaction in the home. *International Journal of Behavioral Development, 9,* 331–341.

Rasmussen, J. (1989). Analysis of Likert-scale data: A reinterpretation of Gregoire and Driver. *Psychological Bulletin, 105,* 167–170.

Roopnarine, J. L., & Field, T. M. (1984). Play interactions of friends and acquaintances in nursery school. In T. Field, J. Roopnarine, & M. Segal (Eds.), *Friendships in normal and handicapped children* (pp. 89–98). Norwood, NJ: Ablex.

Rubenstein, J. L., & Howes, C. (1979). Caregiving and infant behavior in day care and in homes. *Developmental Psychology, 15,* 1–24.

Rubin, K. (1982). Nonsocial play in preschoolers: Necessarily evil? *Child Development, 53,* 651–657.

Rubin, K. H., Maioni, T. L., & Hornung, M. (1976). Freeplay behaviors in middle- and lower-class preschoolers: Parten and Piaget revisited. *Child Development, 47,* 414–419.

Rutter, D., & Durkin, K. (1987). Turn-taking in mother-infant interaction: An examination of vocalizations and gaze. *Developmental Psychology, 23,* 54–61.

Sackett, G. P. (1978). Measurement in observational research. In G. Sackett (Ed.), *Observing behavior: Data collection and analysis methods, Vol. II* (pp. 25–44). Baltimore, MD: University Park Press.

Salisbury, C., Britzman, D., & Kang, J. (1989). Using qualitative methods to assess the social-communicative competence of young handicapped children. *Journal of Early Intervention, 13,* 153–165.

Schaefer, E. (1989). Dimensions of mother-infant interaction: Measurement, stability, and predictive validity. *Infant Behavior and Development, 12,* 379–393.

Schweinhart, L. J. (1993). Observing young children in action: The key to early childhood assessment. *Young Children, 48*(5), 29–33.

Seifer, R., Sameroff, A., Anagnostopolou, R., & Elias, P. (1992). Mother-infant interaction during the first year: Effects of situation, maternal mental illness, and demographic factors. *Infant Behavior and Development, 15,* 405–426.

Shure, M. B. (1993). I can problem solve (ICPS): Interpersonal cognitive problem solving for young children. *Early Child Development and Care, 96,* 49–64.

Sigman, M., & Ungerer, J. A. (1984). Attachment behaviors in autistic children. *Journal of Autism and Developmental Disorders, 14,* 231–244.

Skellenger, A. C., Hill, M. M., & Hill, E. (1992). The social functioning of children with visual impairments. In S. Odom, S. McConnell, & M. McEvoy (Eds.), *Social competence of young children with disabilities* (pp. 165–188). Baltimore, MD: Paul H. Brookes.

Snyder, S., & Sheehan, R. (in press). Program evaluation in early childhood special education. In S. L. Odom & M. E. McLean (Eds.), *Early intervention for infants and young children with disabilities and their families: Recommended practices.* Austin, TX: PRO-ED.

Sparrow, S., Balla, D., & Cicchetti, D. (1984). *Vineland Adaptive Behavior Scales.* Circle Pines, MN: American Guidance Service.

Spieker, S. J. (1986). Pattern of very insecure attachment found in samples of high-risk infants and toddlers. *Topics in Early Childhood Special Education, 6*(3), 86–99.

Stern, D. (1974). Mother and infant at play: The dyadic interaction involving facial, vocal, and gaze behaviors. In M. Lewis & L. Rosenbaum (Eds.), *The effect of the infant on its caregiver* (pp. 187–213). New York: John Wiley.

Strain, P. S. (1983). Identification of social skill curriculum targets for severely handicapped children in mainstreamed preschools. *Applied Research in Mental Retardation, 4,* 369–382.

Strain, P. S., & Shores, R. E. (1977). Social reciprocity: A review of research and educational implications. *Exceptional Children, 43,* 526–530.

Strain, P. S., & Timm, M. A. (1974). An experimental analysis of social interaction between a behaviorally disordered preschool child and her classroom peers. *Journal of Applied Behavior Analysis, 7,* 583–590.

Suen, H. K., & Ary, D. (1989). *Analyzing quantitative behavioral observational data.* Hillsdale, NJ: Lawrence Erlbaum.

Tremblay, A., Strain, P. S., Hendrickson, J. M., & Shores, R. E. (1981). Social interactions of normally developing preschool children: Using normative data for subject selection and target behavior selection. *Behavior Modification, 5,* 237–253.

Vanderbilt/Minnesota Social Interaction Project (S. Odom and S. McConnell, Eds.) (1993). *Play time/social time: Organizing your classroom to build interaction skills.* Tucson, AZ: Communication Skill Builders.

Wedell-Monig, J., & Lumley, J. (1980). Child deafness and mother-child interaction. *Child Development, 51,* 766–774.

Yoder, P. (1987). Relationship between degree of infant handicap and clarity of infant cues. *American Journal of Mental Deficiency, 91,* 639–641.

Zarling, C., Hirsch, B., & Landry, S. (1988). Maternal social networks in full-term and very low birthweight preterm infants. *Child Development, 59,* 178–185.

Zigler, E., & Trickett, P. K. (1978). IQ, social competence, and evaluation of early childhood intervention programs. *American Psychologist, 33,* 789–798.

CHAPTER

14

Assessing Play Skills

Karin Lifter
Northeastern University

Because play activities are an integral, pervasive, and seemingly natural part of young children's lives, supporting all aspects of development, there has been increasing—and wide-ranging—attention to the use of play for assessment and programming efforts. Play is used or recommended as an activity base for the assessment of other developmental areas (Fewell & Kaminski, 1988) and forms the basis for play-based transdisciplinary assessment (Linder, 1993a). Advantages include assessment of spontaneously occurring behaviors in a natural environment, adaptability for use by professionals across disciplines, and potential involvement of family members (see Chapter 3).

Educators and therapists use play as a fundamental part of any preschool curriculum. Play comprises an important framework for developmentally appropriate practice in early childhood education (Bredekamp, 1987) and is used as a medium for intervention in early childhood special education, serving as an activity base for embedding objectives (Bricker & Cripe, 1992; Fox & Hanline, 1993) such as language and social goals (Matson, Fee, Coe, & Smith, 1991; McEvoy, Nordquist, Twardosz, Heckaman, Wehby, & Denny, 1988; Strain & Odom, 1986; Warren, 1992; Warren, Yoder, Gazdag, Kim, & Jones, 1993) and in support of incidental teaching procedures (Hart & Risley, 1968; Hart & Risley, 1975; McGee, Krantz, & McClannahan, 1985).

Play can also be viewed as a legitimate curricular domain in its own right, in contrast to its use as an activity base for assessment and intervention purposes. Because play activities are enjoyable, facilitate development, and increase opportunities for normalized interactions (Wolery & Bailey, 1989), intervention goals may focus specifically on learning to play as well as support of other goals.

The importance of play in children's lives is derived from two historical traditions using play as windows to how children feel and what they know. In the first tradition, play was regarded as "the royal road to the unconscious," as researchers and clinicians examined children's play activities for their affective content (e.g., the upsets surrounding family conflicts played out with doll figures). The results contributed to psychoanalytic theory and to the clinical procedures underlying play therapy, an approach used to reveal children's emotional conflicts and to help them rework those conflicts (Axline, 1947; Erikson, 1950; Freud, 1965; Klein, 1955).

In the second and more recent tradition, researchers have examined the play activities of children without disabilities as a way to understand cognitive development (i.e., knowledge of objects and events) and to determine a child's developmental level (Belsky & Most, 1981; Fein, 1981; Fenson, Kagan, Kearsley, & Zelazo, 1976; Garvey, 1977; Lifter & Bloom, 1989; McCune, 1995; Nicolich, 1977; Piaget, 1962). Similar descriptions were later extended to the play of children with disabilities (Beeghly, Weiss-Perry, & Cicchetti, 1990; Fewell & Kaminski, 1988; Hill & McCune-Nicolich, 1981; Ungerer & Sigman, 1981; Wing, Gould, Yeates, & Brierley, 1977). These efforts yielded normative data regarding play activities and a series of developmentally ordered taxonomies of play and provided a basis for diagnostic instruments to assess developmental progress. The results contributed to developmental theory and to the theoretical relationships between cognition and other developmental domains (i.e., language, affect, and social development) (Lifter & Bloom, 1989; Nicolich, 1977; Ungerer & Sigman, 1981). While the foregoing clinical/psychoanalytic and descriptive/cognitive traditions have been separate historically, contemporary work is centered on their convergence and their mutual influence in the developing child (Bloom, 1993; Lifter, in press; Slade & Wolf, 1994).

Obviously, how play is regarded and understood will influence and frame assessment and intervention questions. Play activities can be viewed broadly, as a pervasive activity base for assessment questions, programming goals, and therapeutic play interventions surrounding emotional conflicts. Play activities also can be viewed from the more circumscribed perspective of play as a window to knowledge of objects and events. This latter view, derived from the descriptive/cognitive tradition, focuses attention on what children are doing when they play and the functions play serves for them. On the one hand, it considers play as pure assimilation and as a "transformation of the world to meet the demands of the self" (Elkind, 1990, p. 15). On the other hand, it considers play as the "work" of childhood (Montessori, 1967), through which children learn about objects and events, learn language, and learn to engage in a variety of interactions with caregivers and peers. It is this circumscribed view of play that is the focus of this chapter and that frames the assessment and intervention questions that will be addressed for young children with special needs. Comprehensive reviews of play and play assessment are readily available (Bretherton, 1984; Rubin, Fein, & Vandenberg, 1983; Schaefer, Gitlin, & Sandgrund, 1991).

Assessing play skills centers on assessing children's actions with objects, whether alone or with caregivers or peers, assuming that what children do with objects indicates what they know about objects and what they are in the process of learning. Consequently, plans for interventions focus on facilitating children's use of play to learn about objects and events, in addition to the use of play for enjoyable purposes and increasing normalized interactions.

This chapter begins with a working definition of play followed by a brief review of studies describing the play of children with and without disabilities. The descriptive studies are used to define play and are foundational for understanding the role of play in the lives of young children and the methods used to assess play to develop intervention goals. Selected instruments for assessing play are presented with recommendations for their use. Finally, current and future directions for play assessment and intervention are discussed.

DEFINITION OF PLAY

In contemporary United States culture, when we talk about children's play, we usually mean play with objects, rough-and-tumble play, or gross motor play in an open area, whether alone or with peers or caregivers. Play with objects, the focus of this chapter, often means play with conventional toys (e.g., blocks, toy vehicles, dolls), but includes any kind of objects (e.g., pots and pans; sticks and stones). The fundamental assumption is that the nature of play materials does not direct what children do with them; rather, it is what children *know* about objects and events that directs the quality of their play activities (Lifter & Bloom, 1989). In other words, the behavior is appropriate to the toy object (i.e., "stimulus-appropriate") rather than dominated by the particular characteristics of the toy (i.e., "stimulus-dominated") (Weisler & McCall, 1976).

In the first edition of this volume, Wolery and Bailey (1989) defined play as "active engagement and interaction with an object or in an activity that appears to be intrinsically motivated, spontaneously performed, flexible, and accompanied by positive affect" (p. 431). This definition stands, certainly in defining play for assessment purposes, and is as viable today as it was several years ago.

Central to this definition is that the activities are *spontaneously performed.* Play is assimilation (Piaget, 1962) and proceeds "by maintenance or exercise of activities for the mere pleasure of mastering them" (p. 89). Attention to means prevails over attention to ends, allowing for *flexibility.* Variations in play themes occur according to the wishes of the player. Given this perspective, play activities reveal what children know or have mastered and are displayed in what they spontaneously do with objects; they are not actions that are prompted by someone else. Included is the idea of free choice in that children are free of external constraints in the selection of play activities and enjoy what they are doing when they play. Play is otherwise known as a "happy display of known actions" (Piaget, 1962).

Active engagement refers to animated attention to the activities of play, in contrast to boredom and inactivity (Garvey, 1977). Attending behaviors, which include the tracking activities observed in a young infant, provide sensorimotor feedback that helps children stay involved in the activities. Active engagement also relates to the "organism-dominated" nature of the activities (Rubin et al., 1983) in that the child directs the activities at hand.

Finally, that play activities are *intrinsically motivated* refers to "behavior neither governed by appetitive drives nor by compliance with social demands or inducements external to the behavior itself" (Rubin et al., 1983, p. 698). Children play simply because they seem to want to; play activities are not a result of externally imposed constraints or prospects of reward.

The reality of the foregoing features for defining play is revealed in the brief review of the descriptive studies that follows.

DESCRIPTIVE STUDIES OF PLAY

When children are playing alone or with their peers or caregivers, what they are doing with objects can be examined from cognitive and social perspectives. From a cognitive view, questions include: Are they attending to objects? Are they picking up, banging, and mouthing objects, or exploring them in various ways? Are they moving objects from place to place and in and out of various containers? Are they caring for dolls by feeding and dressing them? Are they rolling trucks along highways, getting some gas for their vehicles and fixing them along the way? Are they pretending they are on a visit to the doctor? Or are they on a trip to some imaginary land? From a social perspective, questions include: Are children engaging a caregiver in an activity with objects centered on pointing, showing, and giving behaviors? Are they playing alone, alongside a peer, or in some form of interaction with a peer? Or are they negotiating roles to decide who is going to be what, and who is going to do what?

Using these perspectives and questions, distinctly different behaviors can be identified from samples of children's play activities. Repeated sampling of the same child allows judgments to be made about newly learned behaviors, about the complexity of development, and about the order in which behaviors emerge. Measuring different play behaviors also assists in understanding the relationships between different types of play and in identifying changes in the behaviors and relationships over time.

Three tactics—identifying different categories of behavior, understanding the order in which different behaviors emerge, and measuring changes in behaviors and categories over time—underlie the majority of the analyses contained in the descriptive studies of play. These studies also produced taxonomies (classifications) of play activities that are the basis for many current play assessment instruments. This section briefly reviews the procedures used in those descriptive studies, presents various taxonomies of play, and summarizes the play characteristics of children with and without disabilities. Finally, the theoretical and practical implications of the descriptive studies are discussed.

Procedural Commonalities: What Was Done

Similarities among the descriptive studies include naturalistic samples of play activities, use of longitudinal or cross-sectional designs, analyses of spontaneously occurring activities, categorization and measurement of play, and statistical analyses to establish and verify developmental order. All but the last of these procedures are usually used in assessing play skills.

Naturalistic samples of play Samples of play activities were usually collected under unstructured, naturalistic conditions, affording opportunities for the spontaneous occurrence of behaviors, free of externally imposed constraints. These conditions commonly consisted of providing groups of toys to the child and the child's mother or other familiar caregiver with a general request to play with the toys for some continuous period of time. Toys were usually selected to allow manipulative and pretend play activities. In some studies, the investigators' modeling of certain play activities were included (Fenson & Ramsay, 1980; Ungerer & Sigman, 1981; Watson & Fischer, 1977). The observations were videotaped or collected using a checklist of behaviors and an interval recording technique.

Longitudinal versus cross-sectional designs In longitudinal descriptive designs, samples of play were taken from the same child over a period of time (e.g., 12 months as in Lifter & Bloom, 1989; Nicolich, 1977). Advantages of this practice included the detailed analyses of change in a child over time, such as the emergence of new categories of play and change in the relative frequency of play across the categories. Disadvantages included the length of time required to collect the data and the fact that few children could be followed so intensively. Cross-sectional designs, in contrast, permitted the collection of play samples from a greater number of children, collected essentially at the same time, with the children grouped according to age. Disadvantages included a lack of continuity in information about a single child over time.

Distinction between spontaneous and imitative behaviors Given that attention was centered on what children did with toys and their active engagement with objects, a distinction between spontaneous behaviors and activities that were imitations of a model was usually made, with analyses focused on the frequency and variety of spontaneous behaviors. These distinctions are easily seen in videotaped observations.

Categorization of activities The process of organizing different play behaviors into categories of activities was required to develop taxonomies (see examples in Table 14.1). Schemes for categorizing play activities have consisted of predetermined schemes (e.g., Belsky & Most, 1981; McCune, 1995; Nicolich, 1977), schemes that evolved from the observations (e.g., Fenson et al., 1976), or some combination of each (e.g., Lifter & Bloom, 1989). A predetermined scheme was based on either a theoretical framework that was validated with empirical observations (Lifter & Bloom, 1989; Nicolich, 1977; Watson & Fischer, 1977) or one that validated a derived scheme (e.g., Belsky & Most, 1981). Other schemes were derived from the observations and then set into a theoretical context.

For example, Nicolich (1977) defined and measured the levels of play described by Piaget (1962) and detailed children's progress through these levels. Lifter and Bloom (1989) limited their analyses to play activities in which the child related one object to another, derived from Piagetian notions of reversibility in the construction of reality (Piaget, 1954). They focused on acts of construction (i.e., moving two objects together to form a configuration) and then identified change over time in these activities.

Determination of developmental order and developmental change The determination of developmental order presented in

TABLE 14.1
Sample of Taxonomies of Play Activities Identified from the Play of Children Without Disabilities

Study, Design, Ages	Categories Identified
Belsky & Most (1981) cross-sectional: 40 infants, between 7½ and 21 months, with 4 infants at each 1.5 month interval beginning at 7½ months	**mouthing** indiscriminate mouthing of materials **simple manipulation** manipulation of a general sort (turns object over) **functional** manipulation appropriate to object (spins wheels on cart) **relational** brings objects together inappropriately (touches spoon to stick) **functional-relational** integrates objects in appropriate manner (sets cup on saucer) **enactive naming** approximate pretense (touches cup to lips) **pretend self** apparent pretense directed to self (brings cup to lips & tilts head back to drink) **pretend other** pretense directed toward other (feeds doll with spoon) **substitution** using object in a creative manner (feeds doll with stick as if bottle) **sequence pretend** linking different pretense schemes (stirs spoon in cup, then drinks) **sequence pretend substitution** linking schemes, adding object substitution (feeds self with spoon, then stick) **double substitution** two materials transformed in a single act (treat stick as person, and give it a drink from seashell)
Fenson et al. (1976) cross-sectional: 7, 9, 13, and 20 months, with 11 to 20 children in each group	**banging** banging two objects together **relational acts** combining or relating of 2 objects • **grouping** • **simple** (inappropriate, such as touching spoon against pot) • **accommodative** (appropriate, such as lid on pot) **symbolic acts** include eating, drinking, pouring, stirring, spooning **sequential acts** occurrences of 2 or more responses in sequential order

TABLE 14.1
Continued

Study, Design, Ages	Categories Identified
Lifter & Bloom (1989) longitudinal: 14 children, observed from 9 to 24 mos (see also Bloom, 1993) Play activities examined at two language transitions: First Words and the Vocabulary Spurt	**given** recreation of the same relations in which the objects were introduced to the child (nests the nesting cups) **imposed: general** made use of general physical properties of objects that afforded containment and support **imposed: specific** made use of more particular properties of objects in relation to one another • **inanimate surrogate** particular properties of inanimate objects (stringing beads; rolling truck on highway) • **animate surrogate** use of replica person or animal (feeding doll with spoon; putting boy figure on a horse)
Nicolich (1977) longitudinal: 5 children observed from 14 to 27 months (see also McCune, 1995)	**presymbolic** shows understanding of object use (comb to hair) **autosymbolic** child pretends in self-related activities (eats from empty spoon) **single scheme symbolic game** extends symbolism beyond own actions (feeds doll) **combinatorial symbolic games** • **single** 1 scheme related to several actors (child drinks, gives doll drink) • **multischeme** several schemes related in sequence (feeds, washes, puts doll to bed) **planned symbolic games** indicates pretend acts planned beforehand (finds blanket, then looks for doll to cover it)
Piaget (1962) longitudinal	**practice games** preverbal development (ritual actions taken out of context, e.g., lie down to sleep at sight of pillow) **symbolic games** implies representation of the absent object (e.g., pretend to sleep with pillow substitute) **games with rules** necessarily implies social or interindividual relationships and adherence to regulations imposed by group

TABLE 14.1
Continued

Study, Design, Ages	Categories Identified
Ruff & Lawson (1990) longitudinal: with 67 children observed at 1, 2, and 3.5 years of age; also cross-sectional study of 48 children, with 16 each at 2.5, 3.5, and 4.5 years of age	**casual attention** doing things with objects but not necessarily attending to them in a focused way; also included talking to an interactant, moving eyes around toy collection, laughing and smiling, stereotyped repetitive activity, and simply looking at toys without engaging in any activity **focused attention** deliberate manipulation of the object, such as turning it around or fingering different surfaces, with interest in the activity along with gaze at the object; also included looking toward a particular location and activity with relatively serious, interested expression
Smilansky (1968; 1990) 4- to 6-year-old children	**functional play** sensory-motor practice games consisting of repetitive movements with or without objects **constructive play** goal directed play that includes some representational capacities, with materials as the focal point of attention (e.g., builds a "castle") **symbolic play** • **dramatic play** children take on roles in which they pretend to be someone else, with focus on roles and themes, and not on materials • **sociodramatic play** dramatic play that "involves the cooperation of at least two children and the play proceeds on the basis of interaction between the players acting out their roles, both verbally and in terms of acts performed" (p. 19) **games with rules** formal organized and rule-bound play (e.g., simple circle games to team games)
Watson & Fischer (1977) cross-sectional: 36 children, with 12 each at 14, 19, and 24 months of age	**self as agent** infant puts head on pillow to pretend to go to sleep **passive other agent** infants put doll on pillow **passive substitute agent** infant puts block on pillow to pretend **active other agent** infant has doll lie down on pillow to go to sleep, attributing action to doll

Note: The play categories presented here are summarized versions of what appeared in the respective published reports. The interested reader is urged to consult the published reports.

the taxonomies was generally verified by some form of statistical analyses, such as scalogram analyses, analysis of variance, rank order statistics, and changes in relative distribution of categories over time (Belsky & Most, 1981; Lifter & Bloom, 1989). For example, Belsky and Most (1981) reported that the scale that they had derived and tested in their cross-sectional study formed the properties of a Guttman scale. They concluded that the early levels in the scale emerge prior to the later levels in the scale, forming a developmental sequence of play activities.

Taxonomies of Play Categories: What Was Found

Summary of changes in play The early descriptive studies generated a variety of overlapping taxonomies of play activities to describe what children without disabilities did when they played and how that changed over time. The taxonomies presented in Table 14.1 yield the following general description. Play activities begin with infants focusing their attention on the objects available for play and simple manipulation of objects (e.g., mouthing, banging). Play becomes increasingly complex over time as children put toys together in various ways (e.g., relational acts; imposed: general constructions) that begin to exploit their specific properties in relation to one another (e.g., imposed: specific). With development, children go beyond the manipulative characteristics of toys to respect their conventional properties and to embed pretend schemes into ongoing activities (e.g., animate surrogate; autosymbolic and symbolic schemes; passive other agent). Eventually, children take on various roles and enact various themes that they play out in coherent sequences (e.g., planned symbolic acts). Symbolic activities develop further to include dramatic activity and sociodramatic activity as children assume various roles, with or without other children. Eventually they participate with others in games with rules and adhere to the regulations imposed by the group.

Developmental changes were identified in the emergence of different categories of play over time and from changes in the relative distribution of the categories. Belsky and Most (1981) reported a decreasing trend in undifferentiated exploration (mouthing and simple manipulation, combined); a curvilinear trend in transitional play (relational, functional-relational, and enactive naming, combined); and an increasing trend in decontextualized pretend play (pretend self, pretend external, substitution, sequence pretend, and sequence substitution combined). They interpreted the trend in transitional play as linking early exploration with more advanced forms of pretend play. Similar results were reported by Lifter and Bloom (1989): imposed: general relations decreased; imposed: specific relations increased; and given relations stayed essentially the same. Changes in the relative distribution provide information about the developmental course of categories of play activities. Such results illustrate that some categories are replaced by other categories in development and lend a cautionary note to the straightforward use of developmental sequences for identifying objectives for intervention.

The shift from manipulative to conventional or symbolic activities has been used to infer developments in representation and symbolization. These changes are supported by and informed by developments in language and the ability to appreciate and model the activities of others (Fein, 1981; Garvey, 1977).

For example, Lifter and Bloom (1989) reported that the children's early constructions consisted of very general relations (i.e., imposed: general, such as moving a variety of objects in and out of containers) and constructions for which there was considerable perceptual support (i.e., given relations, which re-created the presentation configuration of objects, such as putting a puzzle piece back into a puzzle frame). With development, the children increasingly took into account the specific physical and conventional characteristics of objects in their constructions (i.e., imposed: specific), such as putting a bead on a string and extending a spoon to a doll's mouth to feed it. Children's early constructions were interpreted as evidence of their ability to think about objects as separate entities, which is central to the development of object permanence. The increase in imposed: specific relations was interpreted as developments in representational abilities required to understand and remember the specific characteristics of objects underlying, also known as developments in object knowledge.

In addition, changes in play corresponded to specific changes in children's language behaviors. Achievements in the ability to construct relations between objects, as measured by increases in the frequency and variety of given and imposed: general constructions corresponded to the children's transition to first words. Achievements in the ability to demonstrate knowledge of the particular physical and conventional characteristics of objects (measured by increases in the frequency and variety of imposed: specific constructions) corresponded to the transition to the vocabulary spurt, marked by a sudden increase in the children's use of conventional words to describe objects and events. The two play-language clusters occurred independently of the children's ages.

Developmental changes have also been identified in the way children spontaneously concentrate and sustain attention in play, which are related to developments in play per se (Ruff & Lawson, 1990). In their examination of focused attention in play for children 12 months to 4.5 years of age, Ruff and Lawson noted that their results "reflect developmental trends for more focused, effortful attention and not for attention generally" (p. 91). They suggested that the increases in focused attention are related to the increasing cognitive demands of increasingly complex play.

The play of children with disabilities
Following the descriptive studies of the play of children without disabilities, many studies examined the play of children with disabilities. Similar categories of activities and the same sequence of emergence were identified for children with varying disabilities (see Table 14.2). The differences observed among children with disabilities and between children with and without disabilities were differences more of quantity and timing rather than in the qualitative nature of the activities (Fewell & Kaminski, 1988; Field, Roseman, DeStefano, & Koewler, 1982) and point to the importance of descriptors of disability that transcend categories of disability (Kopp, 1983; Lifter, 1992).

The quality of play of children with disabilities is obviously related to the nature of their impairment (Fewell & Kaminski, 1988; Ungerer & Sigman, 1981). Children with hearing impairments usually develop a wide variety of manipulative activities, but slow down during the transition to symbolic activities, because of difficulties with their communicative expressive and receptive abilities. Children with visual impairments are affected from the start in their limited ability to reach out and explore their environments, which, in turn, impedes development in cognitive abilities (Fraiberg, 1977; Rogers, 1984). Children with physical impairments are limited in their ability to move around and work with toy materials; often their play is less involved. Physical requirements result in less enthusiasm for play (Fewell & Kaminski, 1988). Children with specific language impairments are often delayed in developments in symbolic play (Terrell, Schwartz, Prelock, & Messick, 1984; Westby, 1980). Children with Down syndrome progress "through the same developmental sequences of decentration, decontextualization, and integration in object and social play that characterize the play

TABLE 14.2
Sample of Taxonomies of Play Activities Identified from the Play of Children Developing with Disabilities

Study, Disability Group	Categories Identified
Hill & McCune-Nicolich (1981) 30 children with Down syndrome, 20 to 53 months of age, with mental ages ranging from 12 to 26 months (sequence supported by scalogram analyses)	**presymbolic scheme** demonstrates knowledge of function of object (touches comb to hair) **autosymbolic scheme** demonstrates simple acts of self-pretend (uses empty cup for drinking) **single-scheme symbolic games** extends symbolism beyond self • includes other participants (feeds mother or doll) • pretends at activities of others (cleans the floor) **combinatorial symbolic games** • single scheme applied to several participants (feeds self, then doll) • two successive actions are played (feeds doll, then grooms doll)
Ungerer & Sigman (1981): 16 children with autism, 39 to 74 months of age, with mental ages ranging from 18 to 38 months	**simple manipulation** mouthing, waving, banging **combinations** touching, banging 2 objects together; stacking objects; container/contained relations **functional play** self-directed (brushing own hair); other directed (brushing other's hair); object directed (placing top on teapot) **symbolic** substitution: use of 1 object as if different (e.g., teacup as telephone); agent play (use of doll as independent agent); imaginary play (creation of objects or people having no physical representation, e.g., making pouring sounds).

development of nonhandicapped children in early childhood," but do so at a slower pace (Beeghly et al., 1990, p. 345), with symbolic play level more highly correlated with mental age than with chronological age (Hill & McCune-Nicolich, 1981). The play of children with autism or with autistic-like features is often described as stereotypic and lacking in flexibility and symbolic qualities (Ungerer & Sigman, 1981; Wing et al., 1977). Children with severe retardation suffer from limited attending skills that affect their exploratory behavior and their ability to sustain attention to play activities (Wehman, 1977). Children who were born prematurely often have difficulties with sustaining attention that will affect their early exploration of objects in play (Ruff, 1988). (See Bretherton, 1984; Field et al., 1982; Quinn & Rubin, 1984; and Rubin et al., 1983 for reviews).

Social categories of play Related but historically earlier work on play taxonomies includes Parten's work on social categories of play (Parten, 1932). Rather than using play as a window to developments in cognition, she examined the development of social behavior during preschoolers' play activities and devised the taxonomy presented in Table 14.3. She also examined the quality of social interactions for four groups of children, from less than 2 years of age to 4 years, 4 months. Except for the "Unoccupied" category, the categories presented in the taxonomy were observed in essentially all the children's play, with participation in the most social categories occurring most frequently among the older children. Thus, while Parten's social taxonomy is not necessarily a developmental sequence, the more socially involved categories are associated with older ages and hence developmental progress.

Parten's categories are still used to investigate various aspects of social play, for example the relation of social play to companion status in play (Guralnick & Groom, 1987). Advantages of Parten's taxonomy include the fact that an analysis of the social-interactive quality of play can be performed independently of, and then integrated with, an analysis of the kinds of play activities a child engages in, following the taxonomies presented in Table 14.1. Such analyses await further research.

Theoretical Implications of the Descriptive Studies

The descriptive studies provided empirical support for developmental theory. Theoretical assumptions about developments in knowledge, representation, and the symbolic function were validated with the developmental change observed with the decrease in manipulative activities and increase in symbolic activities. The same developmental sequences were also identified in the play of children with disabilities, although the relative slowness of progress in their play was used to elucidate symbolic deficits (Beeghly et al., 1990; Rogers, 1984; Sigman & Mundy, 1987).

Assessing cognitive development through play activities also permitted investigation of how change in cognition related to change in language for children with and without disabilities with the identification of specific corre-

TABLE 14.3
Parten's Categories of Social Participation in Play

Category	Definition
unoccupied behavior	child does not play but is occupied with watching things of momentary interest
solitary play	child plays alone and with different toys from those children in close proximity
onlooker	child watches other children at play, stands or sits within speaking distance, and often talks to children being observed
parallel activity	child plays independently but with toys that will bring him or her closer to others; child plays beside but not with other children
associative play	children exchange materials and conversation about the common activity, and bring other children into the activity, but each child engages in what he or she wishes
cooperative or organized supplementary play	one or two children direct the activities of the others and organize the group for some purpose, necessitating a division of labor and an organization of roles; accordingly, children either belong or do not belong to the group

spondences between play and language (Bloom, Lifter, & Broughton, 1985; Kennedy, Sheridan, Radlinski, & Beeghly, 1991; Lifter & Bloom, 1989; McCune-Nicolich, 1981; Ungerer & Sigman, 1981; Wing et al., 1977). There is general agreement that developments in play are related to developments in cognitive, language, and social skills for children with disabilities (Fewell & Kaminski, 1988; Odom & Ogawa, 1992) just as they are for children without disabilities.

Practical Implications of the Descriptive Studies

The results of the descriptive studies have also contributed to the practices underlying early childhood education and early childhood special education.

Early childhood education Developmentally appropriate practice (DAP) was derived in reaction to a "trend toward increased emphasis on formal instruction in academic skills" (Bredekamp, 1987, p. 1; 1993). This reaction led early childhood educators to turn to the individual learner in the context of the developmental/cognitive theoretical framework, resulting in "child-directed" approaches to learning, and a shift from outcomes to process in emphasizing the learning that should take place. The descriptive studies of play were undertaken within the same developmental/cognitive theoretical framework and provided normative data for what children do when they play. The studies contributed to the reaffirmation of play in the early childhood classroom, with play regarded as an important activity base for providing child-directed opportunities for learning.

Smilansky's work (1968) had a particularly strong impact on early childhood education. She organized Piaget's constructivist perspective on play into a practical system that teachers could use in studying children's play, which was, for example, integrated into the Cognitively Oriented Curriculum/High Scope Curriculum (Monighan-Nourot, 1990). However, while preschool classrooms usually include areas for sociodramatic play, little work has been done in facilitating children's play within the early childhood education framework (Smilansky, 1990), although this may be changing with the increased attention to play by the National Association for the Education of Young Children.

Early childhood special education
The taxonomies of play generated from the descriptive studies contributed three basic functions to early childhood special education. First, they provided a basis for the assessment of play activities; second, they allowed for descriptive analyses of what children with disabilities do when they play in order to identify areas of need; and, third, the resulting descriptions framed questions of assessment and intervention in play.

Basis for assessment of play activities Aside from their descriptive usefulness, "most assessment procedures adopt various taxonomies of play and attempt to determine the occurrence or nonoccurrence of the included categories" (Wolery & Bailey, 1989, p. 432), hence the usefulness of taxonomies for assessing play skills, determining the kinds of play activities children know about, and setting goals for intervention.

Most play assessment instruments do indeed use taxonomies derived from the descriptive studies (Schaefer et al., 1991). These assessments are used to determine developmental progress and/or to link assessment with intervention for identifying play goals. The origins of the categories used in two current play assessment instruments (Lifter, Edwards, Avery, Anderson, & Sulzer-Azaroff, 1988; Linder, 1993a), presented in Table 14.4, and some of the categories used in the Play Assessment

Scale (Fewell, 1994) can be found in the taxonomies presented in Table 14.1. The taxonomies also have provided categories of activities from which to derive curricula of play activities for intervention purposes.

Descriptions of play of children with disabilities While the play of children with disabilities has been described using the same play categories identified for children without disabilities, their play is often characterized as less developed in frequency and variety. Instead of an enjoyable, intrinsically motivating activity to be engaged in with their peers, play seems to be like real work, a struggle for many. It is characterized by greater amounts of manipulative activities over longer periods of time, less developed pretend activities, little or no role-playing, and limited social interaction (Fewell & Kaminski, 1988; Rogers, 1988; Wehman, 1977). Thus, regarding the functions play serves in development, many young children with disabilities do not take part in play as an enjoyable activity, do not use play as an activity base for learning that would facilitate development, and do not use play to increase normalized interactions with caregivers and peers—issues that have guided questions for assessment and intervention.

Framing questions of assessment and intervention Two important purposes of assessment in serving children with disabilities—to assess for eligibility for services and to assess for intervention planning—guide the assessment of play and, accordingly, the selection of assessment instruments.

Eligibility In assessing for eligibility, many states require a determination of developmental delay, stated in terms of number of months or percentage of chronological age (see Chapter 1). For such questions, age equivalences are needed from an assessment. The advantage of using play to assess for eligibility is that it circumvents many of the problems with currently available standardized assessments of cognitive development: dependence on language for administration and dependence on elicited, in contrast to spontaneously occurring, behaviors. However, current play assessment instruments are not norm-referenced, and/or they have not been norm-referenced on a group of children with similar disabilities. Plans are under way, however, to standardize the Play Assessment Scale, which does provide age equivalences (Fewell, 1994).

Intervention Questions of assessment for intervention take a different focus; they center on regarding play as a curriculum of activities for young children within which various questions linking assessment to intervention can be addressed. Questions of intervention focus on the three functions of play in development: to serve as an enjoyable activity, to facilitate development, and to increase normalized interactions with caregivers and peers. The three functions can be described separately, but actually mutually influence one another in development. Descriptors of current level of performance regarding these goals may be conceptualized within a developmental framework and have to do with determining what the child knows, where the child is in the process of learning, and what the child may or may not be ready to learn in the near future.

Enjoyable activities One goal of intervention is to increase a child's repertoire of enjoyable activities. Here, current level of performance has to do with what the child is interested in or what the child spends the most time doing. This information is useful if you want to increase a child's repertoire of enjoyable activities and/or increase the time a child can spend independently engaged in play activities. The assessment of enjoyable activities is straightforward: It consists simply of the activities that children spend their time doing. A variety of measures of play activities will reveal the favored ones.

A potential problem with the straightforward assessment of enjoyable activities for some children with disabilities has to do with whether the children play at all and/or whether their play activities are intrinsically motivated. Intrinsic motivation is related to knowing about what can be done with objects; accordingly, the lack of play activity may be misinterpreted as lack of interest in the play materials.

Facilitation of development A second goal of intervention is to facilitate development, for which current level of performance is conceptualized in relation to a developmental framework. The assumption is that a child's current level of performance in play can be located at a certain point on a developmental continuum, and interventions can be designed to move him or her forward from that point. This requires procedures for determining what the child knows, what he or she is in the process of learning, and what the immediate next steps would be. Goals to facilitate development might include targeting activities the child is in the process of learning and those that would be next in the sequence, in contrast to activities the child already knows. Goals may also include shifting the relative proportion of categories of activities in relation to one another, decreasing the occurrence of relatively simple activities and increasing the occurrence of the developmentally more complex activities.

A related goal may be to increase a child's attention to play activities. As described by Ruff and Lawson (1990), developmental increases in sustained, focused attention are related to the increasing complexity required by the play activities. Their results suggest that increases in focused, as opposed to casual, attention are related to activities the child in is the process of learning, in contrast to those that have already been mastered.

Coordinated with the use of play to facilitate new learning about objects and events is using play to facilitate developments in language and social interaction. The descriptive studies of play demonstrated that developments in play were linked with developments in language and social competence. These results suggest that interventions in play, centered on teaching about objects and events, may also serve to facilitate developments in other domains. Such interventions, which take place in a social context, on an individual basis with a teacher or caregiver, or in the context of a group of peers, afford many opportunities for hearing about the objects and events of play and for sharing information about the objects and activities involved. Whether play activities the child knows or those he or she is in the process of learning best serve language and social goals awaits further research.

Increase opportunities for normalized interaction A third goal of intervention is to increase a child's opportunities for normalized interactions with caregivers and peers. For this purpose, activities are shifted away from play per se to an emphasis on the social activities that surround and take place in the context of play. This requires that the child know how to play at least at some level that can be sustained in a social context. Parten's (1932) play categories (presented in Table 14.3) are useful for such purposes. Current level of performance would focus on measuring the different categories of social interaction the child engages in, just as for the descriptive categories of play. Goals may include facilitating social interactions at the level higher than the child's predominant mode. What remains unspecified in current work is the interactive relationship between level of social interaction in play as a function of the child's level of competence in the play activities supporting the social interaction. It may be that relatively complex social interactions are supported by play actions that are well known by the child in contrast to play activities that he or she is in the process of learning.

SELECTED PLAY ASSESSMENT INSTRUMENTS

A brief description of three play assessment instruments is presented in relation to the central questions of assessment and intervention. They are also described according to their relevance to the key components of assessment presented in Chapter 3: family involvement, cross-disciplinary collaboration, and assessment in natural environments. Schaefer et al. (1991) includes a comprehensive review of play assessment instruments, although the assessments he reviewed are not traditionally those used in early childhood special education.

The Play Assessment Scale (PAS)

The Play Assessment Scale (PAS) developed by Rebecca Fewell (Fewell, 1994; Fewell & Rich, 1987) consists of a 45-item sequence that begins with activities that a 2-month-old child would perform (e.g., tracking objects) and goes through to activities at about the 36-month-old level (e.g., pretend play activities around object substitution). Some items appear in the play taxonomies presented in Table 14.1 (e.g., acts on self with 2 or 3 objects; makes doll act as though doll is able to perform actions independent of child). Other activities are derived from additional perceptually and cognitively based activities (e.g., holds, visually examines toys; purposely completes two-step problem-solving task for solution with novel toy).

The PAS may be administered by a parent, a teacher, a researcher, or other familiar adult in any comfortable setting. Approximately four of the eight specified sets of toys, selected according to the child's estimated age, are presented to the child under two conditions. The first concerns the assessment of spontaneously occurring play behaviors; the second is focused on the quality of the child's actions following verbal, physical, and a combination of verbal and physical prompts. Procedures include the determination of basal and ceiling scores.

A key factor in this assessment and others is that the behaviors of interest are not specific actions with specific toys, but a range of activities that provide evidence for knowledge of a particular category of perceptual or cognitive activity. Thus, activities with a variety of different toys could qualify for a positive response to a particular item on the scale, allowing for flexibility in administration, which is a definite advantage in a play context. The drawback is that the examiner needs to understand fully the nature of the activity being assessed so that examples of which activities qualify for passing an item can be readily identified.

The PAS includes the translation of a child's raw score on the assessment to a play age. Plans are under way to standardize this instrument (Fewell, 1994), which would make the PAS especially useful for establishing a norm-referenced play age and for capitalizing on the advantages of using a play assessment instrument to determine eligibility for services.

The PAS may be administered by a family member in a natural environment. The incorporation of cross-disciplinary collaboration is not specified, but it appears that the activities that take place in the assessment context would provide information for professionals from a variety of disciplines. While specific procedures for identifying goals for intervention are not provided, goals may be derived from a distinction among activities that the child does, those that he or she is learning to do, and those that are not being used by the child (Fewell & Rich, 1987).

Transdisciplinary Play-Based Assessment and Intervention

Linder has provided a comprehensive body of work surrounding transdisciplinary play-based assessment (TPBA) (Linder, 1993a) and transdisciplinary play-based intervention (TPBI) (Linder, 1993b). Much of it attends to the use of play activities to obtain assessment information from a variety of perspectives and then to develop intervention activities linked to the assessment goals, much like a curriculum-based approach. Linder (1993a) is careful, however, to distinguish the TPBA as a process assessment; it is not a standardized, norm-based assessment nor is it a checklist of developmental skills. It is heavily influenced by the developmental/cognitive theoretical framework.

While much of the TPBA system attends to play as a larger system for the assessment of developmental functioning, the chapter on "Observation of Cognitive Development" includes a section on categories of play. The taxonomies used for this purpose are presented in Table 14.4 and consist of four categories of actions on objects (i.e., exploratory or sensorimotor play, relational play, constructive play, and dramatic play), a games-with-rules category, and a rough-and-tumble play category. These categories were derived directly from the play taxonomies used in the descriptive studies.

Compared with several of the taxonomies presented in Table 14.1, the categories of play Linder uses are relatively broad. However, also included in the chapter "Observation of Cognitive Development" are sections for the assessment of attention span, early object use, symbolic and representational play, imitation, problem-solving approaches, discrimination/classification, one-to-one correspondence, sequencing ability, and drawing ability. Of these additional areas, early object use and symbolic and representational play are most relevant to the categories of play examined in the play studies. While Linder does not delineate specific subcategories for these domain areas, she provides descriptions of activities involving early object use (e.g., primary circular reactions; exploring characteristics of individual objects; combining schemes into relational play), play activities involving symbolic object use (e.g., pretend activities centered on one's own body versus those directed to others or to dolls), and symbolic play roles (e.g., making dolls enact various roles in play). Age correspondences are provided for many categories of activities.

The procedures of TPBA consist of six phases of flexibly administered unstructured and structured activities in which the child plays alone, with a parent/caregiver, and with a peer. TPBA may be administered by a family member and takes place in the natural environment of the classroom. The assessment system was specifically designed to be transdisciplinary.

In each section, links from assessment to intervention are suggested. For example, in the categories of play section, Linder (1993a) highlights the importance of observing the child's primary mode of play to understand developmental level, to identify a child's preferences, and to make recommendations for play activities at home. These suggestions appear to be in accord with increasing play as an enjoyable activity. At the same time, the examples she provides include facilitation of development (e.g., progress in language) as a result of facilitating play.

The TPBI (Linder, 1993b) was specifically designed to link assessment to intervention. Recommendations for intervention appear to be specifically designed for clinical situations and include facilitating the level of play observed in addition to encouraging a higher level of play. Intervention procedures consist of building on what the child initiates and/or modeling activities for the child to imitate. See McWilliam (1994) for a more detailed review of the Linder system.

The Developmental Play Assessment (DPA) Instrument

The Developmental Play Assessment (DPA) instrument (Lifter et al., 1988) consists of a developmental sequence of categories of play activities, which span the developmental period from 8 months to 6 years of age, and procedures for determining a child's current level of performance in that sequence. The sequence (presented in Table 14.4) was based on several descriptive studies of play among children with and without disabilities, with the categories

TABLE 14.4
Taxonomies Used in Play Assessment Instruments

Instrument	Categories
Developmental Play Assessment (DPA) Instrument Lifter, Edwards, Avery, Anderson, & Sulzer-Azaroff (1988) (see also Lifter et al., 1993)	Level and categories: I: **indiscriminative actions** no differentiation among objects (mouths all objects) II: **discriminative actions** actions specific to single objects (rolls ball; squeezes soft toy) III: **presentation** re-creation of presentation relations (reassembles set of nesting cups) **general combinations** general, container/contained relations (puts blocks and figures into box) **pretend self** pretend action to self ("eats" with spoon) IV: **specific physical** configuration respecting particular physical attributes (puts bead on string) V: **child as agent** extends action to doll or other (gives doll a drink from cup) **specific conventional** configuration respecting particular conventional attributes (puts cup on saucer; saws wood with saw) VI: **single scheme sequences** extends same action to two or more figures (brushes doll's hair, then own) **substitutions** uses one object to stand for another (puts bowl on head for a hat) VII: **doll as agent** attributes animacy to figure (moves driver doll to lift blocks into truck) **multischeme sequences** extends different but related actions to same figure (feeds and washes doll)

and order of emergence identified in Lifter and Bloom (1989) (see Table 14.1) forming the foundation for the sequence.

The procedures used in the DPA are based on procedures of behavioral assessment (Powers & Handleman, 1984) and parallel those used for naturalistic assessment of language (Bloom & Lahey, 1978; Lahey, 1988). They include the collection of a 30-minute videotaped sample of unstructured play in which the child plays sequentially with four groups of toys in the presence of an adult (e.g., teacher, researcher). The toys were selected based on their manipulative and pretend play possibilities. The adult does not direct the play, but is responsive to the child's initiations, comments descriptively on what the child does with the toys (e.g., "You have a cup," after the child

TABLE 14.4
Continued

Instrument	Categories
	VIII: **sociodramatic play** adopts familiar roles in play theme (plays house, assigning various roles) **thematic fantasy play** adopts roles of fantasy characters (plays super heroes, assigning various roles)
Transdisciplinary Play Based Assessment Linder (1993a)	• **exploratory or sensorimotor play** "play . . . for enjoyment of physical sensations . . . (repetitive motor movements such as pouring water in and out of containers . . . climbing up and down steps") • **relational play** use of objects for intended purposes (use of "brush for the hair . . . pumping the handle on a top") • **constructive play** creation of something with objects ("building a fence with blocks or making a face from clay") • **dramatic play** "involves the child pretending to do something or be someone . . . (drinks from a cup . . . brushes his or her teeth with a finger . . . has dolls pretend to feed the animals") • **games-with-rules play** involvement in "an activity with accepted rules or limits" that are either preset or made up • **rough-and-tumble play** "boisterous and physical" play ("can include such things as running, hopping, tickling, playful 'punching,' or rolling around on the floor")
Ruff & Lawson (1990)	**Focused attention** "duration of time the infant looks at the object and simultaneously engages in some deliberate manipulation of it" • turning the object around; • fingering surfaces and details of the object

Note: The categories presented here were taken directly from the published versions of the assessment instruments. In each case, the categories were derived from previous descriptive studies, and their origins are listed in the published reports.

picks up a cup), and repeats what the child says (child says "dog" while pointing to a puzzle piece, the adult says "Yes, that's a dog").

The DPA can easily be adapted so that a family member can administer the assessment. The basic requirement is that the adult does not model or prompt any activities, but is responsive to the child's initiations. The assessment takes place in a natural environment (i.e., the child's home or classroom). While not systematized at this point for cross-disciplinary collaboration, the DPA allows for evaluation from several different perspectives (i.e., language, social, motor) because of the natural inclusion of communicative, social-interactive, and motoric behaviors in the videotape.

The play sample is coded in a three-step process. First, the videotaped observation is examined to note the occurrence and frequency of discrete play behaviors (e.g., child places one nesting cup into another; child extends spoon to a doll's mouth). Second, the data are reorganized into categories of activities, according to the definitions presented in Table 14.4. At this point, particular attention is paid to (a) the number of different play activities that represent a particular category (e.g., putting a puzzle piece into the puzzle frame and nesting the cups are two different types of "presentation" activities), and (b) the frequency of each play action (e.g., the child's putting a puzzle piece into the puzzle six times yields a frequency of six for that exemplar of "presentation" activities).

The final step is a determination of the child's current level of performance in play, described in terms of mastery, emergence, or absence, and defined according to the number of types and frequency of play activities that fall within the category. *Mastery* is defined as the occurrence of at least four different types of that category of activity, with an overall frequency of at least 10 for the combined types. Mastery is required for progress through the developmental sequence and is assumed to be a measure of what the child knows. *Emergence,* which is defined as the occurrence of at least two different exemplars from a category, with an overall frequency of at least four activities for the category, is assumed to be a measure of what the child is in the process of learning. *Absence* is defined as fewer than two different exemplars of a category, and, depending upon placement in the developmental sequence, indicates activities that are the "next step" for an intervention or that await further learning.

An initial validation study with three preschoolers with developmental disabilities contrasted their acquisition and generalization of developmentally appropriate (DA) compared with age appropriate (AA) play activities (Lifter, Sulzer-Azaroff, Anderson, & Cowdery, 1993). For this early study, the DA activities identified with the DPA were defined as those that were absent but were the next step beyond mastered and emergent activities in the developmental sequence. The contrasting AA activities, which were derived from samples of play from the children's nondisabled peers, represented a category of play more advanced than the DA activities. The results demonstrated faster acquisition and greater generalization for the DA play activities, in contrast to the AA play activities, providing preliminary support for the identification of play activities based on developmental readiness.

In a second related study, only DA activities were taught to preschoolers with autism and autistic-like behaviors, but two different teaching methods were used (Lifter, Anderson, Sulzer-Azaroff, Burger, & Campbell, 1994). The children learned the targeted play activities regardless of the method used, providing additional support for using the DPA to identify play objectives for intervention.

Ongoing intervention studies from this research group, entitled PROJECT PLAY,[1] are centered on (a) determining which levels of performance in play (i.e., mastered, emergent, next step) best support specific goals of intervention, and (b) the impact of learning to play on progress in other developmental domains (e.g., language, social interaction). Plans are under way for the development of a simplified, but more structured, version of the DPA, negating the need to videotape the behaviors. The disadvantage will be the lack of a permanent record to examine play in relation to competence in language and social interaction. Currently, activities used to address the intervention targets are generated through exam-

[1]PROJECT PLAY: Using Play to Teach About Objects, Events, and Language is supported by the U.S. Department of Education, Office of Special Education Programs (US#H023A30050).

ples of the different categories of play activities. To systematize the link between assessment and intervention, a companion curriculum of play activities is being developed.

Play Curricula

A number of commercially produced curricula are currently available that include sets of activities centered on play and procedures for tracking a child's progress in those activities. These curricula tend to be based on skills derived from either norm-referenced developmental assessment instruments, such as the Bayley Scales of Infant Development (Bayley, 1969), or from a variety of criterion-referenced instruments; they usually are not linked to a research base about play. These curricula are useful in supporting play as an enjoyable activity and in increasing normalized interactions with caregivers and peers. Their specific roles in facilitating development are less clear. The advantages of the play assessment instruments described earlier center on their relationship to a large research base about what children with and without disabilities do when they play, how what they do changes over time, and how these changes are related to progress in language and social interaction. They provide a developmental coherence and an important basis of validity to play activities that may be used to inform assessment and intervention in play. Much still needs to be done, however, in documenting the success of play interventions and the links of those successes to particular assessment and intervention activities.

CURRENT AND FUTURE DIRECTIONS IN PLAY ASSESSMENT AND INTERVENTION

Assessment

Current directions Instruments assessing play are currently used to determine eligibility for services and to develop goals for intervention. These instruments, which are informed by a research base grounded in developmental theory, constitute informal assessment instruments, although the PAS should be available in a standardized form in the near future (Fewell, 1994). The informality of the instruments, however, allows for assessment of spontaneously occurring behaviors in a natural environment, the inclusion of family members in the assessment process, and, in a number of cases, cross-disciplinary collaboration, all factors that have emerged as recommended practices in the assessment of young children (see Chapter 3). While formal data are not available at present, validity is generated through the links each instrument has to the descriptive studies of play.

Limitations and future directions

There are several limitations to the current assessment instruments. First, the taxonomies and sequences of activities forming the basis for an assessment rest on the quality of the descriptive studies on which they were based and their theoretical underpinnings. While the descriptive studies were undertaken with rigor and detail, they were developed within the developmental/cognitive theoretical framework and generally did not take into account the role of culture in play development. Consequently, there is a need for a new wave of descriptive studies. Because much contemporary work in children's play is centered on the convergence and mutual influence of the clinical/psychoanalytic and the developmental/cognitive approaches in understanding children's play activities (Bloom, 1993; Lifter, in press; Slade & Wolf, 1994), new descriptive studies should be undertaken within this integrative framework. Further, in developing taxonomies of children's play activities, it is important to sort out which kinds of activities are universal to all children and which kinds of activities may be culture-specific. Certainly, as children learn to talk about what they are doing with caregivers and peers, the symbolic and conventional activities that are influenced by culture will influence the nature of play activities demonstrated. Descriptive studies and the assessments derived from them would be enhanced with consideration of the interaction of personal, familial, societal, and cultural factors in development, as in an ecological model (Vazquez Nuttall, 1992).

Second, the contexts in which play assessments take place should be expanded. Linder's (1993a) assessment is unique in including a peer. Since goals of intervention include increasing normalized interactions with peers, assessment in play should include play with the child's peers.

Because links to intervention goals are central to the usefulness of assessing play skills, assessment instruments should specify what those connections are. Specific links from assessment to intervention goals are offered in the Developmental Play Assessment (DPA) instrument (Lifter et al., 1988), but these links are presented more generally in the other instruments described (Fewell & Rich, 1987; Linder, 1993a). At the same time, evidence supporting the links of assessment to intervention goals that can be, and are, acquired and generalized is clearly needed, and, at present, is in short supply.

Intervention

Current directions Studies centered on interventions in play have been mixed regarding their links to various assessment instruments. One line of investigation, derived from the behavioral/interventionist tradition, has centered on teaching toy play activities to children with developmental disabilities to provide an activity that competes with the occurrence of maladaptive behaviors (Eason, White, & Newsom, 1982; Favell, 1973; Koegel, 1974; Murphy, Calias, & Carr, 1985; Murphy, Carr, & Calias, 1986; Wehman, 1975) or to increase levels of appropriate play (Haring, 1985). These studies have demonstrated considerable success in increasing children's toy play repertoires. The selection of target play activities was not linked to a specific developmental assessment of play but, in general, to choosing appealing or specifically designed toys.

A second line of investigation, which was undertaken within the developmental/cognitive tradition (Smilansky, 1968, 1990), centered on interventions in sociodramatic play for children from economically disadvantaged families and documented the effect of such interventions on success in school (Smilansky, 1990). Positive effects included better verbal skills and increases in interactive play for the participating children. Smilansky concluded that these changes were a function of appropriate adult intervention in children's play. She also expressed dismay that despite the positive nature of the foregoing results as a function of intervention, teachers in early childhood settings noted that they do not intervene in children's play.

A third and more recent line of investigation has attempted to integrate information on changes in play from the developmental/cognitive tradition with procedures of teaching from the behavioral/interventionist tradition. Children's developmental levels in play (i.e., current level of performance) were taken into account in the selection of target play activities (Goldstein & Cisar, 1992; Kim, Lombardino, Rothman, & Vinson, 1989; Lifter et al., 1994; Lifter et al., 1993), or minimum levels of competence in language were required for instruction in symbolic or sociodramatic play (Stahmer, 1995; Thorp, Stahmer, & Schreibman, 1995). Related studies have identified differences in success rates in learning specific categories of play as a function of children's mental ages (Murphy et al., 1985). Kim et al. (1989) selected symbolic play activities to teach to children with mental retardation on the basis of activities that were slightly more advanced than those observed in baseline, matched against a derived developmental sequence. Their results supported increases in the quantity and quality of symbolic play activities as a result of their intervention. In the Lifter et al. 1993 and 1994 studies, the play activities taught to preschoolers with developmental disabilities were derived explicitly from the DPA tool and were identified as activities the children were ready to learn (e.g., activities at the emergent or next step absent level). The results support the usefulness of integrating developmental readiness with behavioral/intervention procedures in the design of play intervention programs.

Limitations and future directions

There are several limitations of current intervention studies leading to directions for future research. First, more empirical studies are needed to document the effectiveness of linking assessment in play to benefits from a play intervention program. In that regard, the play activities targeted for intervention need to be tied with increased specificity about the child's current level of performance in those activities (e.g., mastery, emergence, next-step level).

Second, future intervention studies need to examine and document the impact of learning to play on other developmental domains (i.e., language and social development). If interventions in play serve to facilitate development, empirical evidence is needed to document increases in a child's knowledge of objects and events, as well as impacts of play interventions on other developmental domains (e.g., language and social interactions).

Third, studies examining interventions in play, including those that use play in the service of goals in language and social interaction, should take into account the covariation among play, language, and social interactions in development. It may be that relatively complex social interactions or language functions are supported by play activities that are well known by the child (i.e., mastered activities) in contrast to those that the child is in the process of learning. The nature of such interactions and their implications for intervention await further research.

Finally, family members need to be consulted in the play activities targeted for intervention. Goals of intervention in play, just like any goals of intervention, need to be determined in the context of the needs and desires of the family and their larger sociocultural system.

SUMMARY OF KEY CONCEPTS

- Assessment and intervention of play depends on whether play is viewed broadly as an activity for asking assessment questions and implementing interventions or in a more circumscribed manner as a window to children's knowledge of objects and events. The latter theme is adopted in this chapter.
- Definitions of play center on children being actively engaged in spontaneous activities that appear to be intrinsically motivated. A fundamental assumption is that it is children's knowledge and not the nature of play materials that directs the quality of their play.
- Descriptive studies of play were based on analyses of naturalistic samples of spontaneous play activities that were categorized, measured, and arranged into developmental sequences.
- Descriptive studies produced taxonomies of play activities that were later used in various assessment instruments and revealed developmental relationships among play, language, and social development.
- The purpose of the assessment (i.e., determining eligibility or planning services) guides the selection of play assessment instruments.

- Intervention in play focuses on three functions of play: (a) to serve as an enjoyable activity, (b) to facilitate development, and (c) to increase normalized interactions with caregivers and peers.
- Children's current levels of performance in play can be categorized in three descriptions: (a) what the child knows, (b) what the child is in the process of learning, and (c) what the child may or may not be ready to learn in the near future.
- The advantages of play assessment include measuring spontaneously occurring behaviors in the natural environments, the inclusion of family members in the assessment process, and cross-disciplinary collaboration. Limitations include a dearth of information on the role of culture in play and a limited knowledge base of the links from assessment to intervention in play.
- The advantages of intervention in play include its pervasiveness in the lives of young children and its links to developments in language and social interaction. Studies are needed to examine the impact of learning to play on developments in knowledge of objects and events and on other developmental domains.

REFERENCES

Axline, V. M. (1947). *Play therapy.* Cambridge, MA: Riverside Press.

Bayley, N. (1969). *Bayley Scales of Infant Development.* New York: The Psychological Corp.

Beeghly, M., Weiss-Perry, B., & Cicchetti, D. (1990). Beyond sensorimotor functioning: Early communicative and play development of children with Down syndrome. In D. Cicchetti & M. Beeghly (Eds.), *Children with Down syndrome: A developmental perspective* (pp. 329–368). Cambridge, England: Cambridge University Press.

Belsky, J., & Most, R. K. (1981). From exploration to play: A cross-sectional study of infant free play behavior. *Developmental Psychology, 17,* 630–639.

Bloom, L. (1993). *The transition from infancy to language: Acquiring the power of expression.* New York: Cambridge University Press.

Bloom, L., & Lahey, M. (1978). *Language development and language disorders.* New York: John Wiley.

Bloom, L., Lifter, K., & Broughton, J. (Eds.). (1985). *The emergence of early cognition and language in the second year of life.* New York: John Wiley.

Bredekamp, S. (1987). *Developmentally appropriate practice in early childhood programs serving children birth through age 8.* Washington, DC: National Association for the Education of Young Children.

Bredekamp, S. (1993). The relationship between early childhood education and early childhood special education: Healthy marriage or family feud? *Topics in Early Childhood Special Education, 13*(3), 258–273.

Bretherton, I. (1984). *Symbolic play.* Orlando, FL: Academic Press.

Bricker, D., & Cripe, J. J. W. (1992). *An activity-based approach to early intervention.* Baltimore, MD: Paul H. Brookes.

Eason, L. J., White, M. J., & Newsom, C. (1982). Generalized reduction of self-stimulatory behavior: An effect of teaching appropriate play to autistic children. *Analysis & Intervention in Developmental Disabilities, 2,* 157–169.

Elkind, D. (1990). Academic pressures—Too much, too soon: The demise of play. In E. Klugman & S. Smilansky (Eds.), *Children's play and learning* (p. 15). New York: Teachers College Press.

Erikson, E. H. (1950). *Childhood and society.* New York: Norton.

Favell, J. (1973). Reduction of stereotypes by reinforcement of toy play. *Mental Retardation, 11*(4), 21–23.

Fein, G. G. (1981). Pretend play in childhood: An integrative review. *Child Development, 52,* 1095–1118.

Fenson, L., Kagan, J., Kearsley, R. B., & Zelazo, P. R. (1976). The developmental progression of manipulative play in the first two years. *Child Development, 47,* 232–236.

Fenson, L., & Ramsay, D. (1980). Decentration and integration of the child's play in the second year. *Child Development, 51,* 171–178.

Fewell, R. (1994, December). *Play assessment workshop.* Presented at International Conference on Young Children with Special Needs, St. Louis, MO.

Fewell, R. R., & Kaminski, R. (1988). Play skills development and instruction for young children with handicaps. In S. L. Odom & M. B. Karnes (Eds.), *Early intervention for infants and children with handicaps: An empirical base* (pp. 145–158). Baltimore, MD: Paul H. Brookes.

Fewell, R. R., & Rich, J. S. (1987). Play assessment as a procedure for examining cognitive, communication, and social skills in multihandicapped children. *Journal of Psychoeducational Assessment, 2,* 107–118.

Field, T., Roseman, S., DeStefano, L., & Koewler, J. (1982). The play of handicapped and nonhandicapped children in integrated and nonintegrated situations. *Topics in Early Childhood Special Education, 2*(3), 28–38.

Fox, L., & Hanline, M. F. (1993). A preliminary evaluation of learning within developmentally appropriate early childhood settings. *Topics in Early Childhood Special Education, 13*(3), 308–327.

Fraiberg, S. (1977). *Insights from the blind.* New York: Basic Books.

Freud, A. (1965). *Normality and pathology in childhood.* New York: International Universities Press.

Garvey, C. (1977). *Play.* Cambridge, MA: Harvard University Press.

Goldstein, H., & Cisar, C. L. (1992). Promoting interaction during sociodramatic play: Teaching scripts to preschoolers and classmates with disabilities. *Journal of Applied Behavior Analysis, 25,* 265–280.

Guralnick, M. J., & Groom, J. M. (1987). Dyadic peer interactions of mildly delayed and nonhandicapped preschool children. *American Journal of Mental Deficiency, 92*(2), 178–193.

Haring, T. G. (1985). Teaching between-class generalization of toy play behavior to handicapped children. *Journal of Applied Behavior Analysis, 18,* 127–139.

Hart, B., & Risley, T. (1968). Establishing use of descriptive adjectives in the spontaneous speech of disadvantaged preschool children. *Journal of Applied Behavior Analysis, 1,* 109–120.

Hart, B., & Risley, T. (1975). Incidental teaching of language in the pre-school. *Journal of Applied Behavior Analysis, 8,* 411–420.

Hill, P., & McCune-Nicolich, L. (1981). Pretend play and patterns of cognition in Down's syndrome children. *Child Development, 52,* 611–617.

Kennedy, M. D., Sheridan, M. K., Radlinski, S. H., & Beeghly, M. (1991). Play-language relationships in young children with developmental delays: Implications for assessment. *Journal of Speech & Hearing Research, 34,* 112–122.

Kim, Y. T., Lombardino, L. J., Rothman, H., & Vinson, B. (1989). Effects of symbolic play intervention with children who have mental retardation. *Mental Retardation, 27*(3), 159–165.

Klein, M. (1955). The psychoanalytic play technique. *American Journal of Orthopsychiatry, 25,* 223–237.

Koegel, R. (1974). Increasing spontaneous play by suppressing self-stimulation in autistic children. *Journal of Applied Behavior Analysis, 7,* 521–528.

Kopp, C. (1983). Risk factors in development. In M. Haith & J. Campos (Eds.), *Infancy and the biology of development* (pp. 1081–1188). New York: John Wiley.

Lahey, M. (1988). *Language disorders and language development.* New York: Macmillan.

Lifter, K. (1992). Delays and differences in the development of preschool children. In E. V. Nuttall, I. Romero, & J. Kalesnik (Eds.), *Assessing and screening preschoolers: Psychological and educational dimensions.* Boston: Allyn and Bacon.

Lifter, K. (in press). Review of *Children at play: Clinical and developmental approaches to meaning and representation* (A. Slade & D. P. Wolf, Eds. New York: Oxford University Press, 1994.) *Contemporary Psychology.*

Lifter, K., Anderson, S. R., Sulzer-Azaroff, B., Burger, J., & Campbell, S. (1994). *Joining in the fun: Facilitating acquisition and generalization of sim-*

CHAPTER

15

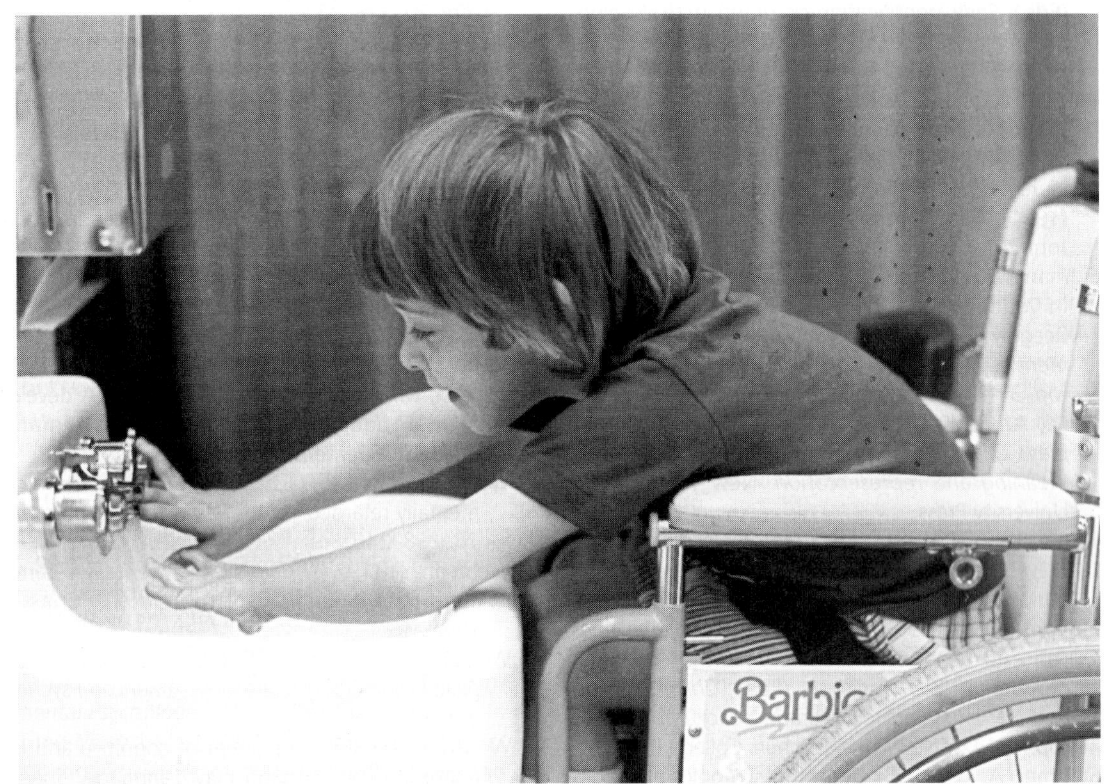

Assessing Adaptive Behavior

Eva M. Horn
Amy Childre
Peabody College of Vanderbilt University

The ways in which young children complete tasks that reflect chronological-age group expectations can be broadly conceptualized as adaptive behavior. Identification of levels of adaptive development in young children is important for two distinct reasons. Adaptive development is one of the five areas used to determine if a child can be labeled developmentally delayed (the other four are cognitive, physical, communication, and social-emotional development) (Individuals with Disabilities Education Amendment, 1991). Second, identification of specific strengths and needs as well as a comprehensive view of the child's status in adaptive development can help to guide program planning. This chapter describes (a) the rationale for assessing development in this domain; (b) critical dimensions of adaptive development in the early childhood years, including a definition and subdomains representative of the area; (c) procedural considerations in identifying the child's developmental status in terms of adaptive behavior; (d) methods of assessment; and (e) information on using assessment data for planning instruction.

RATIONALE FOR INCLUSION OF ADAPTIVE BEHAVIOR ASSESSMENT

Adaptive behavior is a concept that has held a critical role in assessment of persons with disabilities for many years (Harrison, 1987). This role is particularly evident in the area of eligibility evaluation. The assessment of adaptive behavior is generally required before an individual may be classified as having mental retardation and, increasingly, before other disabilities are diagnosed (Frankenberger, 1984). The inclusion of adaptive behavior as a criterion for defining developmental disability marked a pronounced shift in societal attitudes and values concerning mental impairment (Brown & Snell, 1993). This new view required the assessment to include measures that gave a clearer view of an individual's capabilities by including functioning under realistic situational demands. The shift reflects a more practical approach to the education of persons with disabilities. With adaptive behavior rather than I.Q. as a primary measure of competence, the focus for education becomes the acquisition of skills that will ensure functioning across appropriate environments and the provision of support or adaptations to ensure success (Luckasson et al., 1992).

In the field of early childhood special education, the broader concept of adaptive behavior has been less evident, particularly in intervention planning. Narrower definitions and terms like *self-care* or *self-help skills* are typically used. For example, many early intervention curricula (e.g., Hawaii Early Learning Profile and Activities, Furuno et al., 1979; The Carolina Curriculum for Preschoolers with Special Needs, Johnson-Martin, Attermeier, & Hacker, 1990) and texts (e.g., Allen & Hart, 1984; Bailey & Wolery, 1992) include a self-care domain rather than an adaptive behavior domain. In Part H of P.L. 99-457 (The Infant/Toddler Programs of the Education for All Handicapped Children Act of 1986) self-help was included as an area of development for both assessment and intervention. With the 1991 amendments (P.L. 102-119, Individuals with Disabilities Education Act), the term was changed to *adaptive development.* A broad definition should be applied. Adaptive behavior as a curriculum domain should include skills that reflect chronologically age-appropriate skills for meeting the demands of the child's multiple unique environments.

Several rationales for including adaptive behavior in early childhood curricula can be offered. First and foremost, independent participation in normal environments is an anticipated outcome of early intervention (Bailey & Wolery, 1992; Peterson, 1987). Children who can dress, feed, and toilet themselves are obviously more independent than children who cannot. Similarly, children's acquisition of these skills should decrease caregiving demands. All children require caregiving, but a child with disabilities may have more intense and enduring needs (Dyson & Fewell, 1986). Further, many of the behaviors defined as adaptive, such as social adjustment and personal/social responsibility, address important socially acceptable behaviors. Acquisition of these skills results in a child appearing more normal, thus promoting meaningful inclusion in community settings.

Some characteristics of adaptive behaviors also provide logical support for their place in early childhood curricula. Many adaptive behaviors are acquired during early childhood; mastery of these skills is part of daily routines for all children. In addition, the development of these skills takes a long time and reflects a hierarchical sequence of simple to complex. For example, the skill area of eating may proceed as follows: smoothly sucks from nipple, pulls food off spoon with lips, feeds self finger foods, scoops food from dish with spoon, and finally uses appropriate mealtime behaviors, including social graces.

Many adaptive behaviors are visible skills (e.g., putting on clothing, using the toilet, occupying oneself) and their acquisition is obvious. Attainment of these adaptive behaviors may have an immediate, concrete impact, particularly from the family's perspective. Other skills are related to safety issues, such as appropriate behaviors on trips into the community with family or other adults (e.g., holding the adult's hand when walking across the street). A few skills may even have an immediate economic benefit. For example, toileting and eating regular food eliminates the need for the more expensive infant diapers and foods.

A final rationale for the inclusion of the adaptive behavior domain is the impact of independent functioning on the child's sense of competence and self-concept. Consider the sense of personal accomplishment embodied by a toddler proudly proclaiming, "I did it!" upon pulling off his or her shirt or other article of clothing. This image illustrates the tremendous impact mastery of these skills can have on a child's sense of self-worth. Conversely, lack of independence may lead to learned helplessness and passivity (Seligman, 1975).

CRITICAL DIMENSIONS OF ADAPTIVE BEHAVIOR DEVELOPMENT

Adaptive behavior is a dynamic construct, influenced by cultural norms and age-related expectations (Horn & Fuchs, 1987). The construct emphasizes the capacity to respond to demands of the immediate environment and the community. A person judged as "adaptive" in one setting (community) may not necessarily be evaluated similarly in another place. The nature of these demands also changes as an individual progresses through the life cycle. For the young child, adaptive behavior encompasses skills such as walking, talking, and basic self-care. For the school-age child, it reflects the capacity to understand and respond appropriately to the social rules of various settings, including school, community, and home. For the adult, adaptive behavior includes the ability to hold a job, maintain a residence, contribute to family life, and so forth. Adaptive behaviors at one developmental level are qualitatively different from those at another level. In short, adaptive behavior is relative and dynamic, rather than absolute and static (Horn & Fuchs, 1987).

Defining Adaptive Behavior for the Early Childhood Years

Any definition of adaptive behavior must take the perspective of not considering it a single entity but a composite of a wide range of abilities that are dependent on one's age, environment, and cultural group at any moment (Luckasson et al., 1992). The Task Force on

Recommended Practices of the Division for Early Childhood (DEC) of the Council for Exceptional Children (CEC) provided the following definition of adaptive behavior from an early childhood perspective:

> Adaptive behavior consists of changes in children's behavior as a consequence of maturation, development and learning to meet increasing demands of multiple environments. Independent functioning in these environments is the long-term goal. Instruction requires accommodating and adapting to support the specific strengths of individual children. Comprehensive intervention should address the following subdomains: self-care, community self-sufficiency, personal-social responsibility, and social adjustment. (DEC Task Force on Recommended Practices, 1993 p. 89)

Each of these subdomains can be further specified, in terms of the expectations in the early childhood years. In early childhood, the self-care subdomain addresses dressing/undressing, eating/feeding, toileting, and grooming (e.g., handwashing, facewashing, toothbrushing). These sets of skills make up the abilities needed for independent functioning in relation to basic needs such as food and warmth. Community self-sufficiency refers to skills that promote age and culturally appropriate functioning with adult supervision in community environments such as restaurants, neighborhoods, and recreational areas. For example, the child might sit quietly through a religious service, occupying herself in a quiet activity and requesting only minimal attention from her parents. Basic skills in personal/social responsibility include basic environmental interactions, self-directed behaviors, independent play/self-occupation, peer cooperation and interaction, and the assumption of responsibility (e.g., demonstrates caution, avoids dangers). Finally, the subdomain of social adjustment includes behaviors such as the ability to adjust to new situations, regularity of behavior patterns (e.g., eating, sleeping), general disposition, tendency to stick to tasks despite obstacles, attention span and degree of distractibility, and amount of stimulation necessary to evoke a response.

Although this chapter focuses on the assessment of adaptive skills, it is clear that these skills are highly related to other areas of development. For example, acceptable eating behaviors include a variety of social and communication skills as well as the more obvious gross and fine motor skills. Further, critical skills of several of the subdomains are directly addressed in other developmental domains. For example, peer cooperation and interaction, a component of the personal/social responsibility subdomain, is clearly an important skill area in the social development domain. An implication of this overlap is not to remove it from consideration in adaptive behavior assessment but rather to highlight the importance of conducting comprehensive assessments that do not artificially splinter skills into measurable units. In beginning the assessment process with any child, the whole child perspective must always be kept at the forefront of our efforts.

Characteristics and Implications for Assessment

Certain characteristics of adaptive behavior have implications for the assessment process. Since adaptive behaviors are tied to the context in which they are used and focused on performance over time rather than one-time performance, more indirect measurement methods are used. Unlike standardized tests that an evaluator conducts in a test session with a child, many adaptive behavior assessments rely on information from an informant, usually a primary adult or caregiver who is familiar with the child's typical behaviors in multiple real-life settings (Sattler, 1992).

With adaptive behavior, a child's ability to perform a particular skill is insufficient if he or she fails to use the skill as needed. For example, the preschool child may be able to furnish his or her first and last name and street address in opening circle, but, when lost, may not be able to respond to the question "Where do you live?" To detect this an evaluator might need to directly observe the child for an extended period of time. Therefore, in place of direct observation in every setting, evaluators rely on multiple methods and multiple informants in a true team effort. The following sections provide more detailed examples of the link between adaptive behavior characteristics and assessment.

Contextual nature of adaptive behaviors As previously stated, adaptive behavior relates to the "fit" of the child within and across settings. That is, can the child meet the demands of the many current and future settings he or she encounters? The behaviors used to assess competence in adaptive behavior at a specific chronological age are identified from an analysis of the unique needs and lifestyle of the child and his or her family, peers, and community. Similarly, adaptive behaviors are typically a part of regularly occurring events that focus on socially prescribed habitual behaviors (e.g., which food requires the use of utensils in eating and which utensil). This requires that the child learn the cultural expectations of self-care and self-sufficiency necessary in group settings inside and outside the home. Exactly what skills are learned is determined by the culture of the subsettings in which the family and the child participate on a regular basis. Finally, there is significant variance in normal developmental sequences with heavy cultural influence (e.g., movement from breast milk or formula to solid food has varied across generations, regions, and/or nationalities from as early as 6 weeks to as late as 2 years).

An implication of the contextual nature of adaptive behaviors is that the members of the assessment team must develop a broad picture of the child's everyday contexts, including specific family, cultural, and community expectations for adaptive competence for his or her chronological age group. Families tend to be the primary facilitators of learning in many environments and activities in which young children participate on a daily basis (e.g., home, community, mealtimes, bathing, dressing) (Shelton, Jeppson, & Johnson, 1987). The young child's acquisition of adaptive behaviors is embedded in the family's routines and their expectations. Further, since family members usually provide the most consistent support over time and have the broadest and most continuous picture, it follows that they should best know their child's strengths and needs that impact his or her fit in and across settings. In addition to providing valuable information, they can validate information collected from other sources. Interviews and discussions with the family can be particularly valuable, in that they provide an opportunity for parents to indicate the adaptive behaviors they consider to be instructional priorities. Thus, they should be the primary source for identification of skills, priorities, and contexts for assessment and subsequent intervention. (See the section on assessment planning in Chapter 3 for further information.)

Adaptive development in the early childhood years As noted earlier, adaptive behaviors are acquired throughout the early childhood years. Within each of the subdomains, acquisition represents a hierarchical sequence from simple to complex. This sequence typically reflects changes in the amount of adult support needed and the efficiency of completing the task. For example, in feeding, initially the infant is totally dependent on the adult to obtain nutrition and is relatively slow in sucking the liquid from the nipple; he or she rapidly gains independence in latching onto the nipple and more efficiently sucking while maintaining a faster pace and losing less liquid. This development of greater independence continues, with the preschooler being able to pour milk from a pitcher (as long as it is not too full) into a glass with minimal spillage.

This characteristic has three implications for the assessment team. First, members must be competent in assessing skills across the full early childhood age range. Second, members of the team must be knowledgeable of normal development sequences. Further, they need to understand the significant variations in normal developmental sequences and the heavy cultural influence across generations, regions, and/or nationalities on these time frames. Finally, because independence and efficiency are heavily influenced by opportunities for repeated practice, the evaluator needs to be able to determine the probable cause of the absence of a skill. For example, does the child fail to score on "uses fork" because she does not have the fine motor coordination to handle the task or is it because she has had limited exposure both at home and in preschool?

Low-frequency behaviors Some important adaptive behavior skills are used with relatively low frequency; nevertheless, these skills must become habitual to be truly functional. That is, they must be performed fluently in response to natural cues, maintained by natural consequences, and performed in varied settings and circumstances. This implies that the early childhood professional may need to change the traditional assessment and instruction contexts to reflect the diversity of settings in which the skills naturally occur (e.g., home, community, preschool). In addition, the assessment team may need to adapt their schedules in order to increase the opportunities for observing these skills within the context of routines. Children must be given real-life opportunities to demonstrate habitual, generalized responses to natural cues provided across multiple current and future environments. The assessment team must not only assess presence or absence of the adaptive behavior skill but also fluency, generalization, and maintenance. This characteristic highlights the importance of eliciting input from the family since they can provide information that cannot be collected easily through direct observation or testing (Turnbull & Turnbull, 1990).

Chains of physiological and learned behaviors Many adaptive behaviors require physiological maturity and learned behavior (e.g., feeding skills, toileting). These skills are not discrete behaviors but rather a sequence of behaviors that result in a complex function (e.g., toileting requires the physiological ability to hold and release urine, going to the toilet, removing clothing, sitting, etc.). The assessment team must be skilled in analyzing the component parts of complex skills and appropriately assessing the child's current developmental and physiological status in relation to each of these component parts. They must first determine if the required physiological components are present (e.g., equilibrium responses to maintain relaxed sitting on the toilet seat). If they are absent, the team should determine if adaptations can be provided that will bypass the component (e.g., adaptive positioning device) or if strategies can be developed to allow the child to learn to perform the component (e.g., intervention for teaching equilibrium responses).

Summary Adaptive behaviors are important skills for children to learn. The specific characteristics of these skills require consideration in the assessment of current functioning and future needs (Luckasson et al., 1992). First, skill levels should be determined in the context of natural environments typical of the individual's age group. Second, assessment must consider and make necessary adaptations for diversity in language or culture and for limitations and/or challenges. Third, strengths and limitations may coexist even within a single adaptive area for the young child. Finally, gains in quality of life and independence in functioning generally occur for persons with disabilities when they are provided with appropriate supports over time.

PROCEDURES FOR ASSESSING ADAPTIVE BEHAVIOR DEVELOPMENT

This section includes the following segments: (a) discussion of multiple data collection methods; (b) summary of specific instruments available for assessing adaptive behaviors; and (c) specific assessment issues relevant to each of the subdomains. This last segment includes examples of the range of skills within each subdomain as well as specific recommended practices for assessing these subdomains.

Data Collection Methods

As mentioned earlier, more indirect strategies are used as the primary method of data collection in assessing adaptive behavior development. Rather than conducting direct testing, observations in natural contexts and interviews with significant adults are the primary sources of information. There are several approaches to determining what to ask or what to look for, including developmental scales, criterion-referenced lists, and ecological inventory methods.

Developmental scales Developmental scales are based on the normal sequence of development. Skills are sequenced according to the age at which they are acquired by typically developing children. There are several advantages to using these scales for assessing adaptive development in young children. Developmental test items are written in observable terms, aiding in the reliable determination of the presence or absence of the skill. The scales can also be re-administered periodically as a measure of child change.

Since skills are listed in chronological order, they may provide information for determining the next skill to teach; the item following the last item passed in a subdomain becomes the target for instruction. These scales also provide extensive listings of skills within the various subdomains, reducing the risk of overlooking an important skill. The developmental age equivalents provided for clusters of skills assist teachers in determining whether skills targeted for intervention are developmentally appropriate given the child's chronological age. For example, the teacher of an 18-month-old toddler would recognize that it is not developmentally appropriate to expect the child to eat her peas with a fork. Finally, because developmental sequences across various domains are familiar to many disciplines, they may facilitate communication between disciplines.

There are, however, some potential problems associated with using developmental scales, particularly in the area of adaptive development. An obvious one that has already been noted is the significant variation in developmental sequelae of some skills due to the current tendency toward child rearing from a cultural, geographic, and generational perspective. Further, some adaptive behaviors appearing on developmental scales may be irrelevant in certain populations. An obvious example would be the use of a fork for a child living in China. For a child with specific sensory or motor disabilities, developmental items may need to be adapted so that the disability does not prevent assessment of the specific skill of interest.

Other disadvantages relate to the use of the information obtained. Skills within and across subdomains may be seen in isolation. For example, the visual skill "scans objects," which is often assessed using the red ring, takes on more meaning in the context of scanning to find your toothbrush. Similarly, the purpose for including certain elements may not be obvious. Some items are listed on developmental scales because of their high reliability at certain ages (White, 1985). For example, the item "separates easily from caregiver," which is often included in the social adjustment subdomain, is not intended to address a lack of attachment by the child but rather the child's ability to handle transitions and to self-regulate. Further, the assumption is often made that if the item is on an assessment it must be meaningful for instruction. For example, the 3-month item "roots toward food or object infrequently" (Johnson-Martin, Jens, Attermeier, & Hacker, 1991) does not readily translate into an objective. The sequences of items on many scales may not be the best teaching sequences, especially for children with sensory and motor disabilities. For example, a child with a vision impairment would not necessarily go from "chews with a rotary/side-to-side action" (9-month item in feeding) to working on "feeds self with fingers" (the next item in feeding) (items from Johnson-Martin et al., 1991). The child may be able to chew food for quite some time before he or she is able to handle the visual-motor task of finding the food, picking it up, taking it to his or her mouth, and biting off a piece. Further, many sequences have large gaps between items (e.g., "identifies familiar objects by their use" and "identifies big and small") (Newborg, Stock, Wnek, Guidubaldi, & Svinicki, 1988). With each of these examples, misinterpretations could lead to an inaccurate picture of the child's abilities and to inappropriate instruction.

Developmental scales can serve an important role in the assessment process; however, the members of the assessment team must carefully evaluate the relevance of particular items for each child and each family. The child's age, interest, motor or sensory disabilities, and home and community environments must be considered in the assessment process and in the interpretation and use of results.

Criterion-referenced lists of adaptive behavior Criterion-referenced assessments measure a child's performance as compared with a predetermined level of mastery, or criterion. Items are drawn from an analysis of functional skills thought to be essential for young children to function independently and to cope with environmental demands. The focus on functional skills and abilities enhances the likelihood that each test item is an appropriate intervention target (Salvia & Ysseldyke, 1991).

Several important advantages to criterion-referenced tests enhance their appropriateness in the adaptive behavior domain. The preferred method of collecting assessment data is through observation of the child in familiar and typical settings, which allows the assessment team to collect critical information about the responses the child uses in a functional manner and when and how they are used. In addition, most lists provide multiple-level scoring to reflect different levels of proficiency in using the skill. Since a standard presentation format does not have to be maintained, the evaluators are encouraged to find and use adaptations to assist the child in accomplishing the functional outcome. Freedom and flexibility in modifying items or modifying the criteria for "correct" are acceptable because the assessment results are not for comparative purposes, but instead are used to generate appropriate interventions (Berk, 1988).

Another distinction between norm-referenced and criterion-referenced assessments is the breadth of the domain that is covered (Mehrens & Lehmann, 1991). The former typically survey broader domains and age spans, providing a sampling of skills within each. Criterion-referenced lists have fewer domains and/or age ranges but attempt to provide a comprehensive listing of skills with smaller increments to allow small changes to be reflected. Further, some criterion-referenced tests present items reflecting conceptual or response classes instead of singular, specific exemplar skills (Bricker, 1993); for example, an item might ask about adjustment to transitions, rather than "separates easily from caregiver."

The primary disadvantage of most criterion-referenced lists is that they do not provide norms for the test outcomes, which may be necessary for some aspects of eligibility determination, program evaluation, or progress monitoring. They also do not completely address the issue of contextually specific skills, which is often the case for adaptive behavior development. Skills on the lists may still not be relevant to the individual child and family contexts because they are generated to reflect the skills of large population groups and geographic areas.

Ecological inventories Like criterion-referenced tests, ecological inventories examine the environment to determine needed skills; rather than using commercially available lists of skills, the current and future environments relevant to the particular child are analyzed (Brown et al., 1979). Consequently, the process is completely individualized. The purposes are to identify functional routines and activities across germane settings, such as home, preschool, and community. Subsequently, measures are taken to estimate the child's abilities to participate in specific routines and activities in those settings. Assessment and curricular content are identified by assessing the skill requirements of relevant environments. Thus, the environment is the source of the skills listed as well as the assessment site.

The information to identify and analyze routines and activities is collected by direct observation and interviews with significant individuals in the child's life, including the family, who can describe the child's present level of participation in daily routines and activities. The ecological inventory process is child-, family-, and culture-specific. The routines, activities, and skills identified reflect a child's capabilities, interests, and temperament. The uniqueness of each family and child is reflected. The routines and activities will vary from one child to another depending on such characteristics as family members present in the home, work and/or school responsibilities, social/recreational interests and preferences, interpersonal needs and strengths, and so on. Finally, cultural diversity will be reflected in the family's lifestyle and similarly seen in the daily routines from which the assessment content is drawn. For example, family culture will influence family members' roles (who does which chores), routines (in terms of meals and sleeping), and the extent and type of participation in social and/or religious events.

The ecological inventory strategy first discussed by Brown and his colleagues (Brown et al., 1979) is comprised of five phases. The purpose of the first phase is to associate current level of functioning with major activities or settings, such as home living, leisure activities, and community life. In the second phase, current and future places where the child might participate (living, learning, and playing) are identified. For example, the child might currently attend a parents-day-out program three days a week but next year will be attending a five-day-a-week preschool program. The changes in expectation for participation in this program would need to be addressed.

The third phase of the ecological inventory involves identification of subsettings in which the child currently participates or may in the future. The family's home, for example, can be divided into bedroom, bathroom, kitchen, and living room; skills necessary for adaptive functioning in each of these subsettings can then be identified. The fourth phase requires an inventory of each subsetting. Examples of important activities for a bathroom subsetting include bathing, toothbrushing, toileting, and picking up towels, toys, and so forth. Following identification of important activities with subsettings, the activities must be translated into teachable units or task-analyzed into precise sequences of behaviors. The fifth and final phase is to assess the child's performance of these sequences of behaviors. Based on the results of this assessment, an instructional program is designed and implemented. Using an ecological inventory approach and a "current versus subsequent" setting orientation helps members of the team identify skills that are most functional and relevant to the child and the family.

The primary disadvantages of ecological inventories relate directly to their primary advantages, that is, to their flexibility and individualization. This assessment process does not offer structure or specific guidelines for the identification of skills. Although the process ensures identification of skills relevant to the individual, the skill sequences identified by two teams may be very different. For example, a team led by a speech therapist or someone with extensive training in communication might identify many communication opportunities in their inventory. A second team, led by a physical therapist or someone with extensive training in working with children with physical disabilities, might focus on challenges of the physical environment and issues of access and control.

Furthermore, teams need to be sure that ecological inventories identify not only the observable activities and skills that are associated with competent performance in natural environments, but also related skills that may not be so apparent. For example, in addition to communication and motor skills used at mealtime, more subtle social skills, such as smiling at the waitress and making eye contact with your companions at a restaurant, may not be identified. These skills are not critical to the performance of the activity but nonetheless are important to a socially appropriate performance. Similarly, some skills may not be identified because they do not occur at the same time and place as the actual activity. Telling your parents about all the fun things that happened at your friend's birthday party or planning your own party based on your friend's party might not be identified in an ecological inventory. Providing more structure and systematization to guide the identification of skills by the team would begin to address some of these concerns.

Summary of data collection methods

At best our assessment results are educated guesses based on as much data as can be collected in the available time (McCormick, 1990). They give an idea of what the child can and cannot do and what seem to be the child's most critical needs in order to participate in current and future environments. If this information is generated from a developmental scale or set of predetermined criterion-referenced lists, the goals will typically be the next skills in whatever sequence is used. If, on the other hand, we use an ecological inventory process, goals will be based on their relevance to the child's daily activities and settings and will be directed at maximizing participation in ongoing tasks.

Used alone, either approach leaves us short of important information; used together they complement one another. For example, the ecological inventory could be used to identify the activities and routines (e.g., mealtimes, free-play, community trips) the child needs to learn in order to participate in important natural environments such as home or preschool. A developmental list or criterion-referenced list could be used to identify the specific skills across domains that are naturally embedded in these routines and that the child needs for successful, appropriate participation. Next, these skills lists could be validated by checking their appropriateness in the multiple natural settings in which they will be applied. Finally, the lists could be used to assess the child's status and needs for instruction.

Instruments for Assessing Adaptive Development

Assessment instruments including norm-referenced, developmental, and/or criterion-referenced scales for evaluating a young child's adaptive development are available commercially. As indicated earlier, in terms of early childhood curricula and texts, assessment tools in early childhood also use a variety of terms for skills that relate to adaptive behavior development (e.g., self-help, self-care, coping, personal/social responsibility). Measures of adaptive behavior development are also included as domains within multidomain assessment instruments (e.g., Battelle Developmental Inventory) or as instruments developed specifically to measure adaptive behavior (e.g., Vineland Adaptive Behavior Scales).

Global assessments embedding adaptive development measures Several multidomain assessments address adaptive behavior development. Although the goal of assessment is to gain a better understanding of the whole child, it is necessary to break the task into manageable pieces. Many global assessments offer subtests that are defined by the domains each attempts to measure. For example, the Assessment, Evaluation, and Programming System (AEPS) (Bricker, 1993) includes fine motor, gross motor, adaptive, cognitive, social-communication, and social skills, whereas the Learning Accomplishment Profile (LAP) (Nehring, Nehring, Bruni, & Randolph, 1992) includes fine and gross motor, language, self-help, and social-cognitive skills. These instruments do not necessarily include the same domains nor do they necessarily define the domains in the same way. For example, the AEPS measures feeding, personal hygiene, and undressing as strands in the adaptive behavior domain. The Battelle Developmental Inventory (Newborg et al., 1988), on the other hand, includes attention, eating, dressing, personal responsibility, and toileting in the adaptive behavior domain.

Some of the available multidomain assessments for young children that include adaptive behavior strands are presented in Table 15.1. Also included in this table is the terminology used by that instrument to label the domains relevant to adaptive behavior.

Specific measures of adaptive behavior A number of instruments that are specifically focused on adaptive behavior development in young children are available. A brief listing appears in Table 15.2. More detailed reviews of four representative scales of adaptive behavior development in young children (birth to 8 years) follow.

The Adaptive Behavior Scale–School Edition: 2 (ABS-S:2) (Lambert, Leland, & Nihira, 1993), a recent revision of the American Association on Mental Retardation Adaptive Behavior Scales–School Edition (Lambert, Windmiller, Tharinger, & Cole, 1981), is intended for school-age children from 3 to 16. It is divided into two parts. Part One focuses on personal independence, coping skills, and daily living skills by assessing the following nine domains: (a) independent functioning (i.e., self-care, using transportation and other public facilities); (b) physical development (i.e., physical and motor abilities); (c) economic activity (i.e., managing money and being a consumer); (d) language development (i.e., receptive and expressive language in social situations); (e) numbers and time (i.e., basic mathematical skills); (f) prevocational/vocational activity (i.e., skills related to school and job performance); (g) responsibility (i.e., accountability for actions, belongings, and duties); (h) self-direction; and (i) socialization. Part Two focuses on social maladaption. The behaviors that are examined are divided into seven domains: (a) violent and antisocial behavior; (b) rebellious behavior; (c) untrustworthy behaviors (i.e., stealing, lying, cheating, showing disrespect for public and private property); (d) stereotyped and hyperactive behavior; (e) eccentric behavior; (f) withdrawn behavior; and (g) disturbed

TABLE 15.1

Multidomain Assessments That Include an Adaptive Behavior Domain

Title	Source	Age Range	Type	Adaptive Domain Addressed
Assessment, Evaluation, and Programming System (AEPS) (1992)	Paul H. Brookes Publishing Co., P.O. Box 10624, Baltimore, MD 21285-0624	birth to 3 years	criterion-referenced, developmental	adaptive: feeding, personal hygiene, undressing
Battelle Developmental Inventory (BDI) (1984)	Riverside Publishing Co., 8420 Bryn Mawr Rd., Chicago, IL 60031	birth to 8 years	norm-referenced	adaptive: attention, eating, dressing, personal responsibility, toileting
Brigance Diagnostic Inventory of Early Development–Revised (1991)	Curriculum Associates, 5 Esquire Rd., North Billerica, MA 01862	birth to 7 years	criterion-referenced	adaptive (self-help)
Carolina Curriculum for Infants and Toddlers with Special Needs (1991)	Paul H. Brookes Publishing Co., P.O. Box 10624, Baltimore, MD 21285-0624	birth to 24 months	developmental, criterion-referenced	self-help: eating, grooming, dressing
Carolina Curriculum for Preschoolers with Special Needs (CCPSN) (1990)	Paul H. Brookes Publishing Co., P.O. Box 10624, Baltimore, MD 21285-0624	2 through 5 years	developmental, criterion-referenced	self-help: eating, dressing, grooming, toileting; responsibility, self-concept
Child Development Inventory (CDI) (1991)	Behavior Science Systems, P.O. Box 1108, Minneapolis, MN	15 to 72 months	norm-referenced	self-help
Developmental Profile II (DPII) (1986)	Western Psychological Services, 12031 Wilshire Blvd., Los Angeles, CA 90025	birth through 12 years	norm-referenced screening	self-help
Diagnostic Inventory for Screening Children, 2nd Ed. (DISC) (1988)	Kitchener Waterloo Hospital, 835 King St. West, Kitchener, Ontario N2G 1 G3	birth through 5 years	norm-referenced screening	self-help
Early Learning Accomplishment Profile (1978) (E-LAP)	Kaplan School Supply Corp., 1310 Lewis-Clemmons Rd., Lewisville, NC 27023	birth to 36 months	criterion-referenced	self-help
HELP for Special Preschoolers (1987)	VORT, PO Box 60132, Palo Alto, CA 94306	3 through 6 years	criterion-referenced	self-help
Hawaii Early Learning Profile (HELP) (1988)	VORT, PO Box 60132, Palo Alto, CA 94306	birth to 36 months	criterion-referenced	self-help
Kent Infant Development Scale (KIDS) (1985)	Developmental Metrics, 126 West College Avenue, P.O. Box 3178, Kent, OH 44240	birth through 12 months	norm-referenced	self-help
Learning Accomplishment Profile–Diagnostic Edition (LAP–D) (1978)	Kaplan School Supply Corp., 1310 Lewis-Clemmons Rd., Lewisville, NC 27023	birth through 6 years	developmental, criterion-referenced	self-help

TABLE 15.2
Adaptive Behavior Scales for Young Children

Title	Source	Age Range	Subtests
AAMD Adaptive Behavior Scale–School Edition: 2 (ABS–S:2) (1993)	Pro-Ed, 8700 Shoal Creek Blvd., Austin, TX 78758-6897	3 to 16 years	A norm-referenced scale that evaluates personal independence: independent functioning, physical development, language development, economic activity, language development, numbers and time, prevocational-vocational activity, responsibility, self-direction, socialization, social maladaptation: violent and anti-social, rebellious, untrustworthy, stereotyped and hyperactive, eccentric, withdrawal, disturbed behavior.
Adaptive Behavior Inventory for Children (ABIC) (1977)	Psychological Corporation, 55 Academic Court, P.O. Box 839954, San Antonio, TX 78283	5 through 11 years	A norm-referenced inventory measuring student role performance in the family, the community, the peer group, nonacademic school settings, earner/consumer activities, and self-maintenance.
Adaptive Behavior Inventory (ABI) (1986)	PRO-ED, 8700 Shoal Creek Blvd., Austin, TX 78758-6897	5 through 18 years	A norm-referenced inventory with subscales in self-care, communication, social skills, academic skills, and occupational skills.
Balthazar Scales of Adaptive Behavior (1973)	Consulting Psychologists Press, 577 College Ave., Palo Alto, CA 94306	childhood to adult-hood	A criterion-referenced test that includes two major subscales: self-care and social behavior.
Checklist of Adaptive Living Skills (CAL) (1991)	DLM Teaching Resources, P.O. Box 4000, Allen, TX 75002	infants through adult	A criterion-referenced checklist divided into four domains: personal living skills, home living skills, community living skills, and employment skills.
Early Coping Inventory (ECI) (1988)	Scholastic Testing Service, 480 Meyer Rd., Bensenville, IL 60106	4 to 36 months	A criterion-referenced scale covering the domains of sensorimotor organization, reactive behavior, and self-initiated behavior.
Pyramid Scales (1984)	PRO-ED, 8700 Shoal Creek Blvd., Austin, TX 78758-6897	childhood through adult	A criterion-referenced checklist that includes subdomains of sensory skills (tactile, vision, auditory), gross motor, eating, fine motor, toileting, dressing, social inter-action, washing and grooming, receptive and expressive language, recreation and leisure, writing, domestic, reading, vocational, time, money, numbers.
Scales of Independent Behavior (SIB) (1984)	DLM Teaching Resources, P.O. Box 4000, Allen, TX 75002	infant through adult	A norm-referenced scale of skills needed to function independently in home, social, and community settings.
Vineland Adaptive Behavior Scales (1984)	American Guidance Service, P.O. Box 190, Circle Pines, MN 55014-1796	birth to 18 years	A norm-referenced scale with subtests in communication, daily living skills, socialization, and motor skills.

behavior. The ABS-S:2 is administered as an interview. Raw scores are converted to standard scores with a mean of 10 and a standard score of 3. Scores are converted to quotients that have a mean of 100 and standard deviation of 15. Percentiles are also available.

The Checklist of Adaptive Living Skills (CALS) (Moreau & Bruininks, 1991), a criterion-referenced checklist of approximately 800 items in the areas of self-care, personal independence, and adaptive functioning, was developed to measure the adaptive behavior development of infants through adults. The CALS is divided into four domains: (a) personal living skills; (b) home living skills; (c) community living skills; and (d) employment skills. Each of these domains is organized into 24 specific skill strands. Each item covers a range of behaviors; items are arranged in order of difficulty. The scale is administered as an interview and takes approximately 60 minutes to complete. Because it is a criterion-referenced checklist, the scale may be readministered periodically. Scoring requires simply checking items the child can perform independently according to the criterion.

The Early Coping Inventory (ECI) (Zeitlin, Williamson, & Szczepanski, 1988), which assesses the coping and adaptive development of young children between the ages of 4 and 36 months, contains 48 items that are divided into three major categories: (a) sensorimotor organization (i.e., regulation of psychophysiological functions and integration of sensory and motor processes); (b) reactive behaviors (i.e., responses to the demands of the physical and social environment); and (c) self-initiated behavior (i.e., self-directed behaviors intended to meet personal needs and to interact with objects and people). The inventory is completed through direct observation of the child. The evaluator rates the child on a 5-point scale according to the level of effectiveness, ranging from 1 (the behavior is not effective) to 5 (the behavior is consistently effective across situations). Raw scores on each of the categories are converted to effectiveness scores, which are used to compute the adaptive behavior index. A coping profile for the child can also be developed. The Coping Inventory (Zeitlin, 1985) is available for children 3 through 16 years of age and is similar in organization and administration to the ECI.

The Vineland Adaptive Behavior Scales (Sparrow, Balla, & Cicchetti, 1984) is one of the most widely used instruments for evaluating adaptive behavior. There are three separate versions of the scales: a survey form, an expanded form, and a classroom edition. The survey form is designed to obtain an overview of adaptive behavior and covers the age range of birth through 18 years. The expanded form is a comprehensive diagnostic instrument that provides in-depth information across a large sample of behaviors (577 items) and also covers the birth through 18 years age range. The classroom edition addresses adaptive behaviors in classroom and school settings for children 3 through 12 years of age.

All the scales cover four adaptive behavior domains: (a) communication (i.e., receptive, expressive, written); (b) daily living skills (i.e., personal, domestic, community); (c) socialization (i.e., interpersonal relationships, play and leisure time, coping skills); and (d) motor skills (i.e., gross and fine). The scales are conducted as a general interview with a primary caregiver who knows the child well. The survey form and classroom edition take from 20 to 60 minutes; the expanded form takes from 60 to 90 minutes. Scoring procedures take 10 to 15 minutes and yield a standard score for each domain and a composite score. The scales also include an optional maladaptive behavior scale.

ASSESSMENT ISSUES WITHIN EACH SUBDOMAIN

In this last section concerning procedures for assessment of adaptive development, some attention will be given to each of the subdomains of adaptive behavior as presented in the DEC Recommended Practices (i.e., self-care, community self-sufficiency, personal-social responsibility, and social adjustment) (DEC Task Force on Recommended Practices, 1993). Specifically, examples of the range of skills within each subdomain will be provided as well as recommended practices in conducting assessments in these subdomains.

Self-Care

In early childhood, self-care refers to dressing/undressing, eating/feeding, toileting, and grooming (e.g., handwashing, facewashing, toothbrushing). By the age of 5, most children have learned basic self-care skills (Johnson-Martin et al., 1990). All of the discrete behaviors in this subdomain are related to other areas of development. For example, dressing is more than putting on a shirt. It requires discriminating the front from the back, determining the appropriateness of the shirt for the weather, and control over a range of refined motor abilities.

Self-care skills involve a number of discrete behaviors tied together (e.g., putting on pants requires a sequence of placing the pants, putting one leg in, the other leg, pulling them up, fastening, and zipping). Many assessments provide lists of skills (e.g., takes off shirt, puts on shirt, fastens shirt) and provide a binary system (yes/no) to record whether the child can or cannot do the behavior. The problem is that this gives very little information as to why the child is unable to complete the skill. Additionally, even if the child can accomplish the task, no information is gained as to the fluency of the child's response. Furthermore, many lists provide only one sequence of steps, although many self-care skills can be accomplished using a variety of sequences (e.g., taking off a T-shirt can be done by one arm at a time; crossing the arms, grasping the bottom edge of the shirt and pulling it over your head; or using one arm over the back and pulling it over the head). Because all of these approaches have the same end result, none is right or wrong. Some, however, may be easier for an individual child at a particular point in time. Using predetermined lists does not allow the assessment team to address these issues. Lists can serve as guides but should be individualized to address the abilities and disabilities of the child in order to provide the information needed to develop an appropriate intervention. Table 15.3 provides a list of potential skills and suggested sequences across the major areas of self-care. This list is not intended to be comprehensive nor does it break the skills down into their smallest components.

Dressing/undressing and grooming

The assessment of behaviors in this strand requires flexibility by the assessment team. Direct observation should be conducted at natural times when the skill is needed (e.g., removing shoes to settle down for naptime), in natural contexts (e.g., brushing teeth at the bathroom sink, not at a water fountain), and using real materials (e.g., shirt or jacket rather than a buttoning board). After completing the assessment, the team should have answers to the following questions: (1) Can the child perform the task (e.g., take T-shirt off)? (2) If yes, can the child do this fluently and across multiple settings and materials? (3) If no, why not? What piece is missing from the sequence or chain of behaviors? and (4) What adaptations either in materials or strategy could correct this? A decision tree that provides a sequence of questions to be addressed, strategies for getting those answers, and subsequent questions to ask dependent on the initial answer could help to guide the assessment process of these chained behaviors. Table 15.4 provides such a decision tree or assessment heuristic for dressing/undressing and grooming, but could easily be applied to the assessment of other chained behaviors.

TABLE 15.3
Example Skills Across Major Self-Care Skill Areas

Skill Area	Examples
Dressing/undressing	Cooperates in dressing/undressing (e.g., holds arm out for sleeve, foot out for shoe) Removes loose clothing (e.g., mitten, hat, untied shoes) Unfastens clothing zipper that has a large pull tab Puts on sock, loose shoes, and "stretch pants" Puts on all clothes unaided, except for fasteners Undoes fasteners (e.g., large buttons, snaps, shoelaces) Zips front-opening clothing such as jacket Selects and matches clothing appropriate for weather conditions and specific activities
Grooming	Enjoys playing in water Cooperates in handwashing and drying Wipes nose, if given tissue Washes and dries hands and face without assistance Brushes teeth Runs brush or comb through hair Bathes self
Toileting	Usually indicates need to toilet, rarely has bowel accident Urinates in toilet Has bowel movement in toilet Anticipates need to toilet Cares for self at toilet (may need assistance wiping after bowel movement) Wipes and flushes after toileting Cares for clothing before and after toileting
Eating/feeding	Smoothly sucks from nipple Munches food, chewing up and down Pulls food off spoon with lips Chews with rotary/side-to-side action Feeds self with fingers Brings spoon to mouth and eats food off it Holds and drinks from cup Scoops food from dish with spoon Uses fork Gets drink unassisted (e.g., turns tap on and off) Spreads with knife Uses napkin to wipe fingers and mouth Uses appropriate mealtime behaviors, including social graces

TABLE 15.4
Heuristic for Assessing Chained Dressing/Undressing and Grooming Skills

Step	Assessment Task	Question Being Asked	Dimension Being Measured	Result	Next Step in Process
1	Teacher gives child opportunity to do entire task without assistance and in any sequence that will result in desired effect (e.g., take off or put on garment).	Can child complete the entire task? (i.e., take off or put on specific garment)	Accuracy	*No*. Child cannot complete entire task correctly.	Go to Step 2
				Yes. Child completes task accurately.	Go to Step 7
2	Teacher determines whether child has prerequisite skills to do task.	Does child have prerequisite skills?	Presence of prerequisite behaviors and their adequacy	*No*. Prerequisite skills not adequate.	Go to Step 3
				Yes. Prerequisite behaviors present and adequate.	Go to Step 4
3	Teacher searches and tests for task-modifications that will eliminate need for standard prerequisite behaviors.	Can task-modifications be found to eliminate need for standard prerequisite behaviors?	Accuracy with task-modifications being used	*No*. Task modifications not found.	Teach prerequisite skills
				Yes. Need for prerequisite behaviors is eliminated, but child does not do skill accurately.	Go to Step 4
				Yes. Need for prerequisite behaviors is eliminated and child does skill accurately.	Go to Step 7
4	Teacher observes child attempt behavior and notes what type of error keeps child from completing entire task.	What type of error is occurring?	Type of error	Latency error—child can do steps but latency between responses is too long/short.	Identify the level of assistance needed and initiate teaching to eliminate errors
				Topographical error—child incorrectly does specific responses in chain.	Go to Step 5

5	Teacher lists topographical errors and searches for and tests adaptations that will eliminate errors.	Can adaptations eliminate topographical errors?	Accuracy with adaptations being used	*No*. Adaptations cannot be found to eliminate topographical errors.	Go to Step 6
				Yes. Adaptations eliminate topographical errors.	Go to Step 7
6	Teacher searches for and tests sequences to eliminate topographical errors.	Can a different sequence eliminate topographical errors?	Accuracy with different sequence of steps	*No*. Different sequences do not eliminate errors.	Identify level of assistance needed and teach responses where errors occur
				Yes. Different sequences eliminate topographical errors.	Go to Step 7
7	Teacher observes child do skill to determine whether it is done quickly enough.	Is child fluent in doing the skill? (i.e., can child do it quickly)	Duration or rate of skill completion	*No*. Child does skill too slowly.	Teach to increase fluency
				Yes. Child does skill quickly.	Go to Step 8
8	Teacher interviews parents or observes in generalization situations.	Does child perform the skill across needed situations?	Accuracy and fluency	*No*. Child does not do skill in generalization settings.	Teach to facilitate generalization
				Yes. Child does skill in generalization situations.	Monitor for maintenance

Toileting

The typical timeline for accomplishing toilet training is highly variable, with some children being trained well before 2 years while others are 3 or even 4 years old. Muscle control is obviously needed to control elimination. In addition, the behavioral control to stop an interesting activity to attend to toileting needs may be difficult for the young child. Snell (1993) suggests the following three criteria for initiating toilet training: (a) the child has a relatively stable pattern of urination and bowel elimination rather than a random pattern throughout the day; (b) the child has periods of 1½ to 2 hours of dryness; and (c) the child is chronologically 2.5 years old or older. As with many other adaptive behaviors, toileting is learned in a logical developmental sequence, building on certain earlier skills. Assessment for readiness may begin with determining if the child has an awareness of wet or soiled pants, by observing whether he or she shows discomfort or somehow indicates that he or she wants clean clothing.

As the child matures, the time between elimination increases, and the child can begin to learn to "hold it" between adult-initiated trips. The best way to determine whether this is occurring is to collect data on the child's elimination patterns. Probably one of the more common methods for doing this is to use a time-sampling recording system. A data collection sheet for recording this information is shown in Figure 15.1. The child is checked periodically, every 20 or 30 minutes. This information is recorded across several days to determine the child's usual pattern. It is important at this time of "training" for the adult to be aware of subtle signals that the child needs to void and to take him or her to the toilet at these times. He or she will soon begin to associate the physical sensation with the need to use the toilet.

Training can be viewed as a three-level process: (a) when taken to the toilet the child will urinate and/or have a bowel movement in the toilet; (b) the child indicates the need to void and requests assistance or goes independently to the toilet; and (c) the child recognizes the need to void, goes alone, removes and replaces clothing, cleans self, and flushes the toilet. Although the third level is the ultimate goal, each level represents a number of complex skills, and success depends on the child's physical and social maturity.

Eating

Eating is much more than a means of ingesting adequate nutrition in a safe manner; it can be a pleasant and naturally reinforcing event. Ultimately, children should be able to eat unassisted in a range of settings (e.g., home, a school cafeteria, restaurants). Eating skills assessment should address the following aspects: (a) adequate nutritional intake; (b) skill level related to food and liquid intake; (c) skill level in feeding independently; (d) eating preparation (e.g., serving one's plate); (e) table manners; (f) maintaining conversations; and (g) clean-up activities (e.g., clearing one's plate, wiping the table clean).

Feeding Adequate nutritional intake can be problematic for young children with disabilities, particularly those with physical disabilities or other chronic health impairments (Eicher, 1992). These potential problems may be related to the child's particular diagnosis (e.g., metabolic disorders, inadequate food intake due to oral motor impairments), the side effect of medication, specialized diets, or behavioral factors (Brizee, Sophos, & McLaughlin, 1990; O'Brien, Repp, Williams, & Christopherson, 1991; Sobsey, 1983). These threats to nutritional intake can lead to malnutrition, obesity, constipation, and other problems. Professionals should be aware of nutritional screening procedures and be able to recognize indications of need for further nutritional assessment. Brizee and her colleagues provide a helpful guide for

Name: ____________________ Month: ____________________

Date	1	2	3	4	5	6	7	8	9	10	11	12	13	14	15	16	17	18	19	20	21	22	23	24	25	26	27	28	29	30	31
7:00–7:30																															
7:30–8:00																															
8:00–8:30																															
8:30–9:00																															
9:00–9:30																															
9:30–10:00																															
10:00–10:30																															
10:30–11:00																															
11:00–11:30																															
11:30–12:00																															
12:00–12:30																															
12:30–1:00																															
1:00–1:30																															
1:30–2:00																															
2:00–2:30																															
2:30–3:00																															
3:00–3:30																															
3:30–4:00																															
4:00–4:30																															
4:30–5:00																															
5:00–5:30																															
5:30–6:00																															
6:00–6:30																															
6:30–7:00																															
7:00–7:30																															
7:30–8:00																															
8:00–8:30																															
8:30–9:00																															

Coding Symbols:

√ = Dry Pants
O = Urination off Potty
⊗ = Urination on Potty
△ = Bowel Movement off Potty
△ (with X) = Bowel Movement on Potty
△ (with ⊗) = Urination and Bowel Movement on Potty
X = On Potty; Nothing
M = Meal Given to Child
• = Liquids Given to Child

Daily Comments:

FIGURE 15.1
Data collection sheet for collecting data on children's patterns of urination and defecation
Source: From *Toilet Training the Handicapped Child* by H. D. Fredericks, V. Baldwin, D. N. Grove, and W. G. Moore, 1975, Monmouth, OR: Instructional Development. Copyright 1975 by H. D. Fredericks. Reprinted by permission.

collecting relevant dietary information (Brizee et al., 1990). Information germane to nutritional screening includes (a) interviews with caregivers; (b) recordings of changes in height or weight and in appearance of gums, teeth, hair, and skin; and (c) reviews of health and medical records. Before beginning eating or feeding programming, young children should be seen by a physician to rule out possible organic causes for the eating problems (O'Brien et al., 1991). Further, if there are any indicators of threats to the child's nutritional status, a nutritionist should be included on the team.

Effective eating depends on the following steps: (a) the ability to take in food, form a bolus, and swallow; (b) the absence of aspiration into the airway; (c) the lack of reflux of food once it enters the stomach; and (d) the normal digestion and movement of food through the intestines (Eicher, 1992). Problems can occur at one or more of these steps.

Transdisciplinary teamwork is required to assess and plan for interventions. Professionals from different disciplines (e.g., educators, occupational therapists, physical therapists, speech pathologists, and nurses) have expertise that should be considered in mealtime assessment and planning. Parents and other primary caregivers must be included, since they typically know the child and the history of interventions better than any other team member, and since they generally participate in feeding the child most of the time.

Assessment requires both a determination of the child's current skills and the skills critical to improving the child's oral motor functioning. Several assessments of oral motor development and early feeding skills are available (e.g., Oral-Motor Feeding Rating Scale, Jelm, 1990; Pre-Feeding Skills, Morris & Klein, 1987). Assessment and subsequent intervention planning must address the following nine general categories: (a) positioning of the child; (b) food type and texture; (c) utensils; (d) feeding schedule; (e) feeding environment; (f) food presentation; (g) amount of physical assistance needed; (h) sensory sensitivity; and (i) oral-motor status (Eicher, 1992; Morris & Klein, 1987; Orelove & Sobsey, 1991).

Programs to promote feeding for a young child with a disability may often require a number of creative approaches and the involvement of several different professionals and family members. When effective, these methods enable the child to receive the necessary combination of nutrients, fluids, and oral-motor stimulation to help them grow, remain healthy, and develop new skills.

Self-feeding More has been written about the specialized training of oral-motor skills in feeding than training self-feeding skills (Orelove & Sobsey, 1991). Basic self-feeding includes handling finger foods, drinking from a self-held cup, and eating with a spoon. Each of these skills involves a fairly long chain of discrete responses by the child. A task analysis may be useful in assessing exactly what step in the sequence needs work and support.

The first level in moving to independence in self-feeding is the predictably messy stage of eating finger foods. It provides opportunities to practice skills necessary for utensil use and simultaneously continue to refine oral-motor skills. The young child picks up food and thus practices and refines his or her grasp and hand-to-mouth movement in combination with gumming, sucking, chewing, and swallowing of many soft foods. In planning assessment of current skill levels, a teacher or caregiver must determine which piece of the "eating finger food chain" is missing or weak—finding the food, grasping, lifting to mouth, opening mouth at the appropriate time, leaving food in mouth, chewing, and/or swallowing. Furthermore, the teacher or caregiver may determine how the child handles larger food (tears it into smaller bites or bites off smaller pieces); how messy the child is; and what causes the messiness (e.g., too much food in the mouth). The determination of missing or weak skills/links in the chain allows the identification of skills for training.

Once the child can move food from the table to the mouth, the teacher or caregiver can provide self-feeding or drinking opportunities with utensils and a cup. Coordinating arm, hand, head, and mouth movements can be a challenge. Spoon use is the simplest of the utensil skills, followed in difficulty by eating with a fork, using a knife for spreading, and using a knife and fork for cutting. Spilling and messiness are typical well into the latter part of early childhood. If excessive spilling and messiness continue as the child becomes more proficient in eating, observation can assist in determining when the "error" occurs (e.g., while scooping something out of the bowl) and why (e.g., poor lip closure around the spoon in removing food). Once the problem is identified, adjustments in the equipment or instruction can be made.

Eating and mealtimes, as previously noted, involve more than just getting the food to one's mouth and consuming it. Preschool children can participate in mealtime preparation (e.g., serving one's plate), using appropriate table manners (e.g., discriminating between finger food and utensil food, using a napkin), maintaining a conversation (e.g., turn-taking, appropriate volume, not talking with food in the mouth), and clean-up activities (e.g., clearing one's plate, wiping the table clean). These activities are best assessed and taught within the natural flow of the mealtime settings in which the child participates (e.g., home, visiting relatives or friends, preschool, restaurant, fast food).

Community Self-Sufficiency

From a life-span perspective, appropriate use of community resources includes skills such as traveling in the community; grocery and general shopping at stores; obtaining services from community businesses such as doctors and dentists, clinics, restaurants, and repair shops; using public transportation; using public facilities such as schools, libraries, post offices, and recreational areas; attending church or synagogue; and attending theaters and recreational events (Ford et al., 1989). Related skills include communication of choices and needs, social interaction and behavior in the community, and the use of functional academics.

An instructional emphasis on these skills is appropriate during the early childhood years. However, the degree of independence, the range of settings, and the complexity (e.g., purchasing may involve making a choice between chicken nuggets and a hamburger) is adjusted to reflect developmental, age, and cultural expectations. Thus, community self-sufficiency in an early childhood curriculum includes skills that promote age and culturally appropriate functioning *with adult supervision* in community environments such as restaurants, neighborhoods, and recreational areas.

Skills related to "use of the community" overlap with other subdomains of adaptive behavior (e.g., eating, toileting) as well as with other domains such as cognitive (e.g., problem solving), motor (e.g., mobility), social, and communication. While this overlap is obvious, distinguishing community self-sufficiency as a subdomain is important in terms of measuring competency in a given skill based on the demands of the setting (e.g., eating in a restaurant). Competence requires the ability to change behavior to suit the demands of the setting (Evans, 1991). Thus content must be determined by evaluating the community environments of the young child, the child's access to them, and the demands for appropriate participation.

The actual as well as the future community environments that the infant or toddler is apt to encounter must first be indexed. Then specific areas of each environment, the age-appropriate activities that occur there, and the

are applied, their success in managing specific stressors, and how the child appears to feel about the effectiveness of their efforts. Based on this information, interventions can be planned to enhance the effectiveness of the child's coping strategies.

Summary of Assessment Issues in Subdomains

The conceptual framework that drives assessment across the subdomains of adaptive behavior (i.e., self-care, community self-sufficiency, personal-social responsibility, and social adjustment) is a functional ecological approach (DeStefano, Howe, Horn, & Smith, 1991; McDonnell & Hardman, 1988). Several common themes are identified with this approach: (a) assessment items are referenced to the unique needs and lifestyle of the child, family, peers, and community; (b) assessment emphasizes skills that reflect increases in the child's ability to interact with the world; (c) assessment emphasizes skills that are useful immediately and in the future; and (d) assessment is conducted in multiple daily family and child routines and activities. The characteristics of the skills in these subdomains readily allow the application of this model. However, there are many differences among cultures as to the value placed on these skills and expectations for when they should be acquired (Peterson & Haring, 1989). How important these skills are at different ages and how they are supported varies among families within and across cultures. The acquisition of these skills is deeply embedded in the family's unique preferences and expectations. Thus, the specific behaviors at any given developmental stage that determine competence in adaptive behavior should be identified from an analysis of the unique needs and lifestyles of the child, family, peers, and community.

USE OF ASSESSMENT INFORMATION

One of the most challenging tasks facing the assessment team is drafting goals/outcomes for intervention. First, all of the assessment information must be assembled, summarized, and interpreted. The focus is not on the scores or developmental age equivalent, but on what the child knows and can do and how the child interacts with his or her environment. For young children our assessments should yield (a) the specific skills the child has mastered in the relevant subdomains; (b) skills that are in the process of being acquired; (c) skills needed to meet the demands of current environments; (d) the environments/settings that provide sufficient opportunity and support for learning the skill; and (e) related services, equipment, and aids that will facilitate the child's learning the skill. The goal is to select adaptive behaviors for instruction that increase the young child's participation and independence. Even if the child is taught an alternative way of completing the task (e.g., self-catheterization for toileting), the outcome should address maximizing independence.

To establish goals in the adaptive behavior domain, the team must first summarize the skills the child currently demonstrates in relation to the level of proficiency and the demands of the environments in which he or she participates. In addition, members of the team should consider the child's chronological age, the manner in which peers perform the task, and the settings in which the skills will be used. Goals should reflect typical expectations for the child's chronological age. Independent toileting in the community, for example, is not considered developmentally appropriate for a young child. Children in this age group usually receive help from their parents in public toilets, from getting the door open and locked to getting on and off the toilet and reaching the soap and hand dryer.

As teachers begin implementing instruction it becomes important that opportunities are presented to learn and master skills that meet social expectations. While adaptive behavior skills are critical and should be taught when they are needed, they are used at a relatively low frequency. Related to this characteristic is the fact that skills must become habitual to be truly functional. They must be performed fluently in response to natural cues, maintained by natural consequences, and performed in varied settings and circumstances. This implies that the interventionist may need to change the traditional instructional settings to reflect the diversity of settings in which the skills naturally occur (e.g., home, community, and preschool). In addition, the intervention team may need to make adaptations in schedules to increase the opportunities for practicing these skills within the context of routines. Children must be given real-life opportunities to practice and thus establish habitual responses to natural cues provided across multiple current and future environments.

In conclusion, the adaptive behavior domain is an important part of the early intervention endeavor. Providing instruction requires that professionals and/or caregivers accommodate and adapt to support the specific strengths of individual children and their families. Competent independent functioning is the long-term goal.

SUMMARY OF KEY CONCEPTS

- Adaptive behavior as a curriculum domain should include skills that reflect chronologically age-appropriate behaviors for meeting the demands of the child's multiple unique environments.
- Children's acquisition of adaptive skills leads to (a) increased independence in everyday environments, (b) decreased caregiving demands, (c) more meaningful inclusion in community settings because the child may appear more "typical" and less different, and (d) positive impacts on the child's sense of competence and self-concept.
- Any definition of adaptive behavior must take the perspective of not considering it a single entity but a composite of a wide range of abilities that are dependent on one's age, environment, and cultural group at any moment.
- Comprehensive assessment and intervention in the adaptive behavior domain should address the following subdomains: self-care, community self-sufficiency, personal-social responsibility, and social adjustment.
- The self-care domain addresses dressing/undressing, eating/feeding, toileting, and grooming (e.g., handwashing, facewashing, and toothbrushing).
- Community self-sufficiency refers to skills that promote age- and culture-appropriate functioning with adult supervision in community environments such as restaurants, neighborhoods, and recreational areas.
- Basic skills in personal/social responsibility include basic environmental interactions, self-directed behaviors, independent play/self-occupation, peer cooperation and interaction, and the assumption of responsibility (e.g., demonstrates caution, avoids dangers).
- The subdomain of social adjustment includes the ability to adjust to new situations, regularity of behavior patterns (e.g., eating, sleeping), general disposition, tendency to stick to tasks despite obstacles, attention span and degree of distractibility, and amount of stimulation necessary to evoke a response.

- The conceptual framework that should drive assessment across the domains of adaptive behavior should address the following themes: (a) assessment items are referenced to the unique needs and lifestyle of the child, family, peers, and community; (b) skills that reflect increases in the child's ability to interact with the world are emphasized; (c) skills that are useful immediately and in the future are stressed; and (d) assessment is conducted in multiple daily family-and-child routines and activities.

REFERENCES

Allen, K. E., & Hart, B. (1984). *The early years: Arrangements for learning.* Englewood Cliffs, NJ: Prentice Hall.

Bailey, D. B., & Wolery, M. (1992). *Teaching infants and preschoolers with disabilities* (2nd ed.). Englewood Cliffs, NJ: Merrill/Prentice Hall.

Berk, R. A. (1988). Criterion-referenced tests. In J. P. Keeves (Ed.), *Educational research methodology and measurement: An international handbook* (pp. 365–370). Oxford: Pergamon Press.

Brizee, L. S., Sophos, C. M., & McLaughlin, J. F. (1990). Nutrition issues in developmental disabilities. *Infants and Young Children, 2*(3), 10–21.

Bricker, D. (1993). *Assessment, Evaluation, and Programming System (AEPS) for Infants and Children.* Baltimore, MD: Paul H. Brookes.

Brown, L., Branston, M. B., Hamre-Nietupski, S., Pumpian, I., Certo, N., & Gruenwald, L. (1979). A strategy for developing chronological-age-appropriate and functional curricular content for severely handicapped adolescents and young adults. *Journal of Special Education, 13*(1), 81–90.

Brown, F., & Snell, M. (1993). Meaningful assessment. In M. Snell (Ed.), *Instruction of students with severe disabilities* (4th ed.) (pp. 61–98). Englewood Cliffs, NJ: Merrill/Prentice Hall.

DEC Task Force on Recommended Practices. (1993). *DEC recommended practices: Indicators of quality in programs for infants and young children with special needs and their families.* Reston, VA: Council for Exceptional Children.

DeStefano, D. M., Howe, A. G., Horn, E. M., & Smith, B. A. (1991). *Best practices: Evaluating early childhood special education programs.* Tucson, AZ: Communication Skill Builders.

Dyson, L., & Fewell, R. R. (1986). Stress and adaptation in parents of young handicapped and nonhandicapped children: A comparative study. *Journal of the Division of Early Childhood, 10*(1), 25–34.

Eicher, P. M. (1992). Feeding the child with disabilities. In M. L. Batshaw & Y. M. Perret (Eds.), *Children with disabilities: A medical primer.* Baltimore, MD: Paul H. Brookes.

Evans, I. M. (1991). Testing and diagnosis: A review and evaluation. In L. H. Meyers, C. A. Peck, & L. Brown (Eds.), *Critical issues in the lives of people with severe disabilities* (pp. 25–44). Baltimore, MD: Paul H. Brookes.

Ford, A., Schnorr, R., Meyer, L., Davern, L., Black, J., & Dempsey, P. (1989). *The Syracuse Community-Referenced Curriculum Guide.* Baltimore, MD: Paul H. Brookes.

Frankenberger, W. (1984). A survey of state guidelines for identification of mental retardation. *Mental Retardation, 22,* 17–20.

Fredericks, H. D., Baldwin, V., Grove, D. N., & Moore, W. G. (1975). *Toilet training the handicapped child.* Monmouth, OR: Teaching Research.

Furuno, S., O'Reilly, K. A., Hosaka, C. M., Inatsuka, T. T., Allman, T. L., & Zeisloft, B. (1979). *Hawaii Early Learning Profile and Activities.* Palo Alto, CA: VORT.

Harrison, P. L. (1987). Research with adaptive behavior scales. *Journal of Special Education, 21*(1), 37–68.

Horn, E., & Fuchs, D. (1987). Using adaptive behavior in assessment and intervention: An overview. *Journal of Special Education, 21*(1), 11–26.

Individuals with Disabilities Education Act Amendments. (October 7, 1991). Washington, DC: U.S. Government Printing Office.

Jelm, J. M. (1990). *Oral-Motor/Feeding Rating Scale.* Tucson, AZ: Therapy Skill Builders.

Johnson-Martin, N. M., Attermeier, S. M., & Hacker, B. (1990). *The Carolina Curriculum for Preschoolers with Special Needs.* Baltimore, MD: Paul H. Brookes.

Johnson-Martin, N. M., Jens, K. G., Attermeier, S. M., & Hacker, B. (1991). *The Carolina Curriculum for Infants and Toddlers with Special Needs* (2nd ed.). Baltimore, MD: Paul H. Brookes.

Jones, H. A., & Warren, S. F. (1991). Enhancing engagement in early language teaching. *Teaching Exceptional Children, 23*(4), 48–50.

Lambert, N. M., Leland, H., & Nihira, K. (1993). *Adaptive Behavior Scales–School Edition: 2.* Austin, TX: Pro-Ed.

Lambert, N. M., Windmiller, M., Tharinger, D., & Cole, L. (1981). *AAMR Adaptive Behavior Scale–School Edition.* Monterey, CA: CTB/McGraw-Hill.

Luckasson, R., Schalock, R. L., Coulter, D. L., Snell, M. E., Polloway, E. A., Spitalnik, D. M., Reiss, S., & Stark, J. A. (1992). *Mental retardation: Definition, classification, and systems of support* (9th ed.). Washington, DC: American Association on Mental Retardation.

McCormick, L. (1990). Extracurricular roles and relationships. In L. McCormick & R. L. Schiefelbusch (Eds.), *Early language intervention: An introduction* (2nd ed.) (pp. 261–302). Englewood Cliffs, NJ: Merrill/Prentice Hall.

McDonnell, A., & Hardman, M. (1988). A synthesis of "best practice" guidelines for early childhood services. *Journal of the Division for Early Childhood, 12,* 328–341.

McGee, G. G., Daly, T., Izeman, S. G., Mann, L. H., & Risley, T. R. (1991). Use of classroom materials to promote preschool engagement. *Teaching Exceptional Children, 23*(4), 44–47.

McWilliam, R. A. (1991). Targeting teaching at children's use of time: Perspectives on preschoolers' engagement. *Teaching Exceptional Children, 23*(4), 42–43.

McWilliam, R. A., & Bailey, D. (1992). Promoting engagement and mastery. In D. B. Bailey & M. Wolery (Eds.), *Teaching infants and preschoolers with disabilities* (2nd ed.) (pp. 229–255). Englewood Cliffs, NJ: Merrill/Prentice Hall.

Mehrens, W. A., & Lehmann, I. J. (1991). *Measurement and evaluation in education and psychology.* Fort Worth, TX: Holt, Rinehart, & Winston.

Moreau, L. E., & Bruininks, R. H. (1991). *Checklist of adaptive living skills.* Allen, TX: DLM Teaching Resources.

Morris, S. E., & Klein, M. D. (1987). *Pre-feeding skills.* Tucson, AZ: Therapy Skill Builders.

Nehring, A. D., Nehring, E. F., Bruni, J. R., & Randolph, P. L. (1992). *Learning Accomplishment Profile–Diagnostic Standardized Assessment.* Lewisville, NC: Kaplan School Supply.

Newborg, J., Stock, J., Wnek, L., Guidubaldi, J., & Svinicki, J. (1988). *Battelle Developmental Inventory (BDI).* Allen, TX: DLM Teaching Resources.

O'Brien, S., Repp, A., Williams, G. E., & Christopherson, E. R. (1991). Pediatric feeding disorders. *Behavior Modification, 15,* 394–418.

Orelove, F. P., & Sobsey, D. (1991). *Educating children with multiple disabilities: A transdisciplinary approach* (2nd ed.). Baltimore, MD: Paul H. Brookes.

Peterson, N. (1987). *Early intervention for handicapped and at-risk children.* Denver, CO: Love.

Peterson, A. L., & Haring, K. (1989). Self-care skills. In C. Tingey (Ed.), *Implementing early intervention* (pp. 243–263). Baltimore, MD: Paul H. Brookes.

Salvia, J., & Ysseldyke, J. (1991). *Assessment.* Boston: Houghton Mifflin.

Sattler, J. M. (1992). *Assessment of children* (3rd ed.). San Diego, CA: Author.

Seligman, M. E. (1975). *Helplessness: On depression, death and development.* San Francisco: W. H. Freeman.

Shelton, T. L., Jeppson, E. S., & Johnson, B. H. (1987). *Family-centered care for children with special health care needs.* Washington, DC: Association for the Care of Children's Health.

Snell, M. E. (1993). *Instruction of students with severe disabilities* (4th ed.). Englewood Cliffs, NJ: Merrill/Prentice Hall.

Sobsey, R. J. (1983). Nutrition of children with severely handicapping conditions. *Journal of the Association for Persons with Severe Handicaps, 8*(4), 14–17.

Sparrow, S. S., Balla, D. A., & Cicchetti, D. V. (1984). *Vineland Adaptive Behavior Scales, Interview*

Edition. Circle Pines, MN: American Guidance Service.

Turnbull, A. P., & Turnbull, H. R. (1990). *Families, professionals, and exceptionality: A special partnership.* Englewood Cliffs, NJ: Merrill/Prentice Hall.

Whaley, K. T., & Bennett, T. C. (1991). Promoting engagement in early childhood special education. *Teaching Exceptional Children, 23*(4), 51–54.

Williamson, G. (1994). Assessment of adaptive competence. *Zero to Three, 14*(6), 28–33.

White, O. R. (1985). The evaluation of severely mentally retarded individuals. In B. Bricker & J. Filler (Eds.), *Severe mental retardation: From theory to practice* (pp. 161–184). Reston, VA: Council for Exceptional Children.

Zeitlin, S. (1985). *Coping Inventory.* Bensenville, IL: Scholastic Testing Service.

Zeitlin, S., & Williamson, G. G. (1994). *Coping in young children: Early intervention practices to enhance adaptive behavior and resilience.* Baltimore, MD: Paul H. Brookes.

Zeitlin, S., Williamson, G. G., & Szczepanski, M. (1988). *Early Coping Inventory.* Bensenville, IL: Scholastic Testing Service.

CHAPTER

16

Using Assessment Information to Plan Intervention Programs

Mark Wolery
Allegheny-Singer Research Institute

Assessment is a means to an end rather than being an end in and of itself. We conduct assessments for specific purposes, and the information that is gathered through the assessment process should be used. A good assessment is useless unless it is translated to answer the questions related to the reasons for which it was conducted. The purpose for which assessments are conducted determine, in large part, the manner and nature of the data that are collected, which in turn influence how that information can and should be used. Several purposes exist for assessing children, including screening their developmental abilities, determining whether they are eligible for specialized services, making diagnoses, monitoring their progress, and planning intervention programs. Much of this text focuses on gathering information for planning intervention programs for children, and, in this chapter, procedures are described for using that information to develop working intervention plans. The chapter does not address how the family portions of intervention plans are devised; that information was presented in Chapter 8 and is available from other sources (e.g., Bailey, 1988; Dunst, Trivette, & Deal, 1994; Kozloff, 1994a; McGonigel, Kaufmann, & Johnson, 1991).

This chapter contains four major sections. In the first, information is provided on how to describe assessments in written form. In the second section, the types of information needed to plan meaningful intervention programs are described. The third section describes considerations and guidelines for translating assessment information into intervention plans. The final section describes guidelines for implementing plans into ongoing child-care programs and home environments.

WRITING REPORTS FROM INTERVENTION PLANNING ASSESSMENTS

Writing assessment reports for intervention planning is a skill that requires considerable work and practice. The written assessment report is a document from which intervention programs are derived, but it also serves other functions, such as communicating with other team members and professionals, specifying the best estimation of a child's abilities at a given point in time, and as a record against which later performance can be compared. The report should be accurate, clear, objective, and detailed. Although numerous formats exist for writing assessment reports, some types of information are critical. (It should be noted that the information that follows is designed for instructional program planning assessments and not for screening reports, which would be briefer, or diagnostic reports, which have a different function.) Instructional program planning assessment reports should include identifying information about the child and the assessment, background information, methods of assessment, results of the assessment, and recommendations.

Identifying Information

This section includes information about who was assessed, who conducted the assessment, and when and where it occurred. It should appear first in the written report and include the child's full name; agency/client number, if applicable; important demographic information (e.g., age; sex; date of birth; current placement, if any; diagnosis); and the parents' names and addresses. The person who initiated the referral and the reason for the referral should be noted, as well as the assessor's name and title, the setting in which the assessment occurred, dates of the assessment activities, and reference citations of tests that were used.

Background Information

This section provides historical information about the child; it should be a relatively brief narrative summary. For diagnostic assessment reports, this section may be much more comprehensive. Three things should be addressed: the child's birth and medical history, developmental history, and educational experiences. The source of the information also should be noted in this section; for example, parental interviews or review of records. The birth and medical history section should identify whether the pregnancy was difficult and what complications, if any, occurred; whether the birth was full-term or premature; whether it was characterized by any unusual events and what they were; and whether the child has a history of any medical treatment and the nature of that treatment. The developmental history should describe the age at which the child achieved important developmental milestones, and, if appropriate, when the parents suspected that difficulties might exist. The educational history section should be a record of the child's intervention contacts since birth and should include a listing and brief description of the services he or she has received.

Methods

This section should be written in narrative form and should include several subsections. The *tests and scales* used during the assessment should be listed, when and by whom they were administered should be recorded, and the purpose of each should be described. The *observational* procedures should be described in terms of who conducted observations, when and where they occurred, and what domains were observed. When the setting for the observation is described, it should include a brief description of how many children were present, and so on, to give a flavor for the context in which it took place. *Interviews* with others should be described in terms of who was interviewed and their relationship to the child, who conducted the interview, and the topic of the interview. Finally, *environmental assessments* should be described, including which environments were assessed, what measures were used, when they occurred, who conducted them, and the purpose of the assessments.

Results of Assessment Activities

This section can be the most difficult to write, and considerable care should be taken to describe the following information: skills the child does independently; skills the child does with support, adaptation, and/or assistance; the type of assistance, support, and/or adaptation needed; skills the child does not have; variables that may influence how intervention is designed; stimuli that appear to hold reinforcing value; and results of using, even briefly, any instructional or therapeutic strategies. When describing the child's performance, the conditions under which it occurred or did not occur should be included. For example, saying the "child requested cookies" is inadequate because several questions remain. What was occurring when she requested the cookies? Had she already eaten a cookie? Were cookies visible? Describing the conditions presents a more complete and meaningful picture of the child's performance. Generally, this section should be organized by curricular area. Tables that list the three types of skills (independent, supported, did-not-do) can be included, but the conditions must be written on the tables if they are to be useful. As noted earlier, this must be an accurate, objective description of the child's performance; inferences should not be included here or should be identified as such.

Recommendations

This section should summarize the primary abilities of the child and the areas of need. It also should include suggestions about (a) the need for additional assessment activities, (b) potential long-term goals, and (c) potential intervention strategies, as well as a listing of any variables that would influence how the intervention should be implemented.

When writing assessment reports, interventionists should write to communicate with multiple audiences, including their team members, the child's parents, professionals to whom the child might be referred, and future caregivers. This requires use of clear, objective, jargon-free prose. Further, reports should be written sensitively, because they will be available to family members. This does not mean that the hard issues should be ignored but that the conclusions should be described, qualified, and supported by the information gathered in the assessment activities. Finally, clear delineation of facts from assumptions should be made. Both may be included, but assumptions should be labeled as such.

INFORMATION NEEDED TO PLAN MEANINGFUL INTERVENTION PROGRAMS

Intervention and early education programs for infants, toddlers, and preschoolers with developmental delays and disabilities vary from daily interactions between professionals and the child/family in developmental child-care centers to intermittent interactions in weekly home or clinic visits (Bailey & Wolery, 1992; Stayton & Karnes, 1994). The contact between the child and the professional members of the intervention team in even the most intense programs may only be 5 or 6 hours per day. Nearly all children spend most of their time outside of "formal" intervention time. However, they continue to interact with their social and physical environments and to learn from those interactions. This fact holds two major implications for planning interventions. First, the adults and the settings in which the child regularly spends time are the "true" or actual interventionists and intervention contexts, whether planned or not. Young children's learning is not restricted to contacts with teachers and therapists in centers or in their homes; it potentially occurs whenever a child interacts with the environment. The "interventions" children experience are beyond their contacts with professionals. Thus, a variety of individuals need to be aware of and able to use the intervention procedures that are planned. Second, the intervention plan should be designed to address the child's full day in whatever settings he or she spends regular amounts of time. This does not mean that there is active programming throughout the entire day; rather, it means that the intervention strategies and procedures should be appropriate for use in any context in which the child regularly spends time. Further, the intervention plan must be designed with knowledge of and accommodation to the activities, routines, and resources (human and otherwise) that are in the child's environments.

To plan interventions that will address these realities, the team needs four broad types of information. These are (a) information about the child's functioning and his or her interactions with the environment, (b) information about the environments in which the child spends time and about his or her regular schedule, (c) detailed information about several dimensions of the settings that are selected as intervention environments, and (d) information about the family's concerns and priorities for the child. Without information in these four broad areas, the intervention plan is not likely to be successful and may not be implemented consistently. More specific types of information in the four broad areas are identified in the following paragraphs.

Information About the Child

Throughout this text, several measurement strategies are described for gathering information on infants and young children; these strategies include tests of various types, rating scales, observational procedures and systems, interview protocols, and so forth. When planning the intervention program, this information should be organized into meaningful categories so that it can inform the planning process. Four useful categories are (a) the child's developmental abilities and functional performance (i.e., independence and mastery of his or her unique environments); (b) the child's developmental and functional skill needs; (c) the child's usual interaction patterns with the animate and inanimate environment; and (d) the effects of various supports, assistance, and intervention strategies. This information is gathered by a team of individuals (professionals and family members) over time, using multiple measurement strategies in all relevant settings and with input from all relevant caregivers.

The specific types of developmental abilities and needs that should be identified and procedures for assessing them are described by developmental domain in Chapters 10 through 15. Many of these procedures also are useful in identifying a child's functional abilities and needs in terms of independence and mastery of his or her environments. The information on developmental and functional abilities and needs is summarized to guide the team in identifying goals for intervention and for capitalizing on the child's abilities when addressing his or her needs. In short, the team must have information about what the child can do and does and about what he or she needs to learn to do.

The information on a child's usual patterns of interacting with the social and physical environments involves a number of issues. The team needs information on the child's interaction patterns with peers and with adults (Chapter 13) and on how he or she plays with toys and with others (Chapter 14). The team also needs information about the child's style of interacting and level of activity. The style issues deal with such constructs as persistence, problem solving, sustained attention to toys and other objects in the environment, duration and nature of engagement with the environment, the extent to which he or she is easily distracted, whether he or she imitates adults and peers, and compliance with routines and adult requests. It also involves identifying preferences for different toys and materials, interests that appear to be stable, and events and activities that appear to function as reinforcers. For infants and children with severe disabilities this may involve an assessment of their behavioral states to identify the stability and shifts between states and strategies for consoling children when they are upset and fussy (Guess, Roberts, Siegel-Causey, & Ault, 1993; Guess, Siegel-Causey, Roberts, & Guy, 1993). All of this information is needed because it provides important clues about how to organize intervention environments and about the types of interventions that may and may not be successful.

In addition, the team needs information about the effects of assistance, support, and intervention strategies. The assessment activities should result in information about what the child does under usual conditions and what he or she can do when assistance or support is provided. Vygotsky (1978) referred to this as the "zone of proximal development." The assistance and support may take a variety of forms such as adaptive and assistive devices and adult help, which includes such things as verbal prompts, gestural prompts, models, and physical assistance (Wolery, Ault, & Doyle, 1992). Knowing the amount and type of assistance needed by a child to perform a given skill provides information about whether that skill is a legitimate goal for intervention *and* about what strategies may be successful during intervention. For example, two children may not be able to put on their coats. One child can do it successfully if she is given a small amount of physical assistance with getting her arm through the second sleeve, but the second child requires substantial physical assistance on all steps. Knowing this information is likely to lead the team to conclude that putting on a coat is a legitimate goal for the first child but not for the second. Further, they may conclude that the strategy for teaching the first child to put on her coat should involve partial physical prompts.

Information About Environments and Schedules

When teams plan interventions that are relevant to a child's entire day, they need information about the environments in which the child spends time and about when time is spent in those environments. There is tremendous variability in terms of the environments in which young children spend time due to the structure of families (e.g., single parents) and employment demands (e.g., families in which all adults work outside of the home). The variability often is due to the nature of the intervention program (e.g., half-day center-based programs or programs that offer services on selected days of the week). Some children spend nearly all of their time in a single home environment; for others, the major environments may be a center-based intervention program and their homes. Many children, however, spend time in their homes, in a center-based intervention program (e.g., half-day kindergarten), and in a child-care program or family daycare arrangement. Some children may have two home environments that are important; for example, when parents are separated and have joint custody, or when they are cared for by a grandparent or other relative. As a result, teams cannot assume that the child has one or two critical environments such as a home and an early childhood program; they should identify all of the settings in which the child spends substantial amounts of time during a week.

In addition, the team needs to get information on the child's schedule. This should include the time spent in each setting from morning until bedtime. When collecting this information, the team should identify (a) the amount of time spent in each environment, (b) the times when the child goes from one setting to another, and (c) the general and usual routines that occur in each setting. These routines include such things as meals, dressing/undressing, naps, play time, and so on. For example, some children sleep at home, awake, get dressed, eat breakfast, and then go to a classroom program; however, other children may sleep at home, be awakened and taken to a grandmother's house for breakfast and dressing before going to a classroom program. Knowing when various routines occur gives the team information that is useful for (a) deciding whether an environment should be selected as an intervention environment, (b) planning when particular goals can be addressed in context, and (c) identifying who will need to use the intervention practices and strategies. Sometimes the most difficult part of intervention planning is not identifying the important goals or the desirable intervention strategies, but determining how so many different adults can be encouraged and supported in carrying out interventions (i.e., working together rather than working at cross-purposes). Identifying the settings in which a child spends time, the amount of time spent in each setting, the times when the child moves from one setting to another, and the routines in each setting is critical information in planning an intervention program.

Information About Specific Dimensions of Intervention Environments

After identifying the settings in which the child spends time, the daily schedule (which may vary from day to day), and the routines in each setting, the team can determine which settings can be selected as intervention environments. In settings where the team decides intervention is possible, they should gather information about (a) the physical dimensions and organization of the settings, (b) the sequence of activities and routines in each setting, (c) the usual roles of adults in those activities and routines, and (d) the structure of the activities and routines (Wolery, 1994). Sample questions the team should ask about each of these dimensions are presented in Figure 16.1. This information is needed for selecting times in which particular goals can be addressed, identifying which strategies are most likely to be used, and determining who needs to use those strategies.

The primary means of collecting information to answer the questions in Figure 16.1 are interviewing the family (and other caregivers as appropriate) and direct observation in the selected settings. Both strategies probably

Physical Dimension and Organization

- What materials and toys are in each environment?
- How are those toys and materials organized and placed about the room?
- Can the child access all areas and materials and if so, how?
- How much space is available, and how many children and adults are in it?
- What adaptations of equipment and materials, if any, are needed?
- Are there elements of the physical environment that are unsafe for this child?

Temporal Organization of Activities and Routines

- How are activities and routines scheduled within the setting?
- How long does each activity/routine last?
- What basic care routines (meals, toileting, dressing) occur in the setting?
- How much control does the child have over the sequence of activities/routines?

Adults' Roles in Activities/Routines

- For each activity/routine, what do adults do in relation to the child/children?
- When do adults observe children, interact directly with them, take care of other tasks (e.g., material preparation, planning, meal preparation, etc.)?
- When, if ever, do adults lead activities (e.g., read a story, circle time)?
- How do adults interact with children (e.g., tend to direct child's play, respond to child's play, play with the child)?
- What types of verbal exchanges (e.g., questions, commands, comments, conversations) do adults have with the child/children?

Activity/Routine Structure

- How does the child get into and out of each activity/routine?
- How does the child know what is expected in each activity/routine?
- What is the child expected to do in each activity/routine?
- How many other children participate in each activity/routine?
- What toys/materials, if any, are used in each activity/routine?

FIGURE 16.1

Sample questions about dimensions of intervention settings

Source: From "Implementing Instruction for Young Children with Special Needs in Early Childhood Classrooms" (p. 153) by M. Wolery, in M. Wolery and J. Wilbers (Eds.) *Including Young Children with Special Needs in Early Childhood Programs,* 1994, Washington, DC: National Association for the Education of Young Children. Copyright 1994 by the National Association for the Education of Young Children. Reprinted by permission.

should be used. Interviewing family members will secure their perspective of the settings, and direct observation will likely result in unique conclusions that are useful for planning intervention. For example, after observation, the team may conclude that the family daycare setting is not a desirable context for promoting acquisition of particular skills but may be an ideal context for promoting generalization of skills learned in the home or classroom.

Information About Family Concerns and Priorities

Practices for identifying family concerns and priorities are described in Chapter 8; they are not reiterated here. Further, as noted throughout the other chapters, families often have key information about children's abilities and needs. Family participation in intervention planning is critical for three decisions that must be made: determining the goals of intervention, selecting the intervention strategies and practices, and determining when and where selected interventions should be used for the identified goals. Families are likely to participate more in these decisions when they participate in earlier assessment activities. In seeking family participation in these decisions, teams need to be sensitive to cultural (Lynch & Hanson, 1992) and linguistic differences (Barrera, 1993; DeGangi, Wietlisbach, Poisson, Stein, & Royeen, 1994).

TRANSLATING ASSESSMENT RESULTS INTO INTERVENTION PLANS

In the following sections, guidelines for developing intervention plans are presented, then procedures and issues are discussed for three planning activities, which include identifying intervention goals, translating those goals into intervention objectives, and selecting potential intervention strategies.

General Guidelines

Involve families in preparing the plan

Parents should be involved in preparing intervention plans because they have a large stake in the outcome of the plan, they may have unique information about what is possible in some of the environments, they may have information about their child that is unknown to professionals, and it provides them with opportunities to engage in collaborative problem solving with professionals (Salisbury, 1992). Family members can play several roles during the planning process. They can verify the validity of the conclusions made by professionals about the child's abilities and needs. They can provide information about what they believe the child needs to learn, about which goals are the most important for their child, about which intervention strategies are acceptable to them, and about which intervention strategies are likely to be used in various settings. Strategies for soliciting family involvement in planning intervention include sharing information with them, involving them in the initial assessment activities, building relationships with them during the assessment process, scheduling planning meetings at times and in locations convenient for them, being flexible in terms of modes of communication (telephone, meetings, etc.), listening to and addressing their concerns, presenting them with choices when open-ended questions result in deferral to professionals, providing them with information about the content and procedures of meetings well before the meetings occur, using jargon-free language, conducting meetings in an informal but efficient manner rather than in an officious manner, limiting the number of professionals at meetings to avoid overwhelming families with large numbers, and being prepared for meetings. Implicit in these strategies is the assumption that developing an intervention plan is not an activity that occurs in one meeting around a table with multiple assessment reports. Rather, it involves an ongoing dialogue among the members of the team, including the family.

Involve the entire team in preparing the plan In addition to family members, all team members should be involved in the process of developing the intervention plan (McGonigel, Woodruff, & Roszmann-Millican, 1994). It is especially critical that the individuals who will be expected to implement the plan are involved in its development. For example, if some of the intervention plan will take place in a child-care program, a representative of that program, ideally the child's primary caregiver, should be involved in developing the plan. Bruder (1994) describes strategies for promoting teamwork among groups of professionals.

Comply with legal guidelines for preparing the plan An Individualized Family Service Plan (IFSP) is required for an infant or a toddler who receives early intervention services, and an Individualized Educational Program (IEP) is required for a preschooler with disabilities who receives special education and related services. Even if these formalized plans were not required, analyzing assessment information to form intervention plans is a defensible professional practice. Both the IFSP and the IEP have specific requirements about the types of information that should be included on them, which are shown in Table 16.1. Likewise, both the IFSP and IEP have general procedures that should be followed in their development, including basing goals on assessment information, involving families, attending to linguistic and cultural differences, and attending to due process procedures. In addition, some states or local agencies may have specific procedures that must be followed in developing the IFSP or the IEP. The team needs to become familiar with these processes and comply with them or work to change processes that are not conducive to developing meaningful intervention plans. Unfortunately, the requirement to develop IFSPs and IEPs does not guarantee that meaningful intervention plans are developed or that the plans are carried out.

Consider the veracity of the assessment results The assessment results are the foundation on which the intervention plan is developed. Faulty assessment data will likely result in a faulty intervention plan. Faulty assessment results can occur for a number of reasons, for example, faulty assessment information may simply be incomplete. When conducting an assessment, the team must balance the need for more information against the time and effort required to secure that information. As decisions are made, the team should be extremely aware of how complete their information is. If they realize that their information is incomplete, two strategies are defensible. First, they can postpone making decisions and conduct more assessment activities. Second, they can make an initial decision, but also decide that as intervention is implemented additional information should be collected to evaluate that decision. For example, if a child has been observed to assess her levels of social play and it appears that she engages primarily in parallel play rather than social play (e.g., cooperative or associate play), the team may decide to identify social play as an intervention goal. However, they may have little information on the child's sharing and social exchanges during play. By intervening to promote social play, they can monitor the effects of the intervention and decide whether the goal is appropriate or whether other goals should be established on related skills.

Sometimes the findings from different assessment activities may produce apparently contradictory conclusions. For example, in the home, the child may be engaged with toys at appropriate levels and for extended periods of time; however, observations in the child-care program may indicate low levels of

TABLE 16.1
Required Components of the IFSP and IEP

	Individualized Family Service Plan (IFSP)		Individualized Education Program (IEP)
1.	A statement of the infant's or toddler's present levels of physical development, cognitive development, communication development, social and emotional development, and adaptive skills, based on acceptable objective criteria.	1.	A statement of the child's present levels of educational performance, including academic achievement, social adaptations, prevocational and vocational skills, psychomotor skills, and self-help skills.
2.	A statement of the family's resources, priorities, and concerns relating to enhancing the development of the family's handicapped infant or toddler.	2.	A statement of annual goals which describes the educational performance to be achieved by the end of the school year under the child's individualized education program.
3.	A statement of the major outcomes expected to be achieved for the infant and toddler and the family, and the criteria, procedures, and timelines used to determine the degree to which progress toward achieving the outcomes is being made and whether modifications or revisions of the outcomes or services are necessary.	3.	A statement of short-term instructional objectives, which must be measurable intermediate steps between the present level of educational performance and the annual goals.
4.	A statement of specific early intervention services necessary to meet the unique needs of the infant or toddler and the family, including the frequency, intensity, and method of delivering services.	4.	A statement of specific educational services needed by the child (determined without regard to the availability of services), including a description of a. all special education and related services which are needed to meet the unique needs of the child, including the type of physical education program in which the child will participate, and b. any special instructional media and materials which are needed.
5.	The projected dates for initiation of services and the anticipated duration of such services.	5.	The date when those services will begin and length of time the services will be given.
6.	The name of the case manager from the profession most immediately relevant to the infant's or toddler's and family's needs who will be responsible for the implementation of the plan and coordination with other agencies and persons.	6.	A description of the extent to which the child will participate in regular education programs.
7.	The steps to be taken supporting the transition of the handicapped toddler to services provided under part B to the extent such services are considered appropriate.	7.	A justification of the type of educational placement that the child will have.
8.	A statement of the extent to which services will be provided in natural environments.	8.	A list of the individuals who are responsible for implementation of the Individualized Education Program.
		9.	Objective criteria, evaluation procedures, and schedules of determining, on at least an annual basis, whether the short-term instructional objectives are being achieved. (*Federal Register*, 41[252], p. 5692)

engagement that is intermittent and fleeting. This apparent contradiction may be a result of a number of factors, such as the materials/toys available, the child's familiarity with the settings, or differences in how engagement was measured in the two contexts. When contradictory findings arise, the team needs to determine if there are defensible explanations for the differences and whether those explanations lead to intervention goals or the skill should continue to be monitored to determine if a goal should be established at a later time. In the example noted above, the team may decide that the low levels of engagement in the child-care program might have been due to lack of familiarity with the setting. In such cases, the team may decide to monitor the child's engagement, and if it does not change as she becomes more familiar with the classroom, a goal could be established and a specialized intervention developed.

Some assessment reports include statements about children's abilities or needs, but do not describe the conditions from which the findings were derived. For example, a report might state the a child cannot put on his shoes. However, if the types of shoes used, the stability of the position in which the child was seated when trying to put on his shoes, and the assistance that was provided are not described, the finding that the child could not put on his shoes is relatively meaningless. The conditions under which such summary statements are made must be described to plan meaningful intervention programs.

Some assessment information may be faulty because of lack of reliability. Such problems can occur in nearly every stage of the assessment process, including the measure itself, the manner in which the measure is used, and the way the results are scored. If reliability problems are apparent, they should be corrected. Data collected from unreliable measurement should not be used in making decisions about intervention programs.

In addition, some information may come from assessments that have validity problems. In general, the most important validity issue with instructional program planning assessments is construct validity (i.e., the degree to which the measurement procedures assess the phenomenon that is intended). Lack of construct validity can occur with observational measurement as well as with tests. For example, if a team was concerned about whether a child initiated social interactions to peers, this skill could be assessed through direct observation in a play setting. If initiations were defined only as speaking to other children (asking questions, suggesting play themes, etc.), the observation may not be valid, because initiations can occur in many different ways, such as giving a peer a toy, touching the peer, looking at the peer and smiling, gesturing, and so forth. A nonverbal child could engage in frequent initiations, but a definition of initiations that included only verbal behavior would lead to the conclusion that the child was not initiating interactions. Thus, all conclusions about children's performance should be analyzed for the degree to which the measure on which it is based is indeed a valid indication of the presumed skill.

Consider the plan to be a tentative guide for intervention Although a great deal of effort goes into the development of an intervention plan, it should be viewed with a healthy degree of skepticism. Children's development is complex, and a range of factors (including disabilities) can influence development substantially. Thus, despite the best efforts of team members to conduct thorough assessment activities, intervention plans may require adjustment as they are implemented. In Chapter 17, issues related to monitoring the effects of intervention plans are described. The plan should not be viewed as a rigid and unchangeable document; it is a dynamic document that helps guide the intervention efforts, and the team should expect to make modifications and adjustments as it is implemented.

Identifying Intervention Goals

Developing intervention plans requires teams to summarize the assessment results into goal statements, determine the intent of each goal, and make decisions about the relative value or priority of the identified goals. These three tasks are described below.

Summarizing assessment results into goal statements Goal statements are simply short sentences that identify the desirable outcomes of the intervention. Examples are "Ashton will play independently with toys," "Juana will feed herself with a spoon," and "Kenton will carry on conversations with his peers." Three strategies for summarizing assessment results into broad goal statements are used by many intervention teams.

Perhaps the most frequently used strategy in early intervention and education is the *developmental approach*, which is based on the assumption that the development of children with special needs roughly follows a course similar to the development of children without disabilities. This approach leads teams to assess children's abilities in all relevant developmental domains, then draw conclusions about their current level of development. Two types of information are used to devise the intervention goals. First, most children will be developmentally less advanced in some areas or domains than others, and goals are written for the areas in which they are less advanced. Second, the next skills in the sequence of development across all domains may be identified as intervention goals. The developmental approach has some inherent appeal. If used appropriately, broad developmental goals can be identified, and developmental gains can be demonstrated.

The developmental approach has been criticized, however, on many grounds, especially that teams tend to identify the "next items on the test" as the goals of intervention (Goodman, 1992; Johnson & Johnson, 1994). This practice raises the question "Should we teach to the test?" In the case of screening and diagnostic tests, the answer is definitely "No." In the case of other tests (e.g., criterion- and curriculum-referenced tests), the question is stated inappropriately and should be "Should we teach from test results?" The answer to this question is "Yes, but . . . " "Yes," because there is no other reason to conduct assessments for intervention planning than to use the results to plan the targets and methods of intervention. The answer is "Yes, *but* . . . " because there are many inappropriate ways to use test results. For example, a common practice is to assess children with criterion- or curriculum-referenced tests, identify all the skills the child can do in each domain, then target the first items the child failed as the primary intervention goals or objectives. This practice is inappropriate for several reasons: (a) many of these measures have items that were not developed as instructional goals; (b) adjacent items on many tests are not related to the same skill; (c) the sequences of items on many tests may not be the best teaching sequences, especially for children with sensory and motor disabilities; and (d) many of the sequences may have large gaps between items. This practice also does not take into account prerequisite skills needed for some skills and the relationships of skills in one developmental area to those in another.

In addition, the answer to the question is "Yes, but . . . " because a child's failure on an item from criterion- and curriculum-referenced tests simply serves as a prompt to ask a series of questions:

1. What is the intent of the items the child failed, or what are these items designed to measure?
2. Are these intents important developmental constructs or skills that the child should acquire?

3. Why did the child fail these items, and what does that say about the child's overall competence in this and other areas?
4. Why are these skills important to this individual infant or child?
5. Does the infant or child need this skill to be more independent in the environments in which he or she functions or will be expected to function in the future?
6. What are the prerequisite behaviors for performing this skill, and does the child have those prerequisites?
7. How does performance on this skill relate to other domains in this or other developmental areas?
8. Is this skill an important prerequisite to other skills?
9. Should the focus of this skill be on acquisition, fluency, maintenance, or generalization?

Answers to these and related questions allow teams to make appropriate decisions based on testing and assessment results. Clearly, the process is much more complex than teaching the next item on a test. Test results should be supplemented with information taken from other measurement strategies such as direct observation and interviews. For general discussion and critique of the developmental approach see Barnett, Macmann, and Carey (1992).

Another approach to summarizing assessment information is called the *functional approach*. The assessment results with this approach are summarized around two basic themes: age-appropriateness and independence (Rainforth, York, & Macdonald, 1992). The individual items on developmental scales are not considered as critical, but the data are organized around major developmental skills (e.g., achieving mobility, establishing sustained attention and interaction with objects, imitating peers, etc.). Emphasis is placed on ensuring that children are engaged in chronologically age-appropriate activities. The skills needed for participation and independence in those activities often become the goals of intervention. The assessment results also are organized around independence on basic skills, particularly those focusing on activities of daily living, independent living (for older children), and leisure or recreational skills. Examples of such skills are playing with toys independently, feeding oneself with utensils, being toilet trained, putting on and taking off one's clothing, and so on.

The functional approach also has some appeal. If used appropriately, it allows the team to identify goals that are developmentally useful, are age-appropriate, and may have immediate benefits for the child and the child's family and caregivers. That is, if the goals are met, children should become more independent and competent in the settings in which they live and spend time. The primary disadvantage is the lack of an adequate framework for conceptualizing goals for infants and toddlers with special needs.

In the third approach, which is a variation and an extension of the functional model and is called the *ecological approach*, the team summarizes the assessment data around children's current *and* future environments. Teams using this approach start by identifying a desirable future for the child. The following questions are recommended to help teams with this process:

> Who is the [child]?
>
> What are the [child's] interests and strengths?
>
> What are the [child's] greatest challenges?
>
> What is a desirable future . . . the dream for the [child]?
>
> What is the nightmare . . . the future to be avoided?
>
> What are this [child's] greatest needs? (Rainforth et al., 1992, p. 75, words in brackets changed from *student* to *child.*)

These questions are based on a process called "Making Action Plans" (MAPS) (Falvey, Forest, Pearpoint, & Rosenberg, 1994). After envisioning a future for the child, teams using the ecological model identify the current and future environments and the demands/requirements of those settings for participation. Priority environments are selected, and priority activities and routines in those settings are identified. The skills needed in those priority activities and routines become the intervention goals (Rainforth et al., 1992).

Goals are identified that will allow the child to be more independent in those environments, to have more mastery of those environments, to have more control over what occurs in those environments, to develop social relationships with others in those environments, and to fit more appropriately and smoothly into those environments. Rather than analyzing the assessment results by developmental domains as in the developmental approach or age-appropriateness as in the functional model, the results are analyzed by each environment and the activities and routines in those environments. For example, the home environment may be divided into the dining area, the bathroom, the area of the house where leisure activities occur (e.g., family room), the child's sleeping area, the yard, and any other area of the home in which the child might spend time. The activities and demands that occur in each area are identified. For example, in the child's sleeping area, the activities might be dressing, going to bed at night, a story-time routine, and so forth. Other environments in which the child spends time are also analyzed in this manner. If the child is transported a great deal from environment to environment, the team might even analyze this "environment." For example, are there things that can be done to help the child entertain himself or herself while in transit? This approach also is useful in helping children adapt to integrated contexts in which the demands of the classroom may be focused on children with typical development.

Two variations or specific techniques in the ecological model deserve mention: the PASSKey model (Barnett, Ehrhardt, Stollar, & Bauer, 1994) and template matching (Ager & Shapiro, 1995; Cone, 1987). The PASSKey model is based on ecobehavioral analysis and on ecobehavioral consultation. It involves using interviews to identify important planned activities. Those activities are then observed through systematic sampling. Keystone behavior (skills that serve as prerequisites to other skills or skills on which other important skills depend) are selected from observations, the research literature, and consultation with the caregivers. Scripts are devised to assist caregivers in implementing intervention plans, the implementation of the interventions is measured, adjustments are made, and finally the intervention is evaluated. The PASSKey model is particularly useful for addressing problems that teachers, family members, and others might encounter with the child.

Template matching involves using ecobehavioral assessment procedures (Greenwood, Carta, & Atwater, 1991) to measure the performance of successful children in important environments and identify the relationships between their behavior and various environmental events and variables. The environments and environment-behaviors relationships of the target child also are assessed with the same ecobehavioral procedures. The two sets of data are then compared to identify differences in the environmental variables and events across settings. Based on these differences, adjustments are made in the child's environment. The primary utility of template matching appears to be preparing children to transition to new environments (Ager & Shapiro, 1995).

As with the other approaches, the ecological approach has considerable merit. It allows the team to develop goals that should produce immediate and long-term benefits for the child and the family. It involves planning for children in their current situations as well as in the future. Perhaps the major weakness of the approach is that important developmental skills may be overlooked.

Each of these three approaches (developmental, functional, and ecological) has advantages and disadvantages. It is important to note that they are not mutually exclusive; for example, combinations of the developmental and ecological approaches can be used. Regardless of the approach or combination of approaches used, the team should identify all relevant intervention goals for the child.

Determining the intent of each goal

Once goals have been identified, the team should analyze each one to determine its purpose or intent. Many important skills (especially cognitive, communication, and social skills) needed by infants and young children can be performed by multiple behaviors; others (e.g., self-care skills) should be performed by a relatively limited range of behaviors. For example, initiating social interactions can be performed by speaking to other people, touching them, giving them a toy, or making eye contact with them and looking expectantly at them. Each of the behaviors separately and in combination may result in an interaction starting. Often the more important goal is for the child to get the interactions started; the precise behaviors the child uses to do so are of less importance. Similarly, a child may request a drink of water in a number of ways, such as using a full sentence ("Please give me a glass of water"), using two words ("Want wa-wa"), using one word ("Wa-wa"), pointing at the sink without speaking, taking an adult's hand and leading him or her to the sink, and so forth. In each case, the child may be successful in getting a drink.

Other skills can be performed by fewer behaviors or by a small range of acceptable behaviors. For example, a child could use her fingers or a spoon and fork to feed herself. She could also get the food into her mouth by lifting the plate and letting it slide in, or by putting her face down into the plate. However, the most acceptable behavior usually is using utensils.

In all three of these examples (initiating social interactions, requesting a drink, and self-feeding) there is a behavior and an effect of the behavior. White (1980) referred to this relationship as the *form versus function* issue. The form is the behavior; the function is the effect of the behavior. Each behavior is thought to produce an effect, and each effect is actualized by a behavior. For some goals, the form (behavior) is important, as in the case of self-feeding; for other goals, the effect is more important, as in the case of initiating social interactions with peers or requesting a drink.

Neel et al. (1983) suggest that assessment information should address form and function and that the results should be analyzed in terms of both. They present several potential combinations that would lead to very different intervention procedures, and these are presented in Table 16.2. For example, if a child's social interaction skills were analyzed, two important functions would be initiating interactions and responding to others' initiations. A child may have multiple and adequate forms for initiating interactions and limited forms for responding to others' initiations. In such a case, an appropriate goal would be to increase the number of forms (behaviors) for responding to initiations by peers. On the other hand, the child who requested a drink by using one word ("Wa-wa") has a function (requesting drinks) but has limited forms. The goal of intervention would be to increase the number of forms or to teach more advanced and socially accepted forms.

Analyzing each goal in terms of its intent (i.e., form and function) holds important implications for planning interventions. It provides guidance on how instructional objectives should be written (i.e., with prescribed behaviors or with a range of acceptable behaviors); it helps ensure that the objectives will result in more adaptive performance in naturalistic contexts; and it helps focus the team on relevant intervention strategies. Drasgow and Halle (1995) discuss the implications of the form and

TABLE 16.2
Potential Combinations of Form and Function and Resulting Intervention Focus

Forms	Function	Potential Intervention Focus
Adequate	Multiple	Continue monitoring child's performance
Adequate	Limited	Teach new functions using existing forms and promote maintenance of existing functions
Limited	Multiple	Teach new forms for existing functions and promote maintenance of existing forms
Limited	Limited	Teach new functions with existing forms and teach new forms with existing functions
No identifiable form	No identifiable function	Teach new forms and new functions

function issue as it relates to developing communicative interventions.

Making decisions about the relative priority of each goal If the assessment activities are thorough and comprehensive, teams are likely to identify more goals than it is possible to address. To prevent this, goals should be categorized by their relative importance. Although no firm and hard categories exist, three appear useful: critical goals, valuable goals, and desirable goals. Although this three-tier hierarchy seems relatively straightforward, teams may find that it takes considerable discussion and judgment to place each goal into one of these categories.

The judgments of family members should carry substantial weight in categorizing the relative value of goals, but other factors also should be considered. Generally, goals should be given more importance if they allow the child to gain access to or be maintained in inclusive settings. Likewise, goals should be given more importance if they allow the child to learn skills that will result in learning other skills. For example, learning to imitate one's peers allows the child to learn from observing the behavior of others. Goals should be given more importance if they reduce the possibility of the child's being stigmatized. For example, if a child is not toilet trained but is moving into a kindergarten placement, goals related to toilet training may take on added value. Frequently, goals that increase the ease with which the child can be cared for also deserve higher status. For example, if a child is extremely fussy and cries a great deal, a legitimate goal is to assist the child in quieting. Finally, goals should be given more value if they are useful (functional) in multiple environments in which the child spends time.

Identifying the relative value of goals will assist team members in making decisions about how their time and effort should be distributed. Teams can also use this classification to ensure that high-priority goals are addressed at multiple points throughout each day. This categorization of goals also provides guidance to team members in terms of which goals require more extensive monitoring as the intervention plan is implemented.

Translating Goals into Intervention Objectives

After goals are identified through summarizing the assessment results, analyzing the intent of the goals, and determining their relative priority, short-term instructional objectives for each goal should be developed. A common procedure for doing this is task analysis. In this section, the steps for conducting task analyses are described, then issues around writing instructional objectives are discussed.

Task Analysis

Task analysis is a *process* by which large goals are broken into smaller objectives and sequenced for instruction. Task analysis also is a *product;* the written result from conducting a task analysis is a product called a *task analysis.* This product is a list of short-term objectives that lead directly from the child's current level of performance to the long-term objective. It is not a set of teaching procedures or set of activities; rather it is a list of child behaviors that lead to the more advanced behavior in the long-term goals.

Task analysis is a fundamental means of analyzing (into smaller units) curriculum content that is too large to be learned at once. Conducting task analyses is an important teacher competency and may be related to the amount children learn (Fredericks, Anderson, & Baldwin, 1979). The steps for conducting task analyses are straightforward; Wolery, Bailey, and Sugai (1988) present five.

Step 1: Specify the long-term objective and look for related sources The objective to be task analyzed should be specified precisely. The teacher should then look to various curricular guides for information concerning this objective. Over the past 20 years, hundreds of task analyses have been written, and many of them are found in curricula and other texts on teaching children with disabilities. While task analysis is a method for individualizing curriculum content, there is little need to write new task analyses for skills that already have been analyzed by someone else. However, teachers need the skill of analyzing objectives because published task analyses may not be available or may not be successful with a particular child for an important objective. In most cases, skills can be analyzed in a number of sequences. No one task analysis is necessarily correct, and the interventionist should attempt to find the one best suited to the child's learning patterns and current environment.

Thiagarajan (1980) has described a procedure for adapting previously written task analyses for individual children. This involves making adjustments in the entry point into a sequence of steps, adjusting the size of the steps (making them larger or smaller), adjusting the assistance children need to perform different steps, and adjusting the behaviors by which children show they have acquired the content of the task analysis.

Step 2: Break the long-term objective into steps or break the behavior into smaller behaviors At this point in the process, the teacher is not concerned with how to teach the skill or how many steps are involved in the task analysis. Rather, he or she should attempt to break the skill into a few meaningful behaviors. Several means exist for doing this.

First, find a person who can do the skill competently, watch her do it, and write down the behaviors she does. Depending on the complexity of the task being analyzed, the teacher may have to watch the person do the skill several times to identify all of the small subtle behaviors involved. Competent performers do skills quickly, and the teacher may have to ask the person to do the behavior more slowly. Second, the teacher can do the behavior himself and write down the steps as they are done. Again, several repetitions may be needed, and doing the task slowly may be of benefit. These two methods are particularly useful for task analyzing skills that are composed of chains of motor responses, such as playing with certain toys, dressing/undressing, self-feeding, and riding a tricycle.

The two methods just described are not very useful for analyzing skills such as making a greeting response, matching shapes, or naming the letters of the alphabet. For such skills, teachers should use a third method: logical analysis. With logical analysis, teachers "think through tasks" to identify the behaviors and discriminations needed to perform the skill correctly. For example, a logical analysis of naming objectives would involve visual discrimination of the target objects from other similar objects, "matching" the object to the correct name from the infinite number of possible names, and then accurately saying the name.

Fourth, teachers can identify and use the sequences through which typical children acquire a given skill. The assumption of this method is that children learn complex behaviors sequentially, starting with the simplest behaviors and progressively moving toward more difficult responses. Thus, teachers merely determine the course through which a skill is acquired normally and write down the steps. Cohen and Gross (1979a, 1979b) described numerous sequences using this method across a number of different curricular domains. This method is inappropriate when the identified sequences are impossible for the child to do because of a disability.

Fifth, teachers can use a levels-of-assistance approach to break skills into steps. The process involves specifying the different amounts of help that a child might need at various points in learning a specific skill. For example, if a child can perform the target skill only when given a physical prompt, the steps of the task analysis might include doing it in response to partial physical prompts, a full model, a partial model, and without assistance. A similar approach is to increase the complexity of the conditions in which the child performs a skill. For example, if a child currently will greet one teacher, the steps of the task analysis might specify a number of different people and situations in which a greeting response is appropriate. When using this method, which is particularly useful when analyzing generalization tasks, all the possible situations in which the behavior might be needed should be listed.

Step 3: Eliminate unnecessary and redundant behaviors When skills are task analyzed, unnecessary steps may be listed and should be eliminated in the written task analysis. Likewise, if the same behavior occurs several times, it should be listed only once.

Step 4: Sequence the steps for teaching After behaviors have been listed and unnecessary and redundant steps have been eliminated, the remaining behaviors should be sequenced for teaching. The two primary methods for sequencing skills for teaching include sequencing by temporal order and sequencing by difficulty. *Temporal order* involves listing the steps in the sequence in which they will be performed when the skill is completely learned. This is a particularly useful method for chained skills (e.g., putting on clothing, brushing teeth) or for behaviors that occur during large routines (e.g., preparing to go home, mealtime routines). Because it is desirable to teach such skills during naturally occurring routines, specifying the skills to be learned in temporal order is helpful. Sequencing by *difficulty* is more useful with responses that do not occur in chains or larger routines. Teachers must consider the difficulty in actually producing each response and the difficulty of the discriminations associated with those responses. When skills are broken into different behaviors, using the levels-of-assistance method, sequencing by difficulty can be easily accomplished.

Step 5: Specify prerequisite behaviors Most task analyses include some behaviors that must be acquired before the easiest step of the task analysis can be performed. If the target child cannot perform the prerequisite behaviors, instruction should be delayed on the task analysis until the prerequisite behaviors are acquired.

These five steps have been used repeatedly and successfully to develop task analyses of skills across different types of content. To decrease the effort expended in teaching, teachers should retain copies of successful task analyses. If a task analysis was successful with one child, it may well apply to another. Therefore, teachers should compile a task-analysis "bank." Also, teachers who use task analysis frequently accumulate several different task analysis patterns into which they can fit similar content. For example, to name pictures of common objects, the steps of the task analysis might be (a) to imitate verbally the name of the picture, (b) to match the picture to an identical picture in the presence of three distractors, (c) to identify receptively the picture when given the name, and (d) to identify the picture verbally. This structure of verbal imitation, matching, receptive identification, and expressive labeling could fit other areas, such as naming objects, naming letters of the alphabet, reading sight words, and naming numerals. When teachers are aware of these task-analysis patterns, writing new task analyses can be accomplished quickly.

Writing Instructional Objectives

Several sources have described procedures for writing instructional objectives (Mager, 1962; Wolery et al., 1988; Vargas, 1972), which involves specifying the behaviors to be performed, identifying the conditions under which performance will be measured, and identifying the level (criterion) at which the behavior must be performed before it is said to have been learned. Objectives should be written because they are required by law, provide a focus for instruction, are a standard against which progress can be monitored, and can be used to communicate information to others.

A *behavior* is a movement, has a beginning and an end, is repeatable, and can be measured reliably by two or more individuals. Further, behaviors have a variety of dimensions, such as their accuracy, rate, latency, duration, and intensity. Teams must identify the most appropriate dimension when writing objectives. In addition, they must identify whether the function or the form of the skill is more important. As described earlier, the form may be important with some objectives, but function may be more important with others. When function is identified, then a list of appropriate forms should be generated.

Conditions in instructional objectives refer to the materials, task directions, and situations in which the behavior must be performed. Careful specification of the conditions allows for consistent measurement of the effects of the instruction. When specifying conditions, those that will exist in generalization settings should appear in the objective, or separate generalization objectives should be written.

Criterion statements in objectives tell how well the child must perform the skill. Criterion statements serve several functions: (a) They set a goal toward which teachers, families, and children can work; (b) they tell the teacher when to move on to other skills; and (c) they provide a standard against which progress can be monitored. Too often the criterion portion of objectives is written without sufficient thought. Because of the important functions that criterion statements serve, they should be written with care. Consideration should be given to several issues. The dimension (accuracy, rate, combination of accuracy and rate, duration, etc.) of behavior that is most important should be measured. This may change as instruction progresses. For example, initial focus may be on accuracy, and as it is established, the focus may switch to a combination of rate and accuracy. Consideration also should be given to how well the behavior must be performed before it will be useful to the child. This ability can be determined by measuring how well children who competently perform the behavior do it. An average of this measurement can then be used in the criterion statement. For example, the teacher could measure how long it takes typical children to brush their teeth, calculate an average time, and use that interval in the criterion statement for a target child. Consideration should be given to identifying the minimum level that will result in enjoyment of the skill or the minimum level needed to move on to the next skill or environment. Consideration also should be given to the form in which the criterion is written. If percentage is written into the criterion statement, then the number of opportunities on which the percentage is calculated also should be listed. For example, 100% could be one correct response out of one opportunity, or 10 out of 10, or 100 out of 100. When writing the criterion statements, teachers should always check them and ask "What does this really mean?"

In addition to these considerations, the team should ensure that objectives exist for all phases of instruction (Kozloff, 1994a). Children's performance can be conceptualized as progressing through five phases: acquisition, fluency, maintenance, generalization, and adaptation (Haring, Liberty, & White, 1980). Acquisition, the first phase, refers to learning the basic requirements of a skill. Objectives that target acquisition frequently focus on the accuracy of a response. The second phase of learning, fluency (or proficiency), refers to how quickly or smoothly the child performs skills. Fluency objectives frequently have rate or duration-per-occurrence measures in the criterion statements. Maintenance refers to continued performance of a skill in conditions similar to training; generalization refers to performance of acquired skills in situations other than the instructional conditions. For example, children need to apply and use skills when other people are present, in other settings, and with other materials. Billingsley (1984) analyzed IEPs of students with severe disabilities and found that few objectives targeted generalization of skills. Adaptation refers to the child's ability to modify the skill to perform it when the conditions in which it is needed change. A good rule of thumb is that no objective should be considered mastered until (a) it is performed fluently and over time for the persons who taught it in the situations in which it was learned, (b) when it is performed for some other individual at a needed time in a situation different from the instructional setting, and (c) when it is performed spontaneously when needed in a situation other than the instructional environment.

Selecting Potential Intervention Strategies

In addition to identifying the intervention goals and translating them into instructional objectives, teams must select from the wide range of intervention practices and strategies that can be used to address the goals of infants, toddlers, and preschoolers with special needs. These include the guidelines for developmentally appropriate practices (Bredekamp & Rosegrant, 1992) and a number of specialized practices and strategies, which are described in detail in a number of relevant texts. For general information on a wide range of strategies see Barnett and Carey (1992); Bricker and Cripe (1992); Bailey and Wolery (1992); Brown, Thurman, and Pearl (1993); Gable and Warren (1993); Linder (1993); Odom and McLean (in press); Raver (1991); Wolery, Ault, and Doyle (1992); and Wolery and Wilbers (1994). Odom, McConnell, and McEvoy (1992) describe interventions for addressing social competence and social skills; Warren and Reichle (1992), Kaiser and Gray (1993), and Fey, Windsor, and Warren (1995) present information on practices and strategies for addressing communication skills.

When selecting interventions, three general guidelines should be followed. First, the practices and strategies that are selected should be likely to be effective; they should result in the child's meeting the objectives that the team has specified on the intervention plan. Second, they should be likely to be used. The ideal strategy or practice requires minimal adaptations of ongoing activities and routines and minimal changes in the styles of interacting and roles that adults assume in those activities. When more than one strategy will be effective, the persons who will be using the strategy should be given choices about which one they prefer. Usually, they are more likely to use practices they have chosen over those that are imposed on them. Third, the selected practices and strategies should be as naturalistic as possible. When several strategies may be effective in helping a child achieve the objectives that have been established, the strategy that seems most like what occurs in the natural environment should be used.

IMPLEMENTING INTERVENTION PLANS

General Guidelines for Implementing Interventions

After instructional objectives have been written, the team needs to schedule when and in which contexts intervention should be implemented. Six general guidelines should be followed in scheduling the instruction (Wolery, 1994). Implicit in these guidelines is the fundamental assumption that intervention for infants and young children with special needs should be integrated into their daily activities. The intervention strategies should not, in most cases, be implemented at separate and specialized times; rather they should be embedded into the naturally occurring interactions with adults and peers and the ongoing daily activities and routines (Bricker & Cripe, 1992). Another implicit assumption is that children's environments should be responsive to their behavior and should be designed to promote child-initiated activities (Bailey & McWilliam, 1990; Dunst, Lowe, & Bartholomew, 1990). Ensuring that children's social and physical environments are responsive means that some adjustments may be necessary in adults' interaction patterns, the physical environment, and the daily schedule. Adults must be knowledgeable of children's goals, observe their activities, and take advantage of all the opportunities that naturally occur to support and reinforce their performance and use of targeted goals.

Promote both participation and independence When implementing intervention, the team needs to establish a balance between two foundational assumptions. First, children should participate in the activities and routines that are planned for their peers (e.g., siblings, classmates at a child-care program, etc.). Second, teams should promote children's independence and mastery of their environments. In many cases, meeting both assumptions can be achieved without difficulty, and participation in regularly planned and ongoing activities and routines provides multiple opportunities to promote independence. When a child's disabilities appear to preclude participation, the team should seek to identify and use adaptations in the activities to ensure that the child with special needs is supported while participating (Baumgart et al., 1982; Ferguson & Baumgart, 1991). Children should not be excluded from activities and routines because of their ability levels, and they should not be put into situations in which they fail and their inabilities are highlighted to their peers. Thus, careful planning is needed to adapt activities and routines or to provide direct assistance at key times to ensure active participation.

Address each goal multiple times throughout the day Unlike instruction for older elementary school children, intervention on critical goals for infants, toddlers, and preschoolers with special needs must be addressed at multiple occasions throughout the day (Bricker & Cripe, 1992; Wolery, 1994). This guideline has two direct implications for planning instruction. First, planned opportunities for acquiring each critical goal should be interspersed throughout the child's day; the team should devise intervention plans for times outside of their own direct contacts with the child. Second, the persons who interact and care for the child must be cognizant of critical goals and take advantage of each teachable moment or opportunity to support the child's learning and development—even when that opportunity was not scheduled or planned.

1. Down the left-hand column of the matrix, list the events (activities, etc.) in which the child will participate during the day. The events should be listed in the order in which they occur daily.
2. Below each listing in the left-hand column of the matrix, list the location of each event. The listing should include the entire day. The purpose is to provide instruction in all relevant locations.
3. Also in the left-hand column of the matrix, list the time that each activity will start and its expected duration each day.
4. Also in the left-hand column of the matrix, list the name of the adult who is responsible for implementing the instruction; if peers also are used, then they should be listed here as well.
5. Across the top of the matrix list all of the skills that have been identified for instruction. Each column should include one behavior.
6. In the cells of the matrix, list the materials and specialized instructional strategies that will be used. If a skill is not addressed during a given event or time, then that cell should be left blank.
7. Check the matrix to ensure that skills will be taught by different adults using a variety of materials and settings to facilitate generalization.

FIGURE 16.2

Guidelines for using an activity/routine-by-goal matrix

Note: Adapted from "Applications of the Individualized Curriculum Sequencing Model to Learners with Severe Sensory Impairments" (pp. 260–266) by E. Helmstetter and D. Guess, in L. Goetz, D. Guess, and K. Stremel-Campbell (Eds.) *Innovative Program Design for Individuals with Dual Sensory Impairments,* 1987, Baltimore, MD: Paul H. Brookes.

Source: From "Implementing Instruction for Young Children with Special Needs in Early Childhood Classrooms" (p. 157) by M. Wolery, in M. Wolery and J. Wilbers (Eds.), *Including Young Children with Special Needs in Early Childhood Programs,* 1994, Washington, DC: National Association for the Education of Young Children. Copyright 1994 by the National Association for the Education of Young Children. Reprinted by permission.

Address multiple goals within the same activity Because intervention strategies and practices are, for the most part, embedded into ongoing activities and routines, each activity and routine may provide opportunities to address multiple goals almost simultaneously (Bricker & Cripe, 1992). For example, snack time provides opportunities to practice drinking from a cup; it can also provide opportunities to use requesting skills, conversational skills with peers, and motor skills during snack preparation or cleanup. Ideally, each activity and routine would set the occasion to address multiple goals.

Use an activity/routine-by-goal matrix To accomplish the previous two recommendations (i.e., promote use of each important goal in multiple activities throughout the day, and promote use of multiple goals in each activity and routine), the use of an activities/routines-by-goal matrix is recommended (Bricker & Cripe, 1992). This matrix is an organizational tool to assist teams in planning when each goal will be addressed throughout the day, ensuring that each activity and routine is used to address goals, and identifying times for monitoring children's progress. Guidelines for using the matrix are presented in Figure 16.2.

Embed instructional opportunities into existing activities and routines.
To teach peer imitation to young children with autism, five progressive time-delay trials were dispersed throughout daily art activities. The trials were not implemented one after another, but were implemented when the peer was doing a unique behavior that could be imitated and when it did not interfere with the child's ongoing behavior. All children learned to imitate their peer's behavior (Venn, Wolery, Werts, et al., 1993).

To teach picture naming to young children with and without developmental delays, constant time delay was interspersed throughout the day in a variety of activities. The trials were implemented so as not to interfere with children's ongoing behavior. At least 15 minutes occurred between trials. All children learned to name the pictures (Chiara, Schuster, Bell, & Wolery, in press).

Adjust activities by changing what children do in them.
To increase children's social interactions during free-play periods, the nature of what children did during group activities was adjusted. Specifically, group affection activities (games and songs that increased physical contact and interaction) were used. This resulted in increased social contact during free-play (McEvoy et al., 1988).

To teach various preacademic skills, teachers dispersed single, brief instructional trials at the beginning of in-class transitions. The children quickly acquired the targeted skills (Werts, Wolery, Holcombe-Ligon, Vassilaros, & Billings, 1992; Wolery, Doyle, Gast, Ault, & Simpson, 1993).

Adjust activities/routines by adapting the materials and their access.
To increase the amount of social play during free-play periods, teachers provided toys that were more likely to promote social interactions. Providing these toys resulted in increased social contact (Rettig, Kallam, & McCarthy-Salm, 1993).

To increase opportunities for children to initiate communicative behaviors, teachers placed some toys on a "must-ask shelf." To gain access to these toys, children were required to ask an adult for them. The teachers then used incidental teaching and saw increases in children's communicative behaviors (Hart & Risley, 1975).

FIGURE 16.3
Recommendations for adjusting activities/routines
Source: From "Current Practices with Young Children Who Have Disabilities: Placement, Assessment, and Instructional Issues" by M. Wolery, M. G. Werts, and A. Holcombe, 1994, *Focus on Exceptional Children, 26*(6), p 11. Copyright 1994 by Love Publishing Company. Reprinted by permission.

Adapt ongoing activities/routines as necessary Often, but not always, participation in ongoing activities and routines with attention to children's goals will be sufficient to allow children to acquire and use the skills the team has decided are important. However, in many cases, the activities and routines will need to be adapted. These adaptations or modifications are designed to increase the likelihood that children will acquire and use the skills the team has determined are critical. Several potential guidelines are possible. These are provided in Figure 16.3, with examples from the research literature.

Adjust activities/routines by providing additional opportunities to respond.
To teach preacademic behaviors, individualized constant time-delay trials were interspersed with other circle-time activities. Children with developmental delays acquired the targeted skills (Fleming, 1991).

Use shorter but more frequent activities to increase opportunities for instruction.
To teach self-feeding, more meals were provided each day and the amount of food provided at each meal was decreased. Teacher prompting with graduated guidance in this arrangement resulted in rapid increases in children's self-feeding behaviors (Azrin & Armstrong, 1973).

Adjust activities by changing the rules of access to particular areas.
To increase children's contact with a classroom area they avoided and to decrease the number of area switches, children were required to go to the area they avoided each time they wanted to switch areas. This resulted in increased engagement in the avoided area and reduced the number of task switches (Jacobson, Bushell, & Risley, 1969; Rowbury, Baer, & Baer, 1976).

Adjust activities by changing the social composition or rules of social activities.
To increase the amount of social contact between children, structured play activities with defined roles and routines were used. This resulted in more social initiations and responses to children with disabilities (DeKlyen & Odom, 1989).

To increase the number and rate of turn-taking in conversational exchanges, a highly loquacious child was seated next to a child with speech and language impairment during snack and meals. This physical proximity resulted in increased turn-taking (Wolery, Anthony, Heckathorn, Filla, & Bell, 1993).

Adjust activities by training peers to engage in facilitative behavior.
To promote requesting behaviors in children with severe disabilities, their peers without disabilities were taught to use the mand-model procedure. The peers were taught to use the procedure in separate sessions, but implemented it during snack activities (Venn, Wolery, Fleming, et al., 1993).

To increase the amount of social interactions between children with and without disabilities, typically developing peers were taught to initiate social exchanges with their peers. This resulted in increased social interactions between children (Odom, Hoyson, Jamieson, & Strain, 1985).

FIGURE 16.3
Continued

Monitor the implementation and effects of intervention As noted previously, the intervention plan should be viewed as a tentative guide for designing intervention strategies and practices. Adjustments to the goals are likely as the plan is validated through implementation and as children make progress. Thus, regular monitoring of the effects of intervention is required (Kozloff, 1994b). (A detailed discussion is presented in Chapter 17.) Because interventions are implemented during ongoing interactions, activities, and routines, the possibility that intervention practices and strategies will be used incorrectly or inconsistently is high. Thus, implementation of the intervention practices and strategies should be monitored (Barnett et al., 1994). This topic also is discussed in Chapter 17.

SUMMARY OF KEY CONCEPTS

- Assessment information should be collected to make specific decisions, and the decisions that need to be made influence how the information is collected and how it is used.
- Written reports of assessment activities should include the identifying information, background information, methods used in the assessment, results of the assessment, and recommendations.
- To plan meaningful interventions, teams need information on children's developmental abilities, their independence in relevant environments, their usual interaction patterns, and the effects of various supports and assistance.
- To plan meaningful interventions, teams need information about the environments in which children spend time, such as the schedule of activities and the social and physical structure of those environments.
- To plan meaningful interventions, teams need information about the priorities and concerns of families.
- When planning interventions, teams should involve families in the planning, involve all team members, be aware of and comply with relevant legal guidelines, evaluate the trustworthiness of the assessment information, and view the plan as tentative.
- Teams, in conjunction with families, should identify long-term goals, conduct task analyses, write short-term objectives, and devise plans for implementing intervention to accomplish the goals and objectives.
- When planning implementation of intervention, teams should promote both participation and independence, address each goal multiple times throughout the day, address multiple goals within the same activity, and use an activity/routine-by-skill matrix to organize instruction.
- Intervention to address children's goals should be embedded into the ongoing daily routines and activities children experience.

REFERENCES

Ager, C. L., & Shapiro, E. S. (1995). Template matching as a strategy for assessment of and intervention for preschool students with disabilities. *Topics in Early Childhood Special Education, 15,* 187–218.

Azrin, N. H., & Armstrong, P. M. (1973). The "mini-meal": A method for teaching eating skills to the profoundly retarded. *Mental Retardation, 11,* 9–13.

Bailey, D. B. (1988). Considerations in developing family goals. In D. B. Bailey & R. J. Simeonsson (Eds.), *Family assessment in early intervention* (pp. 229–249). Englewood Cliffs, NJ: Merrill/Prentice Hall.

Bailey, D. B., & McWilliam, R. A. (1990). Normalizing early intervention. *Topics in Early Childhood Special Education, 10*(2), 33–47.

Bailey, D. B., & Wolery, M. (1992). *Teaching infants and preschoolers with disabilities* (2nd ed.). Englewood Cliffs, NJ: Merrill/Prentice Hall.

Barnett, D. W., & Carey, K. T. (1992). *Designing interventions for preschool learning and behavior problems.* San Francisco: Jossey-Bass.

Barnett, D. W., Ehrhardt, K. E., Stollar, S. A., & Bauer, A. M. (1994). PASSKey: A model for naturalistic assessment and intervention design. *Topics in Early Childhood Special Education, 14,* 350–373.

Barnett, D. W., Macmann, G. M., & Carey, K. T. (1992). Early intervention and the assessment of developmental skills: Challenges and directions. *Topics in Early Childhood Special Education, 12*(1), 21–43.

Barrera, I. (1993). Effective and appropriate instruction for all children: The challenge of cultural/linguistic diversity and young children with special needs. *Topics in Early Childhood Special Education, 13,* 461–587.

Baumgart, D., Brown, L., Pumpian, I., Nisbet, J., Ford, A., Sweet, M., Messina, R., & Schroeder, J. (1982). Principle of partial participation and individualized adaptations in educational programs for severely handicapped students. *Journal of the Association for the Severely Handicapped, 7*(2), 17–22.

Billingsley, F. F. (1984). Where are the generalization outcomes? (an examination of instructional objectives). *Journal of the Association for the Severely Handicapped, 9,* 186–200.

Bredekamp, S., & Rosegrant, T. (Eds.) (1992). *Reaching potentials: Appropriate curriculum and assessment for young children* (Vol. 1). Washington, DC: National Association for the Education of Young Children.

Bricker, D., & Cripe, J. J. W. (1992). *An activity-based approach to early intervention.* Baltimore, MD: Paul H. Brookes.

Brown, W., Thurman, S. K., & Pearl, L. F. (1993). *Family-centered early intervention with infants and toddlers: Innovative cross-disciplinary approaches.* Baltimore, MD: Paul H. Brookes.

Bruder, M. B. (1994). Working with members of other disciplines: Collaboration for success. In M. Wolery & J. Wilbers (Eds.), *Including children with special needs in early childhood programs* (pp. 45–70). Washington, DC: National Association for the Education of Young Children.

Chiara, L., Schuster, J. W., Bell, J., & Wolery, M. (in press). Comparison of distributed trials and small group instruction with constant time delay. *Journal of Early Intervention.*

Cohen, M., & Gross, P. (1979a). *The developmental resources: Behavioral sequences for assessment and program planning* (Vol. 1). New York: Grune & Stratton.

Cohen, M., & Gross, P. (1979b). *The developmental resources: Behavioral sequences for assessment and program planning* (Vol. 2). New York: Grune & Stratton.

Cone, J. D. (1987). Intervention planning using adaptive behavior instruments. *Journal of Special Education, 21,* 127–148.

DeGangi, G. A., Wietlisbach, S., Poisson, S., Stein, E., & Royeen, C. (1994). The impact of culture and socioeconomic status on family-professional collaboration: Challenges and solutions. *Topics in Early Childhood Special Education, 14,* 503–520.

DeKlyen, M., & Odom, S. L. (1989). Activity structure and social interactions with peers in developmentally integrated play groups. *Journal of Early Intervention, 13,* 342–352.

Drasgow, E., & Halle, J. W. (1995). Teaching social communication to young children with severe disabilities. *Topics in Early Childhood Special Education 15,* 164–186.

Dunst, C. J., Lowe, L. W., & Bartholomew, P. C. (1990). Contingent social responsiveness, family ecology, and infant communicative competence. *National Student Speech Language Hearing Association Journal, 17,* 39–49.

Dunst, C. J., Trivette, C. M., & Deal, A. G. (1994). *Supporting and strengthening families: Vol. 1. Methods, strategies and practices.* Cambridge, MA: Brookline.

Falvey, M. A., Forest, M., Pearpoint, J., & Rosenberg, R. L. (1994). Building connections. In J. S. Thousand, R. A. Villa, & A. I. Nevin (Eds.), *Creativity and collaborative learning: A practical guide to empowering students and teachers* (pp. 347–368). Baltimore, MD: Paul H. Brookes.

Ferguson, D., & Baumgart, D. (1991). Partial participation revisited. *Journal of the Association for Persons with Severe Handicaps, 16,* 218–227.

Fey, M. E., Windsor, J., & Warren, S. F. (1995). *Language intervention: Preschool through the elementary years.* Baltimore, MD: Paul H. Brookes.

Fleming, L. (1991). *Using constant time delay during circle time.* (Unpublished doctoral dissertation, University of Kentucky, Lexington.)

Fredericks, H. D., Anderson, R., & Baldwin, V. (1979). The identification of competency indicators of teaching of the severely handicapped. *American Association for the Education of the Severely and Profoundly Handicapped Review, 4,* 81–95.

Gable, R. A., & Warren, S. F. (1993). *Strategies for teaching students with mild to severe mental retardation.* Baltimore, MD: Paul H. Brookes.

Goodman, J. F. (1992). *When slow is fast enough: Educating the delayed preschool child.* New York: Guilford.

Greenwood, C. R., Carta, J. J., & Atwater, J. (1991). Ecobehavioral analysis in the classroom: Review and implications. *Journal of Behavioral Education, 1,* 59–77.

Guess, D., Roberts, S., Siegel-Causey, E., & Ault, M. M. (1993). Analysis of behavior state conditions and associated environmental variables among students with profound handicaps. *American Journal on Mental Retardation, 97,* 634–653.

Guess, D., Siegel-Causey, E., Roberts, S., & Guy, B. (1993). Analysis of state organizational patterns among students with profound disabilities. *Journal of the Association for Persons with Severe Handicaps, 18,* 93–108.

Haring, N. G., Liberty, K. A., & White, O. R. (1980). Rules for data-based strategy decisions in instructional programs. In W. Sailor, B. Wilcox, & L. Brown (Eds.), *Methods of instruction for severely handicapped students* (pp. 159–192). Baltimore, MD: Paul H. Brookes.

Hart, B., & Risley, T. R. (1975). Incidental teaching of language in the preschool. *Journal of Applied Behavior Analysis, 7,* 411–420.

Jacobson, J. M., Bushell, D., & Risley, T. R. (1969). Switching requirements in a Head Start classroom. *Journal of Applied Behavior Analysis, 2,* 43–47.

Johnson, J. E., & Johnson, K. M. (1994). The applicability of developmentally appropriate practice for children with diverse abilities. *Journal of Early Intervention, 18,* 343–346.

Kaiser, A. P., & Gray, D. B. (1993). *Enhancing children's communication: Research foundations for intervention.* Baltimore, MD: Paul H. Brookes.

Kozloff, M. A. (1994a). *Improving educational outcomes for children with disabilities: Principles for assessment, program planning, and evaluation.* Baltimore, MD: Paul H. Brookes.

Kozloff, M. A. (1994b). *Improving educational outcomes for children with disabilities: Guidelines and protocols for practice.* Baltimore, MD: Paul H. Brookes.

Linder, T. W. (1993). *Transdisciplinary play based intervention: Guidelines for developing a meaningful curriculum for young children.* Baltimore, MD: Paul H. Brookes.

Lynch, E. W., & Hanson, M. J. (1992). *Developing cross-cultural competence: A guide for working with young children and their families.* Baltimore, MD: Paul H. Brookes.

Mager, R. (1962). *Preparing instructional objectives.* Belmont, CA: Fearon.

McEvoy, M. A., Nordquist, V. M., Twardosz, S., Heckman, K. A., Wehby, J. H., & Denny, R. K. (1988). Promoting autistic children's peer interaction in an integrated early childhood setting using affection activities. *Journal of Applied Behavior Analysis, 21,* 193–200.

McGonigel, M. J., Kaufmann, R. K., & Johnson, B. H. (Eds.). (1991). *Guidelines and recommended practices for the Individualized Family Service Plan* (2nd ed.). Bethesda, MD: Association for the Care of Children's Health.

McGonigel, M. J., Woodruff, G., & Roszmann-Millican, M. (1994). The transdisciplinary team: A model for family-centered early intervention. In L. J. Johnson, R. J. Gallagher, & M. J. LaMontagne (Eds.), *Meeting early intervention challenges: Issues from birth to three* (2nd ed.) (pp. 95-131). Baltimore, MD: Paul H. Brookes.

Neel, R. S., Billingsley, F. F., McCarty, F., Symonds, D., Lambert, C., Lewis-Smith, N., & Hanashiro, R. (1983). *Impact curriculum.* U.S. Department of Education (Contract No. 300-80-0842). Seattle, University of Washington, College of Education.

Odom, S. L., Hoyson, M., Jamieson, B., & Strain, P. S. (1985). Increasing handicapped preschoolers' peer social interactions: Cross setting and component analysis. *Journal of Applied Behavior Analysis, 18,* 3–16.

Odom, S. L., McConnell, S. R., & McEvoy, M. A. (1992). *Social competence of young children with disabilities: Issues and strategies for intervention.* Baltimore, MD: Paul H. Brookes.

Odom, S. L., & McLean, M. (in press). *Recommended practices in early intervention/education.* Austin, TX: Pro-Ed.

Rainforth, B., York, J., & Macdonald, C. (1992). *Collaborative teams for students with severe disabili-*

ties: Integrating therapy and educational services. Baltimore, MD: Paul H. Brookes.

Raver, S. A. (1991). *Strategies for teaching at-risk and handicapped infants and toddlers: A transdisciplinary approach.* Englewood Cliffs, NJ: Merrill/ Prentice Hall.

Rettig, M., Kallam, M., & McCarthy-Salm, K. (1993). The effect of social and isolate toys on social interactions of preschool-aged children. *Education and Training in Mental Retardation, 28,* 252–256.

Rowbury, T. G., Baer, A. M., & Baer, D. M. (1976). Interactions between teacher guidance and contingent access to play in developing preacademic skills of deviant preschool children. *Journal of Applied Behavior Analysis, 9,* 85–104.

Salisbury, C. L. (1992). Parents as team members: Inclusive teams, collaborative outcomes. In B. Rainforth, J. York, & C. Macdonald (Eds.), *Collaborative teams for students with severe disabilities: Integrating therapy and educational services* (pp. 43–66). Baltimore, MD: Paul H. Brookes.

Stayton, V. D., & Karnes, M. B. (1994). Model programs for infants and toddlers with disabilities and their families. In L. J. Johnson, R. J. Gallagher, & M. J. LaMontagne (Eds.), *Meeting early intervention challenges: Issues from birth to three* (2nd ed.) (pp. 33–58). Baltimore, MD: Paul H. Brookes.

Thiagarajan, S. (1980). Individualizing instructional objectives. *Teaching Exceptional Children, 12,* 126–127.

Vargas, J. S. (1972). *Writing worthwhile behavioral objectives.* New York: Harper & Row.

Venn, M. L., Wolery, M., Fleming, L. A., DeCesare, L. D., Morris, A., Sigesmund, M. H. (1993). Effects of teaching preschool peers to use the mand-model procedure during snack activities. *American Journal of Speech-Language Pathology, 2*(1), 38–46.

Venn, M. L., Wolery, M., Werts, M. G., Morris, A., DeCesare, L. D., & Cuffs, M. S. (1993). Embedding instruction in art activities to teach preschoolers with disabilities to imitate their peers. *Early Childhood Research Quarterly, 8,* 277–294.

Vygotsky, L. S. (1978). *Mind and society.* Cambridge, MA: Harvard University Press.

Warren, S. F., & Reichle, J. (Eds.) (1992). *Causes and effects in communication and language intervention.* Baltimore, MD: Paul H. Brookes.

Werts, M. G., Wolery, M., Holcombe-Ligon, A., Vassilaros, M. A., & Billings, S. S. (1992). Efficacy of transition-based teaching with instructive feedback. *Education and Treatment of Children, 15,* 320–334.

White, O. R. (1980). Adaptive performance objectives: Form versus function. In W. Sailor, B. Wilcox, & L. Brown (Eds.), *Methods of instruction for severely handicapped students* (pp. 47–69). Baltimore, MD: Paul H. Brookes.

Wolery, M. (1994). Implementing instruction for young children with special needs in early childhood classrooms. In M. Wolery & J. Wilbers (Eds.), *Including children with special needs in early childhood programs* (pp. 154–166). Washington, DC: National Association for the Education of Young Children.

Wolery, M., Anthony, L., Heckathorn, K., Filla, A., & Bell, R. (1993). *Promoting preschoolers' conversations at snack and mealtimes.* Unpublished manuscript.

Wolery, M., Ault, M. J., & Doyle, P. M. (1992). *Teaching students with moderate and severe disabilities: Use of response prompting strategies.* White Plains, NY: Longman.

Wolery, M., Bailey, D. B., & Sugai, G. M. (1988). *Effective teaching: Principles and procedures of applied behavior analysis with exceptional students.* Boston: Allyn and Bacon.

Wolery, M., Doyle, P. M., Gast, D. L., Ault, M. J., & Simpson, S. L. (1993). Comparison of progressive time delay and transition-based teaching with preschoolers who have developmental delays. *Journal of Early Intervention, 17,* 160–176.

Wolery, M., & Wilbers, J. S. (1994). *Including young children with special needs in early childhood programs.* Washington, DC: National Association for the Education of Young Children.

CHAPTER

17

Monitoring Child Progress

Mark Wolery
Allegheny-Singer Research Institute

Several of the chapters in this text describe considerations, methods, and instruments for conducting assessments to plan and design intervention programs for infants and young children with developmental disabilities and delays. A temptation exists to think that when the plan is developed, the early intervention team should stop assessing and focus on intervention activities. In part, this is true; however, assessment is never really completed. Each interaction with children provides an opportunity to gather information for making decisions about their progress and program (to continue assessing them). In this chapter, such assessments are referred to as *monitoring*. Initially, the purposes of monitoring are described, and then general considerations or guidelines for conducting monitoring assessments are presented. The next section addresses approaches used in monitoring children's performance, and the final section addresses issues related to monitoring intervention plans. Throughout the chapter, emphasis is placed on monitoring as an ongoing assessment activity rather than a periodic event that occurs every six months or annually.

PURPOSES OF MONITORING

Three broad purposes of monitoring assessments can be proposed: (a) to validate conclusions from an initial assessment, (b) to develop a record of progress over time, and (c) to determine whether to modify or revise the intervention plan. These purposes are discussed in the following paragraphs.

Validate Conclusions from Initial Assessment

Usual practice involves gathering information from multiple sources using multiple measurement strategies to devise an intervention plan for a young child. After the information is collected, the team analyzes it and makes conclusions and decisions about the goals and objectives that are appropriate and about the intervention practices that are likely to be effective in achieving those goals. However, the conclusions based on the assessment information may be faulty for a number of reasons. Development is complex, children change with time, and disabilities can produce effects on children's development that are difficult to identify. Further, children's behavior can vary considerably, depending on the social and physical contexts in which it occurs. Thus, assessment information gathered from certain contexts may produce conclusions that do not reflect children's performance in other situations. For example, some children's communicative and social behavior may be quite different when they are in familiar as compared with unfamiliar situations. Conducting assessments in natural contexts and seeking validation from family members during the assessment process may minimize but not completely control for the variations in the effects of different contexts. Finally, despite substantial progress, our measurement procedures and instruments are imperfect. Thus, it is quite possible that some of the goals and objectives that are established and some of the interventions that are planned may be based on incomplete or faulty conclusions and assumptions about the child. Rather than accepting that errors are unavoidable, teams should monitor children's progress and use the results of that monitoring to make judgments about the adequacy of the initial intervention plan, and, when indicated, revisions should be made in the plan. Such monitoring should occur during the initial weeks after a plan is first implemented.

In terms of goals and objectives, errors occur on a continuum. At one extreme are goals that are already within the child's repertoire—that is, the team has established a goal for a child that he or she has already achieved. At the other extreme are goals that are inappropriate for the child—that is, the team has set unrealistic goals that are simply beyond the child's capabilities; at some later date, those goals may be appropriate, but currently they are not. Of course, errors in goals also occur between these two extremes. In all cases, however, it is important not to waste the child's and the family's time and energy addressing goals that are either already met or that are impossible to meet in the short term. Whether the plan needs a formal revision is a judgment call, but one that should be made by the entire team through formal or informal discussions.

Errors in the plan in terms of intervention practices also are likely. Many early intervention practices have some efficacy data indicating that they were effective in promoting desirable changes in young children's behavior during experimental studies (for summaries of the intervention literature, see Bailey & Wolery, 1992; Barnett & Carey, 1992; Kaiser & Gray, 1993; Odom, McConnell, & McEvoy, 1992; Odom & McLean, in press; Wolery & Wilbers, 1994). However, for very few of our intervention strategies and practices do we have precise information about (a) the conditions that must be in place to increase the probability of the intervention "working," (b) the prerequisite skills young children need to benefit from the practice or strategy, and (c) the levels of implementation required in order for the intervention to produce maximal benefits. As a result, intervention practices and strategies are selected based on less than complete information. Such conditions, of course, increase the probability that some of the selected strategies and practices may not be effective. To guard against this possibility, teams should monitor children's performance, and, based on the results, make judgments about the adequacy of the intervention strategies and practices.

Develop a Record of Progress

A second function of monitoring is to collect a record over time that describes the child's progress and achievements. This record is important from several perspectives. It can provide a record of the level of accountability for the team. It can alert the team that the child has achieved the major goals of the intervention plan, and a new plan is needed. The record can provide team members and families with concrete evidence that progress is being made, that achievements have occurred, and that celebration of accomplishments is in order. The record of progress can also alert the team to the areas in which changes are not occurring as anticipated. As a result, the team can refocus efforts to address high-priority concerns. This may involve collecting more precise information about the child's progress that can in turn lead to modifications of interventions. Finally, the record of progress can be used to make predictions about future progress. An old and well-established principle of human behavior is that current performance is a good predictor of future performance, given, of course, that situations in which it occurs remain relatively unchanged (White & Haring, 1980). Having substantial information about how the child currently functions allows us to make informed assumptions about how that child will function in the immediate future. Such information may be useful in making decisions about changes in programs and placements.

Determine Whether to Adjust Intervention Practices

A primary function of monitoring assessments is to make adjustments in intervention practices and strategies. To fulfill this function, teams must address two issues: deciding whether changes are needed and deciding what changes to make. Information collected through ongoing monitoring can often be used to assist the team in addressing both issues.

Deciding whether changes are needed

To make this determination, monitoring

information should be collected on the child's usual patterns of performance. Four patterns are possible in the monitoring data (information). First, the child may be making steady-to-rapid progress. In such cases, the team will likely conclude that all is well and no adjustments are needed in the intervention plan. When steady progress is occurring, the team should systematically monitor whether the child generalizes (transfers, uses) the skill when and wherever it is appropriate and needed (Billingsley, Burgess, Lynch, & Matlock, 1991; Warren, 1985).

Second, the monitoring information may indicate that no changes are occurring in the child's performance. Given that the team, including the family, has decided and continue to conclude that change is desirable or critical, such cases are relatively straightforward. The intervention practices, contexts, or strategies should be changed.

The third and fourth possibilities, however, call for more careful deliberation by the team. In some cases, the monitoring information will indicate that progress is being made, but that progress is slow or changing only slightly. For other children, the information may indicate that their performance is highly variable. On some days, it appears that substantial progress is being made; on other days, it appears that no progress or perhaps even regression is occurring. With these two patterns (slow change and variable performance), the team members must determine whether to make modifications in the intervention. They need to take into account the child's previous learning or developmental patterns, contextual factors that may be affecting performance (particularly if performance is variable), and any other information that is relevant. Once a decision is made that modification in the intervention plan is needed, the second issue, deciding what to change, becomes the focus of deliberations.

Deciding how to modify the intervention While it is easy to see how monitoring children's progress can lead to information for making the decision that changes are or are not needed, it is often less obvious how information collected from regular monitoring can be used to determine what modifications in interventions should occur. However, in context, such potential is more obvious; consider the following examples.

. . . .

Hoi's intervention team identified using 2- and 3-word statements with agent-action and agent-action-object structures as an intervention goal. They decided to use incidental teaching (Kaiser, Yoder, & Keetz, 1992; Warren, 1992) as an intervention strategy during free-play time in the classroom to teach this goal. The incidental teaching procedure involves the adult responding to Hoi's initiations and providing a request for more elaborate language (and assistance, if necessary) after each initiation. Over a couple of weeks, they monitored his use of the identified language forms and noted no increases. However, they also noted that on several days he made no initiations and on the remaining days he made only one initiation. Since the procedure is used only after his initiations, the monitoring data suggest that they need to restructure the free-play to increase his initiations. Thus, the monitoring data showed that he was not making progress (indicated that a change was needed); and the monitoring data showed that the intervention, incidental teaching, was not being used frequently because Hoi was not initiating (identified the change that was needed in the intervention plan). Thus, they could restructure the free-play session to provide more opportunities for Hoi to initiate and thereby experience the incidental teaching procedure.

. . . .

Latasha's intervention team set playing with classmates as an intervention goal. As strategies, they decided to ensure that she was in play areas with socially responsive and playful peers, and that she had several "social" as compared with "isolate" toys available (Odom & Strain, 1984; Rettig, Kallam, & McCarthy-Salm, 1993). Over a couple of weeks, the team collected monitoring information and found that she had many opportunities to play with peers, but she rarely did so. They also noted that she frequently took toys from peers and never offered them toys. Thus, they determined that teaching her to share would assist her in playing with others, and they decided to use a peer-assisted intervention (Kohler & Strain, 1990) to help her learn to share. In this case the monitoring data indicated that a change was needed and that an additional intervention was needed to teach sharing to make it more likely that Latasha would play with her peers.

. . . .

The intervention team for Jorge and Emily identified peer imitation as a goal for both children. They decided to use time delay in the context of art activities to teach peer imitation (Venn et al., 1993). Time delay involves providing children with opportunities to do the target behavior (in this case, imitate a peer) and then provides them with the assistance (prompts) needed to do the behavior. Over repeated opportunities, the assistance is delayed for a few seconds after the opportunity is provided (Wolery, Ault, & Doyle, 1992). For Jorge and Emily, when the teacher noted a peer doing a distinct behavior during art activities, she said to Jorge or Emily, "See what (peer's name) is doing; you do it." She then assisted the child in doing what the peer was doing. Over time she faded her assistance. After a couple of weeks, the monitoring data indicated that neither Jorge nor Emily were imitating their peers independently. For Jorge, the monitoring information indicated that he rarely looked at the peer when the teacher asked him to; clearly, he could not learn to imitate his peer if he did not see what the peer did. As a result, the intervention team decided to have the peer call Jorge's name and model the behavior only after Jorge looked at the peer. Because Emily looked at the peer, but consistently responded incorrectly (did not imitate) before the teacher provided assistance, the team decided to provide the assistance more quickly and to fade it more slowly. In both cases, the monitoring information suggested a change was needed and provided guidance in what changes were potentially useful.

. . . .

Carie's intervention team identified increasing her engagement during story time as an intervention goal. The interventions they identified for promoting engagement were reading storybooks that had repetitive language and reading with animation and active participation by the children (Wolery & Wolery, 1992). After a couple of weeks of monitoring, it appeared that Carie was engaged for about half the time, and her levels of engagement were not increasing. Thus, a change was needed. Two other conclusions were drawn from the monitoring information. It appeared that when the teacher asked the children a question about the story or encouraged them to say some of the repetitive words in the story, Carie would be more attentive for a few seconds. In addition, she was more engaged at the beginning than at the end of each story. The teacher decided to read shorter stories and to gradually increase the length and to add more questions and opportunities for children to respond toward the end of those stories.

. . . .

uals for monitoring behavior. The plan should specify who is responsible for monitoring each objective.

The plan should also specify the situations in which monitoring should occur. While this must include the setting, it should also include other important aspects. For example, in monitoring children's self-feeding behaviors, clearly a mealtime setting is appropriate. Whether the child is hungry and has preferred food available, however, also are relevant factors that would influence self-feeding behavior. When possible, these conditions should be identified in the monitoring plan.

The frequency with which monitoring should occur will vary from objective to objective. The general rule is that monitoring should occur regularly and often enough to have sufficient information for making decisions, but no more frequently than is necessary. This issue is discussed in more detail below; however, a general schedule for monitoring should be established when making a monitoring plan.

Because monitoring information is collected to make decisions, the analysis of the information is important. While a variety of individuals may collect the information, someone should be responsible for reviewing the information and summarizing it. For example, teachers and parents may collect information on a child's communication goals, and the speech-language pathologist could review that information and make judgments, in consultation with others, about whether modifications are needed in the intervention practices.

Monitoring Activities Should Consider Contextual Factors

To be meaningful, monitoring activities should occur in authentic, realistic situations in which the behaviors of the goals and objectives are relevant and needed (Haring, 1992), and factors that are likely to influence the occurrence of the behavior should be recognized. Communicative skills are likely to be dependent on the availability and responsiveness of communicative partners and interesting events; play skills are likely to vary by the availability and novelty of toys; social interactions are likely to vary by the availability and responsiveness of interactive partners. Thus, identifying the situations in which monitoring occurs is an important decision. Also, when interpreting monitoring information, variations in relevant factors and their influence on children's behavior should be considered.

Monitoring Should Address Multiple Persons' Perspectives of Progress

Because children's behavior is only functional and meaningful in context and because most behaviors are needed in multiple situations, input is needed in the monitoring system from different individuals. Important perspectives are those of the family, of the educational staff, and of the therapists who work with the child. Thus, well-developed monitoring systems seek input from multiple people who interact and observe the child in different situations and settings.

Monitoring Should Occur Regularly and Frequently

As noted previously, monitoring should take place regularly and often enough to secure the information needed to make valid decisions, but no more often than is necessary. Generally, but not always, more accurate decisions are made when more information is available (Munger, Snell, & Loyd, 1989); however, a balance must be established between the demands of monitoring multiple goals and providing responsive and defensible interventions and child care. For some goals, daily monitoring may be needed; for others, weekly monitoring is adequate; for still others, monitoring every two weeks is sufficient. The frequency of monitoring depends on many factors, such as the importance of the goal, the degree to which progress is being made, and other demands that exist on caregivers.

More-frequent monitoring should occur for high-priority goals Goals are not equal; some goals are more important than others. Because more monitoring information often results in more-accurate decisions, more monitoring should occur on important goals. For example, in describing interventions for moving children who are dependent on gastrostomy-tube feeding to oral feeding, Luiselli and Luiselli (1995) recommend that monitoring occur each time the child is fed orally. Less-frequent monitoring, however, can be used with less important goals. The importance of goals, of course, is established by the team.

More-frequent monitoring should occur for goals on which decisions are needed Decisions need to be made when the information that is being gathered indicates children's progress is not occurring, is slow, or is variable. In such cases, more-frequent monitoring may be needed to identify the modifications that should be made in the intervention. Also, after modifying an intervention, more-frequent monitoring should occur to evaluate the effects of those changes.

Monitoring Should Be Purposeful

Monitoring is done for three purposes: to validate the initial assessment, to develop a record of progress over time, and to make decisions about whether and what modifications are needed in intervention strategies and practices. These purposes should be kept in mind when developing and implementing a monitoring plan. Collecting volumes of monitoring information but not using it to make decisions is no more defensible than not collecting monitoring data. The information that is collected should be used.

To be useful, however, monitoring is like other assessment practices: The measurement procedures must be both valid and reliable. Validity, as discussed above, deals with the extent to which the measurement procedures match the intent of the objectives and the extent to which the measurement occurs in authentic contexts. Reliability refers to the consistency of the information that is collected. With direct observational data, estimates of reliability are usually obtained by having two or more persons observe the same events and independently but simultaneously score or record those events. Interobserver agreement percentages are then calculated (Tawney & Gast, 1984). To increase the probability of reliability, several issues are important. The behavior being observed must be defined precisely, the measurement procedures should be relatively simple to use, and the conditions under which the data are collected should be free of major distractions for the observers. As a rule, it is better to have less data that are reliable than to have volumes of unreliable data.

Summary

When monitoring children's progress, several guidelines are important. The goals and the objectives are the basis for developing a valid monitoring plan, but certain general aspects of children's behavior (e.g., engagement and social contact) also should be monitored even when they are not specific goals on a child's intervention plan. A monitoring plan should be developed and implemented. The monitoring should occur in contexts that are authentic, should include the perspectives of multiple individuals, and should occur regularly and frequently. The monitoring should be done in a purposeful way, keeping in mind the decisions that need to be made.

APPROACHES TO MONITORING

There are at least three broad approaches to monitoring children's progress. These include narrative descriptions and judgment-based assessments, work samples, and direct observation. Emphasis is placed in this section on direct observation because of its utility; however, each approach is defensible and useful to early intervention personnel.

Narrative Descriptions and Judgment-Based Monitoring

Narrative descriptions technically are a type of direct observation, and many judgment-based measures are based on observations. However, these two approaches are discussed separately from direct behavioral observation because of the type of information gathered and differences in recording procedures. A complete monitoring system is likely to use narrative descriptions, judgment-based measures, and direct observation in conjunction with clinical judgment (LeLaurin, 1990) to gather and interpret information for making decisions about modifying intervention programs.

Narrative descriptions Narrative descriptions include three types of observational recording systems: anecdotal records, running records, and specimen descriptions (Thurman & Widerstrom, 1990). Anecdotal records are used frequently in many professions to record observations of various kinds, and they include written descriptions of events that may provide information on children's progress. Such notes can be written for each objective on a regular basis and thereby provide a summary of the child's progress over time. Anecdotal records are particularly useful when the team is attempting to determine what aspects of the intervention to change, because these records can provide information about the context in which the intervention is used, the child's reaction to the intervention, and the accuracy with which the intervention practice or strategy is used. Thurman and Widerstrom (1990) recommend the following guidelines when using anecdotal records: (a) the anecdote should be written soon after the event occurs; (b) the basic action or flavor of the event and the key persons should be described; (c) the setting, time, and activity should be listed; (d) the sequence of the event should be described (beginning, middle, and end); and (e) the main event, specific information about the main event, and qualitative description of the event should be included. Anecdotal reports can be collected efficiently and with little effort; however, they are open to observer bias and inaccurate inference.

Running records, which are less episodic than anecdotal records, involve recording all of the child's behavior and the relevant events for a period of time and provide a more complete picture of the situation than anecdotal records (Thurman & Widerstrom, 1990). When one is conducting a running record, the times and places of observation should be selected purposefully, and the setting and situation should be described. The primary body of the running record is a thorough description of what the child does and how he or she does it. Events that result in changes in child behavior are recorded as well as events that should but do not result in changes. The behavior of others that is directed toward the child should be described thoroughly. Any inferences or interpretative statements should be noted as such. When running records are used, they should be transcribed into a usable form soon after completion of the observation. Transcription is facilitated by listing three columns: antecedent events, child behavior, and consequent events. The primary use of running records in monitoring children's progress is in collecting information for specific problem solving. For example, if other monitoring methods have indicated that a child is not making the expected progress, and the team has little information about why progress is not occurring, collecting a running record may be useful. Running records typically are not useful for routine monitoring because of the extensive time demands in collecting them and because adults cannot engage in other activities while doing a running record.

Specimen descriptions are similar to running records and follow similar procedures. However, specimen descriptions are designed to portray specific episodes or a series of episodes. Thus, the description is tied more to a given event than to all the behavior that may occur, as in a running record. More objective descriptions are written than with anecdotal records. The advantage of specimen descriptions is that information can be collected on specific events or episodes. The disadvantages are similar, however, to those of running records.

Judgment-based assessment Judgment-based assessment refers to "the formal use of structured, quantified judgment to (a) complement norm- and curriculum-based measures, (b) measure ambiguous child characteristics, and (c) serve as a vehicle for team decision making" (Neisworth & Fewell, 1990, p. ix). Judgment-based assessments can involve rating of almost an endless array of factors, including children's developmental skills, their interests, their temperament, their progress on goals, and many others (Fleischer, Belgredan, Bagnato, & Ogonosky, 1990). These measures often involve rating scales that provide quantitative information about respondents' perceptions. Issues to consider in developing and evaluating rating scales for judgment-based measures are described by McCloskey (1990).

As noted earlier, a useful monitoring system should include the perspectives of all the individuals who have sustained contact with the child. A primary advantage of judgment-based measures is that they are designed to collect such perceptions. The purpose, of course, is not to determine who is correct but to obtain a broad picture of the child's progress in different contexts (Neisworth & Fewell, 1990). Another advantage of judgment-based assessment measures is that they allow some level of measurement on important qualities that are difficult to measure.

Work Samples and Portfolio Assessments

The demands for accountability in education coupled with the weaknesses of many group-administered standardized tests has produced an emphasis on performance assessment (Poteet, Choate, & Steward, 1993). One reaction to this state of affairs at the elementary-school level has been to use portfolio assessments, which are compilations of children's permanent products over time that show both progress and the richness of their work (Graves & Sunstein, 1992; Hills, 1992).

Meisels (1993) describes a performance assessment system for use in early childhood and early elementary grades. This system, called the Work Sampling System™, contains three components: "(1) developmental checklists, (2) portfolios, and (3) summary reports" (Meisels, 1993, p. 36). The checklists are completed by teachers based on their observations and knowledge of each child and are not designed to be used as tests. The portfolios include "core" items and "other" items. The core items are products of the child's work that are collected in several areas at least three times each year. Other items vary by child and by date of collection. Because many young children's key activities do not result in permanent products, photographs of achievements are recommended (Poster, Johns, Abrams, & Freund, 1994); of course, video or audio recordings also can be used. The summary reports are written narratives completed by the teacher, based on observations that describe the child's performance in each domain. The summary reports are conducted three times a year (Meisels, 1993).

Although performance assessment through direct observation in naturalistic contexts has been used a great deal in early childhood special education, the use of portfolio assessments and procedures such as the Work Sampling System™ (Meisels, 1993) remains relatively unstudied. However, such procedures may be valuable in monitoring performance, particularly when used in conjunction with more frequently used direct observation of specific skills and intervention goals.

Direct Behavioral Observation

Using direct observation to monitor children's progress has a rich history in the science of human behavior (Bijou, Peterson, Harris, Allen, & Johnston, 1969). For more complete discussions, see White and Haring (1980), Wolery et al. (1988), Cooper, Heron, and Heward (1987), and Cooper (1980). Journals that include studies employing single subject designs (e.g., *Journal of Applied Behavior Analysis, Journal of Behavioral Education,* and many others) provide many examples of using direct observation to measure children's behavior over time. Employing direct observation in monitoring children's behavior involves at least five steps: (1) defining behaviors and identifying their relevant dimensions, (2) selecting data collection systems and designing data collection sheets, (3) selecting times and situations for observations, (4) checking the accuracy of the data collection, and (5) summarizing the data and making decisions.

Defining behaviors and identifying their relevant dimensions As noted earlier, the goals and objectives of the intervention plan are the base from which monitoring systems are developed. Goals often are written in a general sense and do not define precisely the behaviors the team wants the child to achieve. When preparing to monitor goals, teams need to consider whether the actual behavior (form) or the effect of the behavior is of primary concern (White, 1980). *Form* refers to the specific behaviors performed by the child and the *effect* (also called *function*) refers to the outcome of those behaviors. A behavior, of course, is an event that involves movement, has a definite beginning and end, can be performed repeatedly, and can be measured reliably. The effect or function is the result of doing the behavior. For some goals, the effect may be critical and the behavior used to cause the effect will be less important. For example, if a goal is to initiate social interactions, the important issue is whether the social interaction gets started (i.e., the effect). If a child starts the interaction by calling a peer's name, giving the peer a toy, suggesting a play theme, or touching the peer, the result or effect may be the same—an interaction is started. Thus, the behavior used may be of less importance. In other cases, the behaviors used may be important and the effect less so. For example, in self-feeding, a child who uses finger feeding has the effect (i.e., getting food from the table to his mouth); however, using a spoon (specific behavior) may be a legitimate goal. In this case the behavior rather than the effect is important. In fact, in such situations, the goal is to replace an old behavior that accomplishes the effect (i.e., using finger feeding to get food into the mouth) with a new behavior (using a spoon) that has the same effect.

Thus, the team must make decisions about what will be measured. If the effect is to be measured, that effect needs to be defined precisely, and the range of behaviors that can be used to cause the effect should be identified. In cases where the behavior is important, the dimension of the behavior to be measured must be identified. Each behavior has a number of different dimensions (characteristics) that can be measured; these include its frequency, intensity, duration, latency, endurance, and accuracy.

Frequency (or *rate)* refers to how often a behavior occurs. (Rate technically refers to how often a behavior occurs for a given time period.) *Intensity* refers to the amount of force with which the behavior occurs. *Duration* refers to the length of time a given behavior lasts. *Latency* refers to how long it takes a child to initiate a behavior once a cue has occurred. *Endurance* refers to the length of time a given behavior can be repeatedly performed. Another related dimension of behavior is *accuracy,* which refers to the extent to which a child's behavior conforms to the defined topography of a given behavior. For example, accuracy is particularly important when measuring preacademic and language behaviors. If an interventionist is attempting to teach a child to name common objects, the accuracy of naming is more important than the frequency, intensity, latency, duration, or endurance.

When defining a behavior for monitoring intervention effectiveness, the appropriate dimension should be selected and measured. When selecting the dimension, two questions should be asked. First, if the child is to be more independent, developmentally advanced, or more socially acceptable, which dimension(s) of the behavior should be changed? Second, which dimension can be measured most accurately and easily? For example, if a child is hitting others with his fist, the frequency and intensity of the hitting should be changed to make the child more socially acceptable. The duration of the hits, latency from some cue, endurance, and accuracy of hits are less important dimensions. When frequency and intensity are applied to the second question, the frequency of hits is measured more easily and accurately than the intensity.

The important dimension for measurement will vary from behavior to behavior. For example, accuracy may be most important with a naming task, frequency with an aggressive behavior, intensity with a behavior such as speaking loudly enough, duration with behaviors such as eye contact or holding up one's head, latency with behaviors such as responding to others' initiations, and endurance with behaviors such as walking or other responses that must be performed repeatedly.

Selecting data-collection systems and designing data-collection sheets Five different data-collection systems that are often used in monitoring children's progress are event sampling, time sampling, category sampling, levels of assistance recording, and task-analytic recording (Wolery et al., 1988). In this section, these systems are described and examples of data-collection sheets are presented. The team should use these sheets or construct others that are useful and efficient for their monitoring purposes.

Event sampling *Event sampling* refers to situations in which the team records the occurrence of the behavior of interest; the adults are cued to respond when the behavior occurs. The simplest form of this system is when an adult records a tally each time a behavior occurs; for example, counting the number of hits, correct responses, toys with which the child plays, persons to whom the child initiates, steps taken, and bites taken. This system is best used with behaviors that have a definite beginning and end and are relatively brief (i.e., have a stable and short duration). The behaviors are recorded or counted as they occur. For some behaviors, permanent products may occur as a result of the child's behavior. Examples of permanent products are art work (e.g., painted or drawn pictures), soiled diapers, toys put on shelves during cleanup, and a puzzle put together. In many cases, these can be counted after the behavior occurs.

Several issues should be addressed when designing event-sampling recording systems. The behavior that constitutes the event must be defined. This definition of the behavior should be precise so that no questions exist about what is being measured. In addition, the team should be sure to consider the dimension of behavior (accuracy, frequency, duration, latency, intensity, endurance) that is most relevant and easily recorded. Collecting data and interpreting them for each of these dimensions requires slightly different procedures. Accuracy data are frequently collected during instructional sessions when children have an opportunity to respond to target stimuli. In such cases, responses are recorded as correct or incorrect based on specific definitions, and data are analyzed in terms of percentage correct and incorrect. Percentage is calculated by dividing the number of each type of response by the number of opportunities provided. Percentage data have some distinct advantages. They are easy to calculate, especially when the number of opportunities are 5, 10, 20, 25, 50, or 100. Because most people readily understand percentage data, the results of the observation are easily communicated to others. However, percentage data have limitations; the primary one is that an artificial ceiling is placed on performance. For example, two students could be at 100% correct, but one could have performed the same number of responses in half the time required by the other. Many behaviors must be performed quickly to be useful to children. Percentage data do not provide information on the response speed. To deal with this problem, the rate of responding can be calculated with accuracy data. *Rate* refers to the number of responses that occur in a given time period, for example, a week, a day, or a minute. Using a minute as the time unit is useful because it is sensitive to change and can be recorded quickly; however, any standard period can be used if data are collected for the entire period. Rate is calculated by dividing the number of responses (e.g., number correct) by the number of time units (e.g., minutes). Thus, with accuracy data, correct and error rates can be calculated as well as percentage. Another disadvantage of using percentage data is that they may be insensitive measures unless a large number of opportunities are provided. For example, if only five opportunities are provided, each response is worth 20 percentage points. A rule of thumb is that percentage should not be used unless there are at least 20 opportunities to respond. However, many examples exist in the literature in which as few as 10 opportunities existed.

Frequency data can be collected on almost any discrete behavior, but it is important that the behavior be of consistent duration. For example, frequency data could be collected on the number of crying episodes displayed by an infant, but the duration of episodes could vary considerably. For example, on one day the infant could cry three times and each episode could last 30 to 40 minutes. On another day the same infant could cry six times with each episode lasting about 2 minutes. Although the infant had more episodes of crying on the second day, the crying behavior would likely be a greater problem on the first. Frequency data can be recorded in a number of ways, including putting a tally mark on a data-collection sheet, using a golf counter or other counting device, or putting a bean in a jar on the shelf. The number of ways to record frequency data is limited only by an interventionist's creativity. What is important is that an accurate record be maintained with minimum effort and time. When frequency data are being collected, the duration of the observation session also should be recorded. To say that a child displayed three social initiations on one day and six on another is not useful unless the time allowed on both days was equal. By recording the length of the observation, frequency data can be meaningfully interpreted. When the length of the observation is known, the data can be converted to rate. Further, dividing the observation into several intervals will help in interpreting the data. For example, if the interventionist is going to count the number of initiations during a 20-minute free-play period, the observation could be divided into ten 2-minute intervals, allowing the interventionist to determine when during the 20 minutes the initiations occurred.

Duration data, which can be collected on most behaviors occurring for longer than a few seconds, require each response to be timed. Although any clock can be used, stopwatches greatly increase the precision with which data are collected. Duration data can be analyzed in three ways: total duration, duration per occurrence, and percent of time. *Total duration* refers to the total amount of time an infant or child engages in the target behavior during the observation session. Some stopwatches are designed to start and stop and start again without being reset. The teacher simply starts and stops the watch each time the behavior occurs and then reads the time at the end of the session. *Duration per occurrence,* which refers to the average length of time that the child engages in the behavior, requires the teacher to record the duration of each instance of the behavior and divide the total time by the number of occurrences. *Percent of time* refers to the percentage of the session in which the student performs the behavior. When data are collected so that the average duration per occurrence is recorded and the length of the observation session also is recorded, then each of the three types can be calculated.

Latency data also require the interventionist to time the behavior, and use of a stopwatch is recommended. The timing should occur from the end of the cue to the initiation of the response. As with duration, the total latency for an observation session or the average latency per occurrence can be calculated. Generally, the average latency is more meaningful because the measure is tied to the number of cues provided. Latency data may be used to collect important assessment information.

Intensity or magnitude of a response is relatively difficult to measure for most responses. Exceptions include such things as how high or how far a child can jump. In most cases, however, measurement of intensity requires special instrumentation such as noise or pressure gauges. As a result, intensity is rarely measured. Similarly, endurance data, although infrequently used in early childhood settings, can be collected in a number of ways. For example, an interventionist can time how long a child repeatedly can perform a discrete behavior such as running. Other ways to determine endurance are through measures of distance and use of special instrumentation.

In addition to defining the behavior and considering the important dimension of behavior, event-sampling systems should be well calibrated (White & Haring, 1980). This issue is important when monitoring intervention effectiveness. A *well-calibrated system* is one in which each occurrence of the behavior represents relatively equal amounts of the behavior. For example, if the teacher is monitoring a child's ability to work puzzles, the number of pieces inserted or the number of puzzles completed could be counted. The number of pieces would be a better measure, because one puzzle might have four pieces and another might have sixteen. If only the number completed were counted, the two puzzles would represent very different amounts of the behavior. A well-calibrated system also is sensitive to change; that is, it should detect small changes in the behavior. Interventionists should be careful to select behaviors that are relatively easy to record, particularly when the effects of intervention are being monitored. If the requirements of monitoring are costly in terms of interventionists' time and effort, it is likely that relatively little monitoring will occur, ineffective intervention will continue longer than necessary, and changes in behaviors being taught will not occur as frequently as possible.

Data-collection sheets, which are simply the forms on which the record of the observation is written, must be designed. Tawney and Gast (1984) state that data-collection sheets should contain three types of information: situational, performance, and summary. *Situational information* refers to data that establish who was observed, what behavior was measured, when the observation occurred, and who conducted it. Specifically, it should include the child's name, date, activity, beginning and ending times of the observation, instructional strategies being used, behaviors that are targeted for observation, and the observer's name. *Performance information* refers to the actual record of behavior that is generated from the observation. This section of the data sheet varies considerably, depending on the type of data being recorded. For example, if data are being collected to monitor the effects of a direct instruction program, correct responses, error responses, and no responses may be counted. The data-collection sheet could have a column for each of these types of responses, and when one of them occurred, a check could be placed in the appropriate column. However, if data were being collected on the frequency with which an infant spits up, a space for tally marks may be sufficient. The third type of information that should be included on the data-collection sheet is *summary data.* This section, at a minimum, should include the total time of the observation, totals for the data recorded (by type, if used), and anecdotal comments made by the observer to explain the data or to describe a related event or issue. Summary data are important because they will reduce the time required to analyze performance across a number of days and will be useful for transferring that data to graphs. Examples of event-sampling data-collection sheets for frequency (occurrence) and accuracy data are shown in Figure 17.1, data sheets for duration are shown in Figure 17.2, and data sheets for latency are shown in Figure 17.3. These data sheets are samples; interventionists should design their own to match their situation but should be sure that the three components are included.

Time-sampling Unlike event-sampling, in which the occurrence of a behavior cues the interventionist to record the response, time cues recording in *time-sampling systems.* The interventionist records which response occurred at a given time. Time-sampling procedures, like event sampling, can be used with discrete behaviors (e.g., behaviors of relatively short duration) or with categories of behaviors. In its simplest form, time sampling involves the interventionist's recording at prespecified times whether a behavior is or is not occurring. For example, the interventionist may check the infant at 9:00 and record whether she is asleep or awake or may see which toddlers are playing with toys. The advantages of time-sampling procedures are that they can be used with behaviors that are difficult to count or time and that the same behavior of several children can be collected at once.

Using time-sampling procedures requires some of the same considerations as event sampling; however, some special considerations also exist. The behaviors to be measured should be defined, and the relevant dimensions of those behaviors should be identified.

The type of time-sampling procedure also should be selected. At least three types have been described: momentary, partial-interval, and whole-interval time sampling (Cooper et al., 1987). With these procedures, the observation session is divided into intervals. With *momentary* time sampling, the observer records at a specific time whether the behavior is occurring. For example, the 5-hour day may be divided into twenty 15-minute intervals. If the day began at 8:00, the observer would check the target child at 8:00, 8:15, 8:30, 8:45, 9:00, and so on. At each time (e.g., 8:15), the observer would record whether the behavior was occurring *at that instant.* With the *partial-interval* method, the observation period would be broken into intervals, and the observer would observe for the entire interval (e.g., from

FORM A

Name ______________ Date: ______

Behavior/Objective: ______________

Time ______ to ______ Total Time: ____

Observer: ______________________

Trial	C	E	*No Response*
1			
2			
3			
4			
5			
6			
7			
8			
9			
10			
Total #/%	/	/	/

Comments: ______________________

FORM B

Name ______________ Date: ______

Behavior/Objective: ______________

____

Observer: ______________________

Day	*Time Observed*	*Record of Behavior*	*#*	*Rate*
Mon.				
Tues.				
Wed.				
Thurs.				
Fri.				

Comments: ______________________

FORM C

Name ______________ Date: ______

Behavior/Objective: ______________

Time ______ to ______ Total Time: ______

Observer: ______________________

Occurrences

Comments: ______________________

Total # of occurrences: __________

Rate of occurrences: __________

FORM D

Name ______________ Date: ______

Behavior/Objective: ______________

Time ______ to ______ Total Time: ____

Observer: ______________________

Occurrences

Trial	*Response*
1	
2	
3	
4	
5	

Trial	*Response*
6	
7	
8	
9	
10	

Total Correct ______________

Total Errors ______________

Correct Rate ______________

FORM E

Name ______________ Date: ______

Behavior/Objective: ______________

Time ______ to ______ Total Time: ______

Observer: ______________________

Occurrences

2-min Interval	*# of Behavior*	*Rate*
Total		

FIGURE 17.1

Examples of event-sampling data-collection sheets for frequency and accuracy data

Note: Form A could be used to record the accuracy of students' responses; the teacher would place a check in the appropriate column for each trial. Form B could be used to record frequency (rate) for 5 days; the teacher would place a tally mark for each occurrence of behavior. Form C could be used to record frequency (rate); the teacher would place a tally mark for each occurrence of the behavior. Form D would be used for accuracy data; the teacher would mark + for correct, – for error, and 0 for no response. Form E could be used to record the rate of behavior during four 2-minute intervals; the teacher places a tally mark for each occurrence of behavior during each interval.

FORM A

Name ______________ Date: _______

Behavior/Objective: _______________

Time ____ to ____ Total Time: _______

Observer: _______________________

Start Time	*Stop Time*	*Total*

Comments: _____________________

Total Number of Occurrences: _______

Total Duration: ____________

Average Duration per Occurrence: ____

FORM B

Name ______________ Date: _______

Behavior/Objective: _______________

Time ____ to ____ Total Time: _______

Observer: _______________________

Occurrence	*Time*

Comments: _____________________

Total Number of Occurrences: _______

Total Duration: ____________

Average Duration per Occurrence: ____

FIGURE 17.2

Examples of two event-sampling data-collection sheets for duration data

Note: In Form A, the start and stop time of each occurrence is recorded; in Form B only the duration is recorded per occurrence. With both, the total duration, average duration, and percent of time can be calculated.

8:00 to 8:15 and from 8:30 to 8:45). If the behavior occurs during the interval, it is scored as having occurred. With the *whole-interval* method, the observation period is also divided into intervals, and the observer must watch for the entire interval. However, for a behavior to be scored as occurring, it must occur for the *entire* interval. The whole-interval method tends to underestimate the true occurrence of a behavior, and the partial-interval method tends to overestimate the occurrence. Both of these procedures are quite demanding on teacher-time because the teacher must observe for the entire interval. However, when observation sessions are short (e.g., 10 minutes), these sampling methods can be used. The momentary time sample is probably the easiest and most useful when teachers are monitoring the effects of intervention, because they can be involved in other activities between observation points. This method, however, is not sensitive to behaviors that last for relatively short durations.

FORM A	**FORM B**
Name ____________ Date: ______	Name ____________ Date: ______
Cue: ____________	Cue: ____________
Behavior: ____________	Behavior: ____________
Objective: ____________	Objective: ____________
Observer: ____________	Observer: ____________

Cue Time	*Initiate Behavior*	*Total*

Cue Number	*Latency*
1	
2	
3	
4	
5	
6	
7	

Form A	Form B
Comments: ____________	Comments: ____________
Total Number of Cues: ____________	Total Number of Cues: ____________
Total Latency: ______	Total Latency: ______
Average Length of Latency: ______	Average Length of Latency: ______

FIGURE 17.3

Examples of two event-sampling data-collection sheets for latency data

Note: In Form A, the time the cue was presented and the time the behavior was initiated are recorded; in Form B, the number of cues and the length of the latency are recorded.

With each of these methods, the data are analyzed in terms of the percent of intervals in which the behavior occurs.

Selecting a time-sampling procedure requires consideration of the duration and frequency of the behavior and the length of the observation interval. If a behavior is of short duration, the partial-interval method should be used, although long intervals will overestimate the behavior's occurrence. If the behavior is of long duration, momentary time sampling or the whole-interval method should be used. The average duration of the behavior should be considered when the whole-interval method is used, and the observation interval should be similar to the average duration. For behaviors that occur frequently and are of moderate or variable duration, the momentary method is

Name ______________________ Date: ______________________

Behavior: ____

Objective: ____

Observer: ________________ Observation Time: __________ to __________

Minute 1:

Intervals

1	2	3	4	5	6

Minute 2:

Intervals

1	2	3	4	5	6

Minute 3:

Intervals

1	2	3	4	5	6

Minute 4:

Intervals

1	2	3	4	5	6

Minute 5:

Intervals

1	2	3	4	5	6

Minute 6:

Intervals

1	2	3	4	5	6

Minute 7

Intervals

1	2	3	4	5	6

Minute 8:

Intervals

1	2	3	4	5	6

Minute 9:

Intervals

1	2	3	4	5	6

Minute 10:

Intervals

1	2	3	4	5	6

FIGURE 17.5

Example of partial-interval or whole-interval time-sampling data-collection sheet

Note: Each minute of a 10-minute observation session is divided into six 10-second intervals. The teacher records whether behavior occurred or did not occur by marking 0 for occurrence and N for nonoccurrence.

ior can be detected. For example, Tina's aggressive behavior may vary with her play behavior. When she engages in play she appears to be less aggressive; when she is not playing, her aggressions increase. Brian, on the other hand, appears to be more aggressive when the frequency of social initiations from other children increases. Category-sampling procedures allow interventionists to identify such relationships, develop intervention plans based on them, and monitor the effects of the intervention. For example, with Tina, the interventionist should develop a plan to increase her engagement with toys rather than use a punishment procedure to decrease her aggression. Similarly, Brian's teacher should teach him to respond positively to peers' initiations. Category-sampling procedures also allow interventionists to measure the effects of the behavior of one person on another. For example, in parent/infant interactions, the behaviors of the parent and the infant each may influence the behavior of the other. An interventionist may have a hypothesis that an infant is more fussy and less playful when the parent is more directive. The interventionist could measure four categories of behavior: parental directiveness, parental responsiveness, child play behavior, and fussiness. Such data could indicate whether the hypothesis about parental directiveness and child behavior appears to be true and allow an appropriate intervention to be developed.

When category systems are used, interventionists must choose between event- or time-sampling procedures. Children's responses prompt recording with event-sampling procedures; time prompts recording with time-sampling procedures. With category sampling, time-sampling methods are more frequently used, but exceptions occur. Category sampling may be used in an event-sampling format when a child displays a category of behavior that requires careful measurement, occurs relatively infrequently, and when multiple behaviors appear to produce the same effect. For example, a child may hit, bite, and pull the hair of other children and may use these actions to express frustration. To ensure that every instance of these behaviors is noted, the interventionist must define each and record them as a category called "aggressive behavior." Similarly, children may be learning specific communicative or social functions, and the interventionist may want a record of the number of requests they make throughout the day. The form of the request or the object being requested may be unimportant. In such cases, the teacher could define behaviors for a "requesting" category and record that category when each request occurs. In both of these examples, the behavior (aggressive behavior or requests) would prompt the teacher to record.

The more usual method of category sampling involves time-sampling formats. For example, the interventionist may be interested in the types of play behaviors being displayed. The categories of different types of play would be developed, and a momentary time-sampling procedure in which the type of play is recorded every 20 seconds could be used. When time-sampling procedures are used, some response should be recorded in each interval. When the categories represent a subset of the total possible behaviors, the interventionist should devise a category that would represent the absence of those behaviors. For example, if solitary, onlooker, parallel, associative, and cooperative play were being measured, it is possible that none of these types of play would be observed in a given interval. In such cases a category called "nonplay" behaviors could be used. The percentage of intervals in which this category is marked may be important in specifying the amount of time the child is actually playing.

Data-collection sheets that facilitate easy recording are needed with category sampling procedures and range from relatively simple to quite complex. Two simple data-collection sheets for recording the occurrence of aggressive and disruptive behaviors are displayed in

Figure 17.6. Data-collection sheet A is designed for an event-sampling procedure, and data sheet B is designed for a time-sampling procedure. A more complex time-sampling data sheet for measuring levels of social play is displayed in Figure 17.7. Sometimes data are collected simultaneously on several children and for several behaviors. For example, an interventionist may want to collect data on the percentage of time children are engaged in planned activities, waiting, or behaving inappropriately. A momentary time-sampling procedure could be used. At the designated time, the observer would scan the classroom and record the category for each child. A sample data-collection sheet for this example is shown in Figure 17.8. The times are written on the left-hand column and the children's names are written across the top. At each time, the observer would write a symbol indicating which behavior was being displayed by each child. Although this system may seem complex, interventionists can learn to record such behavior reliably with practice.

Care should be taken when interpreting data from category-sampling procedures. The percentage of intervals that each category was recorded should be calculated and compared across categories. Few norms exist, however, that tell how frequently different categories of behavior should occur. It is unlikely that each category of behavior will occur at the same proportion of time, and it is likely that such equality would be inappropriate. For example, it would be undesirable to have children waiting the same percentage of time that they are engaged in activities; it is also unlikely that all children would be engaged 100% of the time. Thus, professional judgment is required in interpreting the results of category-sampling procedures. As noted earlier, covariation of different behaviors can be detected with category-sampling procedures. Many times this covariation cannot be noted by analyzing the totals of the observation session but requires analysis of patterns of behavior throughout the observation. If one category frequently is recorded after another, then some sequential pattern may be present.

Levels-of-assistance recording In *levels-of-assistance recording,* which is a variation of event sampling, the occurrence or nonoccurrence of the behavior is noted at different levels of support. This type of data collection is useful in monitoring objectives for which adults are providing support for children's performance of specific skills; the goal generally is to increase independence, and a measure of the extent to which independence is being achieved is the degree of support provided by the adult. Support or assistance can take many forms, such as adaptive or assistive devices or direct assistance from an adult. The type of support varies based on the behavior being assessed and the context in which it is used.

Some common types of teacher assistance are verbal cues, gestural prompts, models, partial physical prompts, and full physical manipulations (Wolery, 1994a). Verbal cues may include specific instruction on how to do the behavior, instruction on how to do part of a behavior, rules that help the child do the behavior, and indirect verbal cues such as hints. Gestural prompts are arm and facial movements that communicate to the child that specific behavior is wanted. Models are demonstrations of the behavior to be performed and may be motor or verbal behavior. Partial physical prompts are nudges, pushes, and taps that get the child to do the behavior, and full physical manipulations involve the adult holding the child's hands and actually putting him or her through the desired actions.

When monitoring a skill through levels of assistance, the amount of help required is usually recorded. For example, Deon is learning to put on his coat. When he is getting ready to go out to play, the adult could monitor the amount of help required to allow him to do each step of putting on his coat. This could be

FORM A

Name ________________ Date: ________ Observer: ____________

Aggressive Behaviors: ______________________________

Disruptive Behaviors: ______________________________

Time ____________ to ______________ Total Time: ____________

Time	*Activity*	*Aggression*	*Disruption*
	Total		

Comments: ______________________________

FORM B

Name ________________ Date: ________ Observer: ____________

Aggressive Behaviors: ______________________________

Disruptive Behaviors: ______________________________

Time ____________ to ______________ Total Time: ____________

Time	*Activity*	*Aggression*	*Disruption*
9:05			
9:10			
9:15			
9:20			
9:25			
9:30			
9:35			
9:40			
9:45			
9:50			
9:55			
10:00			
Total			

Comments: ______________________________

Percent of Intervals of Aggression __________

Percent of Intervals of Disruption __________

FIGURE 17.6

Examples of category-sampling data-collection sheets for two types of responses: Aggressive behaviors and disruptive behaviors

Note: The sheet in Form A is designed for use with an event-sampling procedure. The teacher would write the time the aggressive or disruptive behavior occurred, note the activity that was occurring, and then put a check mark in the appropriate column. The sheet in Form B is designed for use with a time-sampling procedure. The teacher would observe at each interval, and note whether aggression or disruption occurred.

Name ______________________ Date ______________________

Area: ______________________ Activities: ______________________

Types of Play

Time	*Solitary*	*Onlooking*	*Parallel*	*Associative*	*Cooperative*	*None*
:30						
1:00						
1:30						
2:00						
2:30						
3:00						
3:30						
4:00						
4:30						
5:00						
5:30						
6:00						
6:30						
7:00						
7:30						
8:00						
8:30						
9:00						
9:30						
10:00						
Total % Interval						

√ = occurrence; X = nonoccurrence

Comments: ______________________

____

FIGURE 17.7
Example of a category-sampling data-collection sheet for use with a time-sampling recording system to determine the percentage of intervals in which the student engages in various levels of social play during a 10-minute observation

Name ______________________ Date ______________________

Area: ______________________ Activities: ______________________

Children's Names

Time	*Kim*	*Rodney*	*Hector*	*Ian*	*Larry*	*Dawn*	*Joy*
2:02							
2:04							
2:06							
2:08							
2:10							
2:12							
2:14							
2:16							
2:18							
2:20							
2:22							
2:24							
2:26							
2:28							
2:30							
2:32							
2:34							
2:36							
2:38							
2:40							
Total % Interval							

E = engaged in activities; W = waiting; I = inappropriate behavior

FIGURE 17.8

Example of a category-sampling data-collection sheet for use with a momentary time-sampling recording system to determine the percentage of time children are engaged appropriately in activities, waiting behaviors, and inappropriate behaviors

Note: Children's names are listed across the top of the sheet and observation times are listed on the left-hand side. The teacher records an *E* for engaged in activities, a *W* for waiting, and an *I* for inappropriate behavior for each child and each observation time.

recorded as whether she needs to use a verbal prompt (e.g., "Push your arm all the way out") or physical assistance (e.g., actually helping him get his arm through the sleeve). An advantage of collecting levels-of-assistance information is that data are collected on the amount of help adults provide. In some cases, more assistance is needed; in other cases too much help is provided and independence is pre-empted. Also, some instructional procedures such as the system of least prompts (Doyle, Wolery, Ault, & Gast, 1988), graduated guidance (Bailey & Wolery, 1992), and most-to-least prompting (Wolery et al., 1992) rely on providing different levels of help. Thus, levels-of-assistance recording is useful in monitoring skills being taught with these procedures. Three recording forms for levels-of-assistance data are presented in Figure 17.9. Data Sheet A has space to write down the type of assistance needed across trials. Data Sheet B includes a list of assistance types, ordered from no assistance to the most intrusive level of assistance, and a row of numbers representing trials. The interventionist circles the number that corresponds to the level of assistance needed by the child on that trial. The advantage of Data Sheet B is that it can be used for monitoring during intervention. Data Sheet C is similar, but the levels of assistance are presented in columns across the top. The number of trials are listed on the left-hand side, and the interventionist places a check mark in the level of assistance presented and another symbol in the level at which the child was correct.

Task-analytic recording Task analysis is a process of breaking a skill into teachable parts, and *task-analytic recording* involves recording the child's performance on each step (part) of the skill. Task analysis is often used to develop a hierarchy of skills by difficulty for teaching. One or two skills on the hierarchy are initially taught. When they are mastered, the next most difficult skills are taught. Some skills, however, are chains or sequences of responses—a series of behaviors sequenced together to form a complex skill, such as putting on and taking off clothing, using utensils for eating, setting the table for snack, cleaning up a play area, and making a transition from one play area to the next. As a result, many response chains are highly useful skills and are targets of instruction in early childhood classrooms. Current instructional research indicates that chained skills should be (a) taught using total-task instruction (all steps taught simultaneously) rather than using backward (Kayser, Billingsley, & Neel, 1986) or forward chaining (McDonnell & McFarland, 1988); (b) taught when and where they are needed (Colozzi & Pollow, 1984); (c) taught using flexible and functional step sequences rather than rigid step sequences (Wright & Schuster, 1994); and (d) taught in small groups (two or three children) whose members can observe one another learn the chain (Griffen, Wolery, & Schuster, 1992; Hall, Schuster, Wolery, Gast, & Doyle, 1992) or taught with typically developing children serving as models (Werts, Caldwell, & Wolery, in press). Collecting data on chains taught with total-task and functional step sequences in the natural situations with two or three children adds substantial demands on the adult. Nonetheless, monitoring children's progress is necessary.

In the simplest form, the steps of the response chain (task analysis) are recorded as occurring or not occurring. Unfortunately, failure to do one step of the chain may preclude performance of other steps. For example, failing to put the arm through the sleeve of a front-opening shirt keeps other steps from occurring. Two solutions to this problem are used. First, the teacher completes the step for the child and the step is scored as incorrect. Second, the teacher provides prompts to help the child do the step. The prompts may be in the form of levels of assistance (e.g., if the system of least prompting procedure is used) or a prompt may be used that will ensure a correct response (e.g., if a time delay procedure is

FORM A

Name ______________ Date: ________

Behavior/Objective: ________________

Time ____ to _____ Total Time: ________

Observer: __________________________

Trial	*Write: Level of Assistance Needed*
1	
2	
3	
4	
5	

FORM B

Name ______________ Date: ________

Behavior/Objective: ________________

Time ____ to _____ Total Time: ________

Observer: __________________________

Level of Assistance Needed	*Trial*
Independent	1 2 3 4 5
Verbal Prompt	1 2 3 4 5
Model	1 2 3 4 5
Partial Physical Prompt	1 2 3 4 5
Full Physical Manipulation	1 2 3 4 5

FORM C

Name __________________ Date: __________ Observer __________________

Behavior/Objective: ____

Time __________________ to _____________ Total Time: ________________

Levels of Assistance

Trial	*Independent*	*Verbal Prompt*	*Model*	*Partial Physical Prompt*	*Full Physical Manipulation*
1					
2					
3					
4					
5					
Total					

Comments: ____

FIGURE 17.9

Examples of three data-collection forms for levels-of-assistance data

Note: Data Sheet A has space for the teacher to write the type of assistance needed across trials. Data Sheet B includes a list of assistance types, and a row of numbers representing each trial; the teacher circles the number that corresponds to the level of assistance needed on each trial. Data Sheet C includes the levels of assistance written across the top of the form and the trials on the left-hand side; the teacher checks the level of assistance needed on each trial.

used) (Wolery, Ault, Gast, Doyle, & Griffen, 1990). In the first case, the task-analytic recording is combined with the levels-of-assistance recording procedures. In the second case, the behavior is scored as prompted. Both procedures work well. Because functional rather than rigid sequences should be used, the order in which children complete steps can be recorded by simply numbering the steps on the data sheet as children complete them.

Designing data-collection sheets for task-analytic recording can be difficult; four examples are shown in Figure 17.10. Data Form A is designed for recording only whether the child did each step; this sheet could be used when the teacher was not prompting the child. Data Form B is designed to identify the sequence with which the child does a task analysis. This form would only be used if the child could do all the steps independently, but needed to learn the sequence or order in which to do the steps. Data Form C is designed for use with a prompting procedure that had only one level of prompt. Data Form D is designed for identifying the incorrect steps and the levels of assistance required at each step.

Summary of recording procedures Five different types of recording procedures may be used when monitoring children's performance on target skills. These are event recording, time-sampling recording, category-sampling recording, levels-of-assistance recording, and task-analytic recording. Each of these is useful for different types of skills, and none will be useful for all skills; thus, early intervention teams need to be fluent in using each type of recording when monitoring children's progress.

Selecting times and situations for monitoring As noted previously, monitoring should take place when the skill occurs in the natural environment. Also, it is important to monitor skills in all relevant settings and situations, particularly as the child demonstrates mastery in the instructional context. The frequency of monitoring should be often enough to get adequate information for making decisions, but not so often that it becomes difficult for the team to collect the information.

Checking the accuracy of data collection A pervasive characteristic of the human condition is the tendency to make mistakes; in fact, we are familiar with the saying that "to err is human." Because most monitoring activities are conducted by humans, errors are likely. Kazdin (1977) described two major types of errors: observer bias or expectations and observer drift. *Observer bias* refers to changes in the data collection that occur because of the observer's expectations, feelings, and so on, rather than actual changes in the behavior being observed. Observer bias is particularly likely to occur when monitoring children's progress, because frequently the persons doing the monitoring also are the persons doing the intervention. Most individuals use an intervention with the expectation that it will have positive effects on children's behavior and progress. *Observer drift* refers to unspecified changes in the definitions that the observers apply to data collection over time. Drift also is a particular problem with monitoring, because the nature of monitoring is to collect information over extended periods of time.

To control for these problems, reliability checks can be conducted in which two or more individuals collect data on the same behavior during the same observational sessions, using the same observation methods. Their data are then compared and a percentage of agreement is calculated. Calculating agreement percentages for event sampling data involves dividing the smaller score by the larger and multiplying by 100. With time-sampling and category-sampling data, the records of both observers should be compared at each interval and their responses should be scored as an agreement or

FORM A

Name ________________ Date: ______

Behavior/Objective: ________________

Time ______ to ______ Total Time: ______

Observer: ________________

Steps of Task Analysis	*Response*	
	Correct	*Error*

Comments: ________________

Total Number of Occurrences: ________

Total Duration: ________________

Average Duration per Occurrence: ______

FORM B

Name ________________ Date: ______

Behavior/Objective: ________________

Time ______ to ______ Total Time: ______

Observer: ________________

Steps of Task Analysis	*Write Order Child Did Steps (1 = 1st, 2 = 2nd) 3 = 3rd, etc.)*

Comments: ________________

Total Number of Occurrences: ________

Total Duration: ________________

Average Duration per Occurrence: ______

FORM C

Name ________________ Date: ______

Response Chain/Objective: ____________

Time ______ to ______ Total Time: ______

Observer: ________________

Steps of Task Analysis	*Response*		
	Correct	*Error*	*Prompt*

FORM D

Name ________________________ Date: __________ Observer: ________________

Behavior ____

Steps of Task Analysis	*Trials*			
	1	2	3	4
____________	I V M PP FM	I V M PP FM	I V M PP FM	I V M PP FM
____________	I V M PP FM	I V M PP FM	I V M PP FM	I V M PP FM
____________	I V M PP FM	I V M PP FM	I V M PP FM	I V M PP FM
____________	I V M PP FM	I V M PP FM	I V M PP FM	I V M PP FM
____________	I V M PP FM	I V M PP FM	I V M PP FM	I V M PP FM
____________	I V M PP FM	I V M PP FM	I V M PP FM	I V M PP FM

I = Independent, V = Verbal, M = Model, PP = Partial Physical, FM = Full Manipulation

Circle the level of assistance required for each step.

FIGURE 17.10

Examples of four task-analytic data-collection sheets

Note: In Form A, the observer records only the correctness or incorrectness of each step of the task analysis or response chain. In Form B, the observer records the levels of assistance needed by the child on each step of the chain. In Form C, the observer writes a number for each step in the order in which it occurred (e.g., 1 for first step completed, 2 for second step, 3 for third step, etc.). In Form D, the teacher records whether the child performs each step correctly, incorrectly, or with assistance (prompt).

a disagreement. The number of agreements are then divided by the number of agreements plus the number of disagreements and finally multiplied by 100. Procedures for conducting and calculating reliability estimates are described in detail by Cooper et al. (1987), Tawney and Gast (1984), and Suen and Ary (1989). Conducting reliability checks is difficult and time consuming in some early childhood settings, but it is possible. In part, if the decisions based on the data are critical and if there is a suspicion that bias or drift may be occurring, the reliability checks should be made. Faulty decisions may arise from unreliable data. Retraining observers, clarifying the definitions, simplifying the recording procedures, and practicing with the observation procedures are frequently sufficient strategies for correcting problems of lack of agreement.

Using data to make decisions As stated at the beginning of this chapter, a primary function of monitoring is to make decisions about children's progress and their intervention program. The major decisions are whether a change is needed in the intervention and if so, what change should be made. Interestingly, some research indicates that teachers who frequently collect monitoring data on their students have difficulty knowing how to use that data to make decisions (Farlow & Snell, 1989). Three practices may lend assistance: summarizing the data, graphing the data, and applying data-decision rules.

Summarizing raw data Summarizing data can be quite simple and may involve totalling the results of each observation; calculating the percentage, rate, or total time; and ordering the data in the sequence in which they were collected (e.g., by date). When categories of behavior are measured, the summaries should be calculated for each category of behavior. When changes in the situations under which the data were collected are known, they should be identified and the resulting data should be marked to help in the interpretation of the data.

Task-analytic data present particular problems in data summary (Haring & Kennedy, 1988). If one calculates only the percentage of correctly completed steps, that information does not indicate which steps are problematic and what types of decisions need to be made to correct the problem. As a result, the summary of task-analytic data should retain data on each step of the response chain (Snell & Loyd, 1991). A summary format that preserves and summarizes the data is presented in Figure 17.11. This format allows the team to collect the data, summarize them, and graph them on the same sheet. In addition, the types of errors that occur can be recorded and analyzed (Ault, Gast, Wolery, & Doyle, 1992).

Graphing data to assist in making decisions Some research indicates that experienced teachers can analyze data and make decisions based on graphed and ungraphed data (Snell & Loyd, 1991; Utley, Zigmond, & Strain, 1987). However, other research indicates that children may make more progress when their teachers graph the monitoring data rather than simply collecting and recording it (Fuchs & Fuchs, 1986). For communication among team members, graphs are quite helpful. Several sources describe procedures for graphing data in different formats (Parsonson & Baer, 1992; Tawney & Gast, 1984; White & Haring, 1980). In general, graphing data requires minimal extra time, and the potential benefits are well worth the effort—particularly when important decisions are being made about altering children's intervention programs.

Data decision rules Although it appears that some experienced teachers use rules to make decisions from their data, they tend to use fewer rules and have fewer rules available when the data indicate that their children are not making progress (Farlow & Snell, 1989). To assist teams in making consistent decisions based on particular findings from their monitoring data, sets of data decision rules have been developed (Haring & Liberty, 1990; Liberty & Haring, 1990) for promoting initial learning of skills (acquisition) and for promoting fluent performance (Liberty & Haring, 1990); these are shown in Figure 17.12. Some research indicates that when teachers use decision rules, their students evidence additional achievement (Browder, Demchak, Heller, & King, 1989).

Data decision rules also have been developed for promoting generalization of skills across a number of relevant dimensions such as settings, people, objects and materials, and time (Haring & Liberty, 1990). These rules are shown in Table 17.1. The research also supports the use of these rules; more generalization occurs when the rules are applied (Liberty, Haring, White, & Billingsley, 1988). Belfiore and Browder (1992) found that if teachers were taught to monitor their own instructional decisions, they were more consistent in using the data decision rules.

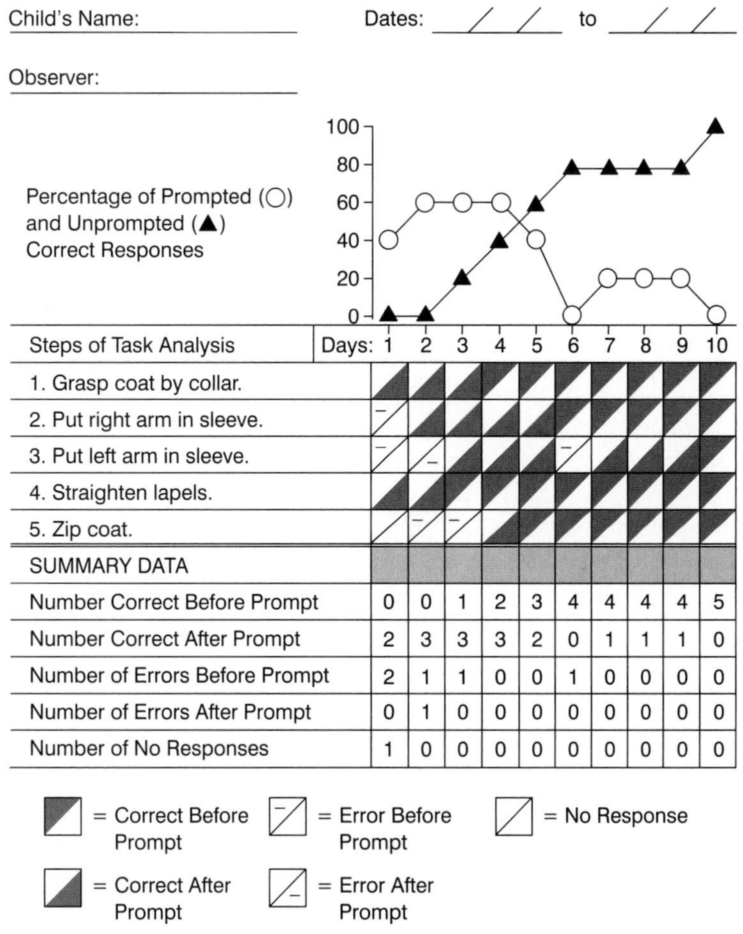

Child's Name: ______ Dates: __/__/__ to __/__/__

Observer: ______

Steps of Task Analysis	Days: 1	2	3	4	5	6	7	8	9	10
1. Grasp coat by collar.										
2. Put right arm in sleeve.										
3. Put left arm in sleeve.										
4. Straighten lapels.										
5. Zip coat.										
SUMMARY DATA										
Number Correct Before Prompt	0	0	1	2	3	4	4	4	4	5
Number Correct After Prompt	2	3	3	3	2	0	1	1	1	0
Number of Errors Before Prompt	2	1	1	0	0	1	0	0	0	0
Number of Errors After Prompt	0	1	0	0	0	0	0	0	0	0
Number of No Responses	1	0	0	0	0	0	0	0	0	0

= Correct Before Prompt
= Error Before Prompt
= No Response
= Correct After Prompt
= Error After Prompt

FIGURE 17.11

Sample data sheet and graph for task-analytic data

Note: The top portion is a line graph of the data; the middle portion is the data-collection sheet, with symbols provided for recording the child's data; the lower portion is a summary of the data.

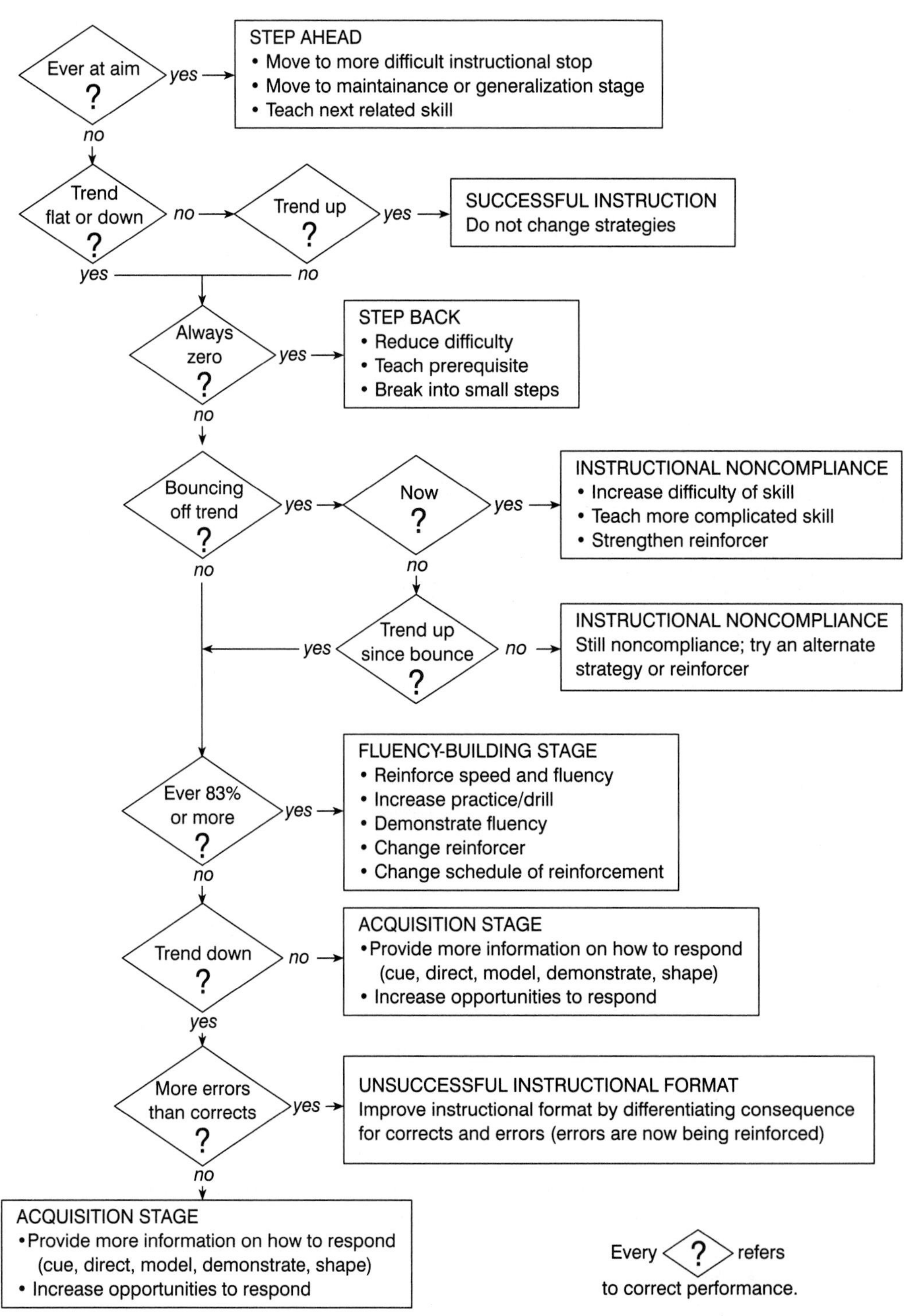

FIGURE 17.12

Data decision rules for analyzing data on acquisition and fluency programs

Source: From "Introduction to Decision Rule Systems" by K. A. Liberty and N. G. Haring, 1990, *Remedial and Special Education, 11*(1), pp. 32–41. Copyright 1990 by PRO-ED, Inc. Reprinted by permission.

As a whole, these studies argue for the regular monitoring of children's progress, summarizing the data, graphing it, and applying rules to the patterns that exist in the data. Two qualifications, however, should be noted. First, the research on teachers' interpretation of monitoring data and on teachers' use of data decision rules has occurred with older students; it has not been studied in early childhood contexts. Second, teams should bring all the knowledge they have about children and about how the children are performing to the issues of interpretation and analysis of monitoring data.

INTERVENTION MONITORING

The previous sections have discussed monitoring children's progress to make decisions about whether it is adequate and to determine what changes are indicated in the intervention plan. Such monitoring is based on the assumption that the intervention is being used accurately and consistently. Unfortunately, this may not always be the case; a child's lack of progress may be due to inaccurate or inconsistent use of interventions (McConnell, McEvoy, & Odom, 1992; Peterson & McConnell, 1993). The practice of monitoring intervention usage is known as *treatment integrity* or *procedural fidelity* (LeLaurin & Wolery, 1992). In short, it involves collecting data on the degree to which the intervention is used as planned.

The rationale for monitoring interventions is relatively straightforward. If the intervention is being monitored and slippage or incorrect implementation begins to occur, that slippage can be identified and corrected (Wolery, 1994b). If incorrect use of the intervention is allowed to continue, the child's progress may be affected negatively. Some research appears to support this contention. For example, McEvoy, Shores, Wehby, Johnson, and Fox (1990) taught teachers to use social skill interventions, collected data on the teachers' use of the interventions, and measured the time children spent in social interaction during play time. Teachers who used the interventions often compared with those who did not had increases in the amount of time children spent in social interactions. Although these data are correlational, some experimental studies of intervention strategies have occurred. For example, Wilbers and Wolery (1994) implemented the constant time delay in two conditions: one with high levels of correct use on all aspects of the strategy and one with high levels of correct use on all but one aspect of the strategy (i.e., the length of the delay interval). Interestingly, no major differences existed between the two conditions in either condition. However, in another study of intervention integrity with the constant time delay strategy, the prompt was delivered inconsistently in one condition and delivered correctly in another (Holcombe, Wolery, & Snyder, 1994). Although one of the five children was not affected, the others were. For most children, learning was much slower when the prompt was used inconsistently; for one child, no learning occurred when the procedure was used incorrectly. Similarly, another study that used a prompt fading procedure to teach children to make transitions between activities provides support for using interventions correctly (Venn, Wolery, Morris, DeCesare, & Cuffs, in press). During baseline conditions, the teachers prompted children a great deal, but children did not make transitions independently until teachers began to fade the prompts systematically. Thus, using prompting may be ineffective unless the prompts are faded.

Procedures for measuring the implementation of interventions have been described (Wolery & Holcombe, 1993). Three major decisions are encountered when planning to monitor

TABLE 17.1
Data Decision Rules for Generalization

	Question	Procedures	Answer	Next Step/Decision
A.	Has skill generalized at the desired level in all target situations?	Probe for generalization in all desired situations, then compare performance with criteria (IEP objective).	yes	1 SUCCESSFUL INSTRUCTION • Step ahead to a more difficult level of skill • Choose a new skill to teach EXIT sequence
			no	CONTINUE with question B.
B.	Has skill been acquired?	Compare performance in instructional situation with criteria for acquisition or performance levels specified in IEP objective. Answer yes if student has met performance levels in training situation but not in generalization.	yes	CONTINUE with question C.
			no	2 SKILL MASTERY PROBLEM • Continue Instruction EXIT sequence
C.	Is generalization desired to only a few situations?	Analyze function of skill in current and future environments available to student.	yes	CONTINUE with question D.
			no	CONTINUE with question E.
D.	Is it possible to train directly in those situations?	Are all situations frequently accessible for training so that training time is likely to be adequate to meet aim date in IEP objective?	yes	3 LIMITED GENERALIZATION SITUATIONS • Train in desired situation • Train sequentially in all situations (i.e., sequential modification) EXIT sequence
			no	CONTINUE with question E.
E.	Is the student reinforced even though he/she does not do the largest skill?	Observe student behavior during probes and note events which follow appropriate, inappropriate, target, and nontarget skills. Determine if those events which should follow the target skills, or have been shown to reinforce other skills, are presented to the student, or available even if he does not respond, or if he does the skill incorrectly, or if he misbehaves.	yes	CONTINUE with question F.
			no	CONTINUE with question H.
F.	Does the student fail to respond and is reinforced?	Answer yes only if the student is reinforced for doing nothing (i.e., accesses reinforcers for "no response").	yes	4 NONCONTINGENT REINFORCER PROBLEM • Alter generalization contingencies
			no	CONTINUE with question G.
G.	Is the behavior reinforced by the same reinforcers as the target skill?	If misbehavior or other behavior accesses same reinforcer available for target skill, answer yes.	yes	5 COMPETING BEHAVIOR PROBLEM • Increase proficiency • Amplify instructed behavior • Alter generalization contingencies EXIT sequence

	Question	Procedure	Answer	Action
			no	6 COMPETING REINFORCER PROBLEM • Alter generalization contingencies EXIT sequence
H.	Did the student generalize once at or close to criterion performance levels and then not as well on other opportunities?	Consider performance in current and past probes. Compare student performance for each response opportunity with performance level specified in objective. If near criterion performance occurred on the first response opportunity, and performance was poor or nonexistent after that, answer yes.	yes	7 REINFORCING FUNCTION PROBLEM • Program natural reinforcers • Eliminate training reinforcers • Use natural schedules • Use natural consequences • Teach self-reinforcement • Teach to solicit reinforcement • Reinforce generalized behavior • Alter generalization contingencies EXIT sequence
			no	CONTINUE with question I.
I.	Did the student respond partially correctly during at least one response opportunity?	Analyze anecdotal data and observation notes from probe.	yes	8 DISCRIMINATION FUNCTION PROBLEM Vary stimuli: • Use all stimuli • Use frequent stimuli • Use multiple exemplars EXIT sequence
			no	CONTINUE with question J.
J.	Did the student fail to perform any part of the target skill?	Analyze student performance during probe situation.	yes	9 GENERALIZATION TRAINING FORMAT • Increase proficiency • Program natural reinforcers • Use natural schedules • Use appropriate natural stimuli • Eliminate training stimuli EXIT sequence
			no	*STOP*. You have made an error in sequence. Begin again at Question A.

Source: From "Decision Rules and Procedures for Generalization" by K. Liberty, in N. G. Haring (Ed.) *Generalization for Students with Severe Handicaps: Strategies and Solutions,* 1988, Seattle, WA: University of Washington Press. Copyright 1988 by Washington Research Organization. Reprinted by permission.

intervention usage; these are deciding what to measure, which measurement procedures to use, and when the measurement should occur. In deciding what to measure, we recommend task analyzing the intervention to identify and define the steps the adult does when using the intervention. This is usually quite simple, but should capture the major decisions that adults make while using the procedure. A number of options exist in terms of measuring intervention usage. Two options that are quite useful are rating scales (for information on constructing rating scales see McCloskey, 1990) and direct observation (LeLaurin & Wolery, 1992). In terms of when to measure the use of the intervention, two conditions should cue the team to start such monitoring. First, if children are not making progress, monitoring the extent to which the intervention is used correctly is appropriate. Second, when informal observations or other information suggests that interventions are being used incorrectly, monitoring should probably occur. In addition to these two conditions, when individuals are initially learning to use a new intervention, collecting monitoring information on their usage and providing feedback is often helpful in establishing more rapid and correct usage.

SUMMARY

Monitoring children's progress is done to validate the results of the initial assessment, to develop a record of child progress, and to determine whether interventions should be changed. When conducting monitoring assessments, the goals and objectives in the intervention plan and selected global aspects of child behavior should be measured. The monitoring plan should specify what will be measured, who will conduct the monitoring, and the contexts in which it should occur. The perspectives of family members and team members who spend time with the child should be solicited, and the contexts in which monitoring occurs should be authentic naturalistic settings. The monitoring should occur regularly and frequently. The monitoring plan may include narrative descriptions, judgment-based assessments, portfolio information, and direct observation. Direct observation is used often, and a variety of data collection systems can be employed. However, the data must be summarized and should be graphed, and data decision rules should be applied. Finally, when children are not making progress, the degree to which the interventions are correctly used should be assessed.

SUMMARY OF KEY CONCEPTS

- Monitoring children's performance should be done for three reasons: to validate the initial assessment information, to develop a record of progress over time, and to make decisions about whether *and* what should be changed in the intervention procedures.
- Children's progress on the individualized goals and objectives should be monitored as well as important indices of child behavior such as engagement, interactions with others, and maladaptive behaviors.
- The monitoring plan should identify the information to be collected, who will collect it, the situations in which it will be collected, how frequently it will be collected, and who will be responsible for analyzing it.
- Monitoring should occur in authentic contexts, include the perspectives of relevant individuals, and occur frequently—more frequently for important goals and for goals on which decisions are needed.

- Broad approaches to monitoring children's progress are narrative descriptions, judgment-based assessments, work samples, and direct observation.
- Narrative descriptions include anecdotal records, running records, and specimen descriptions.
- Judgment-based assessments often involve ratings of children's performance and qualities; they are useful in securing multiple perspectives of children's behavior.
- Work samples are compilations (portfolios) of children's products over time that show progress and the richness of children's behavior.
- Using direct observation and systematic recording to monitor children's progress requires the team to define the behaviors being measured, select relevant data collection systems, select times and situations for observation, check the accuracy of the data collection, and summarize and make decisions based on the data.
- Monitoring using direct observation can include event sampling, time sampling, category sampling, level-of-assistance recording, and task-analytic recording.
- Using data collected for monitoring children's progress is facilitated by summarizing the data, graphing the data, and applying data decision rules.
- In addition to monitoring children's progress, teams should monitor how the intervention strategies and practices are being used.

REFERENCES

Ault, M. J., Gast, D. L., Wolery, M., & Doyle, P. M. (1992). Data collection and graphing method for teaching chained tasks with the constant time delay procedure. *Teaching Exceptional Children, 24*(2), 28–33.

Bailey, D. B., & Wolery, M. (1992). *Teaching infants and preschoolers with disabilities* (2nd ed.). Englewood Cliffs, NJ: Merrill/Prentice Hall.

Barnett, D. W., & Carey, K. T. (1992). *Designing interventions for preschool learning and behavior problems.* San Francisco: Jossey-Bass.

Belfiore, P. J., & Browder, D. M. (1992). The effects of self-monitoring on teachers' data-based decisions and on the progress of adults with severe mental retardation. *Education and Training in Mental Retardation, 27,* 60–67.

Billingsley, F. F., Burgess, D., Lynch, V. W., & Matlock, B. L. (1991). Toward generalized outcomes: Considerations and guidelines for writing instructional objectives. *Education and Training in Mental Retardation, 26,* 351–360.

Bijou, S. W., Peterson, R. F., Harris, F. R., Allen, K. E., & Johnston, M. S. (1969). Methodology of experimental studies of young children in natural settings. *Psychological Reports, 19,* 177–210.

Browder, D. M., Demchak, M. A., Heller, M., & King, D. (1989). An in vivo evaluation of the use of data-based rules to guide instructional decisions. *Journal of the Association for Persons with Severe Handicaps, 14,* 234–240.

Colozzi, G. A., & Pollow, R. S. (1984). Teaching independent walking to mentally retarded children in a public school. *Education and Training of the Mentally Retarded, 19,* 97–101.

Cooper, J. O. (1980). *Measuring behavior* (2nd ed.). Englewood Cliffs, NJ: Merrill/Prentice Hall.

Cooper, J. O., Heron, T. E., & Heward, W. L. (1987). *Applied behavior analysis.* Englewood Cliffs, NJ: Merrill/Prentice Hall.

Doyle, P. M., Wolery, M., Ault, M. J., & Gast, D. L. (1988). System of least prompts: A review of procedural parameters. *Journal of the Association for Persons with Severe Handicaps, 13,* 28–40.

Farlow, L. J., & Snell, M. E. (1989). Teacher use of student performance data to make instructional decisions: Practices in programs for students with moderate to profound disabilities. *Journal of the Association for Persons with Severe Handicaps, 14,* 13–22.

Fleischer, K. H., Belgredan, J. H., Bagnato, S. J., & Ogonosky, A. B. (1990). An overview of judgment-based assessment. *Topics in Early Childhood Special Education, 10,* 13–23.

Fuchs, L. S., & Fuchs, D. (1986). Effects of systematic formative evaluation: A meta analysis. *Exceptional Children, 53,* 199–208.

Graves, D., & Sunstein, B. S. (1992). *Portfolio portraits.* Portsmouth, NH: Heinmann.

Griffen, A. K., Wolery, M., & Schuster, J. W. (1992). Triadic instruction of chained food preparation responses: Acquisition and observational learning. *Journal of Applied Behavior Analysis, 25,* 193–204.

Hall, M. G., Schuster, J. W., Wolery, M., Gast, D. L., & Doyle, P. M. (1992). Teaching cooking skills to students with moderate handicaps in a small group instructional format using constant time delay. *Journal of Behavioral Education, 2,* 257–279.

Haring, N. G., & Liberty, K. A. (1990). Matching strategies with performance in facilitating generalization. *Focus on Exceptional Children, 22*(8), 1–16.

Haring, T. G. (1992). The context of social competence: Relations, relationships, and generalization. In S. L. Odom, S. R. McConnell, & M. A. McEvoy (Eds.), *Social competence of young children with disabilities: Issues and strategies for intervention* (pp. 307–320). Baltimore, MD: Paul H. Brookes.

Haring, T. G., & Kennedy, C. H. (1988). Units of analysis in task-analytic research. *Journal of Applied Behavior Analysis, 21,* 207–215.

Hills, T. W. (1992). Reaching potentials through appropriate assessment. In S. Bredekamp & T. Rosegrant (Eds.), *Reaching potentials: Appropriate curriculum and assessment for young children* (Vol. 1) (pp. 43–63). Washington, DC: National Association for the Education of Young Children.

Holcombe, A., Wolery, M., & Snyder, E. (1994). Effects of two levels of procedural fidelity with constant time delay on children's learning. *Journal of Behavioral Education, 4,* 49–73.

Kaiser, A. P., & Gray, D. B. (1993). *Enhancing children's communication: Research foundations for intervention.* Baltimore, MD: Paul H. Brookes.

Kaiser, A. P., Yoder, P., & Keetz, A. (1992). Evaluating milieu teaching. In S. F. Warren & J. Reichle (Eds.), *Causes and effects in communication and language intervention* (pp. 9–47). Baltimore, MD: Paul H. Brookes.

Kayser, J. E., Billingsley, F. F., & Neel, R. S. (1986). A comparison of in-context and traditional instructional approaches: Total task, single trial versus backward chaining multiple trials. *Journal of the Association for Persons with Severe Handicaps, 11,* 28–38.

Kazdin, A. E. (1977). Artifact, bias, and complexity of assessment: The ABCs of reliability. *Journal of Applied Behavior Analysis, 10,* 141–150.

Kohler, F. W., & Strain, P. S. (1990). Peer-assisted interventions: Early promises, notable achievements, and future aspirations. *Clinical Psychology Review, 10,* 441–452.

Kozloff, M. (1994). *Improving educational outcomes for children with disabilities: Principles for assessment, program planning, and evaluation.* Baltimore, MD: Paul H. Brookes.

LeLaurin, K. (1990). Judgment-based assessment: Making the implicit explicit. *Topics in Early Childhood Special Education, 10,* 96–110.

LeLaurin, K., & Wolery, M. (1992). Research standards in early intervention: Defining, describing, and measuring the independent variable. *Journal of Early Intervention, 16,* 275–287.

Liberty, K. A., & Haring, N. G. (1990). Introduction to decision rule systems. *Remedial and Special Education, 11,* 32–41.

Liberty, K. (1988). Decision rules and procedures for generalization. In N. G. Haring (Ed.), *Generalization for students with severe handicaps: Strategies and solutions.*

Liberty, K. A., Haring, N. G., White, O. R., & Billingsley, F. F. (1988). A technology for the future: Decision rules for generalization. *Education and Training in Mental Retardation, 23,* 315–326.

Luiselli, J. K., & Luiselli, T. E. (1995). A behavior analysis approach toward chronic food refusal in children with gastrostomy-tube dependency. *Topics in Early Childhood Special Education, 15,* 1–18.

McCloskey, G. (1990). Selecting and using early childhood rating scales. *Topics in Early Childhood Special Education, 10,* 65–79.

McConnell, S. R., McEvoy, M. A., & Odom, S. L. (1992). Implementation of social competence interventions in early childhood special education classes. In S. L. Odom, S. R. McConnell, & M. A. McEvoy (Eds.), *Social competence of young children with disabilities: Issues and strategies for intervention* (pp. 277–306). Baltimore, MD: Paul H. Brookes.

McDonnell, J., & McFarland, S. (1988). Comparison of forward and concurrent chaining strategies in teaching laundromat skills to students with severe handicaps. *Research in Developmental Disabilities, 9,* 177–194.

McEvoy, M. A., Shores, R. E., Wehby, J. H., Johnson, S. M., Fox, J. J. (1990). Special education teachers' implementation procedures to promote social interaction among children in integrated settings. *Education and Training in Mental Retardation, 25,* 267–276.

McWilliam, R. A., & Bailey, D. B. (1992). Promoting engagement and mastery. In D. B. Bailey & M. Wolery (Eds.), *Teaching infants and preschoolers with disabilities* (2nd ed.) (pp. 229–255). Englewood Cliffs, NJ: Merrill/Prentice Hall.

Meisels, S. J. (1993). Remaking classroom assessment with the work sampling system. *Young Children, 49,* 34–40.

Munger, G. F., Snell, M. E., & Loyd, B. H. (1989). A study of the effects of frequency of probe data collection and graph characteristics on teachers' visual analysis. *Research in Developmental Disabilities, 10,* 109–127.

Neisworth, J. T., & Fewell, R. R. (1990). Foreword. *Topics in Early Childhood Special Education, 10,* ix–xi.

Odom, S. L., McConnell, S. R., & McEvoy, M. A. (1992). *Social competence of young children with disabilities: Issues and strategies for intervention.* Baltimore, MD: Paul H. Brookes.

Odom, S. L., & McLean, M. E. (in press). *Early intervention for infants and young children with disabilities and their families: Recommended practices.* Austin, TX: PRO-ED.

Odom, S. L., & Strain, P. S. (1984). Classroom-based social skills instruction for severely handicapped preschool children. *Topics in Early Childhood Special Education, 4,* 97–116.

Parsonson, B. S., & Baer, D. M. (1992). The visual analysis of data, and current research into the stimuli controlling it. In T. R. Kratochwill & J. R. Levin (Eds.), *Single-case research design and analysis: New directions for psychology and education.* Hillsdale, NJ: Lawrence Erlbaum.

Peterson, C. A., & McConnell, S. R. (1993). Factors affecting the impact of social interaction skills interventions in early childhood special education. *Topics in Early Childhood Special Education, 13,* 38–56.

Poster, M., Johns, S., Abrams, J., & Freund, C. (1994). The work sampling system implementation at Carnegie Mellon University Child Care Center: Year one reflections. *Pittsburgh Association for the Education of Young Children Newsletter.*

Poteet, J. A., Choate, J. S., & Steward, S. C. (1993). Performance assessment and special education: Practices and prospects. *Focus on Exceptional Children, 26*(1), 1–20.

Rettig, M., Kallam, M., & McCarthy-Salm, K. (1993). The effect of social and isolate toys on social interactions of preschool-aged children. *Education and Training in Mental Retardation, 28,* 252–256.

Sainato, D. M., & Carta, J. J. (1992). Classroom influences on the development of social competence in young children with disabilities. In S. L. Odom, S. R. McConnell, & M. McEvoy (Eds.), *Social competence of young children with disabilities: Issues and strategies for intervention* (pp. 93–109). Baltimore, MD: Paul H. Brookes.

Snell, M. E., & Loyd, B. H. (1991). A study of the effects of trend, variability, frequency, and form of data on teachers' judgments about progress and their decisions about program change. *Research in Developmental Disabilities, 12,* 41–61.

Suen, H. K., & Ary, D. (1989). *Analyzing quantitative behavioral observation data.* Hillsdale, NJ: Lawrence Erlbaum.

Tawney, J. W., & Gast, D. L. (1984). *Single subject research in special education.* Englewood Cliffs, NJ: Merrill/Prentice Hall.

Thurman, S. K., & Widerstrom, A. H. (1990). *Infants and young children with special needs: A developmental and ecological approach* (2nd ed.). Baltimore, MD: Paul H. Brookes.

Utley, B. L., Zigmond, N., & Strain, P. S. (1987). How various forms of data affect teacher analysis of student performance. *Exceptional Children, 53,* 411–422.

Venn, M. L., Wolery, M., Morris, A., DeCesare, L. D., & Cuffs, M. S. (in press). Use of progressive time delay to teach in-class transitions to preschoolers with autism. *Journal of Autism and Developmental Disorders.*

Venn, M. L., Wolery, M., Werts, M. G., Morris, A., DeCesare, L. D., & Cuffs, M. S. (1993). Embedding instruction in art activities to teach preschoolers with disabilities to imitate their peers. *Early Childhood Research Quarterly, 8,* 277–294.

Warren, S. F. (1985). Clinical strategies for the measurement of language generalization. In S. F. Warren & A. K. Rogers-Warren (Eds.), *Teaching functional language intervention series* (pp. 89–122). Austin, TX: PRO-ED.

Warren, S. F. (1992). Facilitating basic vocabulary acquisition with milieu teaching procedures. *Journal of Early Intervention, 16,* 235–251.

Werts, M. G., Caldwell, N. K., & Wolery, M. (in press). The effects of peer models on the observational learning of response chains by students with disabilities. *Journal of Applied Behavior Analysis.*

White, O. R. (1980). Adaptive performance objectives: Form versus function. In W. Sailor, B. Wilcox, & L. Brown (Eds.), *Methods of instruction for severely handicapped students* (pp. 47–70). Baltimore, MD: Paul H. Brookes.

White, O. R., & Haring, N. G. (1980). *Exceptional teaching.* Englewood Cliffs, NJ: Merrill/Prentice Hall.

Wilbers, J. S., & Wolery, M. (1994). *Effects of two methods for delivering the delay interval with time delay.* Manuscript submitted for publication.

Wolery, M. (1994a). Instructional strategies for teaching young children with special needs. In M. Wolery & J. S. Wilbers (Eds.), *Including children with special needs in early childhood programs* (pp. 119–150). Washington, DC: National Association for the Education of Young Children.

Wolery, M. (1994b). Procedural fidelity: A reminder of its functions. *Journal of Behavioral Education, 4,* 381–386.

Wolery, M., Ault, M. J., & Doyle, P. M. (1992). *Teaching students with moderate and severe disabilities: Use of response prompting strategies.* White Plains, NY: Longman.

Wolery, M., Ault, M. J., Gast, D. L., Doyle, P. M., & Griffen, A. K. (1990). Comparison of constant time delay and the system of least prompts in teaching chained tasks. *Education and Training in Mental Retardation, 25,* 243–257.

Wolery, M., Bailey, D. B., & Sugai, G. M. (1988). *Effective teaching: Principles and procedures of applied behavior analysis with exceptional students.* Boston: Allyn and Bacon.

Wolery, M., & Holcombe, A. (1993). *Procedural fidelity: Description, measurement, and an example of its utility.* (U.S. Department of Education, Grant No. H023A10049). Pittsburgh, PA: Allegheny-Singer Research Institute.

Wolery, M., & Wilbers, J. S. (1994). *Including children with special needs in early childhood programs.* Washington, DC: National Association for the Education of Young Children.

Wolery, M., & Wolery, R. A. (1992). Promoting functional cognitive skills. In D. B. Bailey & M. Wolery (Eds.), *Teaching infants and preschoolers with disabilities* (2nd ed.) (pp. 521–572). Englewood Cliffs, NJ: Merrill/Prentice Hall.

Wright, C. W., & Schuster, J. W. (1994). Accepting specific versus functional student responses when training chained tasks. *Education and Training in Mental Retardation and Developmental Disabilities, 29,* 43–56.

AUTHOR INDEX

SUBJECT INDEX